Ancient Maya
Political Economies

D0841226

W. J. Rathje & Luis Rojas, Cozumel Island, Spring 1973.

We dedicate this volume to William L. Rathje in recognition of his revolutionary contributions toward understanding ancient Maya society, which continue to inspire new generations of Mayanists to dig deeply and think big.

Ancient Maya
Political Economies

Edited by

Marilyn A. Masson
and
David A. Freidel

ALTAMIRA
PRESS

A Division of
ROWMAN & LITTLEFIELD PUBLISHERS, INC.
Walnut Creek • Lanham • New York • Oxford

ALTAMIRA PRESS
A Division of Rowman & Littlefield Publishers, Inc.
1630 North Main Street, #367
Walnut Creek, CA 94596
www.altamirapress.com

Rowman & Littlefield Publishers, Inc.
A Member of the Rowman & Littlefield Publishing Group
4720 Boston Way
Lanham, MD 20706

PO Box 317
Oxford
OX2 9RU, UK

Copyright © 2002 by AltaMira Press

All rights reserved. No part of this publication may be reproduced, stored in a retrieval system, or transmitted in any form or by any means, electronic, mechanical, photocopying, recording, or otherwise, without the prior permission of the publisher.

British Library Cataloguing in Publication Information Available

Library of Congress Cataloging-in-Publication Data

Ancient Maya political economies / Marilyn A. Masson, David A. Freidel, Editors.
    p. cm.
Includes bibliographical references and index.
  ISBN 0-7591-0080-2 (hardback : alk. paper) — ISBN 0-7591-0081-0 (pbk. : alk. paper)
  1. Mayas—Economic conditions. 2. Mayas—Politics and government. 3. Mayas—Antiquities. 4. Mexico—Antiquities. 5. Central America—Antiquities. I. Masson, Marilyn A. II. Freidel, David A.
  F1435.3.E27 A53 2002
  320.97281'016—dc21
                                    2002004235

Printed in the United States of America

♾™ The paper used in this publication meets the minimum requirements of American National Standard for Information Sciences—Permanence of Paper for Printed Library Materials, ANSI/NISO Z39.48–1992.

Contents

Preface   vii
David A. Freidel

Chapter 1   Introduction   1
                  Marilyn A. Masson

Chapter 2   The Nouveau Elite Potlatch: One   31
                  Scenario for the Monumental Rise
                  of Early Civilizations
                  William L. Rathje

Chapter 3   The Origins of Maya Civilization:
                  The Old Shell Game, Commodity,
                  Treasure, and Kingship   41
                  David A. Freidel, Kathryn Reese-Taylor,
                  and David Mora-Marín

Chapter 4   The Passage of the Late Preclassic
                  into the Early Classic   87
                  Kathryn Reese-Taylor and Debra S. Walker

Chapter 5   Praise the Ajaw and Pass the Kakaw:
                  Xibun Maya and the Political
                  Economy of Cacao   123
                  Patricia A. McAnany, Ben S. Thomas,
                  Steven Morandi, Polly A. Peterson,
                  and Eleanor Harrison

Chapter 6   Ceramic Exchange in the Late
                  Classic and Postclassic Maya
                  Lowlands: A Diachronic Approach   140
                  Georgia West

Chapter 7 Dynamics of Regional Integration
in Northwestern Belize   197
Lauren A. Sullivan

Chapter 8 At the Crossroads: The Economic
Basis of Political Power in the
Petexbatun Region   223
Antonia E. Foias

Chapter 9 Modes of Exchange and Regional
Patterns: Chunchucmil, Yucatan   249
Bruce H. Dahlin and Traci Ardren

Chapter 10 Praise the Gods and Pass the
Obsidian?: The Organization
of Ancient Economy in San Martín
Jilotepeque, Guatemala   285
Geoffrey E. Braswell

Chapter 11 New Perspectives on the Prehispanic
Maya Salt Trade   307
Anthony P. Andrews and Shirley B. Mock

Chapter 12 Community Economy and the
Mercantile Transformation
in Postclassic Northeastern Belize   335
Marilyn A. Masson

Chapter 13 In Praise of Garbage: Historical
Archaeology, Households,
and the Maya Political Economy   365
Craig A. Hanson

Chapter 14 Perspectives on Economy and Theory 398
Elizabeth Graham

Index   419

About the Authors   433

Preface

David A. Freidel

In March 2001, I opened the *New York Times* Op-Ed page to discover a picture of Fresh Kills, a landscape of garbage ornamented with gulls, emblazoned with "What Happened to My Toothbrush?" The Fresh Kills Landfill, after more than fifty years of use, was finally closing. I was reminded of Bill Rathje's archaeological investigation a little over a decade ago of what he once described as "one of the largest human-made monuments in the world," an artifact "twenty-five times the volume of the Great Pyramid at Giza" (*National Geographic* May 1991: 120). It is fair to predict that until it is mined for its materials in some future world of greater scarcity, it will be as durable a testament to our civilization as the pyramids are to an ancient one. Fresh Kills and other such repositories of the American material world have proven a mine of information for Bill Rathje and his colleagues in The Garbage Project. He once described to me how he went before a Senate committee in jeans, a faux pas excused by then-Senator Al Gore, who said he wished he could work in similar comfort. How an archaeologist who began his career with brilliant and influential models of Maya civilization found himself in the councils of the most powerful people of the modern age is a tale well told in *Rubbish!*, Bill's fine trade book—a worthwhile read for archaeologists interested in educating the public. Why he was before a Senate committee, and why he has been talking over the past twenty years to other politicians both in Washington and throughout the globe, is easier to understand: He commands strategic information about the way contemporary people use the material world.

Studying what we actually do as consumers, rather than what we say we do, has made Rathje unquestionably the most influential archaeologist alive with the decision-makers of America. Unfortunately, Rathje knows better than most that when people understand how they really behave, there is no guarantee that they will adjust "adaptively" on the basis of such knowledge. There are a number of important intervening variables—ideas, values, prejudices, ambitions, politics—between insight and practical response to it. For example, for many of us concepts like recycling and conservation remain abstract admonitions to sustain healthy and ethical behavior, on a par with brushing our teeth regularly. For Bill Rathje, recycling is an idea whose time had better be here. He said,

> I wonder sometimes how future generations will see us when they look at our garbage. I interpret the Classic period of the ancient Maya civilization as one of profligate waste, followed by a period of decline. The Maya woke up and discovered resources were in short supply, and they became very efficient very fast—they recycled, they reused. But it was too late. . . . If we compare our garbage with theirs, I think we can see we're still in a classic phase; that is, we're still discarding tremendous amounts of valuable resources on a daily basis. We have an important opportunity today. We can go into a period of efficiency and pragmatism, and in that way sustain our society in the style to which we've become accustomed for a much longer time. (NGS May 1991: 134)

Bill Rathje and his collaborator Jeremy Sabloff anticipated that the merchants who made Postclassic Cozumel Island a Maya trading center were likewise a pragmatic bunch (Sabloff and Rathje 1975: 9). But even while Rathje and Sabloff focused their field research on discovering the material-behavioral correlates of an economically progressive and resurgent Maya society in the wake of the Classic collapse, they thought about how ideology affected that society. They noted that Cozumel was a shrine center dedicated to the goddess Ix Chel and her oracle:

> From the trading center model it follows that the ability to reconcile conflicts between environmental realities and cultural norms, or between cultural norms held by different merchants is especially important to a trading center. . . . A priest who communicates with his god in dreams, trances, or divination activities is one potential source of change. However, the ultimate form of embedding adaptability into a mythic-religious structure is to have the god, itself, speak at will from its idol directly to its parishioners. Based upon the preceding rationale, it is significant that the Ix Chel "talking idol" was one of a kind in Decadent Period Yucatan and that is was housed on Cozumel. (Sabloff and Rathje 1975: 10)

Actually, the Ix Chel Oracle shrine was not unique. The famous shrine had a life-size hollow idol in which the oracle spoke; as surveyor for the Cozumel Project I discovered a second one. At Rathje's invitation, I presented a paper at a Sunday morning session of the 1973 American Anthropological Association meeting in New Orleans on Structure C-22-41-a, a complex shrine in the Santa Rita Ranch sector of the San Gervasio site zone in the interior of the island. This shrine had a curtain wall with a niche in it directly in front of a small table altar. The oracle could have secreted himself behind the wall and spoken as the effigy of the goddess stood before the supplicant on the altar. As it happened, the previous year when Bill had come down to Cozumel at the end of the first spring season, he had been anxious to get out and see the site of San Gervasio. Bill and his students had arrived right after a hurricane had passed over the island. I told him that the site was not accessible, but he really wanted to get out into the field. So we walked into the Santa Rita sector, the water reaching hip-height on the trail before we got there. I took him directly to the small pyramid housing C-22-41-a and we rested there in the Ix Chel shrine for a few moments before heading on to see the acropolis. The flood did nothing to dampen his enthusiasm. Subsequently, my unexpected interpretation of the shrine at the AAA meetings elicited from him an immediate offer to publish the paper in the project preliminary report, a characteristically generous gesture. But more significantly, Rathje and Sabloff were completely comfortable with the juxtaposition of economic and religious factors conditioning their model of late Maya society on Cozumel Island. They did not find contradictory the propositions that the Postclassic Maya were mercantile pragmatists and devout ritualists. In contrast to some of their contemporaries pursuing cultural ecological models in Maya studies, their approach explicitly proposed that these ancient people could use their ideas to think through solutions to the challenges of their circumstances.

The brilliance of Rathje's original cultural ecology of the lowland Maya, for me, lies not simply in the inversion of the established notion that the resource-redundant and resource-poor lowlands were an environment basically inimical to civilization. Rather it lies in the idea that people invent the institutions and rationales of civilization just as they invent tool technologies—through trial and error to be sure, and for many and various reasons. Still it is invention that is the mother of many human necessities in Rathje's vision. The practical demands of supplying people of the interior lowlands with things they needed may have triggered the process of elite formation his model stipulated. But it was the ability of elites to define themselves as necessary through religious material symbols that kept the ball rolling in the direction of pyramidal social structure. "Selling" elitism through symbols got Rathje lampooned by critics who envisioned intrepid Maya merchants from the lowlands offering a good idea in exchange for a jade boulder. A recent issue of the *New York Times* has a cartoon depicting the U.S. president as Jack in the Bean Stalk story showing his mother a handful of beans labeled "the ABM system" while the mysterious merchant trundles off with the billions the demonstrably impractical system will cost. "They're magic!" exclaims young Jack. Ideas have value in the material world, even when they are not rational or practical.

Now, a generation of scholarship later, we have a different understanding of some of the variables Rathje combined in his model. But some fundamentals endure, in my view, such as the basic cultural geography of the lowlands as core and peripheries (Freidel 1979 to the contrary), and the very notion that there cannot be realistic conceptions of either politics or economics except as they are integrated as political economy. And as Rathje's contribution to this book shows, he remains convinced that in civilization the people in power have opportunities to shape the destinies of their societies. That is not to say that elites necessarily serve the best interests of their societies—he once described Maya elites as "fungal," an appropriate rain forest metaphor. With the idea of free will writ large in the institutions of civilization comes both the chance to find a way to the future that is survivable for the majority and the risk that the elites, in their hubris, will lead their followers into a hell of their own making. The privilege of political economy carries with it the responsibility to make of it an "extrasomatic means of adaptation" (White 1949).

Rathje lives and works in the material world we are shaping, studying it with the disciplined gaze of a forensic scientist evaluating the physical clues of a crime. He discerns some of the unintended consequences of our decisions just as we who study the deeper past see those of ancient potentates. Such a life in the wake of our tsunami of waste might drive one to be blindly cynical, or at least incapacitated with depression, but it seems in Rathje's case to have inspired him to be both an energetic public educator and a believer in the possibility of human enlightenment. Recently he participated in an English translation of the Heart Sutra, the core of the Perfect Wisdom Sutra taught by Shakyamuni Buddha. He said of this work, "Communication is a most precious commodity and the ancient Buddhist Sutras have so much wisdom to give to today's materialistic and ego-centered world" (*The Illustrated Heart Sutra* 1997). There is in this observation an optimism that has likely sustained Rathje as he has taken his experiences and insight to a wide public audience. Relevancy was a rallying cry for Rathje's generation of archaeologists and certainly his archaeology of *us* is relevant. His archaeology of the Maya endures and continues to inspire me. I would like to think that in some important ways Maya archaeology is also becoming relevant—to living Maya people who struggle to rise out of poverty and oppression, to foreigners who are learning that the Maya did not disappear in the ninth-century collapse, to Mayan-speaking scholars who are taking the tools to interpret the past into their own hands as they learn to read and write in the ancient glyphic. There are risks in engaging the real material world of the present armed with archaeology. Be they greed-driven magnates of the wealthy countries or the looters and exploiters of the developing ones, the adversaries are real and well prepared. But I am happy to say that there are more archaeologists in those trenches than when Bill Rathje first decided to work in them.

References

Chung, Tsai Chih
  1997 *The Illustrated Heart Sutra*. Translated by E. E. Ho and W. L. Rathje. Singapore: An Asiapac Publication.
Rathje, William L.
  1991 "Once and Future Landfills." *National Geographic Magazine* 179(5): 116–134.
Sabloff, Jeremy A., and William L. Rathje
  1975 *A Study of Changing Pre-Columbian Commercial Systems: The 1972–1973 Seasons at Cozumel, Mexico*. Monographs of the Peabody Museum No. 3. Cambridge, Mass.: Harvard University Press.
White, Leslie A.
  1949 *The Science of Culture: A Study of Man and Civilization*. New York, Farrar, Straus.

Chapter One

Introduction

Marilyn A. Masson

The organization of Precolumbian Maya political economy was many times reconfigured over a 2,500-year period across the lowlands region. Acknowledging the dynamic variation of economic structures represents a point of embarkation for the essays in this volume, which offer a cross section of perspectives at different scales from points on the Maya map in Yucatan, Belize, and Guatemala. We examine patterns in different regions of the Maya lowlands and highlands, including the Petén, the Petexbatun, northwestern Belize, northeastern Belize, the southern Belize Xibun Valley, the Belize coast, northern Yucatan, and the San Martín Jilotepeque area of highland Guatemala. The majority of Preclassic and Classic period studies in this volume present perspectives from regions peripheral to the Petén core, and are informative about core-periphery relations. Three chapters—by Freidel, Reese-Taylor, and Mora-Marín (chapter 3), West (chapter 6), and Andrews and Mock (chapter 11)—offer broad spatial and temporal evaluations of the political economy of Classic period core centers as well as their relationships with peripheral zones. A Postclassic chapter by Masson (chapter 12) represents a northeastern Belize perspective from an area that was peripheral to the Mayapan core zone in northwest Yucatan. The links between household economy and world systems are examined by Hanson from the Colonial village of Tiquibalón, a settlement that was in close proximity to the center of Spanish rule (chapter 13).

Maya Economy: Autonomous or Centralized?

The term *political economy* traditionally refers to ways in which economic production and exchange are manipulated to support the power of a society's leaders. According to M. Estellie Smith (1991: 34), political economy is defined as "polity-centered, decision-making activities of governing personnel that center around the management of resources deemed germane to the polity's macrosystemic welfare as located in the interdependency of those constituent sectors, groups, and factors that the information selected identifies as relevant to such activities and the aims intended." Economic-based power is rarely solely held by such leaders, however, and a fundamental dialectic is observed within many societies in which factors of relative economic autonomy, entrepreneurship, prohibitive geography, and weak political control increase the social power of secondary elite or commoner factions (Rathje 1972; Mann 1986; Eisenstadt 1981; McAnany 1995; Ehrenreich et al. 1995). A consideration of the relationship between political power and material extraction, production, and exchange can be complex, as economic activities have the potential to empower a variety of social groups (McGuire 1992: 132; McAnany 1995; Sheets 2000). Economic power is not solely limited to the politically dominant. Such a dialectical approach acknowledges the fundamental contradictions within social relations, and the fact that social forms carry the seeds of their own transformations (McGuire 1992: 98). Sullivan's chapter in this volume identifies patterns in ceramic offerings that signal the increased autonomy and empowerment of local elites in northwestern Belize over time during the Classic period as their political affiliation with the Petén core cities dissipated (chapter 7).

Within the Maya area, recent analyses have emphasized the relative autonomy of communities in the countryside in modes of local production and exchange, suggesting that the activities of such communities were of little concern to self-exalting elites who dwelt at urban centers (Rice 1987; Ball 1993: 248; McAnany 1993, 1995; King and Potter 1994; Potter and King 1995). A disjunctive view has emerged of Maya economies, in which the utilitarian realm of everyday commodity production and exchange is perceived to operate rather autonomously from a prestige economy of gift exchange that supported the authority of kings (McAnany 1993: 70–71; Ball 1993: 248, 264). Political centers have been considered consumers of everyday pots, stone tools, and perishable mundane items made by commoners (Rands and Bishop 1980: 42; Fry 1980; Rice 1987; Ball 1993).

McAnany (1989: 365) characterizes the economic structure of Classic Maya polities as a "ring model," in which central cities were consumers of products manufactured in communities distributed around the centers (following Rands and Bishop 1980; Rice 1987). She contrasts this with a "core" model common to highland Mexico polities, where more production takes place within urbanized central cities (McAnany 1989: 365). The mechanisms for exchange by which city dwellers acquired such items are not well understood.

Few would dispute that most production of utilitarian commodities took place in the context of Maya households during all time periods (Freidel 1981: 377; McAnany 1993: 81; 1995; Ball 1993: 265), though the composition of Maya households was quite heterogeneous (McAnany 1993, 1995). Not all production occurred in the countryside as suggested by evidence for craft specialization and farming within some Maya political centers (Chase et al. 1990; Sheets 2000: 223). Previous studies have made important contributions toward understanding the economic empowerment and production autonomy of certain Maya countryside producers. They significantly refine the linear evolutionary notion that political centralization is necessarily accompanied by centralized economic control of production characteristic of more complex civilizations (Freidel 1981; McAnany 1989: 354). More distributional studies of everyday commodities are needed to investigate the integration of utilitarian and luxury economies between political centers and dispersed residential producer communities and the ways that these economies supported political regimes. Rather than representing a "simpler" form of economic organization, Freidel argues that the range and magnitude of production in the Classic Maya realm was substantial and effective and that achieving vertical and horizontal integration despite residential dispersion represents a system of intricate complexity (1981: 377). He argues persuasively that production in dispersed residential localities does not signal a high degree of domestic autonomy as is often assumed. Sheets (2000) recently published a similar argument for southeastern Mesoamerica.

Markets

The disjunctive view supposes that market functions were not well developed for Classic period Maya society as evidence for production centralization at major centers is lacking. A comparison of published data on pottery distributions in the Maya lowlands is offered here by West (chapter 6) to argue that major political centers did host regional markets for their subordinate centers and supporting communities. She further suggests that through such markets, everyday items were distributed through exchange. She further suggests that evidence for Carol Smith's (1976) solar-type marketing systems has been overlooked. Arlen Chase also finds evidence for a solar marketing organization in the settlement of Caracol (1998), based on a system of causeways that linked the city's peripheral producers and traders from other cities to the site core.

The suggestion that southern lowland centers hosted markets is compatible with the pilgrimage-market fair model proposed by Freidel (1981) that was based on analogies to other societies in world history as well as contact period Yucatan. Large open plazas at Maya political centers were probably the locus of important political and ritual events documented in royal texts. However, as Freidel (1981) and Dahlin and Ardren argue in chapter 9, such events drawing large numbers of people together represented prime opportunities for exchange, including market exchange. The symbiotic nature of ritual and economic events involving the exchange of items essential to daily life should not be underestimated as has been demonstrated on a smaller scale for Trobriand society (e.g., Earle 1982: 79). The difficulty of identifying a market-based economy from market facilities at archaeological sites is a methodological issue with which Mesoamericanists have long wrestled (Hirth 1998; Millon et al. 1973; Sharer 1994: 456). However, the view that political elites hosted markets at urban centers where specialists from surrounding communities could exchange utilitarian pottery and other items in the absence of strong elite control of economic production is accepted by some Maya scholars based on analogy to contact period and contemporary market systems in the Maya area (Freidel 1981; Sharer 1994: 67, 456). Large open plazas are often considered possible marketplaces (Sharer 1994: table 14.1; Smith and Masson 2000: 114). Rather than controlling production, Maya political elites may have focused on controlling certain types of distribution through the operation of regional markets (Freidel 1981: 377). Sponsorship of markets does not represent centralized redistribution in the collection, housing, or distribution of various utilitarian craft or subsistence goods by elite leaders. Instead, such a system would have been fluid and offered elites opportunities for tribute extraction or taxation of merchants, retailers, and other participants.

Utilitarian and Luxury Items

Distribution studies of local, regional, and distant resources in household consumption contexts represent a valuable tool for evaluating material dependencies that reflect market exchange. An important new distributional model proposed by Hirth (1998) suggests that household artifact distributions reflect the accessibility of distant objects gained through participation in open market networks. Outlining a distributional approach, Hirth predicts that greater participation in market exchange by households of both commoners and elites will result in more homogenous artifact assemblages among these social classes than in other types of systems, such as prestige-goods economies that circulate valuables primarily among elites. Other scholars also predict that more open market exchange economies involving both utilitarian and luxury items will result in more even distributions among households of different status. For example, Blanton et al. (1996) equate this trend with "corporate" political economies that downplay the conspicuous display of personal authority (and its material symbols) by politically ambitious individuals. In these economies, the distribution of luxury items is not as strictly controlled by elites. Hirth's model is borne out in the archaeological data of Aztec period households in Morelos (Smith 1999), a society known to have had a high level of market exchange from historic sources. The household inventories of Classic period Ceren (Sheets 2000: 223) also suggest that commoners had some access to valuables through market exchange.

The distributions of utilitarian and luxury commodities provide us with a key for reconstructing the material relations of ancient economies. In the Maya area, further intersite examinations of quantified data sets are needed to aid regional scale syntheses. These patterns must be carefully considered and compared, as luxury items are likely to be found regularly in nonelite contexts due to recycling, scavenging, or trickle down effects in societies that are focused on either prestige-based economies or market exchange. Few rural sites or small Preclassic or Classic period house mounds are excavated in the Maya area without a piece of obsidian, greenstone, marine shell, or a finely decorated potsherd being found (e.g., Freidel 1986; Sheets 2000). This effect is also a characteristic of prestige-goods economies (Muller 1997; Earle 1997). How are we to distinguish between highly stratified societies in which poorer social classes may have possessed fewer resources for purchasing nonessential valuables in the marketplace and prestige goods economies in which elite gift-giving systems limited the ability of nonelites to obtain valuables? This distinction is complicated by the fact that elite gift exchange can persist even in state market societies. Simply documenting presence/absence distributions of luxury items in nonelite contexts is insufficient for making such distinctions. The systematic documentation and comparison of relative frequencies of artifact classes is needed, with particular attention to raw material sourcing and the degree of specialized production (West, chapter 6 this volume; Sheets 2000). Such data can permit the evaluation of links between production and distribution that reflect the degree and type of market development (Hirth 1998), along with a consideration of other archaeological features such as storage facilities in redistributive state societies.

Distributional studies also reflect the relative value of artifacts and imply their mechanisms for exchange. Apical concentrations of luxury items are well documented for Classic period Maya sites, as in the case of obsidian at Tikal (Rathje 1973; Moholy-Nagy 1975; Rice 1984) and other centers (Sidrys 1976: table 1). Rice (1987a) notes that obsidian changes in value over time, and in the Terminal Classic and Postclassic periods, it is more evenly distributed among elite and commoner households at both politically central and rural sites in the Petén region. Foias' chapter in this volume reviews ethnohistoric data for the role of Postclassic period elites in Maya economy, in which regional lords derived their income primarily from the produce of their own slave-operated orchards, tribute and gifts of basic items exacted for their services, and their distant trade in high-value items. These references imply that market exchange was not under the direct dominion of elites, and that an additional realm of local and regional exchange existed in tandem with elite trading and tributary mechanisms. Although tribute is the most well-documented form of economic exchange for Classic and Postclassic period Maya polities due to hieroglyphic texts (see McAnany et al., chapter 5; Foias, chapter 8), elite distant trading, local exchange, and regional exchange probably formed equally important components of complex regional economic systems.

It is also difficult to distinguish tribute from trade in the archaeological record (O'Brien 1991: 160). Brumfiel (1991: 177) agrees with Hassig (1985: 85) that tribute and trade should be regarded as functionally alternative or complementary mechanisms that rely on military and market systems respectively to obtain nonlocal goods, though these can obviously be extended to local goods as well. These scholars have argued over whether the Aztec city of Tenochtitlan was primarily a production center and supplier of goods or, instead, an administrative center, a role that has been assigned to Classic period Maya cities as well (Ball 1993). Brumfiel (1991: 178) argues that Tenochtitlan functioned in both capacities. Aztec kings controlled high level markets that were held near their palaces, perhaps profiting from these by demanding tribute from vendors (Brumfiel 1991: 191). Such a system is also plausible for Classic period Maya centers. McAnany and colleagues (chapter 5 this volume) discuss textual evidence for Classic period Maya royals receiving cacao as tribute, however, they acknowledge that it is difficult to know to what degree cacao was brought into elite centers through either tribute or trade at various points in time as glyphic testimonies are rare. They suggest that production locales may reflect this system by their degrees of impoverishment (tribute) or affluence (trade).

Systems of Value and Exchange

Intersecting Spheres of Exchange

Chapter 3 in this volume (Freidel, Reese-Taylor, and Mora-Marín) revises our understanding of Maya luxury goods, and these authors view these items as the most highly valued commodities in a total economic system. They discuss the link between marine shell and jade objects with prestige and authority, and argue that this link was part of the valuation process in which symbolic importance affected the currency value of these items. In the economic systems of most societies, the value of an item increases with the costs of long-distance transport or the costs of an involved manufacturing process (Weigand et al. 1977; Renfrew 1977; Blanton et al. 1993: 29; Smith n.d.). Providing additional support to the observations of Freidel and colleagues (chapter 3 this volume), Foias describes the use of cacao and shell currencies in the Postclassic and early Colonial periods. Lower value commodities of regional or local origin were also an integral part of these economic systems. Commodities of varying value extended from cacao and shell luxury items all the way down to the agrarian base at this late point in Maya history (Foias, chapter 8 this volume). Smith (n.d.) outlines three useful ways of classifying Postclassic commodities throughout Mesoamerica, including function, economic value, and social context of use. Within this latter classifications are necessities, widely used (nonessential) goods, special use goods, and luxuries (Smith n.d.). His classification underscores the complexity of commodity categories, values, and exchange.

Classic Maya luxury and utilitarian economies were probably linked in important ways (Sheets 2000). Classic and Postclassic elites received both subsistence and luxury items in tribute and trade from their supporting communities or from parties external to the polity (Foias, chapter 5 this volume; McAnany et al., chapter 8 this volume). A recent study of household production and exchange from Ceren provides evidence of mutual commoner-elite dependencies and suggests that commoners had significant bartering power for goods traded in by elites (Sheets 2000).

Sponsored production and prestigious gift exchange clearly formed one dimension of the economic power base of Classic Maya kings (Ball 1993; McAnany 1993; Reentz-Budet 1994). Postclassic Maya lords continued this practice on a less conspicuous scale in conjunction with market-oriented production and trade (Masson 2000; Foias, chapter 8 this volume). Through tribute, the sponsorship of market events, and probably through direct purchasing or barter, elites of the Classic and Postclassic probably stimulated important aspects of production in spheres within and outside of gift exchange (Graham, chapter 14 this volume). Improved insight into ancient Maya political economies will result when methods to archaeologically identify mechanisms of exchange are further refined. It is also important to consider that multiple, overlapping spheres of exchange existed in the variable and complex economic systems of Maya polities.

Elsewhere in Mesoamerica, overlapping spheres of exchange have been identified for Aztec society (Berdan 1977). Reciprocity, redistribution, and market exchange can coexist within a single state economy (Whitecotton and Pailes 1986: 185; Sheets 2000). Long-distance trade in luxury items that enhances the prestige of elites is but one important aspect of a market economy (Whitecotton and Pailes 1986: 186). Distinguishing luxury from essential items is a problem that is shared by world systems theorists outside of Mesoamerica (Whitecotton and Pailes 1986: 186) and Schneider (1977: 22–24) attacks Wallerstein's (1974) distinctions of staple versus luxury items. For central Mexico, Berdan (1980) and Brumfiel (1980, 1983) propose that exchange in luxury items paved the way for trade in more essential commodities. Whitecotton and Pailes (1986: 188) hail Berdan's (1980) study for demonstrating how the desire to obtain luxury items stimulated local production of subsistence items and cotton. Berdan also documents a variety of market forms and exchange that varied from small-scale, local interaction to large-scale foreign interaction (1988: table 9.1). At some markets, subsistence items and craft goods were exchanged, while others specialized in particular products, such as wood at Coyoacan or salt at Miahuatlan (Berdan 1988). The value of commodities in the Aztec realm was affected by the intensity of effort put into their production as well as the degree to which their production was limited to particular locations (Smith n.d.). Utilitarian products that were not generally available in all areas represented greater opportunities for mercantile profit and were transported over great distances along with high value goods (Berdan 1988). Berdan's study illustrates important connections between luxury and essential commodity production and exchange, which some economic archaeologists have characterized as a false dichotomy (Peregrine 1992).

Market Variation in the Contact Period Mayan Realm

During the contact period, the Maya area had a complex system of local and regional markets and various types of merchants (Freidel 1981; Feldman 1978; Berdan, Masson, and Gasco n.d.), and this variation provides a glimpse of possible systems that may have existed earlier in Maya history. Petty vendors sold small amounts of their household surplus subsistence items, raw materials, or craft items in local markets, petty traders operated on a local level, regional merchants transported bulk commodities like cacao or cotton, professional merchants traveled great distances in the exchange of precious items, and administrative officials collected tribute from polities under their domain (Berdan, Masson, and Gasco n.d.; Roys 1957: 61; Feldman 1978: 11). Resource heterogeneity across the Maya lowlands fueled this exchange system. Coastal polities provided salt, fish, and marine shell to the interior in exchange for game, produce, and cotton (Landa 1941: 40). Northeastern Belize territories specialized in cacao, honey, beeswax, wild vanilla, achiote, and cotton and textile production, Petén polities embroidered cloth, and produced dyes, honey, beeswax, and copal, and vicinities like Bacalar specialized in wood products and canoe-making (Piña Chán 1978; Jones 1989: 103–106). Raw materials such as cotton were also valuable, and while weaving was common at communities throughout the lowlands, not all areas were suitable for cotton growing. In the Aztec realm, Berdan (1988) documents stages of elaborate textile production at locales that imported cotton for weaving industries. Similarly, people at northeastern Belize sites obtained whole marine shells for ornament manufacture. Masson's chapter in this volume (chapter 12) illustrates variation in local production at two communities in Belize, based on microregional resource heterogeneity. While Late Postclassic Maya economies were more commercialized and more international than in preceding periods, the roots of this complex system of community specialization in production and cultivated intersite dependencies through local and regional market exchange may lie in the Classic period as some scholars have argued (Freidel 1981; Blanton et al. 1993).

A common characteristic of market systems in general is that there are a variety of market locations and types. The value of goods offered at such places contributes to the formation of a market hierarchy, where fewer places, such as political centers, offer a broad range of goods and more common markets offer mundane items only (Blanton et al. 1993: 30). Blanton et al. (1993: 182) argue that the limited distribution of large utilitarian pots and the wide distribution of serving vessels at Tikal points to the existence of both local and regional markets with which this site was connected. Some specialized commercial centers, such as Ecab, are identified during the Postclassic period (Blanton et al. 1993: 196), and towns such as Chauaca and Conil were market towns where trading represented the major activity (Freidel 1981: 381). Dahlin and Ardren argue in this volume that Chunchucmil was a Classic period market town and Arlen Chase makes the same case for Caracol (1998).

Exchange Goods Values

Exchange goods such as obsidian changed in value over time in the Maya area, as transport costs were reduced and mechanisms for their exchange were altered (Sidrys 1977: table 1; Rice 1987; Zeitlin 1982; McKillop 1989: 44, 51). It is thus important to evaluate the value of individual types of goods according to their specific temporal context and the regional system in which they were exchanged. Understanding local resource availability is essential for assessing the degree to which items could only be made in certain places (Rathje 1972). The variation in availability of selected goods in the Maya area is outlined in table 1.1. As McGuire (1989) notes, the more unevenly resources are distributed, the more likely communities will be dependent on others for items critical to their basic maintenance. Rathje (1972) initially argued this point for lowland Mesoamerican civilizations.

Table 1.1 Example of Goods of Different Availability and Value in the Maya Lowlands.

Local goods	Regional goods	Distant goods utilitarian	Distant goods luxury
(made in quantity within most regions)	(not made or unevenly made in all regions, exchanged between regions within lowlands)	(made outside of lowlands)	(made outside of lowlands)
chert/chalcedony tools	Colha chert/ chalcedony tools (or other sources such as Xkichmook or El Pedernal) Colha chert eccentrics	obsidian	obsidian
limestone manos and metates	basaltic or granitic ground stone (from Maya Mountains)	basaltic or granitic ground stone	
forest products and game	forest products and game (dyes, wood, copal, bark paper, medicine, hides, meat, bone, feathers, honey)		
	Greenstone (from Maya Mountains)		greenstone or jade
pottery	trade pottery or gift cotton fish marine shell and coral (Caribbean or Gulf) cacao	trade pottery or gifts	trade pottery or gifts marine shell (Pacific)
		volcanic ash temper	metals or turquoise

The context of artifact recovery must be considered in assessing the meaning of differential artifact distributions and value systems. Archaeologists analyzing household and ritual assemblages have struggled with the categories of "ritual" and "utilitarian" as these overlap considerably (Masson 1999). For example, as McAnany notes in this volume, water jars are essential components of cave rituals in the Belize valley, and offerings of food and drink at ritual events throughout the Postclassic Maya codices and in murals of Tulum illustrate the use of ollas and serving dishes alongside incense burners (Masson 2000). While incense burners exhibit limited distributions at archaeological sites, utilitarian vessels cross both domestic and ritual contexts (Masson 1999).

Ceramicists conducting type/variety analysis also note that domestic wares are found in both elite and commoner contexts, while whole elaborate polychrome vessels are more commonly found in elite ritual funerary or cache contexts. Sullivan's chapter (chapter 7) describes some unique funerary vessels associated with Early Classic period burials in northwestern Belize. Other funerary vessels from these contexts exhibit important similarities to Petén core sites such as Uaxactun, Tikal, and Rio Azul that reflect networks of elite political alliance, emulation, or gift-giving. Decreased interregional integration and changing political alliances are implied by ceramic changes that Sullivan observes in the Late Classic period. Similarly, Cerros' political and economic position within the southern lowlands declined with political cycles in the Petén core (Reese-Taylor and Walker, chapter 4 this volume). The El Mirador-Uaxactun affiliation of this Late Preclassic center contributed to its demise in the Early Classic period as alliances shifted following Tikal's emergence as a dominant power. In the Petexbatun region, Foias observes an important temporal pattern (chapter 8). As political structures collapsed at the end of the Classic period, production of elite serving wares decreased while the manufacture of common household types endured for a longer period. The different social contexts of the production and use of these common pottery types are reflected in the more stable manufacturing trends of vessels produced by nonelites. These studies illustrate regional variation in ceramic economies and how they were linked to political actions of elites.

Lithic artifacts also exhibit varying consumption patterns that are reflected in frequencies of tools made of local, regional, and distant raw materials. Fine chert tools are commonly found in decreasing quantities at communities located at increasing distances from their sources in the Maya area. While local lithic resources were available in a patchwork fashion in the Maya lowlands and these were commonly used for daily tasks (Fedick 1991; Ford and Olson 1989: 194; Rovner 1975: 165), the quality of these outcrops was highly variable (Potter 1993). Formal lithic tools found at northern Belize sites were made primarily at the site of Colha, located in this region. Colha tools were broadly distributed throughout the Maya lowlands, though they were less common outside of northern Belize and southern Quintana Roo (Shafer and Hester 1983; Hester and Shafer 1994; Rice 1987: 216–217). Colha tools were also manufactured and distributed for two primary consumer purposes, utilitarian activities (celts, adzes, blades, smaller stemmed blades) and ritual activities (eccentrics, large stemmed blades) as Hester and Shafer (1994) and Gibson (1989) observe. Tools from Colha found at sites outside of the northern Belize region were embued with greater value, as they are primarily distributed in elite contexts (Gibson 1989: 132; Potter 1993).

Ford and Olson (1989: 206–207) suggest that political centers such El Pilar may have had more specialized or centralized chert tool production than smaller centers in the Belize valley. In this case, the use of local resources varied according the position of local communities in regional political hierarchies. More work is needed to gather a sample of comparative domestic assemblages from different types of sites in order to reconstruct the complex relationships that existed between specialization, political rank, and use of local resources. Ground stone artifacts also exhibit parallel variation in quality and quantity of raw material and types across the lowlands (Rathje 1972). Locally available limestone metates are found at many sites, but basaltic or granitic manos and metates are also common throughout all periods and many of these have been sourced to the Maya Mountains (Graham 1987: 12; chapter 14 this volume). Some areas, like those of southern Belize, did not have locally available chipped stone and were dependent on external exchange (Graham, this volume). Even where local materials are available, the presence of fine quality nonlocal chert or ground stone tools at many sites indicates that these products were desired and obtained (Rathje 1972). Unfortunately, while some commodities that were exchanged across the lowlands region may be tracked in this manner, others are not detectable archaeologically, such as hides, wood, bark, textiles, salt, cacao, cotton, and other products.

Core-Periphery Dynamics

In outlining the "core-buffer model" to explain the rise of the largest Maya kingdoms in the Petén core region, Rathje (1972) suggested that demands for nonlocal utilitarian items such as coastal salt, basaltic or granitic metates, and obsidian in the Petén zone where these resources were unavailable led to the rise of organizational hierarchies in an attempt to gain control over distant exchange networks. Core centers invented hierarchical structures and elite culture that were emulated in less-developed buffer or peripheral zones. Social and political affiliation with centers of innovation encouraged smaller centers at key nodes in buffer zone areas to cooperate in exchange with core cities. As Rathje noted, buffer zones were located either in areas of greater environmental diversity or they were spatially closer to such areas. Buffer zone populations were thus in an advantageous position to obtain exotic items not available in the interior pockets of the Petén jungles. He saw the rise of Maya civilization as contingent upon building these core-buffer economic and political relationships.

Critics (e.g., Marcus 1983: 477, 479) of Rathje's model were quick to point out that Petén settlements could have been capable of self-sufficiency through the use of the inland salt source Salinas de Nueve Cerros or by using the ash of burnt palms to produce salt. Andrews and Mock (chapter 11 this volume) suggest such sources were inadequate for the entire Maya lowlands. The use of local chipped stone and limestone manos and metates to a considerable degree suggests that people at sites in the interior Petén region could have lived without obsidian or basalt metates to maintain themselves. As Rathje (1972: 389) notes, however, this is a moot point as occupants of Petén sites (particularly political elites) desired nonlocal items whether or not they could have lived without them. Such created consumer demands formed an important part of the political economy of Maya core cities and their hinterlands of all periods as Rathje argued (1972).

Subsequent studies, such as Freidel, Reese-Taylor, and Mora-Marín's chapter in this volume (chapter 3), build on Rathje's model by pointing out that Petén elites were intent on obtaining valuable items such as shell, jade, and obsidian for purposes other than utilitarian household maintenance. The rise of powerful core centers was linked to the invention or reinvention of ideological structures and their symbols (Rathje 1972, chapter 2 this volume). Freidel et al. argue that the importation of exotics (shells and jade) from zones outside of the central lowlands was integral to the creation and dissemination of kingly power in the form of social as well as economic currency. Rathje's chapter in this book outlines a model for the social reproduction of emerging core elites in the form of architectural symbols of power, or "monstrous visual symbols." This model parallels patterns of materialization of power observed for other complex societies (DeMarrais et al. 1996; Earle 1997). The currencies discussed by Freidel et al. represent portable symbols of this same kingly ideology. The status conferred on them as well as their distant origin and scarcity resulted in their position as the most valuable of economic currencies.

Braswell's perspective (chapter 10) offered here from communities in the Maya highlands, suggests that commodity exchange relationships were not always symmetrical. Obsidian-exporting settlements near San Martin Jilotepeque exhibit little evidence of materials gained in exchange from the Maya lowlands, despite evidence that lowlands sites were the primary consumers of their products.

The degree to which coastal salt production provided an essential condiment for inland centers has been the topic of considerable debate, as the manufacture of this resource is clearly visible archaeologically at coastal sites (Andrews 1983; Valdez and Mock 1991; Kepecs 1998) but is essentially invisible in consumer contexts. As Andrews and Mock point out (chapter 11 this volume), however, the scale of salt production facilities from the Late Preclassic forward is strongly indicative of a consumer demand that far exceeded the population of nearby coastal settlements. These authors argue that inland urban centers were the likely consumers of this product. They do not claim that inland communities were incapable of making some salt as observed in the highlands today. However, the quality of coastal salt, as these authors argue, is far superior and continues to be broadly desired in Mexico for this reason. Complex economic systems create consumer demands that transcend issues of local self-sufficiency, often to a considerable extent.

Temporal Trends in Maya Political Economy

Much more is known of political dynamics in the Maya lowlands (Freidel 1981; Marcus 1993; Matthews 1991; Martin and Grube 2000) than of the economic foundations of power. Ceramic stylistic patterns indicate some important temporal trends that reflect changes in production and economic affiliation associated with the rise of Late

Preclassic and Classic period states. It has long been noted that Late Preclassic ceramic type groups exhibit broad similarities across the lowlands (Willey 1991; Gifford 1976; Rice 1981), and political power may have been concentrated at fewer, larger central state nodes at this time. Larger sites such as El Mirador in the Petén and Lamanai in Belize appear to have had fewer competitors on the same scale compared to the later proliferation of major centers in the Classic period. Does the widespread extent of Chicanel sphere ceramics imply broader networks of exchange and social affiliation associated with a less-fragmented political landscape (Willey 1991; Masson 2001)? It is difficult to answer this question based on current data, as economic studies at a range of households and communities of different status have not yet been synthesized for this period. It is clear, however, that in the southern lowlands, the hierarchical development of Rathje's "core" Petén zone was established at this time, as well as its economic trade relationships with coastal sites such as Cerros. Colha was mass-producing utilitarian tools and making eccentrics for a large network of eastern lowland consumers during the Late Preclassic (Shafer and Hester 1983; Hester and Shafer 1994). The highly valued currencies of shell, jade, and obsidian were associated with early elite contexts by this time, along with other trappings of Maya kingship (Freidel and Schele 1988; Schele and Freidel 1990).

The Classic period political landscape marks the development of a greater number of competing political centers, and efforts to consolidate power through intersite alliances are documented (Schele and Freidel 1990; Martin and Grube 2000). Ceramic style zones begin to shrink into regional pockets surrounding these alliance networks, and greater diversity is found in ceramic types between regions and within the assemblages of particular regions (Rice 1981, 1989; Masson 2001; Fry 1990) that may reflect the increased diversification of social roles in more hierarchical kingdoms (Rice 1981). The emergence of multiple ceramic style zones around clusters of city-state networks may suggest a fragmentation of larger regional exchange networks, as I have argued elsewhere (Masson 2001), following Willey (1991), Ball (1993), and Fry (1990). Earlier in time, the emergence of a greater number of competing Middle Preclassic Olmec centers in Veracruz is noted by Stark (1997) to correlate with shrinking ceramic style zones as well. Stark acknowledges the possibility that political competition contributed to the development of more insular style zones and the economic networks that they may parallel. McAnany (1989: 360) suggests that toward the latter half of the Classic period, entrenched local kingdoms may have commissioned the production of their own locally produced prestige goods, relying less on materials gained from distant sources. This argument follows Rathje's (Rathje 1973; Rathje et al. 1978) initial identification of this pattern based on the analysis of funerary offerings. Such a trend may also indicate a more insular aspect of Late Classic political economy that parallels the shrinking ceramic style zones.

The development of multiple regional style zones during the Maya Classic period may thus reflect an important aspect of production and exchange patterns, particularly of common utilitarian ceramics. Quantitative data is not yet available that will permit the assessment of parallel trends in lithic technology. This trend could be the result of political activities, such as warfare, that affected local production patterns, defined regional social boundaries more distinctly, and inhibited trade with other regions. It may also reflect a greater political role in organizing exchange mechanisms. If the development of solar market places at central political centers occurred as West (chapter 6 this volume) suggests, then exchange transactions would have become more centralized within the political heart of regional boundaries, and other exchange mechanisms that crosscut political boundaries may have been suppressed. These suggestions can be tested with further quantitative comparisons of artifact distributions.

The Terminal Classic period has been characterized as a time of transition for the southern lowlands (Rice 1987; Fry 1989; Masson and Mock n.d.) and the regionalization of ceramic styles continues to mark this period as it did in the preceding Classic periods (Rice 1989; Fry 1989; Masson 2001). During this time, external influences from the Gulf Coast and the northern lowlands appear in ceramic assemblages of some southern and eastern lowland sites (Sabloff 1970; Masson and Mock n.d.; West, chapter 6 this volume). Coastal trade also becomes more important with the rise of the northern center of Chichen Itza (McKillop 1989: 51, 1996; Dreiss and Brown 1989: 84). Kepecs argues that during the Terminal Classic/Epiclassic period in the northern Maya lowlands, Chichen Itza may have taken a more centralized role in sponsoring the production and distribution of utilitarian ceramics (Kepecs 1998). West concurs with this argument (chapter 6), but notes that it is a singular development within the Maya area. Kepecs and colleagues (Kepecs et al. 1994) effectively argue that Chichen Itza forged a military and economic empire in northern Yucatan at this time that surpasses the integration achieved by earlier Maya states.

The centralizing effects of this city's activities on economic production are perhaps explained by its greater degree of power consolidation.

In the Late Postclassic period, a great degree of uniformity in ceramic styles across regions is once again observed, particularly in Quintana Roo and northern Belize (Sanders 1960; Sabloff and Rathje 1975; Rathje 1975; Rathje et al. 1978; Connor 1983; Masson 2000, 2001). These ceramics share important similarities with those of Mayapan and its allied territories of northern Yucatan (Freidel and Sabloff 1984; Connor 1983; Peraza 1993). While evidence for centralized production has not been presented for this period, uniform attributes do imply widespread trading interactions along coastal networks. As Sabloff and Rathje (1975) argue, maritime transport networks helped to break down barriers of distance making far-flung bulk trade in utilitarian items possible between regions to an extent not previously observed. It is during this period that highland Guatemala obsidian is most common at lowland Maya sites at all levels in the settlement continuum (Rice 1984; McKillop 1996; Braswell n.d.; Masson and Chaya 2000; Masson 2000). This trend reflects the reliance on a distant commodity gained through trade for common daily tasks in Maya households. Historic records indicate that lowland territories produced various combinations of local commodities, including dyes, canoes, bark paper, cacao, honey, cotton, textiles, animal products, and salt for exchange in maritime and overland networks. Each territory specialized in particular combinations of these products according to its local resources (Scholes and Roys 1948; Piña Chán 1978).

As the ceramic trends imply, changes in production and distribution of daily items was seriously affected by political dynamics. The types of interaction elites entertained with polities outside of their realms paved the way for or obstructed the flow of particular items from other regions and from distant lands. Utilitarian and luxury good Maya exchange was linked to political activities in complex ways. The chapters in this volume explore some of this variation, and offer approaches to studying the integrated economies of commoners and elite members of Maya society.

Scale and the Analysis of Maya Economies

The analysis of Maya economies, even at the local level, involves a consideration of scale as goods obtained through exchange reflect interaction within local, regional, and distant realms. Local studies are critical for defining regional variation in interaction among settlements of different rank and function. It is also important to consider larger world contexts and social processes that affected local production and exchange economies. Rathje's core-buffer model represents a landmark attempt to identify general processes that linked the political economies of the Petén core to those of the less hierarchical surrounding zones of the Maya lowlands. As McAnany et al. (chapter 5) and Hanson observe (chapter 13) observe, this model anticipated later world systems approaches in Mesoamerican archaeology. Rathje examined relationships between core and hinterland (or peripheral) zones within specific regions and between regions within a larger Mesoamerican economic interaction sphere and this approach has been highly productive in the works of later scholars (Blanton and Feinman 1984; Kepecs et al. 1994; Kepecs and Kohl n.d.; Smith and Berdan 2000, n.d.). Core-periphery studies are of intrinsic value to archaeologists interested in broader contexts of local site developments, particularly once these concepts are freed from Wallerstein's original definition of world systems development as specifically tied to the rise of capitalism in the western world (Champion 1989; Smith and Berdan 2000). The development of interdependent distant economies can be studied among societies of lesser complexity and scale (Peregrine 1992; Champion 1989). Blanton et al. (1993: 219–224) argue that Wallerstein's classifications of world empire (a world system dominated by a single polity) and world economy (a set of interlinked regional economies under the domain of sovereign states) do not apply to Mesoamerica, except for the Late Postclassic period. In this period, they suggest that a world economy develops. They make this claim based on the lack of prior evidence for interregional dependencies in items essential for daily life, and they argue that prestige-goods exchange systems among elites were the primary basis for interregional interaction prior to the Late Postclassic. In some cases, obsidian exchange may be an exception to this pattern (Whitecotton and Pailes 1986: 192; Blanton et al. 1993: 221). Blanton et al. further propose that within regions (such as smaller scale Classic period polities within the Maya lowlands), prestige-goods exchange was not the sole basis of the economy, and that market-oriented exchange in bulk items probably was probably common. Distance and limitations on transport were the primary curtailing factors for the development of interregional or long distance exchange dependencies in bulky utilitarian items (Claessen and van de Velde 1991: 16). For this reason, prestige-goods exchange forms the basis of many early state long distance economic exchanges (Claessen and van de Velde 1991: 14–15), although portable essentials like salt or obsidian can become incorporated into such networks.

While Champion (1989) and McGuire (1986: 245) note that peripheral areas are often understudied compared to core areas, this pattern does not hold true for the Maya area. Much archaeological research on Maya economy has been performed in areas like Classic period Belize, which was peripheral relative to the Petén core. However, core-periphery relationships need greater attention and several chapters in this volume examine the changing nature of this phenomenon (chapters 4, 5, 7, 10, 11, and 12). McAnany et al.'s investigation of the cacao-producing settlements of the Belize Xibun Valley attacks a difficult archaeological problem for the Maya area (chapter 5). Inscriptions and art of the Classic period attest to the high value of cacao in elite exchanges, and contact period Maya economies relied on currencies such as textiles, cacao, copper bells, beads, and *Spondylus* shells. Cacao is difficult to detect archaeologically at both production and consumption localities. As the Petén core environment was less suitable for cacao production at Spanish contact and Belize valleys like the Xibun are known to have grown this cash crop at this time, these scholars seek to define the relationship between the Xibun and its powerful neighbors to the west.

Hanson's chapter also embraces a world systems framework to explain local changes in household economics at a Colonial period settlement in northern Yucatan. It is clear from his analyses that the impacts of the Spanish conquest in Mesoamerica and the Colonial period world system of interaction are profoundly mirrored within the small microcosm of domestic units at Tiquibalón. His study underscores the appropriateness of utilizing household archaeology for reconstructing the effects of larger world processes on communities enjoined into those worlds. Hanson follows up on another seminal work by Rathje (1983), who advocates the analysis of household data in order to understand the economic organization of societies.

Maya Economy and Social Transformation

Sabloff and Rathje's work on the Postclassic period (Sabloff and Rathje 1975; Rathje 1975) focused on the development of Maya mercantile society that was facilitated by maritime trading networks around the coast of the Yucatan peninsula. Their model has significantly revised understanding of Postclassic period social developments through reinterpreting signs of political decentralization and deflation in the scale of social hierarchy. They revised descriptions of Postclassic society as a devolved product of earlier civilization, arguing instead that the Postclassic Mayan realm was a transformed society that offered more fluid opportunities for social mobility and entrepreneurship than its Classic period predecessors. In their view, Postclassic production modes were efficient, and elaborate investments in monuments glorifying monolithic individual kings were no longer believed to be essential for social maintenance. Along with Malcolm Webb (1964), these scholars suggested that the surplus of social energies was reinvested into the trading efforts of merchants operating at various scales. This mercantile environment resulted in a greater distribution of resources (i.e., trade items and profits from them) more broadly across all sectors of the population. Comparisons with maturing Old World civilizations also identify the development of extensive, decentralized networks with open market exchange in some regions (Webb 1964; Mann 1986; Masson 2000). Eisenstadt (1981) attributes the breakdown in core areas of political power in part to rising power among nonpolitical, autonomous mercantile or literati sectors, and Rathje (1972) acknowledged this dynamic in his delineation of the core-buffer model to explain the Petén decline.

At the end of the Classic period, the breakdown of southern kingdoms was reflected in hieroglyphic evidence for the rising power of secondary elites at various kingdoms such as Yaxchilan, Copan, and the Petexbatun (Schele and Freidel 1990). Increased autonomy of secondary elites may also be reflected in general trends that occurred in the Terminal Classic transition from Classic to Postclassic society in the Maya lowlands. These trends include the following: trade networks became outward-looking, smaller rural sites had greater access to distant objects, ceramic production became more autonomous and regionalized, funerary offerings of the elite became less sumptuous and consisted of more locally made items, and many centers suffered from warfare and destruction (Rathje 1973; Rice 1987; Fry 1989; Demarest 1997). Increasing commercialization of the economy and more open market systems accompany the collapse of strong centralized states in the Old World, and Blanton et al. (1993: 212–213) argue that this trend is also observed for Postclassic Mesoamerica. Along with Jeremy Sabloff, William Rathje has helped advance the understanding of the Maya Classic-to- Postclassic transition by comparing this development to parallel cases in world history. The analysis of political economies continues to have much to contribute to explaining fundamental social transformations in Maya history.

References

Andrews, Anthony P.
1983 *Maya Salt Production and Trade*. Tucson: University of Arizona Press.
Ball, Joseph W.
1993 "Pottery, Potters, Palaces, and Polities: Some Socioeconomic and Political Implications of Late Classic Maya Ceramic Industries." Pp. 243–272 in *Lowland Maya Civilization in the Eighth Century A.D.*, edited by Jeremy Sabloff and John Henderson. Washington, D.C.: Dumbarton Oaks.
Berdan, Frances F.
1977 "Distributive Mechanisms in the Aztec Economy." Pp. 91–101 in *Peasant Livelihood: Studies in Economic Anthropology and Cultural Ecology*, edited by Rhoda Dow Halperin. New York: St. Martin's.
1980 "Aztec Merchants and Markets: Local-Level Economic Activity in a Nonindustrial Empire." *Mexicon* 2: 37–41.
1988 "Principles of Regional and Long-Distance Trade in the Aztec Empire." Pp. 639–656 in *Smoke and Mist: Mesoamerican Studies in Memory of Thelma D. Sullivan*, edited by J. Kathryn Josserand and Karen Dakin. Oxford: British Archaeological Reports, International Series No. 402.
Berdan, Frances F., Marilyn A. Masson, and Janine Gasco
n.d. "An International Economy." In *The Postclassic Mesoamerican World*, edited by Michael E. Smith and Frances F. Berdan. Salt Lake City: University of Utah Press, forthcoming.
Blanton, Richard E., and Gary M. Feiman
1984 "The Mesoamerican World System." *American Anthropologist* 86: 673–682.
Blanton, Richard E., Gary M. Feinman, Stephen A. Kowalewski, and Peter N. Peregrine
1996 "A Dual-Processual Theory for the Evolution of Mesoamerican Civilization." *Current Anthropology* 37(1): 1–14.
Blanton, Richard E., Stephen A. Kowalewski, Gary M. Feinman, and Laura M. Finsten
1993 *Ancient Mesoamerica: A Comparison of Change in Three Regions*, 2d ed. Cambridge: Cambridge University Press.
Braswell, Geoffrey E.
n.d. "Postclassic Mesoamerican Obsidian Exchange Spheres." In *The Postclassic Mesoamerican World*, edited by Michael E. Smith and Frances Berdan. Salt Lake City: University of Utah Press, forthcoming.
Brumfiel, Elizabeth M.
1980 "Specialization, Market Exchange, and the Aztec State: A View from Huexotla." *Current Anthropology* 21: 459–478.
1983 "Aztec State Making: Ecology, Structure, and Origin of the State." *American Anthropologist* 85: 261–284.

1991 "Tribute and Commerce in Imperial Cities: The Case of Xaltocan, Mexico."
Pp. 177–198 in *Early State Economics*, edited by Henri J. M. Claessen and Pieter
van de Velde. Political and Legal Anthropology Volume 8. New Brunswick:
Transaction Publishers.

Champion, Timothy C.
1989 "Introduction." Pp. 1–21 in *Centre and Periphery: Comparative Studies in
Archaeology*, edited by Timothy C. Champion. London: Unwin Hyman.

Chase, Arlen F.
1998 "Planeación Civica e Integración de Sitio en Caracol, Belize: Definiendo
una Economía Administrada del Periodo Clasico Maya." Pp. 26–44 in *Los
Investigaciones de la Cultura Maya* 6 (Tomo I). Campeche, Mexico: Secud,
Universidad Autonoma de Campeche.

Chase, Diane Z., Arlen F. Chase, and William A. Haviland
1990 "The Classic Maya City: Reconsidering the 'Mesoamerican Urban Tradition.'" *American Anthropologist* 92: 499–506.

Claessen, Henri J. M., and Pieter van de Velde
1991 "Introduction." Pp. 1–29 in *Early State Economics*, edited by Henri J. M.
Claessen and Pieter van de Velde. Political and Legal Anthropology Volume
8. New Brunswick: Transaction Publishers.

Connor, Judith G.
1983 "The Ceramics of Cozumel, Quintana Roo, Mexico." Ph.D. dissertation,
University of Arizona. Ann Arbor: University Microfilms.

Demarest, Arthur A.
1997 "The Vanderbilt Petexbatun Regional Archaeological Project 1989–1994:
Overview, History, and Major Results of a Multi-disciplinary Study of the
Classic Maya Collapse." *Ancient Mesoamerica* 8(2): 209–227.

DeMarrais, Elizabeth, Luis Jaime Castillo, and Timothy Earle
1996 "Ideology, Materialization, and Power Strategies." *Current Anthropology*
37: 15–31.

Dreiss, Meredith L., and David O. Brown
1989 "Obsidian Exchange Patterns in Belize." Pp. 57–90 in *Prehistoric Maya
Economies of Belize*, edited by Patricia A. McAnany and Barry L. Isaac. Research in Economic Anthropology Supplement 4. Greenwich, Conn.: JAI
Press.

Earle, Timothy K.
1982 "The Ecology and Politics of Primitive Valuables." Pp. 65–83 in *Culture
and Ecology: Eclectic Perspectives*, edited by John G. Kennedy and Robert B.
Edgerton. Special Publications of the American Anthropological Association
No. 15. Washington, D.C.: American Anthropological Association.
1997 *How Chiefs Come to Power*. Stanford: Stanford University Press.

Ehrenreich, Robert M., Carole L. Crumley, and Janet E. Levy, editors
1995 *Heterarchy and the Analysis of Complex Societies*. Arlington, Va.: Archeological Papers of the American Anthropological Association Number 6.

Eisenstadt, Shmuel N.
1981 "Cultural Traditions and Political Dynamics: The Origins and Modes of
Ideological Politics." *British Journal of Sociology* 32: 155–181.

Fedick, Scott
1991 "Chert Production and Consumption among Classic Period Maya House-holds." Pp. 103–118 in *Maya Stone Tools*, edited by Thomas R. Hester and Harry J. Shafer. Madison, Wis.: Prehistory Press.

Feldman, Lawrence H.
1978 "Moving Merchandise in Protohistoric Central Quauhtemallan." Pp. 7–17 in *Mesoamerican Communication Routes and Cultural Contacts*, edited by Thomas A. Lee and Carlos Navarette. Papers of the New World Archaeological Foundation No. 40. Provo, Utah: New World Archaeological Foundation.

Ford, Anabel, and Kirsten Olson
1989 "Aspects of Ancient Maya Household Economy: Variation in Chipped Stone Production and Consumption." Pp. 185–214 in *Prehistoric Maya Economies of Belize*, edited by Patricia A. McAnany and Barry L. Isaac. Research in Economic Anthropology Supplement 4. Greenwich, Conn.: JAI Press.

Freidel, David A.
1981 "The Political Economics of Residential Dispersion Among the Lowland Maya." Pp. 371–382 in *Lowland Maya Settlement Patterns*, edited by Wendy Ashmore. Albuquerque: University of New Mexico Press.
1986 "Terminal Classic Lowland Maya: Successes, Failures, and Aftermaths." Pp. 409–430 in *Late Lowland Maya Civilization: Classic-to- Postclassic*, edited by Jeremy A. Sabloff and E. W. Andrews, V. Albuquerque: University of New Mexico Press.

Freidel, David A., and Jeremy A. Sabloff
1984 *Cozumel: Late Maya Settlement Patterns*. New York: Academic Press.

Freidel, David A., and Linda Schele
1988 "Kingship in the Late Preclassic Lowlands: The Instruments and Places of Ritual Power." *American Anthropologist* 90: 547–567.

Fry, Robert E.
1980 "Models of Exchange for Major Shape Classes of Lowland Maya Pottery." Pp. 3–18 in *Models and Methods in Regional Exchange*, edited by R. E. Fry. SAA Papers No. 1. Washington, D.C.: Society for American Archaeology.
1989 "Regional Ceramic Distributional Patterning in Northern Belize: The View from Pulltrouser Swamp." Pp. 91–114 in *Prehistoric Maya Economies of Belize*, edited by Patricia A. McAnany and Barry L. Isaac. Research in Economic Anthropology Supplement 4. Greenwich, Conn.: JAI Press.
1990 "Disjunctive Growth in the Maya Lowlands." Pp. 285–300 in *Precolumbian Population History in the Maya Lowlands*, edited by T. Patrick Culbert and Don S. Rice. Albuquerque: University of New Mexico Press.

Gibson, Eric C.
1989 "The Organization of Late Preclassic Maya Lithic Economy in the Eastern Lowlands." Pp. 115–138 in *Prehistoric Maya Economies of Belize*, edited by Patricia A. McAnany and Barry L. Isaac. Research in Economic Anthropology Supplement 4. Greenwich, Conn.: JAI Press.

Gifford, James C.
1976 *Prehistoric Pottery Analysis and the Ceramics of Barton Ramie in the Belize Valley*. Volume 18. Memoirs of the Peabody Museum of Archaeology and Ethnology. Cambridge, Mass.: Harvard University.

Graham, Elizabeth A.
1987 "Terminal Classic to Early Historic Period Vessel Forms from Belize." Pp. 73–98 in *Maya Ceramics*, edited by Prudence Rice and Robert Sharer. Oxford: BAR International Series 345, Great Britain.

Hassig, Ross
1985 *Trade, Tribute, and Transportation: The Sixteenth Century Political Economy of the Valley of Mexico*. Norman: University of Oklahoma Press.

Hester, Thomas R., and Harry J. Shafer
1994 "The Ancient Maya Craft Community at Colha, Belize, and Its External Relationships." Pp. 48–63 in *Archaeological Views from the Countryside: Village Communities in Early Complex Societies*, edited by G. M. Schwartz and S. E. Falconer. Washington, D.C.: Smithsonian Institution Press.

Hirth, Kenneth
1998 "The Distributional Approach." *Current Anthropology* 40: 520–527.

Jones, Grant D.
1989 *Maya Resistance to Spanish Rule: Time and History on a Colonial Frontier*. Albuquerque: University of New Mexico Press.

Kepecs, Susan
1998 "Diachronic Ceramic Evidence and Its Social Implications in the Chikinchel Region, Northeast Yucatan, Mexico." *Ancient Mesoamerica* 9(1): 121–136.

Kepecs, Susan, Gary M. Feinman, and Sylviane Boucher
1994 "Chichen Itza and Its Hinterland: A World Systems Perspective." *Ancient Mesoamerica* 5: 141–158.

Kepecs, Susan, and Phillip Kohl
n.d. "Conceptualizing Macroregional Interaction: World Systems Theory and the Archaeological Record." In *The Postclassic Mesoamerican World*, edited by Michael E. Smith and Frances F. Berdan. Salt Lake City: University of Utah Press, forthcoming.

King, Eleanor, and Daniel Potter
1994 "Small Sites in Prehistoric Maya Socioeconomic Organization: A Perspective from Colha, Belize." Pp. 64–90 in *Archaeological Views from the Countryside: Village Communities in Early Complex Societies*, edited by G. M. Schwartz and S. E. Falconer. Washington, D.C.: Smithsonian Institution Press.

Landa, Friar Diego de
1941 *Landa's Relaciones de las Cosas de Yucatan*, translated by Alfred Tozzer. Papers of the Peabody Museum of Archaeology and Ethnology 18. Cambridge, Mass.: Harvard University.

Mann, Michael
1986 *The Sources of Social Power, Volume I: A History of Power from the Beginning to A.D. 1760*. Cambridge: Cambridge University Press.

Marcus, Joyce
1983 "Lowland Maya Archaeology at the Crossroads." *American Antiquity* 48: 454–488.

1993 "Ancient Maya Political Organization." Pp. 111–184 in *Lowland Maya Civilization in the Eighth Century A.D.*, edited by Jeremy A. Sabloff and John Henderson. Washington, D.C.: Dumbarton Oaks.

Martin, Simon, and Nikolai Grube
2000 *The Chronicles of Maya Kings and Queens.* London: Thames and Hudson.

Masson, Marilyn A.
1999 "Postclassic Maya Ritual at Laguna de On Island, Belize." *Ancient Mesoamerica* 10: 51–68.
2000 *In the Realm of Nachan Kan: Postclassic Maya Archaeology at Laguna de On, Belize.* Boulder: University of Colorado Press.
2001 "Changing Patterns of Ceramic Stylistic Diversity in the Pre-Hispanic Maya Lowlands." *Acta Archaeologica* 73: 1–30.

Masson, Marilyn A., and Henry Chaya
2000 "Obsidian Trade Connections at the Postclassic Maya Site of Laguna de On, Belize." *Lithic Technology* 25: 135–144.

Marilyn A. Masson, and Shirley Boteler Mock
2001 "Maya Cultural Adaptations from the Terminal Classic-to-Postclassic Period at Lagoon Sites in Northern Belize as Reflected in Changing Ceramic Industries." In *The Terminal Classic in the Maya Lowlands: Collapse, Transition, and Transformation*, edited by Don S. Rice, Prudence M. Rice, and Arthur A. Demarest. Boulder, Colo.: Westview Press, forthcoming.

Matthews, Peter
1991 "Classic Maya Emblem Glyphs." Pp. 19–29 in *Classic Maya Political History: Hieroglyphs and Archaeological Evidence*, edited by T. Patrick Culbert. Cambridge: Cambridge University Press.

McAnany, Patricia A.
1989 "Economic Foundations of Prehistoric Maya Society: Paradigms and Concepts." Pp. 347–372 in *Prehistoric Maya Economies of Belize*, edited by Patricia A. McAnany and Barry L. Isaac. Research in Economic Anthropology Supplement 4. Greenwich, Conn.: JAI Press.
1993 "The Economics of Social Power and Wealth among Eighth-Century Maya Households." Pp. 65–90 in *Lowland Maya Civilization in the Eighth Century A.D.*, edited by Jeremy Sabloff and John Henderson. Washington, D.C.: Dumbarton Oaks.
1995 *Living with the Ancestors: Kinship and Kingship in Ancient Maya Society.* Austin: University of Texas Press.

McGuire, Randall H.
1986 "Economies and Modes of Production in the Prehistoric Southwestern Periphery." Pp. 243–269 in *Ripples in the Chichimec Sea: New Considerations of Southwestern-Mesoamerican Interactions*, edited by F. J. Mathien and R. H. McGuire. Carbondale: Southern Illinois University Press.
1989 "The Greater Southwest as a Periphery of Mesoamerica." Pp. 40–66 in *Centre and Periphery: Comparative Studies in Archaeology*, edited by Timothy C. Champion. London: Unwin Hyman.
1992 *A Marxist Archaeology.* San Diego: Academic Press.

McKillop, Heather

1989 "Coastal Maya Trade: Obsidian Densities at Wild Cane Cay." Pp. 17–56 in *Prehistoric Maya Economies of Belize*, edited by Patricia A. McAnany and Barry L. Isaac. Research in Economic Anthropology Supplement 4. Greenwich, Conn.: JAI Press.

1996 "Ancient Maya Trading Ports and the Integration of Long-Distance and Regional Economies: Wild Cane Cay in South-Coastal Belize." *Ancient Mesoamerica* 7: 49–62.

Millon, Rene, R. B. Drewitt, and George L. Cowgill

1973 "The Teotihuacan Map." In *Urbanization at Teotihuacan, Mexico*, vol. 1, part 2, edited by Rene Millon. Austin: University of Texas Press.

Moholy-Nagy, Hattula

1975 "Obsidian at Tikal, Guatemala." *XLI Congreso Internacional de Americanistas, Actas*, vol. 1. Mexico City: Congress.

Muller, Jon

1997 *Mississippian Political Economy*. New York: Plenum Press.

O'Brien, Patricia J.

1991 "Early State Economics: Cahokia, Capital of the Ramey State." Pp. 143–176 in *Early State Economics*, edited by Henri J. M. Claessen and Pieter van de Velde. Political and Legal Anthropology Volume 8. New Brunswick: Transaction Publishers.

Peraza Lope, Carlos Alberto

1993 *Estudio y Secuencia del Material Cerámico de San Gervasio, Cozumel*. Tésis Profesional, Universidad Autonoma de Yucatán, Merida, México.

Peregrine, Peter N.

1992 *Mississippian Evolution: A World-system Perspective*. Madison, Wis.: Prehistory Press.

Piña Chan, R.

1978 "Commerce in the Yucatec Peninsula: The Conquest and Colonial Period." Pp. 37–48 in *Mesoamerican Communication Routes and Culture Contacts*, edited by T. A. Lee and C. Navarrete. Papers of the New World Archaeological Foundation 40. Provo, Utah: Brigham Young University.

Potter, Daniel R.

1993 "Analytical Approaches to Late Classic Maya Industries." Pp. 273–298 in *Lowland Maya Civilization in the Eighth Century A.D.*, edited by Jeremy Sabloff and John Henderson. Washington, D.C.: Dumbarton Oaks.

Potter, Daniel R., and Eleanor M. King

1995 "A Heterarchical Approach to Lowland Maya Socioeconomies." Pp. 17–32 in *Heterarchy and the Analysis of Complex Societies*, edited by R. M. Ehrenreich, C. L. Crumley, and J. E. Levy. Arlington, Va.: Archeological Papers of the American Anthropological Association Number 6.

Rands, Robert L., and Ronald L. Bishop

1980 "Resource Procurement Zones and Patterns of Ceramic Exchange in the Palenque Region, Mexico." Pp. 19–46 in *Models and Methods in Regional Exchange*, edited by Robert E. Fry. SAA Papers No. 1. Washington, D.C.: Society for American Archaeology.

Rathje, William L.
1972 "Praise the Gods and Pass the Metates: A Hypothesis of the Development of Lowland Rainforest Civilizations in Mesoamerica." Pp. 365–392 in *Contemporary Archaeology: A Guide to Theory and Contributions*, edited by Mark P. Leone. Carbondale: Southern Illinois University Press.
1973 "Classic Maya Development and Denouement: A Research Design." Pp. 405–454 in *The Classic Maya Collapse*, edited by T. Patrick Culbert. Albuquerque: University of New Mexico Press.
1975 "The Last Tango in Mayapan: A Tentative Trajectory of Production-Distribution Systems." Pp. 409–448 in *Ancient Civilization and Trade*, edited by J. A. Sabloff and C. C. Lamberg-Karlovsky. Albuquerque: University of New Mexico Press.
1983 "To the Salt of the Earth: Some Comments on Household Archaeology among the Maya." Pp. 23–34 in *Prehistoric Settlement Patterns: Essays in Honor of Gordon R. Willey*, edited by Evon Vogt and Richard Leventhal. Albuquerque: University of New Mexico Press.
Rathje, William L., David A. Gregory, and Frederick M. Wiseman
1978 "Trade Models and Archaeological Problems: Classic Maya Examples." Pp. 147–175 in *Mesoamerican Communication Routes and Culture Contacts*, edited by T. A. Lee and C. Navarrete. Papers of the New World Archaeological Foundation 40. Provo, Utah: Brigham Young University.
Reentz-Budet, Dorie
1994 *Painting the Maya Universe: Royal Ceramics of the Classic Period.* Durham, N.C.: Duke University Press.
Renfrew, Colin
1977 "Alternative Models for Exchange and Spatial Distribution." Pp. 71–90 in *Exchange Systems in Prehistory*, edited by T. K. Earle and J. E. Ericson. New York: Academic Press.
Rice, Prudence M.
1981 "Evolution of Specialized Pottery Production: A Trial Model." *Current Anthropology* 22(3): 219–240.
1984 "Obsidian Procurement in the Central Petén Lakes Region, Guatemala." *Journal of Field Archaeology* 11: 181–194.
1987 "Economic Change in the Lowland Maya Late Classic Period." Pp. 76–85 in *Specialization, Exchange, and Complex Societies*, edited by E. M. Brumfiel and T. K. Earle. Cambridge: Cambridge University Press.
1989 "Ceramic Diversity, Production, and Use." Pp. 109–117 in *Quantifying Diversity in Archaeology*, edited by Robert D. Leonard and George T. Jones. Cambridge: Cambridge University Press.
Rovner, Irwin
1975 "Lithic Sequences from the Maya Lowlands." Ph.D. dissertation, University of Wisconsin, Madison.
Roys, Ralph L.
1957 *The Political Geography of the Yucatan Maya.* Washington, D.C.: Carnegie Institute of Washington. Publication 613.

Sabloff, Jeremy A.
1970 "Type Descriptions of the Fine Paste Ceramics of the Bayal Boca Complex, Seibal, Petén, Guatemala." Pp. 357–404 in *Monographs and Papers in Maya Archaeology*, edited by William R. Bullard. Papers of the Peabody Museum of American Archaeology and Ethnology Volume 61. Cambridge, Mass.: Peabody Museum, Harvard University.

Sabloff, Jeremy A., and William L. Rathje
1975 "The Rise of a Maya Merchant Class." *Scientific American* 233: 72–82.

Sanders, William T.
1960 *Prehistoric Ceramics and Settlement Patterns in Quintana Roo, Mexico.* Contributions to American Anthropology and History 12(60). Washington, D.C.: Carnegie Institute of Washington. Publication 606.

Schele, Linda, and David A. Freidel
1990 *A Forest of Kings.* New York: William Morrow.

Schneider, J.
1977 "Was There a Pre-Capitalist World System?" *Peasant Studies* 6: 20–29.

Scholes, Frances V., and Ralph L. Roys
1948 *The Maya Chontal Indians of Acalan-Tixchel: A Contribution to the History and Ethnography of the Yucatan Peninsula.* Washington, D.C.: Carnegie Institute of Washington. Publication 560.

Shafer, Harry J., and Thomas R. Hester
1983 "Ancient Maya Chert Workshops in Northern Belize, Central America." *American Antiquity* 48(3): 519–543.

Sharer, Robert J.
1994 *The Ancient Maya.* Fifth Edition. Stanford: Stanford University Press.

Sheets, Payson
2000 "Provisioning the Ceren Household: The Vertical Economy, Village Economy, and Household Economy in the Southeast Maya Periphery." *Ancient Mesoamerica* 11: 217–230.

Sidrys, Raymond V.
1976 "Classical Maya Obsidian Trade." *American Antiquity* 41: 449–464.
1977 "Mass-distance Measures for the Maya Obsidian Trade." Pp. 91–107 in *Exchange Systems in Prehistory*, edited by Timothy K. Earle and Jonathon E. Ericson. San Francisco: Academic Press.

Smith, Carol A.
1976 "Exchange Systems and the Spatial Distribution of Elites: The Organization of Stratification in Agrarian Societies." Pp. 309–374 in *Regional Analysis*, vol. II, edited by Carol A. Smith. New York: Academic Press.

Smith, M. Estellie
1991 "The ABC's of Political Economy." Pp. 31–74 in *Early State Economics*, edited by Henri J. M. Claessen and Pieter van de Velde. Political and Legal Anthropology Volume 8. New Brunswick, N.J.: Transaction Publishers.

Smith, Michael E.
1999 "Comment on Hirth's 'The Distributional Approach.'" *Current Anthropology* 40: 528–529.

n.d. "Key Commodities." In *The Postclassic Mesoamerican World*, edited by Michael E. Smith and Frances F. Berdan. Salt Lake City: University of Utah Press, forthcoming.

Smith, Michael E., and Frances F. Berdan
2000 "The Postclassic Mesoamerican World System: Position Paper." *Current Anthropology* 41: 283–286.
n.d. "Spatial Structure of the Mesoamerican World System." In *The Postclassic Mesoamerican World*, edited by Michael E. Smith and Frances F. Berdan. Salt Lake City: University of Utah Press, forthcoming.

Smith, Michael E., and Marilyn A. Masson
2000 *The Ancient Civilizations of Mesoamerica: A Reader*. Malden, Mass.: Blackwell.

Stark, Barbara L.
1997 "Gulf Lowland Settlement in Perspective." Pp. 278–309 in *Olmec to Aztec: Settlement Patterns in the Ancient Gulf Lowlands*, edited by Barbara L. Stark and Philip J. Arnold III. Tucson: University of Arizona Press.

Valdez, Fred, Jr., and Shirley B. Mock
1991 "Additional Considerations for Prehispanic Saltmaking in Belize." *American Antiquity* 6(3): 520–525.

Wallerstein, Immanuel
1974 *The Modern World-System*, vol. 1. Oxford: Oxford University Press.

Webb, Malcolm C.
1964 "The Post-Classic Decline of the Petén Maya: An Interpretation in Light of a General Theory of State Society." Ph.D. dissertation, University of Michigan, University Microfilms, Ann Arbor.

Weigand, Phil, Garman Harbottle, and Edward Sayre
1977 "Turquoise Sources and Source Analysis: Mesoamerica and the Southwestern U.S.A." Pp. 15–34 in *Exchange Systems in Prehistory*, edited by T. K. Earle and J. E. Ericson. New York: Academic Press.

Whitecotton, Joseph W., and Richard A. Pailes
1986 "New World Precolumbian World Systems." Pp. 183–204 in *Ripples in the Chichimec Sea: New Considerations of Southwestern-Mesoamerican Interactions*, edited by Frances Joan Mathien and Randall H. McGuire. Carbondale: Southern Illinois University Press.

Willey, Gordon R.
1991 "Horizontal Integration and Regional Diversity: An Alternating Process in the Rise of Civilizations." *American Antiquity* 56(2): 197–215.

Zeitlin, Robert N.
1982 "Toward a More Comprehensive Model of Interregional Commodity Distribution: Political Variables and Prehistoric Obsidian Procurement in Mesoamerica." *American Antiquity* 47: 260–275.

Chapter Two

The Nouveau Elite Potlatch: One Scenario for the Monumental Rise of Early Civilizations

William L. Rathje

Virtually all theories of the rise of civilization, whether they focus on agricultural intensification, warfare, trade, or ideology, are fundamentally functional and hinge on some prime cause. Rarely do theories focus on the process by which centralization occurs. This chapter combines the potlatch "waste" enigma as described by Boas and explained by Codere into a model that outlines the nature of one mechanism through which resources and power were centralized within the world's first civilizations. The starting point is Big Man systems.

Pioneer anthropologist Franz Boas helped to add a new word to the English language—"potlatch," meaning to give away and/or intentionally destroy valuable resources in order to gain status. Boas' study of the Northwest Coast Kwakiutl defined the classic "Big Man" system. Although Big Man potlatches are now known worldwide, the post-contact Northwest Coast is the only locale where potlatches regularly incorporated wanton destruction of resources. As a result, the post-contact Kwakiutl potlatch is a "waste" enigma (see Trigger 1990: 124–128; Zipf 1949): Why make a public display out of the destruction of large quantities of valuables?

for Gordon R. Willey

Most popular theories of the rise of civilization are fundamentally functional and rarely focus on the process by which the centralization of resources and authority come about, especially with respect to the actions or agendas of individuals or specific institutions (for exceptions see Flannery 1972; Yoffee 1993; and Clark and Blake 1994). One key exception is Hayden and Gargett's model (1990) of the "emergence of individual power." Starting from their model, this chapter attempts to use an explanation of the Kwakiutl "waste" enigma to outline one mechanism—the *nouveau elite potlatch*—through which labor, resources, and power may have become centralized in some of the world's first civilizations. The goal of describing this mechanism is to make a small contribution to a social evolutionary theory that links archaeological issues to archaeological data (see Yoffee 1993).

The theoretical structure of the *nouveau elite potlatch* mechanism fits congenially within Hayden and Gargett's 1990 model, especially as expanded by Clark and Blake (1994) to outline "the development of hereditary rank distinctions." The model begins with a few givens: that high-yield resources have been identified by the subject society and that ambitious political actors play key roles through self-interest "based upon culturally bound rational choice . . . which in the case of the early development of hereditary ranking was very likely a Big Man strategy of competitive generosity." In such cases, "competition for 'prestige' consists of rivalry for continual public recognition by supporters" together with access to their labor and resources (Clark and Blake 1994: 18, 21). "Simply put, followers tag along because they benefit from doing so, retaining the option of shifting their loyalty," and the most successful competitors for power "are those who provide the most physical, social and/or spiritual benefits to the most people on the most reliable basis." And finally, according to the model, competitors capitalize upon "*innovation and risk taking*" (Clark and Blake 1994: 19, 21 [emphasis mine]; see also Hayden and Gargett 1990: 13).

Brunton (1975: 556) argued that to understand the origins of hereditary social stratification, we need to "examine whether the main wealth items can be controlled and given limited circulation and convertibility . . . *This control is a cultural act.* . . . Where conditions are such that [competitors] can *act to limit strategic . . . items and pre-empt others from gaining access to them*, then the stage is set" (emphasis mine). Many of the cultural acts that serve to limit access to wealth have archaeological implications. One set of such acts centers on *social production,* defined by Brookfield (1972) as *the objectification of labor in basically noneconomic forms with social and ideological signifi-cance*—a temple, a burial, a scepter, ritual paraphernalia—what Binford (1962) called *socio-technic* and *ideo-technic* artifacts.

There seem to be at least two basic modes of handling the generation and disposal of social production, one that emphasizes the circulation of labor and strategic goods and one that places a far greater emphasis on limiting access to them. The first form of handling social production, a *social production dispersal* system, is usually typified by smaller societies and involves individual sponsorship of reciprocal exchanges and a resultant dispersal of wealth throughout such societies, albeit through the hands of many individuals who are economically and politically advantaged. For example, among Big Men in Melanesia, arm-shells and other status items are not usually held as one individual's or group's private property; instead, many are continually redistributed at public ceremonies, thereby giving competitors temporary access to power as its material symbols pass through their hands.

The second social production format, an *embedding* system, is typi-fied by larger societies and involves community participation in the building of public spaces and temples or the burying of important personages or objects. In contrast to dispersal regimes, within an embedding system great caches of labor and resources are implanted (or trapped) in material extravaganzas that (1) by the act of their creation decrease the access of potential competitors to both labor and resources, and (2) from that time on continually legitimize the prestige and authority of the elite who constructed them (see Kirch 1990). Conspicuous consumption centers, such as Teotihuacan and Tikal in Mesoamerica, are literally classic examples.

These two patterns of handling social production are elements in contrasting systems where power is more achieved and dispersed in a relatively fluid ranking system versus ascribed and centralized in a more rigid system of social stratification (see Fried 1967). I believe that the link between different uses of social production and differ-ent sociopolitical systems is crucial to understanding both (see Rathje 1978).

The crux of my argument is that the beginnings of a social pro-duction embedding system—in the form of supplying facilities and accouterments for community feasts—can take place conveniently within the parameters of a dispersal system. Once labor and resource embedding actions are introduced into a society, Big Men are free to compete by withdrawing as much labor and material as they possibly can from the reach of other Big Men and into material symbols of community ideology, thus limiting the competition for power to a smaller pool of Big Men who become a *nouveau elite*.

The starting point for an explicit model of the *nouveau elite potlatch* mechanism is the nature of the Big Man dispersal system.

1. At a large public feast, Big Man 1 gives Big Man 2 resources collected by Big Man 1's followers. At the same ceremony, Big Man 2 redistributes many of the resources to his followers. And, of course, everyone has a jolly-good time feasting.

2. A few years later, Big Man 2 collects similar resources from his followers and, at another public ceremony, gives Big Man 1 double or more the resources back.

3. In this exchange, each Big Man receives heightened status.

4. The key to the competition between Big Man 1 and Big Man 2 is the concept of "interest," or return on the resources that were "potlatched" in the first feast. If Big Man 2 cannot return considerably more resources than he received, then he loses position and Big Man 1 alone gains status as well as the allegiance of some of Big Man 2's followers.

While this structure of Big Man dispersal patterns may theoretically work well for the maintenance of society because of the broad-based movement of resources, what about the drives and desires of individual Big Men to expand power and control, to leave a lasting legacy, and, perhaps, even to hand down status to offspring?

Individual Big Men do have options to control the outcome of competitive feasts. The most certain means is for Big Man 1 to give Big Man 2 fewer resources than required to invest in an appropriate return potlatch. But Big Man 1 must not act like a cheapskate and hoard resources—since it is mainly in the act of "giving away" that one receives status—and at the same time, Big Man 1 must use the "withheld" resources in a way that encourages his followers to do more work, while also attracting additional followers to his camp.

How could a Big Man implement this strategy without violating community sensibilities?

The Kwakiutl provide a telling example. In an elegant study, Codere argues that before the arrival of Europeans, potlatches involved little or no destruction of resources (see Piddocke 1969). When European-introduced diseases wiped out nearly three-fourths of the Kwakiutl population, the resources/per person ratio skyrocketed and every Kwakiutl could afford to be a Big Man. How could the ranks of Big Men be kept limited in this condition? Codere believes that the answer Big Men found was to reduce "overabundance" by destroying resources.

Using a similar rationale, there is another type of scheme that would seem to work even better. Rather than take resources out of the hands of competitors by destroying them, another option is to turn them into social production and embed them in material symbols of community—a temple, ceremonial grounds, a carved stone monument, a lavish burial or cache—what Roland Fletcher (1977) calls a Monstrous Visual Symbol or MVS (see also Johnson 1989). An MVS acts both to take labor and resources out of the reach of competitors and to create a material focus for future community feasts and ceremonies, thereby also creating a large material symbol of the status of the Big Man who embedded them. No waste. Big Man 1 would give gifts to Big Man 2 and at the same time give a mega-social production gift to the community at large that represents both Big Man 1 and Big Man 2 and their followers. Using this strategy, Big Man 1 gives Big Man 2 resources to invest in a return feast, but no additional resources to invest in creating his/her own social production gift to the community.

This type of embedding strategy on the part of several Big Men would quickly thin the ranks of their competitors to those who were able to continue the embedding competition without being given enough resources at potlatches to both return gifts to another Big Man and give the community an MVS gift at the same time. Once social production embedding begins in earnest, the Big Men who were still able to participate would become an internally competitive *nouveau elite*.

There are several good reasons for these *nouveau elite* to choose to compete by embedding social production:

1. One motivation for social production withdrawals on the part of *nouveau elite* is a belief in their societies' cosmology and ideology and a certainty that their actions are serving the gods/ancestors as well as all of the living members of their social group.

But pious actions do have behavioral and material, as well as ideological, repercussions:

2. By embedding resources into *social production* symbols of power, Nouveau Elite 1 gives a tangible MVS to the whole community,

including Nouveau Elite 2's followers, *without any of the resources involved in its production going through the control of Nouveau Elite 2.*

3. At the same time, Nouveau Elite 1 takes large quantities of resources out of the competitive system by embedding them in social production so they cannot be used by anyone else to outdo him/her at a community ceremony.

4. Further, Nouveau Elite 1's lasting MVS memorializes its ideological subject of veneration, the community at large, and, in the process, Nouveau Elite 1 himself (see Wilson 1988: 134–135).

I am not suggesting that embedding social production was necessarily a conscious strategy on the part of the *nouveau elite* to gain increased social and political position. Nonetheless, it seems clear that giving spiritual piety material form is one fast-track to temporal power.

When this pattern takes shape, *nouveau elites*, especially those who are both pious and ambitious, would begin to redirect substantial resources from competitive dispersal to competitive embedding in a struggle to personally exploit as many resources as possible in their catchment of power. This would mean bigger and bigger social production trappings at fewer and fewer centers, until one set of elites manages to establish their control over the vast majority of available labor and materials. At this point the *nouveau elite* become a hereditary *aggrandizing elite* and proceed to redirect labor and resources into infrastructures to maintain control, increase the production of local resources, and compete for resources and power with other elites at a distance (see Kolb 1997 for a specific example).

I am from the old school that aims to test models of societal change against expectations of what should be found in the archaeological record. The *nouveau elite potlatch* mechanism of social change is not easy to test since the material remains of social production are also the tangible correlates of social complexity in general.

One obvious (and, sad to say, circular) expectation is that the first examples of social production in early civilizations would be temples, ritual offerings, and burials symbolic of community ideology and cohesion. But all complex societies construct such monuments. How then will the remains of social production potlatches be identified in societies transitional between ranking and true stratification?

If, in fact, contending *nouveau elites* were attempting to heighten their status vis-à-vis rampant competitors through the acquisition and use of manpower and material, those who were successful would have had to embed grandiose quantities of social production in support of their community's ideology. The positive effect for the most "generous" of the *nouveau elite*, though it might have been unintentional, would be to deny huge quantities of labor and material to their competitors. Once a hereditary aggrandizing elite is stabilized, however, social production would be largely redirected from the unbridled embedding of resources and labor into community ideology (see Trigger 1990: 127) toward instead building infrastructure to maintain control and to increase local production to compete with other elites long-distance; in other words, the result would be fewer and smaller local MVSs (see Childe 1945: 17–18).

This rationale leads to an expectation that is, at least to me, clearly counterintuitive: The earliest artifacts of social production should be among the more grandiose and labor intensive ever produced by a particular culture. The Maya Lowlands and particularly the Mirador Basin provide one case example. The region was settled about 750 B.C. (J. E. Clark pers. comm. 2000). By 700–600 B.C. a large village center of at least 50 hectares appeared at Nakbe, one which holds the earliest nonresidential platforms and plazas known in the Mirador Basin (Clark et al. n.d.). Associated with these is dense refuse complete with anthropomorphic figurines that appear to have been intentionally broken during what has been interpreted as ritual use (Hansen 1997). This whole complex suggests to me a long series of conspicuous-consumption Big Man potlatches, with just the beginnings of competitive embedding (see Hill 1999 for another, even clearer example of the same process).

By 500 B.C. Nakbe had become an "impressive capital center" with carefully planned arrangements of pyramids, temples, elevated causeways, public plazas and buildings, and elite domestic dwellings that rivaled the greatest contemporary centers elsewhere in Mesoamerica (Clark et al. n.d.). These Middle Preclassic remains of social production could be the results of actions by innovators among the *nouveau elite* taking risks and making considerable efforts to competitively embed labor and resources.

As Clark and associates report (n.d.: 1), by the Late Preclassic period (ca. 300 B.C. to A.D. 150), "the Mirador Basin became a region of unprecedented architectural constructions, witnessing the erection of the most massive stone superimposed buildings ever built in the Maya area." Along with an exponential rise in the sheer scale of embedded social production came a parallel rise in what the excavators label "conspicuous consumption." For example, large limestone façade blocks (90 X 45 X 45 cm) were positioned with their short faces out, in effect doubling the number of cut stones needed to cover a structure if the blocks' long faces had been turned out instead. At the same time, "the production of lime appears to have been deliberately expensive and wasteful of resources, and the stucco so procured was used almost wantonly—or at least ostentatiously" (Clark et al. 1998: 13).

Nothing at any later Maya sites ever rivaled the sheer scope of the social production embedded at Preclassic Mirador. The *nouveau elite* there seem to have become—for a time—a hereditary aggrandizing elite through their ultra-grandiose trappings of labor and resources for the glory of the gods/ancestors, of society in general, and, of course, of the elite's key relation to both heaven and earth.

The point of these largest of Lowland Maya remains of embedded social production is not only that they were constructed, but that these very early MVS entrapments—built less than 400 years after the first public structures were raised—are more grandiose than anything the Maya built throughout the following 1,300 years in far more populous areas. All of the first civilizations seem to follow a similar pattern of incredibly large and early investments in social production—in the New World consider the stone heads, monstrous terraces, and serpentine caches of Mexico's Olmec (see Clark 1997), and Peru's gargantuan Initial Period ceremonial complexes at Paraíso, Huaca Florida, and Sechin Alto on the coast (see Hass et al. 1987), followed by the semisubterranean labyrinth built in the Early Horizon at Chavín de Huántar in the highlands. These are all evidence of the potlatch syndrome among *nouveau elites*.

Of course, these MVSs were key psychological foci of social organization. But they were also a key material factor in societal change—in this case, limiting access to labor and resources and thereby centralizing power into fewer hands. That is why the post-contact Big Men who Boas observed destroyed so many material goods in potlatches—*to make those goods that were left in circulation far more valuable.*

As someone in our contemporary society might say to the competition, *"Use it or lose it."* I believe it is now time to see the building of MVSs not only as symbols of the centralization of power and resources, but also as material social production whose generation played a crucial role within the origin of the world's first civilizations.

Note

I am deeply indebted to the following colleagues for critiques, comments, sources, and information: an anonymous economist, Anthony P. Andrews, Lewis Binford, John Carpenter, John E. Clark, George L. Cowgill, Barry Cunliffe, Brian Fagan, Kenneth Feder, David Freidel, George Gumerman, Brian Hayden, Warren Hill, David Johnson, Vincent LaMotta, Marilyn Masson, John T. Murphy, David A. Phillips Jr., Klavs Randsborg, Guadalupe Sanchez Miranda, Wolfgang Schliedt, Justine Shaw, MasaKazu Tani, Bruce Trigger, Gordon Willey, and Norm Yoffee. Each made significant contributions to any merit this chapter has.

References

Binford, Lewis R.
  1962 "Archaeology as Anthropology." *American Antiquity* 28: 217–225.
Brookfield, H. C.
  1972 "Intensification and Dis-intensification in Pacific Agriculture: A Theoretical Approach." *Pacific Viewpoint* 13: 18–29.
Brunton, Ron
  1975 "Why Do the Trobriands Have Chiefs?" *Man* 10: 544–558.
Childe, V. Gordon
  1945 "Directional Changes in Funerary Practices during 50,000 Years." *Man* 4: 13–19.
Clark, John E.
  1997 "The Arts of Government in Early Mesoamerica." *Annual Reviews in Anthropology* 26: 211–234.
Clark, John E., and Michael Blake
  1994 "The Power of Prestige: Competitive Generosity and the Emergence of Rank Societies in Lowland Mesoamerica." Pp. 17–30 in *Factional Competition and Political Development in the New World*, edited by E. M. Brumfiel and J. W. Fox. Cambridge: Cambridge University Press.
Clark, John E., Richard D. Hansen, and Tomas Pérez
  n.d. "Maya Genesis: Towards an Origin Narrative of Maya Civilization." Unpublished manuscript.
Flannery, Kent V.
  1972 "The Cultural Evolution of Civilizations." *Annual Review of Ecology and Systematics* 3: 399–426.
Fletcher, Roland
  1977 "Settlement Studies (Micro and Semi-micro)." Pp. 47–162 in *Spatial Archaeology*, edited by D. L. Clarke. New York: Academic Press.
Fried, Morton H.
  1967 *The Evolution of Political Society: An Essay in Political Anthropology.* New York: Random House.
Haas, Jonathan, Susan Pozorski, and Thomas Pozorski, eds.
  1987 *The Origins and Development of the Andean State.* Cambridge: Cambridge University Press.

Hansen, Richard D.
  1997 "Ideología y arquitectura: poder y dinámicas culturales de los Mayas Preclásicos de las Tierras Bajas." Palenque, Mexico: *2a Mesa Redonda de Palenque*.
Hayden, Brian, and Rob Gargett
  1990 "Big Man, Big Heart? A Mesoamerican View of the Emergence of Complex Society." *Ancient Mesoamerica* 1: 3–20.
Hill, Warren D.
  1999 *Ballcourts, Competitive Games, and the Emergence of Complex Society*. Ph.D. dissertation, University of British Columbia, Vancouver.
Johnson, Gregory A.
  1989 "Dynamics of Southwestern Prehistory: Far Outside—Looking In." Pp. 371–390 in *Dynamics of Southwest Prehistory*, edited by L. S. Cordell and G. J. Gumerman. Washington, D.C.: Smithsonian Institution Press.
Kirch, Patrick V.
  1990 "Monumental Architecture and Power in Polynesian Chiefdoms: A Comparison of Tonga and Hawaii." *World Archaeology* 22(2): 207–222.
Kolb, Michael J.
  1997 "Labor Mobilization, Ethnohistory, and Archaeology of Community in Hawai'i." *Journal of Archaeological Method and Theory* 4(3/4): 265–285.
Piddocke, Stuart
  1969 "The Potlatch System of the Southern Kwakiutl: A New Perspective." Pp. 130–156 in *Environmental and Cultural Behavior*, edited by A. P. Vayda. Austin: University of Texas Press.
Rathje, William L.
  1978 "Melanesian and Australian Exchange Systems: A View from Mesoamerica." *Mankind* 11: 165–174.
Trigger, Bruce G.
  1990 "Monumental Architecture: A Thermodynamic Explanation of Symbolic Behaviour." *World Archaeology* 22(2): 119–132.
Wilson, Peter J.
  1988 *The Domestication of the Human Species*. New Haven, Conn.: Yale University Press.
Yoffee, Norman
  1993 "Too Many Chiefs? (or, Safe Texts for the '90s)." Pp. 60–79 in *Archaeological Theory: Who Sets the Agenda*, edited by N. Yoffee and A. Sherratt. Cambridge: Cambridge University Press.
Zipf, George K.
  1949 *Human Behavior and the Principle of Least Effort*. Cambridge, Mass.: Addison-Wesley.

Chapter Three

The Origins of Maya Civilization: The Old Shell Game, Commodity, Treasure, and Kingship

David A. Freidel, Kathryn Reese-Taylor, and David Mora-Marín

In the Relacion of Campocolche . . . we read of presenting an idol "some green stones which they call tun and others which they call kan which are red and these red ones are of value and precious because with them they buy that for which they have need." It may well be that the red beads were of shell. —Alfred M. Tozzer, "Landa's Relacion de las Cosas de Yucatan"

The money which they used was little bells [of copper] . . . and they were valued according to their quantity or size; . . . [also certain] red [shells] which they bring from outside these provinces, [of which they make strings like] the beads of a rosary. —Alfred M. Tozzer, "Landa's Relacion de las Cosas de Yucatan"

Introduction

William Rathje provided Maya archaeology with a powerful and productive vision of Maya geopolitical development that wrapped practical material transactions in ideologically inspired values, or "praise the gods and pass the metates." A challenge to elite who controlled both the places of public performance and the flow of wealth was to ensure that what vassals, clients, and subjects regarded as wealth was definitive of political relationships with rulers—that is, they could receive such goods or be required to deliver them. Such a strategy required both definitions of value by elite through performance and display and control of trade or the means of production. Stephen Houston, in a recent review of Maya glyphic decipherment, observes of the Classic period Maya: "Tribute was shown as heaps of textiles or neat packages that contain green feathers . . . paired *Spondylus* shells, and bundles of chocolate beans" (Houston 2000: 173). Historical descriptions of Maya commerce from the time of the Spanish arrival, like those quoted at the outset of this chapter, make clear that these people, among others in Mesoamerica, used currencies in their transactions (Millon 1955; Freidel 1986). Currencies are fungible commodities—that is, commodities which can be exchanged broadly for other things. Robert McC. Adams (1976) noted that fungibility is correlated with generality of distribution. In the case at hand, *Spondylus* beads have a much wider distribution in the archaeological record of the Maya than do whole *Spondylus* shells. It is reasonable to surmise that beads were more fungible than were shells.

The ancient Maya used a wide variety of shell species for artifacts and adornments (Andrews 1969; Moholy-Nagy 1985, 1989). Recently, Isaza Aizpuruia and Patricia McAnany (1999) have written a thorough and insightful analysis of the production and use of shell artifacts in Middle and Late Preclassic contexts at the site of K'axob in northern Belize. Our principal focus in this chapter is the site of Cerros, directly north of K'axob on the New River and likely the major Late Preclassic trading center in its vicinity. Aizpuruia and McAnany demonstrate that local shell ornament production and use was quite important at K'axob in the Middle Preclassic and Late Preclassic periods. Indeed, K'axob evidently had access to marine shells by means of trade even before the rise of Cerros as a major trading port toward the end of the Late Preclassic period. These scholars come to the following conclusion concerning the developmental patterns in shell use at K'axob: "Variation in quantities of shell beads interred with Formative burials indicate the variety of identities of varying status that existed during the early and late facets of the Chaak'kax [Middle Preclassic] and K'atabche'kax [Late Preclassic] complexes. This fluidity is replaced, however, during terminal K'atabche'kax times by shell artifacts that diacritically mark positions of status and authority. Shell continued to express identity, but within an increasingly formalized authority structure in which ritual performance played a key role" (Aizpuruia and McAnany 1999: 125).

At Cerros, where the shell evidence is more meager than at K'axob (Garber 1989), we think we can substantiate the merit of Aizpuruia and McAnany's conclusions concerning the engagement of shell in the evolution of political power. We review the symbolic manipulation of shell as wealth and commodity as attested in art, architecture, inferred royal performance, and formal caching behavior. But Aizpuruia and McAnany also confirmed another temporal trend in the Maya use of shell. It is at the end of the Late Preclassic period that *Spondylus*, a rare and precious shell, comes into the record at K'axob. Hattula Moholy-Nagy (1989) observed that *Spondylus* comes into the record at Tikal in the Late Preclassic period as well. Here we explore the prospect that with the rise of formal governments in the Late Preclassic Maya lowlands, *Spondylus* was introduced as a new exotic commodity to reinforce relationships between rulers and their followers, and became, over time, a widespread currency in the form of beads. Aizpuruia and McAnany point out that shell beads lend themselves to interchangeability (1999: 124). We would go further and postulate that Maya political economies, from the Preclassic onwards, involved commodity trade over distance that moved not only practical necessities, but also exotics and labor-invested goods that were used for currencies in the ordinary transactions of everyone on the social ladder. These currency goods included small ornaments made of jade and shell, which were universally valued in part because they were directly linked to the sources of cosmic power flowing through rulers and other mediators with the supernatural world.

William Rathje participated in the discovery of some important materials on Cozumel Island. One day in the spring of 1973, he walked into the Harvard Arizona Cozumel Project patio and regarded one of the crew wearing a jade Olmec head as a pectoral. He literally fell flat on his behind in astonishment. That head, broken off a figurine in antiquity and recycled as a *hunal*, a jewel of kingship, was found in the grave of a Terminal Classic lord who also took with him some very nice worked *Spondylus* shell ornaments and a variety of Early and Late Classic partial ceramics. Alberto Ruz L., who visited the site at the time, quipped that the project had exposed a real ancient collector. But the *Spondylus* and the jade were in association as a chest pectoral arrangement. And these two commodities have a very long history together in Maya civilization, beginning in the Late Preclassic period as observed by Hattula Moholy-Nagy (1989). Richard Hansen (1990a) has long championed the transaction in shell as a key feature of the original economies in Petén. In his work at Nakbe, he found clear evidence of Middle Preclassic shell importation from the coast and also the production of standard shell items, small pendants, or pierced shell fragments made of *Strombus*. Other shell species are represented in Middle Preclassic contexts, but significantly *Spondylus* is absent until the Late Preclassic (Richard Hansen, pers. comm. 2000).

In light of the work done by scholars expert in the distribution of shell in Maya archaeological contexts, it should not have surprised us that *Spondylus* comes in the record significantly in the Late Preclassic period, long after less rare and more local species of shell. In addition to the archaeological record, both the iconographic and epigraphic data of the Preclassic substantiates this conclusion. We discerned that *Spondylus* was introduced into the Maya ideological system in the Late Preclassic period as part of a major redefinition of political and economic power that legitimated the social order governed by kings (Freidel and Schele 1988). We do not doubt that Rathje (1972) was prescient in his view that such ideological machinations originated in Petén; but it is equally clear and significant that *Spondylus* was not only new to the Maya system, but derived from its peripheries—namely the Pacific (primarily) and the Caribbean (evidently in smaller quantities). It was, in our opinion, the strategic melding of such distant and precious materials as *Spondylus* and jade with a central and compelling new power controlled by the high elite that made the old shell game work so well. This is a strategy clearly articulated in the theoretical work of Mary Helms (1993).

With regard to Rathje's (1972) original schema, we find productive his basic hypothesis of a Maya lowland world effectively divided into core and peripheral regions. What we would add, as would other colleagues like Patricia McAnany in her treatment of cacao (chapter 5), is that the strategic commodities were by no means confined to the basics—salt, basalt, and so forth—in exchange for idea-laden craft items as originally proposed by Rathje. We think that ideologically charged commodities of great significance, namely money—red shell, green stone, cacao beans primary among the known Maya currencies at the time of the Spanish arrival—were integral to the trade in all goods and services.

However, we do not wish to propose that Mesoamerican economies were static from Preclassic to Postclassic times. On the contrary, if we are on the right track, then *Spondylus* beads did not begin to play that role until the Late Preclassic period (and metal bells and axes as currency came in at the end of the Classic period). Nevertheless, we think both the forms and the contexts of the preciosities will eventually prove to be commensurate with currency-based systems found elsewhere in the world. So the lowland Maya rulers were challenged to keep the trade routes from Petén to the periphery open throughout their history, not only to get the salt to sweating workers in their realms, but also to facilitate the regular exchange of goods and services among them (Freidel 1986).

Jade, *Spondylus*, and Ideology

Spondylus joined greenstone and jade, already established media for treasure, wealth, and exchange (see Dalton 1976 for a discussion of treasure, primitive valuables, and primitive money). First, looking at jade as supernaturally charged treasure, Virginia Fields (1989, 1991) showed that the Olmec and Middle Preclassic elite generally invented the ideological significance of greenstone as a source of water and food (ideas sustained into the Aztec period), specifically sprouting maize, and they displayed this symbol as a diadem jewel on their rulers. Jade and greenstone were thus anchored into the hopes and needs of farmers in ways that promoted the desirability of the material among them. The Maya would call the sprouting jewel and its variants the *hunal*, Oneness, with other related names in the Classic texts (Schele and Mathews 1998). The Olmec jade from Cozumel was clearly used as this icon by the Maya personage who took it with him. Indeed, it has the trifoil headdress design diagnostic of the later *hunal* forms of the Maya world (figure 3.1). So the Late Preclassic Maya did not invent the packaging of jade and greenstone in power, they segued from the Olmec in this regard. Jade and greenstone do occur in documented Middle Preclassic lowland Maya contexts, but as beads rather than as elaborated carvings (Freidel 1992), and this suggests its introduction as an Olmec currency before its elevation to a Maya symbol of treasure. Should such carvings be found in Middle Preclassic Maya contexts, we would anticipate that they would fall into the established parameters of the Olmec or Middle Formative Ceremonial Complex (Reilly 1994). So jade preceded *Spondylus* in the lowland Maya record, and when *Spondylus* came in, it was coupled with jade (Moholy-Nagy 1989), which likely functioned in bead form as an established currency for long-distance exchange.

The Late Preclassic Maya committed to kingship through a dramatic increase in the media registering ideologically legitimated

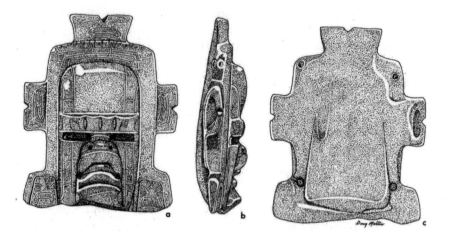

Fig. 3.1. Olmec style jade head found in a Late Classic burial, courtesy of the Harvard Arizona Cozumel Project, illustration by Doug Mellis.

political power, particularly decorated architecture (Freidel 1979, 1980; Hansen 1990b, 1998), and through adherence to new major symbols of power, particularly the Principal Bird Deity, a god anchored iconographically in the Scarlet Macaw (Cortez 1986; Kappelman 1997).

The Maya, and other successor communities to the Middle Preclassic Olmec in southeastern Mesoamerica, combined these new ideas and media with existing ones. Exactly how (through commerce, war, or both) remains to be elucidated, but these emerging rulers certainly appropriated the *hunal* diadem jewel and related *ajaw* pectoral forms from the Middle Preclassic kings of the Olmec civilization (Freidel 1990; Freidel and Suhler 1995). They did not just borrow carved greenstone in the form of heirlooms, but they also produced it in a style that imitated Olmec conventions. *Spondylus* was another new medium for the insignia of the emerging Late Preclassic political order.

Performing Value, *Spondylus*, and Jade in the Late Preclassic Cerros Façade

This Late Preclassic era of innovation is illustrated in the buildings and artifacts discovered at Cerros in Belize (Freidel 1979, 1980; Freidel and Schele 1988; Garber 1981, 1989; Reese 1996; Reese-Taylor n.d.). Particularly on Structure 5C-2nd (figure 3.2 a–d), we discovered giant masks wearing flanged crowns decorated with insignia. On this

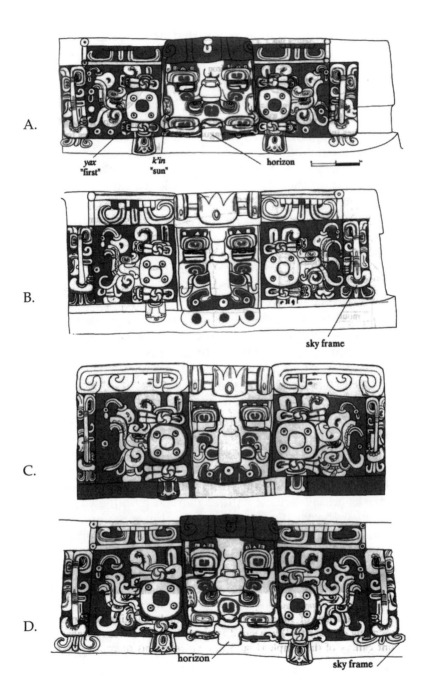

A.

yax   *k'in*
"first"   "sun"   horizon

B.

sky frame

C.

D.

horizon   sky frame

Fig. 3.2. Restoration drawings of the four panels of Structure 5C-2nd at Cerros, drawings by Linda Schele and Barbara MacLeod.

façade, there are iconographic motifs that, on the basis of both shape and color, can be identified as *Spondylus* shell. Others, also on the basis of shape and color, might be identifiable as jade. Moreover, the program as a whole has a celestial theme, which can be identified with the death and resurrection of the Maize god (Reese 1996). The introduction of *Spondylus* as a preciosity is very much connected to this performance program, and both *Spondylus* and jade (Fields 1991; Taube 1998) retained this connection through the Classic period.

Our analysis will be iconographic, but we also rely upon the fundamental premise that the Late Preclassic Maya were employing glyphic notational principles derived from an ancestral Middle Formative Olmec semasiographic script (Justeson and Mathews 1991). In simple terms, the iconographic and glyphic semantic domains still displayed significant overlap in the Late Preclassic period, and we can create bridging arguments in the identification of *Spondylus* and jade symbols in primarily iconographic programs like the Cerros façade by reference to semantic, structural, and iconographic patterns in the Preclassic and Classic scripts. Because we are essentially reading the Structure 5C-2nd façade using iconographic, epigraphic, and behavioral arguments simultaneously, we must attempt to explore all of these issues together in the context of what Clifford Geertz (1973) dubbed "thick description" of the façade.

The Cerros Structure 5C-2nd façade was intentionally preserved by burial during the Late Preclassic period under Structure 5C-1st. It consists of four vertical panels of elaborate modeled and painted stucco over stone armatures, two on the elevated building platform and two on a lower terrace. The composition displays four monumental deity masks wearing the flanged headdress of Maya rulership. The lower masks are jaguarian creatures marked with the *k'in* (day, sun) glyph on their cheeks. We will return to the lower monumental masks after dealing with the upper masks and elements of the flanged helmet, as these are most germane to the identification of *Spondylus* and jade imagery. The upper masks can be identified as sacred birds on the basis of their long, curved beaks and other diagnostic features (Reese 1996: 100, n.d.). While both of these masks bear connections to the Principal Bird Deity, named *Itzam-Ye* or *Mut Itzamna* (Schele and Mathews 1998) during the Classic Period, we suggest that these masks represent in fact two connected divinities, the Principal Bird Deity, on the eastern side, and the Water Fowl on the western upper panel (Reese 1996).

There are several important clues, which distinguish these otherwise quite similar images. First of all, the eastern mask has a painted motif below its chin that is painted red and has a trilobate shape. This shape is diagnostic of the pendant worn by the Principal Bird Deity beginning in the Late Preclassic period, as seen, for example on Kaminaljuyu Altar 10 and on the great mask of Structure H-Sub 12 at Uaxactun (Valdés 1995). This motif is lacking from the western mask, which has a neck and shoulder outlined in red paint on beige background. We will return to this pendant in a moment.

Secondly, the western mask has a distinctive top-line panel design flanking it to either side. While the eastern top-line panel carries the J-scroll and bracket motif which is regularly found in Late Preclassic compositions in southeastern Mesoamerica (Quirarte 1974), the western mask is flanked in the top-line panels by in-curving gum brackets which are normally found on baselines in Late Preclassic (figure 3.3a), and antecedent Middle Preclassic (figure 3.3b) art (Quirarte 1974; Norman 1975; Reilly 1994). Study of the emergence of writing from pictographic icons in southeastern Mesoamerica (Stross 1990; Justeson and Kaufman 1993) shows that this in-curving gum bracket came to be read logographically as *NAS* ("earth, land") and phonetically as *na* in Epi-Olmec writing (figure 3.3c), based on *na: s* from proto-Mije-Soquean, meaning "land" or "earth." This icon, in early Mayan script, became the phonetic symbol T23 *na* (figure 3.3d). While T23 *na* was used only phonetically in Classic Mayan inscriptions, we have examples of the top part of the symbol still functioning iconographically as a base line in Mayan art (figure 3.3e), in the glyph T529 *WITZ* "mountain" (figures 3.3f, g) and sporadically in the form of T23 *na* itself (figure 3.3h). In the 5C-2nd composition, the presentation of this baseline "earth" symbol in the top-line is appropriate to the Water Fowl. This bird, anchored into the cormorant (Schele and Miller 1986: 55), represents the fishing bird, which can dive beneath the calm surface of lakes and rivers and stay submerged for long periods of time. The calm, flat surface of water, *nab* in Mayan languages, represents the surface of the Otherworld (Freidel, Schele, and Parker 1993), and the capacity of the Water Fowl to dive into that world of gods and ancestors and return to this one is its major metaphorical feature (Reese 1996: 103). The western mask carries an eroded symbol painted in black on its snout that appears to be the glyph *akbal*, darkness. This same symbol occurs in the Classic period on a water jar in Creation-era scenes, and it also adorns the snout of the

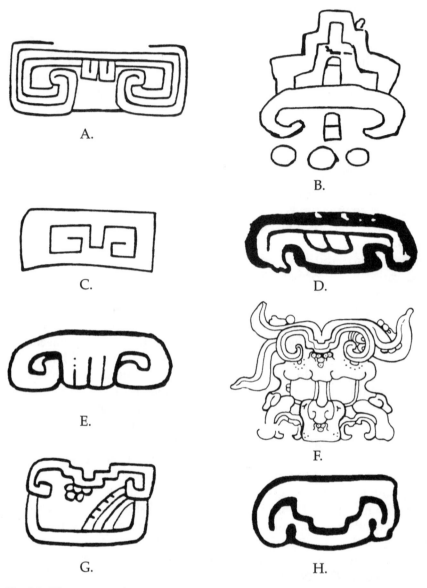

Fig. 3.3. Illustrations of Preclassic icons by David Mora-Marín: a) Late Preclassic J-Scroll and Bracket motif, b) Middle Preclassic Gum Bracket motif on the Creation Plaque, c) Gum Bracket in Proto-Mije-Soquean script (logographic NAS, phonetic Na), d) T23 Na in Classic Mayan script, 3) Gum Bracket as a baseline motif in Classic Mayan art, f) Clefted Gum Bracket as cleft in iconographic Witz Mountain (Palenque), g) T529 Witz Mountain Glyph in Classic Mayan script, h) T23 Na as logograph for Witz Mountain in Classic Mayan art.

Celestial monster in many cases. The Celestial monster is a source of the waters of the primordial deluge (Freidel, Schele, and Parker 1993).

Moving between the waters of the underworld and the trees representative of the sky, the Water Fowl performs the journey of death and resurrection. It remained associated with the resurrection of the Maize god in the Classic period. On the Panel of the Foliated Cross at Palenque, for example, the Water Fowl, masked as the Principal Bird Deity, *Itzam-Yeh*, is perched on top of the Maize plant symbolic of the reborn Maize god. Along with the capacity to change form (to shape-shift in epi-Olmec pre-Mije-Soquean, to conjure one's spirit companion or *way* in Classical Mayan, Houston and Stuart 1989), this journey was one of the critical feats of legitimation for rulers, beginning in the Middle Preclassic period (Justeson and Kaufman 1993; Reilly 1994, 1996; Kappelman 1997; Reese 1996).

Returning to the eastern upper mask on the 5C-2nd façade, there is a trilobate motif painted on the chin that resembles the trilobate pendant regularly worn by the Principal Bird Deity. There is a second trilobate motif in red paint below the mask, on the area of the neck. Kappelman (1997: 71) suggests that the pendant is a cut shell resembling a cut shell finial worn in the headdress of the Bird. There is reason to think that this trilobate pendant is indeed a shell, but our iconographic argument has to first place that trilobate pendant into a larger category of such trilobate motifs. Another trilobate motif on the Cerros façade occurs generally on the ear-flare assemblages that mark the flanges of the typical Maya royal headdress and that flank the main masks. The motif in question occurs on the 5C-2nd façade descending from the bottom of the overall ear-flare assemblage (figure 3.4 a, b). The artists who created the façade had some latitude in both modeling elements in stucco and painting them, or just painting them, so there is variability in the expression of the motif. The preservation is also variable, with both of the descending motifs on the upper west panel destroyed and only one on the upper east panel preserved. However, where preserved, the motif is consistently painted red on its interior, is trilobate, and has circular balls attached to the lobes and/or painted onto them. In this last respect, these trilobate motifs resemble even more closely the general design of the pendant worn by the Principal Bird Deity.

The trilobate motifs on the Cerros ear-flare assemblages are by no means unique. Indeed, they are integral to one of two standard expressions of the Late Preclassic ear-flare assemblages in southeastern Mesoamerica (the other expression is a single curving element).

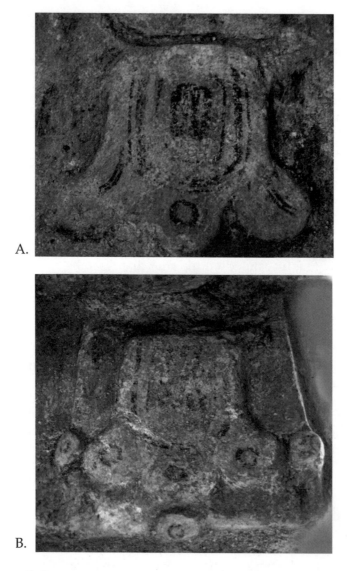

A.

B.

Fig. 3.4. Shell tassel elements from the ear flare assemblages of the lower east (A) and lower west (B) panels of Structure 5C-2nd.

Altar 10 of Kaminaljuyu, for example, depicts the Principal Bird Deity wearing the same basic ear-flare assemblage as found on the 5C-2nd façade, including this trilobate motif (figure 3.5a); the Late Preclassic Maya ruler incised on the obverse of the Dumbarton Oaks

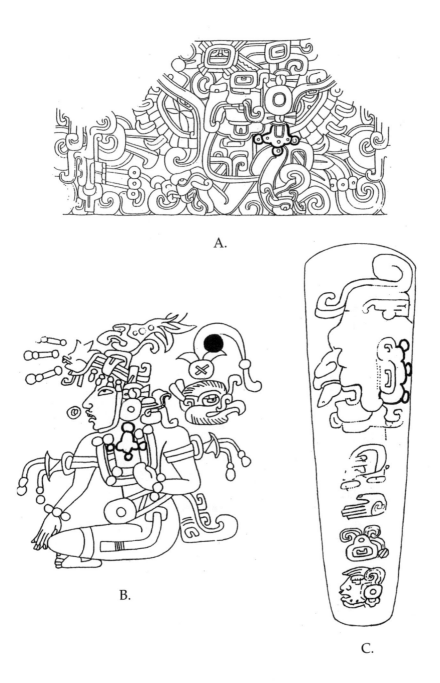

Fig. 3.5. A) Altar 10 of Kaminaljuyu,; B) Obverse, Dumbarton Oaks Plaque; C) Kendall Axe. All illustrations by David Mora-Marín.

pectoral (figure 3.5b) also wears this trilobate motif on his ear flare (Schele and Miller 1986: plate 32a). In some cases, however, this trilobate motif becomes the central element of the ear flare itself. This is found on the Kendal Axe incised image of *Chak* (Schele and Miller 1986: 227), a Late Preclassic expression from Belize (figure 3.5c). A related expression occurs monumentally on Structure 34 at El Mirador (Hansen 1990a). In that case, the ear flares are not only trilobate, but appear to be jaguar paws ending in claws. There are Early Classic examples of feline *Chak* masked personages wearing this trilobate ear flare on lowland Maya monuments, such as El Zapote Stelae (Schele and Grube 1998: 91). The structural positioning of the trilobate motif as the ear flare itself provides the segue to identifying it as shell. The ear flare of *Chak* has been long identified as made of shell (Schele and Miller 1986: 49). That shell can be depicted as trilobate, as spiked, or as sprocketed in Classic iconography. One of the relatively consistent features of the Classic Maya *Chak* ear flare is its decoration with dots or circles directly on the lobes, spikes, or sprockets; this is also a consistent feature of the trilobate motifs found in the Late Preclassic contexts discussed here, including the proposed pendant below the chin of the upper east mask of 5C-2nd.

While the kind of shell is difficult to determine from the iconography, two observations lend support to the identification as *Spondylus*. First, the motifs in question on the 5C-2nd façade are outlined in black, but their interiors are painted red (other available colors being black and yellow), and that is the characteristic color of *Spondylus*. Second, the one example of actual *Chak* ear flares occurring as artifacts that we know about were discovered in a fourth-century A.D. royal tomb at Yaxuna in Yucatan (figure 3.6; Suhler 1996; Suhler and Freidel 1998). In that case, the flares adorning the headdress of the ruler were of the sprocketed variety with incised circles, and they were made of *Spondylus*.

Returning to the descending motif on the ear flare assemblages on Structure 5C-2nd, there is variation, but the four examples on the lower panels contain a black painted u-shaped element within a black-line circular cartouche. This cartouched u-shaped element composition also occurs within the trilobate motif elsewhere in the Late Preclassic, as on the Principal Bird Deity depicted on Kaminaljuyu Altar 10. Such cartouched u-shaped elements also occur elsewhere on the 5C-2nd façade. We agree with Stuart (1995) and other scholars who have identified this element as a symbol for jewel or bead (figure 3.7b). The color of the u-shaped element contrasts with the red

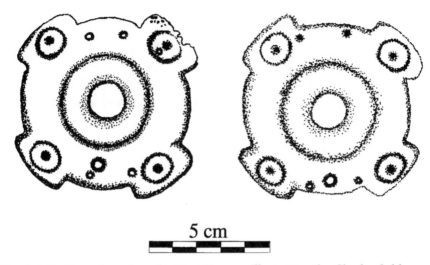

5 cm

Fig. 3.6. Shell ear flares from Bu 23 at Yaxuna. Illustrations by Charles Suhler.

background on the trilobate motif. This depiction of a jade bead as an icon is evidently associated with rulership, for in the context of emerging Late Preclassic period writing systems the cartouched u-shaped element was part of the original form of the T533 *AJAW* and T168: 518 *AJAW* "lord, ruler" glyphs (figures 3.7a); the association may be reflected linguistically in the Tzeltalan term **äjäw*, "venerated or sacred object" (Kaufman and Norman 1984: 115). So this element could convey the meaning of a jade bead or an *AJAW* glyph. For our purposes, both of these meanings are relevant and linked. We would posit that this particular version of the trilobate motif depicts a jade bead, signaling rulership, within a *Spondylus* shell. Using *Spondylus* as a "jewel box" for jade is a pattern documented at some sites with the advent of the Classic period, such as Copan.

Another motif on the 5C-2nd façade that may represent *Spondylus* is the so-called "flame brow" (figure 3.8). These are large, outset oval panels over smaller, L-shaped inset "squint" or oval eye panels on the main masks. Above the flame-brow panels and attached to them are rectangular "sprockets" or triangular "spikes." And attached to the oval panels on the outer edge are P-shaped elements. Flame-brow eye compositions in this general form are found throughout Late Preclassic southeastern Mesoamerica. They occur, for example, on the masks of Uaxactun Structure H-Sub-12 (Valdés 1995), the masks of the Pyramid at Acanceh in Yucatan (Quintal Suaste 1998), Altar 10 Kaminaljuyu, and Izapa Stela 2 (Kappelman 1997), to name some

A.

B.

C.

D.

E.

Fig. 3.7. a) T168:518 *AJAW* "lord ruler" glyphs, b) cartouched ᴜ-shaped element as iconographic bead in a trilobate tassel composition that reads as a variant of the T168:518 *AJAW* glyph, c) early T533 *AJAW* glyph, d) Late Preclassic Mayan *AJAW* glyph with sprockets and "p" element of the flame brow motif, e) Late Preclassic Mayan *AJAW* glyph with the "p" element of the flame brow motif. Illustrations by David Mora-Marín.

Fig. 3.8. Flame brow on the upper east mask, Structure 5C-2nd.

monumental expressions with good context. The 5C-2nd flame brows are all painted with a series of cartouches in red on beige, with a red-painted u element at the center. Three of the four masks have flame brows displaying two "sprockets" flanking a "spike," while the upper east mask just has the two sprockets. Natural representations of *Spondylus* shells later in the Classic period emphasize their red color and their spikes, which extend beyond the oval shape of the shell when viewed from the interior perspective. Kent Reilly (pers. comm. 2000) pointed out to us that "slim," the famous Middle Preclassic greenstone sculpture, carries such a spiked oval incised on one thigh, an image he would identify as *Spondylus*. Moreover the sprockets are the double merlon motif of Olmec iconography. While the sprocketed shape is one variant of the shell ear flare of *Chak* in the Classic period, it is unclear whether they correlate to a natural referent on *Spondylus* shells; it is possible that the sprockets, which come in twos, may correspond to the two teeth of a bivalve shell located on the side of the beak.

We posit that these flame brows may also represent *Spondylus*. To get to that conclusion, we have to move through the Late Preclassic Maya inscriptional system into the Classic one, and from stylized notation back into fully iconic notation. The developmental direction may seem counterintuitive, but we think that the connections are productive. To begin, the flame-brow motif is used in conjunction with a Late Preclassic Mayan variant of *AJAW* in a manner that suggests it conveys the Classic period concept of *k'uh-ul*, "divine" or "holy," yielding *k'uh-ul-ajaw*, "divine lord" (figure 3.9), the standard epithet of rulers in the Classic period, particularly in the southern lowlands. The structural substitution here is between the Late Preclassic flame-brow motif and the Classic period "water group" prefix (Thompson 1950). Significantly, both of these motifs are essentially icons or logographs in the writing system. The water-group prefix (figure 3.10 a, b) takes a variety of forms (Mathews 1991: 24). Commonly it has a band of dots along the side, surmounted by another element or motif. The dots have been variously identified as water, blood, maize kernels, incense, and divination pebbles. The most common element surmounting the dots is either a K'an Cross (figure 3.11a) or a shell (figure 3.11b); T503 *IK'*, "wind" (figure 3.11c), used as a label on jade tinklers and bone rattles, among other musical instruments (Mora-Marín 1997, 2001; Taube 2001); jade ear flares (figure 3.11d); and obsidian cores (figure 3.11e), all of them precious materials from which beads and bead assemblages can be crafted. In fact, the most generic form of the water-group prefix, T32 (figure 3.10b), is a plain beaded necklace, which has previously been identified with blood. The shell, we suggest, is a more literal representation of the shell that comprises the flame brows as seen on 5C-2nd at Cerros. The K'an Cross is a reference to the name *k'an*, applied to red shell beads at the time of the Spanish arrival in Maya country. Those red shell beads were likely made from *Spondylus*. Why such shells might be used to convey the notion of holiness, divinity, or soul force is another matter, to which we will return shortly. Finally, the u-element at the center of the brow motif again likely represents a bead. The red color of these particular u-elements may signal that they are *Spondylus* rather than jade.

The bird masks on the upper terrace of Structure 5C-2nd wore diadem bands with three motifs attached to them (figure 3.12). Only on the eastern side was this composition sufficiently preserved to

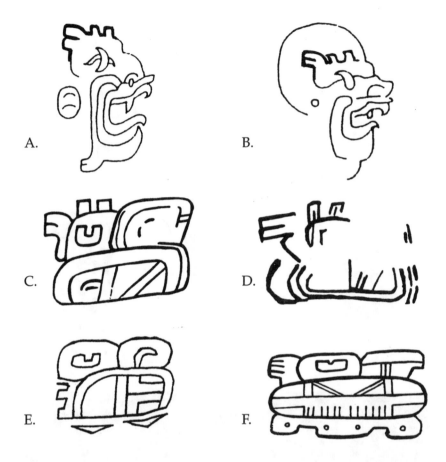

Fig. 3.9. a) Olmec flame brow motif, b) Olmec flame brow motif, c) Late Preclassic Maya *AJAW* with flame brow motif, d) Late Preclassic Maya *AJAW* with flame brow motif, e) Late Preclassic Maya *AJAW* with flame brow motif, f) flame brow *AJAW* glyph in "Sky Lord" epithet. All illustrations by David Mora-Marín.

Fig. 3.10. Water group prefix illustrations.

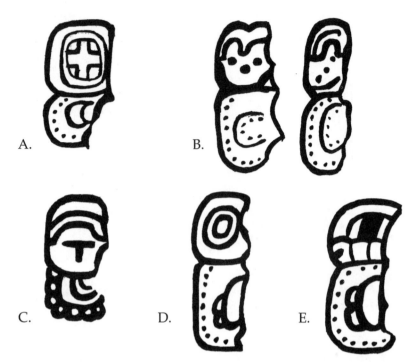

A.   B.

C.   D.   E.

Fig. 3.11. Motifs from the water group prefix.

Fig. 3.12. Detail photograph of the upper east mask on Structure 5C-2nd showing diadem band with three motifs.

confirm this design. This tripartite crown resembles the crown found carved onto the head of the fuschite mask discovered in Bu 85 at Tikal. In that case, the central motif on the crown is trifurcate, a nonanthropomorphic variant of the *hunal* insignia of rulership. It seems likely that the 5C-2nd crowns also sported *hunal* insignia. These insignia are painted red, and like the flame brows, the preserved examples of these have concentric circles painted on them as if to depict the convex surface of a shell. The known corpus of Late Preclassic diadem jewels shows them to be chiefly made of jade or greenstone. However, there are some shell examples of bib-helmet diadem jewels, although we cannot confirm that any are made of *Spondylus*. The Selz Foundation Yaxuna project did discover two royal crowns made of cut rectangles of *Strombus*, but these were white and designed to enhance the color of the white cloth band on which *hunal* jewels were also sewn. So if the crowns of the upper masks were intended to convey the idea of *Spondylus*, it would seem that they were expressions of the link between *Spondylus* and rulership, and not a literal representation of artifacts. A Terminal Preclassic monumental effigy censer found at Kaminaljuyu is relevant here. Parsons (1986) noted the similarity of the headband to that of the fuschite mask in Tikal Bu 85. The central of three diadem insignia is a cartouched U-element; the flanking elements are compact versions of the flame-brow motif under consideration (Parsons 1986: figure 128), which we are positing is *Spondylus*.

Turning to other possible representations of jade, cartouched U-elements painted in black occur in two other contexts in addition to the depending motif at the bottom of the ear-flare assemblages. There are such U-element motifs in the mouths of the lower jaguarian masks, and there are some painted on panels attached to the ends of knot tassels on the eastern side ear-flare assemblages. Those glyph-like icons were read YAX, "blue/green" or "first," by Linda Schele (Freidel and Schele 1988), and AJAW by Virginia Fields (1989). We think that the AJAW reading has more general support as the cartouched U-element generally has that meaning in Late Preclassic inscriptions. However, the particular cartouches are elaborated with scrolls and loops, which may complicate their significance. In the case of the mouth motifs, the U-elements are depicted upside down, and they may thus represent fangs. It is worth noting, however, that placing a greenstone jewel in the mouth of deceased individuals before burial is a documented Maya practice (Taube 1998, 2001).

The ear-flare assemblage on Structure 5C-2nd is typical in the presence of two knot elements, one above and one below the ear flare proper (figure 3.13). Each knot has directly above it a curved element decorated with concentric lines. Previously, Freidel (1985) has identified these motifs together as representative of the knot with infixed mirror grapheme used in the Classic Mayan writing system to signify the headband tied on by lords in accession rituals (the *hunal* headband). We now think it more likely that these knots symbolize that the insignia on the ear-flare assemblage are normally bundled and are here revealed in ritual performance. This more literal reading of the ear-flare assemblage goes further: The ear flare itself is shaped like a flaring, rimmed offering plate of the kind actually used in conjunction with Structure 5C-2nd. A lip-to-lip cache of such plates, in red and beige ceramic, was placed at the base of the stairway when the building was carefully buried under Structure 5C-1st. It is possible, if this analysis is on the right track, that the mirror elements are likewise symbolic of mirror materials, such as volcanic hematite, pyrite, or liquid mercury. Moreover, the elements surmounting the mirror element on the ear flares, a vertical and a scroll element

Fig. 3.13. Detail of the lower east panel of Structure 5C-2nd, showing ear flare assemblage.

previously identified by Freidel (1985) as the smoke of K'awil's forehead axe, might also signify literal artifacts. In this case, it is notable that the vertical elements have a modeled groove in the stucco, and painted in red along that grove are spikes. This combination may signify the stingray spine blood-letter. The accompanying curl might represent blood or perhaps a feather. The prospect that the vertical elements might be spines, combined with the identification of the depending elements as *Spondylus* shell, invites consideration of the ear-flare assemblage as representative of the complex of vessel and materials called the Quadripartite Badge (Greene Robertson 1974) and identified by Freidel, Schele, and Parker (1993) as a major portal to the Otherworld, the *Ol*, or heart-place portal. Supporting the idea that the ear flare is a portal, it is decorated with four circles embossed in stucco relief, painted with black outlines and black dots at their centers. These circles, along with the inset red-painted center of the flare, create the quincunx pattern associated since Middle Preclassic times with the defining of portals to the Otherworld and the centering of sacred space to generate the axis mundi (Reilly 1994, 1995; Freidel and Schele 1988). Karl Taube (2001) has more recently argued that the flare with four bosses as found on ear-flare assemblages reads, as in the writing system, *be /bi*, meaning "path." This glyph is commonly used to denote the path to the Otherworld in Maya texts.

The bosses on the ear flares are actually part of a category of modeled and painted dots on the 5C-2nd façade, usually outlined in black on beige and containing a black center. These dots sometimes have depending pear-shaped ovals attached to them. Such ovals have black loops in them, giving them a "fat" u shape. These compound dots are attached to the mouths and nostrils of profile polymorphs that are adjacent to the ear flares, and they function iconographically like the dots and "bones" before the nostrils of people in Classic Maya art. Taube (2001) connects these Classic nose beads to the notion of spirit and breath conveyed by jade beads. The same argument might be used in the case of these Late Preclassic examples. One of these compound dot motifs occurs on the headdress of the lower west jaguarian mask. There the background color is not beige, but a distinct yellow. In addition to meaning "red shell bead," *k'an* also means "yellow" and "precious." Other dots are scattered randomly in the red background of the panels, analogous to the scattering of "precious" elements in some Classic period compositions, such as the sarcophagus of K'inich Janab Pakal II of Palenque. On Structure 6B at Cerros, slightly later than Structure 5C-2nd, there is a profile polymorphic image painted in a more complex polychrome (figure 3.14). The snout of the polymorph is decorated with dots; two are painted green and one yellow. The upturned snout of the creature is sprocketed, painted red, with dots decorating the ends of the sprockets. The polymorph is at the base of an ear-flare assemblage for a monumental mask, structurally the same position as the trilobate motif on the 5C-2nd façade. Possibly it represents a personified cut *Spondylus* shell with precious beads on it.

The overall composition of the Structure 5C-2nd façade suggests that it was a place for performance celebrating the resurrection of the Maize god (Reese 1996). The detailed iconographic discussions and demonstrations of this hypothesis are given by Reese-Taylor (Reese 1996; Reese-Taylor n.d.). They follow and extend discussions of Maya celestial iconography outlined in Maya Cosmos by Linda Schele and Werner Nahm (Freidel, Schele, and Parker 1993; Schele 1992). Here we just summarize the conclusions of those arguments. As discussed above, we would identify the upper bird masks as known Maya supernaturals, *Itzam-Ye* and the Water Fowl, and these have possible celestial references in the Ursa Major and Cassiopeia constellations, respectively (see also Kappelman 1997). In similar fashion, we think an argument can be made to identify the lower jaguarian masks with

Fig. 3.14. Detail of the facade of Structure 6B, showing the sprocketed profile polymorph motif of the ear flare assemblage.

specific supernaturals, Yax Balam, younger of the Classic period Maya hero twin sons of the Maize god, and the Waterlily Jaguar. We propose that these supernaturals have celestial referents in the constellations in the area of Capricorn/Aquarius and Leo, respectively, on the ecliptic (Reese 1996). The former identification of a jaguarian constellation was proposed by Nahm (cited in Freidel, Schele, and Parker 1993; Schele 1992). The white stairway between the mask panels, in this interpretation, symbolized the Milky Way in its two north-south orientations, the *Wak Chan Ahaw* (Six or Stood-up Sky Lord) and the *Na Te' K'an* (First Tree K'an) as identified by Linda Schele (Freidel, Schele, and Parker 1993).

The Milky Way rotates through the night sky and, according to Schele, symbolizes different important supernaturals in the story of the death and resurrection of the Maize god as it rotates. The following rendition of that story varies from that given in Maya Cosmos in ways outlined in Freidel (1996) and Freidel and MacLeod (2000). The nightly cycle of the Milky Way forms the two major episodes in this story on the nights of August 13 and February 5. Beginning at dusk on August 13, the *Wak Chan Ahaw* World Tree, pregnant with the Maize god, rotates to become the Celestial Monster pouring out the waters of the cosmic deluge (breaking the waters preceding birth); then a celestial canoe carries the Maize god to the center of the sky (the vulva in presentation of the baby's head in birth); then the canoe sinks, rotating to become the *Na Te' K'an*, the Maize god as the Foliated Cross Maize plant above the ecliptic, and the celestial umbilicus connecting the sky to the earth below the ecliptic (see Kappelman 1997 on the celestial umbilicus imagery). On February 5, the Milky Way starts at dusk as the *Na Te' K'an* image of the Maize god, rotates and falls into the western sky, goes into the underworld as a rim of light centered on the southern horizon, framing the dark center of the sky, the Ek Wayeb or dark transforming/dreaming place marking the sacrificial death of the Maize god in the underworld. Finally, the Milky Way rotates back up into the vertical position as the *Wak Chan Ahaw*, the World Tree pregnant with the Maize god. As Reese-Taylor (Reese 1996) described in her dissertation, during the rotational cycles of the Milky Way, the previously described constellation-supernaturals are also rotating, appearing and disappearing in conjunction with the Milky Way. When the Milky Way is in the *Na Te' K'an* north-south position, Cassiopeia is north of it near the horizon, as depicted on the panel of the Foliated Cross at Palenque. When the Milky Way is in the *Wak Chan Ahaw* north-south position, Ursa

Major is in the north above it. Both of the lower jaguarian masks are marked with *k'in* (sun) glyphs on their cheeks. When the *Na Te' K'an* expression of the Milky Way rises at dawn on the morning of August 13, Leo is the constellation that will take the sun through its day journey. Similarly, when the *Wak Chan Ahaw* rises at dawn on February 5, the constellation Capricorn/Aquarius carries the sun. In sum, the masks on Structure 5C-2nd, when combined with the elongated white stairway, provide a performance space for rulers to dance as the Maize god in celestial space and time. In light of the dynamic field of heavenly bodies implicated in the façade program and stairway, it is hardly surprising that the structure is oriented precisely to true north.

The images of the divinities on Structure 5C-2nd are adorned with symbols of preciousness and royalty, which, we have suggested, refer to *Spondylus* and jade as media for treasure, wealth, and exchange. Jade is *yax*, the color of the center, color of the mountain of sustenance (*yax hal witz nal*, Schele and Freidel 1990), the adjectival qualification of founding dynasts in the Classic Maya world (e.g., Yax K'uk' Mo' of Copan). It is symbolic of life-giving water, of growing green Maize, and the primary color of the *hunal* jewels of royalty. Recall that the Preclassic glyph for *AJAW* is derived from an image of a precious bead. *Hun Nal Ye*, the Classic Maya name for the Maize god, can mean one maize revealed (or kernel, or tooth, Freidel, Schele, and Parker 1993). Barbara MacLeod (Freidel and MacLeod 2000) posits that the name reads *Hun Ye Nal*, one breath of maize. It might best read *Hun Nal Ye*, one maize breath, where it is a pun on *Hunal Ye*, oneness breath, where the *hunal* jewel is usually made of jade. Stephen Houston and Karl Taube (2001) have recently reviewed the correlation between jade jewels and breath in Maya thought, art, and artifactual contexts (e.g., a jade bead in the mouth of the deceased). The *Hun Nal Ye* name of the Maize god, we suggest, might be reduced metaphorically to a jade jewel (see Taube 1998 for related arguments). Jade as treasure signified the Maize god and royalty.

A parallel argument can be made for *Spondylus*. As a jewel, *Spondylus* is *k'an*. This word means yellow, precious, and red shell bead in Mayan languages such as Yucatec. As a symbol, the K'an Cross denotes the birthplace of the Maize god in Classic Maya iconography. Specifically, there are several examples in the corpus of Classic Maya painted vases of the K'an Cross marking the turtle carapace from which the Maize god is reborn. The most dramatic image is the Foliated Cross, where the Maize plant form of the Maize god emerges from a personified K'an Cross. It is this image that is explicitly named *Na Te' K'an*, First Tree K'an. As Grube and Martin (2001) observed, the tree is a metaphor for family or dynasty in the Classic Maya culture, as in our own. They identified two examples of Tikal kings being in "tree" places (denoted variously 13 or 14, possibly the number of lineages contributing to the Tikal dynasty, Grube and Martin 2001: ii–17). Using this metaphor, the *Na Te' K'an* may refer to the Maize god as the founder of the first Maya lineage, derived from the K'an Cross. The physical referents of the K'an Cross are likely various, including a mythical creation place (Freidel 2000), but we argue that they include *Spondylus*. There is a distinctive girdle ornament worn by the Maize god, called the Xok Shell girdle (Miller 1974), which is a *Spondylus* shell surmounted by a supernatural's face. The size and location of the girdle ornament, directly over the genitalia, make its identity as a symbol of the female womb reasonable. While it is worn by royal women, and by the Moon goddess, its association with the reborn dancing Maize god is most common. We do not find this association at all problematic. The Creation texts at Palenque make clear that the *Wak Chan Ahaw* and the Maize god are one and the same personage (Freidel and MacLeod 2000). Previously we have suggested that the *Wak Chan Ahaw* is the Milky Way pregnant with the Maize god. Quirigua Stela C declares that another birthplace of the Maize god, the Three Stone Place, is established by the command of the *Wak Chan Ahaw* (Freidel, Schele, and Parker 1993). That statement makes unequivocal that the Maize god is alive and active before he is reborn. We think that the Xok Shell girdle symbolizes the womb out of which the Maize god was reborn. Significantly, there is in Classic Maya Stela portraits of Maya kings a common structural substitution for the Xok Shell girdle motif in this genital area, with a loin cloth marked as the World Tree, the same tree which is the *Wak Chan Ahaw*. The *Spondylus* shell is implicated in the metaphors of rebirth of the Maize god.

In the iconography of the Classic period, the Maize god is depicted being born out of a skull, and this imagery has been used to argue conceptual continuity between the Classic Creation story and the story as given in the K'iche' Popol Vuh, in which the Maize god is beheaded and his head, hung on a tree, engenders his twin sons, who eventually bring him back to life. Other contemporary Maya, such as the people of Santiago Atitlan (Carlsen and Prechtel 1991) have a myth of a pregnant World Tree, which is the source of humanity and all other things imbued with soul. We think that the Atiteco myth cycle may have retained a version of the Creation which includes the pregnant *Wak Chan Ahaw* World Tree, while the K'iche' myth has retained a version including the skull out of which the Maize god is reborn. No doubt there were variations on the Creation story in antiquity as there are among Maya groups today. There is a northern lowland Classic period image of the Maize god being born out of a large round object marked *AJAW* (Kerr 634), and this would appear to be a precious jewel. This jewel, jade or *Spondylus*, attests to the basic "entanglement" (Aizpuruia and McAnany 1999) of commodity and ideologically charged ritual performance designed to declare preciousness and value. "Dead Presidents and Living Queens," Stanley Loten once remarked at a Dumbarton Oaks conference (pers. comm. 1989), grace currencies of our continent today; Jade and *Spondylus* artifacts for the ancient Maya, even ostensibly plain beads, were similarly vested with the blessings of rulership.

Jade and *Spondylus* Artifacts in Ritual Contexts: Defining Treasure

Some cached offerings from Late Preclassic Maya contexts contain jade and *Spondylus* materials arranged in ways that reinforce their association with royal ritual performances of supernatural communion with gods, including the Maize god. Hammond (1987) and Justeson, Norman, and Hammond (1988) have offered detailed comparative analyses of three elaborate Late Preclassic caches from Belize that all contain jade artifacts and *Spondylus* shells. These are Cache 1 from Structure 6B at Cerros (Freidel 1979; Freidel and Schele 1988), the evidently cenotaphic tomb 1 at Pomona containing the Pomona monumental ear flare (Kidder and Ekholm 1951), and the Nohmul Structure 110 cache (Hammond 1974). Of these caches, Cerros Cache 1 is the only one to have a verifiable spatial arrangement of contents. The vessel containing the Nohmul cache was crushed at the time of discovery and the spatial pattern of contents thus destroyed. The description of the Pomona tomb 1 spatial arrangement, which we summarize below, was put together by Justeson, Norman, and Hammond from Kidder and Ekholm's report and unpublished notes by Kidder (Justeson, Norman, and Hammond 1988). On the summit of Structure 6B at Cerros, adjacent to Structure 5C-2nd and southwest of it, the first Cerros Project found the Late Preclassic royal jewels in Cache 1 (Freidel 1979). The green stone jewels, including ear flares and pectoral and diadem ornaments, were accompanied by four

Spondylus shells, mother-of-pearl cutouts in the shape of shells, and elements for mosaic mirrors made of crystalline volcanic hematite (figure 3.15; Garber 1989). In addition, the cache included jade beads and small fragments of jade suitable for mosaic jewelry. The main materials were evidently carefully arranged. The four smaller diadem jewels were in the approximate intercardinals and the larger pectoral head face-up in the center. Above the pectoral head was a single jade ear flare. The four *Spondylus* shells were situated above the jade artifacts inside the bucket. The complex pattern suggests that all these materials were originally wrapped in a bundle of some kind of material (Freidel, Schele, and Parker 1993: 244). If this were the case, the material was completely decayed by the time of discovery. The postulated bundle was placed inside a large ceramic bucket with a plate lid. Ritualists placed four drinking cups around the bucket, roughly in the intercardinal points, and put a three-lugged water jar in the southeast position relative to the bucket (figure 3.16). The cups were placed on flat, square ceramic trivets, and had round, worked sherd lids. The offering was buried slightly less than two meters below the

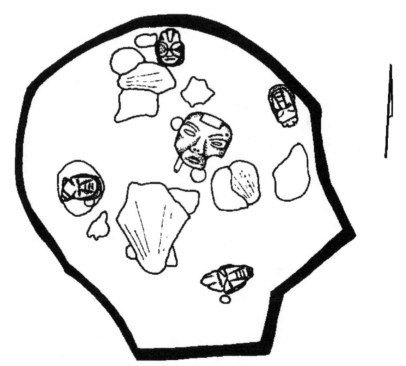

Fig. 3.15. Drawing of the pendants and shells in Cache 1, Cerros.

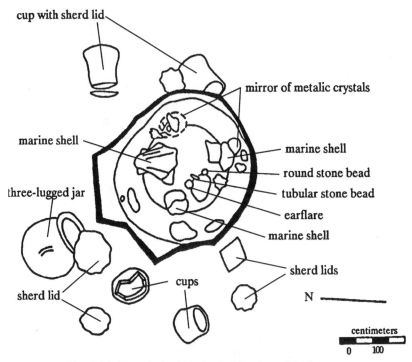

cup with sherd lid

mirror of metalic crystals

marine shell

marine shell

round stone bead

three-lugged jar

tubular stone bead

earflare

marine shell

sherd lids

sherd lid

cups

N

centimeters

0   100

Fig. 3.16. Drawing of Cache 1, Structure 6B, Cerros.

focal point of an open-summited pyramid and it likely defined a portal place for royal communication with supernaturals and ancestors (Freidel, Schele, and Parker 1993, Freidel and Schele 1988).

The central large jade pectoral mask can be identified with the Young Tonsured Lord variant of the Maize god (Taube 1985) by the square tab of hair on his forehead (figure 3.17d). The four diadem jewels (figure 3.17 a–c) include one with the trifurcate headdress of the Jester God/*hunal* royal insignia, derived ultimately from a sprouting Maize seed of Middle Preclassic iconography (Fields 1989). Hammond (1987) has associated the head images with various divinities, especially the Sun god and the Maize god, and these ideas have iconographic merit. Freidel and Suhler (1995) propose that the "butterfly eye" variant of the diadem jewels may relate to the goggle-eyed images of the Classic iconographic program and to Linda Schele's proposed reading for the goggle-eyes on the dynastic founder glyph as *ch'ok*, "bud." The asymmetrical headdress on one of these jewels, identified by Hammond with the Tonsured Maize god, now looks to us very much like a conch shell. The conch shell is a signature in

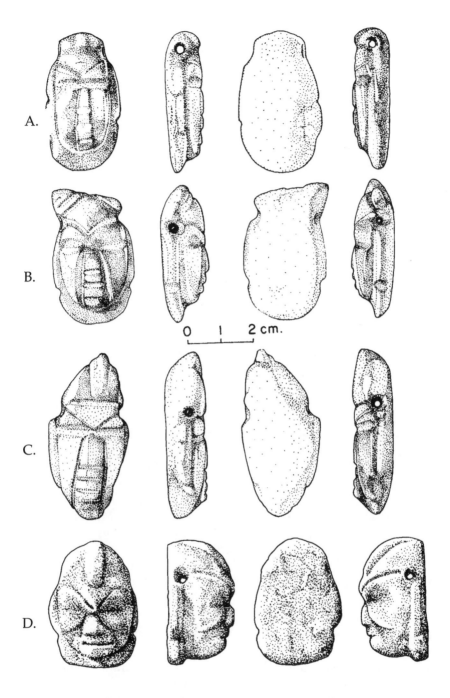

Fig. 3.17 A-D. Illustration of the four diadem pendant jewels from Cache 1 at Cerros.

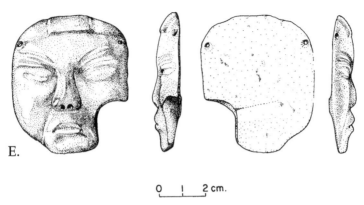

E.

0   2 cm.

Fig. 3.17 E. The pectoral head from Cache 1 at Cerros.

subsequent periods of Maya art of the world-bearing deities, the *Pawatuns*, and of God N, a divinity closely associated with the turtle carapace birthplace of the Maize god. God N, and the *hunal* trifurcate symbol, also function as glyphs in the Late Preclassic writing system. Given the deliberate arrangement of these insignia, it is possible that they were designed to be "read" like the glyphs on the monumental Pomona flare described below. In any case, together the four diadem jewel divinities open the quincuncial aperture to the Otherworld for the face-up central pectoral mask. And they are stylistically comparable to the four pendant heads discovered in the Nohmul cache. The number four is relevant to the Pomona tomb as well: Four small greenstone figurines, of a type called "Charlie Chaplins," were discovered there. These figurines are found, in both jade and *Spondylus*, in other Late Preclassic and Early Classic royal caches. So while the arrangements in the Nohmul and Pomona cases cannot be discerned, the presence of the four images suggests a common pattern of establishing a four-fold sacred space.

The quincuncial pattern is certainly present in the Pomona tomb: The monumental jade flare found there was inscribed with a text that is arranged into the quincunx, with four glyph blocks arranged around the central aperture of the flare (figure 3.18). Justeson, Norman, and Hammond (1988) analyzed this text in great detail and their gloss then was: "The holder of power is the Sun God; the Sun God casts corn to/for the sky god" (1988: 143). Several of their findings stand the test of time. First, glyph blocks B and D are deities, the Sun god and the Maize god, respectively. The sentence "the Sun God casts corn to/for the sky god" still makes sense. What the sky

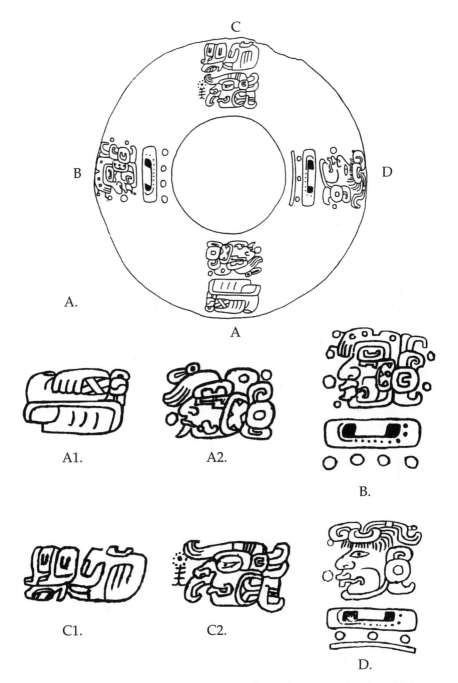

Fig. 3.18. Sentences from the Pomona ear flare. Illustration by David Mora-Marín.

god casts may be subject to modification. Justeson and Norman argued that the Maize god as corn represented what the Sun god cast because it had to be part of that sentence, a three-block sentence, leaving the other sentence, "the holder of power is the Sun God," as the expression of a single glyph block. However, their reasons for considering the Maize god as part of the other sentence are no longer as strong as they were. What they read as "the holder of power" we now read with the opening glyph at AI as *yo-l(e)*, "(it is/was) his/her/its heart," or *y(o)-OL*, "(it is/was) his/her/its heart," "(it is) the heart of." If A1b is a *le* sign, then the first analysis is correct, but if it is a *OL* "heart" logograph, then the second analysis is correct. We think the second analysis is more likely, given an example from the Late Classic recently shown at the Texas Meetings by Stephen Houston and David Stuart of the same sign (A1b) in the spelling of the glyph for "heart" (Stuart, Houston, and Robertson 1999). While they interpret the use of the sign here as phonetic *o* (and therefore as a phonetic complement to the glyph for "heart"), we think it is not an *o* sign at all, but instead the earliest version of the heart glyph. In any case, if we are right, then the glyphic collocation at A1 says: "It is the heart of the Sun god." In other words, we think this sentence of the flare's text is a proprietary statement. The sentence as a single glyph block could read that the flare, as such, is the heart of the Sun god. However, Justeson, Norman, and Hammond excluded the preceding glyph block, the Maize god, from this sentence because they argued that this glyph block D could only make sense grammatically as part of a sentence including glyph block A if D was a possessed noun. In their reading, it could not be possessed and so they excluded it. However, in our reading, there is a statement of possession, namely *y[o*, "his/her/its." Under the circumstances, the preceding Maize god could be the predicate of the clause whose subject might be *y-ohl k'inich-ajaw*: "The Maize God is the heart of the Sun God." This kind of possession is quite normal in the Classic period texts, where "so-and-so is the *y-ajaw* (i.e., the possessed lord) of so-and-so" is a standard statement of subservience and vassalage.

"The Maize God is the heart of the Sun God" makes sense semantically when one considers that *ol* means "heart place portal" (Freidel, Schele, and Parker 1993), so that the intention may be that the Maize god is the portal of the Sun god. A principle image of the portal of the Sun is the Quadripartite Badge. In the image, the glyph for sun and day, *k'in*, is displayed inside the plate carrying the stingray spine and *Spondylus* shell elements. Freidel, Schele, and Parker (1993:

244–45) observed that the incised dedication vessel of Early Classic king *Chak*-Tok-Ich'aak I of Tikal depicted the king as the Maize god cradling the double-headed serpent image of the ecliptic next to the Quadripartite Badge, sun-marked, *Ol*. The vessel contained *Spondylus* figurines, jade, textile (possibly from a bundle), and nine imitation stingray spines. In another Classic period example, king Waxaklajun Ubah K'awil of Copan performs as the Maize god on Stela H while bearing the Quadripartite Badge *Ol* on his back as a burden. As a final example, king Kan B'alam II of Palenque on the panel of the Foliated Cross declares that the Sun god, among several deities, is his *huntan*, his beloved, a relationship normally linking a mother to her child.

There are a number of potential ways this relationship might be analyzed. On Structure 5C-2nd, we posit that the performing ruler took the guise of the Maize god, and that our reading of the lower monumental masks suggests that he performed at dawn on key occasions in the celestial expression of the Creation myth cycle (Reese 1997). Moreover, in the celestial iconography of the Creation, the Quadripartite Badge portal appears as a bulge in the Milky Way marking the conjunction of the ecliptic with the Milky Way at dusk on August 13 and at dawn on February 5. Freidel (Freidel, Schele, and Parker 1993) previously interpreted that "bulge" as the head of the decapitated Maize god hung on the World Tree as related in the Popol Vuh. Here we interpret that "bulge" as the gestating Maize god in the womb of the *Wak Chan Ahaw* World Tree. In light of the depictions of the Maize god reborn from a skull, these are not incompatible ideas. The "heart" of that bulge is the Maize god.

Any interpretation of the second sentence on the Pomona flare is more tentative, since the possible verb, spelled T840-*li-ye*/CHOK, is still undeciphered. The third sign in the verb, T710, has two possible readings: phonetic *ye* and logographic CHOK, "to throw down." The former is more likely in this context, since the latter is signaled by means of a semantic determiner—a series of droplets—which is clearly absent in this instance. An analysis of the text and its various possible interpretations is provided in Mora-Marín (2001), who argues that the most parsimonious syntactic and discursive interpretation for the second clause would yield an intransitive clause such as "He VERBed to/for the Sky God" or "He VERBed in/at the SKY" (if the verb is a root intransitive), or perhaps "It was VERBed to/for/by the Sky God" or "It was VERBed in/at the Sky" (if the verb is a passive or mediopassive). However, if the second Sun god glyph in the text was not an aesthetic license (to allow for the quadripartite pattern of the text), similar to the doubled spelling in Bonampak Stela 2 at G3 of T1.534.533: 24 *u-NIK/NICH-NIK/NICH-li* for *u-NIK/NICH-li/IL*, "the child of [father]," and other similar examples, the sentence might read "The Sun god (is the one who) VERBed to/for the Sky God" or "The Sun God (is the one who) VERBed in/at the Sky," where the location of the action, if "in the sky," may have been the particular the constellation represented by the Deity image. The verb is most likely a positional verb, given that in all instances of T662/840 in later texts it is clear that a locative predication is intended (Justeson, Norman, and Hammond 1988). Whether the repeated Sun God glyph was meant to be read or not, the subject and possibly agent (i.e., doer of action) of the sentence is still likely to be the Sun god. The agent, then, might be the god, or it might be a royal performer entering the sky, which would be commensurate with what we know about early royal performance from such examples as the Hauberg Stela (Schele 1985).

In light of our earlier discussion of the stairway of Structure 5C-2nd as the Milky Way, it is perhaps significant that the "sky" Deity image on the Pomona flare is a long-lipped bird-like being with *akbal*, "darkness," infixed on its cheek. The upper west mask on 5C-2nd has *akbal* on its nose and represents the constellation Cassiopeia as a Water Fowl in our interpretation. Clearly stairways like that on 5C-2nd were designed as places of performance and of sacrifice. Indeed, the first Cerros Project discovered a distinct blackened circle on the summit threshold of the stairway such as might be caused by reverential burning of offerings within a cylindrical effigy censer stand. It is into such censers that Maya kings were depicted as "scattering." One can surmise that the ruler performing as a god on the 5C-2nd threshold was "scattering in the sky" framed by the constellations in the sky above him.

There are other caches of actual artifacts which reinforce the hypothesis we are pursuing that bundled materials could represent in the past what they do for contemporary Maya ritual specialists in many ethographically documented cases, namely the physical symbols of rebirth, resurrection, and renewal of the social and natural orders. The materials we are focusing on are jade and *Spondylus*. No doubt the repertoire of significant materials went far beyond these two categories. We end this discussion of caches with one more salient example. Diane and Arlen Chase (1998) have provided a detailed discussion of early caches at Caracol. Their general observations are entirely commensurate with what we have discerned elsewhere in

Belize: "Early caches from monumental architecture are among the most elaborate encountered at the site. Although their precise contents and layouts vary substantially, one subset of early Caracol caches is easily distinguished from the others: These have contents that are layered, and/or ordered in such a way as to suggest an intentional plan or design reflecting both directional order and placement" (Chase and Chase 1998: 314). There they found Late Preclassic royal materials in a key offering inside Structure A6, the eastern range of an E group (figure 3.19). The cache had been deposited in an open-air intrusive pit. It consisted of a hollowed-out rounded stone sliced in half to form a box. The upper half of the hollowed-out geode had a lid cut out of it. The contents of the stone appeared to be organized carefully and bundled in some kind of cloth: "At the bottom of the stone receptacle was a pool of liquid mercury. Uppermost in the cache was a complete jadeite earflare assemblage. A multitude of malachite pebbles overlay two lip-to-lip *Spondylus* shells, which held other items. Encased within the two halves of the large *Spondylus* shells was a solid jadeite mask covered with red hematite. A jadeite claw pendant was set at its throat and two beads (one jadeite and one shell) were set to its sides as if to form earflares" (Chase and Chase 1998: 315).

The exegesis of this cache can include the following observations: (1) individual stones can represent the Three Stone Place of the Maize god's rebirth (Taube 1998); (2) the A6 cache box is divided into two halves like the carapace and palastron of the turtle from which the Maize god emerges in rebirth; (3) the central jadeite mask was arranged face-up like the Cerros Cache 1 face, and also has the central squared hair tab of the Tonsured Young Lord Maize god; (4) the central mask is framed by three smaller jewels, like the Three Stone Place; (5) the claw jewel reads *tok*, which also means "true," as in the *hal* in *Yax Hal Witz Nal*, the Green True/Corn Cob, Mountain of Maize; (6) the shell bead reads *k'an*, which also marks the rebirth place of the Maize god (and specifically, the royal emblem of Carcol is *K'an tu Mak*, the K'an place in the Turtle Shell); (7) the mask and jewels are encased in *Spondylus* shells, symbolic of the womb from which the Maize god is reborn. Finally, it can be noted that the eastern ranges of deeply ancient E groups at Tikal and Calakmul are places for the burial of Early Classic rulers at those sites. We would identify the Structure A6 cache in question as another cenotaphic expression of Late Preclassic rulership such as described in the case of Cache 1 at Cerros and the Pomona Tomb 1 feature. Diane and Arlen Chase go on to

Fig. 3.19. Late Preclassic Cache from Structure 6A-1st, Caracol, illustration by Joseph Ballay, copyright The Caracol Archaeological Project, by permission of Arlen and Diane Chase.

describe many other relevant cache contexts at Caracol and Santa Rita, demonstrating their thesis that "[j]ust as the placement of structures requires carefully planning in terms of Maya cosmology . . . caches and interments may provide physical representations of the Maya worldview" (Chase and Chase 1998: 303).

Spondylus, jade, and other artifactual materials did not naturally symbolize the Maya order of the cosmos; they were invented as means to do so, or appropriated as such means from predecessors and neighbors in the project of establishing complex society. The whys and wherefores of such developmental dynamics might include both functionalist and exploitative dimensions. Functionally, at the time of the Spanish Conquest, Maya farmers in Yucatan sold part of their maize crops in local markets for currencies like jade and red shell beads (Tozzer 1941: 96). When they needed food and seed grain, they could buy it in the markets with jade and red shell beads. Practically speaking, maize is difficult to store for more than three seasons in the tropics. Maya farmers in Yucatan today store their surplus crops in domesticated animals like cattle, pigs, and horses. When they face hurricanes, prolonged drought, or other sources of crop failure, they cash in their animals for food and seed. Prior to the conquest, markets and currencies provided the means to invest surplus agricultural crops and thus hedge against deprivation and famine. Long-term adaptation to maize farming in the tropical lowlands of Mesoamerica really required this kind of evening out of the natural fluctuations in productivity when long-term storage was not an option, as it was in such societies as ancient Egypt and Mesopotamia. Currency was a viable solution to this general problem, as long as commodities could be moved over distances to offset shortfalls in productivity. There continues to be debate over how much food could be moved over long distances in Mesoamerica, given the constraints of human portage overland (Cowgill 1993). We may never see satisfactory resolution of such arguments given the limitations of archaeology, but long-term transport of food and other agricultural commodities was a fact of the Contact period Mesoamerican economy. No amount of abstract calculation will negate that fact and to ignore it is an invitation to misunderstanding the Precolumbian antecedents to the Contact period institutions. We think that the Preclassic Maya used jade and *Spondylus* and other commodities as currencies, and that governments and elites were complicit in the innovation, celebration, and distribution of these currencies.

In a programmatic exploration of the relationship between the order promulgated by emergent elites, the legitimacy of their rule, and the wealth which provided the means to rule, John Baines and Norman Yoffee (1998) compare the distinct trajectories of early Egypt and Mesopotamia. Order is both cosmic and social, encapsulated in such ideas as *ma'at* in ancient Egypt. In our view, order is evident in the cycles of cosmic rebirth and social reproduction of power performed by the ancient Maya rulers. These cycles were anchored in the metaphor of maize, the fundamental food, and its agricultural cycle. Baines and Yoffee observe that elite control of order is one of the primary means of legitimating privilege: "A major thrust of religion, on which so much of society's resources were expended, was legitimation" (1998: 213). They further observe, with regard to wealth: "Wealth and legitimacy are almost inextricably linked. Wealth, controlled and channeled, can sustain order. Destitution of wealth spells disorder or reversal of order" (1998: 213). We think it is possible, and productive, to identify and analyze the innovations of wealth in ancient Maya civilization, and to understand wealth, treasure, and currency in relation to the legitimacy of elites and rulers, and in relation to the institutions of governance which are, in the last analysis, what set civilizations apart from other forms of society. William Rathje, in his initial models for the origins of Maya civilization, sought the sources in creative responses of people to challenging situations in their natural and social environment. In his chapter in this book, he explores solutions to problems generated in the initial stages of elite formation that had rulers express their wealth, power, and legitimacy in the construction of vast, expensive monuments. We believe such monuments were much more than receptacles for wealth. They were the theaters for advertising the forms of it used by everyone in some measure, for legitimizing the existence of it as the essence of the cosmic order, and inspiring the production of it to reproduce the social order. "High cultures" of this kind, as discussed by Baines and Yoffee, take on lives of their own: "[H]igh culture contains an inner dynamic and a paradox: it seeks to legitimize the whole order of society, along with the role of the elite, as cosmologically just. If it is to do so without simply imposing authority from above, it must offer real or perceived benefits to the rest of society, but those who count most in perceiving the benefits are once again the elite" (Baines and Yoffee 1998: 238). The tensions of this paradox continue to play out in Maya civilization throughout its history subsequent to the Preclassic fluorescence. In such episodes as the ninth-century collapse, the high culture failed. But as Masson reviews in her introduction to this book, the high culture recovered, reinvented by new elites in the Postclassic period. Rathje understood that as well. The trajectory of Maya civilization is complex and multifarious, and continues to the present day.

References

Adams, Robert McC.
  1976 "The Emerging Place of Trade in Civilizational Studies." Pp. 451–464 in *Ancient Civilization and Trade*, edited by Jeremy A. Sabloff and C. C. Lamberg-Karlovsky. A School of American Research Book. Albuquerque: University of New Mexico Press.

Andrews, E. Wyllys IV
  1969 "The Archeological Use and Distribution of Mollusk in the Maya Lowlands." MARI Publication No. 14. New Orleans: Middle American Research Institute, Tulane University.

Aizpuruia, Ilean Isel Isaza, and Patricia A. McAnany
  1999 "Adornment and Identity: Shell ornaments from Formative K'axob." *Ancient Mesoamerica* 10: 117–127.

Baines, John, and Norman Yoffee
  1998 "Order, Legitimacy, and Wealth in Ancient Egypt and Mesopotamia." Pp. 199–260 in *Archaic States*, edited by Gary M. Feinman and Joyce Marcus. A School of American Research Book. Santa Fe: School of American Research Press.

Batten, David C.
  1999 "Horse Power, Wheat, Oats, Maize and the Supply of Cities." *Ancient Mesoamerica* 10: 99–103.

Carlsen, Robert, and Martin Prechtel
  1991 "The Flowering of the Dead: An Interpretation of Highland Maya Culture." *Man* n.s. 26: 23–42.

Chase, Diane Z., and Arlen F. Chase
  1998 "The Architectural Context of Caches, Burials, and Other Ritual Activities for the Classic Period Maya (as Reflected at Caracol, Belize)." Pp. 299–332 in *Function and Meaning in Classic Maya Architecture*, edited by Stephen D. Houston. Washington D.C.: Dumbarton Oaks.

Cortez, Constance
  1986 "The Principal Bird Deity and Early Classic Maya Art." Master's thesis, Department of Art History, University of Texas at Austin.

Cowgill, George L.
  1993 "Comments on Andras Slayter: Long-distance Staple Transport in Western Mesoamerica: Insight through Quantitative Modeling." *Ancient Mesoamerica* 4(2): 201–203.

Dalton, George
  1976 "Karl Polanyi's Analysis of Long-Distance Trade and His Wider Paradigm." Pp. 63–132 in *Ancient Civilization and Trade*, edited by Jeremy A. Sabloff and C. C. Lamberg-Karlovsky. A School of American Research Book. Albuquerque: University of New Mexico Press.

Fields, Virginia M.
  1989 "The Origins of Divine Kingship among the Lowland Classic Maya."
        Ph.D. dissertation, University of Texas at Austin.
  1991 "Iconographic Heritage of the Maya Jester God." Pp. 167–174 in *Sixth
        Palenque Round Table, 1986*, general editor Merle Greene Robertson, volume
        editor Virginia M. Fields. Norman: University of Oklahoma Press.
Freidel, David A.
  1979 "Culture Areas and Interaction Spheres: Contrasting Approaches to the
        Emergence of Civilization in the Maya Lowlands." *American Antiquity* 44:
        5–54.
  1980 "Civilization as a State of Mind: The Cultural Evolution of the Lowland
        Maya." Pp. 188–227 in *Transition to Statehood in the New World*, edited by
        Grant D. Jones and Richard Kraus. Cambridge: Cambridge University Press.
  1985 "Polychrome Façades of the Lowland Maya Pre-Classic." Pp. 5–30 in
        Painted Architecture and Polychrome Monumental Sculpture in Mesoamerica, ed-
        ited by Elizabeth Boone. Washington D.C.: Dumbarton Oaks.
  1986 "Terminal Classic Maya: Success, Failure and Aftermath." Pp. 409–430
        in *Late Maya Civilization: Postclassic Developments*, edited by J. A. Sabloff and
        E. W. Andrews, V. A School of American Research Book. Albuquerque: Uni-
        versity of New Mexico Press.
  1990 "The Jester God: The Beginning and End of a Maya Royal Symbol." Pp.
        67–78 in *Vision and Revision in Maya Studies*, edited by Flora S. Clancy and
        Peter D. Harrison. Albuquerque: University of New Mexico Press.
  1992 "The Jade Ahau: Toward a Theory of Commodity Value in Maya Civili-
        zation." Pp. 149–165 in *Precolumbian Jade: New Geological and Cultural Inter-
        pretations*, edited by Fredrick W. Lange. Salt Lake City: University of Utah
        Press.
  1996 "The Five Portals of the Maya Cosmos: An Hypothesis." SMU Occasional
        Maya Notes 1. Dallas: Southern Methodist University Department of Anthro-
        pology.
  2000 "Mystery of the Maya Façade." *Archaeology* 53(5): 24–28.
Freidel, David A., and Barbara MacLeod
  2000 "Creation Redux: New Thoughts on Maya Cosmology from Epigraphy,
        Iconography and Archaeology." *The PARI Journal* 1(2): 1–8.
Freidel, David A., and Linda Schele
  1988 "Kingship in the Late Pre-Classic Maya Lowlands: The Instruments and
        Places of Ritual Power." *American Anthropologist* 90: 547–567.
  1990 *A Forest of Kings: The Untold Story of the Ancient Maya*. New York: Will-
        iam Morrow.
Freidel, David A., Linda Schele, and Joy Parker
  1993 *Maya Cosmos: Three Thousand Years on the Shaman's Path*. New York: Wil-
        liam Morrow.
Freidel, David A., and Charles K. Suhler
  1995 "Crown of Creation: The Development of the Maya Royal Diadems in
        the Late Preclassic and Early Classic Periods." Pp. 137–150 in *The Emergence
        of Lowland Maya Civilization: The Transition from the Preclassic to the Early Clas-
        sic*, edited by Nikolai Grube. *Acta Mesoamericana* 8. Hamburg: Verlag Anton
        Suarwein.

1998 "Visiones serpentinas y labrintos mayas." *Arqueología Mexicana* VI(34): 28–37.

Garber, James F.
1981 "Patterns of Jade Consumption and Disposal at Cerros, Northern Belize." *American Antiquity* 48(4): 800–807.
1989 *The Artifacts. Archaeology at Cerros, Belize, Central America.* Vol. II. Dallas: Southern Methodist University Press.

Geertz, Clifford
1973 *Interpretation of Cultures.* New York: Basic Books.

Greene Robertson, Merle
1974 "The Quadripartite Badge: A Badge of Rulership." Pp. 77–93 in *Primera Mesa Redonda de Palenque*, Part II, edited by Merle Greene Robertson. Pebble Beach: Robert Louis Stevenson School.

Grube, Nikolai, and Simon Martin
2001 "The Coming of Kings, Writing and Dynastic Kingship in the Maya Area between the Late Preclassic and the Early Classic." *Notebook for the XXV Maya Hieroglyphic Forum at Texas.* Austin: Department of Art and Art History, The College of Fine Arts, and the Institute of Latin American Studies.

Hammond, Norman
1974 "Preclassic to Classic in Northern Belize." *Antiquity* 49: 177–189.
1987 "The Sun Also Rises: Iconographic Syntax of the Pomona Flare." *Research Reports on Ancient Maya Writing 6&7.* Washington D.C.: Center for Maya Research.

Hansen, Richard D.
1990a *Excavations in the Tigre Complex, El Mirador, Petén, Guatemala.* Papers of the New World Archaeological Foundation, no. 62. Provo, Utah: Brigham Young University.
1990b "Proceso cultural de Nakbe y el area del Petén nor-central: Las épocas tempranas." Pp. 81–96 in *V simposio de investigaciones en Guatemala*, edited by Juan Pedro Laporte, Hector Escobedo, and Sandra V. de Brady. Museo Nacional de Arqueología e Historia de Guatemala. Guatemala City: Asociación Tikal.
1998 "Continuity and Disjunction: The Pre-Classic Antecedents of Classic Maya Architecture." Pp. 49–122 in *Function and Meaning in Classic Maya Architecture*, edited by Stephen D. Houston. Washington, D.C.: Dumbarton Oaks.

Helms, Mary
1993 *Craft and the Kingly Ideal: Art, Trade and Power.* Austin: University of Texas Press.

Houston, Stephen D.
2000 "Into the Minds of Ancient: Advances in Maya Glyph Studies." *Journal of World Prehistory* 14(2): 121–201.

Houston, Stephen D., and David Stuart
1989 "The Way Glyph: Evidence for 'Co-essences' among the Classic Maya." *Research Reports on Ancient Maya Writing.* Washington D.C.: Center for Maya Research.

Houston, Stephen D., and Karl Taube
2000 "An Archaeology of the Senses: Perception and Cultural Expression in Ancient Mesoamerica." *Cambridge Archaeological Journal* 10(2): 261–294.

Justeson, John S., and Terrence Kaufman
1993 "A Decipherment of Epi-Olmec Hieroglyphic Writing." *Science* 259: 1703–1711.

Justeson, John S., and Peter Mathews
1991 "Evolutionary Trends in Mesoamerican Hieroglyphic Writing." *Visible Language* 24(1): 88–132.

Justeson, John S., William M. Norman, and Norman Hammond
1988 "The Pomona Flare: A Preclassic Maya Hieroglyphic Text." Pp. 94–151 in *Maya Iconography*, edited by Elizabeth P. Benson and Gillett G. Griffin. Princeton, N.J.: Princeton University Press.

Kappelman, Julia Guernsey
1997 "Of Macaws and Men: Late Preclassic Cosmology and Political Ideology in Izapan-Style Monuments." Ph.D. dissertation, University of Texas at Austin.

Kaufman, Terrence S., and William M. Norman
1984 "An Outline of Proto-Cholan Phonology, Morphology, and Vocabulary." Pp. 77–166 in *Phoneticism in Mayan Hieroglyphic Writing*, edited by John S. Justeson and Lyle Campbell. Institute for Mesoamerican Studies Publication No. 9. Albany: State University of New York.

Kidder, Alfred V., and Gordon F. Ekholm
1951 "Some Archaeological Specimens from Pomona, British Honduras." *Notes on Middle American Archaeology and Ethnology*, No. 102, pp. 125–142. Carnegie Institution of Washington, Department of Archaeology.

Mathews, Peter
1991 "Classic Maya Emblem Glyphs." Pp. 19–29 in *Classic Maya Political History: Hieroglyphic and Archaeological Evidence*, edited by T. Patrick Culbert. A School of American Research Book. Cambridge: Cambridge University Press.

Miller, Jeffrey H.
1974 "Notes on a Stelae Pair Probably from Calakmul, Campeche, Mexico." Pp. 149–161 in *Primera Mesa Redonda de Palenque*, Part I, edited by Merle Greene Robertson. Pebble Beach: Robert Louis Stevenson School.

Millon, Rene F.
1955 "When Money Grew on Trees: A Study of Cacao in Ancient Mesoamerica." Ph.D. dissertation, Columbia University.

Moholy-Nagy, Hattula
1985 "The Social and Ceremonial Uses of Marine Mollusks at Tikal." In *Prehistoric Lowland Maya Environment and Subsistence Economy*, edited by Mary Pohl. Papers of the Peabody Museum of Archaeology and Ethnology, Vol. 77. Cambridge, Mass.: Harvard University.

1989 "Formed Shell Beads from Tikal, Guatemala." Pp. 139–156 in *Proceedings of the 1986 Shell Bead Conference*, edited by Charles F. Haynes III, Lynn Ceci, and Connie Cox Bodner. Research Records No. 20. Rochester, N.Y.: Rochester Museum and Science Center.

Mora-Marín, David
1997 "The Origin of Maya Writing: The Case for Portable Objects." Pp. 133–164 in *U Mut Maya Volume VI*, edited by Tom and Carolyn Jones. Bayside, Calif.: Tom and Carolyn Jones.

2001 "The Grammar, Orthography, Content, and Social Context of Late Preclassic Portable Texts." Ph.D. dissertation, State University of New York at Albany.
Norman, Garth V.
1975 "Izapa Sculpture, Part II: Text." Papers of the New World Archaeological Foundation, No. 30, Part 2. Provo, Utah: Brigham Young University.
Parsons, Lee Allen
1986 *The Origins of Maya Art: Monumental Stone Sculpture of Kaminaljuyu, Guatemala, and the Southern Pacific Coast.* Washington D.C.: Dumbarton Oaks.
Quintal Suaste, Beatriz
1998 "Los Mascarones de Acanceh." *Arqueología Mexicana* 7(37): 14–17.
Quirarte, Jacinto
1974 "Terrestrial/Celestial Polymorphs as Narrative Frames in the Arts of Izapa and Palenque." Pp. 129–135 in *Primera Mesa Redonda de Palenque*, Part 2, edited by Merle Greene Robertson. Pebble Beach: Robert Louis Stevenson School.
Rathje, William L.
1972 "Praise the Gods and Pass the Metates: A Hypothesis of the Development of Rainforest Civilizations in Mesoamerica." Pp. 365–392 in *Contemporary Archaeology: A Guide to Theory and Contributions*, edited by Mark P. Leone. Carbondale: Southern Illinois University Press.
Reese, Kathryn V.
1996 "Narratives of Power: Late Formative Public Architecture and Civic Center Design at Cerros, Belize." Ph.D. dissertation, University of Texas at Austin.
Reese-Taylor, Kathryn
n.d. "Narrative and Sacred Landscape: The Ballcourt Program at Cerros, Belize." *Ancient Mesoamerica* (in press).
Reilly, F. Kent III
1991 "Olmec Iconographic Influences on the Symbols of Maya Rulership: An Examination of Possible Sources." Pp. 151–174 in *Sixth Palenque Round Table, 1986*, general editor Merle Greene Robertson, volume editor Virginia M. Fields. Norman: University of Oklahoma Press.
1994 "Visions to Another World: Art, Shamanism, and Political Power in Middle Formative Mesoamerica." Ph.D. dissertation, University of Texas at Austin.
1996 "Art, Ritual, and Rulership in the Olmec World." Pp. 27–45 in *The Olmec World: Ritual and Rulership*. Princeton: Art Museum, Princeton University.
Schele, Linda
1985 "The Hauberg Stela: Bloodletting and the Mythos of Maya Rulership." Pp. 135–149 in *Fifth Palenque Round Table, 1983*, Vol. VII, general editor Merle Greene Robertson, volume editor Virginia M. Fields. San Francisco: Pre-Columbian Art Research Institute.
1992 *The Proceedings of the Maya Hieroglyphic Workshop*, transcribed and edited by Phil Wanyerka. Austin: Department of Art History, University of Texas.
Schele, Linda, and David Freidel
1990 *A Forest of Kings: The Untold Story of the Ancient Maya.* New York: William Morrow.

Schele, Linda, and Nikolai Grube
1998 *The Workbook for the XVIIIth Maya Hieroglyphic Workshop at Texas.* Austin: Department of Art History, University of Texas.
Schele, Linda, and Peter Mathews
1998 *Code of Kings: The Language of Seven Sacred Maya Temples and Tombs.* New York: Scribner.
Schele, Linda, and Mary Ellen Miller
1986 *The Blood of Kings: Dynasty and Ritual in Maya Art.* Fort Worth: Kimbell Art Museum.
Stuart, David
1995 "A Study of Classic Mayan Inscriptions." Ph.D. dissertation, Vanderbilt University.
Stuart, David, Stephen Houston, and John Robertson
1999 "Classic Mayan Language." In *Notebook for the XXIII Maya Hieroglyphic Forum,*edited by David Stuart, Stephen Houston, and John Robertson. Austin: University of Texas Department of Art History.
Suhler, Charles K.
1996 "Excavations at the North Acropolis, Yaxuna, Yucatan, Mexico." Ph.D. dissertation, Southern Methodist University, Dallas.
Suhler, Charles K., and David Freidel
1998 "Life and Death in a Maya War Zone." *Archaeology* (May/June): 28–34.
Taube, Karl
1985 "The Classic Maya Maize God: A Reappraisal." Pp. 123–133 in *Fifth Palenque Round Table 1983*, general editor Merle Greene Robertson, volume editor Virginia M. Fields. San Francisco: Pre-Columbian Art Research Institute.
1998 "Jade Hearth: Centrality, Rulership, and the Classic Maya Temple." Pp. 427–478 in *Function and Meaning in Classic Maya Architecture*, edited by Stephen D. Houston. Washington, D.C.: Dumbarton Oaks.
2001 "The Classic Maya Gods." Pp. 262–277 in *Maya: Divine Kings of the Rainforest*, edited by Nikolai Grube assisted by Eva Eggebrecht and Matthias Seidel. Cologne: Könemann.
Thompson, J. E. S.
1950 *Maya Hieroglyphic Writing: An Introduction.* Carnegie Institution of Washington Publication no. 589. Washington, D.C.: Carnegie Institution.
1962 *A Catalog of Maya Hieroglyphs.* Norman: University of Oklahoma Press.
Tozzer, Alfred M.
1941 "Landa's Relación de las Cosas de Yucatan: A Translation." *Papers of the Peabody Museum of American Archaeology and Ethnology*, Harvard University, Vol. 98. Reprinted with permission of the original publishers by Kraus Reprint Corporation, New York, 1966.
Valdés, Juan Antonio
1995 "Desarrollo cultural y senales de alarma entre los mayas: el Preclasico Tardio y la transcion hacia el Clasico Temprano." Pp. 71–85 in *The Emergence of Lowland Maya Civilization: The Transition from the Preclassic to the Early Classic*, edited by Nikolai Grube. *Acta Mesoamericana* 8. Hamburg: Verlag Anton Saurwien.

Chapter Four

The Passage of the Late Preclassic into the Early Classic

Kathryn Reese-Taylor and Debra S. Walker

Introduction

From approximately 400 B.C., the beginning of the Late Preclassic period, to A.D. 378, the date that Yax Nuun Ayiin I acceded to the throne of Tikal, the political geography of the southern Maya lowlands changed dramatically. This chapter examines these transformations from the perspective that they were more than just a prelude to the warring superstates of the Classic. We argue that the political maneuvering characteristic of later lowland Maya states was launched during this period and, moreover, that the institution of kingship, in part, developed as a response to this rapidly shifting landscape.

We commence our perusal of the Late Preclassic at the beginning of Cycle 7. We follow Dennis Puleston (1979) in the use of long count dates for organizing our chronology, as it provides a cognitive framework that more closely links the Preclassic with the Classic. To anticipate our conclusion, we make three main points. First, the beginning of Cycle 7 was characterized by relative homogeneity; however, toward the end of this cycle a turbulent period began in which changes occurred rapidly in the political landscape of the southern lowlands. Second, much of this turbulence resulted from competition over control of long-distance trade routes in the wake of El Mirador's demise. Finally, the institution of kingship initially evolved, at least in part, as a means to control long-distance trade, changing in response to shifting political and economic alliances.

We are not the first to recognize an interdependence between expanding trade networks and increasing complexity in the Maya area. In earlier works, William L. Rathje (1971, 1972) proposed that complex sociopolitical organization in the Maya lowlands arose in response to the need for procurement and allocation of basic resources unavailable in lowland rainforests. His hypothesis is founded on the presence of long-distance trade networks. In essence, Rathje suggested that the Maya who lived in the Petén, a core area, traded agricultural produce with coastal groups for salt and with highland Guatemalan groups for commodities such as obsidian blades and metates made of igneous stone. In addition to those items noted by Rathje, further trade in luxury items such as jade, *Spondylus*, cacao, quetzal feathers, and pyrite also fell under the direct control of the elites (Freidel et al., chapter 3 this volume). In the following discussion we use Rathje's model as a point of departure. While some aspects of his core-buffer have changed because of new archaeological evidence, the fundamental concept—that trade was a significant factor in the evolution of complexity in the Maya lowlands—has stood the test of time.

7.0.0.0.0–7.15.0.0.0 (354–58 B.C.)
The Beginning

The beginning of Cycle 7 in 354 B.C. saw a shift in settlement in north-central Petén from Nakbe to the site of El Mirador (figure 4.1). Hansen (1998) notes that the precocious building spree that characterized

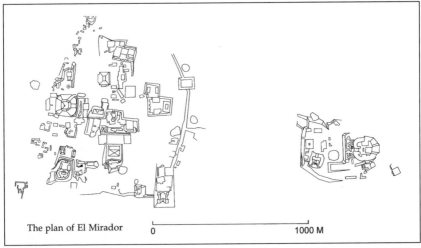

The plan of El Mirador   0   1000 M

Figure 4.1. Map of El Mirador (modified from Price and Feinman 1997: 297).

Nakbe from 600 to 400 B.C. paled in comparison with later accomplishments in north-central Petén. Most of El Mirador's large public buildings were constructed then, including the Tigre and Dante complexes (Hansen 1998). The Tigre Complex alone covered 19,600 sq. meters, an area so massive that it could have effectively encased the North Acropolis, the Great Plaza, and Temples 1 and 2 of Tikal (Hansen 1990a, 1990b, 1998).

Rio Azul elites also constructed monumental architecture during this period (Valdez n.d.). One of the site's earliest known structures, G-103, dates to the Middle Preclassic/Late Preclassic juncture. Structure G-103 iconography does not resemble the large bird and jaguar masks that are hallmarks of their closest neighbors, Nakbe and El Mirador. Instead, according to Valdez (n.d.) and Kappelman (pers. comm. 2001), these façades more closely resemble the iconographic corpus seen on Izapan-style stelae. Further, while the evidence is sparse, there is no indication that Nakbe or its successor, El Mirador, colonized or conquered Rio Azul (Adams 1986, 1987, 1989, 1990, 1999, 2000), supporting the case for complex economic relationships even at this time depth.

Many other sites, including Lamanai (Pendergast 1981) and Uaxactun (Valdés 1987, 1988, 1995), also experienced exponential growth at the beginning of this era, but all appear to be the result of *in situ* development. In addition to the above sites, settlements throughout Petén and northern Belize increased in both number and complexity during Cycle 7 (Coe 1965, 1990; Freidel 1986a, 1986b; Hammond 1973, 1991; McAnany and López Varela 1999; Shafer and Hester 1983; Sullivan 1991). So, what was the catalyst for this transformation of the southern Maya lowlands? Rise in population during the era is well documented, as is the increasing intensification of production (Andrews 1990; Freidel 1978, 1979; Hammond 1985; Houk 1992; Scarborough 1983a, 1983b, 1985; Turner and Harrison 1983). However, this in and of itself may not have been enough to account for the increased social and political complexity of the Late Preclassic. Therefore, what else emerged during Cycle 7?

We argue that the most significant change at this time was that the southern lowlands increased its participation in Mesoamerican long-distance trade networks. Further, trade in precious commodities, such as jade, shell, obsidian, and pyrite, appears to have been under the direct control of elites (Aizpuruia and McAnany 1999; Garber 1983, 1986, 1989). We presume that interregional trade in agricultural products and stone tools was burgeoning given the economic specializations that appear in many smaller settlements, such as K'axob, which has evidence of intense agricultural production (McAnany and López Varela 1999; Turner and Harrison 1983) and Colha, which specialized in stone tool production (Drollinger 1989; Hester and Shafer 1989; Shafer and Hester 1983, 1991). Larger settlements such as Rio Azul also apparently revealed evidence for both specialized lithic tool production and agricultural intensification (Adams 1999; Adams et al. 1988). Indeed, stone tools made of Colha chert were traded as far away as central Petén (Santone 1997: 77). The most commonly produced Late Preclassic Colha tool was the tranchet adze, ideally suited for land clearance, a clear correlate to successful expansionist settlements. Therefore, the development of long distance trade networks, along with the need to manage intensive agricultural systems, may have provided the conditions that lead to the evolution of state-level social and political institutions.

Further, we suggest, along with many others, that large 7th Cycle sites were situated in strategic locations along riverine and overland portage routes to take advantage of this exchange network, which grew exponentially as a result (Rathje 1970, 1971; Pendergast 1981; Hansen 1998). Cerros, located at the mouth of the New River, sat in an ideal location to facilitate coastal to inland trade (Freidel 1979, 1986b; Garber 1986, 1989). Therefore, it should not be surprising that somewhat later, at approximately 100 B.C., Cerros underwent an abrupt expansion wherein large public buildings were constructed over a preexisting village (Freidel 1986b). We suggest that this expansion was a result of El Mirador's efforts to control the New River trade route. Whether people from El Mirador came in and conquered Cerros or a particular lineage was elevated to power through alliance with El Mirador, close ties between Cerros and El Mirador are evident in architectural, iconographic, and ceramic assemblages from both sites.

However, before we turn to specific evidence linking particular sites to each other in early interaction spheres (Caldwell 1964; Freidel 1979), we would like to comment on the relative homogeneity present during Cycle 7. Ties between many larger Late Preclassic settlements are evident in both ceramic and architectural data sets. Richard Hansen's 1998 article neatly outlines the architectural commonalities. Triadic arrangements were present at many sites, including Cerros, Caracol, El Mirador, Lamanai, Nohmul, Tikal, and Uaxactun, to name a few. Equally prevalent are E-groups, notably absent at Cerros and Lamanai, but present at Caracol, El Mirador, Nakbe, Tikal, and Uaxactun. Ball courts proliferate throughout the landscape during

Cycle 7 (Hansen 1998; Scarborough 1991; Scarborough and Wilcox 1993).

The iconographic programs of the 7th *bak'tun* are also consistent. A principal theme consists of birds and jaguars on separate buildings within a single architectural group as seen at Nakbe (figure 4.2), El Mirador, Lamanai, Tikal, and Uaxactun (Reese 1996; Reese-Taylor and Freidel 1998; Schele and Kappelman 2001). Ceramic relationships between northern Belize and the central Petén are likewise strong and well documented. Many ceramicists have noted the similarities between Chicanel ceramic types from sites in northern Belize and those of Tikal, Uaxactun, and Barton Ramie during this era (Robertson-Freidel 1980; Ball 1983; Valdez 1987; Kosakowsky 1987; Reese 1989; López Varela 1996). As we see it, the Petén and northern Belize formed a core area based on riverine trade routes, surrounded by a less developed periphery immediately to the west and south. Successful agriculturalists expanded throughout the southern lowlands,

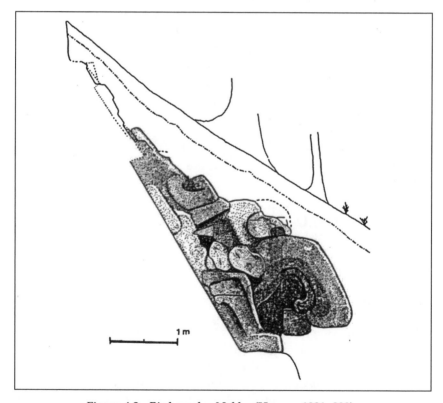

Figure 4.2. Bird masks, Nakbe (Hansen 1991: 223).

following waterways not only to ensure agricultural fertility, but also to facilitate trade and communication between centers. During this era, commodities exchanged included nonstatus goods, which we argue prompted the rise of craft specialization.

It was in the context of exchange systems that kingship was founded, and we concur with Freidel and Schele (1988a, 1988b), Kappelman (1997), Reilly (1994), and others that shamanic performance supplied one of the avenues for the public legitimation of rulership at this time. We further agree with Freidel and Schele (1988b: 93) that these early city-states did not have well-established rules governing succession. We base this on several lines of evidence. First, there were no contemporary portrait masks, inscribed monuments, or other artistic representations of rulers. Instead, iconography focused on the deities themselves, as in bird and jaguar mask programs, emphasizing the supernatural sanctioning of rulership, not the ruler himself. Second, we know of no royal tombs or caches containing overt signatures of kingly office from this era. Therefore, we argue that 7th Cycle kingship was continually negotiated between competing lineages. Furthermore, we suggest that it was this careful balance of power between rulers and lineage heads at various sites that promoted the relative homogeneity in ceramics, architectural programs, and iconographic façades. In sum, from 7.0.0.0.0 to 7.15.0.0.0, a carefully constructed ideology of egalitarianism bound elites throughout the southern Maya lowlands, even in the face of increasingly disproportionate access to wealth and power. While doctrine may have espoused such egalitarian ideology, it is likely that conflict and competition were present, though masked in publicly displayed symbolism.

7.15.0.0.0–8.6.0.0.0 (58 B.C.–A. D. 159)
Interaction Intensifies

By the final *hotun* of the 7th Cycle, the egalitarian ethic was beginning to crumble. During this era, trade intensified dramatically throughout the Maya lowlands as exotic goods associated with the developing institution of kingship began to appear through the miracle of long-distance trade (cf. Helms 1993). Recent investigations have revealed that *Spondylus* entered the southern lowlands at this time and was intimately linked to the institution of kingship (Aizpuruia and McAnany 1999; Freidel et al., chapter 3 this volume; Hansen pers. comm. 2000; Moholy-Nagy 1989). The systematic importation of foreign ceramics also began during this time. Indeed, Usulatan ceramics became the model for a number of local innovations. Notable parallels prevailed in both ceramic and architectural data sets from a network of strategically located sites that indicate an emerging sphere of intensified interaction, with El Mirador as the central node in the network. We note particularly that specific ceramic and architectural affiliations link El Mirador with Cerros, Uaxactun, and several other strategic sites.

First, direct architectural ties connect Cerros to Uaxactun. In a recent article, Reese-Taylor (2001) proposed that both Structure 6 at Cerros and the last construction phase of Group H at Uaxactun functioned as a specific architectural type, the Eight House of the North (figure 4.3). Like triadic groups that represent the Three Stone Place where First Father is reborn, the Eight House of the North is a specific mythic location recorded in Classic texts. At this point, we can confirm the presence of this architectural type only at these two sites during the Late Preclassic. Moreover, Structure 3 complex at Wakna (Hansen 1998, fig. 21) also has buildings located in the cardinal and

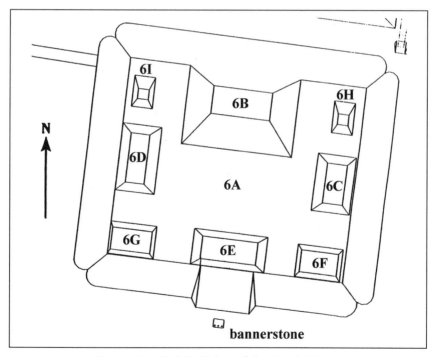

Figure 4.3. Eighth House of the North Place.

intercardinal directions; however, lacking excavation data we cannot establish the contemporaneity or the construction sequence of the complex. Nevertheless, the presence of Wakna Structure 3 implies that similar complexes were built in the north-central Petén, further linking the region to Uaxactun and Cerros.

At Lamanai and Cerros another type of triadic arrangement was constructed. These groups sit on the apex of tall subplatforms, Structure 29A at Cerros and Structure N10-43 at Lamanai. They differ from earlier triadic programs in that they are arranged in a linear fashion (figure 4.4). In both cases flanking structures are so close to the central one that passage between them is somewhat difficult. This rare architectural parallel implies a close link between Cerros and Lamanai, and is interpreted as evidence for increasing interaction between strategic exchange locations, including El Mirador, Uaxactun, Lamanai, Cerros, and Becan. Notably, these sites were situated at significant points on major river and portage routes, implying that control of long-distance trade was the impetus for increased communication.

During this era, iconographic programs found on architecture also changed. Birds and jaguars remained a common motif; it is at this point that jaguar masks appear on Structure 5D-Sub 1-1st at Tikal's North Acropolis (Reese 1996). In general, the complexity of iconographic programs grew and new dimensions of meaning were added.

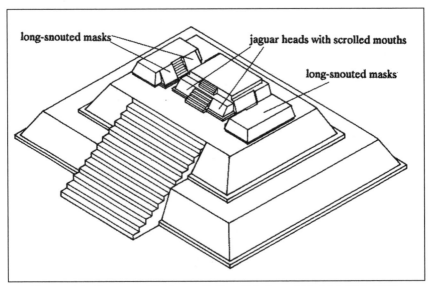

Figure 4.4. Structure 29, Cerros Belize (Schele and Freidel 1990: 125).

The iconographic program on Structure 5C-2nd is the quintessential example of increased complexity. Birds, jaguars, and snakes are depicted for the first time on a single building, with accompanying symbols representing the exotic commodities associated with kingship, jade and *Spondylus* (Freidel et al., chapter 3 this volume). Additionally, references to the office of king, in the form of early *ajaw* glyphs, are integrated into the façades (Fields 1989; Freidel et al., chapter 3 this volume). Moreover, cosmological imagery associates masked façades with constellations in the night sky, thereby identifying the structure as a mythic locale (for a complete discussion of the 5C-2nd façades, see Freidel et al., chapter 3 this volume; Reese 1996; Reese-Taylor 2001, n.d.; Reese-Taylor and Freidel 1998). Specifically, this program replicated the supernatural location where First Father was born and resurrected, in a cycle of birth, death, and rebirth often associated with shamanic transformation (Freidel et al., chapter 3 this volume; Kappelman 1997; Reese 1996). Another iconographic program tied to this era consists of snake and sustenance mountains in various combinations, seen at Uaxactun (figure 4.5), Tikal, and Cerros (Reese 1996; Reese-Taylor and Freidel 1998; Schele and Kappelman 2001). These façades linked directly to mythic locales where First Father had performed paradigmatic acts of creation.

The polyvalent nature of such iconographic programs not only declared them to be sacred space, but also specified particular locales. We suggest that the introduction of mythic locales at this time correlated with shamanic practices among kings. The specificity of the programs laid out performance venues in which kings replicated the actions of First Father (Freidel and Schele 1998; Freidel et al., chapter 3 this volume; Reese 1996; Reese-Taylor 2001, n.d.; Reese-Taylor and Freidel 1998).

Additional architectural façades appear after 8.0.0.0.0 that depict individuals—likely kings—at the sites of Cerros, later at Kohunlich and Tikal, and much later at Lamanai (Pendergast 1981). All of these mask programs are found within triadic groups. However, bird, jaguar, and snake programs, as well as snake and sustenance mountain programs, continue. We propose that this development reflects the changing nature of kingship. Emphasis on shamanic action in the form of an individual reenacting the feats of First Father is, for the first time, augmented by the personal authority of individual rulers.

Not only are rulers depicted on architectural façades of public buildings, but also royal tombs appeared for the first time during this era. Conflating royal tombs with exterior public spaces actually

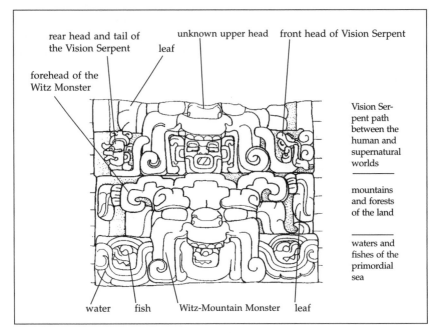

Figure 4.5. Snake and Water Mountain, Uaxactun (Schele and Freidel 1990: 125).

recontextualize the entire notion of public space to center around individual kings, foreshadowing the definition of Classic public spaces (Looper 2001). Thus far, early royal tombs have been identified at Wakna[1] (Hansen 1998), Tikal (Coe 1990; Laporte and Fialko 1995), and Caracol (Chase and Chase 1995). These tombs were dated by ceramic assessment and Carbon-14 (Tikal Burial 85 A.D. 60+/-70, corrected).

Finally, we have clear references to the symbols for kingly office in the form of diadem jewels cached in monumental structures during this era (figure 4.6) (Freidel 1979, 1986b; Freidel and Schele 1988a; Hammond 1974), and in mask programs. Therefore, individual kings are identified both in tombs and on architectural programs reflecting, we would argue, that the office of king was institutionalized near the beginning of Cycle 8, perhaps with ordered rules of succession.

The increase in long-distance trade associated with the rise of institutional kingship is marked by the importation of Usulatan pottery into the southern lowlands from the Maya highlands. Usulatan is a resist double-slipping technique that produces wavy-line designs. Potters from throughout the southern lowlands adapted the style to local production techniques, sometimes using positive painting or

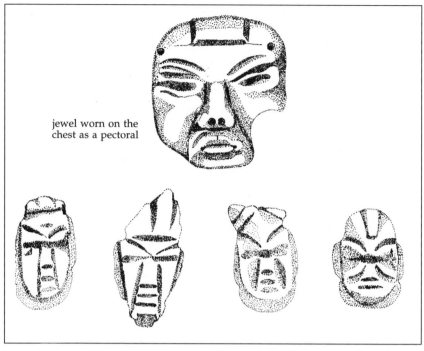

jewel worn on the
chest as a pectoral

Figure 4.6. Diadem jewels, Cerros (courtesy of David Freidel).

zoned incision to produce comparable results. Types such as Sacluc
Black-on-orange and Caramba Red-on-orange are examples of local
modal interpretations.

In addition to long-distance exchange, the distribution of particular ceramic types reflects intensified interaction between specific centers within the lowlands. For example, both the authors (Reese-Taylor
and Walker 2000, 2001) and Robertson-Freidel (1980) have recognized
affinities between Late Preclassic types from Cerros and those from
Becan. One particular type, Zapatista Trickle-on-cream brown, was
common in areas north of the Petén, particularly at the site of Becan
(Ball 1977; Chase and Chase 1995). It has been reported from only two
Late Preclassic centers in the Petén and Belize areas, in small quantities at El Mirador (Forsyth 1989) and in specific contexts at Cerros
(Robertson-Freidel 1980). At Cerros, the type consistently occurred in
one form—a three-handled jug—and was largely restricted to termination deposits on public architecture, implying ritual significance.
Therefore, like the architectural data, the presence of particular ceramic types demonstrates close affiliations linking El Mirador with

areas to the north (Becan) through an intermediary port facility (Cerros).

Increased levels of social interaction also changed the political subtext of ceramics; some vessels became malleable message convey-ors. For example, post-fire-incised graffiti appeared on pots through-out the southern lowlands at this time.[2] Tikal Burial 85 contained a medial flanged Sierra Group bowl with a clear rendering of a scor-pion etched on the vessel interior (Culbert 1993: fig. 7a). At Colha, Belize, two Sierra Group bowls carried versions of the *ajaw* glyph (Valdez 1987: figs. 28, 29). Inclusion of such "tagged" vessels in spe-cial deposits denotes specific ritual function and presages Classic era glyphic statements of function, such as *hawate' sak lak*, for chocolate drinking cup (Freidel, pers. comm. 2001).

Symbolic images represented on pots of this era include the step design and the mat motif. The step design occurred, for example, on a stuccoed fluted urn from Tikal Burial 167 (Culbert 1993: fig. 11b). It became a predominant theme rendered on Protoclassic mammiform tetrapods and Early Classic basal flange bowls, detailed below. Its glyphic counterpart (T-843; c.f. Tikal Stela 31 glyph E5) was literally a staircase to an elevated public building, and it was used to illus-trate the locale of royal public ritual in that era. The mat motif (*pohp* in Mayan), also gracefully rendered on an urn from the same burial (Culbert 1993: fig. 12a), became the glyph for royal place (T-551) in Classic texts. Therefore, it is during this period that we can first be-gin to read pots as text.

Ceramicists have identified more than a dozen modes consistently associated with the intense ceramic interaction of this era. Brady et al. (1999) included discussion of these modes in a recent reexami-nation of the Protoclassic Phase. They argue that what has been called the "Protoclassic" is in reality a constellation of elements superim-posed on an ongoing Late Preclassic ceramic tradition, and we concur. They propose a 400-year span for the Protoclassic, more or less correlated with Cycle 8. We argue that the phenomenon was ultimately political in nature, paralleling increasingly complex times; we subdivide one portion of it to support our arguments below.

To summarize, the period from 7.15.0.0.0 to 8.6.0.0.0 was charac-terized by the introduction of new architectural programs, new icono-graphic programs, and a proliferation of ceramic surface treatments and modes. We argue that these innovations corresponded to increased interaction between specific centers and a change in the institution of kingship. Specific ceramic and architectural affiliations link the sites of El Mirador, Cerros, and Uaxactun. Further, both El Mirador and Cerros seem to share strong ties with the site of Becan to the north. Additionally, architectural and iconographic similarities connect Lamanai and Cerros. We suggest that these five sites may have been closely allied in an effort to control long-distance trade, especially via the New River route. In view of the addition of *Spondylus* shell adornments at this time, the need for coastal ports of trade seems a logical outgrowth.

Significantly, kings are no longer anonymous; we have clear markers for their presence in the form of tombs, portraits on mask façades, and unequivocal *ajaw* glyphs and other symbols later associated with royalty carved or painted on ceramic vessels and integrated into mask programs. In fact, according to retrospective texts, Yax Ehb' Xook founded the Tikal dynasty about this time. Several scholars (Freidel 1995; Martin and Grube 2000; Schele and Mathews 1998) have suggested that his remains are those interred in Burial 85 in the North Acropolis, and we concur.[3]

Concomitant with the increased visibility of the king in the archaeological record was increased diversity in ceramic modes and surface treatments, as if each region was differentiating itself from others. We propose that lineages and nascent dynasties marked powerful relationships through ceramic production and exchange. Researchers first recognized this pattern in Late Classic assemblages, when gifting of elaborate painted ceramic vessels sealed political relationships (Reents-Budet 1994: 303–305; Reents-Budet et al. 1994). During the early part of Cycle 8, the presence of specific types of vessels among grave goods may have marked membership in specific groups or alliances.[4] We further propose that the institution of kingship was developing regulated rules of succession, perhaps as a result of increased administrative functions accompanying growth in long-distance trade. Nonetheless, the shamanic framework underpinning Late Preclassic kingship remained highly visible in public space, indicating that it was still integral to the definition of kingship.

8.6.0.0.0–8.10.0.0.0 (A.D. 159–238)
The Protoclassic Horizon

During the subsequent four *k'atuns*, roughly A.D. 159–238, the political landscape of the southern Maya lowlands changed dramatically. The single greatest factor in this change was a rapid decline and eventual abandonment of El Mirador. Based on comparisons with other cases of rapid and long-term abandonment, Hansen has proposed that the site's decline and eventual collapse resulted from environmental catastrophe that decimated peat bogs surrounding the city, undercutting the subsistence base for people living in the Mirador Basin (Gill 2000; Hansen 1990b). Whatever the cause, we suggest that its collapse resulted in a more decentralized distribution network, as the control that El Mirador exercised over regional trade networks waned.

We propose that El Mirador was virtually abandoned by 8.10.0.0.0 (A.D. 238), based on cessation in monumental construction and a limited presence of Protoclassic Paixbancito Complex ceramics at the site. Hansen (1990a) found evidence that during its final days a large palisade fortified El Mirador's acropolis, built around interior plazas; and the remnant population apparently relocated inside its parapets. He also recovered dart points from the summit of El Tigre, implying warfare. All evidence points to an opponent opportunistically warring against El Mirador when it was already down. The economic and political consequences for trading partners were severe, and some, such as Cerros, never recovered. Others, such as Tikal, struggled to create a new social order, and ultimately succeeded.

While new architectural and iconographic innovations are not apparent, changes did occur in ritual activity associated with public architecture at sites such as Tikal. Excavations in the North Acropolis (Coe 1990) revealed dramatic alterations in its structural arrangement. Masked façades on the north Str. 5D-22-6th-A and south Str. 5D-Sub.3 were defaced, burned, and buried under new staircases; no new masks replaced them until the beginning of the Early Classic. At the south side of the acropolis, Str. 5D-26-3rd was erected, perhaps for defensive purposes, closing off the acropolis and sealing the platform interior where early shrines once sat atop ancestral tombs. Caching ceased for the duration of the era. In all likelihood, the founder's lineage had gone out of favor, perhaps because of kin or political ties to El Mirador.[5]

Further north Cerros was beginning a period of economic hardship. Public construction projects in the central precinct waned, and quality of workmanship declined. Additionally, excavators noted a reduction in the amount of trade items, such as jade and *Spondylus* shell, recovered from the site (Garber 1983, 1986). Elsewhere in the region, the number of hieroglyphic inscriptions found on portable objects increased relative to the early Cycle 8 era. The Kichpanha bone dates to this phase (figure 4.7) (Meskill 1992; Reese 1989), and based

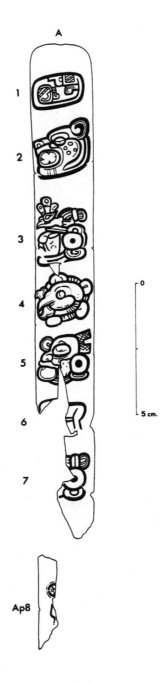

Figure 4.7. Kichpanha Bone (drawn by Peter Mathews).

upon similarities in glyphic form, we suggest that the Dumbarton Oaks pectoral should also be placed in this period.

In dealing with pottery from the middle 8th cycle, researchers have been frustrated by an overabundance of innovation and regionalization of types. Very difficult to isolate stratigraphically, the middle 8th cycle is the core era for Protoclassic pottery, defined herein as the Protoclassic Horizon. As Protoclassic diagnostics have been recovered in association with both Late Preclassic and Early Classic ceramics, spanning over 400 years, the term Protoclassic Horizon is used to isolate the four k'atuns under consideration. We have mustered ceramic evidence linking this era to a crisis-and-response situation, set in motion by the deterioration of El Mirador's economy. As it is so short-lived compared to preceding and subsequent periods, the mid-8th cycle has smaller sample sizes, fewer sealed contexts and more problematic deposits; we consider this reflective of real turmoil, short-lived though it was.

Pottery characteristics of the Protoclassic Horizon embody norms counter to those from the stable Preclassic tradition. Rather than uniformity in technology and vessel form, we see similar stylistic modes expressed on divergent vessel forms and in wide-ranging levels of technological expertise. In short, it has all the characteristics of an economic system in transformation. It is during this era that waxy, dark red Preclassic slips were tossed out in favor of glossier, lighter orange slips, more conducive to painted design. As the importance of the Sierra Red group waned, locally produced redwares proliferated. Across the Petén and into southern Yucatan, economic stresses impacted ceramic production.

The special form most associated with this era is the mammiform tetrapod (figure 4.8). Mammiform tetrapods occur on a wide variety of ceramic types, many locally produced. Pring (1977), Meskill (1992) and Brady et al. (1999) all note the disparity between finely made imports and local reproductions of inferior quality. Indeed, the only widely distributed type is Ixcanrio Orange Polychrome, ranging from the Pasion drainage, across Petén, and into Belize; also rarely in northern Yucatan and south to Honduras (figure 4.9) (Meskill 1992: table 3). While it is likely that they were imported into most of these sites, a specific source is unknown.

Rarely associated with household debris, mammiforms were found in burials and caches, broken in ritual refuse, and uniquely, broken in quantity inside Naj Tunich Cave (Brady et al. 1999). These specific contexts suggest that mammiform tetrapods were used by

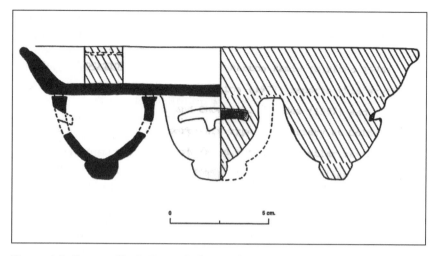

Figure 4.8. Laguna Verde Incised: Grooved-incised Variety, from the site of Kichpanha, Belize (drawing by Frances Meskill 1992).

Figure 4.9. Ixcanrio Orange Polychrome, Mundo Perdido, Tikal (K4877 © Justin Kerr).

ruling elites in situations of political and religious import. Several researchers noted the occurrence of poorly made regional monochrome redware mammiform tetrapods found eroded or broken in debris (c.f. Ball 1982 for Tancah; Forsyth 1989 for El Mirador; Forsyth 1993 for Nakbe; Meskill 1992 for Kichpanha; Walker 1998 for Cerros; Brady et al. 1999 for Naj Tunich). We infer from this that the message delivered by mammiform tetrapods was important enough to replicate for local use.

As a formal mode, mammiform tetrapods add a somewhat puzzling complexity to the mix. We are faced with two distinct problems in dealing with them, what they meant, and why there was so much diversity in their production. As to their meaning, we concur with Meskill's (1992: 152–153) and Brady's (1989) association of mammiform supports with the moon goddess *Ix Chel*. Material evidence supporting this hypothesis was revealed in Brady's work at Naj Tunich Cave, where a high percentage of broken mammiform supports were recovered in association with a wall painting depicting *Ix Chel* embraced by an old god. Meskill (1992: 193) draws on the Dresden Codex as well, noting that *Ix Chel* was depicted as the bearer of the "new day" sign, implying renewal. As the moon goddess, *Ix Chel* symbolized women, monthly cycles, fertility, and birth, concepts that reinforce Meskill's identification.[6] Based on this evidence, we propose that mammiform tetrapod vessels indeed symbolized renewal in the context of a dissolving Mirador state.

An Ixcanrio Orange Polychrome mammiform tetrapod plate excavated from Tikal's Mundo Perdido (figure 4.9) illustrates this political transformation in its elegant iconography. Drawn from centerline cache PNT-010 on Str. 5D-86, it may have been redeposited from disturbed royal tomb PNT-021 (Laporte and Fialko 1990: 40).[7] Str. 5D-86 is the central building in a tripartite E-Group associated with pyramidal 5C-54 to the west. Elements in this scene are found on many simpler mammiform tetrapods, especially scrolls and step designs. Noted in early royal tombs, these elements imply authority and strategic control. As the vessel described here is especially well executed, we suspect that the family that controlled its production, use, and disposition also controlled Tikal at the time. Whether they were locals or intruders is not yet clear.

A second question concerning mammiforms is the extent of their proliferation. Because Ixcanrio Orange Polychrome bowls are generally restricted to high-status deposits, we therefore assume their distribution likewise implies a high level of meaning. In the context of a collapsed Preclassic trading system, their proliferation reflected attempts to renew alliances and reinvent a larger social order. We argue that mammiform tetrapods served as political currency during this era and marked the efforts of an opponent to exert control in the vacuum created by the decline of El Mirador.

Supporting evidence for this hypothesis can be drawn from the difficulty in isolating the Protoclassic stratigraphically. While Meskill (1992) successfully argued for a functionally complete Protoclassic-era assemblage at the site of Kichpanha, this is not the case for most contemporary settlements. Some sites revealed evidence for only a functional subcomplex, such as the burial subcomplex at Colha (Meskill 1992; Potter 1994). Others revealed little or no evidence for Protoclassic ceramics, implying either an absence of settlement or, more likely in our view, a lack of participation in a reinvigorated long-distance exchange environment (Valdez 1998).

The difficulty in isolating a discrete Protoclassic Horizon can be explained if mammiforms symbolized affiliation with a growing web of elite-based exchange networks. Vessels such as these might have been carefully curated during a lifetime, then buried with powerful individuals along with other status goods. The distribution of such pots in the archaeological record, particularly imported Ixcanrio Orange Polychromes, reflected political participation in the burgeoning exchange network. The Protoclassic Horizon in this view revealed economic revitalization in the context of war and defeat. We suggest that the origin of Ixcanrio Orange Polychrome pottery and the core area of a revitalized exchange network are the same.

In sum, the period between 8.6.0.0.0 and 8.10.0.0.0 can be characterized as one of the most turbulent phases in Maya cultural history. The demise of El Mirador caused long-distance trade networks to crumble. Both Cerros and Tikal experience an economic downturn from the collapse of El Mirador in the form of architectural changes, while attempts to fill this void and rebuild a fractured interaction sphere were reflected in the appearance of mammiform tetrapods. Yet cohesion throughout the southern lowlands was not achieved during this period.

8.10.0.0.0–8.17.2.16.17 (A.D. 238–378)
Journey's End: The Early Classic

The next seven *k'atuns* saw an intensification in the struggle to control long-distance trade. Archaeological evidence suggests an increase in military encounters as a new contender, Tikal, grasped for power. In the ensuing conflict some sites, such as Cerros, experience not only economic hardship, but also military defeat, possibly at the hands of Tikal allies in a newly emerging trade network.

During the preceding four *k'atuns*, fierce competition prompted rapid transformation in ceramic technology, but by 8.10.0.0.0 (A.D. 238), pottery production caught up with the market for fine paintable surfaces. A new orange-based Aguila series eventually replaced darker Preclassic slips. Glossy cream and light orange slips, set on well-smoothed, fine paste surfaces, provided ideal venues for polychrome painted designs. Significantly, the basal flange bowl first appeared at about this time. Its exaggerated flange extended the paintable exterior surface, so that more complicated messages might be conveyed. The most widely traded type of basal flange bowl was Dos Arroyos Orange Polychrome (figure 4.10). Together with Balanza Black, these types were relatively long-lived and widely distributed across Petén through Belize's river valleys, and northward into Yucatan.

Also at the beginning of this era, a group of architecturally and materially distinct tombs were built in northeastern Petén and northwestern Belize. Termed Holmul I style for the site in which they were first discovered (Merwin and Vaillant 1932; Willey and Gifford 1961; Kosakowsky 2001), Holmul I style tombs have been reported from

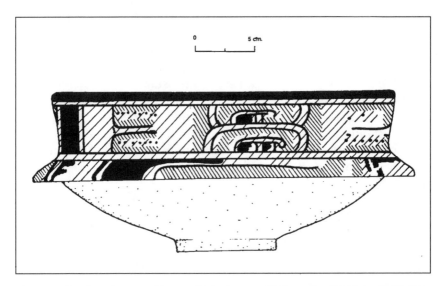

Figure 4.10. Dos Arroyos Orange Polychrome, Kichpanha (McDow 1997: 87).

Nohmul (Hammond 1984), Chan Chich (Houk 1997), and Blue Creek (Guderjan et al. 1996), among other sites. Holmul I burials are distinguished from Protoclassic burials because they contain both Protoclassic Horizon mammiforms and Early Classic diagnostic basal flange bowls, although the latter is a minority type. Most vessels in these tombs were mammiform tetrapods made in a variety of forms and surface treatments, but they also held spouted jars and other specialty and standard forms. These were status burials, accompanied by jade, *Spondylus* shell, and other imports, indicating the individuals interred had access to trade goods during life. We suspect that the diversity in mammiform tetrapod vessels found in a single burial reflected the ad-hoc nature of vessels collected through a *k'atun* or more of long-distance exchange.

Based on the evidence, we concur with Hammond (1984) and others that Holmul I burials cluster around the date 8.10.0.0.0, at the end of the Protoclassic Horizon. We place them at the beginning of the Early Classic, and suggest that the co-occurrence of mammiforms and basal flange bowls coincided with Tikal's rise to power. Further, we hypothesize that the overlap represents a short-lived power struggle in the southern lowlands. As previously stated, we argue that Ixcanrio Orange Polychrome vessels were emblematic of an unknown but powerful earlier site, while Dos Arroyos bowls presaged the entrance of the Tikal dynasty into the fray. We posit that, in the course of a single lifetime, rulers chose Dos Arroyos Orange Polychrome basal flange bowls as the new political currency, replacing Ixcanrio Orange Polychrome mammiform tetrapods. Apparently sites with Holmul I tombs made the shift and thrived at least for the short term in the Early Classic.

During this era, the Mundo Perdido was the seat of power for dynastic rulers at Tikal. According to Martin and Grube (2000), the early king Foliated Jaguar must have been in office about the time of the Holmul I burials. We propose that the development of a new set of symbols associated with basal flange polychromes is linked with him and his heirs, until the end of his lineage in A.D. 378, when the fourteenth successor, Chak Tok Ich'aak I, died in battle (Martin and Grube 2000). Some have suggested that the Mundo Perdido houses Chak Tok Ich'aak I's remains in PNT-019 at Str. 5D-86-7 (Laporte and Fialko 1995), although many unexcavated possibilities exist.[8] As the finest of these basal flange bowls, his lineage or "family pots," traveled with envoys across the landscape, new political relationships were formed with the reigning Tikal dynasty. Such pots often ended up in elite tombs, marking the periphery around the new core of a revitalized trade network. Given the Maya propensity to utilize status objects to invoke and disperse sacred power in Maya buildings, this behavior is not surprising.

It is during this era that we first begin to know Maya kings from contemporary documents rather than retrospective accounts. The earliest long count date is found on Tikal St. 29, at 8.12.14.8.15 (A.D. 292); the illustrated individual, though unidentified, wears *ajaw* insignia. According to Martin and Grube (2000), epigraphic texts inform us that rulers from this era enjoyed only brief reigns. When depicted, early rulers are often shown with the accouterments of war; therefore, the picture that we can reconstruct remains one of political upheaval. At Tikal, for example, Laporte and Fialko (1990: 41) report a set of images illustrating five bound prisoners from Mundo Perdido Str. 5D-86-5. However, after the accession of the eleventh successor, Siyaj Chan K'awil I, in A.D. 298, some amount of stability seems to have been achieved. During his reign, basal flange bowls move throughout the lowlands, and ceramic traits stabilized for the next four *k'atuns*.

After several *k'atuns* of poor quality work and neglect, Cerros experienced a complete cessation in construction in the years just prior to A.D. 400 (Reese 1996). Cerros' ceramic affinities to Becan and northern Yucatan strengthened at this time, a link that was maintained at sites along Chetumal Bay throughout Classic and Postclassic eras. Competition from Santa Rita across the bay (Chase and Chase 1986) likely led to Cerros' downfall, as elites there made new trade alliances at Cerros' expense. Other sites, such as Lamanai and Uaxactun, survived the turmoil and maintained access to the reinvigorated trade network. All of this implies collapse and realignment of a Petén-focused economy with some elites on the periphery lacking the resources to maintain important symbols of power and prestige at their former levels (Reese 1996; Reese-Taylor 1998; Reese-Taylor et al. 1996).

Archaeological evidence at Cerros points to warfare episodes sometime after 8.10.0.0.0. Recent excavations (Walker 1995; Reese-Taylor et al. 1996) revealed destructive events trained on specific and significant targets, such as the bannerstone discovered at the base of Str. 6A and the façades on Str. 6B (Freidel 1986b). Evidence suggests the bannerstone had been shoved off Str. 6A, crushing its northeast edge and resulting in several large cracks now visible on its surface. Likewise, façades on Str. 6B were ripped from their armatures in acts of desecration. Other destructive actions at Cerros included selective burning episodes in the architecture outside of the northern civic zone. Especially significant is burning noted on Str. 21 (Scarborough 1980, 1991), a likely lookout at the site's western edge.

By the end of this era Chak Tok Ich'aak I reigned at Tikal over a burgeoning international network of alliances; however, some may have been militarily enforced. It was probably during his reign that attention once again focused on the long-languishing North Acropolis. About this time pyramidal Str. 5D-22-4th was built with two pairs of masks (Coe 1990), seemingly resanctifying the location after *k'atuns* of disfavor. At its base, excavators located an unusual deposit, PD-87, which contained redeposited remains of Protoclassic-era burials. The rather haphazard assemblage included fragments of three individuals, 22 vessels, and a wide array of status goods. Whatever the purpose of this reinterment, it reflected revamping of Protoclassic-era construction elsewhere in the city.

Subsequently, Str. 5D-22-3rd was erected at the same locus. A cruller-eyed jaguar mask was added at its staircase summit (Coe 1990, fig. 97), emblematic of enduring warfare associated with the reign of Chak Tok Ich'aak I. Tikal St. 39, recently discovered in the Mundo Perdido (Laporte and Fialko 1990), shows him standing atop a captive foreigner at the *k'atun* ending, dated to 8.17.0.0.0, or A.D. 376. Only two years later, he would fall at the hand of a foreign general, forever altering Classic Maya civilization. We, therefore, would characterize the era between 8.10.0.0.0 and 8.17.2.16.17 throughout the central Petén and northern Belize as one of shifting political and military alliances, as various coalitions battled to fill the void left by the El Mirador's collapse.

8.17.2.16.17 5 Kaban, 10 Yaxk'in
The Entrada

Between A.D. 350 and 400 the political landscape was transformed as Tikal acquired a new ally, Teotihuacan. The arrival of the stranger Siyaj K'ak' coincided with the death of Chak Tok Ich'aak I and the defeat of Uaxactun on 8.17.1.4.12 (Jan. 15, 378). Then, on 8.17.2.16.17 (September 12, 379), Yax Nuun Ayiin I, the son of Spearthrower Owl, acceded to the throne of Tikal (Stuart 2000). As recorded on Stela 31, on the same day Yax Nuun Ayiin I grasped them, the 28 provinces[9] under the auspices of Siyaj K'ak' (Stuart 2000). While the reading of this passage is tentative, the consequence of Yax Nuun Ayiin I's accession was unambiguous.

We contend that Yax Nuun Ayiin I, with the support of Teotihuacan, launched a military campaign on multiple fronts to grasp control of much of the Maya lowlands, thus forming a new confederacy of states. Archaeological and epigraphic evidence for this is widespread from Yaxuna (Suhler and Freidel 1998) to Copan (Fash and Fash 2000), and includes the conquest of Rio Azul in the northeastern Petén (Adams 1999) and the mouth of the New River in northern Belize. From approximately A.D. 400–600, the inclusion of Teotihuacan cylinder tripods in royal tombs and caches of member states marked specific membership in the Tikal-Teotihuacan confederacy. These sites are geographically dispersed and include Becan, Bejucal, Copan, Dos Hombres (Lauren Sullivan pers. comm. 2000), El Peru, Lamanai (Graham pers. comm. 2000), Rio Azul, Santa Rita (Chase and Chase 1986), Yaxha, and probably Palenque.

During the final days at Cerros, there is evidence for a large-scale termination event and a subsequent *chak'a* (axing) of the Str. 4B vaulted room. This event consisted of scattering broken pots down the staircase and in front of the Str. 4B façades (Walker 1998). The final event in the site core prior to abandonment consisted of placing Peteltun Modeled censer stands (figure 4.11) on the interior floor of Str. 4B, on which Pochkaak Red-on-orange censer dishes were then stacked. Vault stones were not exposed to censer smoke for long before the vault was collapsed, suggesting a brief time span for the complete event. The act of collapsing a vault is associated with warfare in later times.

Peteltun Modeled censer stands have been identified at only three sites (Walker 1990: appendix): three complete *in situ* examples from Cerros Str. 4B, Chamber 1 (Walker 1998); three complete *in situ* examples from Uaxactun Str. E-VII, Cist 13 (Ricketson and Ricketson 1937); and two examples from Santa Rita Str. 7 (Chase 1988; Chase and Chase 1998: 301, fig. 1) found in secondary context. Similar censers have been reported as a component of the jade cache from Blue Creek (Guderjan et al.1996). Likewise, similar "loop-handled" censers stem from Tikal, associated with the termination of Chak Tok Ich'aak I's building 5D-22-3rd in PD-77 (Coe 1990: 359). The subsequent building, Str. 5D-22-2nd, clearly dates after the entrada, in association with Yax Nuun Ayiin I's activities.[10]

We contend that Peteltun Modeled censer stands left *in situ* at Cerros and Uaxactun marked the final defeat of the last surviving

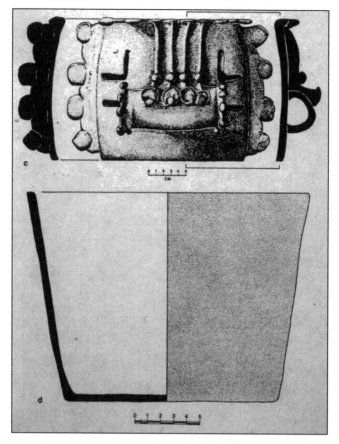

Figure 4.11. Peteltun Modeled Censors, Cerros.

members of the El Mirador alliance. The abrupt vault collapse at Cerros, as well as the provocative presence of Peteltun Modeled effigy censer stands, suggests inimical destruction by outsiders, likely individuals from Santa Rita who left the tell-tale markers of their presence in the form of stacked censers (Reese-Taylor et al. 1996). In secondary context, vessels of this type were recovered from a wall niche in the burial of an elite Early Classic woman at Santa Rita, and may have served to commemorate this defeat. Her tomb is linked to the new Teotihuacan-Tikal alliance by the presence of cylinder tripods as well as other elite goods (Chase and Chase 1986). We speculate that these actions are contemporary with the termination of Tikal Str. 5D-22-3rd, where similar censers were utilized.[11] As considerable textual evidence reliably dates this context to Yax Nuun Ayiin I's early reign, we posit a date of A.D. 380–400 for the site termination at Cerros.[12] With Cerros gone, the last surviving remnant of the El Mirador alliance was out of the way. Tikal, at last, had what it wanted, domination over the long-distance trade network in the Maya lowlands.

Conclusions

It is apparent that the passage from the Late Preclassic into the Early Classic was anything but smooth. Nevertheless, certain definable stages characterized this journey. Kingship emerged during Cycle 7 amidst a backdrop of relative homogeneity in the southern lowlands wherein a doctrinal ideology of egalitarianism among elites was fostered. This cycle was dominated by El Mirador, which established ties to settlements in key locations along important riverine and overland portage routes. By 7.15.0.0.0, long-distance trade and craft specialization increased as El Mirador extended its hegemony over the lowlands by creating an alliance between several city-states in order to control long-distance trade. Concomitantly, the nature of kingship changed and early dynasties were founded. Around 8.6.0.0.0, El Mirador's population declined and it was abandoned. As a result, the long-distance trade network founded and controlled by El Mirador fragmented. The remainder of Cycle 8 was distinguished by rapid change in the political landscape as other sites attempted to reexert control over the area. This was not achieved until the appearance of the Tikal-Teotihuacan alliance, which, through conquest and cooperation, reestablished fragmented long-distance trade networks.

As clearly demonstrated by the above discussion, trade was a compelling force in the development of Maya civilization; the desire to control it drove individual kings to forge alliances and subdue adversaries in attempts to dominate regional interaction spheres. William Rathje understood this and pointed it out to us thirty years ago. Remarkably, it has taken the discipline this long to catch up with him.

Notes

We would like to thank David Freidel for thoughtful comments on earlier drafts of this chapter and Marilyn Masson and David Freidel for the opportunity to present this work in their session honoring William Rathje at the 2000 SAA meetings. Photo credit: Thanks to Justin Kerr of the Maya Vase Project, and FAMSI for its support of the on-line resource.

1. Hansen (1998) dates the three Wakna tombs to the Late Preclassic based upon the presence of three medial flange Sierra Red bowls, one figure-8 shaped Flor Cream bowl, and two Sapote Striated vessels left in the tombs after looting, as well as the identification of Chicanel sphere vessels from the El Mirador collection similar to those found in the tombs by the individual responsible for the looting. Hansen also states that the center tomb at Wakna, likely the royal tomb based upon the amount of jade reported to have been recovered, was identical in construction to PNT-021 from the Mundo Perdido at Tikal. Both tombs have a slab-apex vault that gives the entire tomb construction a pentagonal shape, uncommon during this time period (Hansen 1998: 92–93). The Mundo Perdido tomb was archaeologically excavated and is dated to the Protoclassic based on the presence of two large mammiform tetrapod vessels (Laporte and Fialko 1995: 52–53). In addition, Tikal Burial 85, with a radiocarbon date ranging from 10 B.C. to A.D. 130, has Sierra Red vessels. Given the overlap in ceramic types previously thought to date exclusively to either the Late Preclassic or the Protoclassic (Brady et al. 1999), as well as the possible disturbed nature of the deposits, we consider an early Cycle 7 date for the Wakna tombs to be problematic. Instead we suggest a date after 7.15.0.0.0 for the center tomb at Wakna based on the similarities in morphology and construction techniques with PNT-021 from Tikal.

2. Hansen (personal communication 2001) reports that one sherd from El Mirador has a C_{14} date of approximately 200 B.C.

3. Burial 85 is located in platform 5D-Sub 2-2nd directly in front of Str. 5D-Sub 1-1st. Based on identification of the individual in B-85 as the founder, several caches placed in Str. 5D-22-2nd, directly atop 5D-sub 1-1st, and epigraphic information from Stela 31, Walker suggests that 5D-Sub 1-1st is the location of Tikal's wi-te-na, or root-tree-place, a kind of ancestral shrine. She asserts that the wi-te-na is a real location at Tikal (although see Stuart 2000 for an alternative interpretation), as described on Stela 31, and is the site of Yax Nuun Ayiin I's heir designation ceremony and the location at which he accedes to the throne of Tikal. Furthermore, Walker suggests that two Alta Mira Fluted urns situated at the south end of his tomb are classificatory world trees which indicate a portal location (Walker 1990) that gave the city mythic sanctity as a dynastic seat of power. On one urn rested a Sierra Group bowl etched with a clear scorpion design, referenced in this text, which may recall a mythic action setting up the world tree known in Classic texts (Freidel, personal communication 2001).

4. As Culbert (1993) indicates, the three early Cycle 8 burials at Tikal's North Acropolis share sufficient similarities to suggest real familial relationships. The symbolic content of design on some of these vessels, including Alta Mira Fluted urns and Caramba Red-on-orange bowls, may be associated with this incipient dynasty.

5. We find additional evidence for El Mirador-related elites in Tikal's Burial 125, interred at the base of 5D-22-6th-A. This unique tomb, cut 5 meters below the plaza, held a tall, elderly male apparently buried naked. While lacking grave goods, the construction sequence provided an early Cimi Phase date. His tomb was covered with zapote beams, C_{14} dated to A.D. 35+/-85, although Coe cautions zapote is long-lived and somewhat unreliable. In the shaft above,

excavators discovered 6 distinct layers of reddish brown flint flakes, and above that flint and obsidian concentrations, the earliest use of flint debitage to seal tombs.

Researchers have speculated about the identity of the principal occupant of B-125; we believe he was related to El Mirador's ruling family, and that he was summarily dispatched as a result of war-related activities. One of us (Walker) further suggests that flint chips sealing his tomb comprised debitage from the production of lances used in Protoclassic Horizon battles, perhaps even at El Mirador. A precedent for caching flint debris from lance points is known from Colha (Potter 1994), in which a Terminal Preclassic stemmed macroblade was cached with the flakes struck off it. The blade itself tested positive for human blood.

6. Another set of symbols links the concept of renewal to some unusual mammiform-like tetrapods, the Early Classic peccary head tetrapods (Schele and Miller 1986: plate 105; Freidel et al. 1993: fig. 2:18). In Maya, the word *chel* translates as rainbow, itself a symbol for renewal in many cultures. A rainbow forms an arc across the sky in the presence of the sun, an image depicted in Maya texts as sky bands. The sky band itself has been tied to the sun's ecliptic (Freidel et al. 1993) and therefore to the constellations of the zodiac. One of these constellations, Gemini, has been identified with the Maya constellation called copulating peccaries (Freidel et al. 1993: 82). Further, the mythic locale associated with it in pottery and codex texts is the maize god acting at creation (Freidel et al. 1993: fig. 2:19), thus linking both peccary head tetrapods and mammiform tetrapods to creation and renewal. Of the two, mammiform tetrapods appeared first.

7. First identified at Uaxactun Group E, this architectural type is known to have astronomical associations; one hypothesis is that it demarcates the sun's annual ecliptic from solstice to solstice (Ricketson and Ricketson 1937). Therefore, the representation on this vessel also may depict the Tikal E-Group in action, as the sun rises on an equinox.

8. Laporte and Fialko (1990: 42) report a tetrapod vessel from this burial made of perishable material, of which only the stuccoed tetrapods remain. Uniquely, these four supports are described as human heads. A human head-shaped handle also exists, although the balance had decayed. In view of the meaning proposed for mammiforms earlier, this vessel might illustrate the transfer of that mythical power for renewal and recreation to the Early Classic king buried in PNT-019.

9. The "provinces" reading was suggested by Stan Guenter during a discussion at the 2000 Maya Meetings, University of Texas at Austin. Subsequently Marc Zender (personal communication 2001) has suggested the reading "cultivated lands" for the word *pet*. Both readings connote a type of land. Therefore, we suggest that the passage refers to the actual appropriation of lands.

10. Excavations at Str. 5D-22-2nd and contemporary buildings on the North Acropolis (Coe 1990) revealed several caches containing significant royal materials readily associated with Yax Nuun Ayiin I (glossed First Crocodile), including caches 120, 140, and 186, all of which included the corpses of crocodiles along with myriad other Manik III diagnostics. We suspect this ruler deposited the

series of caches to resanctify the locale, and hearken back to Yax Ehb' Xook, founder of the site. His son, Siyaj Chan Káwiil II, recalled actions of both the founder and Foliated Jaguar in the important history he recorded on St. 31.

11. Coe (1990: 359) notes that the entire base of this staircase "was marked by conflagration" prior to constructing the subsequent building. A loop-handled censer in this setting was discovered half-filled with wood charcoal which dated to 165 B.C.+/-75. We concur with Coe that ancient wood was intentionally used, commemorating the earliest beginnings of Tikal's ancient dynasty

12. Walker (1998) previously proposed a date of 9.0.0.0.0 for this deposit, associating Cerros' demise with the shift to a new Maya millennium, but research undertaken for this paper supported an alternate view. Along with data presented in this chapter, the complete lack of Tzakol III diagnostic cylinder tripods at Cerros lends support to the earlier date.

References

Adams, Richard E. W.
1990 "Archaeological Investigations at the Lowland Maya Site of Rio Azul." *Latin American Antiquity* 1(1): 23–41.
1999 *Rio Azul: An Ancient Maya City.* Norman: University of Oklahoma Press.
Adams, Richard E. W., ed.
1986 *Rio Azul Reports Number 2, The 1984 Season.* San Antonio: University of Texas Center for Archaeological Research.
1987 *Rio Azul Reports Number 3, The 1985 Season.* San Antonio: University of Texas Center for Archaeological Research.
1989 *Rio Azul Reports Number 4, The 1986 Season.* San Antonio: University of Texas Center for Archaeological Research.
2000 *Rio Azul Report Number 5, The 1987 Season.* San Antonio: University of Texas Center for Archaeological Research.
Adams, Richard E. W., William E. Brown Jr., and T. Patrick Culbert
1988 "Radar Mapping, Archaeology, and Ancient Land Use." *Science* 213: 1457–1463.
Aizpuruia, Ilean Isel Isaza, and Patricia A. McAnany
1999 "Adornment and Identity: Shell Ornaments from Formative K'axob." *Ancient Mesoamerica* 10(1): 117–127.
Andrews, E. Wyllys V
1990 "The Early Ceramic History of the Lowland Maya." Pp. 1–19 in *Vision and Revision in Maya Studies*, edited by F. Clancey and P. Harrison. Albuquerque: University of New Mexico Press.
Ball, Joseph
1977 *The Archaeological Ceramics of Becan, Campeche, Mexico.* MARI Publication No. 43. New Orleans: Middle American Research Institute.
1982 "The Tancah Ceramic Situation: Cultural and Historical Insights from an Alternative Material Class." In *On the Edge of the Sea: Mural Painting at Tancah-Tulum, Quintana Roo, Mexico*, edited by A. Miller, Appendix 1. Washington, D.C.: Dumbarton Oaks.

1983 "Notes on the Distribution of Established Ceramic Types in Corozal District, Belize." Pp. 203–220 in *Archaeological Excavations in Northern Belize, Central America*, edited by R. Sidrys. Monograph XVII. Los Angeles: Institute of Archaeology, University of California.

Brady, James
1989 "An Investigation of Maya Ritual Cave Use with Special Reference to Naj Tunich, Petén, Guatemala." Ph.D. dissertation, Dept. of Anthropology, University of California, Los Angeles.

Brady, James E., Joseph W. Ball, Ronald L. Bishop, Duncan C. Pring, Norman Hammond, and Rupert A. Housley
1999 "The Lowland Maya 'Protoclassic': A Reconsideration of Its Nature and Significance." *Ancient Mesoamerica* 9(1): 17–38.

Caldwell, Joseph
1964 "Interaction Spheres in Prehistory." *Illinois State Museum Scientific Papers* 12(6): 133–193.

Chase, Arlen F., and Diane Z. Chase
1995 "External Impetus, Internal Synthesis, and Standardization: E Group Assemblages and the Crystallization of Classic Maya Society in the Southern Lowlands." Pp. 87–101 in *The Emergence of Lowland Maya Civilization: The Transition from the Preclassic to the Early Classic*, edited by Nikolai Grube. *Acta Mesoamericana* 8. Hamburg: Verlag Anton Suarwein.

Chase, Diane Z.
1988 "Caches and Censerware: Meaning from Maya Pottery." Pp. 81–104 in *A Pot for All Reasons: Ceramic Ecology Revisited*, edited by C. Kolb and L. Lackey. Special publication of Ceramica de la Cultura Maya. Philadelphia: Temple University.

Chase, Diane Z., and Arlen F. Chase
1986 *Offerings to the Gods: Maya Archaeology at Santa Rita Corozal*. Orlando: Department of Sociology and Anthropology, University of Central Florida.
1998 "The Architectural Context of Caches, Burials and Other Ritual Activities for the Classic Period Maya (as Reflected at Caracol, Belize)." Pp. 299–332 in *Function and Meaning in Classic Maya Architecture*, edited by S. Houston. Washington, D.C.: Dumbarton Oaks.

Coe, William R.
1965 "Tikal, Guatemala, and Emergent Maya Civilization." *Science* 147: 1401–1419.
1990 *Excavations in the Great Plaza, North Terrace, and North Acropolis of Tikal*, 6 volumes. Tikal Report No. 12, University Museum Monograph 61. Philadelphia: University of Pennsylvania.

Culbert, T. Patrick
1993 *The Ceramics of Tikal: Vessels from the Burials, Caches and Problematic Deposits*. Tikal Report No. 25, Part A, The University Museum. Philadelphia: University of Pennsylvania.

Drollinger, Harold
1989 "An Investigation of a Late Preclassic Maya Chert Workshop from Colha, Belize." Unpublished M.A. thesis, Department of Anthropology, Texas A&M University, College Station.

Fash, William, and Barbara Fash
2000 "Teohuacan and the Maya: A Classic Heritage." In *Mesoamerica's Classic Heritage: Teotihuacán to the Aztecs*, edited by D. Carrasco, L. Jones, and S. Sessions. Boulder: University Press of Colorado.

Fields, Virginia M.
1989 "The Origins of Divine Kingship among the Lowland Classic Maya." Unpublished Ph.D. dissertation, Department of Art History, University of Texas at Austin.

Forsyth, Donald
1989 *The Ceramics of El Mirador, Petén, Guatemala*. El Mirador Series, Part 4, New World Archaeological Foundation. Provo, Utah: Brigham Young University.
1993 "The Ceramic Sequence at Nakbe, Guatemala." *Ancient Mesoamerica* 4(1): 31–53.

Freidel, David A.
1978 "Maritime Adaptation and the Rise of Maya Civilization: The View from Cerros, Belize." Pp 239–265 in *Prehistoric Coastal Adaptations*, edited by B. Stark and B. Voorhies. New York: Academic Press.
1979 "Culture Areas and Interaction Spheres: Contrasting Approaches to the Emergence of Civilization in the Maya Lowlands." *American Antiquity* 44: 36–54.
1986a "Introduction." Pp xiii–xxiii in *Archaeology at Cerros, Belize, Central America, Volume I: An Interim Report*, edited by R. Robertson and D. Freidel. Dallas: Southern Methodist University Press.
1986b "The Monumental Architecture." Pp 1–22 in *Archaeology at Cerros, Belize, Central America, Volume I: An Interim Report*, edited by R. Robertson and D. Freidel. Dallas: Southern Methodist University Press.
1995 Presentation at the Maya Weekend, University of California, Los Angeles.

Freidel, David A., and Linda Schele
1988a "Kingship in the Late Preclassic Maya Lowlands: the Instruments of Power and the Places of Ritual Power." *American Anthropologist* 90: 547–567.
1988b "Symbol and Power: A History of the Lowland Maya Cosmogram." Pp. 44–93 in *Maya Iconography*, edited by E. Benson and G. Griffin. Princeton, N.J.: Princeton University Press.

Freidel, David A., Linda Schele, and Joy Parker
1993 *Maya Cosmos: Three Thousand Years on the Shaman's Path*. New York: Morrow.

Garber, James F.
1983 "Patterns of Jade Consumption and Disposal at Cerros, Northern Belize." *American Antiquity* 48(4): 800–807.
1986 "The Artifacts." Pp. 117–126 in *Archaeology at Cerros, Belize, Central America, Volume I: An Interim Report*, edited by R. Robertson and D. A. Freidel. Dallas: Southern Methodist University Press.
1989 *Archaeology at Cerros, Belize, Central America: Volume III, The Artifacts*. Dallas: Southern Methodist University Press.

Gill, Richardson B.
2000 *The Great Maya Droughts: Water, Life, and Death*. Albuquerque: University of New Mexico Press.

Guderjan, Thomas H., W. David Driver, and Helen R. Haines
1996 *Archaeological Research at Blue Creek, Belize. Progress Report of the Fourth (1995) Field Season*. San Antonio: St. Mary's University.
Hammond, Norman
1973 *British Museum-Cambridge University Corozal Project, 1973 Interim Report*. Cambridge: Cambridge University Centre for Latin American Studies.
1974 "Preclassic to Postclasic in Northern Belize." *Antiquity* 58: 177–187.
1984 "Holmul and Nohmul: A Comparison and Assessment of Two Maya Lowland Protoclassic Sites." *Ceramica de Cultural Maya* 13: 1–17.
1985 "The Emergence of Maya Civilization." *Scientific American* 255(2): 106–115.
1991 *Cuello, An Early Maya Community in Belize*. Cambridge: Cambridge University Press.
Hansen, Richard D.
1990a *Excavations in the Tigre Complex, El Mirador, Petén, Guatemala*. Papers of the New World Archaeological Foundation, No. 62. Provo, Utah: Brigham Young University.
1990b Proceso Cultural del Nakbe y el Area Petén Nor-Central: la Epocas Tempanas. Pp. 81–96 in *V Simposio de Investigaciones Guatemala*, edited by J. P. Laporte, H. Escobedo, and S. V. de Brady. Guatemala City: Museo Nacional de Antropologia e Historia de Guatemala, Associacion Tikal.
1998 "Continuity and Disjunction: The Preclassic Antecedents to Classic Maya Architecture." Pp. 49–122 in *Function and Meaning in Classic Maya Architecture*, edited by Stephen D. Houston. Washington, D.C.: Dumbarton Oaks.
Helms, Mary
1993 *Craft and the Kingly Ideal: Art, Trade and Power*. Austin: University of Texas Press.
Hester, Thomas R. and Harry J. Shafer
1989 "Ancient Maya Craft Community at Colha Belize, and Its External Relations." *Texas Papers on Latin America* 89-11 Austin: Institute for Latin American Studies, University of Texas.
Houk, Brett A.
1992 "Excavations at Nak'nal: Small Site Investigations in the Northeastern Petén." Unpublished M.A. thesis, Department of Anthropology, University of Texas at Austin.
1997 *Report on the Chan Chich Archaeological Project: 1997 Extended Season*. Crystal River, Fla.: Report submitted to Foundation for the Advancement of Mesoamerican Studies.
Kappelman, Julia Guernsey
1997 "Of Macaws and Men: Late Preclassic Cosmology and Political Ideology in Izapan-Style Monuments." Ph.D. dissertation, University of Texas at Austin.
Kosakowsky, Laura
1987 *Preclassic Maya Pottery at Cuello Belize*. Tucson: University of Arizona Press.
2001 "The Ceramic Chronology of Holmul." In *Archaeological Investigations at Holmul, Guatemala: Report of the First Field Season, May-June 2000*, edited by F. Estrada-Belli. Crystal River, Fla.: Foundation for the Advancement of Mesoamerican Studies. Available at www.famsi.org.

Laporte, Juan Pedro, and Vilma Fialko
1989 "New Perspectives on Old Problems: Dynastic References for the Early Classic at Tikal." Pp. 33–66 in *Vision and Revision in Maya Studies*, edited by F. Clancy and P. Harrison. Albuquerque: University of New Mexico Press.
1995 "Un Reencuentro con Mundo Perdido, Tikal, Guatemala." *Ancient Mesoamerica* 6(1): 41–94.

Looper, Matthew G.
2001 "Dance Performances at Quiriguá." In *Landscape and Power in Ancient Mesoamerica*, edited by R. Koontz, K. Reese-Taylor, and A. Headrick. Boulder: Westview Press.

López Varela, Sandra
1996 "The K'axob Formative Ceramics: The Search for Regional Integration through a Reappraisal of Ceramic Analysis and Classification in Northern Belize." Unpublished Ph.D. dissertation, University of London.

Martin, Simon, and Nikolai Grube
2000 *Chronicle of Maya Kings and Queens: Deciphering the Dynasties of the Ancient Maya*. London: Thames and Hudson.

McAnany, Patricia A., and Sandra López Varela
1998 "Re-creating the Formative Maya Village of K'axob: Chronology, Ceramic Complexes, and Ancestors in Architectural Context." *Ancient Mesoamerica* 10(1): 147–168.

Merwin, R. E., and G.C. Vaillant
1932 *The Ruins of Holmul, Guatemala*. Memoirs of the Peabody Museum, Harvard University, Monograph 3. Cambridge, Mass.: Harvard University.

Meskill, Frances
1992 "Ceramics and Context: A Protoclassic Perspective from the Sites of Kichpanha and Colha, Belize." Unpublished M.A. thesis, Department of Anthropology, University of Texas at San Antonio.

Moholy-Nagy, Hattula
1989 "Formed Shell Beads from Tikal, Guatemala." Pp. 139–156 in *Proceedings of the 1986 Shell Bead Conference*, edited by Charles F. Haynes III, Lynn Ceci, and Connie Cox Bodner. Research Records No. 20. Rochester, New York: Rochester Museum and Science Center.

Pendergast, David
1981 "Lamanai, Belize: Summary of Excavation Results 1974–1980." *Journal of Field Archaeology* 18: 29–53.

Potter, Daniel R.
1994 "Strat 55, Operation 2012, and Comments on Lowland Maya Blood Ritual." Pp. 31–38 in *Continuing Archaeology at Colha, Belize*, edited by T. R. Hester. Studies in Archaeology 16. Austin: University of Texas Archaeology Research Laboratory.

Pring, Duncan C.
1977 "The Preclassic Ceramics of Northern Belize." Unpublished Ph.D. Dissertation, University of London.

Puleston, Denny
1979 "An Epistemological Pathology and the Collapse, or Why the Maya Kept the Short Count." Pp. 63–71 in *Maya Archaeology and Ethnohistory*, edited by N. Hammond and G. Willey. Austin: University of Texas Press.

Rathje, William L.
1971 "The Origin and Development of Lowland Classic Maya Civilization." *American Antiquity* 36(3): 275–284.
1972 "Praise the Gods and Pass the Metates: A Hypothesis of the Development of Lowland Rainforest Civilizations in Mesoamerica." Pp. 29–36 in *Contemporary Archaeology*, edited by Mark Leone. Carbondale: Southern Illinois University Press.
Reents-Budet, Dorie
1994 "Collecting Pre-Columbian Art and Preserving the Archaeological Record." Pp. 290–311 in *Painting the Maya Universe: Royal Ceramics of the Classic Maya Period*, edited by D. Reents-Budet. Durham, N.C.: Duke University Press.
Reents-Budet, Dorie, Ronald L. Bishop, and Barbara MacLeod
1994 "Painting Styles, Workshop Locations and Pottery Production." Pp. 164–233 in *Painting the Maya Universe: Royal Ceramics of the Classic Maya Period*, edited by D. Reents-Budet. Durham, N.C.: Duke University Press.
Reese, Kathryn V.
1989 "The Ceramics of Kichpanha, Northern Belize." Unpublished M.A. thesis, Department of Anthropology, Texas A&M University, College Station.
1996 "Narratives of Power: Late Formative Public Architecture and Civic Center Design at Cerros, Belize." Unpublished Ph.D. dissertation, Department of Anthropology, University of Texas at Austin.
Reese-Taylor, Kathryn
1998 "The Way of the Warrior King: Militarism among the Late Preclassic Maya." Paper presented at the 63rd annual meeting of the Society for American Archaeology, March 25–29, Seattle.
2001 "Ritual Circuits as Key Elements in the Design of Maya Civic Centers." In *Heart of Creation: The Mesoamerican World and the Legacy of Linda Schele*, edited by Andrea J. Stone. Tuscaloosa: University of Alabama Press.
n.d. "Narrative and Sacred Landscape: The Ballcourt Program at Cerros, Belize." *Ancient Mesoamerica*, forthcoming.
Reese-Taylor, Kathryn, and David A. Freidel
1998 "The Iconography of Late Preclassic Mask Programs: Examples from Northern Belize." Paper presented at the Quatro Congreso Internacional de Mayistas, August 2–8, Antigua, Guatemala.
Reese-Taylor, Kathryn, and Debra S. Walker
2000 "Boom and Bust! Interaction between Northern Belize and the Central Petén during the Late Formative to Early Classic Transition." Paper presented at the 65th annual meeting of the Society for American Archaeology, April 5–9, Philadelphia.
2001 "The Times They are a Changin': The Body Politic of the Late Preclassic." Paper presented at the 18th Annual Texas Symposium, part of the 2001 Maya Meetings at Texas, March 8–17, University of Texas at Austin.
Reese-Taylor, Kathryn, Debra S. Walker, and Beverly Mitchum
1996 "Inter-Polity Dynamics and the Demise of Cerros." Paper presented at the 61st annual meeting of the Society for American Archaeology, April 10–14, New Orleans.

Reilly, F. Kent III
1994 "Visions to Another World: Art, Shamanism, and Political Power in Middle Formative Mesoamerica." Unpublished Ph.D. dissertation, Latin American Studies Program, University of Texas at Austin.
Ricketson, Oliver, and Edith Ricketson
1937 *Uaxactun, Guatemala, Group E. 1926–1931.* Publication 477. Washington D.C.: Carnegie Institute.
Robertson-Freidel, Robin
1980 "The Ceramics from Cerros: A Late Preclassic Site in Northern Belize." Unpublished Ph.D. dissertation, Department of Anthropology, Harvard University, Cambridge, Mass.
Santone, Lenore
1997 "Transport Costs, Consumer Demands, and Patterns of Interregional Exchange: A Perspective on Commodity Production and Distribution in Northern Belize." *Latin American Antiquity* 8(1): 71–88.
Scarborough, Vernon L.
1980 "The Settlement System at a Late Preclassic Maya Community: Cerros, Northern Belize." Unpublished Ph.D. dissertation, Department of Anthropology, Southern Methodist University, Dallas.
1983a "A Preclassic Maya Water System." *American Antiquity* 48: 720–744.
1983b "Raised Field Detection at Cerros, Northern Belize." Pp. 123–136 in *Drained Field Agriculture in Central and South America.* British Archaeological Reports, Supplemental 189. Oxford: Oxford University Press.
1985 "Resourceful Landscaping: A Maya Lesson." *Archaeology* 38: 58–59.
1991 *Archaeology at Cerros, Belize, Central America. Volume III: The Settlement System in a Late Preclassic Maya Community.* Dallas: Southern Methodist University Press.
Scarborough, Vernon L., and David Wilcox, eds.
1993 *The Mesoamerican Ballgame.* Tucson: University of Arizona Press.
Schele, Linda, and Julia Guernsey Kappelman
2001 "What the Heck's Coatepec? The Formative Roots of an Enduring Mythology." Pp. 29–53 in *Landscape and Power in Ancient Mesoamerica*, edited by R. Koontz, K. Reese-Taylor, and A. Headrick. Boulder: Westview Press.
Schele, Linda, and Peter Mathews
1998 *The Code of Kings: The Language of Seven Sacred Maya Temples and Tombs.* New York: Scribner.
Schele, Linda, and Mary Miller
1986 *The Blood of Kings: Dynasty and Ritual in Maya Art.* Fort Worth: Kimbell Art Museum.
Shafer, Harry J., and Thomas R. Hester
1983 "Ancient Maya Chert Workshops in Northern Belize, C. A." *American Antiquity* 51: 158–166.
1991 "Lithic Craft Specialization and Production Distribution at the Maya Site of Colha." *World Archaeology* 23: 79–97.
Stuart, David
2000 "'The Arrival of Strangers': Teotihuacan and Tollan in Classic Maya History." Pp. 465–513 in *Mesoamerica's Classic Heritage: Teotihuacán to Aztecs,*

edited by D. Carrasco, L. Jones, and S. Sessions. Boulder: University Press of Colorado.

Suhler, Charles, and David A. Freidel
1998 "Life and Death in a Maya War Zone." *Archaeology* 51(3): 28–34.

Sullivan, Lauren
1991 "Preclassic Domestic Architecture at Colha, Belize." Unpublished M.A. thesis, Department of Anthropology, University of Texas at Austin.

Turner, B. L., and Peter D. Harrison
1983 *Pulltrouser Swamp: Ancient Maya Habitat, Agriculture, and Settlement in Northern Belize.* Austin: University of Texas Press.

Valdés, Juan Antonio
1987 "Uaxactún: Recientes Investigaciones." *Mexicon* 8: 125–128.
1988 "Los Mascarones Preclásicos de Uaxactún: el Caso del Grupo H." Pp. 165–181 in *Primer Simposio Mundial Sobre Epigraphía Maya.* Guatemala City: Associacion Tikal.
1995 "Desarrollo Cultural y Senales de Alarma Entre los Mayas: el Preclasico Tardio y la Transcion Hasta el Clasico Temprano." Pp. 71–85 in *The Emergence of Lowland Maya Civilization: The Transition from the Preclassic to the Early Classic,* edited by Nikolai Grube. *Acta Mesoamericana* Vol. 8. Hamburg: Verlag Anton Saurwein.

Valdez, Fred
n.d. "A Preclassic Temple at Rio Azul." Manuscript on file with the author in the Department of Anthropology, University of Texas at Austin.
1987 "The Prehistoric Ceramics of Colha, Northern Belize." Unpublished Ph.D. dissertation, Department of Anthropology, Harvard University, Cambridge, Mass.
1998 "The Chan Chich Ceramic Sequence." Pp. 73–86 in *The 1997 Season of the Chan Chich Archaeological Project,* edited by B. A. Houk. Papers of the Chan Chich Archaeological Project, Number 3 San Antonio: Center for Maya Studies.

Walker, Debra Selsor
1990 "Cerros Revisited: Ceramic Indicators of Terminal Classic and Postclassic Settlement and Pilgrimage in Northern Belize." Unpublished Ph.D. dissertation, Southern Methodist University, Dallas, University Microfilms, Ann Arbor.
1995 "Research at Cerros, Belize: Results of the 1994 Excavation Season." Report presented to the Belize Department of Archaeology, Belmopan, May.
1998 "Smashed Pots and Shattered Dreams: The Material Evidence for an Early Classic Site Termination at Cerros, Belize." Pp. 81–99 in *The Sowing and the Dawning: Termination, Dedication and Transformation in the Archaeological and Ethnographic Record of Mesoamerica,* edited by S. Mock. Albuquerque: University of New Mexico Press.

Willey, Gordon R., and James T. Gifford
1961 *Pottery of the Holmul 1 Style from Barton Ramie, British Honduras.* Papers of the Peabody Museum, Harvard University, Monograph 54. Cambridge, Mass.: Harvard University.

Chapter Five

Praise the Ajaw and Pass the Kakaw: Xibun Maya and the Political Economy of Cacao

Patricia A. McAnany, Ben S. Thomas,
Steven Morandi, Polly A. Peterson,
and Eleanor Harrison

In many parts of the world, river valleys played a key role in the emergence of civilization. The unsurpassed fertility of alluvial soils allowed high levels of productivity and an unprecedented concentration of population, while the waterways themselves provided effective transportation corridors, critical to movement of goods and people. Rivers of the ancient world—the Nile, Indus, Tigris, and Euphrates—come readily to mind, but the rivers of another heartland of civilization—the Maya lowlands—are rarely mentioned except to remark on their near absence. While it is true that river systems are sparse in the karstic terrain of the northern Yucatán and the central Petén, impressive waterways drain both the western and eastern flanks of the Yucatán Peninsula (figure 5.1). The eastern river valleys of the Caribbean watershed are particularly significant because they supported large populations on soils that were capable of producing highly desirable luxury crops—such as cacao—yet monumental architecture and hieroglyphic texts, *sine qua non* of political power in Classic Maya society, are underrepresented, suggesting peripheral political status. What were the political and economic relations between the strategic and fertile eastern river valleys and the centers of political power (Classic period Petén and Postclassic to Colonial period Yucatán)? A core-periphery framework combined with a theory of luxury goods is invoked to examine these questions from the perspective of a Caribbean coastal river valley called the Sibun or Xibun (Jones 1998: map 1; see figure 5.1). Encompassing a study area of 550 sq km, the Sibun River valley of central Belize provides an ideal locale at which to examine Classic to Colonial period core-periphery relations. Cacao is still grown commercially in the valley today, archival records document its production in the valley during the Colonial period, most likely under the *encomienda* system, and the innumerable dry caves and river oxbows offer the potential to recover both macroscopic and microscopic evidence of key cultigens in the deeper past. Two seasons of field work (1997 and 1999) by the Xibun

Figure 5.1. Maya Lowlands with selected archaeological sites and physiographic features.

Archaeological Research Project (XARP) provide a baseline of information from which to approach the political economy of cacao (McAnany 1998; McAnany and Thomas 2001).

Political Economies and Core-Periphery Models

William Rathje (1972) introduced the concept of core-periphery interaction to Maya scholarship. Foreshadowing Wallerstein's (1974) codification of a world system in the context of emergent capitalism, Rathje (1972) modeled the interaction between the core polities of the central Maya lowlands and the peripheral polities to the east and south as one of balanced reciprocity. Ritually saturated cosmology was exchanged for needed supplies such as salt and *metates*. The concept of power differentials or hegemonic overlords was not a part of this discourse nor was the notion that tribute (*i-ka-tsi*, cargo or tribute in Classic Maya texts; Stuart 1997: 9, 1998: 410–414) might have primed the engine that circulated some of the more valuable goods across polity boundaries. Current information on Classic Maya acquisition of luxury goods suggests that tribute played a major role in material transfers of jadeite, cotton, quetzal feathers, and especially cacao from the peripheries to the core (Houston 1997; Miller 1997; Stuart 1998: 410–414). During the last fifteen years, the hieroglyphic compound for cacao (spelled syllabically as *ka-ka-w[a]* or *kakaw*) has been deciphered (Stuart 1988, 1989) and found to be ubiquitous on text bands encircling Classic period cylindrical vessels recovered from tomb contexts. Although such breakthroughs have advanced our knowledge of the demand sector of the luxury economy, particularly in the Petén core area, there have been few parallel breakthroughs in the study of the production sectors of the periphery. Just as Wallerstein (1974) paid scant attention to the transformation of societies outside the core of emergent capitalism, we possess little secure knowledge regarding the structural transformations—both political and economic—of the peripheral production zones (see Champion 1989: 12 and Dietler 1989: 136 for expanded discussion). Also lacking is a secure knowledge base regarding the mechanisms (trade or tribute) responsible for the movement of cacao, and the response of the peripheral zones to the collapse of the Classic dynasties and later European incursions. Such information can only be collected through research in the peripheries. The current Xibun Archaeological Research Project is designed to redress this lacuna and thereby dispel the "black box" aura (Hammond 1991: 259–261) surrounding Maya economic and political relations. This project, furthermore, provides a clear demonstration that effective methods for studying Maya core-periphery relations need to incorporate more than midden debris around palace structures and should embrace a comprehensive, regional approach that includes production locales which are often distant from the regal venues at which consumption occurred.

Peering into the Black Box of Maya Political Economy

Among the ancient states of Mesoamerica, the lowland Maya style of statecraft is singular in its emphasis on named and imaged rulers, some of whom reigned over polities no greater than 30 km in diameter. Recognizing the individual-centered nature of Maya governance, Blanton and colleagues (1996: 2, 4) propose that the power strategy of Classic Maya rulers was exclusionary (as opposed to corporate) with an emphasis on the creation of networks of supply and alliance outside of the polity. This elite strategy of interpolity networking, the authors suggest, was enabled by a Weberian patrimonial rhetoric and a prestige or luxury-goods system (Blanton et al. 1996: 5). In general, items that circulate within a prestige-goods system are difficult to acquire, come from a long distance, involve labor-intensive artistry, or display intrinsically desired properties of color, texture, or durability (Blanton et al. 1996: 12; Brumfiel and Earle 1987; Helms 1993; Miller 1987: 122; Renfrew 1986). For Blanton et al. (1996: 5), the network strategy of power emphasizes prestige items in an effort to reduce competition for power within a polity (by upping the ante) and in order to facilitate successful competition outside of the local domain (in which prestige goods form a type of international currency).

These generalized statements provide a relevant high-level construct for Classic Maya political economy and echo an emphasis on exchange relationships in a neo-Rathjean manner. Both Rathje (1972) and Blanton et al. (1996) focus on the reasons for the emergence of exchange relationships rather than the political conditions of their day-to-day functioning once established. Although Blanton et al. (1996: 3) define political economy as "the interactions of types and sources of power," they do not address the specific power strategies employed in acquiring prestige goods or the conditions under which suppliers within or peripheral to the domain of a ruler might agree to an exchange. This lower tier of prestige-goods theory—the milieu in which propositions meet actual case data—begs to be constructed.

Illuminating the black box of Maya political economy requires the specification of relations of production and transfer framed within relevant historical conditions. For the Maya region, such a framework combines the competitive and acquisitive elements of prestige-goods theory (Friedman and Rowlands 1978) with the explicit power differentials of core-periphery or world systems theory (Blanton and Feinman 1984; Champion 1989; Peregrine and Feinman 1996; Rowlands at al. 1987; Smith and Berdan 2000; Wallerstein 1974; Wolf 1982). Following Champion (1989: 14), the core is assumed to encompass "the net consumers of the products of the periphery, and to be the dominant partners in the network of political relationships of which the exchange may be the visible manifestation, while the peripheries are the net providers and the dominated partners." For the Maya region, the core can be further defined by its active materialization of power (DeMarrais et al. 1996) in the form of massive monumental architecture, hieroglyphic texts, palace courts, and royal tombs that are absent or underrepresented in the peripheries.

In the Maya lowlands, a core of political power was located in the central Petén during the Classic period (A.D. 250–850) and subsequently shifted to northern Yucatán during the Postclassic and Colonial periods. Most polities of the Classic period core area supported a capital with a palace court (Inomata and Houston 2001). Ranked in importance and opulence, the royal courts numbered several dozen during the latter part of the Late Classic (A.D. 650–850). In addition to the acquisition of luxury items as personal accouterments, the palace court had to be supplied with large amounts of food and drink to be used for special banquets and feasts and ritual observances. Cacao was a popular beverage of ritual feasts within palace courts; the means by which palace kitchens acquired their chocolate beans is intimated in the murals of Bonampak, Structure 1, Room 1. An infrared photography project conducted by Mary Miller (1997) has clarified the throne scene on the end wall as a royal family surrounded by five large white bundles, one of which is labeled "five *pih kakaw*" (Houston 1997: 40, 2000). If *pih* stands for a unit of 8,000, as Houston suggests, then 40,000 chocolate beans were contained within these sacks. The placement of the bundles at the base of the throne and the fact that the surrounding walls contain a procession of lords wearing long, white robes—costumes seemingly linked with tribute offering at Yaxchilan and Tikal also (Houston 2000)—indicate that even a small, secondary polity such as Bonampak could command and receive luxury goods in the form of cacao. Stuart (1998:

409–417) has noted the textual association between *ikats* (the tribute glyph) and the glyph for "step" or "ascend." Pictorially, most tribute presentation scenes contain a striking vertical dimension in which the presenter ascends from a much lower position to present a "gift" to a ruler seated on a throne. Such regal locales likely were stages where performances of ritual obeisance and "gift-giving" were enacted. The bundled nature of textual and pictorial references to warfare, conquest, *ikats*, and "stair-climbing" (Stuart 1998: 414–416) point to two very important conclusions relevant to understanding cacao production: (1) Maya hieroglyphs are not mute on the subject of political economy as previously thought, and (2) conquest and tribute extraction were not foreign to Maya statecraft.

Evidence of tribute presentation scenes and of cacao in palace courts of core areas is complemented by agronomic, ethnohistorical, paleo-environmental, and demographic data indicating the difficulty of growing cacao both in the Petén and the Yucatán. The northern Yucatán was simply too dry to grow cacao anywhere but within small, collapsed sinkholes or *rellojadas* (Gomez-Pompa et al. 1990; Perez Romero 1988). While there is sufficient rainfall to grow cacao in the Petén, cacao prefers the lower pH of well-drained alluvial river soils (Muhs et al. 1985: 124) over the sweeter, limestone-derived mollisols of the central Petén. Extracting information from Colonial records, Jones (1989: 102) bluntly states, "Cacao did not grow well in the central Petén, however, and the Itzas and their neighbors had to depend on importation of the product or control over subject populations who could supply them with it."

Cacao blossoms produce only small amounts of large, heavy pollen that are transported laboriously from the stamen to the pistil by a species of midge insects that belongs to the ceratopoginid family and prefer a high-canopy forest habitat (Young 1994: 124–127). Cacao growers today sustain high rates of pollination only when their orchards are small and surrounded by stands of high canopy (Young 1994: 167–172). Cacao's need for conditions that mimic the tropical forest canopy is at odds with both the lower, scrub forests of the northern lowlands and the vegetation communities reconstructed from pollen cores taken from lakes of the Petén. Paleo-vegetation profiles constructed by Brenner et al. (2001: 250–251) suggest that few stands of high canopy remained in that area from the Late Classic through the Postclassic periods. Population estimates gleaned from archaeological survey further suggest densities approaching 150 people per sq km for the central and northern Petén (Turner 1990:

table 15.3). On both ecological and demographic grounds, it seems that cacao production was extremely limited in the core areas. Acquiring sacks of cacao beans either through trade or tribute must have been a high priority of Maya elites from the Classic through the Colonial periods.

During Late Postclassic times, the value of cacao was further codified in terms of equivalencies with other valued commodities such as cotton and thereby took on some of the characteristics of currency. Northern Yucatec Maya were engaged in brisk trade with cacao-producers along the Gulf coast of Tabasco, México, and had established trade relations and some measure of political influence in the cacao-producing valleys bordering the Caribbean Sea (Scholes and Roys 1968: 316). During the earlier Classic period, however, it is not clear whether cacao possessed the same measure of convertibility. Likewise, locales of cacao production and the mechanisms (trade or tribute) by which this valued good was transferred to the palace courts of the Petén are not known. What is known is that proximate sources of cacao were available in the eastern river valleys of central and southern Belize.

Focusing on Production in the Sibun River Valley

One of the primary drainages of Belize, the Sibun River originates in the granitic Maya Mountains of southern Belize through which it has carved a deep gorge. Fed by mountain storms, the course of the Sibun begins at an elevation of 800 meters above sea level and from that point drops precipitously to the limestone plain of central Belize. A rapidly flowing river, the Sibun—once it leaves the confines of the gorge—is prone to overbank events (5 to 8 per year) during which prodigious amounts of alluvium are deposited along its banks, creating natural terraces, levee formations, and an alluvial floodplain suitable for cacao production. At the base of the gorge, the valley opens to form a pocket of rich farm land now planted predominantly in citrus orchards. Flowing from the Maya Mountains to the Caribbean Sea in an east/northeasterly direction, the river's total length exceeds 100 km. The mouth of this perennially flowing waterway is less than 20 km south of the mouth of the Belize River (figure 5.2). From the base of the gorge to a landmark called Gracy Rock, the river flows along the northern edge of the Sibun-Manatee Cone Karst (Miller 1996: 113–114), a limestone formation riddled with complex

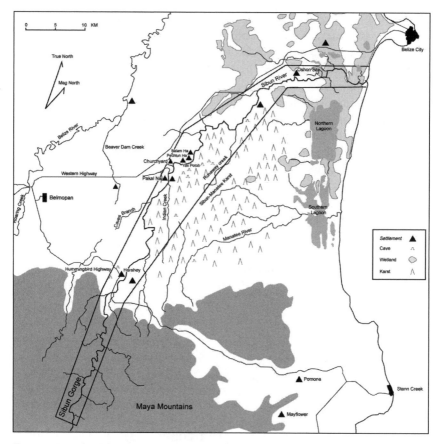

Figure 5.2. The Sibun River Valley showing the location of archaeological sites.

cave systems, many of which contain artifactual deposits from Maya rituals. Downstream, the river slows, widens, and picks up salinity as it nears the salt water of the Inner Channel. The village of Freetown Sibun, on the lower reaches of the river, is situated at a marked transition in the riverine environment. Below Freetown, the height of the river bank drops from over four meters to sea level and the vegetation changes from a community composed of river fig and spiny bamboo, among other plants, to one of predominantly mangrove with an occasional coconut tree. Freetown Sibun also marks the lower end of known ancient Maya settlement.

Citrus and cacao farmers living along the river talk of annual floods during the wet season. While these overbank events fertilize their orchards by leaving behind alluvium, floods also pose a danger since their high energy can induce catastrophic shifts in the meander pattern of the river and result in the loss (or gain) of valuable farm lands. In the middle section of the river, there are frequent overbank events and the tightest meander pattern of any stretch of the river. This sinuosity in addition to the frequency of oxbows (abandoned meander bends) hint at the dynamic hydrological regime of the river. Our survey teams have discovered Maya residential platforms of Late and Terminal Classic construction on the high ground behind many of these oxbows, suggesting that these features may have been part of the active channel when the sites were constructed.

Archival records indicate that the Xibun Maya produced cacao for the tribute economy of Colonial period overlords. Jones (1989) notes that during the seventeenth century a Spanish mission, or *visita*, was built in the Sibun valley that had been parceled into *encomiendas* by the Spanish Crown (G. Jones personal communication, 1997). Cacao production and shipment of a percentage of that production as tribute to Bacalar was the principal *raison d'être* of the *encomiendas*. Active in resistance activities from 1630 to 1638 (Jones 1989: 288), the inhabitants of the mission/cacao *encomienda* at Xibun apparently abandoned the mission town several times (there is one recorded "recapture" event in 1630 [Jones 1989: 289]). During one of their flights, Xibun Maya took with them church ornaments and the bell of the mission church (Jones 1989: 201). Given extant documents, Jones (1989: 288) could not determine the location of the Xibun mission; it now seems likely that the *visita* was located in the rich pocket of alluvium at the base of the gorge. Graham (1994: 324) notes that prior to the development of citrus orchards in the Sibun pocket, the surface was littered with Postclassic incensario fragments; Colonial *encomiendas* often mapped on to pre-existing settlement locales (Graham et al. 1989; Pendergast 1993).

One of the two largest sites in the valley, the Hershey site—so called because it is located in a cacao orchard previously owned by Hershey Foods—is situated in the pocket of fertile land at the base of the gorge (figure 5.2). The large, multi-pyramid Hershey site may be the ancestral site proximate to the Colonial *visita*, much as Indian Church was built on the ancient capital of Lamanai (Pendergast 1993). An intricate, multilevel cave system (Chanona Cave) is located in the limestone hills on the western side of the pocket. Below the confluence of Caves Branch with the Sibun, the northern side of the valley contains a series of settlements documented by representatives of the Belmopan Department of Archaeology, Elliot Abrams (1987), and

XARP survey teams during the 1997 and 1999 field seasons (see McAnany 1998; McAnany and Thomas 2001). These sites include the following: Pakal Na, Churchyard, Pedro's Mound, Yax P'otob, Pechtun Ha, and Balam Ha (figure 5.2). All sites are decidedly residential in focus with a minimal amount of monumental architecture. For the most part, sites consist of 12 to 25 single house platforms arranged in a linear pattern, generally following the 20-meter contour. Low platforms, below 2 m in height, are the norm with important exceptions occurring at Pechtun Ha and Pakal Na. Test excavations into these solo platforms indicate simple, often single-episode, construction histories dating to the Late to Terminal Classic period (Thomas et al. 1998). At Pechtun Ha, however, a large basal platform was constructed and topped with a prismatic pattern of eight structure platforms. This complex is situated on a high terrace overlooking an oxbow locally known as Boat-billed Heron Pond. During the 1999 field season, excavation was conducted in the northern building platform (Structure 109). A midden located off of the southeastern corner of northern Str. 109 yielded tapir and peccary cranial fragments in association with Late to Terminal Classic sherds (Harrison and Acone 2001). This deposit is remarkable because it dates to a time period when widespread protein stress is assumed due to high population levels and diminished forest habitat. Moreover, fauna from large game tends to be associated preferentially with elite residential complexes (Masson 1999); Pechtun Ha is a secondary settlement, at best, within the Sibun valley hierarchy. This deposit may be a clue that deforestation and protein stress, signatures of the Late Classic period in the Petén and elsewhere, may not have typified the Sibun River valley.

To the west of Pechtun Ha, in the center of Pakal Na, three large, linear platforms were configured around a central plaza space. This deviation from low, single platforms may represent an administrative node or simply the residences of a local elite. In the course of excavation in the flat terrain to the west of the largest structure (No. 130), a fired-clay surface (not a house floor) was encountered. Many interpretations of this surface could be offered but, given its proximity to Str. 130 and its prepared and hard-fired surface, this feature may well have been used for drying cacao. Among contemporary Mopan Maya cacao-growers in southern Belize, cacao is dried on concrete pads immediately in front of the main house structure.

Across the river from the middle valley settlements, the karst is riddled with cave chambers; Xibun Maya were active participants in ritual practices undertaken in nearby underground caverns. The well-preserved cave deposits of pottery vessels and large sherds, chipped stone bifaces, polished greenstone celts, and grinding equipment indicate the frequency of pilgrimage to this sacred landscape and hint at a ritual cycle that focused on agricultural concerns (Peterson 2001). Such caves were a key element in the armature of Maya cosmology (Stone 1995), and their association with settlement sites as well as their general significance within Maya conceptions of sacred landscape have long been overlooked (Brady 1997; Brady and Ashmore 1999). The dry caves of the Sibun-Manatee karst also provide a unique opportunity to retrieve botanical remains from ritual practice. As Coe and Coe (1996: 44–45) have noted, cacao is frequently shown in the Postclassic divinatory codices, and Thompson (1956: 101) has discussed the ritual symmetry between chocolate and blood as precious liquids. In a wider sense, the assemblages of well-preserved artifactual and botanical remains deposited within caves are indicative of the materials on hand and available for offertory purposes. The presence of carbon-based pictographs on the walls of several of the Sibun caverns provides an additional opportunity to comprehend the nature of cave ritual as well as collect samples for chronometric analysis.

Immediately downriver from the intensively explored middle section, only limited systematic archaeological recording has been conducted. Farther downriver in the vicinity of the village of Freetown Sibun, however, the second-largest site in the valley—the Samuel Oshon site—can be found (figure 5.2). Mapped during the 1999 field season, the Oshon site contains a core of monumental architecture with two adjoining plazas surrounded by approximately thirty satellite residential platforms. The main precinct is located near an oxbow of the river and peripheral settlement continues to the east along the current course of the river. Preliminary test excavations in the center of the Oshon site uncovered a midden deposit containing over 30 obsidian blades, suggesting that the strategic location of this settlement allowed it to serve as a gateway to the resources of the valley.

Thus far, pottery collected from caves and excavations in the valley settlements dates almost exclusively to the Classic and Epi-Classic periods. A plasma-induced radiocarbon assay on charcoal pigment from a cave pictograph at Actun Ik yielded an age of 1100 +/- 50 years or A. D. 800–900 (CAMS #50930; see Rowe et al. 2001). This Terminal Classic date accords well with the Late to Terminal

Classic ceramics from the settlements and the period of peak demand for cacao.

Modeling the Production of Cacao from the Perspective of the Periphery

If the Sibun River valley was a locale of cacao production during the Classic and Postclassic periods, how was the production organized? Were the residents of the valley engaged in brisk trade in this valuable substance or were they producing at the behest of a distant overlord? Several different production states can be modeled. Here, a construct is presented that attempts to model production dynamically, that is, to allow for variability across space and through time. A basic assumption of this construct is that long-term success in production and trading activities will be manifest in construction and expansion of residences and acquisition of imports. The following two contrastive states regarding the relations of production and exchange can be envisioned:

1. If a luxury crop such as cacao was transferred from a production locale predominantly through trade mechanisms, then said locale should manifest signs of wealth and political autonomy in the form of a high frequency of traded imports, periodic household expansion, and architecture indicative of indigenous power structures;

2. If cacao was transferred from a production locale predominantly through the mechanism of tribute, then the net effect should be a drain of wealth away from the valley and traded imports should be poorly represented, household expansion limited, and political control materialized by vertical linkages to core areas.

These two ideal contrastive states are confounded, however, by the fact that reality seldom operates according to Boolean logic. Moreover, it is recognized that a third condition, some conflation of the two opposing states or an unpredicted condition, may be operating at any point in time or in separate parts of the valley. For instance, if cacao production in the Sibun valley was transferred as tribute to the Petén during the Classic period, then the expected material signature would be one of limited settlement exuberance, limited imports, and limited construction of monumental architecture. In short, much of the wealth of the valley would have been siphoned off in tribute obligations and local power structures would have been depressed. This situation could have changed dramatically (or not at all) after the fall of the Classic period southern dynasties and the shift of power to the north during Epi- and Postclassic times. If tribute relations were relaxed in favor of trade relations with the more distant northern capitals, such as Chichén Itzá, then there might have been an influx of imports such as Ixtepeque obsidian and jadeite, matched by household expansion and the assertion of local power bases in the form of monumental architecture. Possibly, different relations of production and exchange existed in the upper versus the lower portions of the valley.

In the absence of absolute measures of wealth, proxy measures can be invoked including imports such as jadeite, greenstone, obsidian, and exotic pottery (in both cave deposits and settlements); residential growth and elaboration; and construction and expansion of monumental constructions such as pyramids and large plaza groups. Given a spatially diverse sample and sufficient chronological control, temporal and spatial changes should be detectable and potentially provide powerful insight to changes in the relations between core and periphery.

Concluding Thoughts

In the years to come, the fit between the two contrastive states of cacao production (trade as opposed to tribute) and the material remains from survey and excavation in the Sibun River Valley will be evaluated. Just as Wolf's (1982) treatment of the rise of mercantile capitalism shifted focus from the centers of power codified by Wallerstein (1974) to examine the profound effect of an emergent world economy on the mode and relations of production in the periphery—among the "people without history"—so the approach outlined here shifts research focus from the textually rich Maya centers of political power to a "text-free" zone at which production efforts fueled the luxury economy of the centers. In following this paradigm, the deep history of Maya society will become more of a social history. Our understanding of ancient Maya political economy will be transformed from a uni-dimensional focus on core zones of power to a multidimensional comprehension of the conditions under which a locale in the periphery was asked to pass the cacao.

References

Abrams, Elliott M.
1987 *Balam Ha: Preliminary Report of the 1986 Field Season.* Submitted to the Department of Archaeology, Belmopan, Belize.

Blanton, Richard E., and Gary M. Feinman
1984 "The Mesoamerican World System." *American Anthropologist* 86: 673–682.

Blanton, Richard E., Gary M. Feinman, Stephen A. Kowalewski, and Peter N. Peregrine
1996 "A Dual-Processual Theory for the Evolution of Mesoamerican Civilization." *Current Anthropology* 37(1): 1–86.

Brady, James E.
1997 "Settlement Configuration and Cosmology: The Role of Caves at Dos Pilas." *American Anthropologist* 99(3): 602–618.

Brady, James E., and Wendy Ashmore
1999 "Mountains, Caves, Water: Ideational Landscapes of the Ancient Maya." Pp. 124–145 in *Archaeologies of Landscape: Contemporary Perspectives*, edited by W. Ashmore and B. Knapp. Malden, Mass.: Blackwell.

Brenner, Mark, Barbara Leyden, and M. W. Binford
2001 "Recent Sedimentary Histories of Shallow Lakes in the Guatemalan Savannas." *Journal of Paleolimnology* 4(3): 239–252.

Brumfiel, Elizabeth, and Timothy K. Earle
1987 "Specialization, Exchange, and Complex Societies: An Introduction." Pp. 1–9 in *Specialization, Exchange, and Complex Societies*, edited by E. Brumfiel and T. K. Earle. Cambridge: Cambridge University Press.

Champion, Thomas C.
1989 "Introduction." Pp. 1–21 in *Centre and Periphery: Comparative Studies in Archaeology*, edited by T. C. Champion. London: Unwin Hyman.

Coe, Sophie D., and Michael D. Coe
1996 *The True History of Chocolate.* London: Thames and Hudson.

DeMarrais, Elizabeth, Luis J. Castillo, and Timothy Earle
1996 "Ideology, Materialization, and Power Strategies." *Current Anthropology* 37: 15–31.

Dietler, Michael
1989 "Greeks, Etruscans, and Thirsty Barbarians: Early Iron Age Interaction in the Rhone Basin of France." Pp. 127–136 in *Centre and Periphery: Comparative Studies in Archaeology*, edited by T. C. Champion. London: Unwin Hyman.

Friedman, Jonathan, and Michael J. Rowlands
1978 "Notes towards an Epigenetic Model of the Evolution of 'Civilization.'" Pp. 201–276 in *The Evolution of Social Systems*, edited by J. Friedman and M. J. Rowlands. Pittsburgh: University of Pittsburgh Press.

Gomez-Pompa, Arturo, Jose Salvador Flores, and Mario Aliphat Fernandez
1990 "The Sacred Cacao Groves of the Maya." *Latin American Antiquity* 1: 247–257.

Graham, Elizabeth
1994 *The Highlands of the Lowlands: Environment and Archaeology in the Stann Creek District, Belize, Central America.* Monographs in World Archaeology, No. 19. Madison, Wis.: Prehistory Press.
Graham, Elizabeth, David M. Pendergast, and Grant D. Jones
1989 "On the Fringes of Conquest: Maya-Spanish Contact in Colonial Belize." *Science* 246: 1254–1259.
Hammond, Norman
1991 "Inside the Black Box: Defining Maya Polity." Pp. 253–284 in *Classic Maya Political History: Hieroglyphic and Archaeological Evidence*, edited by T. P. Culbert. Cambridge: Cambridge University Press.
Harrison, Eleanor, and Kevin Acone
2001 "Further Investigations at Pechtun Ha: Feasting and Mass Importation of Cave Speleothems." In *Sacred Landscape and Settlement in the Sibun River Valley*, edited by P. A. McAnany and B. Thomas. Albany: State University of New York Institute for Mesoamerican Studies.
Helms, Mary W.
1993 *Craft and the Kingly Ideal: Art, Trade, and Power.* Austin: University of Texas Press.
Houston, Stephen D.
1997 "A King Worth a Hill of Beans." *Archaeology* 50(3): 40.
2000 "Into the Minds of Ancients: Advances in Maya Glyph Studies." *Journal of World Prehistory* 14: 121–201.
Inomata, Takeshi, and Stephen D. Houston, eds.
2001 *Royal Courts of the Ancient Maya, Volume 1: Theory, Comparison, and Synthesis.* Boulder: Westview Press.
Jones, Grant D.
1989 *Maya Resistance to Spanish Rule: Time and Resistance on a Colonial Frontier.* Albuquerque: University of New Mexico Press.
1998 *The Conquest of the Last Maya Kingdom.* Stanford, Calif.: Stanford University Press.
Masson, Marilyn A.
1999 "The Manipulation of 'Staple' and 'Status' Faunas at Postclassic Maya Communities." *World Archaeology* 31: 93–120.
McAnany, Patricia A., ed.
1998 *Caves and Settlements of the Sibun River Valley, Belize: 1997 Archaeological Survey and Excavation.* Submitted to the Department of Archaeology, Belmopan, Belize. On file, Boston University Department of Archaeology.
McAnany, Patricia A., and Ben Thomas, eds.
2001 *Sacred Landscape and Settlement of the Sibun River Valley.* Albany: State University of New York Institute for Mesoamerican Studies.
Miller, Daniel
1987 *Material Culture and Mass Consumption.* Oxford: Basil Blackwell.
Miller, Mary
1997 "Imaging Maya Art." *Archaeology* 50(3): 34–40.

Miller, Thomas E.
1996 "Geologic and Hydrologic Controls on Karst and Cave Development in Belize." *Journal of Cave and Karst Studies* 58(2): 100–120.
Muhs, Daniel R., Robert R. Kautz, and Jefferson J. MacKinnon
1985 "Soils and the Location of Cacao Orchards at a Maya Site in Western Belize." *Journal of Archaeological Science* 12: 121–137.
Pendergast, David M.
1993 "Worlds in Collision: The Maya/Spanish Encounter in Sixteenth and Seventeenth Century Belize." *Proceedings of the British Academy* 81: 105–143.
Peregrine, Peter, and Gary Feinman, eds.
1996 *Pre-Columbian World Systems.* Madison, Wis.: Prehistory Press.
Perez Romero, J. A.
1988 *Algunas Consideraciones sobre Cacao en el Norte de la Peninsula de Yucatán.* Tesis de Licenciatura en Ciencias Antropologicas, Universidad Autónoma de Yucatán, Mérida.
Peterson, Polly
2001 "Shedding Light on Xibalba through Cave Survey and Surface Collection." In *Sacred Landscape and Settlement of the Sibun River Valley,* edited by P. A. McAnany and B. S. Thomas. Albany: State University of New York Institute for Mesoamerican Studies.
Price, T. Douglas, and Gary M. Feinman
1997 *Images of the Past,* Second edition, Mountain View, Calif.: Mayfield Publishing Co.
Rathje, William L.
1972 "Praise the Gods and Pass the Metates: A Hypothesis of the Development of Lowland Rainforest Civilizations in Mesoamerica." Pp. 365–392 in *Contemporary Archaeology: A Guide to Theory and Contributions,* edited by M. P. Leone. Carbondale: Southern Illinois University Press.
Renfrew, Colin
1985 "Varna and the Emergence of Wealth in Prehistoric Europe." Pp. 141–168 in *The Social Life of Things: Commodities in Cultural Perspective,* edited by A. Appadurai. Cambridge: Cambridge University Press.
Rowe, Marvin, Allan B. Cobb, Polly A. Peterson, and Patricia A. McAnany
2001 "Late Classic Pictographs from Actun Ik." In *Sacred Landscape and Settlement in the Sibun River Valley,* edited by P. A. McAnany and B. S. Thomas. Albany: State University of New York Institute for Mesoamerican Studies.
Rowlands, Michael, Mogens Larsen, and Kristian Kristiansen, eds.
1985 *Centre and Periphery in the Ancient World.* Cambridge: Cambridge University Press.
Scholes, Frances V., and Ralph L. Roys
1968 *The Maya Chontal Indians of Acalan-Tixchel.* Second edition (originally published in 1948 in Carnegie Institution of Washington series). Norman: University of Oklahoma Press.
Smith, Michael E., and Frances F. Berdan
2000 "The Postclassic Mesoamerican World System." *Current Anthropology* 41(2): 283–286.

Stone, Andrea J.
1995 *Images from the Underworld: Naj Tunich and the Tradition of Maya Cave Painting*. Austin: University of Texas Press.
Stuart, David
1988 "The Río Azul Cacao Pot: Epigraphic Observations on the Function of a Maya Ceramic Vessel." *Antiquity* 62: 153–157.
1989 "Hieroglyphs on Maya Vessels." Pp. 149–160 in *The Maya Vase Book, Volume 1*, edited by J. Kerr. New York: Kerr.
1997 "Kinship Terms in Maya Inscriptions." Pp. 1–11 in *The Language of Maya Hieroglyphs*, edited by M. J. Macri and A. Ford. Pre-Columbian Art Research Institute, San Francisco.
1998 "'The Fire Enters His House': Architecture and Ritual in Classic Maya Texts." Pp. 373–425 in *Function and Meaning in Classic Maya Architecture*, edited by S. D. Houston. Washington, D.C.: Dumbarton Oaks.
Thomas, Ben, Robert Mack, T. DiPace, Patricia A. McAnany, and Kim Berry
1998 "Settlements in the River Valley." Pp. 19–37 in *Caves and Settlements of the Sibun River Valley, Belize: 1997 Archaeological Survey and Excavation*, edited by P. A. McAnany. Submitted to the Department of Archaeology, Belmopan, Belize. On file, Boston University Department of Archaeology.
Thompson, J. Eric S.
1956 "Notes on the Use of Cacao in Middle America." *Notes on Middle American Archaeology and Ethnology* 128: 95–116.
Turner, Billie L. II
1990 "Population Reconstruction for the Central Maya Lowlands: 1000 B.C. to A.D. 1500." Pp. 301–324 in *Precolumbian Population History in the Maya Lowlands*, edited by T. P. Culbert and D. S. Rice. Albuquerque: University of New Mexico Press.
Wallerstein, Immanuel
1974 *The Modern World System: Capitalist Agriculture and the Origins of the European World-Economy in the Sixteenth Century*. New York: Academic Press.
Wolf, Eric
1982 *Europe and the People without History*. Berkeley: University of California Press.
Young, Allen M.
1993 *The Chocolate Tree: A Natural History of Cacao*. Washington, D.C.: Smithsonian Institution Press.

Chapter Six

Ceramic Exchange in the Late Classic and Postclassic Maya Lowlands: A Diachronic Approach

Georgia West

Much archaeological research in Mesoamerica has focused on determining the extent to which elites administered different types of production in their societies and how administered production related to the broader political economy in which it occurred. This chapter addresses the role of Classic Maya elite monumental centers in lowland regional economies using studies of Maya ceramic production and distribution. The patterns found in these studies indicate that ceramic production during the Classic period was decentralized, taking place at dispersed loci, and distribution spheres tended to be relatively truncated (Hammond and Harbottle 1976; Fry 1980; Rands and Bishop 1980; Beaudry 1984; Hansen et al. 1991; Reents-Budet et al. 1994; Foias and Bishop 1997). I argue that these patterns do not preclude the possibility that some monumental centers were central place nodes of regional market distribution and exchange. The truncated distribution spheres in many areas of the Classic period lowlands would be expected in an area with high levels of interpolity competition (cf. Hodge and Minc 1990) and suggests an economy centered around monumental sites. This idea is supported by the existence of wider ceramic distribution spheres in more peripheral areas of the Classic lowlands, such as Quintana Roo, northern Belize, and the southeastern Maya periphery (Beaudry 1984; Demarest 1988; Rands et al. 1982; Fry 1980; Sidrys 1983a). The apparent absence of intensive and highly standardized ceramic production across the Classic period lowlands does suggest that hinterland communities were poorly integrated into interregional exchange systems. The inhabitants of intersite zones around major centers may have been relatively isolated economically beyond the range of these centers. By comparing patterns of ceramic production and distribution found in the Postclassic periods (Rands et al. 1982; Sidrys and Krowne 1983; Kepecs 1996) with those of the Classic period, it is possible to evaluate the kinds of exchange systems responsible for ceramic distributions in the Classic period, and the role Maya elites may have played in these systems.

The Maya Political Economy: The Role of Elites

Recent evaluations of the Maya economy (Rice 1987a, 1987b; McAnany 1989, 1993; Ball 1993; Potter and King 1995) have used ceramic evidence to argue that elites played a minimal role in the local economy and that Maya centers were indeed little more than "regal-ritual" centers as defined by Fox (1977) and later applied to Mesoamerican urban centers by Sanders and Webster (1988) and Ball (1993). There appears to be widespread agreement (McAnany 1989; Ball 1993; Potter and King 1995) with Rice's statement that Maya economies were more "chiefdom-like than state-like" and that "power rested in the genealogies of the rulers, not in their administration of production and distribution of utilitarian goods within their realms" (Rice 1987b: 514). This statement reflects an either/or attitude recently criticized by Hirth (1996) in an overview of archaeological research in political economy. Hirth cites M. Estellie Smith's observation that "all societies possess organizational structures for accumulation, management, and reinvestment of resources" (Hirth 1996: 206; M. E. Smith 1991). Similarly, Carol Smith argues that stratification in all agrarian societies is, without exception, based on control over scarce resources by select members of that society (Smith 1976). She asserts that control over distribution, rather than control over production, is the critical basis of stratification in agrarian societies (Smith 1976). Given the large-scale investment in monumental architecture and public works evident at some Classic lowland sites, along with the indications of high population densities and the use of intensive agricultural techniques, the idea that elite power rested solely on ideology or genealogy seems unlikely (Chase and Chase 1996; Chase 1998). This chapter thus focuses not on the question of whether Maya elites played a role in the regional economies of their realms, but what that role was and how it changed in the centuries spanning the Classic through the Postclassic periods.

The organization of ancient Maya economy tends to be a highly charged subject, due to the fact that archaeologists tend to associate different systems of exchange with stages of political organization that are perceived as progressing along a linear evolutionary spectrum (Yoffee 1977; Chase and Chase 1996). Looming large in the back of most Mayanists' minds are the examples of the highland states; which McAnany labels the "highland model for the Lowland Maya" (McAnany 1989: 350). Archaeological data from Teotihuacan and the Oaxaca Valley suggest that a major restructuring of production and distribution systems occurred as the Teotihuacan and Monte Alban polities became increasingly powerful and centralized (Cowgill 1997; Spence 1984; Feinman 1982, 1986). Such data in the Maya lowlands are notably absent. Because Mesoamericanists often evaluate political complexity based on indications of economic control by centralized elites (Sanders 1981; Adams and Smith 1981; Freidel 1981), the implications of this discrepancy are that the Maya were evolutionarily retarded (Freidel 1981, citing Willey 1974). A closely related issue is the role of Maya "central places" in regional systems (Marcus 1976). Carol Smith points out that the central place model as originally conceived is based entirely on economic relationships. All other applications, such as Marcus's (1976, 1993), are stretching the model far beyond its relevant applications (C. Smith 1974). Mayanists are concerned with determining the extent to which Maya monumental centers served as economic central places in the regional economy (Rands 1967; Haviland 1970; Fry and Cox 1974; Fry 1979; Marcus 1993; Chase 1998). Sanders and Webster created a flurry of protest (M. E. Smith 1989; Chase et al. 1990) when they relegated most Mesoamerican cities, and all Maya centers, to "regal-ritual" status (Sanders and Webster 1988). Protest against this categorization is still brewing (e.g., McAnany 1993; Potter and King 1995; Chase and Chase 1996).

Yoffee has criticized the typological approach in archaeology for precisely these reasons, arguing that casting socioeconomic functions as strictly linear and hierarchical has created a taxonomic trap for archaeologists (Yoffee 1977). In particular, he notes the tendency of those concerned with the rise of the state to correlate sociopolitical stages with Polyani's (1957) classification of reciprocal, redistributive, and market modes of exchange (Yoffee 1977). In this scheme, redistribution is identified with chiefdoms, and market exchange with states. Yoffee points out that the purpose of such typing seems to be to extrapolate from a single characteristic entire clusters of sociocultural functions thought to categorize a type, whether or not these are indicated in the material record. This act of categorization into stages, Yoffee asserts, tends to make researchers ignore the necessity of exploring subsystemic variability within "stages" and similarities of sociocultural variability across stages. In fact, as many scholars have pointed out (C. Smith 1976; Knapp and Cherry 1994; McAnany 1991), including Polanyi himself (C. Smith 1976, citing Polyani et al. 1957: 334), contrasting forms of economic organization may coexist within any given level of sociopolitical complexity.

This coexistence of differing mechanisms of exchange clearly occurred in Late Postclassic Mesoamerica. According to ethnohistoric accounts, market and middleman exchange was an important part of the Yucatan economy at the time of contact (Tozzer 1941: 95; Piña Chan 1978; Roys 1943). Piña Chan reports that both the "capitals" of jurisdictions, and other strategically placed towns, were centers of commerce and markets (Piña Chan 1978). Market towns tended to be clustered along the coast; markets at inland sites were not reported by the Spaniards (Piña Chan 1978). Interregional exchange was facilitated by middleman traders, and markets were regulated by means of officials who inspected weights and measures and settled litigations (Piña Chan 1978). Landa also describes reciprocal gift exchange and redistributive exchange mechanisms in early Colonial Yucatan (Tozzer 1941: 92, 97). Individuals offered gifts when making visits, and elites regularly held feasts in which they offered gifts of ceramic cups, among other things, to their guests (Tozzer 1941: 92, 97). The economy of the Aztec state was also characterized by both market exchange on a local and interregional level and redistribution among the upper strata of society (Offner 1981a). Although there is debate regarding the relative importance for each of these mechanisms in the working of the state economy (e.g., Carrasco 1981; Offner 1981b), it is clear that both played a role in maintaining an integrated and functioning economy (Berdan 1985; McAnany 1991).

Agrarian Economic Systems:
Bounded Networks and Solar Central Places

Carol Smith's typology of the spatial and economic organization of regional agrarian systems is useful when examining the Maya economy because it articulates the relationship between central places, the role of elites, and the means of exchange within a regional system (C. Smith 1976). While Smith emphasizes that most complex distribution systems are dependent on the coexistence of one or more exchange mechanisms, the economic systems she defines are characterized by one dominant mode of exchange between food producers and non-food producers (C. Smith 1976). Two classes of Smith's regional systems seem relevant to the Maya: the bounded network and the solar central place system (figure 6.1). Both are systems of limited geographic extent in which specialized production is not highly developed. The major differences between the two are their geographic inclusiveness and the primary mechanisms of exchange between food producers and non-food producers. The first type, the Bounded Network system, occurs in a noncommercialized economy. In this system, exchange is organized by the local hierarchy. Trade outside the local system is limited and does not affect the local economy. Households in bounded network economies have direct links to a nodal center to which they offer tribute in exchange for some scarce resource controlled by their overlords. Diversified production is not stimulated due to the isolation of the local system, and most people are engaged in food production on a self-sufficient level.

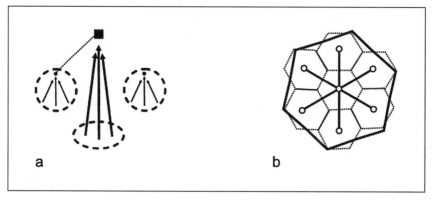

a   b

Fig. 6.1. Selected spatial models for regional agrarian systems (from C. Smith 1976: figure 1): a) Bounded Network System, b) Solar Central Place System.

The lack of commerce in this type of economy disperses elites widely at the centers of small, closed rural systems. The size of these systems is determined by the distance over which elites can control the distribution of the scarce resource that they control (Smith 1976).

In a partially commercialized solar central place system, urban centers are located in the middle of tributary hinterlands, and all rural places are connected to only one of them for marketing (Smith 1976). Through its markets, the central place articulates and organizes exchange among several local systems, and it receives much of the surplus from the peasantry through market exchange rather than direct tribute collection. Settlement pattern analyses of major Classic period Maya sites provide evidence of their centralizing market functions (Chase 1998; Dahlin and Ardren, chapter 9 this volume). The increased complexity of hierarchical organization in solar central place systems, along with the presence of middlemen, allows greater specialization and intensification of trade in the hinterlands. However, peasants are not fully integrated into the regional market economy and thus division of labor does not develop much and is relegated to the few places within regular commuting distance of each market. Moreover, specialization in the production of certain market commodities often occurs on a community-wide, rather than individual, basis (Rands and Bishop 1980). In such economies, peasants are largely self-reliant, but rely on markets for some tools and/or ceremonial goods and perhaps some peasant-produced commodities such as pottery. Because urban dwellers rely on markets for incoming surplus, they must have a monopoly on some market-exchanged commodities, often religious-ceremonial paraphernalia, necessary for peasants (Smith 1976), as Rands and Bishop (1980) suggest for Palenque.

Determining Mechanisms of Exchange in a Regional System

Distribution

In order to evaluate the applicability of Smith's models to lowland Maya economic organization, it is necessary to look not only at patterns of artifact distribution within a region, but also at the organization of production, resource acquisition, and patterns of consumption. Renfrew's (1975) research on the distributional patterns of exchange systems represents perhaps the most systematic attempt to identify mechanisms of exchange in the archaeological record (Sabloff and Lamberg-Karlovsky 1975; Ericson and Baugh 1992; Torrence

1986). Renfrew postulated that artifacts exchanged by distinct mechanisms would display differing distributional fall-off curves in relationship to their source (fig. 6.2; Renfrew 1975, 1977; Torrence 1986: fig. 25). Figure 6.2 shows the shape of Renfrew's predicted fall-off curves for down-the-line exchange (reciprocal), prestige goods exchange, freelance exchange (by means of middlemen), and directional exchange (central place exchange). Unfortunately, as Hodder and

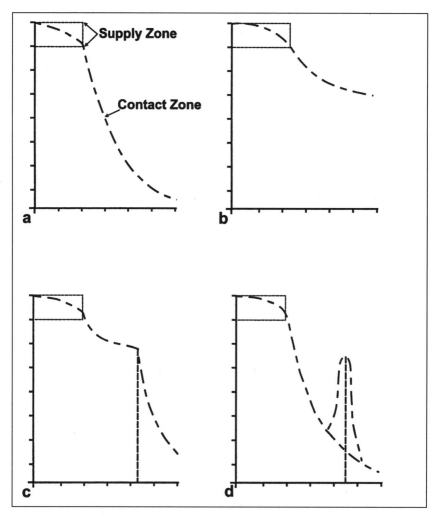

Fig. 6.2. Predicted fall-off curves identified by Colin Renfrew (from Torrence 1986: figure 25): a) down-the-line-exchange, b) prestige-good exchange, c) freelance exchange, d) directional change.

others have pointed out (Hodder 1980; Torrence 1986: 117; Knapp and Cherry 1994: 125), more than one type of exchange may produce similar fall-off curves. The curve representing prestige goods exchange could also represent down-the-line exchange, the freelance model could be duplicated by both middleman or reciprocal exchange, and the directional trade curve is common to both central place market exchange and redistribution (Torrence 1986: 116). Unfortunately, it is precisely the types of exchange that cannot be distinguished in Renfrew's fall-off curves that Smith (1976) uses to discriminate between bounded network and solar central place economic systems. In order to differentiate between alternative modes of exchange, it is thus necessary to examine other factors: in particular, the organization of production, resource acquisition, and artifact consumption patterns.

Production and Specialization

The presence of full-time versus part-time specialization in a sociocultural system has been used by archaeologists to evaluate the level of interdependence, or organic solidarity, of a society (e.g., Sanders and Price 1968; Sanders and Webster 1988; Feinman 1982). Presumably, when full-time specialists are present, one can infer that a well-organized network of exchange exists upon which non-food producers can depend for their subsistence needs (C. Smith 1976). In bounded network systems, specialization is poorly developed (C. Smith 1976). Full-time specialization in solar central place systems is rare due to imperfections of the market system resulting from elite market monopolization and the insularity of regional systems. A dependable flow of subsistence resources throughout a given socio-economic system would be more likely in an economy with fully commercialized market exchange unhindered by a strongly directive administration (C. Smith 1976). Despite its usefulness for evaluating dominant exchange mechanisms within a sociocultural system, differentiating between full- and part-time specialization using archaeological remains is difficult, and although much literature has been dedicated to establishing archaeological methods of identifying levels of specialization, it remains an equivocal task (Costin 1991; Sinopoli 1991).

A less ambiguous measure of production, and one that can shed light on the types of exchange prevalent in a society, is the level of standardization, simplification, and volume of production (Rathje 1975; Rathje, Gregory, and Wiseman 1978; Torrence 1986; Costin 1991).

Standardization and simplification are cost-control devices that may indicate specialized workshops producing relatively high quantities of goods (Rathje 1975; Rathje, Gregory, and Wiseman 1978; Torrence 1986). Such high-volume output would most probably occur in systems where a reliable means of distribution was ensured (C. Smith 1976). Although some scholars have interpreted the presence of standardization and simplification as indicative of a commercialized and competitive economy (Rathje 1975; Torrence 1986), their presence may also indicate centralized control over a region and elite investment in its economy (D'Altroy and Bishop 1990). Mass replication of ceramic goods may occur in both market-based and redistributive economies. However, a means of discriminating between the two is the placement of production loci within the regional system, and the distribution of products from centrally located as opposed to dispersed workshops (Skinner 1985).

The patterns of production and distribution in the Inka and Aztec empires and in the Late Postclassic Oaxaca Valley are illustrative of this point. The administrators of the Inka empire relied primarily on redistributive mechanisms of exchange (Earle and Ericson 1977), whereas Late Postclassic highland Mexico had a flourishing market system (Offner 1981a; Berdan 1985; Blanton 1985; M. E. Smith 1997). Research at a peripheral Andean site in Peru found that most subsistence goods were obtained and consumed locally (Earle and Ericson 1977). The majority of ceramics were locally produced and distributed, both before and after incorporation into the Inka empire. After incorporation into the Inka empire in 1450, 18 percent of the ceramics at the site were imported "imperial-style" ceramics from a state-sponsored workshop (Earle and Ericson 1977; D'Altroy and Bishop 1990). Neutron activation analysis of these imperial-style ceramics suggests that they were produced almost exclusively at two or three centralized workshops rather than at workshops dispersed throughout the empire (D'Altroy and Bishop 1990). In Central Mexico, on the other hand, workshops dispersed throughout the basin of Mexico produced large quantities of Aztec Black-on-orange ceramics for distribution in regional marketing systems (Hodge and Minc 1990). Although a significant quantity of Aztec Black-on-orange III ceramics were produced at a centrally located workshop near Tenochtitlan, the production of which may have been state sponsored, such workshops did not only occur near the administrative core of the state (Hodge and Minc 1990; Hodge et al.1993; M. E. Smith 1996: 129). In the Valley of Oaxaca during the Late Postclassic period, workshops producing the most standardized and widely distributed ceramics were located in areas with less productive agricultural land, not at or near administrative centers (Feinman et al. 1992). This pattern is what one would expect from a highly commercialized economy in a region not unified under a dominant center.

Acquisition of Resources

Elite control over the acquisition of raw materials is a problematic issue in archaeology and, as several scholars have pointed out, few archaeologists have adequately developed methods for identifying elite control of resource acquisition (Torrence 1986; McAnany 1991). More often than not, resource control is assumed rather than empirically demonstrated (Torrence 1986). Distribution of resources is one way to evaluate measures of elite control. For instance, the intersite and intrasite distribution of obsidian cores has been used by Mayanists to assess the role of elites and central places in obsidian procurement from highland sources (Moholy-Nagy 1976; Johnson 1976, 1996; Rice 1984, 1987a; Mallory 1986; Ford et al. 1997). In the central Maya lowlands (figure 6.3), particularly in the Early Classic, cores are concentrated at elite centers, and are often found in special deposits associated with elite activities (Rice 1987a; Moholy-Nagy 1976, 1989). On the other hand, later in time high frequencies of obsidian cores have been found at coastal sites in Belize, where an elite presence is not indicated, suggesting that its inhabitants had access to imported materials brought by middleman traders (McKillop 1989, 1995). In the Copan Valley (figure 6.3), an area closer to the highland Guatemalan obsidian source (Sidrys 1977), obsidian cores are found widely distributed throughout the hinterlands (Mallory 1986; Hendon 1991), suggesting either direct access to the obsidian source, open access through markets, or trade with middlemen. However, the ubiquitous presence of obsidian cores at households of all status levels makes redistribution seem unlikely (Mallory 1986; Hendon 1991; McAnany 1991). The numbers of obsidian sources represented at a site may also indicate its role as a distributive node in the regional economy (Feinman 1982). Both Tikal and coastal sites have a greater diversity of obsidian than secondary and tertiary inland sites, suggesting they were both nodes in the long-distance obsidian exchange network during the Late Classic period (Moholy-Nagy and Nelson 1990; McKillop 1996).

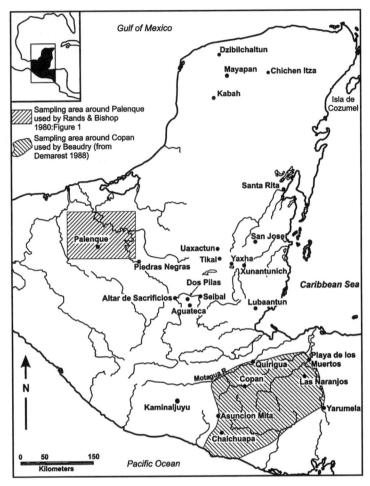

Fig. 6.3. Map of Maya area with sites and sampling areas mentioned in the text.

Consumption Patterns

One way to distinguish between market, redistributive, and/or prestige goods exchange may also be the context of artifact deposition (Knapp and Cherry 1994). Depositional context may signal the social value of an artifact, which aids in identifying the means by which it was exchanged. Prestige goods are characterized by the tendency of individuals not to consume such goods (Knapp and Cherry 1994: 146). Prestige goods are often found in the archaeological record as a result of loss, breakage, or deliberate deposit in mortuary or hoarding contexts (Knapp and Cherry 1994: 146). For example, in ancient Greece metal artifacts occur in a limited range of archaeological contexts (in burials before 750 B.C. and in sanctuaries thereafter), providing strong evidence for gift exchange (Knapp and Cherry 1994: 147). In the Classic period Maya lowlands, the bulk of obsidian has been found associated with special deposits in elite and ceremonial structures (e.g., Moholy-Nagy 1976, 1989; Johnson 1996). In commoner households, however, they are found almost exclusively in midden contexts (Moholy-Nagy 1976; Johnson 1996). This suggests functional differentiation according to status, and may indicate that commoners refrained from placing obsidian out of circulation because of its relatively restricted availability. Nevertheless, the quantities of obsidian found in association with elite burials, including production debris (Moholy-Nagy 1976, 1989; Johnson 1996), suggests that, at least among elites, obsidian was exchanged as a prestige good.

The rate of consumption is also important in evaluating the means of exchange. While redistributive and market exchange are both possible explanations for the presence of obsidian blades at commoner households throughout Tikal and in the intersite areas between Tikal and Yaxha (Ford et al. 1997; Moholy Nagy 1976, 1989), the low quantities of obsidian in all households suggests that this product was not readily accessible. If open market exchange were the means of distribution, one might expect higher rates of consumption at all status levels (M. E. Smith 1997; Hirth 1998). On the other hand, high quantities of polychrome serving vessels found in both commoner and elite contexts in the greater Tikal area, and the consistent distribution of ash-tempered ceramics in households throughout the central lowlands in the Late and Terminal Classic (Fry 1979, 1980; Ford and Glicken 1987; LeCount 1996), suggest that these goods may have been acquired through market exchange or middlemen.

The following sections explore the variables described above in Classic and Postclassic period ceramic exchange systems. In order to address the role of elites and central place exchange in the distribution of these different classes of artifacts, I examine distributional falloff curves, levels of specialized production and mass replication, control over acquisition of resources, and patterns of consumption. Because not all the reviewed studies were designed to explore each of these issues, I concentrate on the variables best addressed by the data produced in each study.

Classic Maya Centers in the Regional Economy: The Ceramic Evidence

Compositional studies of ceramics from the Palenque, Tikal, Petexbatun, and Lubaantun regions (figure 6.3) give an indication of the variability in the role of Classic Maya centers in regional ceramic exchange systems (Hammond 1975; Hammond and Harbottle 1976; Rands and Bishop 1980; Fry 1980; Foias and Bishop 1997). Rands and Bishop's study of the Palenque region used petrographic and chemical analyses to identify clay sources and the paste groups associated with them, and traced paste distributions throughout the 4,500-square-kilometer region (figure 6.3) surrounding Palenque (Rands 1967; Rands and Bishop 1980). Rands and Bishop identified four distinct paste groups associated with three geographic zones: the Micaceous Sierras and General Sierras paste groups from the Chiapas-Tabasco foothills to the west of Palenque, the Plains paste group from the Tabasco-Chiapas plains north of Palenque, and Macropalenque from the immediate Palenque area (Rands and Bishop 1980). The regional distributions of these paste groups, and their distance-decay curve from Palenque, are shown in figures 6.4 and 6.5. These figures suggest that ceramics produced at or near Palenque were largely consumed there and did not circulate widely throughout the surrounding region. On the other hand, ceramics made from the other three paste groups make up a significant proportion of the ceramic assemblage at Palenque, indicating Palenque's role as a consumer in the regional economy (figure 6.6). The three non-Palenque paste groups are also widely distributed at sites throughout the region, suggesting that hinterland communities participated in a lively intraregional exchange of ceramics. Interestingly, the region throughout which the four paste groups are distributed coincides with the area demarcated by the distribution of Palenque's emblem glyph in the Late Classic period, suggesting a correspondence between Palenque's economic and political spheres (Hammond 1982).

These data have been variously interpreted as underlining Palenque's role as a central node in the regional economy (Hammond 1982; Fry 1979, 1980), or as indicating direct, reciprocal exchange between outlying communities (Rice 1987a, 1987b). What makes the data somewhat equivocal is the fact that so few ceramics produced at Palenque entered into the regional system. If individuals from more peripheral locations did not consume Palenque pottery, what goods might they have acquired in exchange for the ceramic goods they

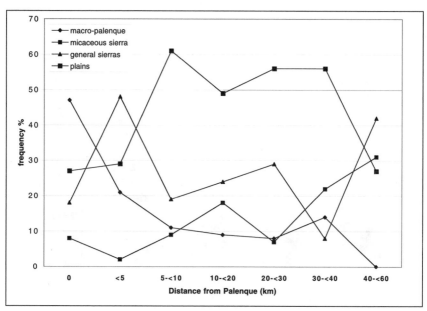

Fig. 6.4. Percentage of the four compositional groups according to distance from Palenque (from Rands and Bishop 1980: figure 10).

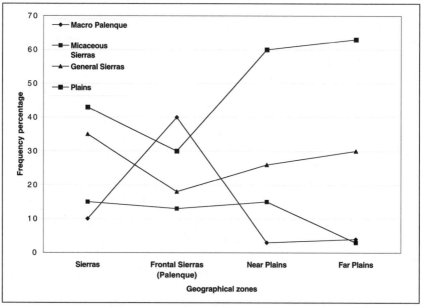

Fig. 6.5. Percentage of the four compositional groups in the Palenque zone (from Rands and Bishop 1980: figure 9).

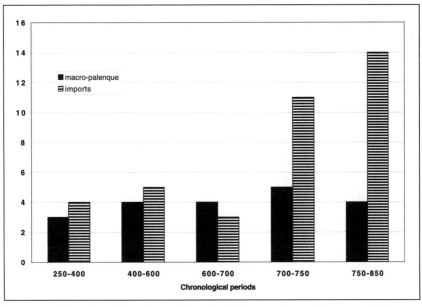

Figure 6.6. Number of locally-produced and imported vessel types at Palenque (from Rands and Bishop 1980: figure 12-16).

supplied? Aside from commodities that are perishable, such as salt, one answer might be ritual paraphernalia. Neutron activation analyses conducted on Late Classic incensario effigy vessel supports collected from sites in the greater Palenque region found that 93 percent of these were produced at or near Palenque (Rands et al. 1978; Bishop et al. 1982). These data suggest that pottery producers may have traded their wares at Palenque, perhaps at periodic markets held during public and religious ceremonial events as Freidel suggests (1981). At such markets they may have purchased effigy censers, the production of which was monopolized by specialists residing at or near Palenque.

Whether the outlying communities exchanged their ceramics through periodic markets at Palenque, by means of itinerant merchants, or in face-to-face direct transactions, is not possible to deduce from the data. It is probable that goods were exchanged in both localized markets, and at central periodic markets, a common pattern in contemporary and historic regional agrarian systems (C. Smith 1974, 1976; Skinner 1985). A certain interdependency between pottery-making communities is indicated by the fact that vessel shape classes are consistently associated with certain paste groups through time

(Rands and Bishop 1980). For instance, narrow-mouth jars in Palenque assemblages are made exclusively with the Plains paste throughout the Classic period (Rands 1967; Rands and Bishop 1980). Serving vessels predominate in the General Sierras and Micaceous Sierras pastes, and utilitarian vessels predominate in the Plains paste (figure 6.7). Moreover, figurines and serving vessels produced with the Plains paste cluster in a distinct chemical grouping (figure 6.7), suggesting that there were clay procurement and production zones in the plains that tended to specialize, perhaps on a local level, in the manufacture of different form and functional classes (Rands and Bishop 1980). This kind of community-level specialization is reminiscent of

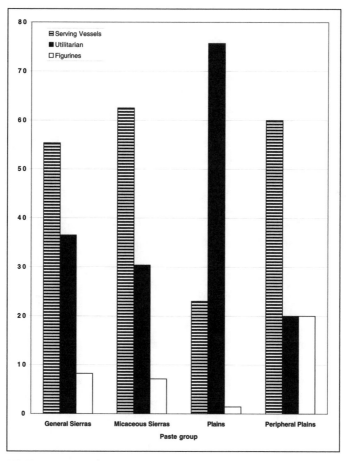

Figure 6.7. Percentage of paste groups across vessel classes (from Rands and Bishop 1980: figure 11).

patterns found in contemporary Guatemala (C. Smith 1974, 1976; Rice 1987a) and is analogous to the part-time community-wide specialization that Smith describes as unique to solar marketing systems (C. Smith 1976). The fact that increasing quantities of Plains ceramics are produced throughout the Classic period, and Palenque consumes greater levels of imported wares in the Late Classic and Terminal Classic periods (figure 6.6), suggests that specialized craft production in rural communities became increasingly important. It is significant to note also that the four paste groups crosscut serving vessels and utilitarian wares, and thus a sharp dichotomy between production and distribution systems of polychromes and utilitarian vessels is not implied.

Fry's (1980) study of Late Classic ceramic exchange at Tikal reveals a more complex pattern. His study is marred by the fact that he did not use petrographic or chemical techniques, and his ceramic groups are based on macroscopic technical and stylistic attributes. The variables used in Fry's landmark study are summarized here in table 6.1. His sample was also taken from a more limited area than Rands', covering only the 123 square kilometers around central Tikal. Fry's study of ceramic standardization indicates that approximately three to five production centers were providing ceramics in each vessel class to the greater Tikal area (Fry 1979, 1980). Figures 6.8, 6.9, and 6.10 illustrate the fall-off curves of vessel classes made with a distinctive paste in the Late Classic period. Fry argues, based on the criteria of abundance and stylistic homogeneity within the shape classes, that these ceramics were produced at a workshop, or workshops, in an intersite area nine kilometers north of Tikal (Fry 1980, 1981). The vases

Table 6.1. Variables used in Fry's Study of Tikal Ceramics 1980.

Technological Variables	Stylistic Variables
Completeness of Firing	Wall Orientation
Differential Firing	Wall Curvature
Fire Clouding	Wall Thickness
Paste Texture	Lip Shape
Temper Frequency	Lip Orientation
Type of Inclusions	Lip Thickness
Frequency of Inclusions- Manganese	Basin Decoration
Frequency of Inclusions-Mica	Basic Decoration-dimensions-depth
	Basin Decoration-dimensions-width
	Neck Height-jars

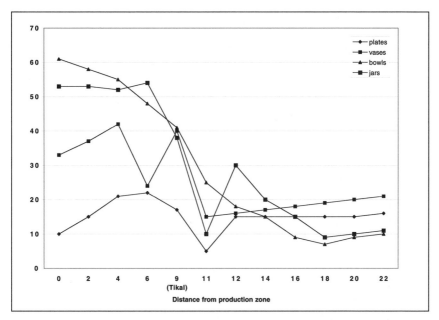

Figure 6.8. Fall-off curves for differing Late Classic shape classes from production center north of Tikal (from Fry 1980: figure 9.4).

and plates represented in the graph are serving vessels, whereas the bowls and jars are utilitarian. As is evident from figure 6.8, the different vessel types have different fall-off curves. The sharp fall-off curve in plates and jars just south of Tikal may suggest competition from another production center. The absence of such a fall-off in bowls and plates suggests that the hypothesized competing production area may not have specialized in these vessel forms (Fry 1981). Overall, serving vessels show a far less steep fall-off curve than the utilitarian bowls and jars, which is what one would expect as serving vessels are smaller and more portable, and thus were likely to be more widely exchanged. The more intensive exchange of serving vessels is also indicated by the fact that they are the most likely pottery class to be imported into the muscavite pottery-producing area (Fry 1980). Locally produced serving vessels are never more than 45 percent of the serving vessel assemblages in this area (figure 6.8).

Although some scholars have interpreted Fry's distributional graph as indicative of redistributive exchange (e.g., Rice 1987a, 1987b; Ball 1993), the multimodality of the curve is reminiscent of Renfrew's (1977) predicted fall-off curve for directional exchange (figure 6.2;

Torrence 1986: fig. 25), which could be caused by redistribution or central place market exchange. It seems most likely that, similar to the Palenque region, the multimodality represents both localized and central place exchange. The interpretations of the curve as redistribution seem based on the assumption that market exchange must be coupled with craft production concentrated in urban centers and centralized in full-time workshops (Rice 1987a; Ball 1993). Both Rands'

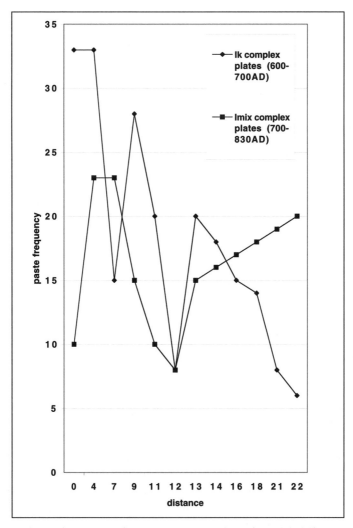

Fig. 6.9. Relative frequency of micaceous paste plates from Tikal (from Fry 1980: figure 3).

and Fry's studies do show a marked absence of centralized and/or intensive ceramic workshop production at urban centers (Fry and Cox 1974; Fry 1979, 1980, 1981; Rands and Bishop 1980). Apparently, mobilization of these basic commodities was not practiced by Palenque's and Tikal's elites. As is indicated from the Inka example, however, centralized control over basic goods production is not necessarily an indication of market exchange (Earle and Ericson 1977).

The ceramic collections from central Tikal contained the greatest heterogeneity as well as the highest quality of ceramic vessels of the

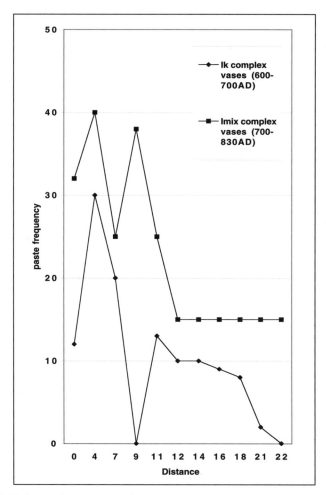

Fig. 6.10. Relative frequencies of micaceous pastes in vase assemblages from Tikal (from Fry 1980: figure 2).

area Fry examined. Measures of artifact heterogeneity at a site are one way of determining a site's role in the regional distribution systems (Blanton 1983; Feinman 1982, 1986) In his study of ceramic production and exchange in the Oaxaca Valley, Feinman compared the number of types at administrative and nonadministrative sites. He found greater heterogeneity in ceramic assemblages at administrative sites during the periods of more intensive centralized administration of regional exchange systems (Feinman 1982, 1986). The high quality and diversity of ceramics in central Tikal is thus a possible indicator of central place status in regional distribution systems.

Although Fry interpreted his own data as indicating, contrary to his expectations, that Tikal was not the locus of a strongly centralized marketing system (Fry 1980), it is this type of pattern that one might expect in a partially commercialized solar central place system as described by C. Smith (1976). In such systems, the bulk of transactions between food producers take place through face-to-face exchange, due to the fact that they are not well integrated into the market system (Smith 1976). The localized distributions of utilitarian ceramics in the Tikal sustaining area suggests that many of these transactions may have taken place by means of direct exchange. On the other hand, the wider distributions of serving vessels suggest that these vessel classes may have been obtained by food producers at centralized markets. Again, this is the pattern noted by Smith in solar central place systems, where peasants obtain some goods locally and more specialized goods at markets (C. Smith 1976). The bulk of transactions between food and non-food producers, on the other hand, takes place through market exchange (Smith 1976). I would argue that the high quality and diversity of ceramics in central Tikal suggest that market exchange was occurring there. Although Fry's study (1980) was limited in areal extent, the frequencies of Imix period ceramics made at the hypothesized production center do not appear to be dropping off at the farthest points sampled by Fry in his survey (figures 6.9, 6.10). This distribution suggests that even more distant sites may also have been consumers of these ceramics.

Hammond's study of Lubaantun ceramics yields a pattern somewhat analogous to that found at Palenque by Rands (Hammond 1975; Hammond and Harbottle 1976). Most ceramics from Lubaantun were made from clays located within six kilometers of the site and were consumed locally (Hammond and Harbottle 1976). The exception to this pattern is Lubaantun-style figurines. Although his data are not published on the figurines, Hammond reports a high level of consistency in their manufacturing technique and design (Hammond 1975: 371–374). The figurines are mold-made, and the majority were found at Lubaantun (Hammond 1975: 371). A concentration of figurines, and all of the figurine molds recovered from excavations and surveys in the region, were found in a provenance near a centrally located plaza (Hammond 1975: 372). A large number of the figurines were found in the areas surrounding Lubaantun, and several were found at sites in the coastal cayes area (Hammond 1975: 373). Although the lack of quantitative data regarding these finds makes any analysis tentative, they suggest that Lubaantun elites controlled the production and distribution of ritual paraphernalia.

It is interesting to note that Lubaantun, a site far smaller and presumably less powerful than Tikal and Palenque, appears to have been more self-sufficient in ceramic production. Apparently the growth of Lubaantun did not greatly affect craft production in the surrounding region. It is possible that low population densities at Lubaantun made it less profitable for more peripheral communities to produce surplus ceramics for trade at the center. It is also possible that populations in or near the larger centers of Palenque and Tikal were engaged in other activities, such as intensified agricultural production, to support denser populations and greater concentrations of non-food producing elites. This change in household activity would lead to greater reliance on ceramic goods produced in the more peripheral communities, a phenomenon that Blanton has described in Central Mexico and China (1985). In any case, variability in consumption patterns is indicated between the larger centers and less populous and/or powerful secondary centers. The data from Palenque and Tikal indicate that inhabitants in the center depended on a steady influx of craft goods produced in outlying communities, whereas the needs of Lubaantun's inhabitants were amply met by local producers.

The pattern at Lubaantun is mirrored at Late and Terminal Classic sites within the Dos Pilas polity (Foias and Bishop 1997). Foias and Bishop's study of ceramics in the Petexbatun found that each large site was more or less independent in its pottery manufacture (Foias and Bishop 1997). However, there does appear to have been a great deal of pottery exchanged between Dos Pilas and Aguateca, suggesting higher levels of economic integration between the two sites (Foias and Bishop 1997). This study is useful in the light it sheds on the role of larger sites within the Petexbatun region, but it is not really comparable to Fry and Rands' studies because it does not undertake a detailed study of ceramic assemblages from intersite areas. In the absence of such data, it is impossible to know the economic relationship of centers with their more immediate hinterlands. However, Foias and Bishop argue that differences in metric attributes between some vessel forms from Dos Pilas, Aguateca, and the small village of Quim Chi Hilan (located south of the previous two sites) suggest that different workshops supplied them (Foias and Bishop 1997). Overall, this study does show a contrast to the widespread intraregional exchange of ceramics that appears to have occurred in the Palenque region, suggesting that competition between sites in the Petexbatun area resulted in truncated exchange networks. This find corresponds to Demarest's characterization of the Petexbatun region as poorly integrated politically, and increasingly torn by intersite conflict (Demarest 1993).

Exchange and Consumption of Maya Polychromes

Several scholars have postulated that the production and exchange of Maya polychrome serving vessels was controlled by elites, perhaps in the form of tethered specialists (e.g., Tourtellot and Sabloff 1972; Adams 1971). As figures 6.7 and 6.9 make clear, however, the same paste groups were used in the production of utilitarian and serving vessels in the Tikal and Palenque areas, suggesting that utilitarian and serving vessel production was not organized differently. Most serving vessels at Tikal were polychromes (Fry 1981), and although the polychrome vessels produced at Tikal appear to have had wider distributions than utilitarian vessels, they do not seem to have been exchanged by means of greatly disparate distribution mechanisms. Access to polychromes does not appear to have been restricted in the Greater Tikal area, at least during the Late Classic period. Serving vessels, the bulk of which are polychromes (Fry 1980, 1981), make up 41 percent (ranging from 26 to 64 percent) of the total assemblage from a stratified random sample of structures from peripheral Tikal and intersite areas near Tikal (Fry 1981). Culbert (1973: 86) reports a similar median of 46 percent from Central Tikal (ranging from 28 to 76 percent). Although access to polychrome pottery most assuredly varied throughout the Maya lowlands (LeCount 1996), other reports confirm that access to polychrome ceramics was not restricted to high-status households or elite centers (Mock 1997; Beaudry 1984; Fry 1979; Hendon 1991; Hansen et al. 1991; Foias and Bishop 1997). The sheer quantity of polychrome ceramics found distributed throughout the greater Tikal area suggest that access to polychromes in the central lowlands may have been determined by exchange at a major center and not by status or kinship affiliation.

Marilyn Beaudry's study of Late Classic polychrome cream paste ceramics in the southeastern lowlands permits a more detailed examination of the structure of polychrome distribution systems (Beaudry 1984). Beaudry conducted stylistic and chemical analyses of Copador and related Late Classic polychromes from sites in western Honduras, western and central El Salvador, and southeastern Guatemala (figure 6.3) to determine the number of production centers, scope of distribution, and levels of standardization and simplification in fine paste polychrome production. Through neutron activation analysis, Beaudry identified two main production areas, a secondary production area with lower output, and a series of ungrouped paste types indicating dispersed household level production (figure 6.11). The two dominant clusters of chemical paste types show a similarity in chemical makeup that led Bishop and Beaudry to conclude that the production centers making these ceramics were located in relatively close geographical proximity (Beaudry 1984). These two areas dominated the production of fine paste ceramics in the Late Classic, and ceramics produced at these centers enjoyed widespread distribution both within the Copan Valley and throughout the southeastern periphery. Forty-one percent of the Late Classic sites in the region Beaudry sampled had Copador ceramics in their assemblages (Beaudry 1984: 210). In the Copan Valley, Copador ceramics were found in 65 percent of all suboperations. Archaeological evidence from the Copan Valley, the Zapotitan Basin, western Honduran sites, far western El Slavador, and the Cerro Grande Basin concurs in finding Copador ceramics distributed in small but consistent frequencies in households of all status levels and sites of all sizes (Demarest 1988). These findings testify to a scale of production that was quite large. Interestingly, the data suggest that while one main production area in the Copan Valley produced ceramics for both export and internal consumption within the Copan Valley, the other center produced Copador ceramics solely for export to El Salvador (figure 6.12) (Beaudry 1984: 243). Such directed output suggests a market-oriented production.

From this distribution data, and a stylistic analysis that measured levels of standardization and simplification (Beaudry 1984: 99–176), Beaudry proposes that producers of Copador specifically designed this type with the aim of widespread distribution to a far-flung

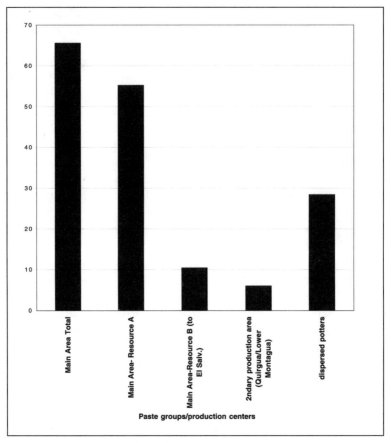

Fig. 6.11. Total frequency output of polychrome production sources (from Beaudry 1984: table 17). Total number equals 201.

consumer base unrestricted by status (Beaudry 1984: 249). Although different polychrome shape classes displayed varying levels of standardization and simplification, Copador, Gualpopa, and Arambala bowls displayed standardized and simplified production methods (Beaudry 1984: 137). Simplification of surface treatment and design is indicated in the pseudoglyphs and elongated figures used to decorate Copador ceramics. These decorative techniques represent a distinct break from previous polychrome traditions in the region (Beaudry 1987, 1988). The easily recognizable and comprehensible motifs may have been designed to communicate to consumers an affiliation with the Maya realm, even if they were only marginally

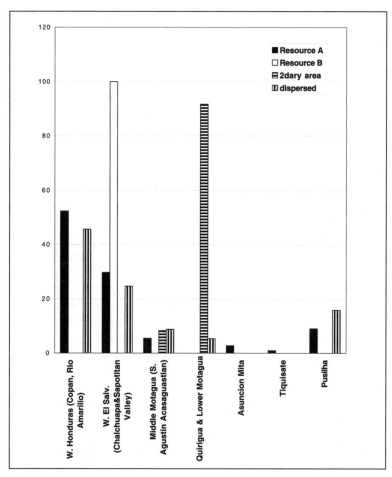

Fig. 6.12. Frequency percentages of Copador polychromes in southeast lowlands (from Beaudry 1984: table 18).

connected to it (Beaudry 1984, 1987, 1988; Demarest 1988). Copador ceramics were also found in ceramic assemblages from houses cutting across all social strata. Such widespread and unrestricted distribution suggests substantial mercantile activity (Beaudry 1984: 210). In Central Mexico, Smith has interpreted the presence of imported polychrome vessels in both elite and commoner contexts as evidence for market exchange (Smith and Heath-Smith 1994; M. E. Smith 1996). The similar distribution pattern of polychromes in the southeastern Maya lowlands points to an analogous mechanism of exchange.

Palace-School Polychrome Ceramics

Ball has postulated a distinction between "village-tradition" and "palace-school" polychrome ceramic systems (Ball 1993: 259). He suggests that village tradition polychromes were produced by the same communities that produced utilitarian ceramics and had a relatively wide distribution (Ball 1993: 259). He argues that "palace-school" polychromes, characterized by considerable iconographic and sometimes epigraphic erudition, may have been produced by attached specialists residing at elite centers (Ball 1993). These more elaborated polychromes were most likely included in reciprocal gift offerings among elites, and played a major role in mortuary offering for members of the elite class (Adams 1971; Fry 1981; Reents-Budet et al. 1994; Ball 1993) Ball has interpreted a concentration of dozens of smashed polychrome vessels found associated with one structure of a palace group at Buenavista as evidence of elite patronage and administration of luxury ceramic production. A termination offering found in association with this concentration, which included a carved statuette of the twin monkey-god patrons of writing, artists, and artisans, lends support to this hypothesis (Ball 1993: 250). Similarly, Coggins has suggested that the residents of patio group 4H-1 in Tikal specialized in producing polychrome cream wares (Coggins 1975: 211). Patio group 4H-1 is located some distance from the center of Tikal, on a small peninsula of land that juts out into the Santa Fe Bajo (Fry 1981). Becker has identified this area as a workshop on the basis of large quantities of pottery, figurine molds, and the presence of such uncommon items as ceramic wall inserts, candlesticks, and pottery masks (Becker 1973: 399). The large quantities of polychrome decorated pottery found in the structure's middens, and the rich burials with additional polychromes found in association with it, led Coggins to believe that the residents were involved in the decoration of polychrome pottery, and may have been attached specialists (Coggins 1975: 211, 429–430).

Other studies of "palace-school" polychrome ceramics have used chemical techniques to trace production and distribution patterns (Hansen et al. 1991; Reents-Budet et al. 1994). Reents-Budet conducted neutron activation analyses (NAA) of seven stylistic groups of polychrome cream ceramics from the Early and Late Classic periods (Reents-Budet et al. 1994). Within all but one group, the patterning of chemical paste composition suggests production at several workshop loci (Reents-Budet et al. 1994). Moreover, the range in stylistic elaboration and quality within each stylistic and chemical group suggests that workshop production was not highly standardized and that the products were intended for consumers of varying status (Reents-Budet et al. 1994). This finding supports Fry's idea that the most elaborate polychrome ceramics may have been produced on a commission basis for elites (Fry 1981). Recent NAA of Codex-style ceramics from Nakbe in the Petén has also identified several paste groups representing more than one locus of production (Hansen et al. 1991). The stylistic variability further suggests various scribes or schools of production. Interestingly, excavations at Nakbe have yielded Codex-style ceramics in nonelite structures both within the site center and in peripheral areas (Hansen et al. 1991). These studies are illuminating in that they point to an absence of highly restricted or workshop organization in the production of "palace-school" serving vessels, despite the high level of craftsmanship evident in the vessels. Moreover, there does not seem to have been a wholly independent organization of production and distribution of "village-school" vs. "palace-school" polychrome ceramics. The evidence for palace-school ceramic production is imprecise at best however, and the fact that most known vessels of this kind are without provenance further complicates the picture (Reents-Budet et al. 1994). The elite-associated contexts of the more elaborate vessels seem to point to a highly restricted exchange of these polychrome types (McAnany 1993; Ball 1993; Potter and King 1995; Reents-Budet et al. 1994; LeCount 1996), but there is no clear evidence that their production was controlled by elites.

Volcanic Ash Tempering of Lowland Ceramics

The studies cited above of ceramic production and exchange all point to a relatively dispersed system, carried out independently of elite control or sponsorship. However, some of the studies also suggest that substantial exchange of ceramics occurred on an intraregional (Fry 1979, 1980, 1981; Fry and Cox 1974; Rands 1967; Rands and Bishop 1980) and interregional (Beaudry 1984) level. I have suggested that some of this exchange may have taken place at periodic markets, perhaps held at centers and sponsored by elites (Freidel 1981). Informal local markets occur in agrarian societies at all levels of complexity (C. Smith 1976; Blanton 1983, 1985; Berdan 1985; Skinner 1985). Based on cross-cultural comparisons, Blanton has described some of the factors that might contribute to a burgeoning market system (Blanton 1983). He points out that early market systems are often generated within peasant communities due to an intensification of agricultural production among peasant households that leads to labor-saving devices, such as buying rather than producing utilitarian goods (Blanton 1983: 53). He also argues that market systems probably originate independently of state or centralized mechanisms (Blanton 1983: 56).

Carol Smith asserts that marketing may occur in both bounded network and solar central place economic systems (C. Smith 1976). Within the latter, elites monopolize the marketing system by various mechanisms, including control over the periodicity of central markets, administration of the types of goods that can be bought and sold there, and taxation (C. Smith 1976). Because this monopolization causes markets to be costly for peasants residing in the hinterlands, they tend to exchange goods among themselves through direct, reciprocal exchange. One difference between the marketing systems found in the two systems of organization is the commoners' access to goods from outside the regional system. In a bounded network system, such goods are unavailable through market exchange, and may only be obtained through some kind of redistributive mechanism flowing from the elite individual to whom commoners owe allegiance (C. Smith 1976). In solar central place systems, there is access to nonlocal goods at the elite-administered central markets or through itinerant merchants radiating out from the center (C. Smith 1976).

Because few nonlocal subsistence goods have been found in the archaeological record of the Classic Maya lowlands, many archaeologists have concluded that a sharp dichotomy existed between the systems of interregional exchange of luxury, or wealth goods, and intraregional exchange of subsistence goods (Potter and King 1995; McAnany 1993; Rice 1987b). Ethnohistoric documents from contact- and colonial period Yucatan, however, record a lively interregional trade in perishable goods such as salt, copal, and honey (Tozzer 1941: 92–97; Piña Chan 1978). Freidel has argued that one way Postclassic elites ensured incoming surplus from the hinterlands was their control over the supply of these commodities at markets (Freidel 1983), a process described by Smith as integral to the functioning of solar central place systems (C. Smith 1976). Because the great majority of the nonlocal subsistence commodities described in the ethnohistoric records are perishable, their role in the regional economies of the Classic Maya lowlands is difficult to determine (Andrews 1980, 1983). The presence of volcanic ash temper in lowland Maya ceramics is therefore of great interest, because it represents one such long-distance import. Its distribution may shed some light on the exchange of long-distance, nonelite goods.

Scholars have intermittently brought attention to the fact that large quantities of ceramics at some lowland Maya sites were tempered with volcanic ash (Shepard 1939, 1964; Simmons and Bren 1979; Jones 1986: 38-56; Ford and Glicken 1987; Kepecs 1996; Kepecs et al. 1994; LeCount 1996). However, despite geological surveys conducted to locate possible sources for volcanic ash in the lowlands, such sources have not been found (Isphording and Wilson 1974; Simmons and Bren 1979; Ford and Glicken 1987). There is currently widespread concurrence that ash temper was imported from the highland volcanic regions (e.g., Jones 1986; Kepecs et al. 1994; Kepecs 1996; Fry 1981; Ford and Glicken 1987; Foias and Bishop 1997). This probability is supported by evidence from the Palenque region, where ash tempering is most frequent in ceramics from sites along the Usamacinta River, which would have had the greatest access to goods traded from the highlands (Rands 1967). The close relationship between the presence of ash temper and the highland-lowland trade networks is supported by the fact that, in northern Yucatan, ash tempering of Terminal Classic/Early Postclassic fine paste and Itza slate ware ceramics ended abruptly by A.D. 1200, along with a steep decline in the occurrence of green obsidian, and the collapse of Chichen Itza, El Tajin, and Tula (Kepecs et al. 1994). In the central lowlands the use of ash temper became increasingly common in the Late Classic period (see figure 6.17), but ebbed after the Terminal Classic (Simmons and Bren 1979: figure 1; Jones 1986: 56). These patterns all suggest that ash temper was not a locally available product, but was brought in through long distance trade networks.

While it is not known why ash temper became so popular among ceramic producers during the Classic period, the fact remains that its use became increasingly common in central lowland ceramic production (Shepard 1939; Simmons and Bren 1979; Jones 1986: 54). Its growing popularity may be attributed to such factors as its ease of preparation, its greater stability under low firing conditions, and the greater strength and uniformity of color and texture in vessels made with volcanic ash (Jones 1986: 42; Ford and Glicken 1987: 484). It may also be that its earlier association with elite polychrome vessels (Jones 1986: 56) may have conferred upon it a social value not measurable in practical terms. Anna Shepard's petrographic analysis of ceramics from San Jose found that although in the Early Classic period ash temper was primarily used for polychrome ceramics (figure 6.13), by the Late Classic (figure 6.14) greater quantities of ash temper were being used for utilitarian monochrome slipped and black wares (Shepard 1939: 99a–c). Ford and Glicken's petrographic analysis of ash-tempered sherds from central Tikal, the Tikal-Yaxha area, the upper Belize River area, Uaxactun, San Jose, and Xunantunich found that their composition was relatively homogeneous, with ash temper making up approximately 20 percent of the sherd content (Ford and Glicken 1987: 485). Taking into account frequencies of ash-tempered vessels found in Late Classic household assemblages, the estimated

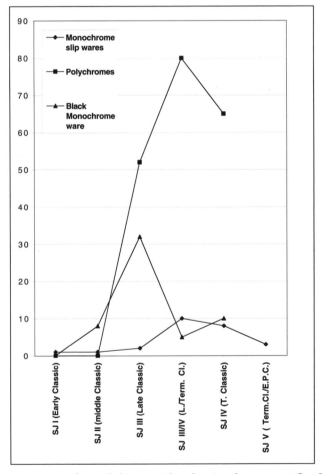

Fig. 6.13. Percentages of vessel classes with volcanic ash temper at San Jose (from Shepard 1939: 99a-c).

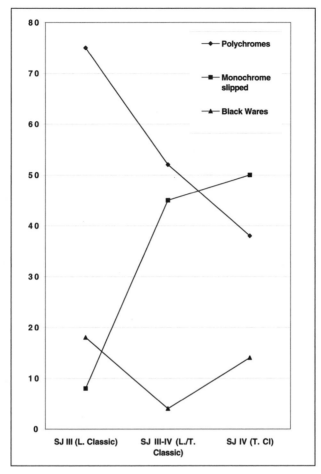

Figure 6.14. Percentage of total ash temper assemblage at San Jose by ware (from Shepard 1939: figure 99d).

population in the central lowlands during this period (200 per square kilometer in the 10,000-square-kilometer Zone Tikal according to D. Rice 1976: 276), and the estimated rate of breakage, Ford and Glicken postulate that central lowland populations may have consumed up to 800,000 kg, or 20,000 40-kg bags, of ash temper per year (Ford and Glicken 1987: 492). Even with a population estimate of 100 persons per square kilometer, demand for ash temper would still be 5,000 40-kg bags per annum.

Some scholars have suggested that ash temper was brought in along the same routes as obsidian and was used as a buffer to prevent damage to the obsidian during the voyage (Simmons and Bren 1979; L. Jones 1986: 55). While this explanation would not be feasible if obsidian macrocores were imported to the lowlands, it would make sense if obsidian was imported in the form of large, prepared cores. The very small quantities of obsidian cortex debris at lowland sites had led many scholars to conclude that obsidian was indeed imported in the form of polyhedral cores (e.g., Moholy-Nagy 1976, 1989). It is significant that ash temper does not occur uniformly throughout the Lowlands. At sites in Petexbatun, ash temper is found in a small minority of vessels (Foias and Bishop 1997). Ash tempered bowls made up 0.1 percent of the utilitarian slipped bowl assemblage at Petexbatun sites (Foias and Bishop 1997). This frequency is low enough to posit that the vessels themselves, rather than the temper, were imported. Ash tempering was more common in polychrome vessels, making up 13.2 percent of these vessels in the early part of the Late Classic from A.D. 600–760 (Foias and Bishop 1997). Neutron activation analysis of these ash-tempered polychromes found that they were produced in the Petén and near the Usumacinta drainage (Foias and Bishop 1997), both areas that may have been central nodes in the highland-lowland trade networks (Sidrys 1976; Dreiss and Brown 1989). Some ceramic assemblages from northern Belize are particularly exceptional for their complete absence of ash temper (L. Jones 1986: 54-55). This absence may be due to the possibility that northern Belize was participating in different long-distance trade networks that did not include the importation of volcanic ash. Obsidian source analyses in this area support the idea that the patterns of obsidian procurement in northern Belize differed from those in the central lowlands (Dreiss and Brown 1989; Dreiss et al. 1993). Sites in northern Belize may have exploited coastal rather than overland trade networks to obtain highland imports (Dreiss and Brown 1989; McKillop 1996), and merchants using this route may not have included ash temper among their merchandise.

While volcanic ash temper may have been brought in from the highlands along with obsidian, its ubiquitous presence in the central lowlands suggests it was distributed by different means. Ford and Glicken's study of ash-tempered pottery from central Tikal, the Tikal sustaining area, the Tikal-Yaxha area, and the Yaxha-Sacnab area suggests that all households in the Late Classic central lowlands had the same vessel inventories with volcanic ash temper, regardless of wealth, status, or distance from centers (Ford and Glicken 1987). This finding is confirmed by LeCount's study of ash-tempered ceramic distributions in and around Xunantunich (LeCount 1996, 1999) (figures 6.15, 6.16; table 6.2). Vessel forms characteristic of the household ash-tempered assemblages in the central lowlands include incurving bowls, narrow orifice jars, and tripod plates (Ford and Glicken 1987).

The strong probability that ash temper was obtained through long-distance networks, and was associated with the trade in obsidian, does not necessarily imply that elites controlled its distribution. However, the break in its occurrence at the end of the Terminal Classic in the central lowlands (Simmons and Bren 1979; L. Jones 1986: 55) suggests that its importation relied on trade networks facilitated by a functioning elite class. Furthermore, polychrome vessels with ash temper in the Xunantunich area were found to be largely restricted to elite contexts (LeCount 1999: 252), suggesting some kind of elite

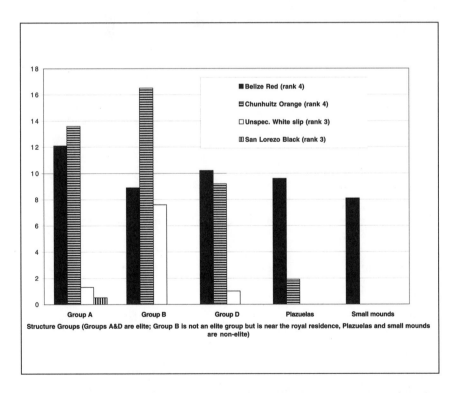

Figure 6.15. Frequency of ash wares at residential groups in Xunantunich and a peripheral hamlet in the Late Classic period (from LeCount 1996: table 6.5; see also LeCount 1999: table 2).

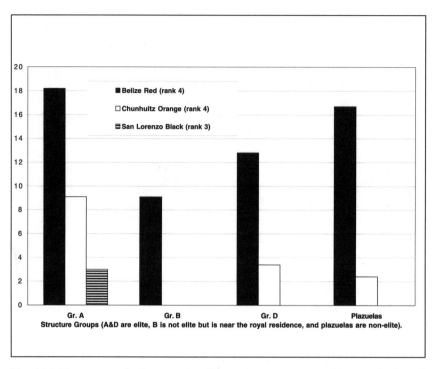

Fig. 6.16. Frequency of ash wares at elite structure groups in Xunantunich and hamlet plazuelas in the Terminal Classic period (from LeCount 1996: table 6.6; see also LeCount 1999: table 3).

Table 6.2. Labor Investment Ranking Scheme for Xunantunich Ceramics (from LeCount 1996: table 6.2)

Distribution	Composition	Surface Treatment	Rank
import	calcite	high	1
import	calcite	moderate	2
local	ash	high	2
local	ash	moderate	3
local	calcite	moderate	4
local	ash	low	4
local	calcite	low	5

control over this resource (figures 6.15, 6.16) The fact that volcanic ash was the dominant temper in polychrome ceramics in the Late Classic period (Jones 1986: 52), as suggested by the example of San Jose (figure 6.14) and other sites, suggests that its importation and use were in response to elite consumer demands, and that its use in utilitarian, nonelite ceramics occurred as a kind of unintended consequence of this demand. The association between Classic lowland elites and importation of ash is further supported by the fact that, while obsidian became increasingly available in the Postclassic period, ash temper never reappeared in the ceramic technology of the central lowlands (Simmons and Bren 1979; Jones 1986; Rice 1980). Its widespread distribution in the central lowlands, and its use in the production of nonelite pottery, suggest that this commodity may have been obtained by commoners at central markets and/or from middlemen radiating out from urban centers. In either case, the ubiquity of ash temper in the central lowlands is indicative of hinterland (areas exporting ash) integration into an exchange system involving long-distance goods obtained through elite-sponsored networks.

Change in Lowland Ceramic Production and Exchange Systems? The Postclassic Period

One obvious way to address the question of the Classic Maya economic organization is to look at how archaeological patterns for the Late Postclassic period correspond with exchange mechanisms described in the ethnohistoric record. In a now-famous model, Sabloff and Rathje argued that the Postclassic period was characterized by growing commercialization and the rise of a merchant class (Rathje 1975; Sabloff and Rathje 1975). Unfortunately, this much-cited model (e.g., Guderjan 1995; Torrence 1986) has never been adequately tested using archaeological evidence. Sabloff and Rathje based their hypothesis on perceived differences in Postclassic ceramics, which they argued became standardized, simplified, and mass produced in the Postclassic, as well as on architectural evidence from Mayapan, the low quality of which they postulated was a purposeful cost-saving mechanism (Sabloff and Rathje 1975; Rathje 1975). While excavations at Cozumel have generally confirmed the growing importance of coastal trade networks in the Postclassic period, they have yielded little data to support or refute Rathje's model of standardization, simplification, and mass replication from a regional scale attribute analysis (Connor 1975; Rathje 1975; Sabloff and Freidel 1975). However, Connor (1983) has documented a high degree of standardization of pottery attributes among the sites of Cozumel Island.

The notion of a Postclassic commercialized economy is based largely on ethnohistoric documents (e.g., Tozzer 1941) or, more accurately, on scholars' interpretations of ethnohistoric documents (e.g., Roys 1943; Piña Chan 1978; Farriss 1984; G. Jones 1989). These scholars describe an economy with flourishing markets at coastal centers and an elite merchant class that administered them (Roys 1943; Piña Chan 1978). They also describe substantial activity by middleman traders who integrated inland communities lacking markets into a broader economy (Piña Chan 1978). Farriss argues that intercommunity exchange in Yucatecan Maya society was a crucial means of communication and integration, and that disruption of local trade during the colonial period was central to dismantling regional links between communities (Farriss 1984). In the Maya highlands, Farriss asserts, local trade was a means by which Maya communities sustained regional networks independently of administrative structures prior to the Colonial era (Farriss 1984). Similarly, Jones argues that Colonial Maya communities in the southern periphery maintained control over exchange networks, providing a means of intraregional communication and integration and permitting these communities to effectively resist Spanish domination (G. Jones 1989).

Is there archaeological evidence to support Sabloff and Rathje's model of economic transformation in the Postclassic period? While the ubiquity of obsidian artifacts found at lowland sites in the Postclassic has been frequently noted, attesting to a change in the nature of obsidian exchange (e.g., McKillop 1995, 1996; Rice 1987b; Masson and Chaya 2000), few compositional studies have been done of ceramic production and distribution to test Rathje's hypothesis. Those studies that have been done are revealing when viewed in this light (Smyth et al. 1995; Kepecs et al. 1994; Kepecs 1996; Shepard 1964; Rands et al. 1982). Extensive chemical analyses of Classic and Postclassic period fine paste ceramics from Seibal, Altar de Sacrificios, Dzibilchaltun, Chichen Itza, Piedras Negras, and other lowland sites (figure 6.17) have been conducted by Rands, Bishop, and Sabloff (Rands et al. 1982). Based on superficial homogeneity, Mayanists had previously believed that these ceramics were produced at one center and widely traded (e.g., Sabloff and Willey 1967). It was the apparent standardized production and widespread distribution of fine paste ceramics that prompted Rathje to hypothesize a shift in ceramic production geared toward mass production and long-distance exchange in the Postclassic period (Rathje 1975: 433).

The results from the neutron activation analysis of fine paste ceramics indicate changes in the production of fine paste ceramics for the periods spanning the Late Classic to the Late Postclassic. The data reveal compositional diversity in Late Classic and Terminal Fine Orange and Fine Gray wares (figure 6.17), suggesting production at several zones or workshops along the Usumacinta (Rands et al. 1982). In fact, the Late and Terminal Classic patterns found for Fine Orange and Fine Gray ceramics are similar to those found for the production of Late Classic polychromes in the southeastern periphery (figure

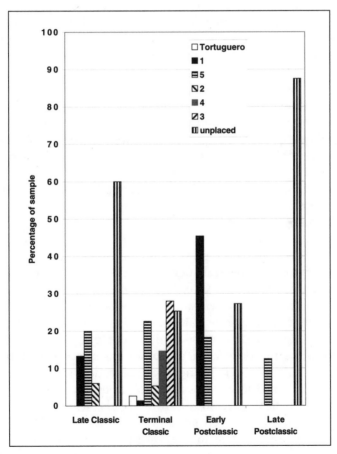

Fig. 6.17. Compositional grouping of Fine Paste ceramics (from Rands et al. 1982: table 12.1-12.7).

6.11). While production of fine paste ceramics in the Terminal Classic became less dispersed, as the decline in the quantities of ungrouped pastes indicates, paste groups from identified production loci were distributed at sites according to geographical proximity (Rands et al. 1982). This pattern suggests a regionalized focus of trade, rather than widespread commerce (Rands et al. 1982). Terminal Classic/Early Postclassic Silho Fine Orange ceramics, which correspond chronologically with Chichen Itza's rise to power, have two dominant compositional groups, suggesting an increased centralization of production and more widespread exchange. In the Late Postclassic, however, production of fine paste ceramics became markedly more dispersed: The assemblage is dominated by ungrouped compositional profiles. While this pattern can be interpreted as supporting Rathje's hypothesized trajectory of mass replication followed by increased local variety, it also indicates a return to the less centralized production that characterized the Classic period. The even more dispersed production of fine paste ceramics indicated for the Late Postclassic period could be interpreted as a response to a more commercialized and competitive economy, but it could also point to less specialized and intensive production than in the Late Classic period. Such a pattern might be expected in a period of reduced political centralization. The critical point is that the organization of fine paste ceramic production in the Late Postclassic period does not seem markedly different from that found in the Late Classic period. The Terminal and Early Postclassic periods, however, may have been a time when major economic changes did occur.

More data is needed before the standardization and distribution patterns of Late Postclassic pottery can be truly assessed. Although production may have been dispersed and not directly controlled by regional centers as in the Classic period, common types of Late Postclassic pottery from Mayapan, the east coast of Quintana Roo, and northern Belize exhibits one pattern that is markedly different from the Late Classic period. There is a high degree of stylistic standardization in forms and decorative attributes observed at sites that suggests the existence of extensive networks of trade and communication that influenced producers across political lines. This trend is not observed in the Late Classic southern lowlands, when stylistic diversity is pronounced between subregions (Masson 2001). Although evidence does not yet exist to suggest that ceramic production was regionally centralized at Mayapan, the emulation of stylistic and functional attributes of this center's utilitarian and ritual wares is clearly observed at east coast and northern Belize communities (Masson 2000).

Evidence found in systematic surveys at the Terminal Classic Puuc site of Sayil provides tantalizing evidence for the possibility that northern Yucatan witnessed a transformation in economic organization during the Terminal and Early Postclassic periods (Smyth and Dore 1992; Smyth et al. 1995). Surface surveys conducted at Sayil have found spatial patterning of artifact assemblages that may indicate ceramic manufacturing activities in one large area of central-west Sayil. In this area, Smyth and Dore found assemblages dominated (more than 50 percent, up to 348 per 3x3-square-meter unit) by a single ceramic ware (Puuc Slate ware), and large quantities of overfired sherds, or "wasters" (up to 245 wasters per 3x3 square meter, Smyth and Dore 1992). Forty-four percent of all Puuc Slate jars collected in the survey were found in this area, as were 22 percent of all bowls (Smyth and Dore 1992). Overfired sherds were not uniformly distributed throughout Sayil and the surrounding survey region (Smyth and Dore 1992). Their concentration in discrete areas of the site suggests these areas were dumping grounds for ceramic production debris. Archaeologists have found such debris to be associated with ceramic production activities at other sites in Mesoamerica, such as Matacapan (Santley et al. 1989). The area that Smyth postulates to be a ceramic production area is adjacent to an architectural group that may have functioned as the site's central marketplace (Tourtellot et al. 1992; Smyth et al. 1995), and it is large enough to suggest production organized at the barrio level (Smyth and Dore 1992).

Neutron activation analysis of Puuc Unslipped, Puuc Slate, Puuc Thin Slate, and Puuc Red found that with the exception of Thin Slate wares, the three types fell into discrete compositional groups (Smyth et al. 1995). Thin Slate wares cross-cut across the three chemical groups (Smyth et al. 1995). This chemical homogeneity points to standardized production, and possible specialization by ware. The widespread distribution of Puuc Slate throughout northern Yucatan and its high level of standardization and superficial homogeneity have led several scholars to suggest widespread exchange of the ware from a few production centers (e.g., Rathje 1975). However, no testing has been done on Puuc Slate wares found outside of Sayil, and thus it is not known whether production at Sayil was aimed at external as well as internal consumption. Nevertheless, the evidence for a ceramic production zone clustered near a major structural group at the site center represents a break from patterns found in the Classic period southern lowlands centers. This unprecedented find may indicate greater investment by elites in the production of ceramics, and/or a structural reorganization of production at Puuc sites.

Paste analysis of ash-tempered Itza slate sherds from Chichen Itza and the Chikinchel region (R. E. Smith 1971; Shepard 1964; Kepecs 1996 and personal communication, 1998) has found that these ceramics are broadly homogeneous in their composition (Kepecs 1996). Such homogeneity suggests standardization in the production of slate wares. Their widespread distribution and ubiquity at sites in Chikinchel, a region that Kepecs argues was under the domination of Chichen Itza (Kepecs et al. 1994; Kepecs 1996), further suggests that these ceramics were "mass produced" during the Itza period. The homogenous composition of Itza slate wares, the scale of its production and distribution, and the cessation of this ware with the decline of Chichen Itza, all indicate that its production may have been administered by the state (Kepecs 1996). At the very least, Chichen Itza's domination over a wide region must have facilitated widespread interregional exchange that made intensified workshop output and greater specialization a profitable endeavor. The significance of far-flung ceramic exchange in the Chichen Itza economy is confirmed by the quantities of Tohil Plumbate imported from the Soconusco region (Shepard 1948; Neff and Bishop 1988). The specialized production of Tohil Plumbate, which was produced largely for export, terminated around 1250 A.D., after the fall of Chichen Itza and contemporary highland Mexican sites (Shepard 1948: 1–4; Neff and Bishop 1988).

Kepecs reports that after Chichen Itza's decline, the production of ceramics in the Chikinchel region became decentralized (Kepecs 1996). Ceramics collected in a full coverage survey at three sites were made with five distinct pastes characterized by a local calcite temper (Kepecs 1996). The distribution of paste types at the three sites suggests that the ceramics were produced locally and exchanged between sites (figure 6.18). Although the dominant paste groups at each site appear to correspond with local clay types (Kepecs, personal communication, 1998), it is possible that the high frequency of "San Fernando" pastes at Emal and San Fernando is indicative of similar clays at the two sites. What is significant about this distribution graph is its similarity to patterns of distribution in the Palenque region during the Late Classic period (figure 6.5). Like the compositional data from NAA analysis of Matillas Fine Orange ceramics (figure 6.17), the data from Chikinchel indicate that ceramic production in the Late

Postclassic period reverted to a Late Classic period pattern of more dispersed production and intraregional distribution. Rathje's hypothesis of local variety deriving from mass replication is therefore not supported. Rather, the data suggest that the standardized, mass production of ceramics that occurred during Chichen Itza's dominance was an aberration in a longstanding lowland Maya tradition of dispersed ceramic production directed toward intersite and intraregional market exchange. Continuity rather than disjunction is implied for the long-term economic organization of the Maya lowlands, and thus

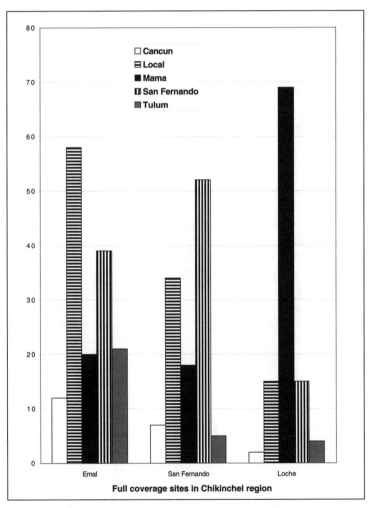

Fig. 6.18. Percentage of Late Postclassic platforms with ceramics in each common paste group (from Kepecs 1996: figure 4).

information found in ethnohistoric documents relating to the Contact period Maya economy may be relevant to the Classic period.

An interesting aspect of these studies is the light they shed on Mayapan's role in the Late Postclassic economy of northern Yucatan. Based on the variability of paste types in the Chikinchel-region ceramics, as well as the high levels of ungrouped Fine Orange pastes, it would appear that Mayapan did not play a role similar to that of Chichen Itza in the regional economy. The variability found in the massive quantities of effigy censers at Mayapan (R. E. Smith 1971: 40) was used by Rathje to support his model of a continued trend toward cost-control mass replication with increased local variety as an end result (Rathje 1975). It is true that no two Mayapan effigy censers have been found that are exactly alike (Sidrys 1983: 245), indicating purposeful individuation in their production. The variability in pastes and attributes found in Late Postclassic sites in northern Belize (Sidrys 1983: 238–265) and coastal Quintana Roo (Sanders 1960) point to localized manufacture. Landa's observation that effigy ceramic production was a common activity in Maya households supports the probability that effigy censer production, at least in the post-Mayapan period, was dispersed rather than centralized or administered (Tozzer 1941: 95). Nevertheless, the spatial distribution of effigy molds suggests that Late Postclassic centers may have played a role in their distribution and production. At least fourteen such molds were found at Mayapan (Smith 1971: figure 66a), and one was found at Santa Rita Corozal (Sidrys 1983: 257). If Mayapan was a center for the production of effigy censers, this pattern is similar to that found at some Classic period lowland sites. As the evidence reviewed above suggests, both Palenque and Lubaantun may have monopolized the production and distribution of ritual paraphernalia (Hammond 1975; Rands et al. 1978).

Discussion

The lack of clarity regarding the economic system of the Classic Maya lowland polities may in fact be the key to understanding it. In cases where elites have centralized control over broad regions, the patterns of artifactual distribution are relatively unambiguous. Often an "imperial" ceramic type is widely distributed throughout the realm, or structural reorganization of the economic system is evident (cf. Feinman 1982; Earle and Ericson 1977; M. E. Smith 1990; Cowgill 1997). The lack of clear distribution patterns for mass-replicated "imperial" ceramics, or evidence for major restructuring of the Classic Maya economy, seems to point unambiguously away from the "strong-state" model proposed by Martin and Grube (2000) and Diane and Arlen Chase (Chase and Chase 1996). Instead, there appears to have been a resiliency in economic structure that, apart from a brief experiment during the heyday of Chichen Itza, continued up until contact with Europeans and beyond. Nevertheless, the evidence for rural craft production and limited distribution spheres does not signify, as some scholars have suggested (Ball 1993; Rice 1987a; Potter and King 1995), that elites at monumental centers did not play a role in integrating the regional economy, or articulating exchange between local systems. There is ample cross-cultural evidence that dispersed, rural production and localized exchange of utilitarian goods is common in both emerging states and contemporary agrarian societies (C. Smith 1976; Brumfiel and Earle 1987; Blanton 1985). During period Ic in the Oaxaca Valley, most craft production was carried on outside of Monte Alban (Marcus 1983; Feinman 1982). Brumfiel points out that in the Central Mexican regions of Xico and Huexotla, proportions of craft producers were not greater in market towns (Brumfiel 1987). In fact, the most convincing evidence for specialized workshop production in Late Postclassic Central Mexico comes from Otumba, a peripheral region of the Aztec empire (Charleton et al. 1991). Specialized craft production in eighth-century China was largely carried out in rural communities for trade at local and regional markets (Blanton 1985; Skinner 1985). Similarly, in early modern England, community level craft production outside of urban centers was common, often stimulated by shortages in land (Thirsk 1961). McAnany's (1993: 40) characterization of Classic period lowland Maya production as "a distinctive, largely autonomous household " phenomenon that was essentially disassociated from central political places is not supported by the evidence I have presented here. Similarly, Freidel finds the dispersed, household-level craft production found in the Classic Maya lowlands to be "unique" (Freidel 1981), though he does suggest that Maya centers were involved in a system of economic change that was highly complex in the need to integrate dispersed production and to facilitate mechanisms for the circulation of essential commodities (Freidel 1981, 1986).

The extensive intraregional exchange carried out in the Palenque region, the widespread distribution of ash temper in the central lowlands, and the concentrated production and wide distribution of Late Classic polychromes in the southeastern periphery, all suggest that the rural inhabitants of these regions were integrated into a specific regional economy centering around lowland centers. Some regions were clearly more integrated than others, as data from Lubaantun and the Petexbatun region indicate. The economic systems around these sites may have resembled more closely Smith's bounded network model (Smith 1976). Tikal seems to have reduced economic competition from nearby centers in the latter part of the Late Classic. This expansion of its economic sphere is indicated by the fact that Ik period (600–700 A.D.) ceramics from the producing center north of Tikal were not consumed in large quantities at Jimbal, a secondary monumental center 20 kilometers north of Tikal, but Imix period ceramics (700–830 A.D.) became a significant portion of its assemblages (figures 6.9, 6.10). Similarly, Late Classic polychromes produced in the Copan Valley were not imported to Quirigua, which may be due to the hypothesized political split between Quirigua and Copan in the Late Classic (Beaudry 1984; Demarest 1988). Instead, a distinct production center, probably located near Quirigua, produced imitation Copador and related polychromes for local consumption (figure 6.12; Beaudry 1984). The regionalized distributions of ceramics in the Classic lowland Maya polities are consistent with patterns found in Aztec city-states before incorporation into the Aztec empire (Hodge and Minc 1990). Hodge and Minc found that Black-on-orange ceramics had distributions roughly corresponding with political boundaries in the period preceding conquest by Tenochtitlan (Hodge and Minc 1990).

The patterns found in the production and distribution of Classic Maya ceramics are not greatly different from those found from the late Prehispanic period, a time during which markets and commerce were a significant part of the economy (Roys 1943; Piña Chan 1978). Ethnohistoric documents suggest that during this period elites monopolized markets at regional centers by controlling the supply of goods obtained through long-distance exchange networks (Piña Chan 1978; Freidel 1983). It is possible that a similar system existed in some Late Classic polities. In the more inclusive of these systems, elites may have ensured hinterland participation in markets held at monumental centers by providing goods whose supply they monopolized, such as ritual paraphernalia, volcanic ash temper, salt, or (in some areas) obsidian cores or blades. Rural communities would have exchanged craft items at these periodic central markets, and among themselves in local markets or direct exchange. Such a system would be commensurate with Smith's model of a solar central place (see also

Chase 1998 for evidence of Classic Maya solar central place economies).

Summary

The organization of ceramic production and distribution in the Maya lowlands strongly indicates that the administration of ceramic production was not an important part of the political economy in the Classic period. Specialized production appears to have been largely autonomous and often took place in rural hinterland communities for trade with centers and other rural communities within the region. The distribution patterns suggest that the regions surrounding Maya centers were economically integrated to a variable degree. Around larger centers, such as Palenque, Tikal, and Copan, central place exchange may have occurred, facilitating exchange between dispersed populations. In turn, elites residing at these centers may have provided certain imported and specialized goods whose supply they monopolized. In the Terminal Classic/Early Postclassic, a restructuring of the economy occurred in the northern lowlands in which ceramic production became centralized and possibly administered by the rulers at Chichen Itza, suggesting greater political centralization and interregional integration. In the Late Postclassic period, the patterns of ceramic production and distribution return to those found in the Late Classic period. Ceramic production was probably dispersed as it was during the Classic period, however, suggesting that the production system operated on a reduced scale. Patterns of production and distribution identified for Late Postclassic ceramics based on a handful of studies suggest that the dispersed nature of Maya lowland pottery-making traditions is a long-term trend that does not exhibit permanent structural transformations.

References

Adams, Richard E. W.
1971 *The Ceramics of Altar de Sacrificios.* Papers of the Peabody Museum of Archaeology and Ethnology 63. Cambridge, Mass.: Harvard University.
Adams, Richard E. W., and Woodruff D. Smith
1981 "Feudal Models for Classic Maya Settlement." Pp. 335–350 in *Lowland Maya Settlement Patterns,* edited by Wendy Ashmore. Albuquerque: University of New Mexico Press.
Andrews, Anthony P.
1980 "The Salt Trade of the Ancient Maya." *Archaeology* 33: 24–33.
1983 *Maya Salt Production and Trade.* Tucson: University of Arizona Press.

Ball, Joseph W.
1993 "Pottery, Potters, Palaces and Polities: Some Socioeconomic and Political Implications of Late Classic Maya Ceramic Industries." Pp. 243–272 in *Lowland Maya Civilization in the 8th Century*, edited by J. A. Sabloff and J. F. Henderson. Washington, D.C.: Dumbarton Oaks.
Beaudry, Marilyn
1984 *Ceramic Production and Distribution in the Southeastern Maya Periphery: Late Classic Painted Serving Vessels*. Oxford: BAR International Series 203.
1987 "Southeast Maya Polychrome Pottery: Production, Distribution, and Style." Pp. 503–524 in *Maya Ceramics: Papers from the 1985 Maya Ceramic Conference*, edited by Prudence M. Rice and Robert J. Sharer. Oxford: BAR International Series 345(i).
1988 "The Function of Non-Functional Ceramics." In *A Pot for All Reasons: Ceramic Ecology Revisited*, edited by Charles C. Kolb and Louanna M. Lackey. Philadelphia: Ceramica de Cultura Maya, Temple University.
Becker, Marshall J.
1973 "Archaeological Evidence for Occupational Specialization among the Classic Period Maya at Tikal, Guatemala." *American Antiquity* 38: 396–406.
Berdan, Frances F.
1985 "Markets in the Economy of Aztec Mexico." Pp. 339–368 in *Markets and Marketing*, edited by Stuart Plattner. Monographs in Economic Anthropology, No. 4. New York: University Press of America.
Bishop, Ronald L., Robert L. Rands, and G. Harbottle
1982 "A Ceramic Compositional Interpretation of Incense-Burner Trade in the Palenque Area, Mexico." Pp. 411–440 in *Nuclear and Chemical Dating Techniques: Interpreting the Environmental Record*, edited by Lloyd A. Currie. Washington, D.C.: American Chemical Society.
Blanton, Richard E.
1983 "Factors Underlying the Origin and Evolution of Market Systems." Pp. 51–66 in *Economic Anthropology: Topics and Theories*, edited by Sutti Ortiz. Monographs in Economic Anthropology, No. 1. New York: University Press of America.
1985 "A Comparison of Early Market Systems." Pp. 399–416 in *Markets and Marketing*, edited by Stuart Plattner. Monographs in Economic Anthropology, No. 4. New York: University Press of America.
Brumfiel, Elizabeth M.
1980 "Specialization, Market Exchange, and the Aztec State: A View from Huexotla." *Current Anthropology* 21: 459–478.
1987 "Elite and Utilitarian Crafts in the Aztec State." Pp. 102–118 in *Specialization, Exchange, and Complex Societies*, edited by Elizabeth Brumfiel and Timothy K. Earle. Cambridge: Cambridge University Press.
Brumfiel, Elizabeth, and Timothy K. Earle
1987 "Specialization, Exchange, and Complex Societies: An Introduction." Pp. 1–9 in *Specialization, Exchange, and Complex Societies*, edited by E. Brumfiel and T. K. Earle. Cambridge: Cambridge University Press.
Carrasco, Pedro
1981 "Comment on Offner." *American Antiquity* 46: 62–68.

Charleton, Thomas H., Deborah L. Nichols, and Cynthia Otis Charleton
1991 "Aztec Craft Production and Specialization: Archaeological Evidence from the City-State of Otumba, Mexico." *World Archaeology* 23: 98–113.

Chase, Arlen F.
1998 "Planeación Civica e Integración de Sitio en Caracol, Belize: Definiendo una Economiá Administrada del Periodo Clasico Maya." Pp. 26–44 in *Los Investigaciones de la Cultura Maya 6 (Tomo I)*. Campeche, Mexico: Secud, Universidad Autónoma de Campeche.

Chase, Arlen F., and Diane Z. Chase
1996 "More than King and Kin: Centralized Political Organization among the Late Classic Maya." *Current Anthropology* 37: 803–810.

Chase, Diane Z., Arlen F. Chase, and William A. Haviland
1990 "The Classic Maya City: Reconsidering the 'Mesoamerican Urban Tradition.'" *American Anthropologist* 92: 499–506.

Coggins, Clemency
1975 "Painting and Drawing Styles at Tikal: An Historical and Iconographic Reconstruction." Ph.D. dissertation, Harvard University, Cambridge, Mass.

Connor, Judith G.
1975 "Ceramics and Artifacts." Pp. 114–135 in *Changing Pre-Columbian Commercial Systems: the 1972–73 Seasons at Cozumel, Mexico*, edited by Jeremy A. Sabloff and William L. Rathje. Cambridge, Mass.: Peabody Museum of Archaeology and Ethnology, Harvard University.
1983 "The Ceramics of Cozumel, Quintana Roo, Mexico." Ph.D. dissertation, University of Arizona.

Costin, Cathy L.
1991 "Craft Specialization: Issues in Defining, Documenting, and Explaining the Organization of Production." Pp.1–56 in *Archaeological Method and Theory Volume 3*, edited by M. B. Schiffer. New York: Academic Press.

Cowgill, George L.
1997 "State and Society at Teotihuacan, Mexico." *Annual Review of Anthropology* 26: 129–161.

Culbert, T. Patrick, editor
1973 *The Classic Maya Collapse*. Albuquerque: University of New Mexico Press.

D'Altroy, Terence, and Ronald Bishop
1990 "The Provincial Organization of Inka Ceramic Production." *American Antiquity* 55: 120–138.

Demarest, Arthur A.
1988 "Political Evolution in the Maya Borderlands: The Salvadoran Frontier." Pp. 335–394 in *The Southeast Classic Maya Zone: A Symposium at Dumbarton Oaks*, edited by Elizabeth H. Boone and Gordon R. Willey. Washington, D.C.: Dumbarton Oaks.
1993 "The Violent Saga of a Maya Kingdom." *National Geographic* 183(2): 95–111.

Dreiss, Meredith L., and David O. Brown
1989 "Obsidian Exchange Patterns in Belize." Pp. 57–90 in *Prehistoric Maya Economies of Belize*, edited by Patricia A. McAnany and Barry Isaac. Research in Economic Anthropology, Supplement 4. Greenwich, Conn.: JAI Press.

Dreiss, Meredith L., David O. Brown, Thomas R. Hester, Michael D. Glascock, Hector Neff, and K. S. Stryker
1993 "Expanding the Role of Trace-Element Studies: Obsidian Use in the Late and Terminal Classic Periods at the Lowland Site of Colha, Belize." *Ancient Mesoamerica* 4: 271–283.
Earle, Timothy K., and Jonathan E. Ericson
1977 "Exchange Systems in Archaeological Perspective." Pp. 3–12 in *Exchange Systems in Prehistory*, edited by Timothy K. Earle and Jonathan E. Ericson. New York: Academic Press.
Ericson, Jonathan E., and Timothy G. Baugh
1992 "Trade and Exchange in a Historical Perspective." Pp. 3–20 in *The American Southwest and Mesoamerica: Systems of Prehistoric Exchange*, edited by J. E. Ericson and T. G. Baugh. New York: Plenum Press.
Farriss, Nancy M.
1983 "Indians in Colonial Yucatan: Three Perspectives, in Spaniards and Indians." Pp. 1–39 in *Southeastern Mesoamerica: Essays on the History of Ethnic Relations*, edited by M. J. Macleod and R. Wasserstrom. Lincoln: University of Nebraska Press.
1984 *Maya Society under Colonial Rule: The Collective Enterprise of Survival.* Princeton, N.J.: Princeton University Press.
Feinman, Gary
1982 "Patterns in Ceramic Production and Distribution: Periods Early I–V." Pp. 181–206 in *Monte Alban's Hinterland, Part 1: The Prehispanic Settlement Patterns of Central and Southern Parts of the Valley of Oaxaca, Mexico*, by Richard E. Blanton, Gary M. Feinman, Stephen Kowalewski, and Jill Appel. Memoirs of the Museum of Anthropology No. 15. Ann Arbor: University of Michigan Press.
1986 "The Emergence of Specialized Ceramic Production in Formative Oaxaca." Pp. 347–374 in *Economic Aspects of Prehispanic Mexico*, edited by Barry L. Isaac. Research in Economic Anthropology, Supplement 2. Greenwich, Conn.: JAI Press.
Feinman, Gary M., Stephen A. Kowalewski, Sherman Banker, and Linda M. Nicholas
1992 "Ceramic Production and Distribution in Late Postclassic Oaxaca: Stylistic and Petrographic Perspectives." Pp. 235–260 in *Ceramic Production and Distribution: An Integrated Approach*, edited by George J. Bey III and Christopher A. Pool. Boulder, Colo.: Westview Press.
Foias, Antonia E., and Ronald L. Bishop
1997 "Changing Ceramic Production and Exchange in the Petexbatun Region, Guatemala: Reconsidering the Classic Maya Collapse." *Ancient Mesoamerica* 8: 275–291.
Ford, Anabel, and Harry Glicken
1987 "The Significance of Volcanic Ash Tempering in the Ceramics of the Central Maya Lowlands." Pp. 490–502 in *Maya Ceramics: Papers from the 1985 Maya Ceramic Conference*, edited by P. M. Rice and R. J. Sharer. Oxford: BAR International Series 345(i).

Ford, Anabel, F. Stross, F. Asaro, and H.V. Michel
1997 "Obsidian Procurement in the Tikal-Yaxha Intersite Region in the Central Maya Lowlands." *Ancient Mesoamerica* 8: 101–110.

Fox, Richard
1977 *Urban Anthropology*. Englewood Cliffs, N.J.: Prentice Hall.

Freidel, David
1981 "The Political Economics of Residential Dispersion Among the Lowland Maya." Pp. 371–384 in *Lowland Maya Settlement Patterns*, edited by Wendy Ashmore. Albuquerque: University of New Mexico Press.
1983 "Lowland Maya Political Economy: Historical and Archaeological Perspectives in Light of Intensive Agriculture." Pp. 40–63 in *Spaniards and Indians in Southeastern Mesoamerica: Essays on the History of Ethnic Relations*, edited by Murdo J. Macleod and Robert Wasserstrom. Lincoln: University of Nebraska Press.
1986 "Terminal Classic Lowland Maya: Successes, Failures, and Aftermaths." Pp. 409–432 in *Late Lowland Maya Civilization: Classic to Postclassic*, edited by Jeremy A. Sabloff and E. W. Andrews V. Albuquerque: University of New Mexico Press.

Fry, Robert E.
1979 "The Economics of Pottery at Tikal, Guatemala: Models of Exchange for Serving Vessels." *American Antiquity*: 44: 494–512.
1980 "Models of Exchange for Major Shape Classes of Lowland Maya Pottery." Pp. 3–18 in *Models and Methods in Regional Exchange*, edited by R. Fry. SAA Papers No. 1. Washington, D.C.: Society for American Archaeology.
1981 Pottery Production-Distribution Systems in the Southern Maya Lowlands." Pp. 145–168 in *Production and Distribution: A Ceramic Viewpoint*, edited by Hilary Howard and Elaine L. Morris. Oxford: BAR International Series 120.

Fry, Robert E., and Scott C. Cox
1974 "The Structure of Ceramic Exchange at Tikal, Guatemala." *World Archaeology* 6(2): 209–225.

Guderjan, Thomas H.
1995 "The Setting and Maya Maritime Trade." Pp. 1–8 in *Maya Maritime Trade, Settlement, and Populations on Ambergris Caye, Belize*, edited by Thomas H. Guderjan and James F. Garber. San Antonio: Maya Research Program.

Hammond, Norman
1975 *Lubaantun: A Classic Maya Realm*. Peabody Museum Monographs, No. 2. Cambridge, Mass.: Harvard University.
1982 *Ancient Maya Civilization*. New Brunswick: Rutgers University Press.

Hammond, Norman, and G. Harbottle
1976 "Neutron Activation and Statistical Analysis of Maya Ceramic Clays from Lubaantun, Belize." *Archaeometry* 18: 147–168.

Hansen, Richard D., Ronald L. Bishop, and Federico Fahsen
1991 "Notes on Codex-Style Ceramics from Nakbe, Peten, Guatemala." *Ancient Mesoamerica* 2: 225–243.

Haviland, William A.
1970 "Tikal, Guatemala and Mesoamerican Urbanism." *World Archaeology* 2: 186–198.
Hendon, Julia A.
1991 "Status and Power in Classic Maya Society: An Archaeological Study." *American Anthropologist* 93: 894–918.
Hirth, Kenneth G.
1996 "Political Economy and Archaeology: Perspectives on Exchange and Production." *Journal of Archaeological Research* 4: 203–239.
1998 "The Distributional Approach." *Current Anthropology* 39: 451–476.
Hodder, Ian
1980 "Trade and Exchange: Definitions, Identification and Function." Pp. 151–156 in *Models and Methods in Regional Exchange*, edited by Robert E. Fry. SAA Papers No.1. Washington, D.C.: Society for American Archaeology.
Hodge, Mary G., and Leah D. Minc
1990 "The Spatial Patterning of Aztec Ceramics: Implications for Understanding Prehispanic Exchange Systems in the Valley of Mexico." *Journal of Field Archaeology* 17: 415–437.
Hodge, Mary G., Hector Neff, M. James Blackman, and Leah D. Minc
1993 "Black-on-Orange Ceramic Production in the Aztec Empire's Heartland." *Latin American Antiquity* 4: 130–147.
Isphording, Wayne C., and Eugene M. Wilson
1974 "The Relationship of 'Volcanic Ash,' SAK LU'UM, and Palygorskite in Northern Yucatan Maya Ceramics." *American Antiquity* 39: 483–488.
Johnson, Jay K.
1976 "Chipped Stone Artifacts from the Western Maya Periphery." Ph.D. dissertation, Department of Anthropology, Southern Illinois University, Carbondale.
1996 "Lithic Analysis and Questions of Cultural Complexity: The Maya." Pp. 159–179 in *Stone Tools: Theoretical Insights into Human Prehistory*, edited by George H. Odell. New York: Plenum Press.
Jones, Grant D.
1989 *Maya Resistence to Spanish Rule: Time and History on a Colonial Frontier.* Albuquerque: University of New Mexico Press.
Jones, Lea D.
1986 *Lowland Maya Pottery: The Place of Petrological Analysis.* Oxford: BAR International Series 288.
Kepecs, Susan
1996 "Native Yucatan and Spanish Influence: The Archaeology and History of Chikinchel." *Journal of Archaeological Method and Theory* 4: 307–327.
Kepecs, Susan, Gary Feinman, and Sylviane Boucher
1994 "Chichen Itza and Its Hinterland: A World-Systems Perspective." *Ancient Mesoamerica* 5: 141–158.
Knapp, A. Bernard, and John F. Cherry
1994 *Provenience Studies and Bronze Age Cyprus: Production, Exchange, and Politico-Economic Change.* Monographs in World Archaeology No. 21. Madison, Wis.: Prehistory Press.

LeCount, Lisa J.
1996 "Pottery and Power: Feasting, Gifting, and Displaying Wealth among the Late and Terminal Classic Lowland Maya." Ph.D. dissertation, Department of Anthropology, University of California at Los Angeles.
1999 "Polychrome Pottery and Political Strategies in Late and Terminal Classic Lowland Maya Society." *Latin American Antiquity* 10(3): 239–258.
Mallory, John K.
1986 "'Workshops' and 'Specialized Production' in the Production of Maya Chert Tools: A Response to Shafer and Hester." *American Antiquity* 51: 152–157.
Marcus, Joyce
1976 *Emblem and State in the Classic Maya Lowlands*. Washington, D.C.: Dumbarton Oaks.
1983 "On the Nature of the Mesoamerican City." Pp. 195–242 in *Prehistoric Settlement Patterns: Essays in Honor of Gordon R. Willey*, edited by Evon Z. Vogt and Richard M. Leventhal. Albuquerque: University of New Mexico Press.
1993 "Ancient Maya Political Organization." Pp. 111–182 in *Lowland Maya Civilization in the 8th Century A.D.*, edited by Jeremy A. Sabloff and John F. Henderson. Washington, D.C.: Dumbarton Oaks.
Martin, Simon, and Nikolai Grube
2000 *The Chronicles of Maya Kings and Queens*. London: Thames and Hudson.
Masson, Marilyn A.
2000 *In the Realm of Nachan Kan: Postclassic Maya Archaeology at Laguna de On, Belize*. Boulder: University Press of Colorado.
2001 "Changing Patterns of Ceramic Stylistic Diversity among the Maya Lowlands." *Acta Archaeologica* 73: 1–30.
Masson, Marilyn A., and Henry Chaya
2000 "Obsidian Trade Connections at the Postclassic Maya Site of Laguna de On, Belize." *Lithic Technology* 25: 135–144.
McAnany, Patricia A.
1989 "Economic Foundations of Prehistoric Maya Society: Paradigms and Concepts." Pp. 347–372 in *Research in Economic Anthropology*, Supplement 4. Greenwich, Conn.: JAI Press.
1991 "Structure and Dynamics of Intercommunity Exchange." Pp. 271–293 in *Maya Stone Tools: Selected Papers from the Second Maya Lithic Conference*, edited by Thomas R. Hester and Harry J. Shafer. Madison, Wis.: Prehistory Press.
1993 "Resources, Specialization, and Exchange in the Maya Lowlands." Pp. 213–246 in *The American Southwest and Mesoamerica: Systems of Prehistoric Exchange*, edited by Jonathon E. Ericson and Timothy G. Baugh. New York: Plenum Press.
McKillop, Heather
1989 "Coastal Maya Trade: Obsidian Densities at Wild Cane Caye." Pp. 17–56 in *Prehistoric Maya Economies of Belize*, edited by Patricia A. McAnany and Barry Isaac. Research in Economic Anthropology, Supplement 4. Greenwich, Conn.: JAI Press.

1995 "The Role of Northern Ambergris Caye in Maya Obsidian Trade: Evidence from Visual Sourcing and Blade Technology." Pp. 163–174 in *Maya Maritime Trade, Settlement, and Populations on Ambergris Caye, Belize*, edited by T. H. Guderjan and J. F. Garber. San Antonio: Maya Research Program.

1996 "Ancient Maya Trading Ports and the Integration of Long Distance and Regional Economies." *Ancient Mesoamerica* 7: 49–62.

Mock, Shirley

1997 "Monkey Business at Northern River Lagoon: A Coastal-Inland Interaction Sphere in Northern Belize." *Ancient Mesoamerica* 8: 165–183.

Moholy-Nagy, Hattula

1976 "Spatial Distribution of Flint and Obsidian at Tikal, Guatemala." Pp. 91–108 in *Maya Lithic Studies: Papers from the 1976 Belize Field Symposium*, edited by Thomas R. Hester and Norman Hammond. San Antonio: University of Texas Center for Archaeological Research.

1989 "Who Used Obsidian at Tikal?" Pp. 379–390 in *La Obsidiana en Mesoamerica*, edited by M. Gaxiola G. and J. Clark. Mexico City: Instituto Nacional de Antropologia e Historia.

Moholy-Nagy, Hattula, and Fred W. Nelson

1990 "New Data on Sources of Obsidian Artifacts from Tikal, Guatemala." *Ancient Mesoamerica* 1: 71–80.

Neff, Hector, and Ronald L. Bishop

1988 "Plumbate Origins and Development." *American Antiquity* 53: 505–522.

Offner, Jerome A.

1981 "On the Inapplicability of 'Oriental Despotism' and the 'Asiatic Mode of Production' to the Aztecs of Texcoco." *American Antiquity* 46: 43–60.

1981 "On Carrasco's Use of 'Theoretical First Principles.'" *American Antiquity* 46: 69–74.

Piña Chan, Roman

1978 "Commerce in the Yucatan Peninsula: The Conquest and Colonial Period." Pp. 37–48 in *Mesoamerican Communication Routes and Cultural Contacts*, edited by Thomas A. Lee and Carlos Navarrete. Provo, Utah: New World Archaeological Foundation, Brigham Young University.

Polanyi, Karl

1957 "The Economy as Instituted Process." Pp. 243–270 in *Trade and Market in Early Empires*, edited by K. Polanyi, C. M. Arensberg, and H. W. Pearson. New York: Academic Press.

Polanyi, Karl, Conrad M. Arensberg, and Harry W. Pearson, editors

1957 *Trade and Market in Early Empires*. New York: Academic Press.

Potter, Daniel R., and Eleanor M. King

1995 "A Heterarchical Approach to Lowland Maya Socioeconomics." Pp. 17–32 in *Heterarchy and the Analysis of Complex Societies*, edited by Robert M. Ehrenreich, Carole L. Crumley, and Janet E. Levy. Archaeological Papers of the American Anthropological Association No. 6.

Rands, Robert L.

1967 "Ceramic Technology and Trade in the Palenque Region, Mexico." Pp. 137–151 in *American Historical Anthropology*, edited by C. L. Riley and W. W. Taylor. Carbondale: Southern Illinois University Press.

Rands, Robert L., and Ronald L. Bishop
  1980 "Resource Procurement Zones and Patterns of Ceramic Exchange in the Palenque Region, Mexico." Pp. 19–46 in *Models and Methods in Regional Exchange*, edited by Robert Fry. SAA Papers No. 1. Washington, D.C.: Society for American Archaeology.
Rands, Robert L., Ronald L. Bishop, and Garman Harbottle
  1978 "Thematic and Compositional Variation in Palenque Region Incensarios." Pp. 19–30 in *Tercera Mesa Redonda de Palenque*, Vol. IV, edited by M. G. Robertson and D. C. Jeffers. Monterey, Calif.: Pre-Columbian Art Research, Herald Printers.
Rands, Robert L., Ronald L. Bishop, and Jeremy A. Sabloff
  1982 "Maya Fine Paste Ceramics: An Archaeological Perspective." Pp. 315–338 in *Excavations at Seibal No. 2: Analyses of Fine Paste Ceramics*, edited by Jeremy A. Sabloff. Memoirs of the Peabody Museum of Archaeology and Ethnology Vol. 15, No. 2. Cambridge, Mass.: Harvard University.
Rathje, William L.
  1975 "The Last Tango in Mayapan: A Tentative Trajectory of Production-Distribution Systems." Pp. 409–448 in *Ancient Civilization and Trade*, edited by Jeremy A. Sabloff and C. C. Lamberg-Karlovsky. Albuquerque: University of New Mexico Press.
Rathje, William L., David A. Gregory, and Frederick M. Wiseman
  1978 "Trade Models and Archaeological Problems: Classic Maya Examples." Pp. 147–176 in *Mesoamerican Communication Routes and Cultural Contacts*, edited by Thomas A. Lee and Carlos Navarrete. Provo, Utah: New World Archaeological Foundation, Brigham Young University.
Reents-Budet, Dorie, Ronald L. Bishop, and Barbara Macleod
  1994 "Painting Styles, Workshop Locations, and Pottery Production." Pp. 164–233 in *Painting the Maya Universe: Royal Ceramics of the Classic Period*, edited by Doris Reents-Budet. Durham, N.C.: Duke University Press.
Renfrew, Colin
  1975 "Trade as Action at a Distance: Questions of Integration and Communication." Pp. 3–59 in *Ancient Civilization and Trade*, edited by Jeremy A. Sabloff and C. C. Lamberg-Karlovsky. Albuquerque: University of New Mexico Press.
  1977 "Alternative Models for Exchange and Spatial Distribution." Pp. 71–90 in *Exchange Systems in Prehistory*, edited by Timothy K. Earle and J. E. Ericson. New York: Academic Press.
Rice, Don
  1976 "The Historical Ecology of Lakes Yaxha and Sacnab, El Peten, Guatemala." Ph.D. dissertation, Department of Anthropology, Pennsylvania State University.
Rice, Prudence M.
  1980 "Peten Postclassic Pottery Production and Exchange: A View from Macanche." Pp. 67–82 in *Models and Methods in Regional Exchange*, edited by Robert Fry. SAA Papers No. 1. Washington, D.C.: Society for American Archaeology.

1984 "Obsidian Procurement in the Central Peten Lakes Region, Guatemala." *Journal of Field Archaeology* 2: 181–194.
1987a "Economic Change in the Lowland Maya Late Classic Period." Pp. 76–85 in *Specialization, Exchange, and Complex Societies*, edited by E. M. Brumfiel and T. K. Earle. Cambridge: Cambridge University Press.
1987b "Lowland Maya Pottery Production in the Late Classic Period." Pp. 525–544 in *Maya Ceramics: Papers from the 1985 Maya Ceramic Conference*, edited by Prudence M. Rice and Robert J. Sharer. Oxford: BAR International Series 345(i).

Roys, Ralph L.
1943 "The Indian Background of Colonial Yucatan." Washington, D.C.: Carnegie Institution.

Sabloff, Jeremy A., and David A. Freidel
1975 "A Model of a Pre-Columbian Trading Center." Pp. 369–408 in *Ancient Civilization and Trade*, edited by J. A. Sabloff and C. C. Lamberg-Karlovsky. Albuquerque: University of New Mexico Press.

Sabloff, Jeremy A., and C. C. Lamberg-Karlovsky
1975 *Ancient Civilization and Trade*. Albuquerque: University of New Mexico Press.

Sabloff, Jeremy A., and William L. Rathje
1975 "The Rise of a Maya Merchant Class." *Scientific American* 233: 72–82.

Sabloff, Jeremy A., and Gordon R. Willey
1967 "The Collapse of Maya Civilization in the Southern Lowlands: A Consideration of History and Process." *Southwestern Journal of Anthropology* 23: 311–336.

Sanders, William T.
1960 *Prehistoric Ceramics and Settlement Patterns in Quintana Roo, Mexico*. Publication 606. Washington, D.C.: Carnegie Institution.
1981 "Classic Maya Settlement Patterns and Ethnographic Analogy." Pp. 351–370 in *Lowland Maya Settlement Patterns*, edited by Wendy Ashmore. Albuquerque: University of New Mexico Press.

Sanders, William T., and Barbara J. Price
1968 *Mesoamerica: The Evolution of a Civilization*. New York: Random House.

Sanders William T., and David Webster
1988 "The Mesoamerican Urban Tradition." *American Anthropologist* 90: 521–546.

Santley, Robert S., Phillip J. Arnold III, and Christopher A. Pool
1989 "The Ceramic Production System at Matacapan, Veracruz, Mexico." *Journal of Field Archaeology* 16: 107–132.

Shepard, Anna O.
1939 "Technological Notes on the Pottery of San Jose." Pp. 251–277 in *Excavations at San Jose, British Honduras*, by J. E. S. Thompson. Publication 506. Washington, D.C.: Carnegie Institute.
1948 *Plumbate: A Mesoamerican Tradeware*. Carnegie Institution of Washington, Publication 609, Washington, D.C.
1964 "Ceramic Development of the Lowland and Highland Maya." Pp. 518–520 in *35th International Congress of the Americanists*. Vol. 1. Mexico, D. F.

Sidrys, Raymond V.
1977 "Classic Maya Obsidian Trade." *American Antiquity* 41: 449–463.
1983 "Late Postclassic Effigy Censers in Northern Belize." Pp. 238–265 in *Archaeological Excavations in Northern Belize, Central America*, edited by Raymond V. Sidrys. Monograph XVII Los Angeles: UCLA Institute of Archaeology.

Sidrys, Raymond V., and Clifford Krowne
1983 "The Aventura Double Mouth Jar." Pp. 221–237 in *Archaeological Excavations in Northern Belize, Central America*, edited by Raymond V. Sidrys. Monograph XVII. Los Angeles: UCLA Institute of Archaeology.

Simmons, Michael P., and Gerald F. Brem
1979 "The Analysis and Distribution of Volcanic Ash-Tempered Pottery in the Lowland Maya Area." *American Antiquity* 44: 79–91.

Sinopoli, Carla M.
1991 *Approaches to Archaeological Ceramics*. New York: Plenum Press.

Skinner, G. William
1985 "Rural Marketing in China: Revival and Reappraisal." Pp. 7–48 in *Markets and Marketing*, edited by Stuart Plattner. Monographs in Economic Anthropology, No. 4. New York: University Press of America.

Smith, Carol
1974 "Economics of Marketing Systems: Models from Economic Geography." *Annual Review of Anthropology* 3: 167–202.
1976 "Exchange Systems and the Spatial Distribution of Elites: The Organization of Stratification in Agrarian Societies." Pp. 309–374 in *Regional Analysis*, Vol. II, edited by Carol A. Smith. New York: Academic Press.

Smith, M. Estellie
1991 "The ABCs of Political Economy." Pp. 31–73 in *Early State Economics*, edited by H. J. M. Claessen and P. van de Velde. New Brunswick, N.J.: Transaction Publishers.

Smith, Michael E.
1989 "Cities, Towns and Urbanism: Comments on Sanders and Webster." *American Anthropologist* 91: 454–460.
1990 "Long-Distance Trade under the Aztec Empire: The Archaeological Evidence." *Ancient Mesoamerica* 1: 153–169.
1996 *The Aztecs*. Malden, Mass.: Blackwell.
1997 "The Aztec Empire and the Mesoamerican World-System." Paper presented at Symposium No. 122 entitled "Imperial Designs: Comparative Dynamics of Early Empires," sponsored by the Wenner-Gren Foundation, Mijas, Spain.

Smith, Michael E., and Cynthia Heath-Smith
1994 "Rural Economy in Late Postclassic Morelos." Pp. 349–376 in *Economies and Polities in the Aztec Realm*, edited by Mary G. Hodge and Michael E. Smith. Institute for Mesoamerican Studies, Albany.

Smith, Robert E.
1971 *The Pottery of Mayapan*. Peabody Museum Papers 66, Vol. 1 & 2. Cambridge, Mass.: Harvard University.

Smyth, Michael P., and Christopher D. Dore
1992 "Large-Site Archaeological Methods at Sayil, Yucatan, Mexico: Investigating Community Organization at a Prehispanic Maya Center." *Latin American Antiquity* 3: 3–21.
Smyth, Michael P., Christopher D. Dore, Hector Neff, and Michael D. Glascock
1995 "The Origin of Puuc Slate Ware: New Data from Sayil, Yucatan, Mexico." *Ancient Mesoamerica* 6: 119–134.
Spence, Michael W.
1984 "Craft Production and Polity in Early Teotihuacan." Pp. 87–114 in *Trade and Exchange in Early Mesoamerica*, edited by Kenneth G. Hirth. Albuquerque: University of New Mexico Press.
Stross, Frederick H., Payson Sheets, Frank Asaro, and H. V. Asaro
1983 "Precise Characterization of Guatemalan Obsidian Sources, and Source Determination of Artifacts from Quiriqua." *American Antiquity* 48: 323–336.
Thirsk, Joan
1961 "Industries in the Countryside." Pp. 70–88 in *Essays in the Economic and Social History of Tudor and Stuart England*, edited by F. J. Fisher. Cambridge: Cambridge University Press.
Torrence, Robin
1986 *Production and Exchange of Stone Tools: Prehistoric Obsidian in the Aegean.* Cambridge: Cambridge University Press.
Tourtellot, Gair, and Jeremy A. Sabloff
1972 "Exchange Systems among the Ancient Maya." *American Antiquity* 37: 126–135.
Tourtellot, Gair, Jeremy A. Sabloff, Patricia A. McAnany, Thomas W. Killion, and Nicholas P. Dunning
1992 *Archaeological Investigations at Sayil, Yucatan, Mexico, Phase II: The 1987 Field Season.* Anthropological Papers. Pittsburgh: University of Pittsburgh Press.
Tozzer, Alfred M.
1941 *Landa's Relacion de las Cosas de Yucatan. A translation edited with notes by A. M. Tozzer.* Papers of the Peabody Museum of American Archaeology and Ethnology 18. Cambridge, Mass.: Harvard University.
Willey, Gordon
1974 "Precolumbian Urbanism: The Central Mexican Highlands and the Lowland Maya." Pp. 95–103 in *The Rise and Fall of Civilizations: Modern Archaeological Approaches to Ancient Cultures*, edited by J. A. Sabloff and C. C. Lamberg-Karlovsky. Menlo Park, Calif.: Cummings.
Yoffee, Norman
1977 "The Decline and Rise of Mesopotamian Civilization: An Ethnoarchaeological Perspective on the Evolution of Social Complexity." *American Antiquity* 44: 5–35.

Chapter Seven

Dynamics of Regional Integration in Northwestern Belize

Lauren A. Sullivan

The data discussed here are from the Three Rivers Region (figure 7.1) located in northwestern Belize and were recovered under the auspices of the Programme for Belize Archaeological Project directed by Fred Valdez Jr. The ceramic data from this region indicate changes in political organization and regional integration between the Early and Late Classic periods. The analysis of ceramic types, vessel forms, and shared motifs demonstrates a high degree of interregional integration during the Early Classic with sites located in northwestern Belize closely tied to Petén sites such as Tikal, Uaxactun, and Rio Azul. By the Late Classic, an increased variability is observed in ceramic distribution and consumption patterns, suggesting changing political alliances and decreasing interregional integration.

The Three Rivers Region is a geographically defined region of 1,600 square kilometers (figure 7.2), which is bounded by the Rio Azul and its associated flood plains on the northern and western margins, the Booth's River on the eastern edge, and the site of Chan Chich which arbitrarily sets the southern border (Adams 1995: 5). The term *region*, as used to label the Three Rivers Region, refers to a geographic and topographically, not politically, defined area. The Three Rivers Region provides us with the opportunity to fill in the blanks regarding the populations living between the major sites of the Petén core to the west, Yucatan to the north, the Belize River Valley to the south, and major sites in Belize to the east.

Fig. 7.1. Location of the Three Rivers Region (illustrated by Brett Houk).

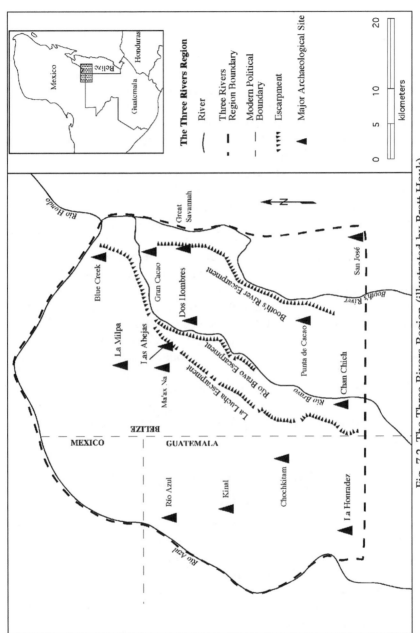

Fig. 7.2. The Three Rivers Region (illustrated by Brett Houk).

The region sits on top of the limestone-derived Yucatan Platform formed during the early Eocene. Three terraces faced by steep escarpments (the Rio Bravo, Booth's River, and La Lucha escarpment) form the dominant topographic features of the area (Lundell 1937; Hartshorn et al.. 1984; Brokaw and Mallory 1993). The rest of the region consists of upland ridges and flat alluvial valleys. These ridges are composed of exposed limestone bedrock carbonate sediments covered by river gravel and moderate to poorly drained smectite clay soils (Dunning 1992). This exposed marly limestone would have provided a readily available source of building material for the ancient Maya, and the chert nodules found within the limestone were also utilized by the Maya in the production of stone tools (Hartshorn et al. 1984; Lewis 1995). The Rio Bravo and Booth's River are the only perennial streams in the region, usually measuring only five meters across. The majority of rainfall in the area drains through the porous limestone bedrock and flows away below ground. Other available surface water is found in aguadas as well as in perennial and seasonal swamps (Hartshorn et al.. 1984; Dunning 1992; Brokaw and Mallory 1993). The vegetation of the region is strongly correlated with its topographic position and corresponding soil conditions, with the principle vegetation types defined as upland forests, escobal bajos, corozal bajos, and tintal bajos (Brokaw and Mallory 1993). The varied tropical forest environment, shallow gradient of soils, and high topographical diversity of this region resulted in a series of different microenvironments. Scarborough et al. (n.d.) suggest that this diversity created a series of resource-specialized communities within these microenvironments that had limited economic and agricultural adaptations to the landscape.

Chronological Background of Three Rivers Region

Ceramic and settlement data suggest that the area was continuously occupied from the Middle Preclassic to the Late Classic with little indication of Postclassic occupation. At this point, there is scattered evidence for habitation beginning in the Middle Preclassic but no evidence of Middle Preclassic architecture. Middle Preclassic occupation has been noted at La Milpa (Hammond and Tourtellot 1993), Blue Creek (Guderjan 1995), and Dos Hombres (Brown 1995; Houk and Brown 1995; Houk 1996).

Late Preclassic settlement indicates a population increase across the region (Sullivan and Valdez 1996). Late Preclassic settlement has been identified at the majority of excavated sites and is characterized by the presence of Chicanel sphere ceramics demonstrating that the Three Rivers Region was part of the widespread homogeneity observed in pottery production throughout the lowlands (Rathje 1977: 375; Kosakowsky 1987; Kosakowsky and Pring 1991; Sullivan and Valdez 1996; Sullivan and Sagebiel in press, Kosakowsky and Sagebiel 1999). Reese-Taylor and Walker (chapter 4 this volume) note the strong connections between northern Belize and the central Petén at this time. Populations seem to have congregated around natural and stable water sources, such as the Rio Bravo and Rio Azul, during this period (Adams 1990, 1995: 6). Late Preclassic structures have been located at Dos Hombres (Brown 1995; Houk 1996) and La Milpa (Guderjan 1995). Other Late Preclassic deposits have been documented at Las Abejas (Sullivan 1997), Blue Creek (Guderjan 1995), Gran Cacao (Levi 1994; Lohse 1995), and Chan Chich (Guderjan 1991; Houk and Robichaux 1996). Mammiform supports have been recovered and in 1998 a Protoclassic tomb was located at Chan Chich indicating that a Floral Park equivalent is also present in the region (Valdez 1998).

Ceramic data suggests a slight population decline during the Early Classic even though the nearby site of Tikal was flourishing. Also noted is a movement of people away from large site centers and into other more intermediary areas (Muñoz 1997; Durst 1998; Pyburn 1998; Hageman 1999). The Early Classic in the Three Rivers Region is distinguished by elaborate ceramics that represent connections to sites outside of the region, and few utilitarian unslipped wares are recovered (Sullivan and Sagebiel 1999a, 1999b, in press). Substantial Early Classic construction has been documented at Rio Azul (Adams 1990, 1995), La Milpa (Guderjan 1995), La Honradez (Von Euw and Graham 1984), and Blue Creek (Guderjan 1995). Early Classic ceramics have also been recovered from Dos Hombres (Brown 1995, Houk 1996; Durst 1998; Sullivan 1998), Las Abejas (Sullivan 1997), Gran Cacao (Levi 1994), and Guijarral (Sullivan 1998).

The Late Classic (Tepeu 2–3) marks the largest population levels in the Three Rivers Region. This population growth coincides with an increase in agricultural-related activities and associated land modification (Lewis 1995; Hughbanks 1995; Walling 1995), an increase in the number of rural communities that developed around larger centers (Robichaux 1995), and an increase in the construction of monumental architecture (Adams 1995). Large sites in the region with significant Late Classic construction include the following: Rio Azul (Adams 1995, 1999), Kinal (Adams 1999; Hageman 1992), La Honradez (Adams 1999), La Milpa (Tourtellot and Rose 1993; Hammond and Bobo 1994), Dos Hombres (Houk 1996), Blue Creek (Guderjan 1995; Guderjan and Driver 1995), Ma'ax Na (Barnhart and Ross 1997; Shaw and King 1997), Chan Chich (Guderjan 1991; Houk and Robichaux 1996), and Gran Cacao (Lohse 1995). Smaller centers include Las Abejas (Sullivan 1997), Guijarral (Hughbanks 1994, 1995), Dos Barbaras (Lewis 1995), El Intruso (Lewis 1995, Muñoz 1997), and El Arroyo (Tovar 1995).

During the Terminal Classic, the city of Rio Azul was burned (ca. A.D. 840) and invaded by peoples from the north (Adams 1990, 1995, 1999). Kinal survived; however, its population declined due to a collapse in food production in the area and its buildings began to deteriorate (Adams 1995). Many rural areas in the region were depopulated by the end of the Terminal Classic (Robichaux 1995; Houk 1996). At La Milpa, there was also a population decline and low-walled buildings were constructed by stones robbed from existing structures (Tourtellot and Rose 1993: 15). Sometimes these buildings were constructed on top of Late Classic plaza surfaces, as was the case with a domestic structure at La Milpa (Structure 86) (Tourtellot and Rose 1993: 15). Similar structures have been found at Dos Hombres (Houk 1996: 124).

Evidence for Postclassic occupation is sparse with no indication of a rural population at this time (Robichaux 1995). Postclassic censers have been found at some of the larger sites including Rio Azul (Houk 1996), La Milpa (Hammond and Bobo 1994), and Dos Hombres (Houk 1996), which may represent Postclassic pilgrimages.

Early Classic Connections

The data under discussion here include ceramics collected from a number of sites ranging from large site centers to small sites to test pits conducted on surveys in more intermediary settlement zones located between centers across the Three Rivers Region (i.e., Dos Hombres, La Milpa, Las Abejas, Dos Barbaras, Guijarral, My Lady, El Intruso, and survey blocks between Dos Hombres and La Milpa). These data suggest close ties in the Early Classic between the Three Rivers Region and Petén sites such as Tikal, Uaxactun, and Rio Azul. This pattern changes by the Late Classic with a high degree of regional independence and internal integration observed according to ceramic production typologies specific to each site (Sullivan and Sagebiel in press).

Data recovered from the regional project originally suggested that there was a drastic population decline in this area during the Early Classic compared to the Late Preclassic; however, through the years a clearer picture has emerged suggesting that the population decline was not as extreme as originally hypothesized. Problems contributing to the detection of Early Classic settlement include the following three patterns: the continued use of Late Preclassic ceramic types in the Early Classic at many sites in the region, making the distinction between Late Preclassic and Early Classic deposits more difficult (Lincoln 1985; Sullivan and Valdez 1996; Kosakowsky and Pring 1991; Kosakowsky and Sagebiel 1999); the location of Early Classic remains under Late Classic and Terminal Classic deposits (Fash and Stuart 1991: 150; Willey and Mathews 1985: 1); and, most recently detected, a movement of people away from large centers and into other areas (Fry 1990; Muñoz 1997; Durst 1998; Pyburn 1998; Hageman 1999). There is evidence of Early Classic monumental construction at only four of the fourteen major sites in the region (Houk in press), including Rio Azul (Adams 1999), La Milpa (Hammond et al.. 1996: 88), La Honradez (Von Euw and Graham 1984), and Blue Creek (Guderjan 1995). There is also evidence for Early Classic construction and occupation away from these main centers, including a group on top of the Rio Bravo escarpment (Hageman 1999), Guijarral (Hughbanks 1994, 1995; Sullivan 1998), El Intruso (Muñoz 1997), and outside of the ceremonial precinct of Dos Hombres (Durst 1998); however, the architecture in these areas is minimal. This trend contrasts to the Late Classic where monumental construction is observed at all of the fourteen known major sites as well as at a number of middle-sized centers and smaller sites.

Evidence for elite populations is found away from site centers where we do not see extensive Early Classic architecture. This evidence is in the form of tombs containing ceramic vessels with symbolic elements that demonstrate ties to large and politically powerful Early Classic sites outside of the Three Rivers Region. In short, the elites were moving away from or to the edge of site centers and were focusing on the reproduction of different ideological elements that denote power and prestige and not on the replication of site plan or temple architecture (as is often observed) as a way to politically align themselves with major centers (Rathje 1971; Houk in press). The major centers I am referring to include Tikal and Uaxactun, both major political forces during the Early Classic. Tikal's influences spread far and wide at this time, as evidenced by inscriptions outside of the Petén core area at Caracol that record the accession of a new king in A.D. 553 under the auspices of a Tikal ruler (Martin and Grube 2000). The connection of sites in the Three Rivers Region with these important sites of the Petén core is observed in the ceramics.

Early Classic Ceramic Data from the Three Rivers Region

The first Early Classic tomb under discussion (Sullivan and Sagebiel 1999a, 1999b, n.d.) was excavated by Jeff Durst (1998) and is associated with the site of Dos Hombres. It was located in Structure B-16 which is part of Courtyard B-4 (Houk 1996; Durst 1998). This structure, which rises approximately 2 meters above the courtyard surface, is part of a small, raised platform group of four structures, which appears to be separate from the primary ceremonial precinct (associated with Group A) and is located 75 meters west of the ball court and sacbe (figure 7.3) (Houk 1996; Durst 1998). Due to the small size and the location of this group away from the main site center, the discovery of the tomb was somewhat of a surprise (Durst 1998). In fact, original descriptions of this courtyard prior to excavation suggested its use as a residential area with possible ancillary structures for cooking and/or storage (Houk 1996). Among the nine vessels recovered from this deposit was a Dos Arroyos Orange-polychrome basal flange bowl covered by a Yaloche Cream-polychrome scutate lid (see Sabloff 1975: 27) with a macaw head handle. The Dos Arroyos bowl is very similar to a vessel recovered from Burial 1 at Uaxactun (Smith 1955: figure 76b5), as noted in the images on the vessel interiors: Both depict a man in profile wearing a headdress (figures 7.4 and 7.5). Similar figures are also noted on the vessel exteriors (figures 7.6 and 7.7): a male figure lying on his stomach with bent knees (Smith 1955: figure 3e). This design was also observed on a sherd from a looted tomb at Chan Chich (B. Houk, personal communication, 1999) and on a sherd from San Jose. The macaw head handle from the lid (figure 7.8) is also similar to a handle from Uaxactun (figure 7.9) (Smith 1955: figure 69b4). This type of macaw imagery was typically used by elites to link themselves with supernatural forces, in this case, the Principle Bird Deity (Schele and Miller 1986; Kappelman 1997; Carmean 1998). A coatimundi effigy

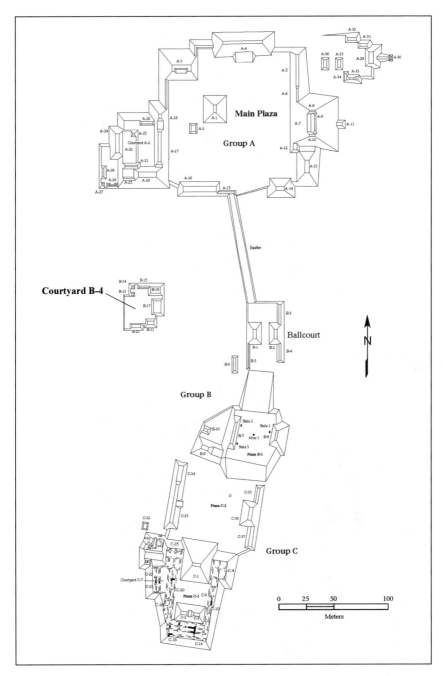

Fig. 7.3. Map of Dos Hombres showing location of tomb (illustrated by Brett Houk).

Fig. 7.4. Interior of Dos Hombres' Dos Arroyos Orange-polychrome bowl (illustrated by Ashlyn Hoffman).

Fig. 7.5. Interior of vessel from Uaxactun similar to vessel in Figure 7.4 (redrawn by Pamela Headrick from Smith 1955: figure 76b5).

Fig. 7.6. Exterior of Dos Hombres' Dos Arroyos Orange-polychrome bowl.

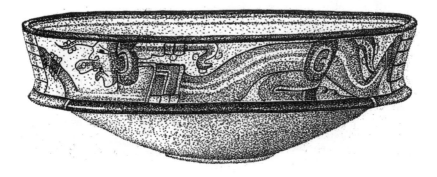

Fig. 7.7. Exterior of vessel from Uaxactun similar to vessel in Figure 7.6 (redrawn by Pamela Headrick from Smith 1955: figure 3e).

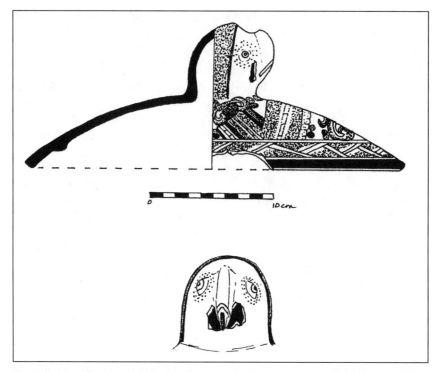

Fig. 7.8. Dos Hombres' Yaloche Cream-polychrome macaw lid (illustrated by Ashlyn Hoffman).

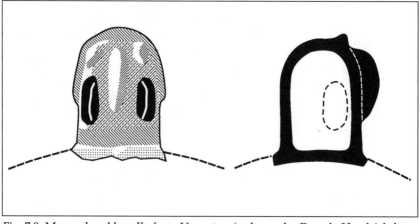

Fig. 7.9. Macaw head handle from Uaxactun (redrawn by Pamela Headrick from Smith 1955: figure 69b4).

vessel (figure 7.10) with a red-and-black mottled slip was among the vessels recovered and is very close to a vessel associated with Burial A22 at Uaxactun (figure 7.11, Smith 1955: figure 5a–d). This type of specialized effigy vessel was not recovered from any other context at the site.

Another Early Classic tomb, excavated by Jon Hageman (1999), was located on top of and at the edge of the Rio Bravo Escarpment, about 2.5 km northwest of Dos Hombres. Among the five vessels recovered (figure 7.12) was a Teotihuacan-style cylinder tripod with a human head handle that is similar to a lid recovered from Burial A 22 at Uaxactun (Smith 1955: figure 1j) and several from Rio Azul (Hall 1989). There were three uniquely shaped effigy vessels in this deposit. The first is anthropomorphic and resembles a shell with a human head and might represent God N (*Pawatun*), who is often shown emerging from a shell (Schele and Miller 1986: 54). As seen with the macaw head handle, this could represent the elites' attempt to reinforce the idea that they could communicate with the Otherworld though the primordial sea (Freidel et al.. 1993: 139). The second effigy vessel, a zoomorphic Orange polychrome jaguar, highlights elite association with the jaguar—an animal that is generally associated with kings (Schele and Freidel 1990). The last effigy vessel recovered from this burial resembles an ocellated turkey. The turkey was often used as an offering and is even depicted in the Dresden Codex where God D (Itzamna) is shown presenting a turkey to the Spaniards (Freidel et al.. 1993: 40).

There was also an Early Classic tomb recovered from the site center of La Milpa; however, the tomb was not associated with any major Early Classic construction. Kerry Sagebiel (Sullivan and Sagebiel 1999a, 1999b) has discussed the ceramics from this tomb and has demonstrated connections with Teotihuacan (in the form of a cylinder tripod), Tikal, and Uaxactun.

The paragraphs above have focused on prestige goods from tomb contexts without much mention of utilitarian wares. This is due to the fact that there are very few utilitarian types associated with the Early Classic in this area. In fact, less than 1 percent of all Early Classic sherds recovered are unslipped utilitarian types (recovered types include Truinfo Striated and Quintal Unslipped). These data demonstrate strong connections (through ideological ties) between the Three Rivers Region and politically powerful sites lying just outside of the area. The region was clearly part of the "Tikal cult" phenomenon that was so widespread during the Early Classic (Rathje 1977).

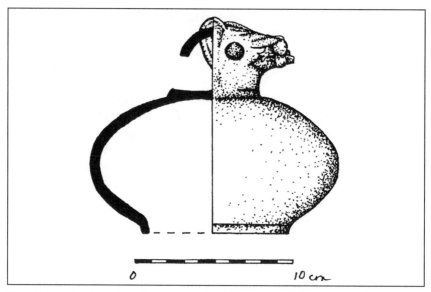

Fig. 7.10. Dos Hombres' coatimundi effigy vessel (illustrated by Ashlyn Hoffman).

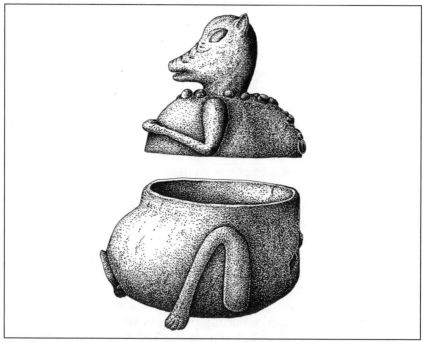

Fig. 7.11. Coatimundi vessel from Uaxactun (redrawn by Pamela Headrick from Smith 1955: figure 5 a–d).

Fig. 7.12. Vessels from tomb on the Rio Bravo Escarpment.

These types of luxury vessels were often gifted between the elite from different sites and represent an integration between the Three Rivers Region and sites outside of the region not seen in later times (Potter and King 1995; Sullivan and Sagebiel in press). In this case, I suggest that the local elite were using these vessels in a "prestige-good system" in an attempt to consolidate political power through social reproduction (Kowalewski 1996: 30; Peregrine 1996: 6; Rathje, chapter 2 this volume). Paste and temper resemble local clay sources, suggesting that many of these tomb vessels may have been locally made; however, the importation of ceremonial symbols and stylistic similarities (if not the actual items themselves) is significant nonetheless (Rathje 1971). As has been suggested for northern Belize (Potter and King 1995), there seem to have been several types of ceramic exchange: locally produced and exchanged utilitarian wares, prestige vessels with restricted local production (i.e., produced just for the elite), and/or vessels produced for elite exchange over greater distances.

Late Classic Independence

During the end of the Early Classic and first part of the Late Classic (Tepeu 1), a population decline is noted throughout the area which is, at least in part, related to Teotihuacan's decline as a political entity as well as the abandonment and destruction of Rio Azul (in A.D. 530) (Adams 1999; Sagebiel 1999). Tikal withdrew from the area and there were no dated monuments erected at the site for 130 years, suggesting that Tikal was at war or isolated from most neighboring sites (Martin and Grube 2000). During this "hiatus" the Three Rivers Region seems to break away from their close association with sites in the Petén core area.

By the latter half of the Late Classic (Tepeu 2–3), there is a population increase, which is reflected in an increase in the number of sites of all sizes as well as an increase in the construction of monumental architecture. Over 80 percent of the ceramics recovered date to this period (Sullivan 1998). Major Late Classic sites in the Three Rivers Region with significant Late Classic architecture include the following: Rio Azul (Adams 1990, 1995, 1999), Kinal (Adams 1990; Hageman 1992), La Honradez (Houk in press), La Milpa (Tourtellot and Rose 1993; Hammond and Bobo 1994: Sagebiel and Kosakowsky 1997), Dos Hombres (Houk 1996; Houk and Brown 1995), Blue Creek (Guderjan 1995; Guderjan and Driver 1995), Ma'ax Na (Barnhart and Ross 1997; Shaw and King 1997), Chan Chich (Guderjan 1991; Houk and Robichaux 1996), and Gran Cacao (Lohse 1995). This increase in monumental architecture clearly contrasts with that of the Early Classic. Based on site planning, Houk (in press) has suggested that the elite of the largest sites (especially La Milpa) broke free from sites outside of the region that had controlled them during the Early Classic, while simultaneously asserting their control over developing sites within the Three Rivers Region.

Concurrent with this reorganization of regional politics was a change in pottery production and distribution. While the Early Classic was distinguished by a low percentage of utilitarian wares and a high percentage of prestige vessels, the Late Classic was distinguished by an increase in the percentage of locally made utilitarian wares and a decrease in the percentage of prestige vessels. The production and distribution system for these Late Classic utilitarian types appears to be organized on a local level and oriented toward local consumption as suggested by paste and temper (Sullivan and Sagebiel in press). Fry proposes a similar system of localized distribution systems for the Tikal area, with the core of Tikal being a consumer of utilitarian vessels and not necessarily the producer (Fry and Cox 1974; Fry 1980; Ball 1993).

Late Classic Ceramic Data
from the Three Rivers Region

The Early Classic tomb vessels discussed above were clearly exclusive, being reserved for elite contexts (in most cases). On the other hand, in the Late Classic we see burial vessels that are not especially distinctive or restricted to burial contexts (Smith 1955; Ball 1993). In fact, Late Classic burials in the region generally yield more utilitarian ceramics and not "prestige" items. One of the two Late Classic burials from the site center of Dos Hombres (in a large range structure) was placed into a floor and had no associated grave goods (Houk 1996). The other Late Classic burial was placed in a lip-to-lip cache consisting of a Cayo Unslipped vessel covered by a Subin Red bowl—both utilitarian rather than exotic types. In fact, these large-mouthed Cayo Unslipped jars are quite common throughout the region in all contexts. Tepeu 2–3 burials from the site of Dos Barbaras also fit this pattern (Lewis, personal communication 2000). Three Late Classic burials were placed directly into the subfloor fill of the largest structure at the site and were not associated with any grave goods. In the same courtyard, three cyst burials were located. Only one of these cyst burials had associated material—in the form of a conch shell ladle (Lewis, personal communication, 2000). There were no vessels recovered with any of these burials, a big departure from the pattern observed in the Early Classic.

Also observed in the Late Classic are utilitarian ceramics in elite, but not necessarily burial, contexts. At Las Abejas two Late Classic caches were found on the center staircase of the largest structure (Sullivan 1997). The first cache consisted of a plain bowl with a small, unslipped plate placed on top. The second cache was an unslipped bowl. Similar caches were also noted at Dos Barbaras (although these vessels were a bit more elaborate, yet still unslipped). It is clear that during the Late Classic more common utilitarian types were being used in elite contexts, a pattern not observed in the Early Classic. Also, these utilitarian types are distributed across a number of different contexts (i.e., not just elite) in the region, ranging from small rural sites to ritual use in large centers. High-quality ceramics (such as Palmar Orange-polychrome and Ticul Thin Slate) are recovered in rural houses as well as in large site centers. Using restricted and symbolic ceramic forms and decoration to express interregional political affiliations, as noted in the Early Classic, does not seem to be important during the Late Classic. Instead, elites adopt other means of expressing their authority (e.g., architecture). There clearly appears to be a change in regional organization through time.

Regional Comparisons

The data presented above is centered around the relationship between the Three Rivers Region and the nearby sites of the Petén core (i.e., Tikal and Uaxactun) with which the most significant interactions and exchanges appear to occur. However, the site of Calakmul cannot be left out of this discussion. Calakmul emerges as a major power in the Early Classic, and is only approximately 50 kilometers northwest of the study area. Martin and Grube (2000) have suggested that southern Maya political organization was centered around the rival sites of Calakmul and Tikal. Calakmul, identified by a serpent-head emblem glyph, was associated with the powerful Serpent Head polity that included Dos Pilas and Caracol. Tikal's decline in power at the end of the Early Classic coincides with Calakmul's first appearance in the glyphic record at A.D. 546 (Martin and Grube 2000). Early Classic ceramics recovered from Calakmul are residential and ritual in nature; however, Carrasco (1996: 49) notes that at this time there is "a greater presence of ceramics, these being produced in sealed contexts, as in Tomb 2 of Structure IV-B and in Tomb 1 in Structure III." The significant point here is that the Early Classic ceramics from Calakmul are a most prevalent form of offerings in elite tomb deposits. During the early Late Classic (A.D. 685), conflicts between these two centers escalated and Tikal eventually defeated Calakmul and experienced a resurgence of regional power (Vargas et al.. 1999). The Late Classic ceramics from Calakmul indicate that the site was part of a large interregional network with ties to the Rio Bec area and not just the Petén core (Carrasco 1996). This pattern does differ from the Three Rivers Region data in that Calakmul seems to be forging connection with sites toward the north. Although Tikal returns to power by the mid-eighth century, there is less evidence for diplomatic alliances between large centers, signaling an increase in warfare and large-scale political unrest (Martin and Grube 2000).

Similar patterns have been observed throughout the Maya area. Along the Belize Coast, Graham (1989) has documented the presence of basal flange polychrome bowls with simple geometric line decoration in Early Classic (Tzakol 3) levels that are replaced in the Late Classic by more utilitarian vessel types thought to be used in salt processing. Likewise, at Santa Rita, the Chases (1989) have observed noticeable differences between the elite and the rest of society during the Early Classic, with the elite associating themselves closely with the Petén core as demonstrated in the ceramics recovered. This pattern changes during the Late Classic when a larger percentage of the population gains access to material items. Reese-Taylor and Walker (chapter 4 this volume) suggest that the fall of Cerros by the end of the Early Classic is due, in part, to the failure of the elite to maintain a connection with the sites of the Petén core, specifically Tikal. In the Belize River Valley at the site of Xunantunich, LeCount (1993) has noted that in the Late Classic ceramic assemblages there is a high degree of similarity in the vessel forms found in elite and nonelite households. There was also no differential distribution of polychrome pottery observed although there was some difference in the distribution of certain symbols across social groups (LeCount 1993). Ball's (1993) work in the Mopan-Macal area and including a range of sites (i.e., Buenavista, Cahal Pech, Guerra, Nohock Ek, and Eden) points strongly toward localized ceramic complexes that can be used to distinguish different Late Classic communities. Ball (1993: 256) concludes that "the absence of larger cohesive ceramic units corresponding to specific Late Classic polities is simply another reflection of the weak politicoeconomic integration characterizing these realms." By the Late Classic there clearly appears to be an increase in local ceramic production and distribution as well as a breakdown of the prestige-good exchange system that characterized the Early Classic. These changes are correlated with a more fragmented political environment.

Conclusions

In conclusion, the Early Classic in the Three Rivers Region is characterized by a consolidation of power in few dominant centers and small pockets of elite forging strong ties with key sites in the core. This strategy coincides with the rise of Tikal's fortunes and may have served as a way for the more rural elite to associate themselves with the powerful rulers of the core area. The population increase of the Late Classic brings with it a number of new sites and a shift in organization, which is, at least in part, based on a struggle for regional independence from the Petén core. This regional independence was manifested in increasing levels of local autonomy and organization as observed in utilitarian pottery production. The population increase would have forced people into all environmental zones (optimal or otherwise), as observed in the Late Classic settlement pattern, and, in many cases, the occupants would have perhaps had fewer options for economic adaptations to local resources (Scarborough et al. in press). Occupants of newly colonized microenvironments may have maximized their economic potential by developing a greater degree of economic specialization in agriculture, pottery, stone tool production (Lewis 1995), or other crafts or types of resource extraction. This situation would have encouraged the development of local networks of exchange, interdependence, and integration on a local and *intra*regional level.

Note

I would like to thank the Government of Belize and the Department of Archaeology for their continued support of the Programme for Belize Archaeology Project (PfBAP) and for allowing us to do our research in their country. I would also like to thank Marilyn Masson, Fred Valdez Jr., Paul Goldberg, Elizabeth Graham, Jon Hageman, Brett Houk, Kathryn Reese-Taylor, and Kerry Sagebiel for their help and assistance with this chapter. Ashyln Hoffman, Brett Houk, and the PfBAP graciously provided the illustrations for this article.

References

Adams, Richard E. W.
1990 "Archaeological Research at the Lowland Maya City of Rio Azul." *Latin American Antiquity* 1: 23–41.
1995 "The Programme for Belize Regional Archaeological Project: 1994 Interim Report, Introduction." Pp. 1–14 in *The Programme for Belize Archaeological Project, 1994 Interim Report*, edited by R. E. W. Adams and F. Valdez Jr. San Antonio: University of Texas, Center for Archaeology and Tropical Studies.
1999 *Rio Azul: An Ancient Maya City*. Norman: University of Oklahoma Press.
Ball, Joseph W.
1993 "Pottery, Potters, Palaces, and Polities: Some Socioeconomic and Political Implications of Late Classic Maya Ceramic Industries." Pp. 243–272 in *Lowland Maya Civilization in the Eighth Century A.D.*, edited by Jeremy A. Sabloff and John S. Henderson. Washington, D.C.: Dumbarton Oaks.
Barnhart, Ed, and Chap Ross
1997 "Survey in the Western Central Region of Programme for Belize, PfB Archaeological Project: 1995 Season." In *The Programme for Belize Archaeological Project: 1995 Interim Report*, edited by F. Valdez Jr. Austin: University of Texas Department of Anthropology.
Brokaw, Nicolas V. L., and Elizabeth P. Mallory
1993 *Vegetation of the Rio Bravo Conservation and Management Area*. Manomet Bird Observatory, Massachusetts, and the Programme for Belize, Belize City.
Brown, M. Kathryn
1995 "Test Pit Program and Preclassic Investigations at the Site of Dos Hombres, Belize." Unpublished Master's thesis, University of Texas at San Antonio.

Carmean, Kelli
1998 "Leadership at Sayil." *Ancient Mesoamerica* 9(2): 259–270.
Carrasco, Ramon
1996 "Calakmul: The Archaeology of a 'Superpower.'" *Arqueología Mexicana* 3: 46–51.
Chase, Diane Z. and Arlen F. Chase
1989 "Routes of Trade and Communication and the Integration of Maya Society: The Vista from Santa Rita Corozal, Belize." Pp. 19–32 in *Coastal Maya Trade*, edited by Heather McKillop and Paul F. Healy. Peterborough, Ontario: Trent University.
Dunning, Nicholas
1992 "Appendix 1: Notes on the Environment and Ancient Agricultural Features at La Milpa and Surrounding Areas, Belize." Pp. 82–102 in *Water Management Studies at La Milpa, Belize*, edited by V. L. Scarborough, M. E. Becher, J. L. Baker, G. Harris, and J. D. Henz. Report submitted to the National Geographic Society, Department of Archaeology, Belize, and Programme for Belize. Cincinnati, Ohio: University of Cincinnati Department of Anthropology.
Durst, Jeff
1998 "Early Classic Iconographic Connections of Dos Hombres and Other Lowland Maya Sites." Paper presented at the 63rd annual meeting of the Society for American Archaeology. Seattle, Washington.
Fash, William L., and David S. Stuart
1991 "Dynastic History and Cultural Evolution at Copan, Honduras." Pp. 147–179 in *Classic Maya Political History: Hieroglyphic and Archaeological Evidence*, edited by T. Patrick Culbert. School of American Research. Cambridge: Cambridge University Press.
Freidel, David, Linda Schele, and Joy Parker
1993 *Maya Cosmos: Three Thousand Years on the Shaman's Path*. New York: William Morrow.
Fry, Robert E.
1980 *Models and Methods in Regional Exchange*. SAA Papers No. 1. Washington D.C.: Society for American Archaeology.
1990 "Disjunctive Growth in the Maya Lowlands." Pp. 285–300 in *Precolumbian Population History in the Maya Lowlands*, edited by T. Patrick Culbert and Don S. Rice. Albuquerque: University of New Mexico Press.
Fry, Robert E., and Scott C. Cox
1974 "The Structure of Ceramic Exchange at Tikal, Guatemala." *World Archaeology* 6(2): 209–225.
Graham, Elizabeth
1989 "Brief Synthesis of Coastal Site Data from Colson Point, Placencia, and Marco Gonzalez, Belize." Pp. 135–154 in *Coastal Maya Trade*, edited by Heather McKillop and Paul F. Healy. Peterborough, Ontario: Trent University.
Guderjan, Thomas H.
1991 "Chan Chich." Pp. 35–50 in *Maya Settlement in Northwestern Belize: The 1988 and 1990 Seasons of the Rio Bravo Archaeological Project*, edited by T. H. Guderjan. Maya Research Program and Labyrinthos, California.

1995 "Aspects of Maya Settlement in Northwestern Belize: The View from Blue Creek." Pp. 13–26 in *Archaeological Research at Blue Creek, Belize. Progress Report of the Third (1994) Field Season*, edited by Thomas H. Guderjan and W. David Driver. San Antonio, Tex.: Maya Research Program and Department of Sociology, St. Mary's University.

Guderjan, Thomas, and W. David Driver
1995 "Introduction to the 1994 Season at Blue Creek." Pp. 1–12 in *Archaeological Research at Blue Creek, Belize. Progress Report of the Third (1994) Field Season*, edited by T. H. Guderjan and W. D. Driver. San Antonio, Tex.: Maya Research Program and Department of Sociology, St. Mary's University.

Hageman, Jon
1992 "The 1991 Test Pit Program at Kinal, Guatemala." Unpublished M.A. report, Department of Anthropology, University of Texas at Austin.
1999 "Ideology and Intersite Settlement among the Late Classic Maya." Paper presented at the 64th annual meeting of the Society for American Archaeology, March 24–28, Chicago, Illinois.

Hall, Grant
1989 "Realm of Death: Royal Mortuary Customs and Polity Interaction in the Classic Maya Lowlands." Unpublished Ph.D. thesis, Department of Anthropology, Harvard University.

Hammond, Norman, and Gair Tourtellot
1993 "Survey and Excavations at La Milpa, Belize, 1992." *Mexicon* 15: 71–75.

Hammond, Norman, and Matthew R. Bobo
1994 "Pilgrimage's Last Mile: Late Maya Monument Veneration at La Milpa, Belize." *World Archaeology* 26: 19–34.

Hammond, Norman, Gair Tourtellot, Sara Donaghey, and Amanda Clarke
1996 "Survey and Excavation at La Milpa, Belize, 1996." *Mexicon* 28(5): 86–91.

Harstorn, Gary, Lou Nicolait, Lynne Hartshorn, George Bevier, Richard Brightman, Jeronimo Cal, Agripino Cawich, William Davidson, Random DuBois, Charles Dyer, Janet Gibson, William Hawley, Jeffrey Leonard, Robert Nicolait, Dora Weyer, Hayward White, and Charles Wright
1984 *Belize: Country Environmental Profile: A Field Study.* USAIS Contract No. 505–0000-C-00-3001-00. Belize City, Belize: Robert Nicolait and Associates.

Houk, Brett A.
1996 "The Archaeology of Site Planning: An Example from the Maya Site of Dos Hombres, Belize." Unpublished Ph.D. dissertation, Department of Anthropology, University of Texas at Austin.
in press "The Ties that Bind." In *Heterarchy, Political Economy, and the Ancient Maya: The Three Rivers Region of the East-Central Yucatan Peninsula*, edited by Vernon L. Scarborough, Fred Valdez Jr., and Nicholas P. Dunning. Tucson: University of Arizona Press.

Houk, Brett A., and M. Kathryn Brown
1995 "Preliminary Investigations at the Site of Dos Hombres, Belize." Paper presented at the 60th annual meeting of the Society for American Archaeology, Minneapolis.

Houk, Brett, and Hubert Robichaux, editors
1996 *The 1996 Season of the Chan Chich Archaeological Project*. Papers of the Chan Chich Archaeological Project, Number 1. San Antonio, Tex.: Center for Maya Studies.

Hughbanks, Paul J.
1994 "Research at Guijarral, 1993." Pp. 96–102 in *The Programme for Belize Archaeological Project: 1993 Field Season*, edited by R. E. W. Adams. San Antonio: University of Texas Press.
1995 "Research at Guijarral (RB-18), 1994." Pp. 73–77 in *The Programme for Belize Archaeological Project: 1994 Interim Report*, edited by R. E. W. Adams and F. Valdez Jr. San Antonio: University of Texas Center for Archaeology and Tropical Studies.

Kappleman, Julia G.
1997 "Of Macaws and Men: Late Preclassic Cosmology and Political Ideology in Izapan-Style Monuments." Ph.D. dissertation, University of Texas at Austin.

Kosakowsky, Laura J.
1987 *Preclassic Maya Pottery at Cuello, Belize*. Anthropological Papers No. 47. Tucson: University of Arizona Press.

Kosakowsky, Laura J., and Duncan C. Pring
1991 "Ceramic Chronology and Typology." Pp. 60–69 in *Cuello: An Early Maya Community in Belize*, edited by N. Hammond. Cambridge: Cambridge University Press.

Kosakowsky, Laura J., and Kerry Sagebiel
1999 "The Ceramic Sequence of La Milpa, Belize." *Mexicon* XXI(6): 131–136.

Kowalewski, Stephen
1996 "Clout, Corn, Copper, Core-Periphery, Culture Area." Pp. 27–37 in *Pre-Columbian World Systems*, Monographs in World Archaeology No. 26, edited by Peter N. Peregrine and Gary M. Feinman. Madison, Wis.: Prehistory Press.

LeCount, Lisa
1993 "Ceramic Research: Initial Investigations into Assemblage Variation." Pp. 219–249 in *Xunantunich Archaeological Project: 1993 Field Season*, edited by R. Leventhal. Los Angeles: University of California Press.

Levi, Laura
1994 "Site Map, Evaluation of Salvaged Ceramics, and Artifact Storage Data, Site RB-43, Programme for Belize Lands." Pp. 1–44 in *The Programme for Belize Archaeological Project: 1993 Field Season*, edited by R. E. W. Adams. San Antonio: University of Texas.

Lewis, Brandon
1995 "The Role of Specialized Production in the Development of Sociopolitical Complexity: A Test Case for the Late Classic Maya." Unpublished dissertation, Department of Anthropology, University of California, Los Angeles.

Lincoln, Charles
1985 "Ceramics and Ceramic Chronology." Pp. 55–94 in *A Consideration of the Early Classic Period in the Maya Lowlands*, edited by Gordon R. Willey and Peter Mathews. Institute for Mesoamerican Studies, Publication No. 10. Albany: State University of New York.

Lohse, Jon C.
1995 "Results of Survey and Mapping During the 1994 PfB Season at Gran Cacao." Pp. 106–114 in *The Programme for Belize Archaeological Project: 1994 Interim Report*, edited by R. E. W. Adams and F. Valdez Jr. San Antonio: University of Texas Center for Archaeology and Tropical Studies.

Lundell, Cyrus
1937 *The Vegetation of Petén*. Publication Number 478. Washington D.C.: Carnegie Institution.

Martin, Simon, and Nikolai Grube
2000 *The Chronicles of Maya Kings and Queens*. London: Thames and Hudson.

Muñoz, A. Rene
1997 "Excavations at RB-11: An Ancient Maya Household in Northwestern Belize." Unpublished Master's thesis, University of Texas at San Antonio.

Peregrine, Peter N.
1996 "Introduction: World-Systems Theory and Archaeology." Pp. 1–10 in *Pre-Columbian World Systems*, Monographs in World Archaeology No. 26, edited by Peter N. Peregrine and Gary M. Feinman. Madison, Wis.: Prehistory Press.

Potter, Daniel, and Eleanor King
1995 "Heterarchical Approach to Lowland Maya Socioeconomies." Pp. 17–32 in *Heterachy and the Analysis of Complex Societies*, edited by Robert M. Ehrenreich, Carole L. Crumley, and Janet. E. Levy. Archaeological Papers No. 6. Arlington, Va.: American Anthropological Association.

Pyburn, K. Anne, Boyd Dixon, Patricia Cook, and Anna McNair
1998 "The Albion Island Settlement Pattern Project: Domination and Resistance in Early Classic Northern Belize." *Journal of Field Archaeology* 25(1): 37–62.

Rathje, William
1971 "The Origin and Development of Lowland Classic Maya Civilization." *American Antiquity* 36(3): 275–285.
1977 "The Tikal Connection." Pp. 373–382 in *The Origins of Maya Civilization*, edited by R. E. W. Adams. Albuquerque: University of New Mexico Press.

Robichaux, Hubert R.
1995 "Ancient Maya Community Patterns in Northwestern Belize: Peripheral Zone Survey at La Milpa and Dos Hombres." Unpublished Ph.D. dissertation, Department of Anthropology, University of Texas at Austin.

Sabloff, Jeremy A.
1975 *Excavations at Seibal, Department of Petén, Guatemala: Ceramics*. Memoirs of the Peabody Museum of Archaeology and Ethnology Vol. 13(2). Cambridge, Mass.: Harvard University.

Sagebiel, Kerry
1999 "The La Milpa Ceramic Sequence: Evidence of Renewal and Growth in the Early Late Classic." Paper presented at the 64th annual meeting of the Society for American Archaeology, Chicago.

Sagebiel, Kerry, and Laura J. Kosakowsky
1997 "On the Frontier: The Ceramic History of La Milpa." Paper presented at the 62nd annual meeting of the Society for American Archaeology, Nashville, Tennessee.

Scarborough, Vernon L., Fred Valdez Jr., and Nicholas P. Dunning
n.d. "The Engineered Environment and Political Economy of the Three Rivers Region." In *Heterarchy, Political Economy, and the Ancient Maya: The Three Rivers Region of the East-Central Yucatan Peninsula*, edited by Vernon L. Scarborough, Fred Valdez Jr., and Nicholas P. Dunning. Tucson: University of Arizona Press, forthcoming.

Schele, Linda, and David Freidel
1990 *A Forest of Kings*. New York: William Morrow.

Schele, Linda, and Mary Ellen Miller
1986 *The Blood of Kings: Dynasty and Ritual in Maya Art*. Fort Worth: Kimbell Art Museum.

Shaw, Leslie C., and Eleanor M. King
1997 "Research in High Places: The Hilltop Center of Ma'ax Na, Belize." Paper presented at the 62nd annual meeting of the Society for American Archaeology, Nashville, Tennessee.

Smith, Robert E.
1955 *Ceramic Sequence at Uaxactun, Guatemala*. Middle American Research Institute Publication No. 20. New Orleans: Tulane University Press.

Sullivan, Lauren A.
1997 "Classic Maya Social Organization: A Perspective from Las Abejas." Unpublished Ph.D. dissertation, Department of Anthropology, University of Texas at Austin.
1998 "Ceramic Analysis in Northwestern Belize: Chronology and Typology." Paper presented at the 63rd annual meeting of the Society for American Archaeology, Seattle, Washington.

Sullivan, Lauren A., and Kerry L. Sagebiel
1999a "The Power of Pottery: A Contextual Analysis of Pottery from Northwestern Belize." Paper presented at the 64th annual meeting of the Society for American Archaeology, Chicago.
1999b "Pottery: A Dynamic Expression of Ideology." Paper presented at the 98th annual meeting of the American Anthropological Association, Chicago.
n.d. "Changing Political Alliances in the Three Rivers Region." In *Heterarchy, Political Economy, and the Ancient Maya: The Three Rivers Region of the East-Central Yucatan Peninsula*, edited by Vernon L. Scarborough, Fred Valdez Jr., and Nicholas P. Dunning. Tucson: University of Arizona Press, forthcoming.

Sullivan, Lauren A., and Fred Valdez Jr.
1996 "Late Preclassic Maya Ceramic Traditions in the Early Classic of Northwestern Belize." Paper presented at the 61st annual meeting of the Society for American Archaeology, New Orleans.

Tourtellot, Gair, and John Rose
1993 *More Light on La Milpa Mapping: Interim Report on the 1993 Season*. Version 2.25. Boston, Mass.: La Milpa Archaeological Project.

Tovar, Lynne
1995 "RB-45: Investigations of Domestic Lithic Technology and Production." Pp. 118–124 in *The Programme for Belize Archaeological Project: 1994 Interim Report*, edited by R. E. W. Adams and F. Valdez Jr. San Antonio: University of Texas Center for Archaeology and Tropical Studies.

Valdez, Fred, Jr.
1998 "The Chan Chich Ceramic Sequence." Pp. 73–86 in *The Chan Chich Interim Report*, edited by Brett Houk. Papers of the Chan Chich Archaeological Project, No. 3. San Antonio, Tex.: Center for Maya Studies.

Vargas, Ramon Carrasco, Sylviane Boucher, Paula Alvarez Gonzalez, Vera Tiesler Blos, Valeria Garcia Vierna, Renata Garcia Moreno, and Javier Vazquez Negrete
1999 "A Dynastic Tomb from Campeche, Mexico: New Evidence on Jaguar Paw, a Ruler of Calakmul." *Latin American Antiquity*: 10(1): 47–58.

Von Euw, Eric, and Ian Graham
1984 *Corpus of Maya Hieroglyphic Inscriptions*, Vol. 5, Part 2. Peabody Museum of Archaeology and Ethnology. Cambridge, Mass.: Harvard University.

Walling, Stanley L.
1995 "Bajo and Floodplain Sites along the Rio Bravo: 1994 Survey and Excavations." Pp. 48–52 in *The Programme for Belize Archaeological Project, 1994 Interim Report*, edited by R.E.W. Adams. San Antonio: University of Texas Center for Archaeology and Tropical Studies.

Willey, Gordon R., and Peter Mathews
1985 "Introduction." Pp. 1–10 in *A Consideration of The Early Classic Period in the Maya Lowlands*, edited by G. R. Willey and P. Mathews. Institute for Mesoamerican Studies, Publication No. 10. Albany: State University of New York.

Chapter Eight

At the Crossroads: The Economic Basis of Political Power in the Petexbatun Region

Antonia E. Foias

Although the most famous and best-known of Mesoamerican civilizations, the Classic period Maya city-states remain obscure in some aspects. Among the most enigmatic issues is the relationship between economic and political power during the Classic period. Located between the Pasion and Chixoy-Salinas river trade routes, the Petexbatun region of the southwestern Petén lies at the crossroads of the Central Petén core and buffer or peripheral zones of the Verapaz and highlands. Thus, it is natural to assume that economic activities such as trade were an important component of Maya polities in this region. Beyond the unrecoverable perishables, such trade included obsidian, nonlocal chert, jade, volcanic stone, marine shell, and pottery. This chapter examines how these items (and in particular pottery) obtained through trade were used to establish and increase political and social power during the Late and Terminal Classic (600– 950 A.D.) in the Petexbatun region.

A major debate in Maya archaeology centers on the political structure of the Classic period (250–950 A.D.): to what degree were Maya states centralized or decentralized (Chase and Chase 1996; Demarest 1996; Fox et al. 1996; Houston 1993; Marcus 1993; Sharer 1993; Stuart 1993)? Variability in political organization may be related to differences in state involvement in economic matters. Unfortunately, the specifics of Classic period Maya economic organization remain little known and scholars argue over the degree to which the ruling class was involved in the management of economic institutions such as craft production and exchange as well as agricultural systems (Henderson and Sabloff 1993; McAnany 1989; Webster 1989). The relationship between political and economic power is crucial to our reconstruction of the nature of Maya states and of the developmental trajectory of this Mesoamerican civilization.

In this chapter, I address the question of the economic basis of political power of Classic period Maya elites from a more general point of view and from a specific case: the Petexbatun region in southwestern Petén, Guatemala (figure 8.1). The economic power of Maya elites can be related to two distinct subsystems, including (1) economic systems that they directly control, and (2) tribute or tax systems that provide economic support for state political structure in many complex societies. Ethnohistorical evidence considered in conjunction with archaeological data provides a more holistic understanding of the economic power of Maya elites during the Classic period, and both will be considered below.

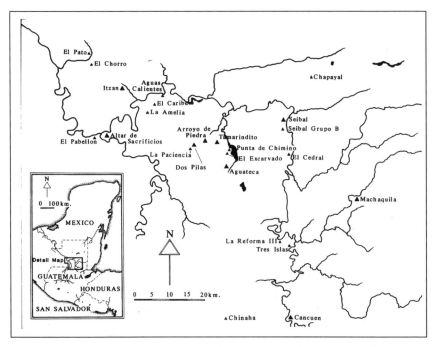

Fig. 8.1. Map of the Petexbatun region (drawn after Mathews and Willey 1991: figure 3.1).

Ethnohistorical Data about the Economy, Tribute, and Elite Control in Contact Period Yucatan

Ethnohistorical evidence about the nature of Yucatecan Maya economy at the time of the Spanish Conquest (Roys 1943; Garza et al. 1983) gives us an image of part-time specialization, variable degrees of community specialization, and some province-level specialization (Piña Chan 1978). These sources also attest to flourishing intraregional and long-distance exchange, major and minor market places (Freidel 1986a), a professional merchant group called the *ppolom*, and the use of cacao beans, shell, or greenstone beads as currency. Some scholars argue that the use of these objects as currency was a late introduction after the arrival of the Spanish (Feldman 1985: 86; Roys 1939: 61; Landa 1941: 95). Community specialization often occurs when a specific raw material is available in quantity nearby (for example, some north Yucatan coast villages adjacent to extensive salt beds engaged in salt making, as Andrews and Mock describe in chapter 11). Community specialization also occurs in geographic locations that influence the demand for specific products. For example, Mazanaho, near Lake Bacalar, specialized in boat building and Sinsimato in the province of Chikinchel specialized in the production of copal gum (Garza et al. 1983; Roys 1939). Lumber and copal were not unique resources concentrated around these communities (both widely available around other lowland communities as well), but they specialized in the production of these items nonetheless. It is important to consider how different Classic period economies were from contact period Yucatan, as argued by Sabloff and Rathje (1975) and Rathje (1975).

However, we find little expression of elite involvement in this economy. Roys remarks that merchants "ranged from the wealthy and noble wholesalers . . . to the petty itinerant who carried his own pack" (1943: 51). Thus, the elites were involved in some exchange. This exchange involved long-distance trade in wealth items, as suggested by the famous story of the survival of the last Cocom, the son of the Mayapan ruler. This son was away from Mayapan on a trading expedition in Honduras when the city fell from power, and from this distant point such trade items as feathers and cacao are described (Landa 1941; Roys 1943: 51). Therefore, the Cocom elites controlled, at least in part, the exchange of these two goods, both of which were prestige items. Cacao was also a currency in Mayapan markets.

The degree of elite control over economic systems can also be reconstructed from the roles and responsibilities of the nobility of sixteenth-century Yucatan as described in ethnohistorical documents. The rulers and administrators, whether *halach uinic* (regional ruler), *batab* (local town lord), *ah cuch cab* (head of town subdivisions or of lineages), *nacom* (war chief), *ah holpop* (overseer in charge of the council house), or *caluac* (tax collector), did not have economic functions beyond collecting tribute. Tribute collection could have varied from minor to substantial. Their duties were political, judicial, and religious (Landa 1941; Roys 1943). Roys lists the sources of income of the *halach uinic* as "the produce of the cacao groves and farms worked by his own slaves," the tribute from the towns of his province, and the gifts he received in his role as judge (1943: 61). These multiple strands of evidence are highly suggestive that the ruler and his political officials controlled only these parts of the economy: the tribute system and probably the long-distance trade in exotics, such as cacao, feathers, greenstone, and marine shell. Roys specifically mentions cacao in his list of the *halach uinic*'s income, implying that the lords had their own treasury of this important good in Yucatan. Although the dry climate precluded the cultivation of cacao on a large scale, humid sinkholes or *aguadas* were ideal for cacao orchards, and these may have been owned by the elite (Roys 1943: 37; Farriss 1984: 180; McAnany 1995: 142). Thus, it is possible that the elites or royal families may have controlled local production of cacao on their own estates (see also McAnany et al., chapter 5 this volume).

The ethnohistorical evidence suggests that the most important economic system controlled by Maya elites was the tribute or tax system. All states have administrative personnel who are not involved in agricultural work (D'Altroy and Earle 1985). These individuals have to be financially supported by the state through systems of tribute or tax (D'Altroy and Earle 1985; Brumfiel and Earle 1987). D'Altroy and Earle have defined two systems of tribute/tax: staple and wealth finance. In staple finance systems, taxes consist of subsistence goods, such as food and cloth; these are then redistributed to the administrative personnel for their necessities. In wealth finance systems, the tax consists of money or some other item that can function to purchase basic necessities (D'Altroy and Earle 1985).

Which type of finance system characterized the Yucatecan Mayas? During the sixteenth century, the Yucatan provinces employed the staple finance. Almost every Relación repeats the same list of tribute: corn, hens, honey, wax, beans, black pepper, and cotton cloth (Garza et al. 1983). The majority of these items are basic subsistence goods. The texts also emphasize how little was demanded in tribute, although military service was an additional burden. The provincial governors, the *batabob*, and possibly another official called the *mayordomo* or *caluac* collected the tribute for the principal governor or *halach uinic* (Garza et al. 1983; Roys 1957; Landa 1941: 27). With this control over local tribute, a *batab* could rebel and establish an independent hegemony. A way to check such fissionary tendencies of the secondary governors was through control of production of prestige or wealth items around the principal ruler, as was the case in Hawaiian chiefdoms and the Inca Empire (Earle 1987). It is quite likely that the same system applied in the Maya case.

Small states did not possess the capacity to manage a system that would have provided for the needs of every administrator. A system of land estates assigned to each official is often observed which allows officials a degree of economic autonomy (Brumfiel and Earle 1987: 6). This tendency is described in the ethnohistorical documents of Yucatan in which several *encomenderos* speak of lands reserved for the *batab*, which were cultivated by the people of the town. The *batab* received no part of the tribute gathered as it was reserved for the *halach uinic* (Garza et al. 1983). However, if the *batab* was independent, he did receive some tribute, while in the Cupul area, a *batab* who controlled several towns demanded more significant tribute in "grain, other produce, and poultry, . . . cacao, cotton mantles, and beads of red shell and green stone" (Roys 1943: 62–63). It is possible that this staple tax system and estates assigned to administrative personnel (elite lineages) existed during the Classic period. This system would have provided a significant financial base to secondary elites who governed the lesser centers within Maya states, allowing them to rebel with relative ease.

A system of monetary tribute and salaried administrators would have permitted more political stability and centralization (Brumfiel and Earle 1987: 6; Claessen 1985). In the sixteenth century, there were goods that functioned as currency: cacao and beads or stones of different colors, or beads of marine shell (Landa 1941: 95). But, the lists of tribute paid by each settlement given in Yucatecan ethnohistorical sources almost never mention cacao or stone/shell beads (Garza et al. 1983; Roys 1943). The exception is in the Cupul area where certain *batabob* who controlled several communities did receive both cacao and greenstone beads in tribute. Therefore, according to the ethnohistorical documents, the general pattern of the Postclassic

Yucatecan tax system does not conform to the second type of wealth finance as defined by D'Altroy and Earle (1985). While evidence may be scant for tribute or tax in the form of these valuables, Freidel and colleagues (chapter 3 this volume) make a strong argument for the use of these items as currencies in the Postclassic period and earlier. Their argument suggests that the economy of the Postclassic was complicated and did not conform strictly to a "staple finance" model.

Ethnohistorical Evidence on Economy and Elite Control in Sixteenth-Century Highland Guatemala

Highland Maya production and exchange were also flourishing at the time of the Spanish Conquest (Feldman 1985). Feldman identifies dual distribution systems, one through markets and a second referred to as "special exchange of the lords" (1985: 21). Markets were common at both major and minor sites, supervised by political authorities that settled disputes (1985: 15). Three types of merchants existed: (1) professional traders who bought in quantity from the manufacturers and sold to other merchants, generally long-distance; (2) petty traders who functioned within one local market district and exchanged one item that they often manufactured themselves; and (3) retailers who sometimes were farmers who sold agricultural surplus, or craftsmen who made their items on request at the market (Feldman 1985: 21). Only professional traders were members of the upper class (Feldman 1985: 21).

Superimposed over market exchange was the second sphere of distribution, which consisted of the "official channel of taxes, fines, and gifts" (Feldman 1985: 21). Different goods circulated in these two spheres of exchange. Wealth or prestige items circulated in the restricted sphere, and subsistence items in the other sphere (Feldman 1985: 23). In contrast to Yucatan, Feldman suggests that different media of exchange were used within these two economic spheres. Within the market exchange, barter was the norm of "maize for beans and beans for cacao, and especially salt in many places is exchanged very high" (Las Casas in Feldman 1985: 23). Within the sphere of valuables, different items were gift-exchanged: "cloaks of cotton for gold and for hand-axes of copper, and gold for emeralds and turquoises and plumes, which are the merchandise most valued" (Las Casas in Feldman 1985: 23). Indeed, these prestige items are identified as the privilege and property of the rulers and nobles: birds, feathers, precious stones, metals, and cacao (Feldman 1985: 23). Within the Guatemalan highlands, communities tended to be specialized. For example, only three towns produced metates in central-eastern Guatemala (Feldman 1985: 51). Exotic goods, defined as items of high value whether of local or nonlocal derivation, were primarily used by the elites, including hide-fur, salt, honey, resin, narcotics, and nonlocal prestige items such as marine shell, cacao, feathers, precious stones, and metal artifacts (Feldman 1985: 73–97). Elites completely controlled the entry of these exotics into local exchange spheres by dominating long-distance networks through which these items were procured (such as gift exchange or operating or sponsoring professional merchant voyages) or by producing these objects on elite estates. For example, the Cakchiquel and Zutuhil lords of highland Guatemala controlled the precious cacao through their ownership of cacao plantations in the piedmont (Vasquez 1937: 44 in Feldman 1985: 86). Thus, in the contact period Guatemalan highlands, there is evidence that elites controlled the production and exchange of prestige items and the tribute system, but many commonly used items were available through open market exchange.

Archaeological Evidence for the Economy and Elite Control from the Petexbatun Region

If we turn to the Classic Period Maya of the southern lowlands, economic evidence is more sparse. The economy was complex and was comprised of the production and exchange of agricultural crops, subsistence items, and craft goods. This chapter focuses on the latter category, craft items. Four aspects of Classic period Maya economy are commonly considered in an extensive body of literature on this topic. These four aspects include: (1) the organization of production (Adams 1970; Becker 1973; Rice 1987a; Abrams 1987; Webster 1989; McAnany 1989; Ball 1993); (2) the scale of exchange at intraregional and interregional scale (Sanders and Price 1968; Shafer and Hester 1983, 1986; McAnany 1989, 1993b); (3) the forms of reciprocity, redistribution and market exchange (Fry 1979, 1980; Tourtellot and Sabloff 1972; Sabloff and Rathje 1975; Rice 1987a); and (4) the degree and forms of elite control over manufacture and exchange.

Many societies from simple to complex recognize valuables apart from subsistence items (Malinowski 1961; Sahlins 1972; Brumfiel and Earle 1987; Clark and Parry 1990; Bohanan 1959), and the Maya were no exception. Brumfiel and Earle (1987: 4) distinguish between wealth items (symbols of status or prestige) and subsistence items (those needed for the livelihood of every individual). The definition of two such levels in Classic period Maya economy has been formalized in the most recent economic models (McAnany 1993a; Ball and Taschek 1992). The political economy for the Maya area has been defined as the production and distribution of wealth or prestige items, while the general economy is defined as the production, exchange, and consumption of utilitarian or subsistence items (Ball and Taschek 1992; McAnany 1993a). The sixteenth-century economy of highland Guatemala (Feldman 1985) is a good analogy for similar dual spheres of subsistence and wealth exchange. Distinguishing between artifacts made for distribution and consumption in either sphere represents the first task necessary for reconstructing such Classic period systems.

Level of Specialization during the Late Classic

The first crucial aspect of the craft economy is the organization of manufacture as expressed in the level of specialization. There are many typologies for the organization of production, especially in the case of pottery (Balfet 1965; Peacock 1981, 1982; Rice 1987b; Costin 1991; Van der Leeuw and Pritchard 1984; Sinopoli 1988). Peacock's typology (1981, 1982) centers on the level of specialization, defining several levels: (1) household production as a part-time activity which serves to supply only household necessities; (2) household industry that is part-time production for consumers outside the household; (3) workshop industry that is either part-time or full-time but forms the main occupation of the household; and (4) nucleated workshops that involve individuals beyond the family, generally producing on a larger scale and located in nonresidential specialized facilities.

It is more difficult to determine archaeologically whether Classic period Maya production was at the level of household industry or household workshop, or of nucleated workshops. The best way to study the level of production is through excavations of the production loci themselves, but very few ceramic workshops are known in the Maya lowlands: one was discovered in the royal palace of Buenavista (Ball 1993), a possible one is observed at Tikal (Becker 1973), and a third is reported from Quirigua (Ashmore 1988). However, recently Dorie Reents-Budet (personal communication 2000) has suggested that the midden of reconstructible polychromes found in the Buenavista palace may be the remains of feasting rather than a workshop due to the absence of wasters in the collection. The rarity of ceramic workshops in the Maya lowlands suggests a low level of household specialization, as large-scale household or workshop industries would have left behind more visible remains (Rice 1985). More lithic workshops have been reported from the Maya region, and these vary in size and complexity (Potter 1993; Shafer and Hester 1983, 1986).

Because of the lack of direct evidence for the scale of production, indirect methods have been used to estimate the level of specialization. One of these methods centers on the standardization of the end products themselves (Benco 1988; Blackman et al. 1993; Costin and Hagstrum 1995; Hagstrum 1985; Longacre et al. 1988). Standardization studies are based on the assumption that full-time specialists producing on large scale will create objects more standardized than those who work part time on a low scale in a domestic context (Rice 1981). This approach has been used in many areas of the world to estimate the scale of ceramic production or the level of specialization (Benco 1988; Costin 1991; Costin and Hagstrum 1995; Feinman et al. 1984; Foias 1996; Foias and Bishop 1997; Hagstrum 1985, 1988; Junker 1993; Longacre et al. 1988; Rice 1981; Sinopoli 1988). Various studies of modern and ancient potters demonstrate that full-time specialists with higher output manufacture ceramics with a coefficient of variation (standard deviation x 100 / mean) of metric morphological attributes between 5 and 10 percent, while part-time potters who produce on a small scale create vessels with a coefficient of variation closer to 15 percent (Benco 1988; Blackman et al. 1993; Longacre et al. 1988; Sinopoli 1988).

I have used standardization to estimate the level of pottery specialization in the Petexbatun region during the Late Classic period (Foias 1996; Foias and Bishop 1997). Metric morphological attributes (diameter, height of vessel or of ridge to rim, wall thickness) were used to calculate the coefficients of variation for the monochrome and polychrome pottery of the Late and Terminal Classic (Foias and Bishop 1997). The resulting coefficients of variation of monochrome types varied between 16.8 and 30.5 percent, while those of the polychromes were lower, between 13.9 and 23 percent (Foias 1996; Foias and Bishop 1997). These high values are closer to the coefficients associated with part-time production on a low scale. This proposition is supported by the neutron activation analysis of the Petexbatun pottery: The high variability in chemical composition indicates that many individuals were involved in pottery production, using highly diverse paste preparation recipes (Foias and Bishop n.d.a). However, a number of scholars (Arnold 1991; Blackman et al. 1993; Costin 1991; Pool 1992) have urged caution in using standardization as an index of production scale, as it may not directly correlate with the level of specialization. Costin (1991) believes that the coefficient of variation gauges the number of potting groups: A high coefficient indicates many producers, while a low coefficient indicates few producers. Thus, the high coefficients of variation of Petexbatun pottery indicate many potters, which characterizes a low scale of production.

A number of technological and chemical features distinguish polychromes from monochromes, leading us to suggest that they were generally produced by different individuals (Foias and Bishop n.d.b). First, Petexbatun polychromes almost never have fire clouds, while among the monochromes they are very common. It is probable that the polychromes were fired with covers or *saggars* to avoid such errors. Second, during the Late Classic, the carbonate nonplastic inclusions are predominantly fine-grained among polychromes, and medium-grained among the monochromes. The difference in the coefficients of variation between the monochromes and polychromes also suggest that there were fewer producers of the latter and more of the former. Finally, neutron activation analysis has confirmed that at Aguateca, polychrome potters used different raw materials from the monochrome producers (Foias and Bishop n.d.b).

Scale of Local and Long-Distance Exchange

The second issue in Classic period Maya economy is the scale of intra- and interregional exchange. It is important to remember that, as described in ethnohistorical documents, exchange in the past included many perishables that we do not recover archaeologically. The majority of trade items in sixteenth-century Yucatan were perishables, such as cotton mantles, honey, salt, fish, and cacao. Furthermore, the southern Maya lowlands of Petén and Verapaz have a number of perishable natural products that are not found in the highlands, and which therefore would have been important trade items. These include jaguar skins, feathers of brilliant colors, hard tropical woods, spices, cacao, cotton, medicines, hallucinogenic drugs, and dyes (Voorhies 1982; Graham 1987; Sharer 1994; McAnany 1993b). Unfortunately, archaeologists only find the nonperishables, and these can give only an estimate of the scale of exchange within a region and between regions.

Neutron activation analyses of a sample of Late Classic polychrome and monochrome pottery from the Petexbatun region permits an estimate of the amount of local and long-distance ceramic exchange. Long-distance pottery imports are very low (some 2 percent) (Foias and Bishop 1997, n.d.a, n.d.b). These are imported from three sources: the Greater Tikal-Uaxactun area, the Greater Motul de San Jose area in Central Petén, and the larger Usumacinta drainage. The majority of these imports are polychrome serving wares including vases, plates, bowls, or beakers. These ceramics are small and open, and therefore represent unsuitable long-distance carrying vessels for large quantities of trade items. Furthermore, their elaborate decoration makes them "hypertrophic" (Clark and Parry 1990) in that they require excessive labor and therefore probably represent status or prestige items. As they are containers of food, their discovery in the Petexbatun implies that a small quantity of food was served in them during feasts as we see depicted in palace scenes painted on these vessels (Reents-Budet 2000). In contrast, the level of intraregional pottery exchange was higher, above 20 percent (Foias and Bishop n.d.a, n.d.b). Both monochromes and polychromes were traded extensively within the Petexbatun region (Foias and Bishop n.d.b). Thus, while long-distance exchange was low scale and consisted of prestige pottery, local exchange in both subsistence and prestige pottery flourished.

Reciprocity, Redistribution, or Market Exchange?

The third issue in Maya economic studies is the type of exchange that dominated in the Classic period: reciprocity, redistribution, or market exchange? I follow McAnany (1993), Ball and Taschek (1992), Abrams (1994), and Feldman (1985) in suggesting that there were different forms of exchange for subsistence and wealth items.

In systems of the political economy, the exchange of prestige items often occurred through gifting or reciprocity. In the conference organized by the Xiu in Mani in 1557 to define the frontiers of the province, each *batab* who attended received gifts of "five four-hundred-piece lots [of cacao] each, five cotton mantles of four breadths each, a string of red beads as long as one's arm, and one score each of green stones" (Land Treaty of Mani, in Roys 1943: 186).

Gifting was clearly an important part of the political structure of Postclassic Yucatan, and it was probably also an important part of Classic period states. The elaborate polychromes that functioned as wealth items (e.g., figure 8.2) are found archaeologically in restricted elite contexts in the Petexbatun region (Foias 1996), suggesting that they were distributed primarily as gifts between elites.

The system of exchange of subsistence items is more difficult to understand for a number of reasons. In sixteenth-century ethnohistorical documents of Yucatan and Guatemalan highlands, it is quite clear that markets were common, and it is possible that they also existed in the Classic period. Unfortunately, it is close to impossible to identify markets archaeologically as they leave no material remains behind. In spite of this, many have suggested that various plazas in the epicenter of Maya cities (such as the East Plaza at Tikal) functioned as markets (Jones 1996; Freidel 1986a). There is some archaeological evidence that supports the existence of markets, but it is rare. For example, the distribution of utilitarian pottery at Tikal indicates the probable existence of various noncentralized markets at different levels of settlement (Fry 1979, 1980). In contrast, Abrams

Fig. 8.2. Example of an elaborate polychrome dish from the tomb of Dos Pilas Ruler 2, Str. L5-1, Dos Pilas, Petexbatun (drawn after S. Houston; courtesy of Vanderbilt University Press).

suggests that exchange was associated with social relations: "some utilitarian artifacts would have been produced by households and exchanged within a reciprocal system; others would have been produced by lineage specialists, and distributed only to the members of the lineage" (1994: 122). In summary, it is probable that the system of exchange of subsistence items was characterized by a combination of simple barter and/or reciprocity based on social relations and noncentralized markets, or a combination of local and regional markets.

Level of Elite Control over Pottery Economy

A final issue surrounding Classic period Maya economy is the degree to which elites controlled the system of production and distribution of goods. The connection between political and economic power in the Classic period is of great importance for understanding the nature of Maya states. Some scholars (Marcus 1976, 1983, 1993; Adams and Jones 1981; Culbert 1988; Chase and Chase 1996) suggest that Maya polities were centralized and that ruling elites controlled the economy at all levels, from the agrarian base to utilitarian and prestige production and exchange. In contrast, others envision the Maya state as small-scale, integrated by religion and kinship with little elite control over the economy (Adams and Smith 1981; Demarest 1992, 1996; Sabloff 1986; Freidel 1986b; Sanders 1981; Ball and Taschek 1991; Fox et al. 1996; Hendon 1991; Abrams 1994).

The majority of archaeological evidence supports a partial control by the elite over a segment of the nonsubsistence economy, specifically, the political economy sphere. Caracol may be the exception, where accumulating evidence suggests that the upper class controlled a larger proportion of the economy, including intensive terrace systems (Chase and Chase 1996). However, in most Classic period Maya states, the upper class controlled primarily the production and exchange of prestige or wealth items, such as elaborate polychrome vases with palace scenes and hieroglyphic texts, shell, and jade (Ball 1993; Ball and Taschek 1992; Reents-Budet et al. 1994; Freidel and colleagues, chapter 3 this volume).

The manufacture of sumptuary goods by artisans was probably sponsored by elite patrons (Ball 1993; Reents-Budet et al. 1994; Inomata 1995). This pattern of elite artisans is identified at the site of Aguateca in the Petexbatun region (Inomata 1995, 1997; Inomata and

Stiver 1998). In the epicenter, elite residences close to the royal palace were associated with workshops of different specialists, including that of a scribe and possible shell artisan, a pyrite mirror maker, and a wood carver. The craft specialization of these nobles was embedded in their social role within the royal court, as seen among the Northwest Coast Native Americans (Ames 1995) and at Tiwanaku (Janusek 1999). Furthermore, Ball (1993) has identified a palace workshop at the minor center of Buenavista, where polychromes were manufactured by elite scribes. My excavations close to the royal palace of Motul de San Jose in Central Petén have discovered a rich pottery midden that included several manufacturing wasters that imply that a polychrome workshop was located nearby (Foias 2000). The artisans who painted these elaborate polychromes were nobles themselves as the title of *ahaw* is included in many of their signatures on the pots (Reents-Budet et al. 1994). The elite status of these artisans who were associated with royal courts indicates that the upper class controlled the production of these prestige objects.

This reconstruction of the elite production of sumptuary goods in the epicenters of Maya cities contrasts strongly with the production and exchange of utilitarian artifacts. Extensive studies of pottery at the major centers of Tikal (Fry 1979, 1980, 1981) and Palenque (Rands and Bishop 1980; Bishop 1994) indicate that utilitarian ceramic manufacture took place outside of these sites, and that the centers themselves were the consumers of these products. I suggest that it would have been very difficult for the elite to directly control the production of utilitarian goods if the workshops were dispersed outside the major centers.

The Petexbatun pottery of the Late and Terminal Classic periods also sheds light on the nature of elite control over the system of pottery production and exchange (Foias 1996; Foias and Bishop 1997, n.d.b). Temporal trends in the pottery system from the Late to the Terminal Classic indicate a pattern of stability in the monochrome utilitarian pottery and a decline in polychrome production (Foias 1996; Foias and Bishop 1997). Political disintegration in the Terminal Classic correlates with a corresponding collapse of the polychrome pottery production system and stability of the monochrome pottery system. This pattern suggests that the elite controlled only the production and distribution of the polychrome and not the entire ceramic economy.

Evidence for Tribute from the Classic Period

As discussed above, a tribute or tax system is integral to the functioning of every complex society. Tribute supports the administrative personnel who are not involved in subsistence pursuits. David Stuart (1995: 356–358) has recently identified several glyphs associated with tribute payment: *patan* (tribute), *u-tohol* (his payment), or *ikats* (burden). These are found on both Classic period polychrome pottery and monuments. On Vessel K1728 (figure 8.3), a tribute payment scene is depicted. The primary lord, Lord Completion Star of Motul de San Jose, receives two lord-scribes, and two bundles are placed behind them. The decipherment of the glyphs *u-tohol*, "his payment" (Reents-Budet et al. 1994) and of *yubte'* "tribute mantle" (Houston in Stuart 1995: 358–359) in the secondary text provides evidence of the existence of tribute during the Classic period. Presumably the bundles hold the tribute payment of cotton mantles. Dos Pilas Hieroglyphic Stairway 1 also shows nobles standing between several bundles (Stuart 1995: 358–359). A vase from Rio Azul shows a number of bundles, some painted with the glyphs *ka-bul*, "our beans" (Houston, personal communication 1999), which may refer to either cacao (Houston, personal communication 1999) or regular beans. It is more probable that the *bul* refers to regular beans, as the Relaciónes Histórico-Geográficas de Yucatan mention that the Indians refer to

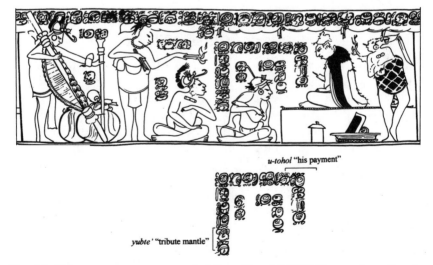

u-tohol "his payment"

yubte' "tribute mantle"

Fig. 8.3. Tribute payment scene painted on Vessel K1728 (drawn from Reents-Budet et al. 1994: figure 5.9).

these frijoles as *bul* (Garza et al. 1983). Other bundles in this scene appear to be tied cotton mantles (Stuart 1995). In several other presentation scenes, bunches of feathers are held by attendants, and feathers were probably another tribute item (Stuart 1995). Stuart (personal communication 1999) also found the glyph *ikats*, "burden," in the carved text of a jade block. He argues that this jade can represent the burden or tribute of one lord to another. Although these decipherments are still preliminary, they offer hints about Classic period tribute systems, and suggest that beans (or cacao), cotton mantles, feathers, and jade were given as tribute. Tribute payments were, therefore, made in both subsistence and wealth goods, although the frequency or quantity of the tribute payments cannot be gauged. While beans and cotton mantles were also part of contact period tribute payments in Yucatan, jade was included less often and feathers were not mentioned. Thus, there were some differences in the tribute systems between the Classic and Postclassic Maya states. However, we do not know if, during the Late Classic, other materials were also given in tribute, such as subsistence foods or prestige items like shell (Freidel and colleagues, chapter 3 this volume) and are simply not reported in our sample of monuments and vases. The tribute payments recorded of both utilitarian items (beans and cotton) and prestige items (jade and feathers) suggest that tribute extraction crosscut both utilitarian and prestige production spheres.

Feasting and the Economic Power of Classic Elites

Although archaeological and ethnohistorical evidence supports partial elite control over the economy, specifically over the production and exchange of prestige or wealth items, this control was linked to the system of feasting which provided occasions for displays, status quests, and distribution of gifts. Feasting is well documented ethnohistorically and ethnographically in the Maya region, and it was probably common during the Classic period (McAnany 1995: 31–33). In a recent publication, Reents-Budet (2000) argues that Late Classic polychrome vessel imagery and archaeological evidence found in Group A at Altun Ha indicate that feasting often took place in the southern Maya cities during the Classic period. Behind one of the main structures in Group A at Altun Ha, a thick midden of polychrome reconstructible vessels was found and Reents-Budet (2000) argues that these are the remains of cycles of feasting by the ruling elites of the site. McAnany has also emphasized the importance of feasting within the cycles of ancestor veneration in Maya culture from the Preclassic period to the present time (1995: 31–33).

Landa (1941) discusses the frequency of feasts given by Yucatecan elites in the sixteenth century. Such feasts were held at significant points in each individual's life, including birth, initiation, betrothal, wedding, and death. These feasts also occurred at important calendrical passages and events related to ancestral or lineage celebrations (Roys 1943: 25–29). Landa (1941: 92) describes feasting in the following manner: "And to each guest they give a roasted fowl, bread and drink of cacao in abundance; and at the end of the repast, they were accustomed to give a manta to each to wear, and a little stand and vessel, as beautiful as possible." Not only was a significant amount of foodstuffs needed to throw such a feast, including the precious cacao, but gifts were given to each of the guests. If the ruler controlled the production or procurement of cacao and the production or procurement of beautiful vases (as suggested above), he then controlled the economy of key commodities necessary for feasting, an activity through which elites (and commoners, too) gained or maintained their social positions. Landa (1941: 92) asserts that each invited guest was expected to subsequently hold his own feast (Roys 1943: 29).

Ethnographically, we know that commoners also engaged in feasting activity, perhaps as much as the upper class. Their feasts may not have been as extravagant as those of the elites, and their gifts may have been of lesser value (Redfield and Villa Rojas 1934). Nevertheless, marriage gifts given by the male's family to the female's were substantial in the twentieth century, described as "a gold chain 'of two loops,' two rings of specified quality, two hair ribbons, one silk handkerchief, several meters of cotton cloth, two or three silver pesos, rum, bread, chocolate and cigarettes" (Redfield and Villa Rojas 1934: 193). Although gold was not used in the Classic period, jade and shell jewelry probably served as equivalent commodities (Freidel and colleagues, chapter 3 this volume). If similar items were given as gifts during marriage ceremonies in the Classic period, it becomes clear that whoever controlled the distribution of jade, shell, and cacao had considerable power over materials necessary for key rites of passage. Elite control over prestige items—jade, polychrome vases, cacao, and so on—gave the ruling class social power that was linked to feasting economies integral to each individual's life, whether elite or nonelite.

Conclusions

When ethnohistorical and archaeological evidence are viewed together, our perspective of Maya economy is more detailed. Most of the archaeological data suggests that most elites of Classic period Maya states primarily controlled the production and exchange of prestige or wealth items and foods, such as jade and marine shell jewelry, elaborate glyphic polychromes, and cacao for political gain (for exceptions, see Chase and Chase 1996). The economic control over prestige items was supplemented by the tribute system that provided elites with an additional source of prestige items and utilitarian or subsistence goods. Establishment of production estates may have also existed in the Classic period (McAnany 1995, McAnany and colleagues, chapter 5 this volume) and these are documented historically for the sixteenth-century Yucatan (McAnany 1995) and the Guatemalan highlands (Feldman 1985). Prestige items that functioned as political and social currency were used in an extensive system of feasting in which elites and nonelites probably participated. Elite control over and manipulation of these prestige items bestowed substantial social and political power on the Classic period Maya aristocracy.

Note

The author would like to thank Drs. Arthur A. Demarest and Ronald L. Bishop for the guidance, support, and opportunity to undertake the Petexbatun ceramic analysis as part of the Petexbatun Regional Archaeological Project, and Vanderbilt University for granting permission to include pottery illustrations. The research presented here was supported by many agencies and individuals, including Vanderbilt University, the Petexbatun Regional Archaeological Project, the National Science Foundation, the Sigma-Xi Scientific Society, the Mellon Foundation, the Smithsonian Center for Materials Research and Education, Dumbarton Oaks, and Williams College. All illustrations were produced by Luis Fernando Luin.

References

Abrams, Elliot M.
  1987 "Economic Specialization and Construction Personnel in Classic Period Copan, Honduras." *American Antiquity* 52(3): 485–499.
  1994 *How the Maya Built Their World: Energetics and Ancient Architecture.* Austin: University of Texas Press.
Adams, Richard E. W.
  1970 "Suggested Classic Period Occupational Specialization in the Southern Maya Lowlands." Pp. 487–498 in *Monographs and Papers in Maya Archaeology*, edited by W. Bullard. Papers of the Peabody Museum No. 61. Cambridge, Mass.: Harvard University.

Adams, Richard E. W., and Richard C. Jones
1981 "Spatial Patterns and Regional Growth among Classic Maya Cities." *American Antiquity* 46: 301–322.
Adams, Richard E. W., and Woodruff D. Smith
1981 "Feudal Models for Classic Maya Settlement." Pp. 335–349 in *Lowland Maya Settlement Patterns*, edited by Wendy Ashmore. Albuquerque: University of New Mexico Press.
Ames, Kenneth M.
1995 "Chiefly Power and Household Production on the Northwest Coast." Pp. 155–187 in *Foundations of Social Inequality*, edited by T. D. Price and G. M. Feinman. New York: Plenum Press.
Arnold, Philip J., III
1991 "Dimensional Standardization and Production Scale in Mesoamerican Ceramics." *Latin American Antiquity* 2(4): 363–370.
Ashmore, Wendy
1988 "Household and Community at Classic Quirigua." Pp. 153–169 in *Household and Community in the Mesoamerican Past*, edited by R. R. Wilk and W. Ashmore. Albuquerque: University of New Mexico Press.
Balfet, Harriet
1965 "Ethnographic Observations in North Africa and Archaeological Interpretations: The Pottery of the Maghreb." Pp. 161–177 in *Ceramics and Man*, edited by F. R. Matson. Chicago: Aldine.
Ball, Joseph W.
1993 "Pottery, Potters, Palaces and Polities: Some Socioeconomic and Political Implications of Late Classic Maya Ceramic Industries." Pp. 243–272 in *Lowland Maya Civilization in the Eighth Century A.D.*, edited by J. A. Sabloff and J. S. Henderson. Washington, D.C.: Dumbarton Oaks.
Ball, Joseph W., and Jennifer T. Taschek
1991 "Late Classic Lowland Maya Political Organization and Central Place Analysis: New Insights from the Upper Belize Valley." *Ancient Mesoamerica* 2: 149–165.
1992 "Economics and Economies in the Late Classic Maya Lowlands: A Trial Examination of Some Apparent Patterns and Their Implications." Paper given at the symposium "The Segmentary State and the Classic Lowland Maya," Cleveland State University.
Becker, Marshall
1973 "Archaeological Evidence for Occupational Specialization among the Classic Period Maya at Tikal, Guatemala." *American Antiquity* 38: 396–406.
Benco, Nancy
1988 "Morphological Standardization: An Approach to the Study of Craft Specialization." Pp. 57–72 in *A Pot for All Reasons: Ceramic Ecology Revisited*, edited by C. C. Kolb and L. M. Lackey. Philadelphia: Temple University, Laboratory of Anthropology.
Bishop, Ronald L.
1994 "Pre-Columbian Pottery: Research in the Maya Region." Pp. 15–65 in *Archaeometry of Pre-Columbian Sites and Artifacts*, edited by D. A. Scott and P. Meyers. Los Angeles: The Getty Conservation Institute.

Blackman, M. James, Gil J. Stein, and Pamela B. Vandiver
1993 "The Standardization Hypothesis and Ceramic Mass Production: Technological, Compositional, and Metric Indexes of Craft Specialization at Tell Leilan, Syria." *American Antiquity* 58(1): 60–80.

Bohanan, P.
1959 "Some Principles of Exchange and Investment among the Tiv." *American Anthropologist* 57: 60–70.

Brumfiel, Elizabeth M., and T. K. Earle
1987 "Specialization, Exchange, and Complex Societies: An Introduction." Pp. 1–9 in *Specialization, Exchange, and Complex Societies*, edited by E. M. Brumfiel and T. K. Earle. Cambridge: Cambridge University Press.

Chase, Arlen F., and Diane Z. Chase
1996 "More Than Kin and King: Centralized Political Organization among the Late Classic Maya." *Current Anthropology* 37(5): 803–810.

Claessen, Henri J. M.
1985 "From the Franks to France—The Evolution of a Political Organization." Pp. 196–218 in *Development and Decline: The Evolution of Sociopolitical Organization*, edited by H. J. M. Claessen, P. Van de Velde, and M. E. Smith. South Hadley, Mass.: Bergin & Garvey.

Clark, John E., and William J. Parry
1990 "Craft Specialization and Cultural Complexity." Pp. 289–346 in *Research in Economic Anthropology*, Vol. 12, edited by Barry L. Isaac. Greenwich, Conn.: JAI Press.

Costin, Cathy L.
1991 "Craft Specialization: Issues in Defining, Documenting, and Explaining the Organization of Production." Pp. 1–56 in *Archaeological Method and Theory*, Vol. 3, edited by Michael B. Schiffer. Tucson: University of Arizona Press.

Costin, Cathy L., and Melissa B. Hagstrum
1995 "Standardization, Labor Investment, Skill, and the Organization of Ceramic Production in Late Prehispanic Highland Peru." *American Antiquity* 60: 619–639.

Culbert, T. Patrick
1988 "The Collapse of Classic Maya Civilization." Pp. 69–102 in *The Collapse of Ancient States and Civilizations*, edited by N. Yoffee and G. Cowgill. Tucson: University of Arizona Press.

D'Altroy, Thomas, and Timothy K. Earle
1985 "State Finance, Wealth Finance, and Storage in the Inka Political Economy." *Current Anthropology* 26: 187–206.

Demarest, Arthur A.
1992 "Ideology in Ancient Maya Cultural Evolution: The Dynamics of Galactic Polities." Pp. 135–158 in *Ideology and Pre-Columbian Civilizations*, edited by A. A. Demarest and G. Conrad. SAR Advanced Seminars Series. Santa Fe: School of American Research Press.
1996 "Closing Comment to Forum on Theory in Anthropology, The Maya State: Centralized or Segmentary?" *Current Anthropology* 37(5): 821–824.

Earle, Timothy K.
1987 "Specialization and the Production of Wealth: Hawaiian Chiefdoms and the Inka Empire." Pp. 64–75 in Specialization, Exchange, and Complex Societies, edited by E. M. Brumfiel and T. K. Earle. Cambridge: Cambridge University Press.

Farriss, Nancy M.
1984 Maya Society Under Colonial Rule: The Collective Enterprise of Survival. Princeton, N.J.: Princeton University Press.

Feinman, Gary M., Stephen Kowalewski, and Richard Blanton
1984 "Modeling Ceramic Production and Organizational Change in the Pre-Hispanic Valley of Oaxaca, Mexico." Pp. 297–333 in The Many Dimensions of Pottery: Ceramics in Archaeology and Anthropology, edited by S. E. Van der Leeuw and A. C. Pritchard. CINGULA 7. Amsterdam: University of Amsterdam Press.

Feldman, Lawrence
1985 A Tumpline Economy: Production and Distribution Systems in 16th-century Eastern Guatemala. Culver City, Calif.: Labyrinthos.

Foias, Antonia E.
1996 "Changing Ceramic Production and Exchange Systems and the Classic Maya Collapse in the Petexbatun Region." Unpublished Ph.D. dissertation, Vanderbilt University. Ann Arbor, Mich.: University Microfilms.
2000 "Entre la Politica y Economia: Resultados Preliminares de las Primeras Dos Temporadas del Proyecto Arqueologico Motul de San José." Pp. 945–973 in XIII Simposio de Investigaciones Arqueologicas en Guatemala, edited by J. P. Laporte, H. L. Escobedo, A. C. de Suasnavar, and B. Arroyo. Ministerio de Cultura y Deportes, IDAEH, Asociacion Tikal, Guatemala.

Foias, Antonia E., and Ronald L. Bishop
1997 "Changing Ceramic Production and Exchange in the Petexbatun Region, Guatemala: Reconsidering the Classic Maya Collapse." Ancient Mesoamerica 8: 275–291.
n.d.a "A Window into Maya Economy: The Production and Exchange of Late and Terminal Classic Pottery in the Petexbatun Region, Petén, Guatemala." In New Horizons for Ancient Maya Ceramics, edited by H. McKillop and S. Boteler-Mock. Under review, University Press of Florida.
n.d.b Ceramics, Production and Exchange in the Petexbatun Region: The Economic Parameters of the Classic Maya Collapse. Petexbatun Regional Archaeological Project, Vanderbilt University Monograph. General editor, A. A. Demarest. Nashville, Tenn.: Vanderbilt University Press.

Fox, John, G. W. Cook, Arlen F. Chase, and Diane Z. Chase
1996 "Questions of Political and Economic Integration: Segmentary versus Centralized States among the Ancient Maya." Current Anthropology 37(5): 795–801.

Freidel, David A.
1986a "Terminal Classic Lowland Maya: Successes, Failures, and Aftermaths." Pp. 409–430 in Late Lowland Maya Civilization, edited by J. A. Sabloff and E. W. Andrews, V., School of American Research, Albuquerque: University of New Mexico Press.

1986b "Maya Warfare: An Example of Peer Polity Interaction." Pp. 93–108 in *Peer Polity Interaction and Socio-political Change*, edited by C. Renfrew and J. Cherry. Cambridge: Cambridge University Press.

Fry, Robert E.

1979 "The Economics of Pottery at Tikal, Guatemala: Models of Exchange for Serving Vessels." *American Antiquity* 44: 494–512.

1980 "Models for Exchange for Major Shape Classes of Lowland Maya Pottery." Pp. 3–18 in *Models and Methods in Regional Exchange*, edited by R. Fry. SAA Papers No. 1. Washington, D.C.: Society for American Archaeology.

1981 "Pottery Production-Distribution Systems in the Southern Maya Lowlands." Pp. 145–167 in *Production and Distribution: A Ceramic Viewpoint*, edited by Hilary Howard and Elaine L. Morris. Oxford: BAR International Series 120.

Garza, Mercedes de la, A. L. Izquierdo, Ma. del Carmen Leon, and T. Figueroa, editors

1983 *Relaciónes Histórico-Geográficas de la Gobernación de Yucatan*. Fuentes Para el Estudio de la Cultura Maya 1, Instituto de Investigaciones Filologicas, Centro de Estudios Mayas. UNAM, Mexico, D.F.

Graham, Elizabeth

1987 "Resource Diversity in Belize and Its Implications for Models of Lowland Trade." *American Antiquity* 52: 753–767.

Hagstrum, Melissa

1985 "Measuring Prehistoric Ceramic Craft Specialization: A Test Case in the American Southwest." *Journal of Field Archaeology* 12(1): 65–75.

1988 Ceramic Production in the Central Andes, Peru: An Archaeological and Ethnographic Comparison." Pp. 127–145 in *A Pot for All Reasons: Ceramic Ecology Revisited*, edited by C. C. Kolb and L. M. Lackey. Philadelphia: Temple University, Laboratory of Anthropology.

Henderson, John S., and Jeremy A. Sabloff

1993 "Reconceptualizing the Maya Cultural Tradition: Programmatic Comments." Pp. 445–468 in *Lowland Maya Civilization in the Eighth Century A.D.*, edited by J. A. Sabloff and J. S. Henderson. Washington, D.C.: Dumbarton Oaks.

Hendon, Julia

1991 "Status and Power in Classic Maya Society: An Archaeological Study." *American Anthropologist* 93(4): 894–918.

Houston, Stephen D.

1993 *Hieroglyphs and History at Dos Pilas: Dynastic Politics of the Classic Maya*. Austin: University of Texas Press.

Inomata, Takeshi

1995 "Archaeological Investigation at the Fortified Center of Aguateca, El Petén, Guatemala: Implications for the Study of the Classic Maya Collapse." Unpublished Ph.D. dissertation, Vanderbilt University. Ann Arbor, Mich.: University Microfilms.

1997 "The Last Day of a Fortified Classic Maya Center: Archaeological Investigations at Aguateca, Guatemala." *Ancient Mesoamerica* 8: 337–351.

Inomata, Takeshi, and Laura R. Stiver
1998 "Floor Assemblages from Burned Structures at Aguateca, Guatemala: A Study of Classic Maya Households." *Journal of Field Archaeology* 25(4): 431–452.
Janusek, John Wayne
1999 "Craft and Local Power: Embedded Specialization in Tiwanaku Cities." *Latin American Antiquity* 10(2): 107–131.
Jones, Christopher
1996 *Excavations in the East Plaza of Tikal*. University Museum Monograph 92. Tikal Reports 16. Philadelphia: University Museum, University of Pennsylvania.
Junker, Laura L.
1993 "Craft Goods Specialization and Prestige Goods Exchange in Philippine Chiefdoms of the Fifteenth and Sixteenth Centuries." *Asian Perspectives* 32(1): 1–35.
Landa, Diego de
1941 *Landa's Relación de las Cosas de Yucatan: A translation with notes by Alfred M. Tozzer*. Peabody Museum Papers vol. 18. Cambridge, Mass.: Harvard University.
Longacre, William, Kenneth L. Kvamme, and Masashi Kobayashi
1988 "Southwestern Pottery Standardization: An Ethnoarchaeological View from the Philippines." *Kiva* 53: 101–112.
McAnany, Patricia A.
1989 "Economic Foundations of Prehistoric Maya Society: Paradigms and Concepts." Pp. 347–372 in *Prehistoric Maya Economies of Belize*, edited by P. A. McAnany and B. L. Isaac. Research in Economic Anthropology Supplement 4. Greenwich, Conn.: JAI Press.
1993a "The Economics of Social Power and Wealth among Eighth-Century Maya Households." Pp. 65–89 in *Lowland Maya Civilization in the Eighth Century A.D.*, edited by J. A. Sabloff and J. S. Henderson. Washington, D.C.: Dumbarton Oaks.
1993b "Resources, Specialization, and Exchange in the Maya Lowlands." Pp. 213–245 in *The American Southwest and Mesoamerica*, edited by J. E. Ericson and T. G. Baugh. New York: Plenum Press.
1995 *Living With the Ancestors: Kinship and Kingship in Ancient Maya Society*. Austin: University of Texas Press.
Malinowski, Bronislaw
1961 *Argonauts of the Western Pacific*. New York: Dutton.
Marcus, Joyce
1976 *Emblem and State in the Classic Maya Lowlands: An Epigraphic Approach to Territorial Organization*. Washington, D.C.: Dumbarton Oaks.
1983 "Lowland Maya Archaeology at the Crossroads." *American Antiquity* 48(3): 454–488.
1993 "Ancient Maya Political Organization." Pp. 111–183 in *Lowland Maya Civilization in the Eighth Century A.D.*, edited by J. A. Sabloff and J. S. Henderson. Washington, D.C.: Dumbarton Oaks.

Peacock, David P. S.
1981 "Archaeology, Ethnology, and Ceramic Production." Pp. 187–194 in *Production and Distribution: A Ceramic Viewpoint*, edited by H. Howard and E. Morris. Oxford: BAR International Series 120.
1982 *Pottery in the Roman World: An Ethnoarchaeological Approach*. London: Longman.
Piña Chan, R.
1978 "Commerce in the Yucatec Peninsula: The Conquest and Colonial Period." Pp. 37–48 in *Mesoamerican Communication Routes and Culture Contacts*, edited by T. A. Lee and C. Navarrete. Papers of the New World Archaeological Foundation 40. Provo, Utah: Brigham Young University Press.
Pool, Christopher A.
1992 "Integrating Ceramic Production and Distribution." Pp. 275–313 in *Ceramic Production and Distribution: An Integrated Approach*, edited by George J. Bey and Christopher A. Pool. Boulder, Colo.: Westview Press.
Potter, Daniel R.
1993 "Analytical Approaches to Late Classic Maya Industries." Pp. 273–298 in *Lowland Maya Civilization in the Eighth Century A.D.*, edited by Jeremy Sabloff and John Henderson. Washington, D.C.: Dumbarton Oaks.
Rands, Robert L., and Ronald L. Bishop
1980 "Resource Procurement Zones and Patterns of Ceramic Exchange in the Palenque Region, Mexico." Pp. 19–46 in *Models and Methods in Regional Exchange*, edited by R. Fry. SAA Papers No. 1. Washington, D.C.: Society for American Archaeology.
Rathje, William L.
1975 "The Last Tango in Mayapan: A Tentative Trajectory of Production-Distribution Systems." Pp. 409–448 in *Ancient Civilization and Trade*, edited by J. A. Sabloff and C. C. Lamberg-Karlovsky. Albuquerque: University of New Mexico Press.
Redfield, Robert, and Alfonso Villa Rojas
1934 *Chan Kom: A Maya Village*. Publication No. 448. Washington, D.C.: Carnegie Institution.
Reents-Budet, Dorie J.
2000 "Feasting among the Classic Maya: Evidence from the Pictorial Ceramics." Pp. 1022–1037 in *The Maya Vase Book*, Vol. 6, edited by Justin Kerr. New York: Justin Kerr Associates.
Reents-Budet, Dorie, Ronald L. Bishop, and Barbara MacLeod
1994 "Painting Styles, Workshop Locations and Pottery Production." Pp. 164–233 in *Painting the Maya Universe: Royal Ceramics of the Classic Period*, edited by D. Reents-Budet. Durham, N.C.: Duke University Press, Duke University Museum.
Rice, Prudence
1981 "Evolution of Specialized Pottery Production: A Trial Model." *Current Anthropology* 22(3): 219–240.
1985 "Maya Pottery Techniques and Technology." Pp. 113–132 in *Ancient Technology to Modern Science*, edited by W. D. Kingery. Ceramics and Civilization, Vol. 1. Columbus, Ohio: American Ceramic Society.

1987a "Lowland Maya Pottery in the Late Classic Period." Pp. 525–543 in *Maya Ceramics: Papers from the 1985 Maya Ceramic Conference, Part II*, edited by P. M. Rice and R. J. Sharer. Oxford: BAR International Series 345(ii).

1987b *Pottery Analysis: A Sourcebook*. Chicago: University of Chicago Press.

Roys, Ralph L.

1939 *The Titles of Ebtun*. Publication No. 505. Washington, D.C.: Carnegie Institution.

1943 *The Indian Background of Colonial Yucatan*. Publication No. 548. Washington, D.C.: Carnegie Institution.

1957 *The Political Geography of the Yucatan Maya*. Publication No. 613. Washington, D.C.: Carnegie Institution.

Sabloff, Jeremy A.

1986 "Interaction among Classic Maya Polities: A Preliminary Examination." Pp. 109–116 in *Peer Polity Interaction and Socio-political Change*, edited by C. Renfrew and J. F. Cherry. Cambridge: Cambridge University Press.

Sabloff, Jeremy, and William L. Rathje

1975 "The Rise of a Maya Merchant Class." *Scientific American* 233(4): 72–82.

Sahlins, Marshall D.

1972 *Stone Age Economics*. Chicago: Aldine.

Sanders, William T.

1981 "Classic Maya Settlement Patterns and Ethnographic Analogy." Pp. 351–369n *Lowland Maya Settlement Patterns*, edited by W. Ashmore. Albuquerque: University of New Mexico Press.

Sanders, William T., and Barbara J. Price

1968 *Mesoamerica: The Evolution of a Civilization*. New York: Random House.

Shafer, Harry J., and Thomas R. Hester

1983 "Ancient Maya Chert Workshops in Northern Belize, Central America." *American Antiquity* 48: 519–543.

1986 "Maya Stone-Tool Craft Specialization and Production at Colha, Belize: Reply to Mallory." *American Antiquity* 51: 158–166.

Sharer, Robert J.

1993 "The Social Organization of the Late Classic Maya: Problems of Definition and Approaches." Pp. 91–109 in *Lowland Maya Civilization in the Eighth Century A.D.*, edited by J. A. Sabloff and J. S. Henderson. Washington, D.C.: Dumbarton Oaks.

1994 *The Ancient Maya*. 5th ed. Stanford, Calif.: Stanford University Press.

Sinopoli, Carla M.

1988 "The Organization of Craft Production at Vijayanagara, South India." *American Anthropologist* 90: 580–597.

Stuart, David

1993 "Historical Inscriptions and the Maya Collapse." Pp. 321–354 in *Lowland Maya Civilization in the Eighth Century A.D.*, edited by J. A. Sabloff and J. S. Henderson. Washington, D.C.: Dumbarton Oaks.

1995 "A Study of Maya Inscriptions." Unpublished Ph.D. dissertation, Vanderbilt University, Nashville. Ann Arbor, Mich.: University Microfilms.

Tourtellot, Gair, and Jeremy A. Sabloff
  1972 "Exchange Systems among the Ancient Maya." *American Antiquity* 37: 126–135.
Van der Leeuw, Sander E., and Alison C. Pritchard, editors
  1984 *The Many Dimensions of Pottery: Ceramics in Archaeology and Anthropology.* CINGULA 7. Amsterdam: Institute for Pre- and Proto-history, University of Amsterdam.
Voorhies, Barbara
  1982 "An Ecological Model of the Early Maya of the Central Lowlands." Pp. 65–95 in *Maya Subsistence: Studies in Memory of Dennis E. Puleston*, edited by K. V. Flannery. New York: Academic Press.
Webster, David
  1989 "Introduction: The House of the Bacabs, Copan, Honduras." Pp. 1–4 in *The House of the Bacabs,Copan, Honduras*, edited by David Webster. Washington, D.C.: Dumbarton Oaks.

Chapter Nine

Modes of Exchange and Regional Patterns: Chunchucmil, Yucatan

Bruce H. Dahlin and Traci Ardren

Introduction

Many Maya archaeologists accept some variant or another of the regal/ritual model as a general representation of the political and economic organization of Classic lowland Maya polities. This is particularly true for investigators of sites that are characterized by large and lavish architecture (Fox 1987; de Montmollin 1989; Sanders and Webster 1988; Hendon 1991; Ball and Taschek 1992; Ringle and Bey 1992; McAnany 1993, 1995; Chase and Chase 1996; Demarest 1996; Fox et al. 1996; Haviland 1997). The regal/ritual model is rich in ethnographic detail relative to most archaeological models, as it derives from ethnohistoric and ethnographic analogies from Africa, Southeast Asia, and South Asia (Southall 1956, 1991; Fox 1977; Ball and Taschek 1992; Marcus and Feinman 1998). It has support in the lowland Maya artistic, hieroglyphic, and architectural patterns, settlement patterns, urban layouts, and by the distribution of some diagnostic artifacts.

A critical feature of the regal/ritual model as it is applied to the lowland Maya is the lack of a well-developed economy. Maya regal/ritual centers were central places in regional settlement hierarchies with respect to political and economic organization. They were primarily loci of consumption and the redistribution of prestige goods and services gained either through elite gift exchanges or through trade with foreigners to the regal/ritual tradition, such as itinerant Putun (or Chontal) Maya or Central Mexicans (Ball and Taschek 1992). In such models, however, Maya cities were not central places with respect to commercial craft production and market trade because evidence for craft specialization within political centers is scarce and appears geared toward production of items that legitimated authority and conferred prestige. Market-oriented production of lower-value utilitarian items, including everyday pottery, stone tools, and raw materials, is not documented at political centers and was dispersed among settlements in the countryside that organized labor primarily at the kin group level (McAnany 1995). Many households were capable of self-sufficiency outside of urban centers, although local production and exchange systems between communities are documented for essential household items (McAnany and Isaac 1989; Rands and Bishop 1980; Rice 1987).

Under grants from the National Science Foundation, the National Geographic Society, and Howard University, mapping, survey, and some excavation data at and around the northwest Yucatecan site of Chunchucmil (figure 9.1) reveals an organization and function that departs significantly from the regal/ritual model. We will present and discuss evidence in this chapter that Chunchucmil derived its unique organizational principles and regional relationships from two different but complementary modes of exchange. The first of these, border market exchange, facilitated long- and medium-distance trade between one of the most vigorous coastal pan-Mesoamerican trade routes and interior Classic Maya sites on the Yucatecan northern plains and Puuc regions. The second, market exchange, facilitated local and short-distance trade in staple items. According to Blanton (1983: 55), a border market involves face-to-face barter (or gift-giving exchanges). Such markets are located along cultural frontiers where people and commodities flow freely across social barriers and where products come from different environmental settings. Our data allow identification of Chunchucmil as a specific kind of border market: It displays all the essential criteria of a gateway community (Hirth 1978; also see Kepecs et al. 1994). The regal/ritual center model assumes that market exchange did not occur because all households were more or less self-sufficient in producing the necessities of life (Blanton 1985; Ball and Taschek 1992). In contrast, at Chunchucmil, market exchange in petty commodities was vital to its very survival.

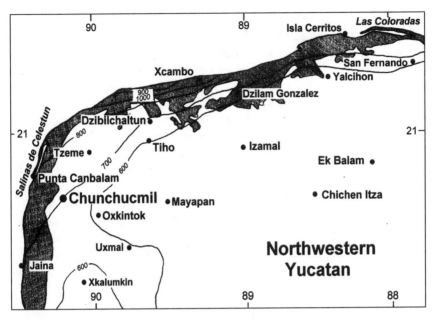

Fig. 9.1. Map of Northwestern Yucatan with the locations of important sites noted in the text. According to INEGI's (1982) thematic map, *Uso Potencial Agricultura*, the shaded area along the coast is unsuited to agriculture due to problems with soil quality and water supply.

The Model of Gateway/Semiperipheral Sites

Border markets are found in much of Mesoamerica, but, except for Chunchucmil, they have not yet been recognized as such in the Maya lowlands. Nor have gateway communities been thus far identified in the Maya lowlands although this robust model has been applied to some of the oldest complex settlements in Mesoamerica. Trade—more precisely, elite gift exchange—was an important organizational link between regions as early as the Early Formative period. Interregional exchanges were accomplished through trading partners who tended to be heads of elite lineages (Flannery 1968; Hirth 1978). By the beginning of the Mesoamerican Middle Formative period, however, elite lineage heads situated at sites standing between important trade routes and more distant centers of consumption for those trade goods began to attract more trading partners. The sites they occupied emerged as specialized nodes of economic activities (Hirth 1978).

Gateways have seven identifying characteristics. First, they are distribution nodes standing between major trade routes and distinct cultural or natural regions, where the flow of merchandise into and out of these regions can be controlled. Second, this is typically along shear lines where cost factors change and where there are economic discontinuities in the free movement of merchandise (Hirth 1978: 38), such as along coastlines or rivers. Third, gateways are located at the edge of their hinterlands rather than in central places. Settlement is therefore asymmetrical or fan-shaped, with the handle of the fan reaching from the trade route to the gateway and sites on the other side of the gateway fanning out across the landscape forming dendritic market networks. Fourth, insofar as gateways function to satisfy demand for commodities through trade, members of its merchant factors operate as middlemen offering wholesale, retail, and service functions. Therefore, they often have facilities that enhance trade and bulk transportation such as streets, canals, way stations (see below), warehouses, and marketplaces. For example, at Chalcatzingo, Grove et al. (1976) found indirect evidence for merchant specialists and large buildings that may have served as specialized trade-related warehouse facilities (Hirth 1978: 44). Fifth, gateways become a price-setting market insofar as dendritic market networks focus or converge on them. Moreover, resident merchant factors operating out of gateways have direct access and can divert at least a share of trade goods for their own consumption rather than passing them on in their entirety to other consumption centers. Therefore, one expects higher levels of consumption of portable wealth items than at regal/ritual centers. Sixth, although it is long-distance trade that creates the asymmetrical and dendritic hinterland settlement distributions, gateways may function as redistributive central places within their own physiographic regions (Hirth 1978: 38). Short-distance markets develop as the value of servicing long- and medium-distance trade reaches or exceeds levels that produce wealth comparable to that generated by the control of agricultural land. In effect, mercantile urban elites exchange part of their wealth with the rural populace who produce for urban markets (Sanders and Webster 1988). Thus, gateways often provide opportunities for commercial production of staples to provision local specialized craft producers and service industries. The distribution of wealth among its social strata may appear more egalitarian than at regal/ritual centers where most wealth is concentrated at the top of the hierarchy. This true petty economy may emerge as a result of overpopulation, that is, a local, urban, and perhaps even regional population that has grown to exceed agricultural carrying capacity. Seventh, a series of gateways develops dynamically along a moving frontier of settlement (such as the nineteenth-century frontier towns that sprang up as the American and Canadian frontier moved progressively westward throughout the Midwest; see Burghardt 1971). Alternatively, if the frontier is stationary and they can retain the ability to control the flows of long-distance trade goods, they continue to perform all of their service functions as a gateway city. In the dynamic situation, as newer gateways develop, settlement distribution in former gateway regions may ultimately approximate the classic central place distribution and hierarchy of centers (Burghardt 1971: 273). On the other hand, a gateway can continue to dominate the regional site hierarchy if the frontier is stationary and its tributary areas remain small and unproductive enough to preclude the support of other competitive central place service sites. We would like to add an eighth characteristic. To the extent that gateways are strategically located along vigorous long-distance trade routes, gateway cities are virtually synonymous with semiperipheral sites in world system parlance (Schortman 1989; Schortman and Urban 1992, 1994; Hirth 1992; Kepecs et al. 1994; Blanton and Feinman 1984; Frank 1991, 1993; Chase-Dunn and Hall 1991; Hall and Chase-Dunn 1993). This means that not only do gateway/semiperipheral sites act as conduits for exotic raw materials and finished goods, they function as both conveyors and filters of foreign ideas that impact heavily on the very structure of their economic, political, social, and ideological institutions. As a result, gateway/semiperipheral sites may have combined traits associated with participation in the Mesoamerican world system with elements derived from the more traditional regional system from which they originated. That is, many cultural patterns may be extraordinary variations on traditional themes but other patterns may be entirely new.

Chunchucmil as a Gateway/ Semiperipheral Site

Landscape and Cityscape

Chunchucmil's cityscape is so different from the typical regal/ ritual pattern that we were first inclined to the hypothesis that it was not even ethnically Yucatecan Maya, but perhaps an extension of the Chontal Maya (Scholes and Roys 1948; Thompson 1970). However, we could find no convincing cultural patterns at any specific site or set of related sites that might have been the source of borrowed traits.

Instead, as survey data accumulated both in the region and in the site proper, they increasingly approximated the gateway model. What follows in this section is an admittedly selective list of traits that suggest the operation of two modes of exchange proposed for Chunchucmil and their importance.

The Gulf Coast participated in one of Mesoamerica's most vigorous Classic period maritime trade routes, connecting nuclear areas in the Mexican highlands and southern Maya lowlands with Yucatan, the Caribbean, and lower Central America (figure 9.1). Chunchucmil had a port facility on the Gulf Coast, Punta Canbala (Andrews 1977, 1990; Dahlin et al. 1998). In addition to having a vast inland market for their goods, coastal traders had at least three other reasons for stopping at Punta Canbalam. First, it was the last protected harbor for at least another 100 kilometers to the north; therefore it would have been an important layover and provisioning port. Second, Punta Canbalam commanded the mouth of the Rio Celestun, a slow-moving, brackish lagoon separating what is now the Celestun peninsula from the mainland. However, these lagoons and low, unconsolidated sand dunes are unstable; periodically today they provide an all-weather protected passage open to canoe traffic all the way to Progreso on the northern coast (Dahlin et al. 1998). Third, Punta Canbalam had its own highly desired product—salt—as it is adjacent to the Celestun Salinas, the second-largest salt works in all of Mesoamerica (A. Andrews 1983; G. Andrews 1997; Dahlin et al. 1998). There can be no doubt that salt was produced in the Celestun Salinas in quantities that exceeded domestic needs (A. Andrews 1981, 1983; G. Andrews 1997; Bezanilla 1995). This trend also characterized the Yucatecan and Belizean coasts (Graham 1987; McKillop 1995, 1996). The Celestun Salinas would have provided the Chunchucmil economic region with considerable wealth. Indeed, Punta Canbalam's artifact inventory is incredibly rich in obsidian of all kinds, jade, and fine foreign ceramics. Merchants from nuclear Mesoamerica wanting only to bring salt home with them needed to go no farther, that is, they need not have gone all the way to the largest Mesoamerican salinas on Yucatan's north coast. Thus, Chunchucmil, with its outlier, Punta Canbalam, not only was situated along a vigorous trade route and stood at a shear line where cost factors could be controlled, it could also have partially controlled long-distance trade in salt.

Chunchucmil is near the geographic center of its economic region. We purposefully defined this 2,500km^2 area so that it would include all of the resource zones within easy reach of Chunchucmil. This potential catchment area is environmentally diverse, with cultivable land to the east and uncultivable but highly productive savanna, estuary, and marine zones to the west (figure 9.2). Chunchucmil could therefore have served a central place function with respect to the collection and distribution of regional resources. That it was a primate city in these service functions is clear from the rather flattened regional settlement hierarchy. There are no sites that resemble Rank II sites in the region, only Rank III and IV sites. Nine Rank IV sites are known in the roughly 1,000km² area to the west, and four of them are on the coast. No less than 32 Rank III and IV sites were recorded within just a 10km radius to the east by the *Atlas Arqueológico del Estado de Yucatan* (Garza and Kurjack 1980) and by our own initial reconnaissance. Presumably, if competing sites developed central place functions in the regional settlement system, another large site

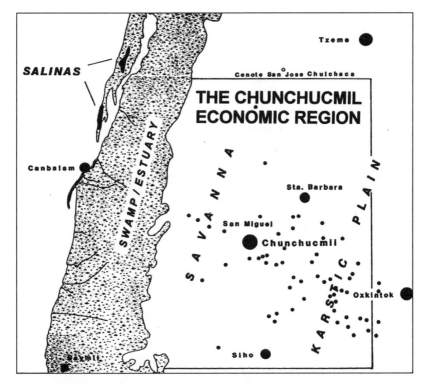

Fig. 9.2. Map of the environmental zones and asymmetrical settlement distribution within the Chunchucmil Economic Region. The large savanna zone grades imperceptibly into the arable karstic plains toward the east and cannot be delimited with a sharp boundary.

would have been located 10 to 15km to the east, surrounded by the overwhelming majority of the region's tributary sites and presumably its agricultural sustaining area. However, Chunchucmil is located as close to the Gulf of Mexico as a large site could possibly be, as the broad band of coastal wetlands could support only small settlements. Sites in the wetlands are confined to constantly shifting beach sands, as at Punta Canbalam, or rare and small microtopographic highs (~0.5m) amid permanent or wet-season floodwater. The terrain surrounding 15Q-f(9):36 (Rancho San Simon), for example, floods annually to a depth of ~80cm for months at a time. Therefore, Chunchucmil is centrally located with respect to the full variety of environmental resources including the western coast and its estuaries, the savanna, and the central and eastern agricultural lands. Some method of collecting and distributing these diverse regional resources would have to be devised and Chunchucmil's location suggests its involvement in these activities.

Settlement therefore is off-center or asymmetrical, and fan-shaped, for both environmental and trade-related reasons. The handle of the fan reached from the salinas and Gulf Coast maritime trade route to the west of Chunchucmil across to cultivable land and a network of sites on the east that extended into the heart of the western northern plains and Puuc zone to the east. It is also clear that Chunchucmil occupied an important position and functioned as a gateway until the moment of its abandonment. Were this not the case, one of several settlement arrangements would have eclipsed it and this would be immediately obvious from settlement survey data (Burghardt 1971: 272–273).

The Chunchucmil Economic Region is physically integrated by several connective features that are readily interpretable as transportation facilities. First, the Gulf Coast is intersected by several natural and man-made channels cut through the swamp/estuary (Dahlin et al. 1998; also see Guderjan 1995 for possible man-made canals in northern Belize). Millet (1981) presents good evidence that these canals were all dug in the historic era. However, Dahlin et al. (1998) argue that it is highly likely that the canals were placed over preexisting natural drainage channels (draining the Yucatan aquifer) and perhaps man-made channels dating to the Classic period. Today, they are navigable for several kilometers, but with a moderate amount of cleaning they would extend for several more kilometers to accommodate cargo canoes and would lower bulk transport costs for at least this part of the journey inland. A second type of transport facility may be represented by four of the six known savanna sites that stretch in a straight line, as if along a trail, from the headwaters of the <13km-long La Venezia canal directly to Chunchucmil. The fact that the surrounding terrain of all four sites floods to such depths in the wet season leads us to the strong suspicion that they were not totally self-sufficient in agriculture and were involved at least part-time (during dry seasons) in servicing caravans of tumpline porters. Similar way stations or *sitios de paso* are strung out in the savanna along the north coast (Miguel Covarrubias, personal communication 1998).

Caravans entering the city took advantage of a third kind of transport facility. Almost all of Chunchucmil's residential zone is laced with property boundary walls *(albarradas)* around residential units. Most of these units use a common wall between them. Settlement packing is so tight, however, that movement within the city could only be achieved by means of a unique network of 3- to 4m-wide *callejuelas*, or streets (figure 9.3). Classic period *callejuelas* have so far only been reported at Dzibilchaltun (Kurjack and Garza 1981: 297) and Coba (Gallareta 1984) but they are a common urban trait at Late Postclassic sites like Mayapan (Bullard 1954) and Tulum (Vargas et al. 1985). Chunchucmil's *callejuelas* wind around residential units or clusters of residential units in the site center, but a few of them radiate out for long distances to the site's hinterlands. This latter radial pattern indicates that at least some *callejuelas* were intended primarily to organize traffic between the heart of the city and destinations beyond the urban core. Mapping and excavations are not yet at a point where we can say that the city developed a sectorial plan (Marcus 2000: 52–54) with distinct central business and manufacturing districts and residential districts stratified by status. However, it is clear that access to open, public spaces in the epicenter was largely unimpeded. On the other hand, urban residents in outer, residential, concentric zones could not go across town easily, as no grid plan or cross-streets exist to facilitate such movement. Access to the radial *callejuelas* as well as to adjacent or nearby residential units could be gained only by climbing over a neighbor's wall or by way of *cul de sacs* or *callejones* that branch off the *callejuelas*. Therefore, if one wanted to go across town, one would have to either trespass through others' yards or go all the way downtown and back out again on another *callejuela*.

There are at least two features of Chunchucmil's *sacbeob* that suggest that they, too, carried rather mundane traffic. The 1km-long Sacbe 1, for example, begins in the heart of the city and ends formally at

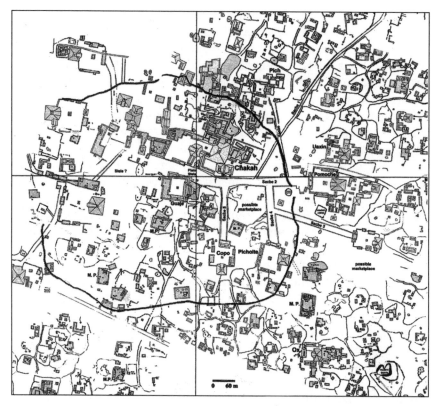

Fig. 9.3. Chunchucmil's urban design, showing some of the city's unusual features, such as *albarradas*, *callejuelas*, *sacbeob*, named patio quadrangle groups, the lack of public ritual spaces, and two of several possible marketplace locations. Mapping of the site center is still in process, so this map is incomplete.

an open space associated with a large (unnamed) temple-dominated residential unit (not shown on figure 9.3), whereupon it connects with a *callejuela* that runs for another 300m into unmapped terrain to the northeast. No doubt it carried pedestrian traffic to the very edge of the city. Sacbe 1 (as well as some other *sacbeob*) also has *albarradas* placed flush against its edge. In other cases, a space, or "'fairway," was left between them, but these *albarradas* indicate that property owners adjacent to *sacbeob* and *callejuelas* felt it necessary to send a message to travelers to "stay out of my yard." Because this feature of walled yards is not typical of most ancient Maya site plans at presumably more homogenous communities, this message may have been sent if routine travelers were strangers to the neighborhoods and communities through which these transportation arteries passed. Thus, the radial pattern of *callejuelas*, *callejones*, and *sacbeob* informs us that the destination of inhabitants and visitors to the city alike was the downtown area and that a significant number of these visitors were probably neither community members nor neighbors.

Who were these visitors to the heart of the city? It is highly unlikely that they came to witness or celebrate communal rituals of the kind implied by the formal open plazas typical of regal/ritual centers, which Demarest (1992, following Geertz 1980) interestingly characterizes as theater states, nor simply to avail themselves of civic offices. While the epicenter does indeed contain open spaces where masses of people could congregate to witness communal rituals, they are decidedly amorphous and have none of the usual architectonic trappings of public ritual spaces. Most are not built up as formal plaza areas; indeed, most of these open spaces occur on open, undulating bedrock pavements that often flood after rains. They are not bounded by impressive temple pyramids or palaces but are often segregated from adjacent residential groups by *albarradas* or the backs of buildings. They are not graced with elaborate and awe-inspiring sculpture; we have seen only one possible plain stela in such places, and while other plain stelae exist at the site, they were all placed in the parochial spaces that we feel were associated with lineage monuments (patio quadrangles). In fact, these expansive central spaces do not even provide particularly good vistas of the temple pyramids where most liturgical dramas in regal/ritual centers usually took place. The backs and sides of the largest central temple pyramids are as likely to be shown to people in these open spaces as the fronts. Indeed, one cannot easily get close to the fronts of pyramids, a matter we will return to later.

Artifacts

Sourcing imported artifacts or their parent materials is obviously an important key in understanding the role of long-distance exchange. Mapping differential patterns of production and consumption in a site's households is also important. So far we have every indication that Chunchucmil enjoyed an extraordinarily high level of prosperity in portable wealth objects. Punta Canbalam's richness is also evident as the site was destroyed by rising sea levels and wave action and its millions of water-worn artifacts have been strewn on the beaches and in the water offshore for a total of 9.8km (Dahlin et al.

1998). Its cultural inventory is incredibly rich in imported exotics, including cherts, obsidians (green, brown, gray, and black), and fragments of mold-made figurines and jades. The surfaces of all ceramics are highly eroded from centuries of weathering in the open sea. Nevertheless, Fernando Robles was able to identify surprising amounts of imported pottery on the basis of pastes alone, such as plumbates and fine oranges and greys, including Silho. Robles also identified large numbers of imported polychromes and other exotics in our surface collection from the heavily looted coastal port of Isla Uaymil. As on the Belizean coast (see McKillop 1996), the richness of Late/Terminal Classic coastal sites strongly indicates that coastal and near-coastal sites benefited from vigorous maritime trade.

Artifacts recovered in very limited excavations in 1998 at Chunchucmil suggest that its urban elites were also well supplied with luxury and utilitarian goods of foreign origin. Test excavations in middens at two modest platform groups suggest that midlevel elites were well supplied with imported marine shell jewelry, a large amount of obsidian (including at least two varieties from Central Mexico), and other imported flaked stone. The wealth of Early Classic Burial 2, for example, far exceeded our expectations for an inconspicuous 2m-high residential mound (Hutson 2000). The occupant of Burial 2 was interred under a thick plaster floor with five elaborate vessels, one of which contained an ancestor bundle. Another vessel was carved with an Early Classic hieroglyphic inscription. Over fifty jade and shell beads were recovered from the burial that was covered in a rich layer of specular hematite. While the vessels appear to be largely regional in manufacture, they represent some of the finest examples of elite wares from the northern lowlands. The iconography of the jades and ceramics demonstrates direct participation in the institutions of Maya elite culture and prestige goods exchange.

Our preliminary data from Chunchucmil represent a variety of residential and elite-oriented contexts. The cultural inventory at Chunchucmil's port facility, Punta Canbalam, and Uaymil (Dahlin et al. 1998) also parallels that of Chunchucmil itself.

A Possible Market Economy

Possible Marketplaces

Chunchucmil's access to diverse environmental zones, its large population, and the fact that its regional agricultural potential was extremely limited (Beach 1998) are factors that strongly suggest it served as a center for the collection and distribution of a variety of foodstuffs and luxury and utilitarian items. While the exchange of these regional necessities can be arranged by a number of exchange mechanisms, we have reason to think that they were circulated by means of a market system. We have therefore been on the lookout for possible marketplaces.

A market economy can operate without marketplaces, but the obvious first place to look for a market economy is in open spaces with easy access. We are exploring the provisional hypothesis that the central open spaces referred to earlier were in fact marketplaces. Some of them were deliberately fashioned but we hesitate to identify them as plazas intended to host congregations witnessing public ceremonies. For example, between the Chakah and Guaje groups (figure 9.3), a 30- to 40m-wide open space exists that was an extension of Sacbe 2. It is here that the previously mentioned stela was found. Similarly, the large block bordered by Sacbeob 2, 4, and 5 was artificially flattened. However, these spaces lack other trappings of a ceremonial plaza and could have hosted market exchange. Other, informally bounded open spaces in the site center could be interpreted as private infields, gardens, orchards, etc., belonging to downtown elite households, except for the fact that *callejuelas* empty into them. Because both types of open spaces were deliberately accessed by *callejuelas* and *sacbeob*, they no doubt served some public functions, but, lacking elaborate architecture, credible alternative hypotheses turn toward the mundane, and given the richness of Chunchucmil's artifact inventory, a marketplace function seems likely.

Agricultural Productivity and Population Estimates

Assessments of population levels, carrying capacity, and subsistence systems in the region are currently being prepared, and our preliminary results are summarized here. Judging from the ubiquity of metates in all residential units, maize was the staple that filled everyone's bellies. However, even under the best of conditions, Chunchucmil's urbanites must have imported maize into the city. Agricultural productivity throughout the surrounding region is among the lowest in the Maya lowlands (Vlcek et al. 1978; Beach 1998) due to a precarious precipitation regime and deficient soils. A total of 640 to 900mm of precipitation is regionally available in an average growing season—a barely adequate amount for maize—and a high percentage is lost in seepage through the permeable limestone bedrock and in evapotranspiration. Therefore, there is a very high mean annual water budget deficit of 600 to 700mm. Rainfall is also unpredictable due to highly localized convectional thunderstorm activity and hurricanes, recurring on average every eight to nine years (INEGI 1983). Moreover, about 80 percent of the present-day landscape has thin to no soil; 50 percent of the landscape is bare bedrock (Isphording and Wilson 1973) and 30 percent has soils that restrict nutrient uptake and soil moisture capacity (Beach 1998). At most, only 20 percent of the contemporary landscape has relatively thick, fertile, black, clay loam and moisture-conserving soils. However, a significant fraction of these superior soils developed just over the last 1,000 years on long-abandoned mounds and plazas. Therefore, something less than 20 percent of the best zonal soils would have been available to the Classic Maya who built and used these buildings. There is no reason to think that growing conditions were any better in the past (Isphording and Wilson 1973; Wilson 1980; Dunning 1992; Farrell et al. 1996; Beach 1998). Paleoecological analyses at Cenote San Jose Chulchaca, 24km north of Chunchucmil, indicate neither significant climate ameliorations nor terrestrial soil loss; soils were as thin and at least as sparse in antiquity as they are today (Isphording and Wilson 1973; Dahlin et al. 1992; Leyden et al. 1996; Beach 1998).

Interestingly, two crops that thrive on the ubiquitous limestone pavements and thin soils in the region are *nopal* (*Opuntia ficus*) and *henequen* (*Agave fourcroydes*). Nopal and henequen have no nutritive value, but other native agaves are rich in sugars (Parsons and Parsons 1990; Evans 1992). However, both nopal and agaves have important commercial products, especially nopal that hosts the *Dactilopius coccus* beetle, the source of the dye cochineal (Borrego E. and Burgos V. 1986). We suspect that both were cultivated in *solares* enclosed by *albarradas*, and the efforts to enclose these spaces indicate that *solares* were economically productive pieces of the landscape.

The generally poor agricultural potential of the region stands in marked contrast with its huge population. This assessment is based on the following reasoning. We have already alluded to the fact that almost all of Chunchucmil's residential groups are surrounded by *albarradas*, or residential boundary walls (also see Magnoni 1995; Dahlin et al. 1998). Among other things, these hard boundaries allow accurate delimitation of residential units so that we can ultimately discriminate who was living with whom as well as calculate the amount of land, types of soils, and access to water and lithic materials within each residential unit. Vlcek et al. (1978) counted ~2,400 *solares* (or yards surrounding domestic buildings; see Goni Motilla 1993) in the central 6km² area, or ~4 solares per ha. Assuming that each solar represents a single household averaging five persons (a commonly used factor, e.g., Becquelin and Michelet 1994, although most solares clearly had more than a single nuclear family), each family in downtown Chunchucmil had ~0.25ha available to it. Since maize productivity in the region is ca. 0.25 to 1.0m tons/ ha and since a Maya family of five consumes a little more than a metric ton of maize per year under subsistence conditions (at Piste and Komchen, see Shuman 1974; in the Puuc, see Smyth 1991), a family's annual requirements are between 1 and 4ha actually under production. Even without subtracting for fallowing and the area taken up by buildings and activity areas (estimated by Killion at ~60 percent of the average solar, 1992: 129–130), an extremely crude (and conservative) estimate of the average family's land needs to be self-sufficient in maize production would be ~4 to 16 times the amount of land in a typical household unit. Either Chunchucmil's urban residents were self-sufficient in outfield production or someone else outside the city was exporting critical surpluses of staple foods to Chunchucmil's urban markets.

Agricultural self-sufficiency in outfield production is problematic. Vlcek et al. (1978) estimated that the population of the central 6km² was ~12,000 (if each 0.25ha solar was occupied by just one household numbering five persons each). They further estimated 8,000 and 18,000 persons in an outer 13km² rural zone, for a greater Chunchucmil population of 20,000 and 30,000 persons and an overall population density of between 1,540 and 2,300 persons per km². Our own reconnaissance and detailed mapping since then indicate that Chunchucmil's Classic period population could be easily twice their figure, but until we can accumulate more accurate figures, we will use the original estimates of Vlcek et al. With an urban population of 20,000 to 30,000, Chunchucmil would have needed a total of 4,000 to 24,000ha of maize under production in any given year. However, fields can only be used for about two years without significant yield declines due to soil nutrient depletion and weed competition and are fallowed for ten to twelve years, although *milperos* have recently reduced fallow times with the advent of chemical inputs. Using chemical inputs and assuming contemporary indigenous fallow practices, then, 240 to 1,680km² of cultivable land would have to have been available to feed Chunchucmil's urban population, but it is doubtful that amount of land was available in the region. Much of the 1600km^2 of the cultivable karstic plains we have defined as our study region was well within the catchment area of other sites like Oxkintok, 26km to the ESE (Misión Arqueólogica de España en México, Proyecto Oxkintok 1987–90), and Siho 17km to the south (Dunning and Andrews 1994). Our provisional estimates of the land needs of Chunchucmil's urbanites are in addition to the land needs of the rural population as well as the populations of scores of secondary and tertiary sites. Moreover, *milpa* productivity today greatly exaggerates Classic period productivity because with virtually no land pressures today's *milperos* have more options and can be selective about where they place their *milpas*. For example, they can maximize fertility and soil depths, avoid planting on the 50 percent of the land that is limestone pavement, and plant in the fertile soils recently developed on abandoned Classic period building slopes.

All of these factors suggest that the region's agricultural carrying capacity was seriously challenged, even given the obvious problems with accurately estimating both archaeological populations and carrying capacities. Even if the threshold between self-sufficiency and dependence on imported staple commodities had not been passed, however, it seems safe to hypothesize that regional agriculture involved both substantial labor investments in intensification and a narrow margin of safety in a densely populated and fluctuating environment leading to considerable subsistence risk. A common risk-minimization strategy in the face of agricultural uncertainty is diversification of crop production in different microenvironmental zones and in nonagrarian pursuits, including craft production (Netting 1990). Moreover, at high levels of agricultural intensification, labor requirements may become so odious that households begin to obtain some desired items from specialists who are more skilled. These specialists can turn out common household products at low enough cost that purchasing them in the market is preferable to making them in the home (Blanton 1983; Hirth 1998). Therefore, strategies of risk reduction and labor-saving practices can lead to market production and exchange.

The Chunchucmil Economic Region was ideally suited to generate a variety of important food stuffs, raw materials, and utilitarian items that could sustain Chunchucmil's urban population. The surrounding 2500km^2 region is environmentally heterogeneous with several closely spaced resource zones, each offering large amounts of high quality nutritional supplements (including protein and fats) and other useful, desirable, or essential raw materials. The 5- to 15km-wide savanna immediately to the west supplies game, fruit and nuts, and cordage materials (palms for roof thatch, vines and grasses for bundling materials, etc.); modern villagers consider savanna forage products critical to their livelihood. The savanna grades into a spring-fed, mangrove-dominated wetland rich in shellfish and game animals (e.g., birds, jaguar, manatee, monkeys, and crocodiles), hardwoods, dyes, and cordage materials. The Gulf Coast is rich in highly valued resources like salt, marine mammals, and abundant fresh- and salt-water fish and shellfish, as well as sting ray spines, decorative feathers, shell, and coral (e.g., Lange 1971). While direct evidence for regional exchange systems is notoriously difficult to identify (Costin 1991), particularly for perishable items, there is at least some evidence at the site of Uaymil. At this location, *manos* and metates in numbers consistent with maize processing for domestic consumption have been found in looters' pits (Dahlin et al. 1998). Uaymil is located deep in the estuary where neither stone nor maize could be obtained locally.

Specialized Production Implied by Metate Distributions

Metates have long been ignored as uninformative in the Maya lowlands, yet we view them as key to understanding one of the unique aspects of Chunchucmil's economy. Takeshi Watanabe and Ramon Carillo Sanchez have begun to recognize a few important patterns in their cultural contexts and forms (Watanabe 2000). For example, unlike at Uaymil, several residential groups at Chunchucmil have far more metates than can be explained on the basis of maize processing for domestic consumption. One platform has 25 metates. High numbers of metates seem to be more common at a kind of architectural grouping called a platform group. It consists of a single, large platform in excess of 20m on a side and 1.5m high. Most platform groups had columns and very fine stonework but they also seem to have disproportionately suffered destruction and stone removal. We do not know why. Some platform groups are integral components of larger elite compounds, others seem to be specialized workshops involving metates. There is also a close association between these metate platforms and the open spaces we are tentatively calling marketplaces. We have found that basin metates, made of limestone boulders but with circular depressions, are more common at household groups while trough metates with a deep rectangular groove are more common at the metate platforms (Watanabe 2000). In any case, it is reasonable to hypothesize that groups that have more metates than would be necessary for maize processing for domestic consumption alone conducted some sort of production for extra-household consumption (Costin 1991). Indeed, metates are general-purpose tools that are almost always used for a variety of productive activities in addition to processing maize, such as preparing dyes, paints, fibers, seeds, and salt (Zier 1981). What was being commercially produced on Chunchucmil's metates is not yet known, but salt, cochineal, cotton seed, fermented beverages, and achiote all seem to be distinct possibilities. Our project ceramicist, Tara Bond, has recognized a disproportionate number of striated jars at metate platforms, implying that these metates were used to grind some bulk substance that was then stored or processed in a liquid form.

Some of the larger residential groups also have one or more circular grinding stones that we are calling querns. The grinding surfaces were deeply worn by a small *mano* used in a circular motion. Some of the substance(s) being milled was trapped between the sides of the *mano* and the grinding-stone walls, thus undercutting the top surface of the grinding stone, and a ~3- to 4cm-wide spillway is invariably found on one side. Querns are sometimes found near metates, but others are found in isolation. Again, we have no idea what they were used for, but some sort of specialized production intended for extra-household consumption is strongly implied.

The majority of metates at Chunchucmil and elsewhere are made from almost any available boulder of the appropriate size and shape. They tend to be large, not easily moved, and made of highly soluble limestone with deeply pitted and eroded surfaces developing over the course of the last 1,000 years. For this reason, wear patterns on metates have rarely if ever been analyzed for clues as to their functions. Chemical analyses of soils taken from around those metates that still appear to be in their original positions are being done by Timothy Beach in an effort to determine what products were processed on metates. Hopefully, palynologist John Jones will soon see if identifiable starch grains are preserved in these same soils.

Finally, a substantial number of metates are quite small (<50kg), finely shaped and finished from a relatively insoluble and predominantly pink crystallized limestone. Considerable labor went into the production of these essentially portable metates, and they seem to be found disproportionately at larger and obviously more elaborate residential groups. Their portability, the labor expended in making them, the uniformity of materials and finishing techniques, and their restricted distribution at wealthy households all suggest that they were made by craftsmen for the market.

An Economic Model of Chunchucmil

There is considerable support for Chunchucmil's function as a gateway city as well as some evidence for its role as a marketplace for local goods. We will further explore in this section how these two modes of exchange articulated with political, social, and other institutions at Chunchucmil. There is a discrepancy between Chunchucmil's huge demographic size (suggesting it may have dominated the surrounding region) and the relative lack of signature features within the site indicating political centralization and hierarchy. The *Atlas Arqueológico del Estado de Yucatan* ranked Chunchucmil as a Rank II site in the regional settlement hierarchy because it lacks the hallmarks of a cultural innovator that normally occupies the apex of a regional hierarchical settlement system. According to this ranking system, either Chunchucmil was a dependent of the closest Rank I regal/ritual center, Oxkintok, or it was a large autonomous exception to their ranking system.

A few elements expressing centrality in urban design and political organization are present but muted at Chunchucmil (Vlcek 1978; Vlcek et al.. 1978; Garza and Kurjack 1980, 1984; Kurjack and Garza 1981). Indeed, Chunchucmil's ~45ha site center is remarkably decentralized. There are simply no focal temple pyramid complexes, no imposing civic buildings, and no great ceremonial plazas specifically designed for witnessing power performances. In contrast, these same hallmarks of power are abundant at demographically smaller neighbors, like Oxkintok, Santa Barbara (10km to the north) and Uaymil in the estuary (Dahlin et al. 1998). Centrality at Chunchucmil is indicated by the presence of moderately large architecture (e.g., 8- to 18.5m-high pyramids), *sacbeob*, the convergence of *callejuelas*, the clustering of patio quadrangles, and a defensive barricade. The barricade is a very small (~1.5m high x 2–3m wide) line of unconsolidated rubble and stone robbed from all nearby buildings, *albarradas*, and *sacbeob*. Despite its 2km length, it was hastily built and clearly reflects a confused amalgam of military considerations and the balance of power between the leading lineages at the final moment of the site's existence, for Chunchucmil was attacked, pillaged, and never rebuilt

(Dahlin 2000). It was clearly not built as a permanent marker, for example, of epicentral sacred space, nor was it built as a permanent defensive feature by specialists who were well versed in the arts of war.

The focal architecture in the epicenter is what we are calling patio quadrangles. Known primarily from the Chenes region to the south at such sites as Xkichmook, Yakal Chen, and Dzehkabtun, patio quadrangles are usually found with a single example near the main temple complexes (Thompson 1898; G. Andrews 1997). We have so far positively identified fourteen of them at Chunchucmil, but there are surely more. Although there is some variation among them, they tend to be a highly formulaic arrangement of range-type structures on three sides of a rectangular patio that is dominated by a temple pyramid on the fourth side and a small performance platform in the middle. A plain stela, altar, and/or banner stone may be found in the patio. Their pyramids are among the largest buildings at the site and it is noteworthy that they front onto completely enclosed patios and not onto large, open plazas. These parochial spaces are much smaller than, and bear little resemblance to, public plazas at typical lowland Maya centers. Moreover, even though these enclosed patios may be approached by *sacbeob*, suggesting some civic or public function, access to them was carefully controlled by narrow openings between buildings. Most of them cluster in epicentral Chunchucmil, but one of them has been mapped as far away as 2km to the south.

Although the structures around the enclosed patio perimeter may have served a residential purpose, domestic activities clearly predominated around smaller and less elaborate buildings in locations behind or to the side of the patio arrangement, judging from metates found here. These private spaces are visually separated from the patio by buildings and from other spaces by *albarradas*. It is readily apparent that there was as much status differentiation within the patio quad's domestic quarters (and among the inhabitants of other large residential units) as between them (see McAnany 1993, 1995). Some patio quads almost certainly housed multi-household groups as their interior spaces are partitioned off by smaller, often partial interior walls. Such partitioning recalls McAnany's argument (1993, 1995) that large and complex residential groups include not only members of the same lineage but perhaps also discrete lineage segments, servants, slaves, serfs, and perhaps visitors. The interior walls seem to symbolically mark and partially restrict interaction between cohabiting groups as well as perhaps work spaces and infield gardens or orchards. There can be little doubt that these quadrangle complexes were the headquarters for some sort of elite corporate group (see de Montmollin 1989; McAnany 1993, 1995), and that the semiprivate spaces of the patios up front were reserved for some sort(s) of formal receptions for invited visitors.

The Chakah Group (figure 9.3) is the largest patio quadrangle at the site and most likely the seat of power for the leading lineage. It has the only ball court in downtown Chunchucmil (another is found at the San Miguel site, 4km to the west) and a complex of courtyards that look suspiciously like administrative buildings. This group also has the tallest structure at the site, which reaches a height of 18.5 meters. This size is not all that impressive for a central pyramid in sites of the northern lowlands, particularly given the enormous size of Chunchucmil's potential labor supply (Kurjack and Garza 1981: 304–305). It is also pertinent that, like other patio quadrangles, its pyramid has absolutely no public access as it faces onto a very private courtyard and away from the largest expanse of public space at the site. The Chakah Group, then, is not very different from other epicentral groups and gives every appearance of being something like a "first among equals"—a relationship to immediate subordinates that Carmean (1998) observed at Sayil—rather than the residence and ritual locus of a highly authoritarian king.

In a seminal paper in economic anthropology, Heider (1969) identifies a pattern of trade across ethnic and national borders (i.e., in border markets) that involves visiting trade institutions. Such trade is generally done by trading partners and transactions are often invested with great fanfare, ceremonialism, feasting, and dancing to extend and symbolize long-term kin-like ties between partners. These rituals emphasize intimate relationships between the parties that are akin to gift-giving in familistic generalized reciprocity (Sahlins 1972) rather than the popular notion of barter and its associated haggling (see Humphery and Hugh-Jones 1992). Such intimate relationships avoid tension and difficulties that are inherent in between-society dealings and in negative reciprocity between strangers. Given all the empirical and suggestive evidence for a heavy involvement in long-distance trade at Chunchucmil, we suggest that the formal spaces in the patio quadrangles were the formal contexts for receiving foreign traders, negotiating trade deals, performing rituals cementing trading partnerships, and bulking or warehousing trade goods. The architecture and activities of patio quadrangle elites no doubt also impressed other competing elite lineages as well as lesser, contributing lineage members who lived in Chunchucmil's hinterlands.

The multiplicity of competing elite factions of roughly equivalent status must have required informal integrating mechanisms. The model of Chunchucmil's political economy that is emerging—and we offer it as a preliminary hypothesis only—is more like a market-oriented corporate state rather than a redistributive theater state. As we are using the term here (which differs in some respects from Blanton's 1998 use of the term), in a corporate state the business of government is business, as opposed to the maintenance of community solidarity in a theater state. The paramount ruler of a corporate state resembles a chairman of the board more than a divine king and master of ceremonies. For example, one of the tasks of any political leader is to keep competition for power, wealth, and status between elite factions within bounds. Given the muted expression of kingly power and authority, however, political issues may have been resolved through negotiation in councils, trade associations, and other institutions. That these elite factions competed for power, status, and wealth is obvious in the conspicuous consumption of personal articles of clothing, jewelry, and even some household articles like finely crafted metates, to say nothing of building ostentatious quadrangular compounds downtown.

We further hypothesize that elite lineage heads competed among themselves by acting relatively autonomously in developing trading partnerships, engaging in wholesaling of long-distance trade items, and/or servicing overland and maritime trading caravans and fleets. This is a common *modus operandi* in relatively decentralized polities comprised of relatively autonomous private entrepreneurs competing for "market share" in wealth and bulk items (Renfrew 1974; Earle 1991; Kristiansen 1991; Claessen and van de Velde 1991). Dalton (1965) provides many ethnographic examples of such systems from the Pacific, China, India, and Africa. Competition among merchant groups for trading partners and market share would have been balanced by the need for cooperation among these same merchant factors to keep the exchange value of trade goods both stable and high. This kind of simultaneous cooperation and competition, or what Brandenburger and Nalebuff (1996) call *co-opetition*, is almost universal in business today. Co-opetition, for example, is why often fiercely competing companies within the same industry form cooperative trade associations. We suggest that the absence of a strong central government at Chunchucmil was based on the mutual benefits involved in co-opetition among its relatively autonomous elite merchant families (also see Kurjack and Garza 1981; Carmean 1998). This polyarchy of elites was capable of maintaining a largely tranquil environment conducive to trade across the region. Under the circumstances, a powerful and generous king may have been expensive and superfluous. Evidence suggests minor failures in this system may have occurred. In the one medium-sized quadrangle excavated so far, we have evidence that the sizable Early Classic constructions were abandoned after 600 A.D., perhaps reflecting the inability of that lineage to compete in a changing economic environment (Ardren 1999).

It is probable that most of Chunchucmil's less prestigious residents were dependent for their livelihood on production for the market and that most food and other necessities were imported from the surrounding countryside and from afar. Given these conditions, we argue that maintaining order and conformity within the city was fundamental to the smooth functioning of the marketplace. With most of the residents embedded in interdependent networks of production and exchange, norms of etiquette and respectful behavior on everyone's part were indispensable.

Although the physical layout of Chunchucmil has no parallel among known Classic period sites anywhere in the Maya lowlands, we suggest that the gateway phenomenon is more general than Chunchucmil. For example, the Yucatan peninsula was fringed by what Dunning and Andrews (1994) refer to as corridor sites. They include, among others, San Fernando, Yalcihon, Dzilam Gonzalez, Dzibilchaltun, Tzeme (Kurjack and Garza 1981), Siho, and Xcalumkin. San Fernando is even connected to Emal, its port on the northern coast, by a ~25km-long *sacbe* that is reminiscent of the connection between Canbalam and Chunchucmil via La Venezia canal and its string of way stations. Like Chunchucmil, most of these sites are found in the densely populated but agriculturally depauperate zone between the coast and the interior reaches of the peninsula. These other possible gateways need not, and do not, look exactly like Chunchucmil. Given the different strategic locations that they occupy along the Yucatecan maritime trade route, and different trading partners whom they encountered, one would expect a great deal of variation in foreign influences, just as there was among the Late Postclassic provinces of the region (Marcus 1993; Kepecs 1998). This would include variations in the modes of governance that were adopted. For example, some Classic sites such as Xcalumkin more closely approximate a regal/ritual center and were probably governed by a stronger, centralized ruler or *Ajaw* who conducted communal rituals for the commonweal from ostentatious pyramid platforms. Other sites like Dzibilchaltun, with its diminutive temple pyramids and plethora of range-type structures fronting onto public plazas, seem to have emphasized civic administration more than religious ideology or mercantilism.

We would also argue that the economic dominance of gateways set up an unusual economic interdependence between sites throughout the northern plains and, as a result, the economic organization of this large region was vastly different than that in other parts of the Maya lowlands. We base this argument primarily on an enormous paradox in northern plains settlement patterns. One of the zones of greatest population (and site) densities known anywhere in the Maya lowlands is located precisely where agricultural productivity is the most severely limited—near the margin between the low deciduous forest and low deciduous spiney forest zones with its deficient rainfall and sparse and thin soils (Flores and Espejel 1994; also see Kurjack and Andrews 1976; Andrews and Andrews 1980; Dahlin 1987, 2000). Recently, U.S.D.A. pedologist Russell Almaraz (personal communication 1998) pointed out another important inconsistency in settlement pattern that offers a resolution to this paradox: Those parts of the northern plains with the least population have the greatest agricultural potentials—the wetter portions of the low deciduous and the medium subdeciduous forest. These lands, with among the lowest population and site densities so far recorded anywhere in the Maya lowlands and an abundance of rainfall (1,000mm) and deep fertile soils, are north of the base of the Sierrita de Ticul. If this pattern holds up, we would argue that high productivity was sustained and substantial surpluses were generated by appropriately observing long fallow cycles. Nowhere is this huge area beyond the bulk transport capabilities of the Maya (see Drennan 1984a, 1984b) or more than 100km from dense population centers. Thus, we would argue that hugely overpopulated gateways relied on underpopulated inland breadbasket zones for critical subsidies of maize, and, with no access to the sea, these same inland breadbasket zones were totally dependent on gateways for marine products such as salt and fish and canoe-borne long-distance trade goods. Gateways prospered and grew well beyond their paltry local and regional carrying capacities precisely because they controlled economic activity along the coast and along overland trade routes.

Finally, there is the matter of Classic period marketplaces, the existence and nature of which are highly controversial. It is probably fair to say that many Mayanists agree with Farriss' comment that all but a small minority of the Maya (living in regal/ritual centers), before or after the conquest, were simply outside a market economy with little to sell and little need to buy (1984: 156). Nevertheless, Landa and Oviedo (Tozzer 1941: n. 424, Roys 1939: 62) report that markets were common on the northern plains during the Conquest and early Colonial periods. Classic period central marketplaces are not common but they have been tentatively identified at Tikal, Quirigua, Coba, Nohmul, Caracol, and Sayil. Peripheral markets with a catchment of ca. 20km or less have been tentatively identified at Tikal and Palenque (McAnany 1993). Even if the existence of Classic period marketplaces and Classic to Postclassic market economies is accepted, it does not necessarily mean that market exchange was in any way critical to the survival of Maya civilization. Arguing against this position is some evidence from Tikal and Palenque that pottery-making was associated with agriculturally marginal lands (Rands and Bishop 1980; Fry 1980; Ball and Taschek 1992), suggesting that production for peripheral markets was a means for some households to manage periodic or chronic food shortages (Rice 1987). Similarly, Dahlin and Litzinger (1986) attempted to show that some households in residential Tikal resorted to producing and marketing fermented consumables during hard times. Thus, it seems increasingly likely that even regal/ritual centers exhibit some reliance on local markets. The question that remains—at least for us—is how frequent and vital this reliance was for most households.

There can be little doubt that the most archaeologically conspicuous Classic Maya economy was the prestige sector with its obsidian, jade, marine shell, and exotic ceramics. However, a legitimate argument can be made that this visibility is because prestige items tend to be made of more durable stuff to improve the "store" (read "storability") of their value. Moreover, their rarity confers greater exchange values relative to something that is common and must be consumed before it decomposes. It is their durability, not necessarily their greater frequency, that makes them more archaeologically visible. On the other hand, items that circulate in petty economies tend to be highly perishable, making them archaeologically invisible. This is even more the case among tropical and subtropical peoples like the Maya whose environments rapidly destroy almost all perishable materials. If prestige economies tend to circulate predominantly durable items and are overrepresented in the archaeological record, and if perishable items circulating in petty economies are grossly underrepresented, then it seems legitimate to hypothesize that durable petty goods that have survived the ravages of time—like chert, utilitarian ceramics, and metates—are "the tip of the proverbial iceberg." Without a vigorous and systematic exploration of petty economies, it would be specious to argue anything else and so far such a study has not taken place. This enormous disparity between what we know peoples in the humid and subhumid tropics routinely use and consume in their day-to-day activities and what is preserved in the archaeological record remains a huge gap in our knowledge about ancient Maya economic organization (McAnany 1993: 65).

While it may make sense to disconnect petty and prestige economies in some archaeological situations (e.g., Brumfiel and Earle 1987; Earle 1982, 1991; Claessen and van de Velde 1991), we don't think it is justified in gateway situations. First, some objects like obsidian apparently circulated in both economic spheres. Second, some items in each sphere probably flowed in parallel fashion, much like the *kula* barter described by Leach and Leach (1983). In this barter system, exchanges of prestige items (*kula* objects) were a pretext for exchanging important petty commodities (e.g., yams). Needless to say, the yams would not show up in the archaeological record but the *kula* objects might. Third, a voluminous trade along the Gulf Coastal maritime trade route would have brought with it service opportunities of all kinds and remuneration in all forms of wealth (Rappaport 1968; Pires-Ferreira and Flannery 1976; Humphery and Hugh-Jones 1992). Food imports from beyond a region (and from within), for example, may have been acquired as direct or indirect payments for portering or bulking wealth and status items. Just this sort of situation might account for the presence of metates at Isla Uaymil. Another "cross-over" opportunity between the two economic spheres might occur when exchange equivalencies are not exact, for example, between foreign-made ceramic vessels (that are variable in quality), and hunks of coral (that are variable in size, luster, etc). Locally produced petty consumables (e.g., salt, cacao beans, cotton mantles, and achiote) could be drawn into such common transactions in the form of "change." Finally, items in one exchange sphere often enter into the other exchange sphere as a matter of necessity. Bohannon (1955) illustrates what is probably a frequent situation in which this kind of "cross-over" occurs. When a Tiv family falls on hard times it exchanges its wealth items for the food it needs, much to its shame (also see Keesing 1983). Due to the increased volume of trade funneled through gateways, this boundary between prestige and petty economic spheres was probably much more permeable and the economies more mixed than is typical of areas dominated by regal/ritual centers.

Conclusions

Located on the geographic and cultural periphery of the regal/ritual tradition, Chunchucmil was a gateway city controlling, and dependent upon, long-distance maritime trade up and down the Gulf Coast, medium-distance trade along inland routes, and short-distance trade circulating goods between its immediate regional environments. The city grew way beyond regional agricultural carrying capacity by drawing in foodstuffs and other utilitarian goods to sustain itself and enrich its leading merchant lineages, and it did so without the help of a powerful centralized authority. Exotic status and authority symbols so necessary to the redistributive and authority structures of regal/ritual centers elsewhere underwrote Chunchucmil's very support and sustenance. We argue that there were several gateway communities in Yucatan where medium- and long-distance trade constituted a vital force that shaped the basic political and economic organization of this entire portion of the northern lowlands. A similar function for trade is observed later on the east coast during the Postclassic period (Rathje and Sabloff 1973; Sabloff and Rathje 1975).

We are left with a number of important unanswered questions. For example, we have not been able to determine in the short time we have been working at the site that any given household was critically dependent on the proceeds from specialized production or marketing activities, or if it was merely moonlighting to obtain desired—as opposed to essential—items (McAnany 1986; Ball and Taschek 1992). Nor can we say whether specialized productive activities were full-time, seasonal, or part-time. We do not know if markets were regular, daily occurrences or if they were held periodically or opportunistically. We also do not know if Chunchucmil's merchant elite merely provided transport or warehousing services for professional, foreign, medium- and long-distance traders or if they were professional middlemen or wholesalers, buying and selling goods before shipping them on to their ultimate destinations. They may also have derived income from levying taxes on caravans, but this has not yet been determined. We feel confident in saying that the data thus far suggest that Chunchucmil actively participated in long-, medium-, and short-distance trade and that this trade was essential in sustaining the community at large.

References

Andrews, Anthony P.
1977 "Reconocimiento Arqueológico de la Costa Norte del Estado de Campeche." *Boletín de la Escuela de Ciencias Antropólogicas de la Universidad de Yucatan* 4(24): 64–77.
1981 "The Salt Trade of the Ancient Maya." *Archaeology* 33(4): 24–33.
1983 *Ancient Salt Production and Trade.* Tucson: University of Arizona Press.
1990 "The Role of Trading Ports in Maya Civilization." Pp. 159–168 in *Vision and Revision in Maya Studies*, edited by F. S. Clancy and P. D. Harrison. Albuquerque: University of New Mexico Press.
1997 "New Perspectives on the Prehispanic Maya Salt Trade." Paper presented at the 62nd annual meeting of the Society for American Archaeology, Nashville.

Andrews, E. Wyllys, IV, and E. Wyllys Andrews V
1980 *Excavations at Dzibilchaltun.* Publication No. 48. New Orleans: Middle American Research Institute, Tulane University.

Andrews, George
1997 *Pyramids and Palaces, Monsters and Masks.* Lancaster, Calif.: Labyrinthos.

Ardren, Traci
1999 "Chunchucmil: A Preliminary Chronology and Summary of Research." Paper presented at the annual meeting of the American Anthropological Association, Chicago.

Ball, Joseph W., and Jennifer T. Taschek
1992 "Economics and Economies in the Late Classic Maya Lowlands: A Trial Examination of Some Apparent Patterns and Their Implications." Paper presented at the Wenner-Gren Segmentary State Symposium at Cleveland State University.

Beach, Timothy
1998 "Soil Constraints on Northwest Yucatán: Pedo Archaeology and Subsistence at Chunchucmil." *Geoarchaeology* 13: 759–791.

Becquelin, Pierre, and D. Michelet
1994 "Demografia en la Zona Puuc: el Recurso del Metodo." *Latin American Antiquity* 5(4): 289–311.

Bezanilla, Clara I.
1995 "Salt-Making in Celestún, Yucatan (Mexico): Contemporary Evidence and Archaeological Problems." B.A. thesis, Institute of Archaeology, University College London.

Blanton, Richard
1983 "Factors Underlying the Origin and Evolution of Market Systems." Pp. 51–66 in *Economic Anthropology: Topics and Theories.* Monographs in Economic Anthropology No. 1, edited by S. Ortiz. Society for Economic Anthropology. Lanham, Md.: University Press of America.

1985 "A Comparison of Early Market Systems." Pp. 399–416 in *Markets and Marketing*. Monographs in Economic Anthropology No. 4, edited by S. Plattner. Lanham, Md.: University Press of America.

1998 "Beyond Centralization: Steps Toward a Theory of Egalitarian Behavior in Archaic States." Pp. 135–172 in *Archaic States*, edited by Gary M. Feinman and Joyce Marcus. Santa Fe, N.M.: School of American Research Press.

Blanton, Richard, and Gary M. Feinman
1984 "The Mesoamerican World System." *American Anthropologist* 86: 673–682.

Bohannon, Paul
1955 "Some Principles of Exchange and Investment among the Tiv." *American Anthropologist* 57: 60–69.

Borrego E., F., and N. Burgos V.
1986 *El Nopal*. Saltillo, Coahuila: Universidad Autonoma Agraria Antonio Narro Buenavista.

Brandenburger, A. M., and B. J. Nalebuff
1996 *Co-opetition*. New York: Doubleday.

Brumfiel, Elizabeth M., and Timothy K. Earle
1987 "Specialization, Exchange, and Complex Societies: An Introduction." Pp. 1–9 in *Specialization, Exchange, and Complex Societies*, edited by E. M. Brumfiel and T. K. Earle. Cambridge: Cambridge University Press.

Bullard, William R., Jr.
1954 "Boundary Walls and House Plots at Mayapan." Pp. 234–253 in *Current Reports*, Vol. 1, No. 13. Washington, D.C.: Carnegie Institution.

Burghardt, A. F.
1971 "A Hypothesis about Gateway Cities." *Annals of the Association of American Geographers* 6: 269–285.

Carmean, Kelli
1998 "Leadership at Sayil: A Study of Political and Religious Decentralization." *Ancient Mesoamerica* 9: 259–270.

Chase, Arlen F., and Diane Z. Chase
1996 "More than Kin and King: Centralized Political Organization among the Late Classic Maya." *Current Anthropology* 37: 803–810.

Chase-Dunn, Christopher, and Thomas D. Hall
1991 *Core/Periphery Relations in Precapitalist Worlds*. Boulder, Colo.: Westview Press.

Claessen, Henri J. M., and Pieter van de Velde
1991 *Early State Economics*. New Brunswick, N.J.: Transaction Publishers.

Costin, Cathy L.
1991 "Craft Specialization: Issues in Defining, Documenting, and Explaining the Organization of Production." *Archaeological Method and Theory* 3: 1–56.

Dahlin, Bruce H.
1987 *Reconstructing Ancient Maya Adaptive Patterns on the Northern Plains of Yucatan, Mexico: 1986 Interim Report*. Washington, D.C.: Sociology/Anthropology Department, Howard University.

2000 "The Barricade and Abandonment of Chunchucmil: Implications for Northern Maya Warfare." *Latin American Antiquity* 11: 283–298.

Dahlin, Bruce H., Anthony P. Andrews, Timothy Beach, C. Bezanilla, P. Farrell, Susan Luzzadder-Beach, and Valerie McCormick
1998 "Punta Canbalam in Context: A Peripatetic Coastal Site in Northwest Campeche, Mexico." *Ancient Mesoamerica* 9: 1–16.
Dahlin, Bruce H., Mark Brenner, Barbara Leyden, and Jason Curtis
1992 "Preclassic and Early Classic Period Climate Change at San Jose Chulchaca, NW Yucatan, Mexico." Paper delivered at the annual meeting of the Society for American Archaeology, Pittsburgh.
Dahlin, Bruce H., and William J. Litzinger
1986 "Old Bottle, New Wine: the Function of Chultuns in the Maya Lowlands." *American Antiquity* 51(4): 721–736.
Dalton, George
1965 "Primitive Money." *American Anthropologist* 67: 44–65.
Demarest, Arthur A.
1992 "Ideology in Ancient Maya Cultural Evolution: The Dynamics of Galactic Polities." Pp. 135–158 in *Ideology and Pre-Columbian Civilizations*, edited by Arthur A. Demarest and Geoffrey W. Conrad. Santa Fe, N.M.: School of American Research Press.
1996 "Comment on: 'The Maya State: Centralized or Segmentary?' by John W. Fox, Garrett W. Cook, Arlen F. Chase, and Diane Z. Chase." *Current Anthropology* 37: 821–824.
de Montmollin, Olivier
1989 *The Archaeology of Political Structure: Settlement Analysis in a Classic Maya Polity.* Cambridge: Cambridge University Press.
Drennan, Robert D.
1984a "Long-Distance Movement of Goods in the Mesoamerican Formative and Classic." *American Antiquity* 49(1): 27–43.
1984b "Long-Distance Transport Costs in Pre-Hispanic Mesoamerica." *American Anthropologist* 86: 105–112.
Dunning, Nicholas
1992 *Lords of the Hills: Ancient Maya Settlement in the Puuc Region, Yucatan, Mexico.* Monographs in World Archaeology No. 15, Madison, Wis.: Prehistory Press.
Dunning, Nicholas, and George F. Andrews
1994 "Ancient Maya Architecture and Urbanism at Siho and the Western Puuc Region, Mexico." *Mexicon* 16(3): 53–61.
Earle, Timothy K.
1982 "The Ecology and Politics of Primitive Valuables." Pp. 65–83 in *Culture and Ecology: Eclectic Perspectives*, edited by J. G. Kennedy and R. B. Edgerton. Special Publication No. 15. Washington, D.C.: American Anthropological Association.
1991 "The Evolution of Chiefdoms." Pp. 1–15 in *Chiefdoms: Power, Economy and Ideology*, edited by Timothy Earle. New York: Cambridge University Press.
Evans, Susan T.
1992 "The Productivity of Maguey Terrace Agriculture in Central Mexico During the Aztec Period." Pp. 92–116 in *Gardens in Prehistory: The Archaeol-

ogy of Settlement Agriculture in Greater Mesoamerica, edited by Thomas W. Killion. Tuscaloosa: University of Alabama Press.

Farrell, Patricia, Timothy Beach, and Bruce. H. Dahlin
1996 "Beneath the Roots of the Chukum Tree: A Preliminary Soil Analysis of the Chunchucmil Region." Yearbook, Conference of Latin American Geographers 22: 41–50.

Farriss, Nancy M.
1984 Maya Society Under Colonial Rule. Princeton, N.J.: Princeton University Press.

Flannery, Kent V.
1968 "The Olmec and the Valley of Oaxaca: A Model for Interregional Interaction in Formative Times." Pp. 79–110 in Dumbarton Oaks Conference on the Olmec, edited by Elizabeth P. Benson. Washington, D.C.: Dumbarton Oaks.

Flores Guido, J. S., and Ileana Espejel
1994 Tipos de Vegetación de la Peninsula de Yucatán. Etnoflora Yucatanense 3. Merida: Universidad Autónoma de Yucatan.

Fox, John W.
1987 Maya Postclassic State Formation: Segmentary Lineage Migration in Advancing Frontiers. Cambridge: Cambridge University Press.

Fox, John W., Garrett W. Cook, Arlen F. Chase, and Diane Z. Chase
1996 "Questions of Political and Economic Integration: Segmentary versus Centralized States among the Ancient Maya." Current Anthropology 37: 795–801.

Fox, Richard
1977 Urban Anthropology. Englewood Cliffs, N.J.: Prentice Hall.

Frank, A. G.
1991 "A Plea for World System History." Journal of World History 2: 1–28.
1993 "Bronze Age World System Cycles." Current Anthropology 34: 383–429.

Fry, Robert E.
1980 "Models of Exchange for Major Shape Classes of Lowland Maya Pottery." Pp. 3–18 in Models and Methods in Regional Exchange, edited by Robert E. Fry. SAA Papers No. 1. Washington, D.C.: Society for American Archaeology.

Gallareta Negrón, Tomas
1984 Coba: Forma y Funcion de una Comunidad Maya Prehispanica. Tesis, Escuela de Ciencias Antropologicas de la Universidad de Yucatan, Merida.

Garza Tarazona de Gonzalez, S., and Edward B. Kurjack
1980 Atlas Arqueológico del Estado de Yucatan. 2 vols. Instituto Nacional de Antropologia e Historia, Centro Regional del Sureste. Mexico D. F.
1984 "Organizacion Social y Asentamientos Mayas Prehispanicos." Estudios de Cultura Maya 15: 19–34.

Geertz, Clifford
1980 Negara: The Theater State in Nineteenth-Century Bali. Princeton: Princeton University Press.

Goni Motilla, G. A.
1993 Solares Prehispanicos en la Peninsula de Yucatan. Tesis, Escuela Nacional de Antropologia e Historia, Mexico D. F.

Graham, Elizabeth
1987 "Resource Diversity in Belize and Its Implications for Models of Lowland Trade." *American Antiquity* 52(4): 753–767.
Grove, David C., Kenneth G. Hirth, David E. Buge, and Ann M. Cyphers
1976 "Settlement and Cultural Development at Chalcatzingo." *Science* 192: 1203–1210.
Guderjan, Tomas H.
1995 "Settlement Patterns and Survey Data." Pp. 9–30 in *Maya Maritime Trade, Settlement, and Populations on Ambergris Caye, Belize,* edited by Tomas H. Guderjan and James F. Garber. Lancaster, Calif.: Labyrinthos.
Hall, Thomas D., and Christopher Chase-Dunn
1993 "The World-Systems Perspective and Archaeology: Forward into the Past." *Journal of Archaeological Research* 1: 121–143.
Haviland, William A.
1997 "On the Maya State." *Current Anthropology* 38(3): 443–445.
Heider, Karl G.
1969 "Visiting Trade Institutions." *American Anthropologist* 71: 462–471.
Hendon, Julia
1991 "Status and Power in Classic Maya Society." *American Anthropologist* 93: 894–918.
Hirth, Kenneth
1978 "Interregional Trade and the Formation of Prehistoric Gateway Cities." *American Antiquity* 43: 35–45.
1992 "Interregional Exchange as Elite Behavior: An Evolutionary Perspective." Pp. 18–29 in *Mesoamerican Elites: An Archaeological Assessment,* edited by Diane Z. Chase and Arlen F. Chase. Norman: University of Oklahoma Press.
1998 "The Distributional Approach: A New Way to Identify Marketplace Exchange in the Archaeological Record." *Current Anthropology* 39(4): 451–476.
Humphery, Caroline, and Stephen Hugh-Jones
1992 *Barter, Exchange, and Value: An Anthropological Approach.* Cambridge: Cambridge University Press.
Hutson, Scott
2000 "Excavations in Albarrada Group Aak." In *Chunchucmil Regional Economy Project Report of the 1999 Field Season,* edited by Traci Ardren. Tallahassee: Department of Anthropology, Florida State University.
INEGI
1982 *Uso Potencial Agricultura.* Merida sheet, 1:1,000,000 scale. Mexico D. F.
1983 *Carta de Transpiración y Deficit de Agua.* Merida sheet, 1:1,000,000 scale. Mexico, D. F.
Isphording, Wayne C., and Eugene M. Wilson
1973 "Weathering Processes and Physical Subdivisions of Northern Yucatan." *Proceedings of the Association of American Geographers* 5: 117–121.
Keesing, Roger M.
1983 *Elota's Story: The Life and Times of a Solomon Islands Big Man.* New York: Holt, Rinehart, and Winston.

Kepecs, Susan
1998 "Diachronic Ceramic Evidence and Its Social Implications in the Chikinchel Region, Northeastern Yucatan, Mexico." *Ancient Mesoamerica* 9: 121–136.
Kepecs, Susan, Gary M. Feinman, and Sylviane Boucher
1994 "Chichen Itza and Its Hinterland: A World Systems Perspective." *Ancient Mesoamerica* 5: 141–158.
Killion, Thomas W.
1992 "Residential Ethnoarchaeology and Ancient Site Structure: Contemporary Farming and Prehistoric Settlement Agriculture at Matacapan, Veracruz, Mexico." Pp. 119–149 in *Gardens in Prehistory: The Archaeology of Settlement Agriculture in Greater Mesoamerica*, edited by T. W. Killion. Tuscaloosa: University of Alabama Press.
Kristiansen, Kristian
1991 "Chiefdoms, States, and Systems of Social Evolution." Pp. 16–43 in *Chiefdoms: Power, Economy and Ideology*, edited by Timothy K. Earle. New York: Cambridge University Press.
Kurjack, Edward B., and E. Wyllys Andrews V
1976 "Early Boundary Maintenance in Northwest Yucatan, Mexico." *American Antiquity* 41: 318–325.
Kurjack, Edward B., and Sylvia Garza T.
1981 "Una Vision de la Geografia Humana en la Region Serrana de Yucatan." Pp. 15–28 in *In Memoria Del Congreso Interno, 1979*. Instituto Nacional de Antropologia e Historia, Centro Regional Yucatan, Merida.
Lange, Frederick W.
1971 "Marine Resources: A Viable Subsistence Alternative for the Prehistoric Maya." *American Anthropologist* 73: 619–639.
Leach, J., and Edmund R. Leach
1983 *A World of Made Is Not a World of Born: Doing Kula in Kiriwina*. Cambridge: Cambridge University Press.
Leyden, Barbara, Mark Brenner, J. Curtis, Dolores Piperno, Thomas Whitmore, and Bruce H. Dahlin
1996 "A Record of Long- and Short-Term Climatic Variation from Northwest Yucatan: Cenote San Jose Chulchaca." Pp. 30–50 in *The Managed Mosaic*, edited by Scott Fedick. Provo: University of Utah Press.
Magnoni, Aline
1995 "*Albarradas* at Chunchucmil and in the Northern Maya Area." B.A. thesis, Institute of Archaeology, University College London.
Marcus, Joyce
1983 "The Nature of the Mesoamerican City." Pp. 195–242 in *Prehispanic Settlement Patterns: Essays in Honor of Gordon R. Willey*, edited by Evon Z. Vogt and Richard Leventhal. Albuquerque: University of New Mexico Press.
1993 "Ancient Maya Political Organization." Pp. 111–184 in *Lowland Maya Civilization in the Eighth Century A.D.*, edited by Jeremy A. Sabloff and John S. Henderson. Washington, D.C.: Dumbarton Oaks.

Marcus, Joyce, and Gary M. Feinman
1998 "Introduction." Pp. 3–13 in *Archaic States*, edited by Gary M. Feinman and Joyce Marcus. Santa Fe, N.M.: School of American Research Press.

McAnany, Patricia A.
1986 "Lithic Technology and Exchange among Wetland Farmers of the Eastern Maya Lowlands." Ph.D. dissertation, Department of Anthropology, University of New Mexico. University Microfilms, Ann Arbor.
1993 "The Economics of Social Power and Wealth among Eighth-Century Maya Households." Pp. 65–89 in *Lowland Maya Civilization in the Eighth Century A.D.*, edited by Jeremy A. Sabloff and John S. Henderson. Washington, D.C.: Dumbarton Oaks.
1995 *Living with the Ancestors: Kinship and Kingship in Ancient Maya Society.* Austin: University of Texas Press.

McAnany, Patricia A., and Barry L. Isaac
1989 *Prehistoric Maya Economies of Belize.* Research in Economic Anthropology Supplement 4. Greenwich, Conn.: JAI Press.

McKillop, Heather
1995 "Underwater Archaeology, Salt Production, and Coastal Maya Trade at Stingray Lagoon, Belize." *Latin American Antiquity* 6: 214–228.
1996 "Ancient Maya Trading Ports and the Integration of Long-Distance and Regional Economies: Wild Cane Cay in South-Coastal Belize." *Ancient Mesoamerica* 7: 49–62.

Millet, C. Luis
1981 "Los Canales de la Costa de Campeche y su Relacion con la Industria del Palo de Tinte." Paper presented at the XVII Mesa Redonda de la Sociedad Mexicana de Antropologia. San Cristobal de las Casas, Chiapas, Mexico, June 21–27.

Misión-Arqueólogica de España en México, Proyecto Oxkintok
1987–1990 *Oxkintok*, 3 volumes. Madrid, Spain: Ministerio de Asuntos Exteriores.

Netting, Robert McC.
1990 "Population, Permanent Agriculture, and Polities: Unpacking the Evolutionary Portmanteau." Pp. 21–61 in *The Evolution of Political Systems*, edited by Steven Upham. Cambridge: Cambridge University Press.

Parsons, Jeffrey R., and Mary H. Parsons
1990 *Maguey Utilization in Highland Central Mexico: An Archaeological Ethnography.* Anthropological Papers No. 80. Ann Arbor: University of Michigan Museum of Anthropology.

Pires-Ferreira, J. W., and Kent V. Flannery
1976 "Ethnographic Models for Formative Exchange." Pp. 286–292 in *The Early Mesoamerican Village*, edited by Kent V. Flannery. New York: Academic Press.

Rands, Robert L., and Ronald L. Bishop
1980 "Resource Procurement Zones and Patterns of Ceramic Exchange in the Palenque Region, Mexico." Pp. 19–46 in *Models and Methods in Regional Exchange*, edited by Robert E. Fry. SAA Papers No. 1. Washington, D.C.: Society for American Archaeology.

Rappaport, Roy
1968 *Pigs for the Ancestors: Ritual Ecology of a New Guinea People*. New Haven, Conn.: Yale University Press.
Rathje, William L., and Jeremy A. Sabloff
1973 "Ancient Maya Commercial Systems: A Research Design for the Island of Cozumel, Mexico." *World Archaeology* 5: 221–231.
Renfrew, Colin
1974 "Beyond a Subsistence Economy: The Evolution of Social Organization in Prehistoric Europe." Pp. 69–95 in *Reconstructing Complex Societies: An Archaeological Colloquium*, edited by C. B. Moore. Supplement to the Bulletin of the American Schools of Oriental Research No. 20. Ann Arbor.
Rice, Prudence M.
1987 "Economic Change in the Lowland Maya Late Classic Period. Pp. 76–85 in *Specialization, Exchange, and Complex Societies*, edited by Elizabeth M. Brumfiel and Timothy K. Earle. Cambridge: Cambridge University Press.
Ringle, William M., and George Bey
1992 "The Center and Segmentary State Dynamics: African Models in the Maya Lowlands." Paper presented at the Wenner-Gren Conference on the Segmentary State and the Classic Maya Lowlands. Cleveland State University.
Roys, Ralph L.
1939 *The Titles of Ebtun*. Publication No. 505. Washington, D.C.: Carnegie Institution.
1943 *The Indian Background of Colonial Yucatan*. Publication No. 548. Washington, D.C.: Carnegie Institution.
Sabloff, Jeremy A., and William L. Rathje
1975 *A Study of Changing Pre-Columbian Commercial Systems: The 1972–1973 Seasons at Cozumel, Mexico*. Monographs of the Peabody Museum No. 3. Cambridge, Mass.: Harvard University.
Sahlins, Marshall
1972 *Stone Age Economics*. Chicago: Aldine.
Sanders, W. T., and D. Webster
1988 "The Mesoamerican Urban Tradition." *American Anthropologist* 90: 521–546.
Scholes, Frances V., and Ralph L. Roys
1948 *The Maya Chontal Indians of Acalan-Tixchel*. Norman: University of Oklahoma Press.
Schortman, Edward M.
1989 "Interregional Interaction in Prehistory: the Need for a New Perspective." *American Antiquity* 54: 52–65.
Schortman, Edward M., and Patricia A. Urban, editors
1992 *Resources, Power, and Interregional Interaction*. New York: Plenum Press.
1994 "Living on the Edge: Core/Periphery Relations in Ancient Southeastern Mesoamerica." *Current Anthropology* 35: 401–428.
Shuman, Malcolm
1974 "The Town Where Luck Fell: The Economics of Life in a Henequen Zone Pueblo." Unpublished Ph.D. dissertation, Department of Anthropology, Tulane University.

Smyth, Michael P.
1991 *Modern Maya Storage Behavior: Ethnoarchaeological Case Examples from the Puuc Region of Yucatan.* University of Pittsburgh Memoirs in Latin American Archaeology No. 3. Pittsburgh: University of Pittsburgh Press.
Southall, Aidan W.
1956 *Alur Society: A Study in Process and Types of Domination.* Cambridge: Heffer.
1991 "The Segmentary State: From the Imaginary to the Material Means of Production." Pp. 75–96 in *Early State Economics,* edited by H. J. M. Claessen and P. van de Velde. New Brunswick, N.J.: Transaction Publishers.
Thompson, Edward H.
1898 *Ruins of Xkichmook, Yucatan.* Publication 28. Chicago: Field Columbian Museum.
Thompson, J. Eric S.
1970 *Maya History and Religion.* Norman: University of Oklahoma Press.
Tozzer, Alfred M.
1941 *Landa's Relacion de las Cosas de Yucatan,* edited and translated by A. M. Tozzer. Papers of the Peabody Museum of American Archaeology and Ethnology Vol. 18. Cambridge, Mass.: Harvard University.
Vargas P., E. P. Santillan S., and M. Vilata
1985 "Apuntas para el Analisis del Patron de Asentamiento en Tulum." *Estudios de Cultura Maya* XVI: 55–83.
Vlcek, David T.
1978 "Muros de Delimitacion Residencial en Chunchucmil." *Boletin de la Escuela de Ciencias, Antropologicas de la Universidad de Yucatan* 28: 55–64.
Vlcek, David T., S. Garza de Gonzalez, and E. B. Kurjack
1978 "Contemporary Farming and Ancient Maya Settlements: Some Disconcerting Evidence." Pp. 211–223 in *Pre-Hispanic Maya Agriculture,* edited by Peter D. Harrison and Billie Lee Turner II. Albuquerque: University of New Mexico Press.
Watanabe, Takeshi
2000 "Form and Function of Metates in Chunchucmil, Yucatan, Mexico." Master's thesis, Florida State University, Tallahassee.
Wilson, Eugene M.
1980 "The Physical Geography of the Yucatán Peninsula." Pp. 5–40 in *Yucatán, A World Apart,* edited by E. Mosely and E. Terry. Tuscaloosa: University of Alabama Press.
Zier, Anne H.
1981 "An Experiment in Ground Stone Use-Wear Analysis." M.A. thesis, Department of Anthropology, University of Colorado, Boulder.

Chapter Ten

Praise the Gods and Pass the Obsidian? The Organization of Ancient Economy in San Martín Jilotepeque, Guatemala

Geoffrey E. Braswell

In 1972, the book *Contemporary Archaeology: A Guide to Theory and Contributions*, edited by Mark Leone, was published. Although the title of this thirty-year-old gem no longer is apt, one contribution to it, "Praise the Gods and Pass the Metates: A Hypothesis of the Development of Lowland Rainforest Civilizations in Mesoamerica," by William Laurens Rathje, still is widely cited today. Three aspects of this work strike me as particularly noteworthy. First, it drew attention to the noneconomic aspects of trade by positing that information, particularly ideology, plays an important role in interaction. Second, it focused not only on the lowlands, where most Maya archaeologists work, but also on the highlands, the location of many important resources exploited in ancient times. A third important contribution was the introduction of core-periphery perspectives on ancient economy. Although there are certain aspects of his hypothesis that I cannot accept—for example, that the highlanders were ideological consumers rather than producers—Rathje's substantivist and interregional approach was a refreshing challenge to both environmental determinism and isolationist models that ignored the importance of the Guatemalan highlands to broader Maya and Mesoamerican economies.

– 285 –

A key resource in Rathje's model—as well as in other economic scenarios (e.g., Santley 1983, 1984, 1989a)—is obsidian, a volcanic glass prized throughout ancient Mesoamerica. Three important obsidian source areas, as well as many more minor sources, are located in the

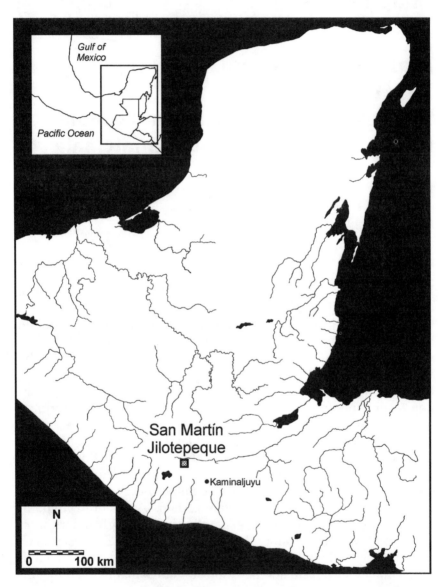

Fig. 10.1. Location of San Martín Jilotepeque obsidian source and settlement region.

highlands of southern Guatemala. One of these is San Martín Jilotepeque (SMJ), department of Chimaltenango, Guatemala (figures 10.1 and 10.2). During the Middle Preclassic period, SMJ was the most important obsidian source in southeastern Mesoamerica, supplying most of the high-quality volcanic glass used in the Maya lowlands, the western highlands, and the Pacific Coast. Material from SMJ was traded as far away as La Venta, where it accounts for more than 28 percent of the Middle Preclassic obsidian at that Olmec site (Hester et al. 1971: table 8, "Chemical Type C"). In later periods, the importance of the SMJ source to the Maya lowlands waned, but it continued to be a critical resource for inhabitants of the southern Maya area.

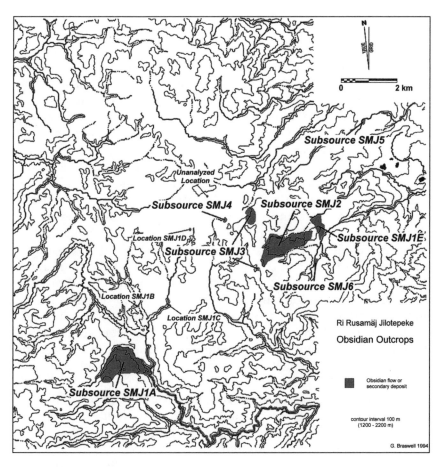

Fig. 10.2. Obsidian outcrops and chemical subsources within the San Martín Jilotepeque source area.

From 1990 to 1993, I directed an integrated program of geological survey, geochemical research, settlement survey, and excavations in and around the SMJ obsidian source (Braswell 1996a, 1998; Braswell and Glascock 1998). My investigations focused on the economic organization of the region. Questions central to the research include: (1) How were production and exchange organized? (2) What was the relationship between settlement, resource exploitation, and social hierarchy in the region? and (3) How did prehistoric production and exchange change over time?

Economic Models

Modes of Production

Two key aspects of any economic system are production and distribution. Santley (1989b, 1994), van der Leeuw (1976), and Peacock (1982) describe three organizational "modes" of production—reflecting increasing levels of production intensity, potential surplus, and specialization—that are relevant to highland Guatemalan archaeology. These are household production, the household industry, and the workshop industry. As with all such typologies, actual cases may not fit a single, ideal type.

The purpose of *household production* is to meet the needs of the household. That is, the level of production is equal to the level of consumption by the household. A farmer carving a digging-stick handle so he can plant maize and a woman weaving clothes for her family on a back-strap loom are examples of household production. Production waste reflects typical household goods in both the types represented and the quantity consumed by members of the household. Product quality is variable, reflecting the skill of individual producers. Since production is aimed at maintenance and demand is low, production events may be very infrequent. For this reason, household production usually occurs as part of typical household routines and often is carried out by women (Arnold 1987; Santley and Kneebone 1993: 39). Thus the context of household production for most nonagricultural goods is the house lot. Production waste is mixed with general household trash and because the level of production is quite low, little may be present. Finally, production loci are scattered throughout the settlement area, creating a pattern of mechanical repetition from house lot to house lot.

In a *household industry*, a small surplus of typical household goods is produced for trade or social purposes. The context of craft production is the house lot, but small, specialized facilities may be built in order to increase productivity. Most potters produce ceramics as a household industry; drying, firing, and storage spaces within the residential compound are examples of such facilities (Arnold 1987). The range of goods that are produced for exchange usually is small, reflecting part-time specialization. Product quality is variable but may be standardized, particularly in households where a relatively large surplus is generated. Refuse from a household industry displays increased production of certain everyday goods, with the result that assemblages look quantitatively—but not qualitatively—different from those of households that do not practice a household industry (Deal 1983; Krotser 1974; Santley and Kneebone 1993). Thus, as the intensity of production increases, a household industry becomes easier to identify in the archaeological record. Production waste may be discarded with general household trash or deposited in small, specialized dumps within or near the house lot. As with household production, production loci are scattered throughout the settlement area.

When production becomes a full-time occupation, a *workshop industry* is present (Santley and Kneebone 1993: 41). Production levels are increased not only by intensification but also by specialization. Full-time specialization may not occur without social stratification because the distribution systems that typify egalitarian and ranked societies are not sufficiently integrated (Smith 1976a). The presence of a workshop industry, then, has definite sociopolitical correlates. The surplus generated by a workshop industry may be manipulated by elite nonproducers as well as by producers.

Production levels in a workshop industry are much higher than in either household mode because producers must meet all their subsistence needs through exchange. Efficiency of production, therefore, is an important factor in a workshop industry. Efficiency may be increased in several ways: "(1) by spatial segregation and routinization of production tasks; (2) by specialization in the manufacture of a limited number of commodity types; (3) by improvements in technology; or (4) by some combination of these" (Santley and Kneebone 1993: 41). The first leads to the creation of workshops, or specialized production loci. These are often, but not necessarily, segregated from household space. The use of space within a workshop may become specialized, with certain rooms or areas set aside for specific purposes or stages of production (Arnold 1987; Santley and Kneebone 1993). One effect of increased efficiency and the routinization of tasks is standardization of the product. When a workshop is removed from a household context, its location may be determined by factors that increase production efficiency. Ease of access to required natural resources, distribution facilities, and disposal sites are examples of such factors. Workshops, therefore, may not be evenly distributed throughout a settlement area, but may cluster in *barrios*. In the case of lithic production, workshops often are found near exploitable outcrops of raw material, or near the residential groups of the elites who control the distribution of raw material and finished products.

Because production levels are high, the waste generated by a workshop industry is too abundant to dispose in residential contexts. Instead, specialized dump sites are used. The distance between specialized disposal areas and residences increases when workshop refuse is potentially hazardous, as is the case with lithic debitage (Santley and Kneebone 1993). Because of segregation from household contexts, an archaeological assemblage recovered from a specialized disposal area does not quantitatively or qualitatively resemble typical household waste. The internal diversity of such an assemblage is low, reflecting tasks related to specialized production and not to the full spectrum of household activities. The examination of such debris is often the easiest way to identify the presence of a workshop industry.

Much has been said about the misidentification of lithic workshops as *contexts* of production (e.g., Clark 1986, 1989a, 1989b; Moholy-Nagy 1990). What should be stressed is that it is not necessary to find the exact location of a lithic workshop to demonstrate the practice of a workshop industry. The identification of a specialized disposal area removed from household contexts is sufficient for this purpose.

The Spatial Organization of Distribution Systems

Smith (1976b) has identified two spatial patterns for uncommercialized economies. These correspond with different types of exchange within the regional system. In *extended network systems*, exchange is conducted between several equivalent spatial units, be they households or communities. Exchange is dyadic and tends to be poorly organized, largely because of the nonhierarchical, almost random pattern of the network. For this reason, there is little feedback between demand, production, and supply (Smith 1976a: 315). In fact, production levels of a given commodity at a particular location often are determined not by demand for that product at another location, but by local demand for the commodity for which it is exchanged (Rappaport 1967). There is little or no specialization in the nodes of an extended network system, and economic integration is minimal. Thus, the household industry is the mode of production generating exchangeable surplus. For these reasons, such systems do not support stratification (Smith 1976a: 315–318). The lack of stratification is reflected in settlement patterns; sites tend to be dispersed evenly across the landscape and show little differentiation in size or function. Although organization is minimal, the open, extended pattern of such systems allows down-the-line exchange over great distances. For this reason, nodes in extended network systems can be considered open corporate communities (Smith 1976a, 1976b). An important archaeological correlate is that imported goods from other regions may be present in such systems, but their distribution does not reflect preferential access or social stratification.

A second distributional pattern is the *bounded network system*. These are well ordered according to a local hierarchy, but exchange outside of the system is very limited (Smith 1976a: 315). Such systems also have been called bounded hierarchical networks (e.g., Santley 1994: 244–245) because of the linkage of households or communities to a nodal center that allocates some degree of specialization. Within the bounded system, exchange has a polyadic aspect, particularly if workshops are present. The majority of the population, however, is engaged in subsistence food production and are not full-time specialists. This not only keeps production levels low, but also limits demand. Furthermore, the lack of articulation and integration of different bounded network systems also acts to keep demand low, prohibiting the development of markets. For this reason, bounded network systems are somewhat more specialized and stratified than extended network economies but also are uncommercialized. In bounded network systems, elites are found at sites dispersed throughout the countryside (organizational nodes) but are not found at the majority of sites (production nodes). Bounded network systems are relatively small. There should be two or three levels in the settlement hierarchy.

The bounded nature of the network implies that such systems form closed corporate groups (Santley 1994: table 1; Smith 1976a: table 2). An important archaeological correlate is that very few imported goods can be found at sites in a bounded network system. Typically, bounded network economies support complex "chiefdoms" and some simple states (Santley 1994; Smith 1976a, 1976b). To the extent that interaction beyond the boundary of the network does occur, exchange is dyadic. Such interregional interaction involves the exchange of small quantities of status goods among elites.

Survey and Excavations in San Martín Jilotepeque

Systematic survey of an area of 138 km^2 surrounding the prehistoric quarries of SMJ discovered 147 sites, including residential locations, quarry-workshops, secondary workshops, and workshop disposal areas. A three-level hierarchy was developed for habitation sites, based on factors including site area and the presence and quantity of

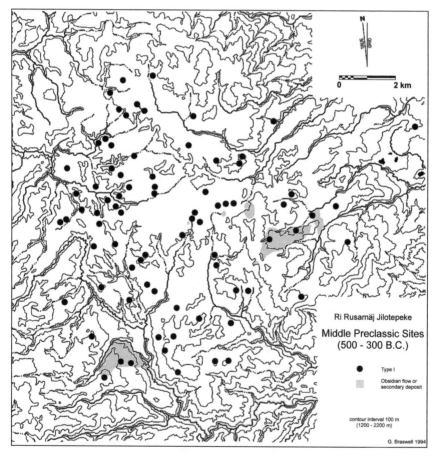

Fig. 10.3. Middle Preclassic settlement in San Martín Jilotepeque.

mounds, sculpture, and imported goods (Braswell 1996a: chapter 5). In addition, test-pitting excavations were conducted in selected habitation and special-function sites.

Middle Preclassic (500–300 B.C.)

Permanent occupation of the region began in the late Middle Preclassic period. A total of seventy-seven habitation sites dating to that period were identified (figure 10.3), and occupation is best characterized as broadly distributed but low in density. No earthen mounds or sculptures date to this period and all habitation sites are small. Most, in fact, probably represent one or two house lots. The two largest sites (measuring 1.0 and 3.3 ha in area) might be small villages, but site formation processes are not well understood and the dispersed pattern of artifacts on the surface may be caused by more recent land-use strategies. It is interesting that these two sites are located in strategic positions. The largest is situated on an open plain ideal for agriculture. The second site is located near the Pachay obsidian quarries, suggesting that obsidian extraction was a motive for settlement. Nearest neighbor analysis indicates that sites are spaced randomly with regard to each other, but a slight tendency for habitation sites to cluster near exploited obsidian quarries was noted (Braswell 1998). Despite the presence of two sites that may have been small villages, the Middle Preclassic settlement hierarchy consisted of only one level, which I call Type I sites.

Test pits in sites with Middle Preclassic components failed to recover imported artifacts. Instead, all ceramics are of a local tradition and belong to the Sacatepéquez complex identified by Shook (1952). Despite many shared similarities with Providencia-phase material from Kaminaljuyu, the Middle Preclassic pottery of SMJ is less diverse and lacks many of the more elaborate forms. Moreover, no ceramics belonging to Pacific Coast traditions were recovered. Given the widespread distribution of SMJ obsidian throughout southern Mesoamerica during the late Middle Preclassic period, the economic isolation of the region is somewhat surprising.

Late Preclassic (300 B.C.–A.D. 250)

Only twenty-four sites dating to the Late Preclassic period were identified (figure 10.4), and Late Preclassic sherds account for just 0.8 percent of the diagnostic ceramics recovered from these sites. It seems likely that this pottery represents lingering Middle Preclassic

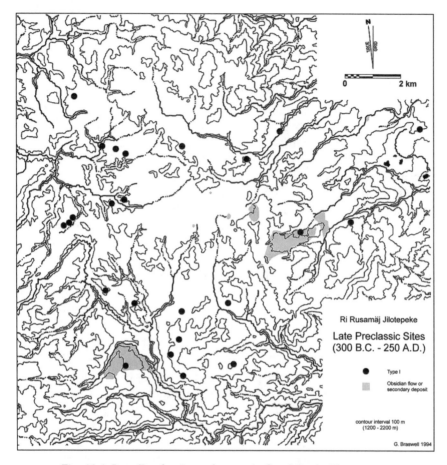

Fig. 10.4. Late Preclassic settlement in San Martín Jilotepeque.

settlement or precocious Early Classic reoccupation. That is, SMJ probably was abandoned for much of the Late Preclassic period. I have
no explanation for the abandonment of the region during this inter-
val, but the decline in the importance of SMJ obsidian in the Maya
lowlands during the Late Preclassic period probably was related to
population loss near the source. As in the Middle Preclassic period,
the settlement hierarchy consisted of only one level, and habitation
sites were positioned randomly with regard to each other on the landscape. No imported artifacts dating to the Late Preclassic period were
recovered, and local ceramics reflect continuing divergence from the
pottery-making tradition of Kaminaljuyu (see Popenoe de Hatch
1997).

In contrast, several large sites with both visible architecture and important Preclassic components are found in the valleys between the modern towns of San Andrés Itzapa, Chimaltenango, El Tejar, and Parramos. The most important sites are Durazno, Cerritos Itzapa, and San Lorenzo (Richardson 1938; Shook 1952). These sites, although located well beyond survey boundaries, are only some 15–20 km south of SMJ. No doubt the rich soils and open, flat plains of the south promoted early intensive settlement, while the poor soils, harsh terrain, and occasional frosts of the SMJ area were inhibiting factors. The chronologies of these early valley sites are not well known. Although all have strong Middle and Late Preclassic components, Classic period ceramics also are found in abundance on their surfaces. Dating

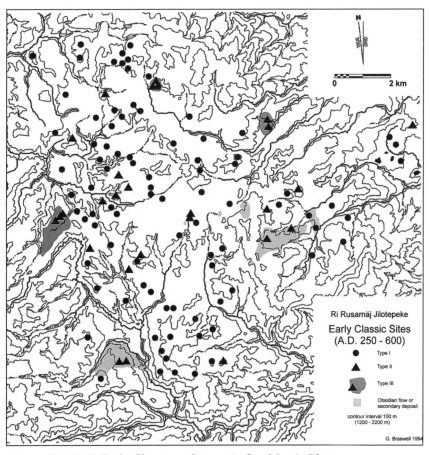

Fig. 10.5. Early Classic settlement in San Martín Jilotepeque.

the construction of the mounds from surface collections, therefore, is problematic. Test excavations were conducted recently at San Lorenzo. Although a Middle Formative burial was discovered at a depth of 3.0–3.4 m below the surface, contexts related to the mound itself were either stratigraphically mixed or inverted (Eugenia J. Robinson, personal communication 1994). The Late Classic seems to have been the period of heaviest occupation in the Itzapa region (Shook 1952). I conducted a brief reconnaissance of Finca Durazno in 1990, and most of the ceramics I found there are Early Classic in date. Thus, although the valleys south of SMJ were inhabited during the Middle and Late Preclassic, it is quite possible that Type II sites did not develop in that region until the Early Classic period.

Early Classic Period (A.D. 250–600)

The Early Classic was a period of heavy occupation (figure 10.5). Elsewhere, I have argued that the new Early Classic settlers of the region were ancestral to the modern Kaqchikel speakers who now occupy this portion of the highlands (Braswell 1996a, 1998; Braswell and Amador 1999; see also Popenoe de Hatch 1997, 1998). A total of 107 habitation sites have Early Classic components, and a three-tiered settlement hierarchy developed during this period. This indicates a qualitative change in the sociopolitical complexity of the SMJ area. In fact, the level of settlement complexity at SMJ during the Early Classic period is greater than in other surveyed areas of the Kaqchikel highlands. Mound architecture and sculpture (Braswell 1996b) first appear in the Early Classic period, as do specialized obsidian activity areas removed from quarry contexts. The largest Type III sites (figure 10.6a), at the top of the settlement hierarchy, consist of multiple courtyard groups and scattered isolated mounds covering areas of 10 to 90 ha.

Nearest neighbor analysis reveals several interesting patterns in the Early Classic data. First, there is a tendency for specialized obsidian activity areas—either off-quarry workshops or, more likely, workshop dumps—to aggregate around the larger and more elaborate Type II and Type III habitation sites. Debitage recovered from these obsidian activity areas is highly specialized, demonstrating the production of bifacially retouched tools on macroblade blanks. Second, Type III sites are regularly spaced between exploited quarries. But Type II sites—intermediate-sized habitation sites with a few imported goods, occasional sculpture, and isolated mounds or a single mound group—show a tendency to cluster near exploited outcrops.

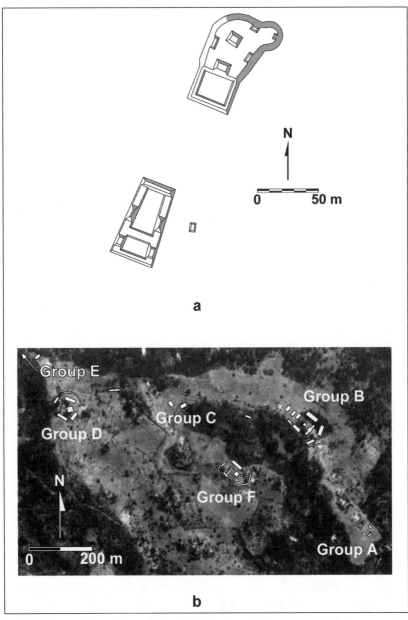

Fig. 10.6. Examples of Type III habitation sites in San Martín Jilotepeque: (a) mound structures at El Perén, a single-component Early Classic site (an additional mound is located southwest of the two groups shown); (b) O'ch'al K'abowil Siwan (Chuisac), showing Postclassic mound structures at the site (Group E is located northwest of the area shown in the photograph).

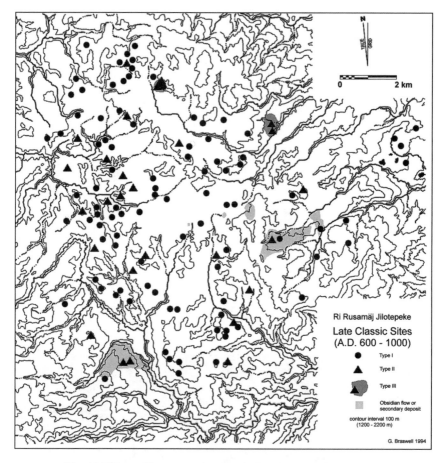

Fig. 10.7. Late Classic settlement in San Martín Jilotepeque.

Construction sequences are not sufficiently fine-grained to determine if these Type II sites began as simpler Type I communities or were founded and built as intermediate-ranked sites. Thus, the clustering of Type II sites around exploited outcrops may suggest an attempt by elites to control obsidian quarries. Alternatively, the inhabitants of Type II sites may have owed their prosperity (relative to that of Type I site occupants) to the proximity of obsidian quarries.

Late Classic (A.D. 600–1000)

The Late Classic was the period of heaviest occupation in the SMJ region. Late Classic components are present at 119 of the 147 sites sampled by the survey (figure 10.7). The three-tiered hierarchy of settlement continued in the Late Classic period, but two of the largest Type III sites, El Perén and Quimal, were abandoned by or shortly after the beginning of the Late Classic. Occupation and construction continued at the third Type III site, La Merced, with the addition of another group of mounds. The erection of tenoned sculpture and blank stelae persisted in the Late Classic period but was less frequent than in Early Classic times.

Nearest neighbor analysis indicates that intermediate-level Type II sites were spaced at regular intervals from the larger Type III sites, something to be expected if they were politically subordinate. Seven off-quarry obsidian activity areas—again, workshops or workshop dump sites associated with biface production—were located within the survey zone. Nearest neighbor analysis demonstrates an extremely strong pattern of aggregation of these activity areas with intermediate-ranked Type II sites, but they are randomly distributed around the Type I and Type III sites. In addition, Late Classic Type II sites tend to cluster near obsidian quarries. Thus, during the Late Classic period, biface production was a specialized activity associated with small mound sites. These intermediate-ranked sites also tend to be located near exploited outcrops.

Postclassic (A.D. 1000–1550)

The transition from Classic to Postclassic is the least understood period in the prehistory of the central Guatemalan highlands. At this time, Kaminaljuyu and the Valley of Guatemala were largely abandoned, but regions to the west, including SMJ, were not. Ceramic and settlement data from SMJ strongly suggest that the Classic to Postclassic transition was gradual, and do not support the arrival of conquering groups. There are very few diagnostic types of the Early Postclassic period, and supposedly diagnostic Late Classic and Late Postclassic wares were found together in middens radiocarbon-dated to the Early Postclassic period (see Braswell 1996a: chapter 6). Moreover, there is a remarkable continuity of settlement between the Late Classic and the Postclassic period; fully 87 percent of the eighty-two Postclassic sites in SMJ also have Late Classic components.

The three-tiered settlement hierarchy continued into the Postclassic period (figure 10.8), although a new paramount site, O'ch'al K'abowil Siwan, emerged as the dominant center (figure 10.6b). O'ch'al, a large site containing at least forty-two mounds and terraces arranged in six groups, is known from ethnohistorical

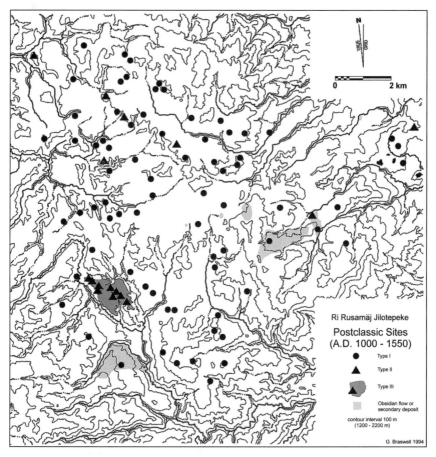

Fig. 10.8. Postclassic settlement in San Martín Jilotepeque.

documents to have been founded by the Xpantzay faction. Later it served as the first capital of the Chajoma', who eventually moved to the site erroneously called "Mixco" Viejo (Carmack 1979). Three obsidian activity areas with Postclassic components were located, and nearest neighbor analysis demonstrates a reversal of Classic period trends. These activity areas tend to aggregate with Type I sites rather than with the larger Type II or Type III sites. Thus, it appears that Postclassic workshop production was more closely associated with small habitation sites lacking mound architecture. Also in contrast with the Classic period, Type II habitation sites are spaced at regular intervals from obsidian quarries, and Type I and III sites appear to be randomly spaced around exploited outcrops.

Conclusions

What do these settlement data tell us about the organization of production and distribution in ancient San Martín Jilotepeque? During the Preclassic period, lithic extraction and production was organized on the household level and distribution was structured as an extended network. During the Classic and Postclassic periods, the economy of SMJ was a bounded network and at least one lithic industry, biface production, was practiced as a workshop industry.

When I began research, I expected to find evidence dating to the Preclassic period for trade with the Gulf and Pacific Coasts and with the Maya lowlands. Following Rathje (1972), I thought I might find items that indicated participation in a cult originating in, or at least with important ties to, these other areas. I even joked about finding an Olmec head or a low-relief sculpture in the pan-Mesoamerican "Olmecoid" style, as have been found at Middle to Late Preclassic sites in the Pacific piedmont of Guatemala. Minimally, I thought I would find evidence of a ranked or stratified society, where social differences were supported by surpluses generated by trading obsidian. Instead, all lines of data support the existence of simple, egalitarian communities in SMJ during the Middle and Late Preclassic periods. Lithic extraction and production were organized at the household level, with only very low levels of part-time specialization. Given the lack of evidence for social stratification—or even data suggesting social ranking—exchange probably was conducted between equal partners. The economic system is best categorized as a simple, extended network system. Compared to much of Middle and Late Preclassic Mesoamerica, SMJ seems to have retained a relatively low level of political, social, and economic complexity. SMJ was not the center of an important chiefdom, as some investigators have suggested.

The implication, then, is that obsidian from the SMJ source probably left the regional system through acts of dyadic exchange conducted in a down-the-line fashion. Given the complete lack of evidence for imported goods and ideas—even from regions as close as the Pacific Coast and the Valley of Guatemala—it does not seem likely that local inhabitants viewed the resource as particularly valuable. Specifically, obsidian was not traded for exotic, status-endowing materials. We may imagine that perishable items and ground stone tools were received from other neighbors in the highlands, but whatever these items were, they do not seem to have been manipulated in ways that bestowed status on their owners. I can see no evidence for even the most incipient of aggrandizing behavior, and prefer to view the Middle to Late Preclassic inhabitants of SMJ as simple farmers who occasionally exchanged obsidian for other quotidian goods produced by their neighbors. Thus, it does not seem likely that demand from outside of the system—which must have been substantial—played any role in determining the organization of obsidian production within SMJ.

Two alternative scenarios require additional exploration. First, access to the quarries may have been open, and parties from other regions may have obtained their obsidian directly from the SMJ source. Although occasional visitors would not have left many traces of their presence, no Preclassic ceramics or other goods produced outside of the region were recovered, even from the comparatively large site of Pachay 2, located next to the most important quarry zone utilized in the Preclassic period. Excavations and survey of that site failed to reveal any traces of a foreign presence, however fleeting. Second, the SMJ region may have been the periphery of a larger chiefdom, centered some 15–20 km to the south. Although there are indications of an important Preclassic occupation in that region, there are as yet no convincing data that settlements were larger or politically more complex than in SMJ itself. A few mounds in the Chimaltenango-Itzapa-El Tejar region may date to the Preclassic, but most appear to have been built during the Classic period. Thus, this second alternative also seems unlikely.

In the Classic and Postclassic periods, the political and economic organization of SMJ was somewhat more complex. A three-tiered site hierarchy existed, and truly stratified society emerged. At least one lithic industry, biface production, was practiced as a workshop industry. Classic period biface workshops are associated with intermediate-rank habitation sites, which usually have at least one mound, perhaps a few pieces of sculpture, and may have obsidian or ceramics imported from another part of the Guatemalan highlands. In addition, intermediate-rank sites seem to cluster near obsidian quarries, suggesting a relationship between status and production.

In the Postclassic period, workshop production was not associated with intermediate-rank sites, but with habitation sites of the lowest tier in the hierarchy. Apparently, specialization in lithic production either no longer presented opportunities for social mobility or no longer was limited to practitioners of elevated status.

What kind of distribution system existed in Classic and Postclassic times? A three-tiered settlement hierarchy is consistent with a bounded network system of the type typically associated with chiefdoms. The lack of long-distance—or even medium-distance—exchange goods in SMJ also is evidence for the existence of a bounded network. Very few imported artifacts were recovered from Classic or Postclassic contexts, and what little that was found came from regions less than 50 km away, such as the Lake Atitlán area and the Valley of Guatemala. An elite burial offering from the late Early Classic Type III site of El Perén, for example, contained locally made pottery, native mica, and a necklace made of clay beads painted green in imitation of jade. Despite the relative proximity of Kaminaljuyu and the central Escuintla region, late Early Classic SMJ did not participate in an interaction sphere in which ideas and goods from central Mexico circulated. There is no *talud-tablero* architecture, no "Teotihuacanoid" ceramics, and no green obsidian from the Pachuca, Hidalgo, source in SMJ. As in earlier periods, the regional economy remained essentially independent.

Alas, Rathje's (1972) core-periphery model of Maya highland-lowland relations is not supported by data from SMJ, although other regions in southern Guatemala may have been more articulated with regional economies to the north. Contrary to Rathje's predictions, there are no imported items suggesting that highland goods were exchanged for lowland esoteric knowledge and symbol sets loaded with ideological content. The pattern of economic autonomy—perhaps best described as relative isolation—from larger trading spheres persisted from Preclassic to Postclassic times. To my knowledge, fragments of just two vessels subject to long-distance exchange have been found at Postclassic sites in the Guatemalan highlands. The only Classic to Postclassic good that may have been imported to SMJ over significant distances was *pom* (copal incense), which I found in many excavated contexts. If the elite of SMJ were passing the obsidian and praising the gods, as posited in Rathje's model, they did so with copious quantities of incense.

References

Arnold, Philip J. III
1987 "The Household Potters of Las Tuxtlas: An Ethnoarchaeological Study of Ceramic Production and Site Structure." Ph.D. dissertation, Department of Anthropology, University of New Mexico. Ann Arbor: University Microfilms.

Braswell, Geoffrey E. .
1996a "A Maya Obsidian Source: The Geoarchaeology, Settlement History, and Ancient Economy of San Martín Jilotepeque, Guatemala." Ph.D. dissertation, Department of Anthropology, Tulane University. Ann Arbor: University Microfilms.
1996b "The Sculpture of San Martín Jilotepeque: Cotzumalguapan Influence in the Highlands or Highland Influence on the Pacific Coast?" Pp. 441–451 in *Eighth Palenque Roundtable, 1993*, edited by Martha Macri and Jan McHargue. San Francisco: Pre-Columbian Art Research Institute.
1998 "La Arqueología de San Martín Jilotepeque, Guatemala." *Mesoamérica* 35: 117–154.
Braswell, Geoffrey E., and Fabio E. Amador Berdugo
1999 "Intercambio y producción durante el Preclásico: la obsidiana de Kaminaljuyu-Miraflores II y Urías, Sacatepéquez." Pp. 905–910 in *XII Simposio de Investigaciones Arqueológicas en Guatemala, 1998*, volumen 2, edited by Juan Pedro Laporte, Héctor Escobedo, and Ana Claudia Monzón de Suasnávar. Guatemala: Museo Nacional de Arqueología y Etnología.
Braswell, Geoffrey E., and Michael D. Glascock
1998 "Interpreting Intrasource Variation in the Composition of Obsidian: The Geoarchaeology of San Martín Jilotepeque, Guatemala." *Latin American Antiquity* 9: 353–369.
Carmack, Robert M.
1979 "La verdadera identificación de Mixco Viejo." Pp. 131–162 in *Historia Social de los Quiches*. Editorial José de Pineda Ibarra, Ministerio de Educación, Guatemala.
Clark, John E.
1986 "From Mountains to Molehills: A Critical Review of Teotihuacan's Obsidian Industry." Pp. 23–74 in *Economic Aspects of Prehispanic Highland Mexico*, edited by Barry L. Isaac. Research in Economic Anthropology Supplement No. 2. Greenwich, Conn.: JAI Press.
1989a "Fifteen Fallacies in Lithic Workshop Interpretation: An Experimental and Ethnoarchaeological Perspective." Paper presented at the Pedro Bosch-Gimpera Symposium on Ethnoarchaeology, August 1988, México, D. F.
1989b "Hacia una definición de talleres." Pp. 213–217 in *La Obsidiana en Mesoamerica*, edited by Margarita Gaxiola G. and John E. Clark. Instituto Nacional de Antropología e Historia, México, D. F.
Deal, Michael
1983 "Pottery Ethnoarchaeology among the Tzeltal Maya." Unpublished Ph.D. dissertation, Simon Fraser University, Burnaby, British Columbia.
Hester, Thomas R., Robert N. Jack, and Robert F. Heizer
1971 "The Obsidian of Tres Zapotes, Veracruz, Mexico." *Contributions of the University of California Archaeological Research Facility* 13: 65–131.
Krotser, Paula H.
1974 "Country Potters of Veracruz, Mexico." Pp. 131–146 in *Ethnoarchaeology*. University of California Institute for Archaeology Monograph 4. Los Angeles: University of California Institute for Archaeology.

Leone, Mark, editor
1972 *Contemporary Archaeology: A Guide to Theory and Contributions*. Carbondale: Southern Illinois University Press.
Moholy-Nagy, Hattula
1990 "The Misidentification of Mesoamerican Lithic Workshops." *Latin American Antiquity* 1: 268–279.
Peacock, D. P. S.
1982 *Pottery in the Roman World: An Ethnoarchaeological Approach*. London: Longman.
Popenoe de Hatch, Marion
1997 *Kaminaljuyú/San Jorge: Evidencia arqueológica de la actividad económica en el Valle de Guatemala 300 a.C. a 300 d.C.* Guatemala: Universidad del Valle de Guatemala.
1998 "Los k'iche's-kaqchikeles en el altiplano central de Guatemala: evidencia arqueológica del período clásico." *Mesoamérica* 35: 93–115.
Rappaport, Roy A.
1967 *Pigs for the Ancestors*. New Haven, Conn.: Yale University Press.
Rathje, William L.
1972 "Praise the Gods and Pass the Metates: A Hypothesis of the Development of Lowland Rainforest Civilizations in Mesoamerica." In *Contemporary Archaeology: A Guide to Theory and Contributions*, edited by Mark Leone. Carbondale: Southern Illinois University Press.
Richardson, Frederick B.
1938 "Study of Maya Sculpture." *Carnegie Institute of Washington Year Book* 37: 20–23.
Santley, Robert S.
1983 "Obsidian Trade and Teotihuacan Influence in Mesoamerica." Pp. 69–124 in *Highland-Lowland Interaction in Mesoamerica: Interdisciplinary Approaches*, edited by Arthur G. Miller. Washington, D.C.: Dumbarton Oaks.
1984 "Obsidian Exchange, Economic Stratification, and the Evolution of Complex Society in the Basin of Mexico." Pp. 43–86 in *Trade and Exchange in Mesoamerica*, edited by Kenneth G. Hirth. Albuquerque: University of New Mexico Press.
1989a "Obsidian Working, Long-Distance Exchange, and the Teotihuacan Presence on the South Gulf Coast." Pp. 131–151 in *Mesoamerica after the Decline of Teotihuacan, A.D. 700–900*, edited by Richard Diehl and Janet C. Berlo. Washington, D.C.: Dumbarton Oaks.
1989b "Residential Site Structure in the Basin of Mexico During the Formative and Classic Periods." Pp. 398–406 in *Households and Communities*, edited by S. MacEachern, D. J. W. Archer, and R. D. Gavin. Calgary: Archaeological Association of the University of Calgary.
1994 "The Economy of Ancient Matacapan." *Ancient Mesoamerica* 5: 243–266.
Santley, Robert S., and Ronald R. Kneebone
1993 "Craft Specialization, Refuse Disposal, and the Creation of Spatial Archaeological Records in Prehispanic America." Pp. 37–63 in *Prehispanic Domestic Units in Western Mesoamerica: Studies of the Household, Compound, and*

Residence, edited by Robert S. Santley and Kenneth G. Hirth. Boca Raton, Fla.: CRC Press.

Shook, Edwin M.

1952 "Lugares arqueológicos del altiplano meridional central de Guatemala." *Antropología e Historia de Guatemala* 4(2): 3–40.

Smith, Carol A.

1976a "Exchange Systems and the Spatial Distribution of Elites: The Organization of Stratification on Agrarian Societies." Pp. 390–474 in *Social Systems,* edited by Carol A. Smith. Regional Analysis, Vol. 2. New York: Academic Press.

1976b "Regional Economic Systems: Linking Geographic Models and Socioeconomic Problems." Pp. 3–63 in *Economic Systems,* edited by Carol A. Smith. Regional Analysis, Vol. 1. New York: Academic Press.

van der Leeuw, Sander E.

1976 *Studies in the Technology of Ancient Pottery.* Amsterdam: Organization for the Advancement of Pure Research.

Chapter Eleven

New Perspectives on the Prehispanic Maya Salt Trade

Anthony P. Andrews and Shirley B. Mock

Ongoing research on the prehispanic Maya salt industry and trade has seen a number of major developments in the last twenty years. In 1980 the senior author concluded an extensive study of the salt industry of the Maya Area (figure 11.1), which included a field survey, ethnographic and historic research on salt production, and a preliminary reconstruction of the industry and trade of this resource from Preclassic times to the present.

That study was primarily focused on the prehispanic period, with an eye to the role it might have played in the development of Maya commercial systems and, by extension, in the rise of Maya civilization. It was, in part, designed to test the hypothesis, proposed by William Rathje (1971), that the long-distance salt trade had played a major role in the development of socio-political complexity in the Maya lowlands. One of the major conclusions that resulted from the study was that the saltworks of northern Yucatán were the main source of supply for the Maya lowlands, and that a long-distance trade in this resource had existed from Preclassic times until the arrival of the Spanish (Andrews 1980a, 1980b, 1984a, 1984b, 1991, 1997).

Since the publication of the study, several investigations have added new data to our knowledge of the Maya salt industry, especi-cïally in Yucatán and Belize. These data offer fresh perspectives on the prehispanic salt trade, and this chapter summarizes and discusses these materials (Andrews 1998).

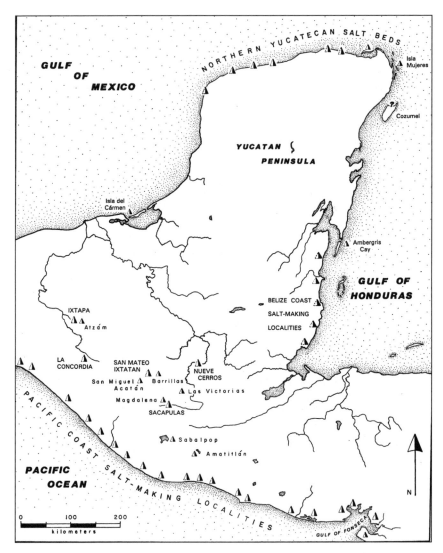

Fig. 11.1. Map of the Maya area, showing location of salt sources.

The *Salinas* of Northern Yucatán

There have been several new studies of the modern saltworks of the north coast of Yucatán. Among the most important are the works of Eduardo Batllori (1992; Batllori et al. 1998) and Luis Marrón Quiroz (1992). The first deals with the *salinas* of the entire north coast, while the second focuses on the saltworks of Celestún.These studies present new information on the ecology, geology, and hydrology of the *salinas*, as well as ethnographic accounts of the salt-making process and production figures.They also discuss the impact of the saltworks on the coastal ecology of the region and the destructive consequences of coastal development on the salt beds, and offer recommendations for mitigating these impacts (see also Aguilar Cordero 1993, 1998; Flores Guido et al. 1995; Loria Palma 1998; Paré and Fraga 1994; and Roche 1998).

The salt industry was an important component of the peninsular economy in historic times, a fact underscored by recent historic research. One of the most prominent works is Ursula Ewald's (1985, 1997) massive survey of the Mexican salt industry from 1560 to 1980; the chapter dedicated to Yucatán explores its role in the historic context of the larger Mexican economy, stressing the importance of Yucatecan salt in silver mining and other industries. These topics are also examined in more detail in José Serrano Catzin's (1986; see also 1995, 1997, 1998) thesis on the nineteenth-century industry, which traces the fluctuations of north coast production to changes in mining technology, trade with Cuba, and peninsular and national political events.

Research on the Colonial period industry is scarce. Two important studies by María Justina Sarabia Viejo explore various attempts by royal authorities and individuals to control the income from the production and trade of this commodity, from 1591 to 1610 (1978), and in 1717 (1994). Another key study, by Alicia Contreras Sánchez (1998), focuses on the Colonial period exports of Yucatecan salt and documents a substantial volume of trade with Veracruz and other Mexican ports along the coast of the Gulf of Mexico, Cuba, Central America, and even New Orleans. Most of this trade, though clearly in violation of laws prohibiting trade between Spanish colonies, was nonetheless sanctioned by local authorities, who undoubtedly derived a profit from its taxation.

Four archaeological projects have recovered new information pertaining to the prehispanic salt industry of the north coast of Yucatan. The first of these is the Isla Cerritos Archaeological Project, which investigated an island port complex at the mouth of the Rio Lagartos, a major artery for the trade of the salt from Las Coloradas. This island served as the main port of the Itzá during the Terminal Classic/Early Postclassic period (ca. A.D. 700–1200), and the data from the project reinforces the notion that Chichén Itzá controlled the saltworks of the north coast during that period; the control of this resource provided it with access to the circumpeninsular commercial trade networks from which it obtained long-distance trade goods from Central Mexico, Guatemala, and Central America (Andrews et al. 1988; Andrews et al. 1989; Andrews and Gallareta Negrón 1986; Gallareta Negrón et al. 1989; Gallareta Negrón and Andrews 1988).

Another nearby investigation, directed by Susan Kepecs, was a survey of the Chikinchel province of northeastern Yucatán, which has the largest salt beds in Mesoamerica. The research included mapping and test excavations at the coastal site of Emal, the main salt-making community and administrative center of the prehispanic industry in this region, as well as a survey of the *salinas* between Las Coloradas and El Cuyo. Kepecs (1990, 1992, 1994, 1997, 1999) confirmed the long sequence of occupation at Emal (from Late Preclassic times to the beginning of the Colonial period) and obtained new evidence of the Itzá control of the *salinas* of Chikinchel (see also Kepecs, Boucher, and Burton 1991; Kepecs and Boucher 1992; Kepecs, Feinman, and Boucher 1994; Kepecs and Gallareta Negrón 1995). It is now evident that much of the wealth of the Itzá capital was obtained through the salt trade. Moreover, both projects recovered long-distance trade goods dating to the Classic period, indicating that the long-distance salt trade was in place during that period.

Another project that included salt-related research is the Chunchucmil Archaeological Project, directed by Bruce Dahlin (Dahlin et al. 1995; see also Ardren 2000). It is probable that the site of Canbalám, located on the northern Campeche coast just south of Celestún, was the port for the Classic inland city of Chunchucmil (Andrews 1990; Dahlin and Ardren 2000), and that the nearby coastal resources—which included the *salinas* of the Celestún peninsula— were a basic component of the city's economy. Large quantities of Fine Orange and Fine Grey ceramics, as well as other long-distance trade goods (moderate quantities of grey, black, and green obsidian, and Tohil Plumbate ceramics) at Canbalám reinforce the notion that it was a major trading port in Classic and Early Postclassic times; these goods were most likely obtained in exchange for salt from Celestún.

The investigations of the Chunchucmil Project also included surveys of the *salinas* of the Celestún peninsula. These surveys produced an apparent paradox: With the exception of one small hamlet (Andrews 1976; Eaton 1978), we have not located any prehispanic settlements on the Celestún peninsula, which is surprising, in view of the large-scale salt-making industry the Spanish reported there in the sixteenth century. This paradox was the subject of a detailed study by Clara Bezanilla (1995), who has explored various explanations for it, including natural and human processes that may have erased traces of prehispanic settlement on the peninsula. Bezanilla's study also contains historic and ethnographic data on the *salinas* of Celestún, and represents an excellent complement to the study of Marrón Quiroz (1992).

The ongoing investigations at the site of Xcambó-Xtampú, directed by Thelma Sierra Sosa, are uncovering some of the strongest evidence for long-distance salt trade in the Classic period (1998, 1999a, 1999b). This site, which is located nine kilometers west of the port of Telchac on the north coast of Yucatán, is currently being mapped and excavated, and appears to be one of the most important sites on the coast. A prehispanic port and salt-making emporium, it was occupied from Late Preclassic to Early Colonial times. The saltworks continued to be exploited in the Colonial period and the nineteenth century, and are still in use today. Excavations have yielded substantial quantities of imported ceramics of the Classic period—from the Gulf Coast and Guatemalan Petén—which clearly suggest that a large-scale exchange network was in place between the north coast and the southern lowlands at this time (Andrews 1983: 27; Sierra Sosa personal communication 2000).

The *Salinas* of El Salvador and Guatemala

The Southern Maya area has seen few salt-related projects in recent years. Andrews has published a synthesis of historic, ethnographic, and archaeological data on the *salinas* of El Salvador from a survey conducted in 1978 (1991). William Fowler (1989) has published additional ethnohistoric materials on the history of exploitation, commerce, and tribute of salt during the early Colonial period. Taken together, these studies document the existence of a salt-making industry all along the Salvadorean littoral, which supplied the interior through trade networks since prehispanic times. Today, El Salvador is the principal salt producer and exporter of Central America.

Three studies have provided new information on the industry in Guatemala. On the Pacific coast, near Ocós, recent excavations by Roger Nance (1992) have documented the existence of a *sal cocida* industry dating to Late Preclassic times. The earthern mounds of discarded sherds used in the salt-making process indicate that salt was obtained by cooking brine, previously filtered through estuary soils, as is still done in some Pacific coastal localities today. The vessel forms were similar to those used in Sacapulas today, as documented in an ethnographic study in recent times by Rubén Reina and John Monaghan (1981).

One of the most important studies of the prehispanic salt industry is the research of Brian Dillon, Kevin Pope, and Michael Love (1988) at the site of Salinas de los Nueve Cerros, in the Alta Verapaz. The salt at this site is produced from a brine spring that flows out of a hill with a subterranean salt dome (Andrews 1980a, 1983; Dillon 1977). Dillon and his colleagues have documented the existence of a *sal cocida* industry during the Late Preclassic and Classic periods. Andrews originally estimated that prehispanic production by boiling brine in large ceramic vessels might have produced 300 tons a year, although he also noted the possibility of supplemental solar salt evaporation of the brine prior to cooking, as suggested by Dillon (Andrews 1980a, 1983). Subsequently, on the basis of an experiment with solar salt evaporation on the salt flats next to the site, Dillon and his colleagues have argued that salt may have been produced directly by solar evaporation, cooking of brine, and/or a combination of both methods. They further estimate that the potential production of the site may have varied from 2,000 to 24,000 tons a year during the Classic period. The wide range of the potential production figures is due to the high precipitation rate in this region, in which it rains almost all year, with only a few dry days in which solar production could take place. Thus, there is no way at present to estimate the varied levels of production from the different production technologies or combinations thereof. Moreover, if solar evaporation was used, it is not known whether the solar-produced brine was strengthened by filtering through salt-laden soils prior to cooking. It is important to note that this reconstruction of the industry is speculative, without supporting historic or archaeological evidence of solar evaporation. The boiling of partially solar-evaporated brine has been reported from El Salvador (Andrews 1980a, 1983, 1991) and the Central Mexican highlands (Apenes 1944; Sisson 1973; Parsons 1994). We currently have no evidence of solar salt production at Salinas de los Nueve Cerros in historic times. The available evidence suggests that all production from the Colonial period to the late nineteenth century was by the *sal cocida* method (Andrews 1980a, 1983). In fact, the last concessionaire of the *salinas*—who closed down his operation in 1937—believed that solar evaporation was not possible at the site, due to the year-round rainy season (Andrews 1983: 99). Nonetheless, we have to consider the possibility of a larger production capability for this source during the Classic period, which could have a major impact on our reconstruction of the salt trade during that period; this will be further discussed below.

The *Salinas* of Coastal Belize

Salt-Making Sites along the North Central Belize Coast

Thomas Gann (1918: 22) provided the first eyewitness account of coastal Maya producing salt by *sal cocida*. He also observed that inland villages obtained it from Yucatán or Guatemala. Unfortunately, Gann did not record the salt-making assemblage or the specific location of the villages. Before 1980, the only know salt sources in Belize were some small lagoons near the northern end of Ambergris Cay, from which the local inhabitants had harvested small amounts of solar salt in historic and recent times (Andrews 1980a, 1983). Since then, several archaeological investigations have uncovered the remains of a large prehispanic *sal cocida* industry all along the Belize coast (figure 11.2). The history of this research is an interesting story in itself (see Mock 1994, 1996, 1998; Vail 1988).

Research on coastal sites began in 1950, when James Bennyhoff and Clement Meighan—graduate students at the time—surveyed several sites along the coast north of Belize City, in the environs of Rocky Point, Salt Creek Lagoon, and Pott's Creek Lagoon, with the intentions of uncovering Postclassic settlements (Mock 1994, 1996, 1998). Among the materials they recovered were large quantities of fired clay cylinder fragments (figure 11.3), in association with even larger quantities of sherds of crude, thin-walled, unslipped vessels, both of unknown function. The purpose of these artifacts was not identified until almost twenty years later.

In 1968 Peter Schmidt, then Archaeological Commissioner of Belize, while inventorying the collections of the Department of Archaeology, noticed several clay cylinders from a coastal collection, possibly that of Bennyhoff and Meighan, and suggested their possible use as supports for brine-cooking vessels (Schmidt, personal communication 1996). Other archaeologists working in Belize were not aware of Schmidt's identification.

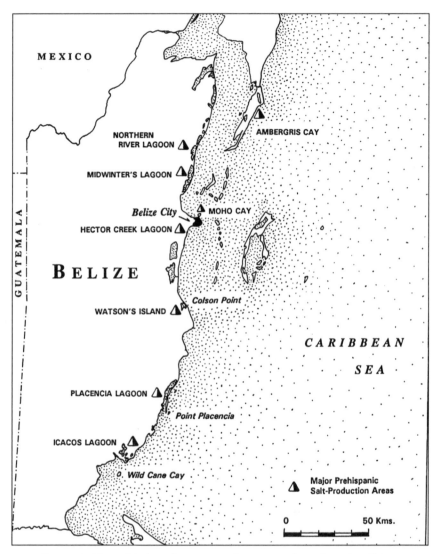

Fig. 11.2. Map of Belize showing prehispanic salt-making localities.

In the course of an investigation of several sites in the Colson Point region in 1975 and 1976, Elizabeth Graham recovered a new ceramic type at the site of Watson's Island, which she named *Coconut Walk Unslipped* (to be referred to as CWU below). These were the same vessels that Bennyhoff and Meighan (1952) had found in 1950, but Graham was not aware of their collection. Graham (1983: 160–161, 381–383, 1994: 155–156) considered several possible functions that

Fig. 11.3. Fragments of clay cylinders, which served as supports for brine cooking vessels. Terminal Classic period, Northern River Lagoon, north coast of Belize. Scale in centimeters. Photo by Shirley Mock (1994: 76, figure 5).

these vessels might have served, including the notion that they may have been used to boil brine; however, when she showed them to the senior author, he dissuaded her from the notion, as the vessels seemed too thin and fragile for salt production. He has since had to eat a fair amount of crow on this matter.

In 1980 Thomas Kelly of the Colha Archaeological Project in northern Belize conducted test excavations at several sites in the vicinity of Northern River Lagoon. Among the materials he recovered were several "puzzling" clay cylinders of unknown function (Kelly 1980). In a second season in 1981, Kelly recorded the presence of these cylinders at five additional sites: Corozalito Northeast, Will Edward's Lagoon, Pott's Creek Lagoon, Pott's Landing, and the Northern River Lagoon site (NRL). He eventually identified the cylinders as supports for brine-cooking vessels (Kelly 1982). The ethnographic study of Reina and Monaghan (1981) has suggested this interpretation, since stones to support brine-cooking vessels were still being used in a similar way at Sacapulas (Andrews 1980a, 1983; Mock 1994).

Later, in 1987, Mock studied Kelly's materials, confirming his identification. She determined that the cylinder fragments occurred in association with the CWU unslipped ceramics noted by Graham (1989) at Watson's Island. All cylinder fragments (approx. 14–33cm x

7 x 9cm; see MacKinnon and Kepecs 1989, 1991; McKillop 1995a, 1995b, 1995c; Mock 1994) display the distinctive red-pink and yellow mottling and lateral splitting characteristic of repeated firings (also see Valdez and Mock 1991). The presence of rounded- or pointed-end fragments suggest that the cylinders were driven into the ground to hold the vessels in some manner (figure 11.4); this method was replicated and found to be satisfactory for the task. By standardizing the lengths, the saltmaker was able to keep the salt vessels at a certain level, thus avoiding any spillage or overheating.

The crude, unslipped, semi-hemispheric CWU bowls from the northern Belize coast have a distinctive orange/pink paste due to complete oxidation and thin walls (3–6mm) with the vessel diameter ranging from 24–30cm. Thin walls would have provided a decided advantage in conducting heat and thus faster cooking, in addition to saving fuel resources (Rice 1987: 228). Under microscopic examination the sherds reveal many horizontal voids due to hasty smoothing of the coils. Rim sherds from NRL suggest two variations of the salt-making vessels: a slightly outflaring, walled vessel and a slightly incurved vessel form with rounded sides—a difference that may be due to individual preferences among on-site potters. Strangely, no obvious bases, curved portions, or reconstructable CWU vessels have been recovered from any site in Belize. This absence may be due to factors of poor preservation (such as the crumbly paste) or local disposal patterns or extraction methods.

Mock (1994) has argued that the vessels, like the salt-making vessels used at Sacapulas, Guatemala, were used both to evaporate

Fig. 11.4. Schematic reconstruction of brine-cooking vessels, with cylinders, sockets and spacers. South coast of Belize, Terminal Classic period. Drawing by Mary Lee Eggart, from Heather McKillop (1995c: 225, figure 10).

the brine and to make salt molds. She proposes that the CWU vessels were discarded after a single use, turned over and hit on the bottom to extract the mold, leaving rim sherds and small crushed bottom sherds to be swept away. Smoothing on the interior of the vessels may have facilitated this process. Given the precious nature of fuel sources at coastal sites with increasing population demands during the Late to Terminal Classic (Mock 1994), it is also unlikely that the vessels were fully fired prior to use (Mock 1994). Incrustations of salt and precipitates collected during the cooking process also would have clung to the vessel, contributing to its deterioration. Disposable, unfired brine-cooking vessels (placed together in groups) are still in use in the Guatemalan highland communities of San Mateo Ixtatán and Sacapulas today, and the debris is swept away after the molds are removed and stored (Reina and Monaghan 1981).

With the intentions of determining both the intensity and temporal range of salt production, Mock (1994, 1996, 1998) conducted fieldwork between 1990 and 1993 as part of the Northern Belize Coastal Project (NBCP), documenting evidence of salt-making activities at six more sites. This brought to eleven the total number of sites with unequivocal evidence of salt-making activities, attested to by the presence of the characteristic clay cylinder fragments and CWU ceramics. Mock (1994) also noted a pattern: the existence of small, isolated, spatially distinct salt-making households or stations dating to the Late to Terminal Classic. She concluded that these subsidiary sites were linked to the larger sites, such as NRL, through the provisioning of salt in return for agricultural products, such as corn, or stone tools.

In all likelihood there were other seasonally specific activities in addition to salt making that we cannot detect in the archaeological record, such as net and rope manufacture or mending, canoe manufacture, or trap and weir construction and maintenance that supplemented salt making and utilized the labor of different genders and age groups. Fishing is one such industry that has been detected at this site (Mock 1994). Production of salt (and the manufacture of the CWU ceramics) probably occurred in the dry season during high salinity, while fishing occurred during both wet and dry seasons depending on the species or spawning habits. During the dry season salt could have been exported easily by land routes. A series of rock-lined causeways radiating out from NRL over the savanna to the west supports the presence of overland routes to maximize trade. However, Mock (1994, 1998, 1999) has argued that rapid transportation of salt, salted fish, or other products to inland sites by boat would have been easier during the rainy season, when the creeks were high and navigable. Today many of the creeks can only be navigated during the rainy season. The NBCP has also revealed additional evidence of rock-lined features such as canals, sea walls, and boat slips in the lagoons that would have facilitated trade by canoe.

The NBCP 1998 field season revealed additional evidence of salt production at three sites in Midwinter's Lagoon: Powell's Ridge, Xibalba (possibly Meighan and Bennyhoff's Salt Creek site) and Saktunja. The latter is situated on a large, working plantation, Cabbage Ridge, located directly south of Northern River Lagoon. The site, like NRL, accessible only by boat, was first singled out in aerial photographs (Craig 1965) as a substantial village. It is one of thirteen sites located on and around Midwinter's Lagoon, distinguished by the large concentrations of CWU ceramics and the expended clay cylinders (figure 11.3) found on the surface. The initial reconnaissance of Saktunja, like NRL, revealed concentrations of house mounds and a disproportionate number of imported goods, in particular, ceramics typical of the Late to Terminal Classic transition. However, the ceramics revealed that Saktunja, unlike NRL, also had a noticable Postclassic presence, which may suggest that populations lingered later at Saktunja than NRL, perhaps as a result of depletion of resources at the latter site.

Considering this preliminary evidence, one of the primary goals of the subsequent NBCP 1999–2000 projects at Saktunja was to examine the ceramic distribution and fine tune the Late Classic to Postclassic transition (A.D. 660–1500) in north coastal Belize. Additional objectives were to collect data pertinent to intra-/intersite socioeconomic relationships and the production of salt. Mock, given the 1993 NBCP evidence of salt-making areas or households on the periphery of Northern River Lagoon, proposed that Saktunja was a subsidiary station to the larger site of NRL. Investigations at such a small, contained site also provide a rare opportunity to fine-tune inland/coastal relationships. The nested array of producer/consumer communities at the Northern River Lagoon is representative of a larger system of coastal and inland sites in north central Belize (Mock 1994, 1999, n.d.a, n.d.b).

One of the most important findings of the NBCP 2000 field season and ongoing analysis is that ceramics associated with salt making date to the Late to Terminal Classic transition, thus anchoring this specialized activity to this time period (Mock 1999). These data support Mock's (1999) previous contention that salt making, at least by *sal cocida*, did not linger into the Postclassic.

Another question that lingered persistently through the NBCP field seasons was whether the salt producers used a preliminary solar evaporative process to maximize production. Certainly given the fact that NRL is an estuarine lagoon today with low salinity, salt-making communities may have chosen to implement this more efficient process. As we have noted, salt making is an old and geographically widespread profession in Mesoamerica, and just as with any craft, the methods and the traditions associated with it were encoded in memory, passed down from generation to generation. Features at Saktunja, such as marl-like features between "fingers" of land and rock alignments, may have been evaporative areas during the dry season as the salt water receded. Further support for this interpretation is found in the discovery of upright expended clay cylinders in this marly matrix on the edges of Hidden Lagoon in the 1999 field season that suggest it was a salt-making zone.

To sum up this brief overview of the history of salt-making research on the northern Belize coast, regardless of size or extent of economic activities, all the sites examined had one thing in common: They seemed to be part of an economic boom during the Late to Terminal Classic Period (ca. A.D. 660–1000). This prosperity is reflected in the abundance of nonlocal ceramics that were accessible to these communities through local and regional exchange networks. Despite their remoteness today, these communities were an integral part of a network of socioeconomic, political, and ideological relationships with inland sites (Graham and Pendergast 1989; Mock 1992, 1993, 1994, 1999, n.d.a, n.d.b).

Salt Making in Southern Coastal Belize

Farther south, on the central coast of Belize, Heather McKillop has reported clay cylinders from a midden on Moho Cay directly east of Belize City; these were associated with materials dating to Middle Classic times, ca. A.D. 500–700 (McKillop 1980; see also Mock 1994). At another nearby site on the mainland near Belize City known as Hector Creek Lagoon (or "Mile 12"), Graham (1989: 152; see also MacKinnon 1989: 193) also has reported both cylinders and CWU sherds. On the central coast, as mentioned above, Graham (1989, 1994) identified CWU ceramics for the first time in 1975–76 at Watson's

Island near Colson Point, where they were dated to Middle and Late Classic times (ca. A.D. 600–900). She also found several clay cylinders at the site, but these were not directly associated with the CWU sherds.

On the lower southern coast, salt-making sites have been identified in two regions. Jefferson MacKinnon and his colleagues have reported thirteen sites in the area around Placencia Lagoon where there is substantial evidence of salt making: remains of thick-walled, globular vessels for cooking brine, clay cylinders, and spacers and sockets. Sockets were used to hold the vessels on top of the clay cylinders, while the spacers served to separate the vessels from one another (figure 11.4). Similar objects have been reported from sites farther south on the coast, as well as from salt-making sites on the Pacific coast of Guatemala (Nance 1992). The Placencia Lagoon region sites with salt-making materials date to the Late and Terminal Classic periods (see MacKinnon 1986, 1989; MacKinnon and Kepecs 1989, 1991; MacKinnon and May 1986; and MacKinnon et al. 1989).

Farther south, beneath the waters of Icacos Lagoon in the Port Honduras/Wild Cane Cay area, Heather McKillop has located the remains of four Late and Terminal Classic period salt-making sites, with materials similar to those found at the sites of Placencia Lagoon (McKillop 1993, 1994, 1995a, 1995b, 1995c, 1996, 1998). These sites were submerged toward the end of the Terminal Classic period, around A.D. 900–1000, when there was a sea-level rise of approximately one meter. McKillop also reports the presence of clay cylinders on several of the offshore cays such as Wild Cane, Frenchman's Green Vine Snake, Tiger Mound, Pelican One Pot, and Moho Cay-Toledo (see also Brandehoff-Pracht 1995). In total, fourteen sites have been reported with salt-making artifacts in this area.

There is also evidence of a prehispanic *sal cocida* industry on Ambergris Cay. CWU ceramics have been reported at two sites near the southern end, Marco Gonzalez and Guerrero (Graham 1983, 1989; Graham and Pendergast 1987, 1989, with cylinders at the latter site) and at four sites on the northern part of the island: San Juan, Ek Luum, Chac Balam, and Santa Cruz (Guderjan 1988, 1993, 1995). Most of these ceramics were recovered from contexts dating to the Late and Terminal Classic periods. Evidently, salt was produced on Ambergris by cooking brine and harvesting solar salt from the northern lagoons. It is most likely that the inhabitants of northern Ambergris Cay were harvesting solar salt from the northern lagoons throughout the prehispanic period; the Spanish reported salt ponds in the lagoons in the sixteenth century (Archivo General de Indias 1565), and solar salt was harvested in more recent historic times as well (Andrews 1983; Guderjan 1995).

In summary, remains of salt-making activities are found at over forty sites along the Belize coast. With the exception of the solar evaporation on Ambergris Cay, prehispanic Maya salt making in Belize was mainly a *sal cocida* industry, indicated archaeologically by the presence of clay cylinders and/or CWU ceramics. The lack of CWU at some sites suggests the possibility that the cylinders were used for other purposes; however, they have not been reported from inland sites. It is notable that all of the salt-making sites on the Belize coast have dates as early as the Middle Classic (ca. A.D. 500), but these sites were most populous during the Late to Terminal Classic time periods (A.D. 600–1000). Mock observes that no concrete evidence of salt making in Postclassic times has been reported archaeologically on the Belizean coast.

There are a number of unresolved issues regarding the prehispanic *sal cocida* industry of the Maya on the coast of Belize, and answers to these questions must be provided to fully reconstruct Maya salt production systems in this area. The major challenge lies in determining the volume of production at the various salt-making localities, a daunting task given the absence of historical or ethnographic data. In order to develop rough estimates of the production at individual sites, we must have a more precise idea of the details of the modes of production. For example, were the Maya cooking estuary water directly, without filtration, or filtering the water through salt flat soils to increase the salinity of the brine prior to cooking? The soil filtration process is well documented along the Pacific coast of Guatemala and El Salvador, and at Sacapulas in the Guatemalan highlands, where it has been in use since prehispanic times (Andrews 1980a, 1983, 1991; Reina and Monaghan 1981). The strongest indication of this technique may be the mounds of leached earth that MacKinnon (1989: 194) has noted around Placencia Lagoon. However, this mode of extraction is not indicated by fieldwork along the northern Belize coast (Mock 1994, 1998). Considering the low return–high energy expenditure of boiling sea water, Mock (1999) has argued for a preliminary solar evaporation process on the northern coast prior to boiling to increase salinity (see, for example, Dillon, Pope, and Love 1988).

Given the possibility that different technologies were used on the southern and northern coasts of Belize, we may also anticipate different yields: Direct boiling of salt water produces tiny quantities, filtering produces much more, and a combined solar-cooking operation produces much higher quantities. Due to the difficulty of tracing these technologies in the archaeological record, it is difficult to calculate the scale of production of different areas and their export potential. To further complicate matters, there is a possibility that different salt-making localities may have employed different production techniques (Mock 1994, 1996, 1998; see also Neely, Caran, and Sorensen 1997 for different salt-making technologies in the Tehuacan Valley). For example, the type of cooking vessels and the sockets and spacers used on the south coast suggest a different production process from the central and northern coasts, where only CWU vessels— without sockets and spacers—were used to cook brine. Valdez and Mock (1991) and Mock (1994) have discussed possible reasons for the absence of the spacers, including the presence of an alternative technology, the sockets and spacers being associated with jar forms, not CWU. Furthermore, the presence of possible leached earth mounds at Placencia Lagoon may indicate the use of soil filtration on the south coast, as opposed to some other process in the north (direct cooking or solar-cooking). Complicating matters further is the possibility not only of regional variation in technique, but of temporal variability as well; different techniques may have been employed in different temporal periods or during different seasons (Mock 1999).

Finally, we need to determine whether all the salt-making sites were engaged in production at the same time. The brine-cooking process uses large quantities of firewood, and the exhaustion of local fuel sources may have forced salt-makers to relocate periodically (Mock 1994: 356). This pattern is documented in the *sal cocida* operations of the Pacific Coast of Central America (Andrews 1980a, 1983, 1991). However, this change would have been gradual, not abrupt, and would be difficult to isolate archaeologically. Mock's (1999, n.d.a, n.d.b) documentation of all salt-making sites on the coast may ultimately provide some patterns to illuminate these settlement changes.

The Prehispanic Salt Trade

In his earlier reconstruction of the Maya salt trade, Andrews argued that the salt beds of northern Yucatán were the main source of supply of salt for the Maya lowlands, and that the long-distance trade of this commodity began in Late Preclassic times. We continue to hold the same general opinion, though in view of the data from recent research, it is now evident that the southern lowlands were not as dependent on northern imports as originally proposed, especially during the Classic period.

A major factor that promoted the emergence of a large-volume, long-distance Maya salt trade is the high level of salt consumption that characterizes the area. Tropical farming societies with low levels of meat consumption typically consume large quantities of salt to meet their minimal physiological need for sodium. In the Maya area, industry data and ethnographic reports spanning several decades indicate a modern per capita consumption of eight grams a day (Andrews 1980a, 1983). Joyce Marcus (1984) has argued that this figure is too high, citing much lower consumption figures for modern industrial and hunter-gatherer societies; however, this is a moot point since the prehispanic and modern Maya have traditionally had a diet low in meat and/or protein, requiring a salt supplement (Andrews 1980a: 75–77, 1983: 18–19; Pohl 1985; Márquez Morfín 1982; White, Healey, and Schwarcz 1993).

Another point that Marcus brings up is that the southern lowlands would not have needed to import salt from northern Yucatán in prehispanic times, as they could have satisfied their needs by obtaining salt from the ash of burnt palms and by acquiring salt from Salinas de los Nueve Cerros, a southern lowland source (1983). Palm ash yields only tiny amounts of sodium, and would therefore not have been a significant source for a population that numbered in the millions (Andrews 1984a). The new potential production figures for Salinas de los Nueve Cerros, on the other hand, do raise the possibility that this source may have supplied a significant portion of the southern lowlands during the Classic period, perhaps the middle and upper Usumacinta basin and adjoining areas. Furthermore, the thriving salt industry in southern and northern coastal Belize may have had the potential to supply large portions of the eastern and southern lowlands with salt during the same period. The question is, then, to what extent could these sources meet the demand of the Classic southern lowlands? And, if the southern lowlands needed additional salt from northern Yucatán, how much? At present, given the uncertainties in quantifying the production levels of Salinas de los Nueve Cerros and the salt-making sites of the Belize coast, there is no way to answer these questions.

In view of the almost unlimited quantities of salt that could be obtained with a minimal labor investment on the north coast of Yucatán (Andrews 1980a, 1983), several scholars have wondered why

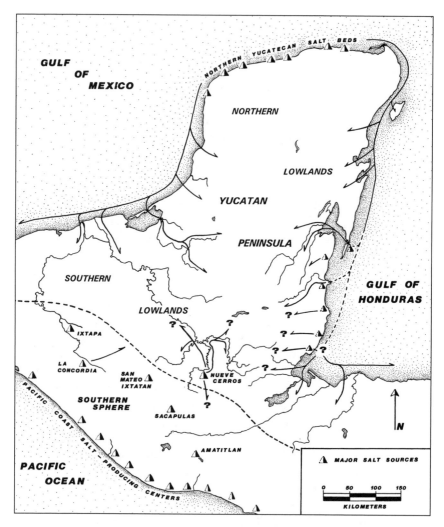

Fig. 11.5. Prehispanic salt trade routes of the Maya area.

a labor-intensive, low-yield *sal cocida* industry arose on the Belize coast. In a previous paper, Mock (1994: 332–342) proposed two factors that likely played a role in the development of this industry: (1) demographic pressure in Classic times created a huge demand for salt in the southern lowlands; it is quite possible that the trade from northern Yucatán could not meet this demand, thus spurring the growth of local industries; and (2) increasing land shortages probably created a disenfranchised population that had to invest in nonagricultural pursuits such as *sal cocida* production. This cheap labor yielded an inexpensive product that could compete with the Yucatecan salt works, where originally low production cost was inflated by long-distance transport costs. In sum, these conditions would have allowed the smaller southern producers to compete favorably against imports from the north.

An impressionistic assessment of the situation would suggest that the Belize and Nueve Cerros production centers were important sources of supply at the regional level (i.e., interior of Belize and Middle and Upper Usumacinta basin) during the Classic period (figure 11.5). It is possible, moreover, that these sources supplied even larger areas of the lowlands, such as the Classic cities of the Petén, thus diminishing their dependence on northern Yucatán.

In view of the archaeological evidence of prehispanic salt production and long-distance trade in prehispanic northern Yucatán, there is little doubt that the long-distance salt trade networks were in place since the Late Preclassic. The recent excavations at the north coast salt-related sites of Canbalám, Xcambó, Isla Cerritos, and Emal, which have yielded significant quantities of imported Gulf Coast and Petén polychromes, obsidian, and jade (which were probably purchased with salt), clearly reinforce the evidence for the existence of the long-distance salt trade in Classic times.

At the end of the Classic period, the southern salt-making industries ceased production. Nueve Cerros was abandoned in the ninth century, and most of the Belizean coastal salt-making activities came to an end around A.D. 900–1000. It is likely that several factors played a role in this process. One factor may have been the collapse and abandonment of some southern cities, leading to the reorganization or even collapse of some trade markets. The availability of fuel may have also drastically limited production and thereby settlement in Belize, as it did at Nueve Cerros. A sea-level rise of approximately one meter in Terminal Classic times may have inundated many salt-making sites on the coast of Belize, disrupting production, lowering estuary salinity, and flooding and diluting salt-impregnated soils (Mock 1994). Evidence suggests that some of the sites such as Marlowe Cay, Rocky Point, and Saktunja (figure 11.2) are former islands that have been incorporated into present day lagoons by complex sedimentation processes and sea-level changes over time.

It is interesting to note that as the southern industry went into decline, Chichén Itzá began its ascent to maximum power and wealth in northern Yucatán. As the senior author has noted elsewhere

(Andrews 1998), its rise may be related to its control of the northern saltbeds. As many of the southern salt markets dwindled with the collapse of the southern lowland cities, the accompanying decline of the Belize coastal industry would have opened up new Postclassic markets in the Petén Lakes district, northern Belize, and the Gulf of Honduras. Supplying these new markets may have been a key ingredient in Itzá commercial expansion (Susan Kepecs, personal communication 1996).

During the Postclassic, the trade of Yucatecan salt spread from the Gulf of Mexico throughout Mesoamerica. With the disappearance of the southern salt-making centers, the Yucatec Maya captured an almost exclusive monopoly of this valuable commodity in the lowlands. Needless to say, this situation was not lost on the Spanish when they arrived in the sixteenth century, and the industry survives as a major staple of the Yucatecan economy to this day.

Conclusions

The view we now have of the prehispanic Maya salt industry and its trade is much more complex than the reconstruction the senior author presented seventeen years ago (Andrews 2000). That reconstruction turned out to be far too simple. The new research in Guatemala and Belize indicates that patterns of production and trade in the Classic period were much more diverse than we originally envisioned. It is now clear that some regions of the southern lowlands had alternate sources of supply and were not exclusively dependent on imports from northern Yucatán.

The challenge for future research will be to determine levels of consumption and production in the southern lowlands during the Classic period, in order to develop a more accurate reconstruction of the trade during that period. As for the Postclassic period, the original model still stands, as the northern Yucatec saltbeds appear to have been the main source of salt for the entire lowlands up until the time of arrival of the Spanish.

Note

Heather McKillop kindly allowed us to reproduce her illustration of salt artifacts in figure 11.4. Various friends and colleagues have provided us with many useful suggestions, salty comments, and unpublished data over the last few years, for which we are most grateful: Mary Andrews, Eduardo Batllori Sampedro, Jodi Brandehoff, Clara Bezanilla, José Enrique Serrano Catzín, Alicia Contreras Sánchez, Bruce Dahlin, Elizabeth Graham, Thomas Guderjan,

Thomas R. Hester, Robert Hill III, Grant Jones, Susan Kepecs, J. Jefferson MacKinnon, Heather McKillop, Jeffrey Parsons, David Pendergast, Juan Carlos Reyes, Peter Schmidt, Thelma Sierra Sosa, and Fred Valdez Jr. Mock acknowledges the contributions and financial assistance of the following: the Colha Regional Project, The National Science Foundation, Foundation for the Advancement of Mesoamerican Studies, and Hilly Martinez of Belize City. She also notes the kind assistance of Dr. Allan Moore and Dr. John Morris of the Department of Archaeology, Belmopan, Belize.

References

Aguilar Cordero, William de Jesús
1993 "Sociedades Cooperativas de Producción Pesquera y la Industria Salinera: Dos formas de apropriación en el ecosistema de la Ría de Lagartos en el Edo. de Yucatán, Méx." Tesis de Maestría en Ciencias Antropológicas, Universidad Autónoma de Yucatán, Mérida.
1998 "Conflictos por el uso productivo de los recursos naturales en una área protegida: industria salinera y productores." Pp. 449–458 in La Sal en Mexico II, edited by J. C. Reyes G. Secretaría de Cultura, Gobierno del Estado de Colima // Universidad de Colima // Dirección General de Culturas Populares B Consejo Nacional para la Cultura y las Artes. Colima.
Andrews, Anthony P.
1980a "Salt-Making, Merchants and Markets: The Role of a Critical Resource in the Development of Maya Civilization." Ph.D. dissertation, University of Arizona, Tucson. Ann Arbor, Mich.: University Microfilms.
1980b "The Salt Trade of the Ancient Maya." Archaeology 33(4): 24–33.
1983 Ancient Maya Salt Production and Trade. Tucson: University of Arizona Press.
1984a "Long-Distance Exchange among the Maya: A Comment on Marcus." American Antiquity 49(4): 826–828.
1984b "A Survey of Maya Salt Sources." Pp. 43–61 in National Geographic Society Research Reports Vol. 16 (1975 Projects). Washington, D.C.: National Geographic Society.
1990 "The Role of Ports in Maya Civilization." Pp. 159–167 in Vision and Revision in Maya Studies, edited by Flora S. Clancy and Peter D. Harrison. Albuquerque: University of New Mexico Press.
1991 "Las salinas del El Salvador: bosquejo histórico, etnográfico y arqueológico." Mesoamerica 21: 71–93.
1997 "La sal entre los antiguos mayas." Arqueología Mexicana V(28): 38–45.
1998 "El Comercio Prehispánico Maya de la Sal: Nuevos Datos, Nuevas Perspectivas." Pp. 1–28 in La Sal en Mexico II, edited by J. C. Reyes G. Secretaría de Cultura, Gobierno del Estado de Colima // Universidad de Colima // Dirección General de Culturas Populares B Consejo Nacional para la Cultura y las Artes. Colima.
Andrews, Anthony P., F. Asaro, H. V. Michel, F. H. Stross, and P. Cervera Rivero
1989 "The Obsidian Trade at Isla Cerritos, Yucatán, Mexico." Journal of Field Archaeology 16(3): 355–363.

Andrews, Anthony P., and Tomás Gallareta Negrón
1986 "The Isla Cerritos Archaeological Project, Yucatán, Mexico." *Mexicon* VIII(3): 44–48.
Andrews, Anthony P., T. Gallareta Negrón, F. Robles Castellanos, R. Cobos Palma, and P. Cervera Rivero
1988 "Isla Cerritos: An Itzá Trading Port on the North Coast of Yucatán, Mexico." *National Geographic Research* 4(2): 196–207.
Apenes, Ola
1944 "The Primitive Salt Production of Lake Texcoco." *Ethnos* 9(1): 25–40.
Archivo General de Indias
1564–65 "Juan Pérez de Tordesillas to gobernador (ca. 1564)." In *Proceso contra Hernando Dorado, 1564–65*. Seville: Archivo General de Indias, Justicia 251.
Ardren, Traci
2000 *Chunchucmil Regional Economy Program: Report of the 1999 Field Season.* Report on file at the Department of Anthropology. Tallahassee: Florida State University.
Batllori Sampedro, Eduardo
1992 *La Actividad Salinera Artesanal en el Estado de Yucatán. Problemática y Perspectivas.* Ms. en el archivo de la CINVESTAV, Mérida.
Batllori Sampedro, Eduardo, José L. Febles Patrón, Cármen Díaz Novelo, and Miguel Briceño Quijano
1998 "Condiciones ambientales relacionadas con la actividad salinera en el estado de Yucatán." Pp. 401–447 in *La Sal en Mexico II*, edited by J. C. Reyes G. Secretaría de Cultura, Gobierno del Estado de Colima // Universidad de Colima // Dirección General de Culturas Populares B Consejo Nacional para la Cultura y las Artes. Colima.
Bennyhoff, James A., and Clement W. Meighan
1952 "Excavations in British Honduras." Manuscript in the files of the Texas Archaeological Laboratory. Austin: University of Texas.
Bezanilla, Clara I.
1995 "Salt-Making in Celestún, Yucatán (Mexico): Contemporary Evidence and Archaeological Problems." B.A. thesis, Institute of Archaeology, University College, London.
Brandehoff-Pracht, Jodi
1995 "Test Excavation at Pork & Doughboy Point, Belize." M.A. thesis, Louisiana State University, Baton Rouge.
Contreras Sánchez, Alicia del Cármen
1998 "La sal en Yucatán durante la epoca colonial." *Revista de la Universidad Autónoma de Yucatán* 205–206: 78–83. Mérida.
Dahlin, Bruce H., Anthony P. Andrews, Timothy Beach, and Valerie McCormick
1995 "Punta Canbalám in Context." Paper presented at the 60th annual meeting of the Society for American Archaeology, Minneapolis.
Dahlin, Bruce H., and Traci Ardren
2000 "Chunchucmil as a Specialized Trade Center." In *Chunchucmil Regional Economy Program: Report of the 1999 Field Season.* Report on File at the Department of Anthropology. Tallahassee: Florida State University.

Dillon, Brian D.
1977 *Salinas de los Nueve Cerros, Alta Verapaz, Guatemala.* Ballena Press Studies in Mesoamerican Art, Archaeology and Ethnohistory, 2. Socorro, N.M.: Ballena Press.
Dillon, Brian D., Kevin O. Pope, and Michael W. Love
1988 "An Ancient Extractive Industry: Maya Salt-Making at Salinas de los Nueve Cerros, Guatemala." *Journal of New World Archaeology* 7(2/3): 37–58.
Eaton, Jack D.
1978 "Archaeological Survey of the Yucatán-Campeche Coast." *Middle American Research Institute*, Pub. 46: 1–67. New Orleans: Tulane University.
Ewald, Ursula
1985 *The Mexican Salt Industry, 1560–1980. A Study in Change.* Stuttgart: Gustav Fischer Verlag.
1997 *La industria salinera de Mexico, 1560–1994.* Mexico: Fondo de Cultura Económica.
Flores Guido, José Salvador, E. Battlori, M. Villasuso Pino, and A. Mendoza Millán, editors
1995 *Marco de Referencia Para el Manejo de la Zona Costera del Estado de Yucatán.* Documento Técnico No. 1. Consejo Estatal de Consultoría Ecológica. Mérida.
Fowler, William R.
1989 *The Cultural Evolution of Ancient Nahua Civilizations: The Pipil-Nicarao of Central America.* Norman: University of Oklahoma Press.
Gallareta Negrón, Tomás, and Anthony P. Andrews
1988 "El proyecto arqueológico Isla Cerritos, Yucatán, México." *Boletín de la Escuela de Ciencias Antropológicas de la Universidad de Yucatán* 15(89): 3–16.
Gallareta Negrón, Tomás, Anthony P. Andrews, Fernando Robles Castellanos, Rafael Cobos Palma, and P. Cervera Rivero
1989 "Isla Cerritos: Un puerto maya prehispánico en la costa norte de Yucatán." *Memorias del II Coloquio Internacional de Mayistas* (Campeche, 1987), I: 311–32. México: Centro de Estudios Mayas, Universidad Nacional Autónoma de México.
Graham, Elizabeth
1983 "The Highlands of the Lowlands: Environment and Archaeology in Stann Creek District, Belize, Central America." Ph.D. dissertation, University of Cambridge, Cambridge. Ann Arbor, Mich.: University Microfilms.
1989 "A Brief Synthesis of Coastal Site Data from Colson Point, Placencia, and Marco González, Belize." Pp. 135–54 in *Coastal Maya Trade,* edited by Heather McKillop and Paul F. Healy. *Occasional Papers in Anthropology.* Peterborough, Ontario: Trent University.
1994 *The Highlands of the Lowlands: Environment and Archaeology in Stann Creek District, Belize, Central America.* Monographs in World Archaeology No. 19. Madison, Wis.: Prehistory Press.
Graham, Elizabeth, and David M. Pendergast
1987 "Cays to the Kingdom." *Royal Ontario Museum Archaeological Newsletter* II(18): 1–4.
1989 "Excavations at the Marco González Site, Ambergris Cay, Belize." *Journal of Field Archaeology* 16(4): 1–16.

Guderjan, Thomas H.
1988 "Maya Maritime Trade at San Juan, Ambergris Cay, Belize." Ph.D. dissertation, Southern Methodist University, Dallas. Ann Arbor, Mich.: University Microfilms.
1993 *Ancient Maya Traders of Ambergris Caye.* Benque Viejo del Carmen, Belize: Cubola Productions.
1995 "The Setting and Maya Maritime Trade." Pp. 1–8 in *Maya Maritime Trade, Settlement, and Populations on Ambergris Caye, Belize,* edited by Thomas H. Guderjan and James F. Garber. Maya Research Program, San Antonio. Lancaster, Calif.: Labyrinthos.
Kelly, Thomas C.
1980 "The Colha Regional Survey." Pp. 51–69 in *The Colhá Project: Second Season, 1980 Interim Report,* edited by Thomas R. Hester, Jack D. Eaton, and Harry J. Shafer. San Antonio: University of Texas Center for Archaeological Research.
1982 "The Colhá Regional Survey, 1981." Pp. 85–97 in *Archaeology at Colhá, Belize: The 1981 Interim Report,* edited by Thomas R. Hester, Jack D. Eaton, and Harry J. Shafer. San Antonio: University of Texas Center for Archaeological Research, and Centro Studi e Ricerche Ligabue, Venezia.
Kepecs, Susan M.
1990 "Preliminary Report on the Chikinchel Survey Project to the Instituto Nacional de Antropología, Mexico City, D. F., and the Centro Regional de Yucatán, Mérida." Manuscript.
1992 "Informe Preliminar al INAH, D.F., y al CRY-INAH, Mérida, Yuc., sobre la Segunda Temporada del Campo del Proyecto Chikinchel, Yucatán, México." Manuscript.
1994 "Northeast Yucatán and the Aztecs: A World Systems Perspective." Paper presented at the 59th annual meeting of the Society for American Archaeology, Anaheim, Calif.
1997 "Native Yucatán and Spanish Influence: The Archaeology and History of Chikinchel." *Journal of Archaeological Method and Theory* 4(3/4): 307–29.
1999 "The Political Economy of Chikinchel, Yucatán: A Diachronic Analysis from the Prehispanic Era through the Age of Spanish Administration." Ph.D. dissertation, University of Wisconsin, Madison. Ann Arbor, Mich.: University Microfilms.
Kepecs, Susan M., and Sylviane Boucher
1992 "Proyecto Chikinchel: pozos de sondeo en Emal, Yucatán." Pp. 162–166 in *Consejo de Arqueología, Boletín 1991.* Instituto Nacional de Antropología e Historia, México.
Kepecs, Susan M., Sylviane Boucher, and James Burton
1991 "The Itzá in Chikinchel: The Politics of Salt." Paper presented at the 47th International Congress of Americanists, New Orleans.
Kepecs, Susan M., Gary Feinman, and Sylviane Boucher
1994 "Chichén Itzá and its Hinterlands: A World Systems Perspective." *Ancient Mesoamerica* 5(2): 141–158.

Kepecs, Susan M., and Tomás Gallareta Negrón
1995 "Una visión diacrónica de Chikinchel y Cupul, Noreste de Yucatán, México." Pp. 275–293 in *Memorias del Segundo Congreso Internacional de Mayistas*. Universidad Nacional Autónoma de México, México.

Loria Palma, José Inés
1998 "El sector social en la producción salinera." Pp. 459–473 in *La Sal en Mexico II*, edited by J. C. Reyes G. Secretaría de Cultura, Gobierno del Estado de Colima // Universidad de Colima // Dirección General de Culturas Populares B Consejo Nacional para la Cultura y las Artes. Colima.

MacKinnon, J. Jefferson
1986 "In Search of the Ancient Maritime Maya." *Wisconsin Academy Review* (June): 22–26. Madison: University of Wisconsin.

1989 "Spatial and Temporal Patterns of Prehistoric Maya Settlement, Procurement, and Exchange on the Coast and Cays of Southern Belize." Ph.D. dissertation, University of Wisconsin, Madison. Ann Arbor, Mich.: University Microfilms.

MacKinnon, J. Jefferson, and Susan M. Kepecs
1989 "Prehispanic Salt-Making in Belize: New Evidence." *American Antiquity* 54(3): 522–533.

1991 "Prehispanic Salt-Making in Belize: A Reply to Valdez and Mock and to Marcus." *American Antiquity* 56(3): 528–530.

MacKinnon, J. Jefferson, Susan M. Kepecs, Gary R. Walters, and Emily M. May
1989 "Coastal Trade and Procurement Sites in Southern Belize: Implications for Yucatecan Salt Production and Circum-Peninsular Trade." In *Memorias del II Coloquio Internacional de Mayistas* (Campeche 1987) I: 703–716. Centro de Estudios Mayas, U.N.A.M., Mexico.

MacKinnon, J. Jefferson, and Emily M. May
1986 "Late Classic Salt Production on Lagoon Shores in the Stann Creek District, Belize, Central America." Paper presented at the 51st annual meeting of the Society for American Archaeology, New Orleans.

Marcus, Joyce
1983 "Lowland Maya Archaeology at the Crossroads." *American Antiquity* 48(3): 454–488.

1984 "Reply to Hammond and Andrews." *American Antiquity* 49(4): 829–833.

1991 "Another Pinch of Salt: A Comment on MacKinnon and Kepecs." *American Antiquity* 56(3): 526–527.

Márquez Morfín, Lourdes, coordinator
1982 *Playa del Cármen. Una población de la costa oriental en el Postclásico [Un estudio osteológico]. Colección Científica*, 119. I.N.A.H., Mexico.

Marrón Quiroz, Luis G.
1992 "Manifestación de Impacto Ambiental. Modalidad General. Operación de la Charca Salinera 'Tanques.,' Mpio. de Calkiní, Campeche." Salinas de Celestún, S.A. Ms. on file, Consultóres en Ecosistemas, S.C., Mérida.

McKillop, Heather
1980 "Moho Cay, Belize: Preliminary Investigations of Trade, Settlement and Marine Resource Exploitation." M.A. thesis, Trent University, Peterborough, Ontario, Canada. Ann Arbor, Mich.: University Microfilms.

1993 "Sea Level Change and Ancient Maya Salt Production in South Coastal Belize." Paper presented at the 92nd annual meeting of the American Anthropological Association, Washington, D.C.

1994 "Traders of the Maya Coast: Five Field Seasons in the Swamps of Southern Belize, 1988–1993." *Mexicon* 16(6): 115–119.

1995a "The 1994 Field Season in South-Coastal Belize." *LSU Maya Archaeology News* 1. Baton Rouge.

1995b "Modeling Classic Maya Settlement and Sea Level Changes in South Coastal Belize." Paper presented at the 60th annual meeting of the Society for American Archaeology, Minneapolis.

1995c "Underwater Archaeology, Salt Production, and Coastal Maya Trade at Stingray Lagoon, Belize." *Latin American Antiquity* 6(3): 214–228.

1996 "Ancient Maya Trading Ports and the Integration of Long-Distance and Regional Economies: Wild Cane Cay in South-Coastal Belize." *Ancient Mesoamerica* 7(1): 49–62.

1998 "Ancient Maya Economic Specialization of Salt Production Revealed by Underwater Excavations, South-Coastal Belize." Paper presented at the 63rd annual meeting of the Society for American Archaeology, Seattle.

Mock, Shirley B.

1992 "Late-Terminal Classic Salt-Making Sites along the Northern Coast of Belize." Paper presented at the annual meeting of the Texas Archaeological Society, Corpus Christi, Tex.

1993 "When It Rains It Pours: Additional Consideration for Salt-Making in Belize." Paper presented at the 58th annual meeting of the Society for American Archaeology, St. Louis, Mo.

1994 "The Northern River Lagoon Site (NRL): Late to Terminal Classic Maya Settlement, Salt-Making, and Survival on the Northern Belize Coast." Ph.D. dissertation, University of Texas, Austin. Ann Arbor, Mich.: University Microfilms.

1996 "Salt: A Mover and a Shaker in Late to Terminal Classic Maya Communities on the Belize Coast." Paper presented at the 61st annual meeting of the Society for American Archaeology, New Orleans.

1998 "La sal como impulsor y agitador en las comunidades mayas al final de la época clásica en las costas de Belize." Pp. 29–41 in *La Sal en Mexico II*, edited by J. C. Reyes G. Secretaría de Cultura, Gobierno del Estado de Colima // Universidad de Colima // Dirección General de Culturas Populares B Consejo Nacional para la Cultura y las Artes. Colima.

1999 *The Northern Belize Coastal Project: 1999 Interim Report*, edited by Shirley Boteler Mock. San Antonio: University of Texas, ITC.

n.d.a "'Pushing the Limits': Terminal Classic Social and Economic Processes on the Belize Coast." Invited paper to be published in *Maya Ceramics: Socioeconomic Processes*, edited by Antonia Foias and Sandra Lopez Varela. Los Angeles: Institute for Archaeology, forthcoming.

n.d.b "Excavating the Terminal Classic to find the Postclassic: Ceramics from Saktunja, Belize." In *New Horizons for Ancient Maya Ceramics*, edited by Heather McKillop and Shirley Boteler Mock. Tallahassee: University Press of Florida, forthcoming.

Nance, C. Roger
1992 "Guzmán Mound: A Late Preclassic Salt Works on the South Coast of Guatemala." *Ancient Mesoamerica* 3(1): 27–46.

Neely, James A. S., Christopher Caran, and Frances Ramirez Sorensen
1997 "The Prehispanic and Colonial Saltworks of the Tehuacan Valley and Vicinity, Southern Puebla, Mexico." Paper presented in the Salt II Session at the 62nd annual meeting of the Society for American Archaeology, Nashville, Tenn.

Paré, Luisa, and Julia Fraga
1994 *La Costa de Yucatán: Desarrollo y Vulnerabilidad Ambiental.* Cuadernos de Investigación 23. Instituto de Investigaciones Sociales, Universidad Nacional Autónoma de México, Mexico.

Parsons, Jeffrey R.
1994 "Late Postclassic Salt Production and Consumption in the Basin of Mexico: Some Insights from Nexquipayac." Pp. 257–290 in *Economies and Polities in the Aztec Realm*, edited by Mary G. Hodge and Michael E. Smith. Studies in Culture and Society No. 6. Albany: Institute for Mesoamerican Studies, State University of New York.

Pohl, Mary, editor
1985 *Prehistoric Lowland Maya Environment and Subsistence Economy.* Papers of the Peabody Museum of Archaeology and Ethnology No. 77. Cambridge, Mass.: Harvard University.

Rathje, William L.
1971 "The Origin and Development of Lowland Classic Maya Civilization." *American Antiquity* 36(3): 275–286.

Reina, Ruben E., and John Monaghan
1981 "The Ways of the Maya. Salt Production in Sacapulas, Guatemala." *Expedition* 23(3): 13–33.

Roche D., Joaquín
1998 "Producción y comercialización de la sal en la península de Yucatán: Un relato testimonial." Pp. 323-330 in *La Sal en Mexico II*, edited by J. C. Reyes G. Secretaría de Cultura, Gobierno del Estado de Colima // Universidad de Colima // Dirección General de Culturas Populares B Consejo Nacional para la Cultura y las Artes. Colima.

Sarabia Viejo, María Justina
1978 "El estanco de la sal en Yucatán (1591–1610)." *Anuario de Estudios Americanos* XXXV: 379–405.
1994 "La real hacienda yucateca en 1717: los asientos de Diego de Santiesteban." *Memorias del Primer Congreso Internacional de Mayistas* (San Cristóbal de las Casas, 1989) III: 280–287. México: Universidad Nacional Autónoma de México.

Serrano Catzín, José Enrique
1986 "Apuntes sobre la industria salinera de Yucatán a mediados del siglo XIX." B.A. thesis in History, Facultad de Ciencias Antropológicas de la Universidad Autónoma de Yucatán, Mérida.

1995 "Aspectos del trabajo, la propiedad y el comercio salinero en Yucatán durante el siglo XIX." Pp. 113–127 in *La Sal en México*, Juan Carlos Reyes, coordinator. Universidad de Colima y Consejo Nacional para la Cultura y las Artes. Colima.

1997 "El comercio de la sal en el siglo XIX: problemas y obstáculos para su desarollo." *Revista de la Universidad Autónoma de Yucatán* 201: 96–106. Mérida.

1998 "Problemas sobre el comercio de la sal yucateca en el siglo XIX." Pp. 225–251 in *La Sal en Mexico II*, edited by J. C. Reyes G. Secretaría de Cultura, Gobierno del Estado de Colima // Universidad de Colima // Dirección General de Culturas Populares B Consejo Nacional para la Cultura y las Artes. Colima.

Sierra Sosa, Thelma Noemí
1998 "Xcambó: Centro Administrativo y Puerto de Comercio del Clásico Maya." Paper presented at the Congreso Internacional de Mayistas, Guatemala.

1999a "Xcambó. Codiciado enclave económico del Clásico Maya." *Arqueología Mexicana* VII(37): 40–47.

1999b "Xcambó: Codiciado Puerto del Clásico Maya." *I=INAJ Semilla de Maíz* 10(Junio): 19–27. Conaculta - I.NA.H, Centro INAH Yucatán, Mérida.

Sisson, Edward B.
1973 *First annual Report of the Coxcatlan Project*. Andover, Mass.: R. S. Peabody Foundation for Archaeology, Phillips Academy.

Vail, Gabrielle
1988 *The Archaeology of Coastal Belize*. Oxford: BAR International Series 463.

Valdez, Fred, Jr., and Shirley B. Mock
1991 "Additional Considerations for Prehispanic Salt-Making in Belize." *American Antiquity* 56(3): 520–525.

White, Christine D., Paul F. Healey, and Henry P. Schwarcz
1993 "Intensive Agriculture, Social Status, and Maya Diet at Pacbitun, Belize." *Journal of Anthropological Research* 49(4): 347–375.

Chapter Twelve

Community Economy and the Mercantile Transformation in Postclassic Northeastern Belize

Marilyn A. Masson

Three influential models proposed by William L. Rathje in 1972, 1975, and 1983 outlined important elements of Maya economic organization that have stood the test of time. The first of these, known as the core-buffer model, examines the development of primary Petén Maya centers through economic and political interaction with resource-rich coastal and highland buffer zones in the Maya area (Rathje 1972; Rathje et al. 1978). The second of Rathje's seminal theoretical contributions is the mercantile model, which he proposed along with Jeremy Sabloff (Sabloff and Rathje 1975; Rathje and Sabloff 1973; Rathje 1975; Rathje et al. 1978). This model offers new interpretations of Postclassic Maya social transformations in light of the amplification of maritime trade networks, bulk transactions, and interregional exchange that altered the political and economic institutions of this period. Rathje's third model (1983) calls for the analysis of household economies, as these form the basic units of regional systems of production and exchange.

These models were path-breaking when they were first published, and twenty-five years of subsequent research have confirmed fundamental premises of Maya political economies that were outlined in these models while refining them with new archaeological data. The essays in this volume are a testimony of the pivotal position that

Rathje's works continue to play in the study of interregional economic interaction in the Maya area. Like most seminal works, many of the details of Rathje's models have been revised and embellished by recent research, but the essential frameworks stand strong and remain useful.

This chapter outlines results of recent research on Postclassic Maya economic development in northern Belize. William Rathje's models provide helpful frameworks for interpreting the diachronic trends of local production and long-distance trade at the island settlements of Laguna de On and Caye Coco. Northeastern Belize is one region where the collapse of southern lowland Classic period Maya civilization was less catastrophic for the demography and prosperity of subsequent populations (Culbert 1988; Masson 1997). This area would have been a Classic period "buffer" zone according to Rathje's (1972) model, due to its distant location from the Petén core, its less-pronounced political development, and its proximity to coastal resources and coastal trade routes. Substantial numbers of thriving communities have been found in northeastern Belize for the Early and Late Postclassic periods (Sidrys 1983; Andrews and Vail 1990; Masson 2000a), and some sites were occupied continually through the Classic to Postclassic transformation (Pendergast 1981; 1985; 1986; Graham 1987; Masson 1997).

The mercantile model represents a landmark effort by Rathje and Sabloff (1975) to account for Classic-to-Postclassic differences in architectural accomplishments through nontraditional modes of assessing the "height" of "civilization." They offer a viable alternative to the aesthetic view of Postclassic society as a "decadent" remnant of former glory based primarily on decreased investment in monumental architecture (Proskouriakoff 1955; Pollock 1962; Willey 1986). These authors observe that more efficient investments of social energy into mercantile development and architectural forms that do not preserve well during the Late Postclassic are the mark of maturing state market-oriented societies in the Maya area and elsewhere in the annals of world history.

Differences are observed in regional demographic trends of collapse between Petén core city-states and zones that were more "peripheral" to the Petén core zone during the Classic period such as northeastern Belize (Culbert 1988; Demarest 1997). Rathje's core-buffer model (1972) provides important insights for explaining the prosperity of northeastern and coastal Belize areas even as the Petén states crumbled. The buffer or peripheral zones of Belize and

Quintana Roo were in a more advantageous geographic position to participate in growing networks of maritime trade. Their location made it easier for traders in these zones to obtain diverse resources of other regions, including those of Honduras, the Guatemalan highlands, and northern Yucatan, as Rathje (1972) notes. These networks of exchange rose in importance and the coast of the Yucatan peninsula became a primary path for commercial interaction during the Postclassic period (Rathje 1972; Sabloff and Rathje 1975; Dreiss and Brown 1989; McKillop 1996). The southern lowland Classic-to-Postclassic transition is marked by the trend of former "buffer" zone regions achieving economic and political independence from the former Petén "core" zones and in the process contributing to the core zone's destruction by strangling its economy as outlined in Rathje's (1972) model. The "organizational advantages" possessed by the Petén core in ideological, political, and economic realms were either now transferred to formerly peripheral locations or they were no longer useful or desired by this time (Rathje 1972).

A third important paper published by William Rathje (1983) calls for the analysis of household assemblages to test models of economic development in the Maya area. Specifically, he advocates a consideration of the following categories of data: the range of labor investments in household architecture, material inventories, the quantity and quality of personal adornments, the amount of imported tools, the range in quality and functions reflected in pottery assemblages, and the health status of domestic groups (Rathje 1983: 27–30).

These approaches have been applied in recent work performed at the communities of Laguna de On and Caye Coco (Masson 1999a, 1999b, 2000a; Masson and Rosenswig 1997, 1998, 1999; Rosenswig and Masson 2000, 2001a, n.d.). Postclassic research at the households of these sites has investigated three particular trends: (1) the long-term development of production and exchange patterns at each community throughout the Late Postclassic period (around A.D. 1100–1517); (2) variation in community scale economies that are tied to their regional political status; and (3) variation in household economic patterns according to status within each community. These three types of data reflect the growth of Postclassic mercantile society in northern Belize and the role of specific communities and individual domestic groups in production and exchange. Two crucial tenets of the mercantile model are as follows: that market exchange was prevalent, and that an entrepreneurial environment encouraged greater overall affluence. For this reason, social distinctions on the scale of those

observed during the Classic period in architecture and lavish posses-
sions were less pronounced for the Postclassic period (Webb 1964;
Rathje 1975). The work at Caye Coco and Laguna de On discussed
here identifies the social and economic characteristics of two communities that were linked to regional commercial development. This
chapter summarizes diachronic trends in settlement and artifact assemblages at these sites and current interpretations of the socioeconomic transformations they represent.

The Sites of Caye Coco
and Laguna de On

Caye Coco and Laguna de On are island settlements on Progresso
Lagoon and Honey Camp Lagoon respectively (figure 12.1). These
lagoons are part of the Freshwater Creek drainage system, one of
several waterways that connects northern Belize to the Caribbean Sea
via a south-to-north route. Both island settlements are thought to have
been the central focus of Postclassic period settlements that also extended along the shores of these lagoons, as they each exhibit greater
architectural elaboration and evidence for ritual activity than their
associated shore settlements (Rosenswig and Masson n.d.; Masson
1999a). Leaders of each lagoon community probably resided on these
island nuclei. Within the region of northeastern Belize, which formed
the southern half of the Chetumal Province during the Postclassic
period (Jones 1989), Caye Coco was one of at least five political centers (Masson 2000a). This island is 400 X 200m (Masson 1999a), on
which large elite residential mounds and a meeting hall are present.
The island of Laguna de On was one-fourth the size of Caye Coco,
and as it lacks mounded architecture, this settlement appears to have
been far less politically significant than Caye Coco. However, substantial construction activity at Laguna de On is represented in terrace
extensions to the island's surface, as well as a linear depression feature that may have been a ballcourt (Masson 2000a). Both sites were
occupied throughout the Postclassic period.

Architecture and Burials
at Caye Coco and Laguna de On

Rathje (1983: 26) advocates comparing the scale of investment in
domestic architecture as one method of assessing interhousehold
wealth differences. Clear differences are seen between Laguna de On

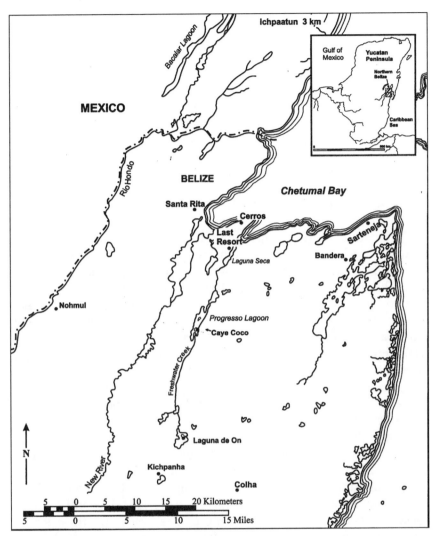

Fig. 12.1. Map showing the location of Laguna de On and Caye Coco in northern Belize.

and Caye Coco, as the former lacks the mounded residential architecture so common at the latter community. Within Caye Coco, however, distinct divisions are not observed in the volume of residential construction (Rosenswig and Masson n.d.). This trend suggests a continuum in the wealth of family groups living on the island as might be expected in a socially fluid, entrepreneurial environment. I have elsewhere noted (1999b, n.d.) that the primary distinguishing factor of Postclassic elite residences at Caye Coco and Laguna de On is their association with ritual facilities or paraphernalia. This trend parallels observations at other Postclassic communities such as Santa Rita (Chase 1986, 1992) and it suggests that the control of ritual knowledge, religious symbols, and ritual activities helped elite social classes to maintain their status during this period. As Chase (1986, 1992) argues, the difficulty in identifying elite social classes by degrees of residential elaboration may attest to a society with fluid social boundaries. It is interesting to note that patterns are more difficult to identify within communities than between them. This may suggest that social stratification was closely tied to communities' positions in regional hierarchies.

The sudden and perhaps simultaneous erection of Caye Coco's mounded residential structures in the middle of the thirteenth century suggests that the site underwent centralizing tendencies at this time. The construction of these platforms may reflect a founding event (Masson 2000b). This trend is similar to patterns observed in the settlement history of Cozumel Island sites that are coeval with the rise of Mayapan to power in northwest Yucatan. Rathje and Sabloff (1973: 225) suggest that the Cozumel administrative bureaucracy became internally strengthened and centralized in response to a general decentralization of economic power structures in the Late Postclassic Maya world (see also Connor 1983; Freidel and Sabloff 1984). The lack of strong external controls imposed on trading activities at Cozumel may have allowed local power to coalesce, according to these authors. Similar processes may have been operating in northern Belize (Masson 2000a, 2000b).

Burial patterns at Caye Coco and Laguna de On, like the architectural construction patterns at Caye Coco, suggest a continuum of social status among residents of these sites. Burials at these settlements are concentrated in discrete family cemeteries that are located in off-mound locations that were probably within residential courtyards (Rosenswig 1998, 2001). Thirty-nine Postclassic burials were excavated at Caye Coco, and twenty burials of this period were excavated at Laguna de On. Most burials do not exhibit dramatic interpersonal differences in grave goods, although more burials have grave goods at Caye Coco (38.7 percent) than at Laguna de On (19 percent). At Caye Coco, two individuals at Cemetery 2 received far more elaborate grave offerings than the others (Rosenswig 2001). One of these was interred with three large incense burners and an olla, a chert knife, and an uncarved stela. The other individual was interred with deer skulls and additional human crania fragments. Ten other burials had offerings of items such as marine shell ornaments, single vessels, a carved bone object, chert cores, and obsidian blades. At Laguna de On, one burial was distinguished from the others by grave goods that included a carved animal femur, a jade bead, a ceramic effigy face, and a vessel (Rosenswig 1998). All other burials at this site had humble offerings such as *Pomacea* (freshwater snail) shells or a single crystal bead. These intersite comparisons highlight the same differences in community status suggested by the architecture at each site. Caye Coco residents were wealthier than those of Laguna de On. At each settlement, the majority of individuals received no grave goods. The majority of individuals with grave goods at each site were buried with local materials or low quantities of exotic materials. At each site, one or two individuals do appear differentiated by their interment with unusual grave goods, but these individuals are not interred in separate, elaborate facilities. Instead, they are located in the midst of cemeteries in which individuals with no grave goods or few grave goods are also found. On a regional scale, the offerings associated with graves at these communities are not elaborate. Richer burials are known from Santa Rita (Chase and Chase 1988), for example, although these do not approach the scale of funerary investment known from the Classic period. These data generally correspond to Sabloff and Rathje's (1975: 80) prediction that mercantile societies might be expected to refrain from investing heavily in funerary rituals in favor of continuing to circulate wealth.

Economic Trends over Time: Caye Coco and Laguna de On

One of Rathje's criteria for reconstructing household economy is the comparison of domestic inventories (1983: 27, 32). These are compared below in two ways—over time and between contemporary domestic areas. These comparisons reflect important similarities and differences in household and community production and exchange.

Excavations around the domestic structures at Caye Coco have revealed some deep (70cm) midden deposits that provide important temporal information on changing artifact patterns. The relative percentage of abundant classes of artifacts from three of these middens (figure 12.2) shows similarities over time—which implies long-term stability of local production and exchange networks. All levels shown postdate A.D. 1100, except for the bar at the top left corner (Suboperation 18, Levels 5–7), which is Terminal Classic/Early Postclassic in date. The proportions of lithic flakes, lithic tools, obsidian blades, and net weights are similar within each location over time for all Postclassic levels. These artifacts were related to everyday activities, and suggest similarities in domestic economy throughout Caye Coco's Postclassic occupation. Furthermore, these trends suggest that little specialization in household activities is reflected by these particular tool inventories. Households were involved in similar activities of self-maintenance.

The Terminal Classic levels (figure 12.2, top graph, far left column) are different in that local chert and chalcedony lithic tools and flakes make up a greater proportion of the assemblage. This trend suggests that local lithic resources were more important in this period, a trend I discuss in more detail below. Fewer faunal resources are present in the Terminal Classic deposit, and this level shares the presence of obsidian blades and net weights with later Postclassic levels shown in figure 12.2.

Artifact categories that are less numerically abundant at the site illustrate some additional interesting temporal differences (figure 12.3). Obsidian blades increase over time from the Terminal Classic through Postclassic levels in Suboperation 18 with a correlating decline in local lithic tools, suggesting an amplification of long-distance exchange networks and a greater dependency on obsidian in the households of this community (see also Masson and Chaya 2000). This pattern represents one highly visible aspect of the involvement of Caye Coco residents in trading activities.

The production of marine shell artifacts increases at Caye Coco from the Terminal Classic through Postclassic periods at Suboperation 18. Marine shellworking debris is found in all three Postclassic middens, although it is more common at Suboperation 31. This midden was adjacent to an elite residential structure, and may reflect an elite focus on shellworking at the site that is also suggested by additional spatial comparisons discussed below. Spindle whorls are also more common in the latest level of Suboperation 31 compared to the other middens. These data provide some indication that certain craft activities increased over time at Caye Coco.

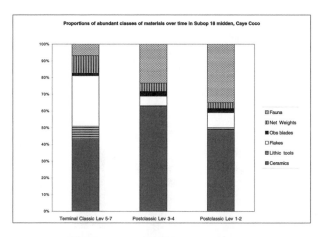

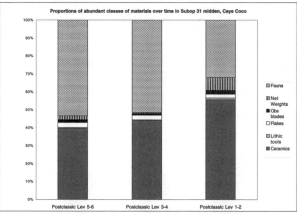

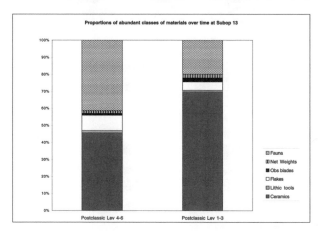

Fig. 12.2. Proportions of abundant classes of materials by level at Caye Coco midden deposits, Suboperations 18 (top), 31 (center), and 13 (bottom).

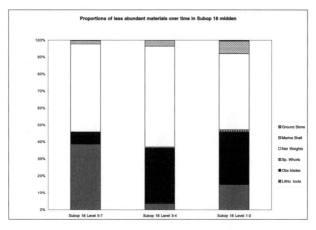

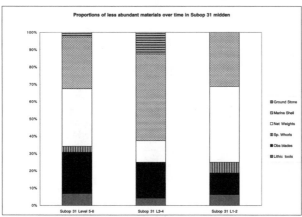

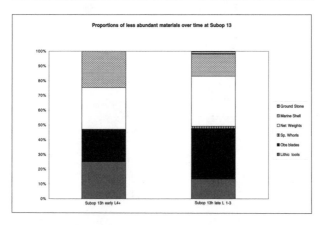

Fig. 12.3. Proportions of less abundant classes of materials by level at Caye Coco midden deposits, Suboperations 18 (top), 31 (center), and 13 (bottom).

Ceramic Trends over Time

Looking at the types of ceramics found in the Suboperation 18 midden over time in figure 12.4, we see a trend of increasing uniformity in production of Postclassic ceramic type groups over time. The homogenous nature of Postclassic ceramic assemblages was recognized by Sabloff and Rathje (1975; Rathje 1975; Rathje et al. 1978) at Cozumel and other east coast Maya sites. They note that common Postclassic ceramic types from different sites exhibited important similarities in form, paste, and surface treatment, and suggested that maritime trade contributed in important ways to these similarities in production templates. They further suggested that Postclassic ceramics may have been mass-produced and widely traded, although more information on paste variation at many sites is needed to test this hypothesis. Their articles primarily refer to Fine Orange and Fine Gray trade wares, but their hypothesis is supported in a study of common Postclassic pottery types at Cozumel (Connor 1983). Connor's ceramic attribute analysis at Cozumel confirms a high degree of uniformity and homogeneity in manufacturing attributes of Late Postclassic pottery (Connor 1983: 356–373). She identified these trends using coefficient equations that measured the similarity and homogeneity over time in assemblages of ceramic attributes. Connor notes that these trends increase over time from earlier assemblages and she attributes this pattern to increasing internal centralized control of production and trade activities within Cozumel communities.

At Caye Coco, a greater diversity of slipped (figure 12.4, top chart) and unslipped (figure 12.4, bottom chart) ceramics is indicated in basal Terminal Classic/Early Postclassic levels of the Suboperation 18 midden. The dominant red-slipped ware is Zakpah Red, characterized by its buff sandy paste, highly eroded slipped surfaces, and its incompletely fired core. Also present are slate or ash-tempered sherds and other eroded red-slipped or black-slipped sherds with sandy or calcite temper. Levels 1–5 show a predominant proportion of Payil or Rita red-slipped sherds. Distinguishing Payil and Rita Red has been difficult at Caye Coco, as the calcite-tempered pastes of these types vary along a continuum. Attributes of form that differentiate these types (Chase 1982) cannot be determined from the fragmented sherds of these middens. Paste and slip categories show increased homogeneity (fewer type groups) in the assemblage over time. The forms within these type groups also show decreased variability over time (Masson and Rosenswig 2001). Specifically, in Payil Red vessels

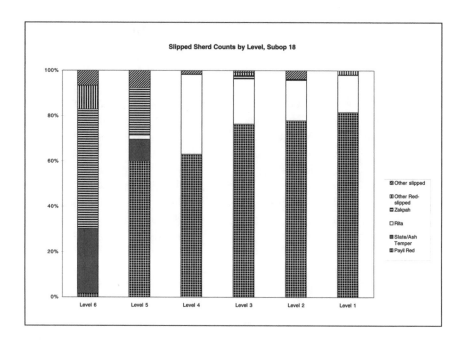

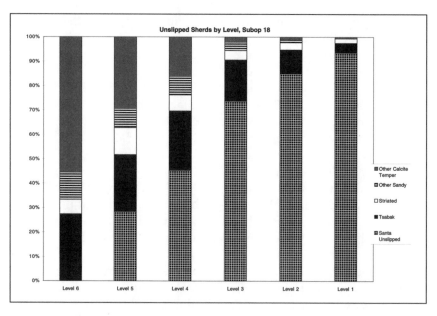

Fig. 12.4. Slipped (top) and unslipped (bottom) sherd counts by type and paste groups in levels of Caye Coco midden (Suboperation 18).

at Caye Coco, the use of fewer rim/lip combinations is observed over time, suggesting that manufacturing techniques became more standardized.

Greater standardization and decreasing numbers of type groups are also indicated in unslipped ceramic temporal trends. A variety of calcite-tempered, striated, and sandy-tempered paste types are present in unslipped types of the lower Terminal Classic/Early Postclassic levels of Suboperation 18, and calcite-tempered Santa Unslipped wares dominate the unslipped assemblage in Postclassic Levels 1–4 (figure 12.4, bottom). Technologically, both slipped and unslipped ceramic type groups improve significantly over time at Caye Coco—as reflected in the quality of their slip (for slipped types), hardness, fineness, and the homogeneity of their pastes. For all types we see a continuum of improvement that also supports the idea of long-term trends of economic growth and stability at this community and standardization of the Postclassic pottery of northeastern Belize. These trends parallel patterns observed in ceramics of this date at Cozumel (Connor 1983) and at Petén Lakes sites (Rice 1980).

Interpreting these data is a challenging enterprise. Sabloff, Rathje, and colleagues (1975, Rathje et al. 1978) attribute this trend to greater mass production and distribution of pottery through trade. A greater degree of interregional integration may have also occurred through trade that might have influenced more widespread stylistic similarities. Smaller numbers of specialists and more tightly regulated manufacturing processes can also create uniform products. Regional studies are needed to compare clay sources and manufacturing attributes between sites before we can fully understand the mode of production for Postclassic pottery.

Figures 12.5 and 12.6 show the distribution of artifact classes by context at Caye Coco. These graphs differ from figures 12.2 and 12.3 as they incorporate a greater number of domestic contexts from Caye Coco, whereas figures 12.2 and 12.3 only present data from middens. The top graphs in figures 12.5 and 12.6 depict mounded architecture, while the bottom graphs compare assemblages from off-mound domestic zone deposits. Obsidian blades, shown in gray at the bottom of each chart, are generally distributed in all contexts at the site. This pattern illustrates the long recognized trend that this material was accessible to all members of Postclassic communities through enhanced distribution and market systems that made this commodity more abundant and affordable (Sidrys 1977; Freidel 1986; Rice 1984: 192; Rice et al. 1985: 602; Rice 1987). Obsidian from Caye Coco is

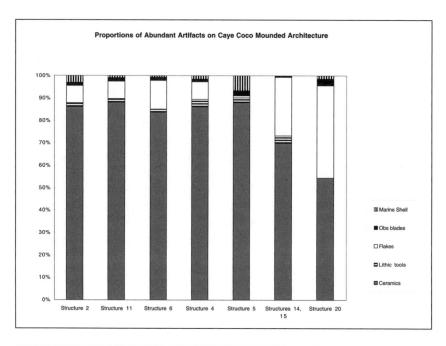

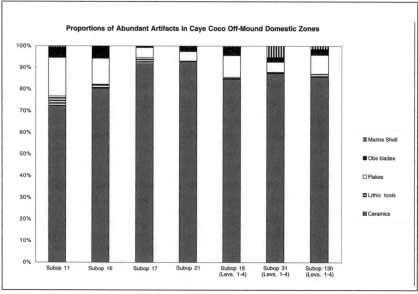

Fig. 12.5. Proportions of abundant classes of artifacts on Caye Coco mounded (elite residential) architecture (top), and in off-mound domestic deposits (bottom). Two off-mound deposits, Suboperations 31 and 13, were near elite residential architecture and may represent associated elite middens.

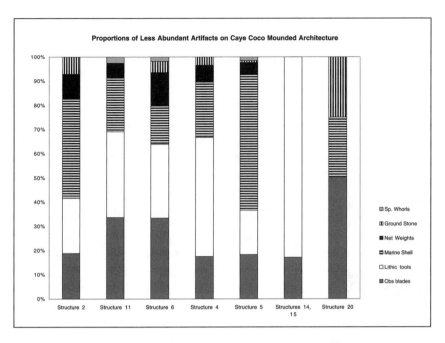

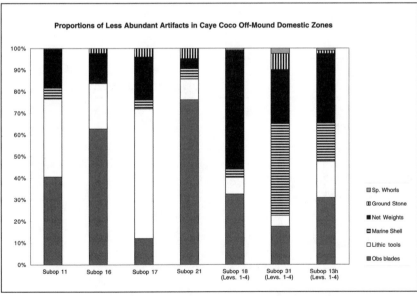

Fig. 12.6. Proportions of less abundant classes of artifacts on Caye Coco mounded (elite residential) architecture (top), and in off-mound domestic deposits (bottom). Two off-mound deposits, Suboperations 31 and 13, were near elite residential architecture and may represent associated elite middens.

primarily from the Ixtepeque source in the Guatemalan highlands (Masson and Chaya 2000; Mazeau 2000).

Other comparisons reiterate the trends observed in middens that were previously presented (figures 12.2, 12.3). Local lithic tools, flakes, ground stone, and net weights are also found in almost all contexts at the site, and ceramics are the most ubiquitous artifact category (figures 12.5, 12.6). Marine shell manufacturing debris is far more abundant at mounded architectural sites or in middens immediately adjacent to them (Suboperations 13, 31). Spindle whorls are found on elite residential mounds (Structures 5, 6, and 11), within their nearby midden deposits (Suboperations 13, 31), and at many off-mound contexts throughout the site (table 12.1).

Table 12.1 provides some additional comparisons of the numbers of craft items and ornaments found at mounded and off-mound contexts at Caye Coco. Only a few items were limited to mounded residential contexts, including stone beads (other than jade), painted plaster, slate, and mica. The slate came from a single structure (Structure 2), and the mica is from only two structures (Structures 6, 11). The latter two items may be related to specific craft industries of elite specialists, along with polished stone, which is more common in these

Table 12.1. Craft items and ornaments at Caye Coco.

	Mounded residential structures	Off-mound contexts
shell bead	6	3
perforated shark tooth	1	1
bone bead	1	9
stone bead	3	0
polished stone	8	2
painted plaster	3	0
pigment	6	7
carved bone	1	20
carved stone	0	3
crystal	0	3
greenstone adze	0	6
jade or greenstone bead	2	2
slate	12	0
mica	2	0
spindle whorls	18	33

contexts. Sixty-three percent of all of the polished stone was from Structure 5, the largest residential mound on the island. Shell beads are also more common on residential mounds. These trends suggest that some of the site's elites or their servants may have engaged in the production of fine quality crafts or arts.

All other items are either equitably distributed or they are more common in off-mound contexts. These include jade or greenstone beads, bone beads, crystals, carved bone or stone, greenstone adzes, pigments, and spindle whorls. Most of these items reflect a range of craft production activities performed in off-mound contexts. Greenstone or jade objects were obtained through exchange, while other items reflect local industries. Greenstone adzes were used in woodworking (Sheets 2000), and like obsidian, these represent both a long-distance trade item and a tool used in local production.

Caye Coco household inventory data can be combined for a composite look at community economic activities. Temporal comparisons for the community of Caye Coco (figures 12.7, 12.8) illustrate few differences from the Early Facet of the Late Postclassic (A.D. 1100–1250) to the Late Facet (A.D. 1250–1500). Abundant artifacts are present in similar proportions during both facets (figure 12.7), although ceramics form less of the assemblage (52 percent) in the Late Facet than in the Early Facet (60 percent). Slight increases in proportions of fauna (28–33 percent), obsidian blades (2–3 percent), and lithic flakes (6–8 percent) are observed over time. Artifacts that occur in lower frequencies (figure 12.8) underscore this pattern for obsidian, which rises from 23 to 32 percent of these artifact classes from the Early to Late Facet. Local lithic tools decrease in popularity over time (17–14 percent), perhaps due to the increased significance of obsidian for this community.

Marine shell ornament production increases (figure 12.8) during the Late Facet as suggested by the proportion of shell debris (8 percent in the Early Facet, 12 percent in the Late Facet). Spindle whorls and ground stone form low proportions of the assemblages of both temporal facets, and net weights comprise less of this sample over time relative to the increases mentioned in obsidian and marine shell debris. The increase in these latter artifacts at the site probably represents an amplification of maritime trading ties through which obsidian was obtained. The increase in marine shell production may reflect the increased need for valuable commodities for exchange as Caye Coco emerged as one of the important political centers in northeastern Belize (Masson 2000b).

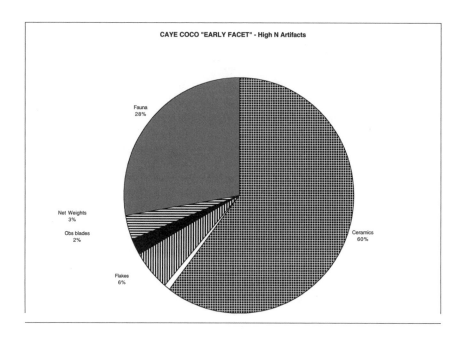

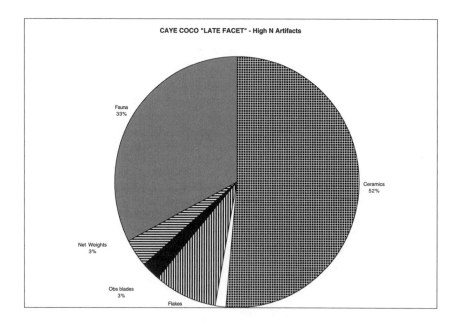

Fig. 12.7. Comparisons of highly similar proportions of abundant classes of artifacts in Early (top) and Late Facet (bottom) deposits of Caye Coco.

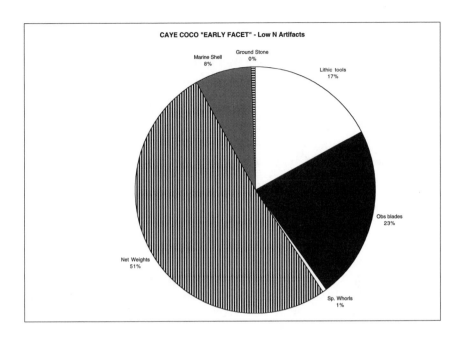

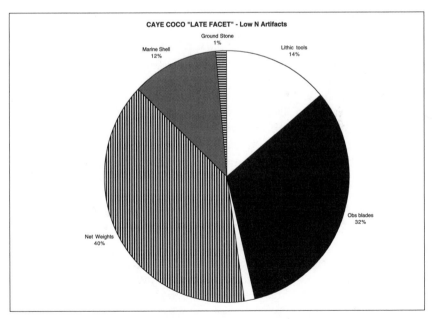

Fig. 12.8. Comparisons of less abundant artifact class proportions in Early (top) and Late Facet (bottom) deposits of Caye Coco. Both obsidian and marine shell increase in relative frequency over time.

Similar comparisons at the site of Laguna de On indicate that almost all artifact classes are equitably distributed among domestic zones at the site (Masson 2000a), including such items as local lithic tools and flakes, obsidian, net weights, ground stone, faunal bone, and ceramics. Like Caye Coco, spindle whorls are found in many contexts at Laguna de On, and they are not more common in upper-status residential deposits. Marine shell-working in the Late Facet of the Postclassic period (A.D. 1250–1500) at Laguna de On is concentrated in elite contexts, and this pattern parallels that observed at Caye Coco (Masson 2000a).

Comparisons of relative artifact classes at Laguna de On and Caye Coco are offered in figure 12.9 to highlight similarities and differences in community economies. Lithic flakes were over twice as common at Laguna de On compared to Caye Coco (figure 12.9, upper), perhaps due to the abundance of chalcedony outcrops near the former site. Laguna de On is thought to have exchanged chalcedony raw materials to other nearby sites such as Caye Coco and Colha (Masson 2000a). Nonobsidian lithic tools are present in similar proportions at both sites (figure 12.9, lower), as are ground stone, exotic (nonlocal) stone ornaments, and net weights. Obsidian is relatively more common at Laguna de On, and marine shell is relatively more common at Caye Coco (figure 12.9). Other measures of comparison indicate that Laguna de On has more obsidian than Caye Coco. Obsidian forms 71 percent of the total assemblage of obsidian and nonobsidian lithic tools at Laguna de On (for both the Early and Late Facets) and 64.4 percent of the Caye Coco sample of lithic tools. The ratio of obsidian to nonobsidian lithic tools at Laguna de On is 2.28 (for both temporal facets), compared to a ratio of 1.81 at Caye Coco (Masson and Chaya 2000).

The greater quantity of marine shell at Caye Coco may reflect this site's function as a political center where multiple elite families resided. It is possible that elites at this site were engaged in or sponsoring the production of shell ornaments for gift or trade exchange. Caye Coco is also located closer to the sea and conch shell was available in the saline waters of Progresso Lagoon and nearby lagoons as well as in the Caribbean. The availability of this resource also probably encouraged a specialization in shell ornament manufacture at households at this site. The other difference in the assemblages of the two sites is the greater proportion of spindle whorls at Laguna de On. The occupants of this site probably grew cotton and manufactured textiles for exchange. Alternatively, perhaps textiles were required of

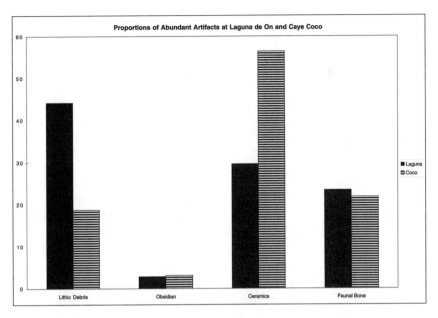

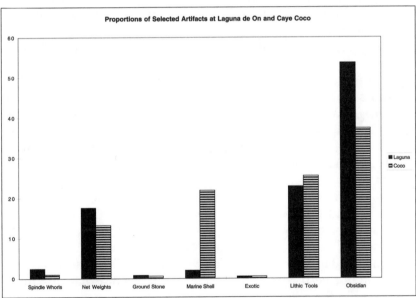

Fig. 12.9. Comparisons of relative proportions of abundant (top) and less abundant (bottom) artifact classes at Laguna de On and Caye Coco. Graphs show a greater quantity of local lithic manufacturing debris at Laguna de On, while both sites have similar proportions of northern Belize lithic tools. More shell-working debris is found at Caye Coco.

Laguna de On in local tribute systems. Tribute demands or a desire to supplement income through selling textiles in the marketplace could have stimulated production at this site. These processes stimulated spinning industries in rural communities of the Aztec empire (Smith and Heath-Smith 1994: 368–369; Smith 1994: 154). Spinning was not an activity restricted to elites in either the Belize communities examined here or in communities studied in the Aztec realm (Smith and Heath-Smith 1994: 357; Smith 1994: 149).

Discussion

Caye Coco and Laguna de On specialized in similar activities of household maintenance and similar types of local and long-distance exchange. Craft production at these communities overlaps, but different emphases are observed. Shared artifact inventories at the two sites are observed in items necessary for domestic maintenance such as ceramics, ground stone, local lithic tools, obsidian, animal resources (faunal bone), and net weights. Lithic tools at both sites include formal objects obtained in trade from the site of Colha (Michaels 1987; Shafer and Hester 1983), located a few kilometers to the southeast of each of these sites. Expedient core and flake tools were made at each community from raw materials available near each lagoon. Symbiotic exchange between communities is implied by their varying quantities of different types of lithic manufacturing debris. Caye Coco has less lithic manufacturing debris than Laguna de On, and its lithic assemblage has a greater proportion of finished formal tools obtained from other sites. An expedient industry of informal tools is observed at Caye Coco, however, indicating that its residents exploited lower quality Progresso cherts.

Craft industries thus varied at these settlements, with spinning and lithic manufacture more common at Laguna de On and marine shell ornament production more common at Caye Coco. Both sites relied more heavily on obsidian than on local lithic tools for daily tasks, despite the fact that this item had to be traded in from a distant Guatemalan source and ample fine quality lithic resources are present in northern Belize. The lack of exclusive or even substantial differences in the distribution of obsidian between these sites or between households at each site implies that both communities, a center and a small village, had access to materials through a market system. This pattern also parallels that observed at other communities in the Aztec realm that were tied into complex Postclassic commercial systems (Smith 1994: 155). It also conforms to expectations of Hirth's (1998) distributional approach for identifying markets through household assemblage analysis (Masson and Chaya 2000). Trends over time at these island communities suggest that from the twelfth through fifteenth centuries, patterns of production and exchange flourished and trade with the vicinities beyond northern Belize (as represented by obsidian) was amplified over time. Many perishable items produced in northern Belize undoubtedly entered into this Maya world of exchange, such as the honey, cacao, and cotton reported in ethnohistoric documents (Piña Chan 1978). Yucatecan salt was also probably exchanged into northern Belize (Andrews and Mock, chapter 11 this volume). Exotic beads and greenstone adzes thought to be from highland Maya sources made their way into these communities in lower numbers than common utilitarian items but are not concentrated in elite contexts (Masson 1999b, 2000). In the Aztec realm, imported exotic beads and other luxury items are also not concentrated in elite contexts (Smith and Heath-Smith 1994: 365; Smith 1994: 153). Evidence for small scale elite craft industries in the production of special artistic items is suggested at Caye Coco by the distribution of materials such as mica, slate, polished stones, and painted plaster (for an Aztec parallel, see Smith and Heath-Smith 1994: 359, 365). The elites of each northeastern Belize site engaged in marine shell ornament production, although this was performed on a greater scale at Caye Coco compared to Laguna de On. Shell items were one currency used for exchange in the Postclassic Maya world (Freidel et al.., chapter 3 this volume; Foias, chapter 8, this volume), and it is probably no coincidence that elites in northeastern Belize were involved in more of its production. Shell ornaments were likely worn by such elites to signify their status, and were probably given away at feasts and calendrical ceremonies hosted by elite families. Such ornaments were also probably produced for exchange either in markets or in transactions with maritime merchants along the coast. Following Freidel and colleagues' argument in chapter 3 of this volume, Caye Coco and Laguna de On elites were, literally, making money in the form of shell currency. Nonelites individuals at these communities were also engaged in this activity, but to a much lesser degree.

From the perspective of Laguna de On and Caye Coco data reviewed here, Postclassic Maya economy in northeastern Belize underwent a stable and long-term development with no major ruptures from the twelfth through fifteenth centuries. From the thirteenth through fifteenth centuries, exchange with the outside world was accelerated, perhaps due to intensified interaction with northern Yucatan through the outreach operations of Mayapan merchant elites. Mayapan's lords took an active interest in cacao production in distant lands, and they disseminated information about cultivation and calendrical ceremonies (Roys 1962: 50, 55–60). The participation of northeastern Belize elites in Mayapan religious/calendrical rituals is reflected in the construction of Mayapan style shrines and the emulation of effigy censer production and use (Masson 1999a), as also noted for Cozumel (Freidel and Sabloff 1984) and the Petén (Rice 1988). The adoption of utilitarian ceramic modes resembling those of Mayapan in Late Facet Postclassic Belize sites is another form of evidence that reflects close economic relationships with the northern city (Chase and Chase 1988; Graham 1987). The exact nature of political and economic relationships of Mayapan and provinces along the east and west coasts of Yucatan, interior zones of Quintana Roo, Campeche, the Petén, and highland Guatemala is not well understood and probably varied considerably over time and space. However, evidence from northeastern Belize suggests that the integrating efforts of this city spurred local elites to consolidate local hierarchies, to promote market and other commercial activities, and to participate in broader networks of economic exchange and ideological interaction (Masson 2000a). If the Cozumel model is correct, it is possible that a lack of direct political or economic control by the Mayapan state created opportunities for internal centralization at production or trading communities of the Late Postclassic (Rathje and Sabloff 1973).

The rise of affluent Postclassic mercantile society, first described by Sabloff and Rathje (Sabloff and Rathje 1975; Rathje 1975), is reflected in northeastern Belize household and community economic patterns. Few differences are observed in exchange items obtained by elites and commoners at Laguna de On and Caye Coco. This observation suggests that an open market system was in operation in which local and distant commodities were widely available for purchase. Elites in these communities promoted ritual calendrical festivities as suggested by shrine features associated with elite residences (Barrett 2000; Masson 1999a). Such calendrical celebrations would have provided opportunity for intercommunity exchange, as Freidel (1981) has suggested in his market fair model. Elites may have also coordinated other types of market events. They invested in the production of local valuables in the form of marine shell. Profits from shell commodities may have helped fund calendrical ceremonies, the construction of ritual facilities, and the construction of elevated residential platforms at Caye Coco. Shell ornaments probably symbolized the prestige of their owners and their circulation probably promoted status hierarchies within and between communities. However, as ethnohistoric documents suggest (see Foias, chapter 8 this volume), this item was also a currency that was integrated into market exchange involving the full array of everyday and luxury items. A higher frequency of spindle whorls suggests that textiles were more commonly made at Laguna de On, perhaps due to tribute burdens or opportunities seized by entrepreneurial occupants of this site. Spindle whorl dimensions do not suggest that different types of cloth were made at the two sites.

The economy of northeastern Belize as observed from these domestic contexts incorporated local, regional, and distant spheres of production and exchange. These spheres overlapped in complex, interrelated ways that are reflected in the assemblages of Postclassic households. Inhabitants of individual communities capitalized on local resources that provided them with particular niches for the production of surplus items in demand throughout these networks of exchange. It is clear from this study that subtle variations in local environments and resources provided the occasion for small-scale production of household surpluses destined for market exchange. The political position of these communities within the regional settlement hierarchy also affected the types of products made, as more marine ornaments were manufactured at Caye Coco, while Laguna de On engaged in more weaving and lithic production. Another example of community specialization is found at the site of Colha, which produced formal lithic tools for exchange in northern Belize and perhaps beyond to more distant provinces during the Postclassic period (Michaels 1987, 1994; Michaels and Shafer 1994).

This analysis of spatial and temporal distributions of household materials represents a preliminary effort to track the development of mercantile society in northern Belize. Further community comparisons are needed to understand the various responses to economic growth and development that affected and integrated many Postclassic provinces.

References

Andrews, Anthony P., and Gabriela Vail
1990 "Cronología de sitios Prehispanicos costeros de la peninsula de Yucatan y Belice." *Boletin de la Escuela de Ciencias Antropologicas de la Universidad de Yucatan* 18: 37–66.

Barrett, Jason Wallace
2000 "Excavations at Structure 5: Postclassic Elite Architecture at Caye Coco." Pp. 31–58 in *The Belize Postclassic Project 1999: Continued Investigations at Progresso Lagoon and Laguna Seca*, edited by R. M. Rosenswig and M. A. Masson. Institute of Mesoamerican Studies Occasional Publication No. 5. Albany: State University of New York.

Chase, Diane Z.
1982 "Spatial and Temporal Variability in Postclassic Northern Belize." Ph.D. dissertation, Department of Anthropology, University of Pennsylvania. Ann Arbor, Mich.: University Microfilms.
1986 "Ganned but Not Forgotten: Late Postclassic Archaeology and Ritual at Santa Rita Corozal, Belize." Pp. 104–125 in *The Lowland Maya Postclassic*, edited by A. F. Chase and P. M. Rice. Austin: University of Texas Press.
1992 "Postclassic Maya Elites: Ethnohistory and Archaeology." Pp. 118–134 in *Mesoamerican Elites: An Archaeological Assessment*, edited by Diane Z. Chase and Arlen F. Chase. Norman: University of Oklahoma Press.

Chase, Diane Z., and Arlen F. Chase
1988 *A Postclassic Perspective: Excavations at the Maya Site of Santa Rita Corozal, Belize.* Monograph 4. San Francisco: Precolumbian Art Research Institute.

Connor, Judith G.
1983 "The Ceramics of Cozumel, Quintana Roo, Mexico." Ph.D. dissertation, University of Arizona.

Culbert, T. Patrick
1988 "The Collapse of Classic Maya Civilization." Pp. 69–101 in *The Collapse of Ancient States and Civilizations*, edited by Norman Yoffee and George Cowgill. Tucson: University of Arizona Press.

Demarest, Arthur A.
1997 "The Vanderbilt Petexbatun Regional Archaeological Project 1989–1994: Overview, History, and Major Results of a Multi-disciplinary Study of the Classic Maya Collapse." *Ancient Mesoamerica* 8(2): 209–227.

Dreiss, Meredith L., and David O. Brown
1989 "Obsidian Exchange Patterns in Belize." Pp. 57–90 in *Prehistoric Maya Economies*, edited by P. A. McAnany and B. L. Isaac. Research in Economic Anthropology Supplement 4. Greenwich, Conn.: JAI Press.

Freidel, David A.
1981 "The Political Economics of Residential Dispersion among the Lowland Maya." Pp. 371–382 in *Lowland Maya Settlement Patterns*, edited by Wendy Ashmore. Albuquerque: University of New Mexico Press.
1986 "Terminal Classic Lowland Maya: Successes, Failures, and Aftermaths." Pp. 409–430 in *Late Lowland Maya Civilization: Classic to Postclassic*, edited by

Jeremy A. Sabloff and E. W. Andrews, V. Albuquerque: University of New Mexico Press.
Freidel, David A., and Jeremy A. Sabloff
1984 *Cozumel: Late Maya Settlement Patterns*. New York: Academic Press.
Graham, Elizabeth A.
1987 "Terminal Classic to Early Historic Period Vessel Forms from Belize." Pp. 73–98 in *Maya Ceramics*, edited by Prudence Rice and Robert Sharer. BAR International Series 345, Great Britain.
Hirth, Kenneth
1998 "The Distributional Approach." *Current Anthropology* 39(4): 451–476.
Jones, Grant D.
1989 *Maya Resistance to Spanish Rule*. Albuquerque: University of New Mexico Press.
Masson, Marilyn A.
1997 "Cultural Transformation at the Maya Postclassic Community of Laguna de On, Belize." *Latin American Antiquity* 8(4): 1–26.
1999a "Postclassic Maya Communities at Progresso Lagoon and Laguna Seca, Northern Belize." *Journal of Field Archaeology* 25: 285–306.
1999b "Postclassic Maya Ritual at Laguna de On Island, Belize." *Ancient Mesoamerica* 10: 51–68.
2000a *In the Realm of Nachan Kan: Postclassic Maya Archaeology at Laguna de On, Belize*. Boulder: University Press of Colorado.
2000b "Segmentary Political Cycles and Elite Migration Myths in the Postclassic Archaeology of Northern Belize." In *The Past and Present Maya: Essays in Honor of Robert M. Carmack*, edited by John M. Weeks. Lancaster, Calif.: Labyrinthos Press.
n.d. "Social and Economic Class Constructs in Postclassic Maya Society." In *Ancient Maya Commoners*, edited by John C. Lohse and Fred Valdez Jr. Manuscript in review. Austin: University of Texas Press.
Masson, Marilyn A., and Henry Chaya
2000 "Obsidian Trade Connections at the Postclassic Maya Site of Laguna de On, Belize." *Lithic Technology* 25: 135–144.
Masson, Marilyn A., and Robert M. Rosenswig
2001 "The Evolution of Postclassic Maya Pottery Traditions in Northern Belize." Paper presented at the Society for American Archaeology meeting, April 21, New Orleans.
Masson, Marilyn A., and Robert M. Rosenswig, editors
1997 *The Belize Postclassic Project: Report of 1996 Investigations at Laguna de On Island*. Institute of Mesoamerican Studies Occasional Publication No. 1. Albany: State University of New York.
1998 *The Belize Postclassic Project: Laguna de On, Progresso Lagoon, and Laguna Seca*. Institute for Mesoamerican Studies Occasional Publication No. 2. Albany: State University of New York.
1999 *The Belize Postclassic Project 1998: Investigations at Progresso Lagoon*. Institute of Mesoamerican Studies Occasional Publication No. 3. Albany: State University of New York.

Mazeau, Daniel E.
  2000 "The Obsidian of Caye Coco." Pp. 145–152 in *Belize Postclassic Project 1999: Continued Investigations at Progresso Lagoon and Laguna Seca*, edited by R. M. Rosenswig and Marilyn A. Masson. Institute of Mesoamerican Studies Occasional Publication No. 5. Albany: State University of New York.
McKillop, Heather
  1996 "Ancient Maya Trading Ports and the Integration of Long-Distance and Regional Economies: Wild Cane Cay in South-Coastal Belize." *Ancient Mesoamerica* 7: 49–62.
Michaels, George H.
  1987 "A Description of Early Postclassic Lithic Technology at Colha, Belize." M.A. thesis, Department of Anthropology, Texas A&M University.
  1994 "The Postclassic at Colha, Belize: A Summary Overview and Directions for Future Research." Pp. 129–136 in *Continuing Archaeology at Colha, Belize*, edited by Thomas R. Hester, Harry J. Shafer, and Jack D. Eaton. Texas Archeological Research Laboratory Studies in Archaeology No. 16. Austin: University of Texas.
Michaels, George H., and Harry J. Shafer
  1994 "Excavations at Operations 2037 and 2040." Pp. 137–154 in *Continuing Archaeology at Colha, Belize*, edited by Thomas R. Hester, Harry J. Shafer, and Jack D. Eaton. Texas Archeological Research Laboratory Studies in Archaeology No. 16. Austin: University of Texas.
Pendergast, David M.
  1981 "Lamanai, Belize: Summary of Excavation Results, 1974–1980." *Journal of Field Archaeology* 8(1): 29–53.
  1985 "Lamanai, Belize: An Updated View." Pp. 91–103 in *The Lowland Maya Postclassic*, edited by A. Chase and P. Rice. Austin: University of Texas Press.
  1986 "Stability through Change: Lamanai, Belize from the Ninth to the Seventeenth Century." Pp. 223–250 in *Late Lowland Maya Civilization: Classic to Postclassic*, edited by J. A. Sabloff and E. W. Andrews, V. Albuquerque: University of New Mexico Press.
Piña Chan, Roman
  1978 "Commerce in the Yucatec Peninsula: The Conquest and Colonial Period." Pp. 37–48 in *Mesoamerican Communication Routes and Culture Contacts*, edited by T. A. Lee and C. Navarrete. Papers of the New World Archaeological Foundation No. 40. Provo, Utah: Brigham Young University Press.
Pollock, Harry E. D.
  1962 "Introduction." Pp. 1–24 in *Mayapan, Yucatan, Mexico*, by Harry E. D. Pollock, Ralph L. Roys, Tatiana Proskouriakoff, and A. L. Smith. Publication No. 619. Washington, D.C.: Carnegie Institute.
Proskouriakoff, Tatiana
  1955 "The Death of a Civilization." *Scientific American* 192: 82–88.
Rathje, William L.
  1972 "Praise the Gods and Pass the Metates: A Hypothesis of the Development of Lowland Rainforest Civilizations in Mesoamerica." Pp. 365–392 in *Contemporary Archaeology: A Guide to Theory and Contributions*, edited by Mark P. Leone. Carbondale: Southern Illinois University Press.

1975 "The Last Tango in Mayapan: A Tentative Trajectory of Production-Distribution Systems." Pp. 409–448 in *Ancient Civilization and Trade*, edited by J. A. Sabloff and C. C. Lamberg-Karlovsky. Albuquerque: University of New Mexico Press.

1983 "To the Salt of the Earth: Some Comments on Household Archaeology Among the Maya." Pp. 23–34 in *Prehistoric Settlement Patterns: Essays in Honor of Gordon R. Willey*, edited by Evon Vogt and Richard Leventhal. Albuquerque: University of New Mexico Press.

Rathje, William L., D. A. Gregory, and F. M. Wiseman
1978 "Trade Models and Archaeological Problems: Classic Maya Examples." Pp. 147–175 in *Mesoamerican Communication Routes and Culture Contacts*, edited by T. A. Lee and C. Navarrete. Papers of the New World Archaeological Foundation No. 40. Provo, Utah: Brigham Young University Press.

Rathje, William L., and Jeremy A. Sabloff
1973 "Ancient Maya Commercial Systems: A Research Design for the Island of Cozumel, Mexico." *World Archaeology* 5: 221–231.

Rice, Don S.
1988 "Classic to Postclassic Maya Household Transitions in the Central Petén, Guatemala." Pp. 227–248 in *Household and Community in the Mesoamerican Past*, edited by Richard R. Wilk and Wendy Ashmore. Albuquerque: University of New Mexico Press.

Rice, Prudence M.
1980 "Petén Postclassic Pottery Production and Exchange: A View from Macanche." Pp. 67–82 in *Models and Methods in Regional Exchange*, edited by R. E. Fry. SAA Papers No. 1. Washington, D.C.: Society for American Archaeology.

1984 "Obsidian Procurement in the Central Petén Lakes Region, Guatemala." *Journal of Field Archaeology* 11: 181–194.

1987 "Economic Change in the Lowland Maya Late Classic Period." Pp. 76–85 in *Specialization, Exchange, and Complex Societies*, edited by E. M. Brumfiel and T. K. Earle. Cambridge: Cambridge University Press.

Rice, Prudence M., Helen V. Michel, Frank Asaro, and Fred Stross
1985 "Provenience Analysis of Obsidian from the Central Petén Lake Region, Guatemala." *American Antiquity* 50: 591–604.

Rosenswig, Robert M.
1998 "Burying the Dead at Laguna de On: Summary of Mortuary Remains from the 1991, 1996, and 1997 Field Seasons." Pp. 149–156 in *Belize Postclassic Project 1997: Laguna de On, Progresso Lagoon, Laguna Seca*, edited by Marilyn A. Masson and Robert M. Rosenswig. Institute of Mesoamerican Studies Occasional Publication No. 2. Albany: State University of New York.

2001 "Burying the Dead at Caye Coco: Summary of Mortuary Remains Excavated in the 1998, 1999, and 2000 Seasons." Pp. 153–176 in *Belize Postclassic Project 2000: Investigations at Caye Coco and the Shore Settlements of Progresso Lagoon*, edited by Robert M. Rosenswig and Marilyn A. Masson. Institute of Mesoamerican Studies Occasional Publication No. 6. Albany: State University of New York.

Rosenswig, Robert M., and Marilyn A. Masson
n.d. "Monumental Architecture and Social Organization at Caye Coco, Belize."
Manuscript submitted to *Ancient Mesoamerica*.
Rosenswig, Robert M., and Marilyn A. Masson, editors
2000 *The Belize Postclassic Project 1999: Continuing Investigations at Progresso Lagoon and Laguna Seca*. Institute of Mesoamerican Studies Occasional Publication No. 5. Albany: State University of New York.
2001 *The Belize Postclassic Project 2000: Investigations at Caye Coco and the Shore of Progresso Lagoon*. Institute of Mesoamerican Studies Occasional Publication No. 6. Albany: State University of New York.
Roys, Ralph L.
1962 "Literary Sources for the History of Mayapan." Pp. 25–86 in *Mayapan, Yucatan, Mexico*, by Harry E. D. Pollock, Ralph L. Roys, Tatiana Proskouriakoff, and A. L. Smith. Publication No. 619. Washington, D.C.: Carnegie Institute.
Sabloff, Jeremy A., and William L. Rathje
1975 "The Rise of a Maya Merchant Class." *Scientific American* 233: 72–82.
Shafer, Harry J., and Thomas R. Hester
1983 "Ancient Maya Chert Workshops in Northern Belize, Central America." *American Antiquity* 48: 519–543.
Sheets, Payson
2000 "Provisioning the Ceren Household: The Vertical Economy, Village Economy, and Household Economy in the Southeast Maya Periphery." *Ancient Mesoamerica* 11: 217–230.
Sidrys, Raymond V.
1977 "Mass-Distance Measures for the Maya Obsidian Trade." Pp. 91–107 in *Exchange Systems in Prehistory*, edited by T. K. Earle and J. E. Ericson. New York: Academic Press.
1983 *Archaeological Excavations in Northern Belize, Central America*. Monograph XVII, Institute of Archaeology. Los Angeles: University of California.
Smith, Michael E.
1994 "Social Complexity in the Aztec Countryside." Pp. 143–159 in *Archaeological Views from the Countryside: Village Communities in Early Complex Society*, edited by Glenn M. Schwartz and Steven E. Falconer. Washington, D.C.: Smithsonian Institution Press.
Smith, Michael E., and Cynthia Heath-Smith
1994 "Rural Economy in Late Postclassic Morelos." Pp. 349–376 in *Economies and Polities in the Aztec Realm*, edited by Mary G. Hodge and Michael E. Smith. Institute for Mesoamerican Studies, Studies on Culture and Society Volume 6. Albany: State University of New York.
Willey, Gordon R.
1986 "The Postclassic of the Maya Lowlands: A Preliminary Overview." Pp. 17–52 in *Late Lowland Maya Civilization: Classic to Postclassic*, edited by J. A. Sabloff and E. W. Andrews, V. Albuquerque: University of New Mexico Press.

Chapter Thirteen

In Praise of Garbage: Historical Archaeology, Households, and the Maya Political Economy

Craig A. Hanson

In a seminal work on the history of science, Kuhn (1970) argued that "paradigms" consisting of cornerstone theories, methods, and experiments define "normal" scientific research. Investigators use these paradigms to refine theories, explain anomalous data, and increase accuracy in predictions. Accordingly, paradigms frame the "preformed and relatively inflexible box" (Kuhn 1970: 24) of problems, questions, and research considered important and legitimate as avenues of investigation for a discipline's practitioners. A "revolution" results from the accumulation of anomalies that cannot be accommodated in the paradigm. In this case, investigators develop speculative theories and methods that lead to new discoveries that inspire the gathering of new evidence, development of new research techniques, and exploration of alternative options in theory and method that are radically incommensurate with the normative ones. These discoveries over time result in a paradigm shift that alters the fundamental concepts underlying research while incorporating the evidence, research, methods, and theories of the passing paradigm. Kuhn's work revolutionized the history and philosophy of science, and his concept of paradigms and paradigm shifts impacted a wide array of other disciplines.

Beginning with the "new archaeology," a paradigm shift in the study of the pre-Hispanic Maya has occurred which, over a period of three decades, has come to revolve around the concept of political economy. This paradigm has superseded its longstanding predecessor that sometimes is referred to in the literature as the Morley model (Fedick 1996: 1–2). The new paradigm explores precisely those theoretical and methodological aspects of its predecessor that were weakly articulated. The economic aspects of pre-Hispanic lowland history were relatively undeveloped in the Morley model in comparison with its emphasis on the social-hierarchical features of the Maya elite as inferred from architecture and inscriptions. The model stressed elite ideology as paramount to Maya community integration and approached the pre-Hispanic economy only indirectly, either in terms of long-distance trade that supplied rulers with status emblems and religious paraphernalia, or in terms of peasant swidden agriculture that supplied the star-struck rulers with nourishment. The inefficiency inherent in the model's conception of overland human carriers as the predominant mode of pre-Hispanic transportation and its supposition of nonexistent or weak local and regional market hierarchies further limited understanding of the impact of economy on political hegemony in lowland Maya history (Pyburn et al. 1998: 39). As a result, Mayanists concentrated entirely on a "prestige" or "luxury" elite item trade; a "staple" or "bulk" commodity trade was rarely considered or conceived. Economy, in summary, was not seen as a "significant part of the process of culture change. The emphasis instead [was] on the traded objects" (Sabloff 1977: 67).

The emerging paradigm can be traced to William Rathje and other members of the "Southwestern School" of Mayanist archaeology and their investigations, beginning in the 1970s, of the pre-Hispanic Maya political economy. Proponents of the paradigm now recognize a variable mosaic of small holders, commodity production, resource and land ownership, settlement agriculture, random-walk trade models, entrepreneurial merchants, and long-distance maritime transport as integral to a complete explanation of Maya lowland (and Mesoamerican) history (Drennan 1984, 1988; Fedick 1996; Hammond 1997; Harrison 1989; Killion 1992a; McAnany 1989, 1993, 1995; Netting 1971, 1993; Phillips and Rathje 1977; Pyburn 1996; Pyburn et al. 1998; Rathje 1971, 1972, 1973, 1975; Rathje et al. 1978; Sabloff 1977; Sabloff and Rathje 1975; Sabloff et al. 1974; Santone 1997; Tourtellot 1988; Wilk 1991). As yet the paradigm lacks a systematically defined theoretical base, but the broad scope of its concerns and the level of detail necessary to substantiate its claims require a coordinated investigation of abandoned Maya communities and a comparative approach to the recovered data.

This contribution proposes both a theoretical and methodological foundation for the paradigm that builds on Rathje's own substantial contributions to it. In the sections that follow I discuss political economy as a concept, Rathje's Core-Buffer Zone model as a type of political-economic analysis that is consistent with world-systems theory, and world-systems theory as it pertains to historical archaeology and the study of Maya (and Mesoamerican) history. I then demonstrate that household archaeology as a research method in the Maya lowlands complements a recent focus on households in world-systems theory. Given the significance of households for both fields, I turn to methods of studying their remains as a prelude to presenting a case study in the archaeological identification of corporate groups at sixteenth-century Ek Balám. I conclude that this identification, in conjunction with organizing principles of world-systems theory, provides a foundation for the emergent paradigm of the pre-Hispanic Maya political economy. Again, the primary purpose of this chapter is the identification of a corporate group in the archaeological record of the Early Hispanic horizon. This methodological step facilitates the identification of corporate groups in the pre-Hispanic archaeological record through the direct historical approach. The significance of this methodological advancement for the emerging paradigm should become apparent during the course of the discussion.

Political Economy and World-Systems Theory

Economy, etymologically, is a Greek word that originally signified "household management" (Groenewegen 1987: 904–905). The concept of *political economy*, on the other hand, originated in the early seventeenth century and was popularized by John Stuart Mill, Adam Smith, and Karl Marx in the nineteenth century. There are as many definitions of political economy as there are political economists. For the present, I take my definition from Mill's ([1848]1965, 2: 21) *Principles of Political Economy* where he defined it rather broadly as the laws of production and distribution. Merging the Greek concept of household management with this definition, I conclude that political economy analyzes the production and flow of goods between households, or, at different scales of analysis, the production and flow of goods between communities, nations, or polities (Phillips and Rathje 1977: 104). The phrase "political economy" has been employed with increasing frequency in Mesoamericanist archaeology generally and Mayanist archaeology specifically during the last decade (Alexander 1999a: 176, 179; Arnold et al. 1993; Blanton et al. 1996; Braswell et al. 2000: 270; Demarest 1996: 822; Freidel 1981, 1983, 1986: 413–415; Henderson and Sabloff 1993: 448; Hicks 1994; McAnany 1993: 83; McCafferty and McCafferty 2000: 42; Pyburn 1996: 242; Pyburn et al. 1998; Santley 1986; Sheets 2000; Webster 1992: 147–150; Willey 1999: 87). Thirty years ago Rathje (1971, 1972, 1973) proposed the Core-Buffer Zone model to explain the origin and historical development of the Maya political economy. Rathje's model has remained "the most comprehensive and explicit" explanation for the rise and maintenance of complex polities in the Maya lowlands (Freidel 1979: 37; Hayden and Cannon 1982: 151; Inomata and Aoyama 1996: 291; Pyburn 1996: 238–239; Willey 1974: 425). Rathje (Rathje et al. 1978: 149) hypothesized that polities emerged in the core area of the Petén because its environment lacked certain essential resources (salt for diet, obsidian for cutting tools, hard stone for grinding tools, ash for pottery temper) necessary for the survival of individual households. Accordingly, more sophisticated political-economic and ideological organization developed in this region to manage both the acquisition of nonlocal utilitarian goods from buffer communities for distribution in the core, and the production of prestige markers in the core for distribution in buffer-zone communities.

Rathje's formulation was contemporaneous with the publication of Frank's (1967) *dependencia*, Braudel's (1972–1973) *Annales*, and Wallerstein's (1974) world-systems theories. Because the similarities of these core-periphery models of dependent development and unequal exchange are much greater than their differences, for present purposes I collapse them into what I will hereafter refer to as *world-systems theory*. World-systems theory developed to explain dependent economic development among polities of the globe beginning in the sixteenth century. Briefly summarizing three decades of research, world-systems theory has postulated a set of nested political and economic "core" and "periphery" interactions in which a metropolitan core extracts raw materials from a geographically remote periphery and returns to it secondary manufactures that often are prestige-enhancing materials. Secondary metropolitan centers are established in the *semiperiphery* to facilitate this exchange. The cumulative surplus value of the transactions accrues at the core, creating a concomitant *underdevelopment* in the periphery. The dynamic interaction between core, semiperiphery, and periphery provides world-systems theory with an explanatory model of historical change.

Typically, world-systems theorists have dealt with the processes of historical capitalism that began in the sixteenth century (Braudel 1980: 96; Frank 1967: 14–15; Hopkins and Wallerstein 1987: 775; Marx and Engels [1846]1977: 57; Meillassoux 1981: 104; Wallerstein 1974: 67; Weber 1978, I: 353–354; Wesseling 1991: 80). World-systems, therefore, has provided a unifying theory for the field of historical archaeology (Deagan 1988: 9; Johnson 1996; Leone 1992: 132; Mrozowski 1993: 107; Schmidt and Patterson 1995: 13; Schuyler 1978: 28, 30). According to James Deetz (1991: 1), historical archaeology investigates "the spread of European societies worldwide, beginning in the fifteenth century, and their subsequent development and impact on native peoples in all parts of the world." However, despite Deetz's and others' assertions to the same effect, neither historical archaeology nor world-systems theory have included specifically pre- or noncapitalist political economies in their formulations and thus made the investigation of this "development and impact" a realizable goal. Leone and Potter (1988: 4–6; Noble 1999: 78; Wolf 1982: 23) have critiqued world-systems theory based on this issue, which also has resulted in much discussion over its applicability to "prehistoric archaeological situations" (Santley and Alexander 1996: 173).

Schneider (1977) was the first to argue for the application of world-systems theory to contexts prior to the sixteenth century. Since then increasing numbers of studies have employed world-systems as an explanatory framework in a variety of historical contexts (Abu-Lughod 1989; Algaze 1993; Denemark et al. 2000; Frank and Gills 1993; Kardulias 1999). In the Maya lowlands, Robert Redfield (1955: 114) first observed that a Maya community was not "fully self-contained. To describe it completely we must reckon with parts of outside communities, or influences from communities that have their centers and their principal being elsewhere than in the village." Redfield (1955: 113–114) specifically identified these influences as emanating from what he called a "world economy," which he understood to mean that "events in one part of the world can affect almost everybody in it. The little community we are likely to study today is not plainly distinct, and is plainly enclosed within other communities with which its fortunes are bound." More recently a number of authorities have advocated world-systems theory in particular regions and/or time periods of Maya and Mesoamerican history (Alexander 1998, 1999b; Blanton and Feinman 1984; Blanton et al. 1992, 1996; Kepecs, Feinman, and Boucher 1994; Knapp 1992; Lange 1986; Rice 1998; Santley and Alexander 1992, 1996; Smith 1992; Whitecotton and Pailes 1986). I contend that Rathje's Core-Buffer Zone model (as well as his model of production and distribution systems [Rathje 1975]) was implicitly a world-systems model that explained how "communities were bound" in the Maya political economy.

Santley and Alexander (1996: 173) have pointed out that part of the problem with the application of world-systems theory to pre- and noncapitalist political economies has been the lack of "specific sets of archaeological correlates with which to monitor variation in world-system structure and the articulations among its parts." Their insight, in combination with Rathje's model, provides a preliminary framework for solving this problem. In the remainder of this contribution I present arguments which demonstrate that household archaeology in the Maya lowlands (Ashmore 1981; Ashmore and Wilk 1988; Wilk and Rathje 1982; Rathje 1983) provides a specific set of correlates with which to monitor the Mesoamerican world-system.

Households as an Institution of the Maya Political Economy

Almost fifty years ago Willey (1953, 1956) introduced the term "settlement pattern" to lowland Maya archaeology. Willey (1953: 1) defined settlement pattern as

> the way in which man disposed himself over the landscape on which he lived. [Settlement pattern] refers to dwellings, to their arrangement, and to the nature and disposition of other buildings pertaining to community life. These settlements reflect the natural environment, the level of technology on which the builders operated, and various institutions of social interaction and control which the culture maintained.

Twenty-five years later, Willey (1981: 386) observed that the study of "lowland Maya settlement patterns" had

> no centralizing problem. As a subfield, "settlement" is still an unformulated branch of Maya archaeology. Investigative strategies have been diverse and often quite specialized. Aims have been unstated, implicit, and sometimes not clearly formulated. They have focused variously on population estimates, subsistence adaptations, micropattern details of

architectural layouts, or macrosettlement problems of site sizes and hierarchies.

In response to Willey's definition and critique, households and dwellings have become *the* "unit of data recovery as well as a unit of analysis" (McAnany 1989: 354; Hirth 1993: 21) in Mayanist settlement studies. Yet despite this focus, and despite significant advances in Mayanist settlement studies by Bullard (1960), Kurjack (1974), Tourtellot (1988) and others, there still exists no unifying premise in contemporary theory for household archaeology other than a "democratizing" (Ashmore and Wilk 1988: 7) study of the "salt of the earth" (Rathje 1983) sectors of a site.

Settlement studies and household archaeology remain "an unformulated branch of Maya archaeology" because Mayanists have investigated settlement *microstructure* and neglected the equally important settlement *macrostructure*. In a seminal publication on settlement archaeology Chang (1968: 7–8; Willey 1981: 394–395) made the critical distinction between a settlement's microstructure and its macrostructure, or the "'within' and the 'beyond' of a community." Chang defined the "cultural and social structure" of a settlement as its microstructure and the wider-scale, higher-order, or more inclusive "cultural and social system" of which the individual settlement was a member as its macrostructure.

> The microstructure is the model for an archaeological community [constructed] on the evidence from an archaeological settlement, whereas the macrostructure is the model for the larger sphere of social/cultural activities (beyond those relevant simply to the community) in which members of the community participate, as well as the sphere of cultural and social influences the community imparts to the outside world during a certain time span. (Chang 1968: 7)

Chang's distinction between the micro- and macrostructure concepts facilitates understanding of the interaction between the dwelling and community, and the world in which they participate.[1] He proposed that analysis of individual settlement patterns and their component dwellings and other features is incomplete; analysis must also include an individual settlement's articulation with the wider "sphere" in which it participated (Parsons 2000: 579–580). For this, Chang specifically stated that a "model," a framework of reference, for the macrostructure is necessary. I propose that it is specifically this model or macrostructure that is lacking in Mayanist settlement studies.

World-systems is a particularly appropriate settlement macro-structure because it is a theory of historical change that examines the production and distribution of goods between households, communities, and nations. Although in early works world-systems theorists focused on the "nations" end of this spectrum, in more recent works they have targeted the role of households in world-systems (Wallerstein, Martin, and Dickinson 1982; Wallerstein and Smith 1992a, 1992b; Smith and Wallerstein 1992; Smith, Wallerstein, and Evers 1984). Households concern world-systems theorists because labor in the periphery creates the surplus that the core extracts and because, although labor is individual, the household regulates its deployment. The household is, therefore, central to the analysis of political economy because households allocate labor. Rathje recognized this point. His model was based on essential household resources and on their procurement in the wider political economy, or, employing Chang's terms, in the settlement micro- and macrostructure. The convergence of household archaeology in the Maya lowlands and households as a pivotal institution in world-systems theory provides fertile ground for both fields of investigation.

The Identification of a
Sixteenth-Century Corporate Group

Archaeological ethnography (more widely known as ethnoarchaeology) and household archaeology are related research methods in Mayanist field investigations (Rathje 1978). Ethnoarchaeology in the Maya area developed specifically to interpret and explain the patterning and variability in material systems associated with pre-Hispanic dwellings. The Coxoh Ethnoarchaeological Project (Hayden 1988; Hayden and Cannon 1982, 1983, 1984) has performed the most intensive and complete study of Maya communities to date and has made several substantive contributions to settlement studies and household archaeology. One contribution, that of the houselot refuse model, has been independently confirmed and used as an analytical tool by investigators across Mesoamerica (Alexander 1999b; Arnold 1990; Deal 1985, 1998; Hayden and Cannon 1983; Killion et al. 1989; Killion 1990, 1992b; Manzanilla and Barba 1990; Santley 1992; Santley and Hirth 1993; Smyth 1989, 1990).

Another of the Coxoh project's contributions has not been so widely employed, although it too has significant methodological implications for settlement studies. I refer to this contribution as the "hierarchy of assemblage reliability." The hierarchy predicts the relative reliability of an artifact assemblage as an inferential tool as a function of its scale of recovery and analysis. The scale ranges from individual artifacts to community-wide assemblages. At the weak end of the scale, Hayden and Cannon demonstrated that attempts to analyze or assign meaning to individual artifacts are futile, chaotic endeavors. They also demonstrated that despite the emphasis in pre-Hispanic Maya archaeology on the individual household and dwelling, the artifact assemblage recovered from the individual dwelling does not yield reliable social, political, economic, or, for that matter, ideological inferences about the household that occupied it. They concluded that

> behavior at the household level is almost as complex as Brownian movement, while at the community level a few simple relationships serve as powerful predictors and interpretive devices with high levels of reliability. If archaeologists are to formulate meaningful statements similar to laws, it is probably at the [corporate or] community level that they will achieve their first and most notable successes. (Hayden and Cannon 1984: 19)

Stated differently, and according to the results of the Coxoh Ethnoarchaeological Project, any attempt to characterize individual household "status" or explain its artifact assemblage based on the random sampling of a few dwellings from a settlement yields conclusions that are, with a high degree of probability, grossly inaccurate. Thus, despite emphasis on the individual household in Mayanist archaeology, inferences about households are only accurate when assemblages are systematically recovered from a large number of dwellings in a systematically defined and operational sample. Only under these conditions are inferences reliable. Individual artifacts and households analyzed in isolation have virtually no meaning. In a very real sense, then, household archaeology and studies of settlement patterns are isomorphic.

Hayden and Cannon did not offer any explicit definition of a community that would facilitate its identification in the archaeological record. They did propose criteria to identify corporate groups in the archaeological record (Hayden and Cannon 1982: 152). Henry Maine ([1861]1960) first employed the term *corporate group*, which since has been defined in many ways. Hayden and Cannon (1982: 133–135) defined it through two features and by way of contrast with a third: first, corporate groups "function as individuals in relation to property" (Goodenough (1951: 30–31); second, members of corporate groups reside together (Engels [1884]1954; Morgan [1881]1965); and, third, corporate groups are not "groups of people who join together for political, religious, or monetary reasons"—these groups Hayden and Cannon (1982: 135) define as "institutions." A corporate group, therefore, is that which has "come into being as a result of strong economic or environmental pressures, and which, as a result, exhibit[s] a recognizable degree of residential coherency among two or more nuclear families within the community" (Hayden and Cannon 1982: 134–135). Hayden and Cannon referred to these entities as "residential corporate groups" and implied that they, in some manner, formed the basis of community.

Hayden and Cannon (1982: 152) proposed nine criteria to identify residential corporate groups in the archaeological record. For the purposes of this contribution I will discuss only two of these: architecture and control of key resources. Of the various criteria, Hayden and Cannon argued that architecture is the most significant. Architecture not only provides the "major criterion for identifying residential corporate groups, but size and complexity of architecture may also provide a good indicator of the strength or coherency of corporate groups" (Hayden and Cannon 1982: 147). Specifically, they found that repetitive patterns in dwellings, multifamily dwellings, and spatial reoccurrence of administrative structures were robust archaeological indicators of residential corporate groups. Although other criteria could provide supporting evidence, strength of patterning in architecture alone provides a relatively accurate measure of corporate group strength.

Control of key resources is another criterion that facilitates identification of corporate groups in the archaeological record because resource control is essential to their formation. Corporate groups form "where access to important resources can be restricted by a few people for use or control by themselves." In these situations, "without adverse repercussions, individuals or cliques will act to gain control of those resources, and restrict access to them. This in turn would render other individuals to greater or less degrees dependent on those persons who controlled resources" (Hayden and Cannon 1982: 149). The formation of corporate groups is directly related to the principle of first occupancy, which states that founders and their successors reside in the oldest, most central and elaborate architecture on the most productive land of a community (Dunning 1995; Ford 1996; Hayden and Gargett 1990; Hauck 1975; McAnany 1995; Rathje, this volume; Schele 1992; Silva-Galdames 1971; Tourtellot 1988; Vogt 1969;

Wilk 1991). Rathje's (1972) Core-Buffer Zone model represents the apical development of corporate groups and the power they wield when they control, by whatever mechanism and in whatever form, the distribution of localized, scarce resources (Freidel et al., chapter 3 this volume). In summary, strong patterning in dwelling architecture and the presence of valuable resources provide a relatively accurate indicator for the presence of a residential corporate group.

Sixteenth-Century Tiquibalón (Ek Balám): History and Method

The sixteenth century is a rosetta stone theoretically, methodologically, and substantially because interpretation of pre-Hispanic Maya history and political economy depends on ethnographic analogy and on the direct historical approach (Fox and Cook 1996; Orme 1973; Proskouriakoff 1950: 1; Steward 1942). If a corporate group can be identified in the archaeological record of the sixteenth century using these criteria, then, according to the procedures of the direct historical approach, the theoretical and methodological bridge is built for their identification in earlier periods across the Maya lowlands. At the same time, according to world-systems theory, by analyzing households a foundation for eliciting the pre-Hispanic Maya political economy is established.

Sixteenth-century archaeological research in the northern Maya lowlands has primarily explored Franciscan chapels.[2] By contrast, my fieldwork investigated the sixteenth-century settlement at the archaeological site of Ek Balám, located 25 km north-northeast of Valladolid. According to extant documents, Francisco Montejo the Younger commended the town and district of Tiquibalón with its eleven towns and their dependencies, farms, and fields to *primero conquistador* Juan Gutiérrez Picón on December 2, 1545. Gutiérrez Picón took formal possession of his grant on March 23, 1546, with Ah Na Cobo Copul, Ah Na Yltiz, Ah Na Cay Copul and Ah Na Chan, lords and principals ("senores y principales") of the *cuchcabal* in attendance (*Archivo General de Indias*, Mexico 145, ff. 24–27). Information contained in these and other sixteenth- and seventeenth-century documents indicate that the Franciscans missionized the community and oversaw the construction of the temporary chapel at Tiquibalón, ca. 1555. After an occupation during the Hispanic horizon that lasted no more than two generations, the friars depopulated the town and the site was abandoned, ca. 1605.

The sixteenth-century settlement was located in the northeast sector of the site just beyond the triple walls that encircled the Late Classic constructions of the monumental center (Bey et al. 1998: 104, figure 3). The chapel (HT01) and nucleus of the Early Hispanic Maya community are located approximately 500 meters east of the largest of these structures (GT01) that forms the north side of the great plaza.[3] Two features characterize the karstic topography of this sector. First, the terrain is relatively level but constantly broken by *altillos* (limestone outcrops or hillocks). The outcrops formed the basal platforms for the settlement's dwellings. The majority of these platforms were very informally constructed in that most of the basal constructions did not have retaining walls and are more accurately defined as *nivelaciónes* (levelings or leveled surfaces) (Gallareta Negrón 1984).

Second, seven *rejolladas* (sinkholes or dolines), which vary dramatically in width, depth, and slope gradient, irregularly ring this sector of the site. The chapel is located just north of the southernmost *rejollada* of this ring. Three *rejolladas* have extensive limestone quarries associated with them; one *rejollada* has a pre-Hispanic, veneer-stone-lined well that reaches to standing water at its bottom. A test excavation adjacent to the well's mouth dated its construction to the Late Classic horizon. The well is the only water source in the eastern zone of the site and must have served the Early Hispanic community. The presence of dense settlement in this *rejollada* zone adjacent to the site center indicates intensive use of these natural features throughout the site's long pre-Hispanic history (Bey et al. 1998).

My definition of the Tiquibalón community was based on a 1573 royal *çédula* which mandated that an indigenous community in New Spain possess a plot of land for houses and public buildings which measured 600 *varas* in all directions from the door of the church (Bushnell 1990: 486; Simpson 1937: 13; Wolf 1959: 164). I used this distance (approximately 500 m) measured from Tiquibalón's chapel to define the community and conducted three-phase fieldwork in three adjacent 500m quadrants (HT, HS, IT) of the site map (Bey et al. 1998: 104, figure 3; Hanson 1995a: 19, figure 4). Phase I investigations included the identification, clearing, and mapping of structures and features within each quadrant. Phase I data recovery also featured systematic limited surface collections (four 2-X-2m recovery units) of each mapped structure. Phase II investigations systematically sampled structures on an intensive basis. Selected structures were gridded into 4m_-units and a 20-percent sample of these units were surface collected while two 1-X-2m units (one unit was located on the upper platform surface and the other on its slope) were excavated to bedrock. Phase III investigations selectively excavated (judgmental sample) particular features and structure types specifically related to the Late Postclassic/Early Hispanic occupation at the site and consisted primarily of shallow trenches and horizontal exposures. The samples from Phases II and III of the fieldwork were stratified according to map quadrant and distance from the chapel (Hanson 1992, 1995a, 1995b, 1997b). These field methods provided the data for the following discussion.

Domestic Site Structure

Approximately 150 structures were mapped in the community with occupations ranging from the Middle Formative through Hispanic horizons. The majority of the structures (over 75 percent) were hypothesized to be homesteads, with ancillary buildings, watchtowers, cists, kilns, and structures of unknown function completing the count (Hanson 1999). Artifact assemblages dated approximately 50 percent of the homesteads to the Hispanic horizon. These dwellings clustered in the *rejollada* zone and artifacts recovered from them included: diagnostic pottery of the Xtabay Hocaba-Tases complex (Mama Red, Tecoh Red-on-buff, Yacman Striated, Navula Unslipped, Chen Mul Modeled); Cizin Chauaca-complex olive jar fragments (Middle Style), Sevilla Blue-on-blue and Columbia Plain majolica, Kraak porcelain, and a type of colono-plainware pottery (including brick) analogous to, but more frequent and diverse than, Smith's (1971) Yuncu Unslipped (Bey et al. 1998); animal and human bone (deFrance 1997); arrow points (and their manufacture debitage) and lithic tools; worked shell, greenstone beads, copper bells, axes, and finger rings, and other items of personal adornment; and, iron hardware, tools, and knife blades. Four silver coins minted in México City in the sixteenth century were also recovered from the site (Hanson 1997b).

Two types of sixteenth-century residential architecture were identified in the survey area. In the first type, which was by far the more frequent of the two, the *nivelación* itself was the only vestigial evidence of the presence of residential architecture. In other words, there were no discernible remains of a superstructure visible on the surface of the *nivelación*. Subsequent horizontal excavation of one of these *nivelaciónes* (HT12) near the chapel, however, revealed unhewn stones immediately beneath ground surface that were laid into two disturbed, but still identifiable, apsidal-shaped patterns. These stones were the remains of frame braces that once supported or reinforced the perishable *pajarique* (pole-and-thatch) buildings typical of traditional Maya dwellings (Wauchope 1938). One of the frame braces was oriented on an east/west longitudinal axis. I infer from this limited sample that *pajarique* dwellings were superstructures on the *nivelaciónes* and that this first type of architecture housed the majority of the community.

The second type of architecture, by contrast, is previously unreported in the northern Maya lowlands but occurs thirteen times in the survey area. The nonperishable remains of this building consisted of a single-course, north-south alignment of stones (referred to hereafter as a "single-line structure") that traversed the upper surface of a *nivelación* or, in one case, a platform. The reutilized veneer building stones of this alignment faced east and the alignment was located near the longitudinal centerline of the upper surface of a *nivelación*. The alignments varied between 7 and 28 meters in length and were interpreted not necessarily as the front walls of a dwelling, but as lines demarcating an interior and exterior. In five cases, an eastward-bowing arc of stones joined the alignment's northern and southern termini (forming a D-shape). This feature was interpreted as a formal patio area (which may have been roofed) lying immediately adjacent to the front of the dwelling. In two cases, flights of laid stone forming staircases accessed this patio area from the surrounding ground level. In a few cases, a line of rubble parallel and to the west of the north-south alignment defined this structure's rear frame brace. Relatively dense concentrations of Cizin-complex artifacts were deposited inside the structure along this line. The type of *pajarique* structure that produced these remains differed from the traditional Maya dwelling; it was made of the same materials, but was distinguished by a limited degree of architectural embellishment.

The first examples of this architectural type were encountered on three of the five platforms that encircle the Tiquibalón chapel at a close distance. Two of these, HT03 (located immediately east of the chapel's atrio) and HT21 (located immediately west of the atrio), were two of the largest and most elaborate examples of this architectural type (in that they also had formal stairways to the patio area). The other eleven examples of this building type were identified subsequently in various states of preservation. Their spatial distribution was not clustered near the chapel as much as it was clustered within the *rejollada* zone. Cizin-complex materials were also clustered in the *rejollada* zone.

A Residential Corporate Group

Three lines of evidence (historical records, resource control and production, and architectural patterning) provide sufficient reason to conclude that members of the community's ranking corporate group resided in the single-line structures at Ek Balám. First, *encomendero* descriptions of Maya dwellings compiled in the *Relaciones Geográficas* from Valladolid verify that *principales* occupied a distinct type of residence. In general, according to these accounts, houses in a Maya community "have the sites of their houses on altillos [tiene los asientos de las casas en altillos]" (*Relaciones de Yucatán* [1579–1580]1898–1900 II: 47; hereafter RYII; author's translations followed by Spanish transcriptions as in the original). The Maya constructed houses of "wood with roofs of palm leaves [madera con unas hojas de palma cubiertas]" (RYII: 213) and "walls made of poles lashed together with vines [las paredes son de palos atados con unos bexucos]" (RYII: 56). "The wood poles and the roof reached to the ground on the west side [lega la madera y la cobija por la vanda del poniente hasta el suelo]" and always "the door of these houses is toward where the sun rises and [the roof of] this side was higher [than the west side] although only so much that one did not have to lower oneself to enter the house [la puerta de estas casas esta hazia donde sale el sol y esta mas alta desta vanda aunque no tanto que no se baxen un poco para entrar en casa]" (RYII: 213). However, *encomendero* Juan de Urrutia observed in his *relación* that the residences "the caciques and headmen had were very splendid, although they were of wood" [los caçiques y principales . . . sus casas, que las tenian muy sumptuosa, aunque de madera] (RYII: 69). Urrutia's statement effectively differentiated Hispanic-Horizon Maya dwellings into two types: although both types of houses were constructed of wood, those of the *principales* were distinct by their relative magnificence.

These descriptions of Maya dwellings in the *Relaciones* and the archaeological remains of single-line structures at Ek Balám bear a strong resemblance each to the other: sixteenth-century dwellings and single-line structures were located on *altillos* and were *pajarique* buildings that faced east, with the front and rear of the dwellings constructed differently. This resemblance permits two inferences to be made. First, single-line structures were, in fact, residences. The convergence of the documentary and archaeological records confirms my original premise regarding their residential function. Second, not only were single-line structures dwellings, they were also residences of community *principales*. The documentary and archaeological records each contain two types of residence (all four of which were primarily pole-and-thatch constructions). Urrutia states that houses of the *principales* were distinct from the remainder of a community's dwellings by their elaboration. The nature of this elaboration is not detailed in the documents, but the existence of the relatively more elaborate single-line structure in the archaeological record confirms, with a high degree of probability, that these were the houses of the *principales*. Indeed, it is quite possible that the specific houses that *encomenderos* described in their texts were the dwellings of Maya *principales*—because they interacted primarily with the *principales* of a community, they were most familiar with their dwellings. Therefore, these contemporary observations may have described specifically the single-line dwellings that belonged to *principales*. *Principales* in a Yucatecan Maya community were often members of the same *deme* (or "house"). A *deme* is a residential corporate group (Lévi-Strauss 1982; Monaghan 1995; Murdock 1949; Restall 1997; Soustelle 1962; Spores 1967; Trigger 1968).

A second line of evidence derives from Stark's (1985: 159) premise that spatial proximity determines which segments of a community controlled resources and production. As discussed above, control of key resources is fundamental to residential corporate groups. The presence of two sixteenth-century Castilian kilns near HT03 and HT21 and the nonrandom spatial distribution of single-line structures in relation to the zone of *rejolladas* substantiate that occupants of single-line structures restricted access to local resources. Two updraft kilns (HT02 and HT15A) of sixteenth-century Castilian (or Moorish) design at Ek Balám further substantiate the control of resources and production by occupants of single-line structures (Hanson 1997a; Lister and Lister 1982: 82). The presence of these kilns in the Tiquibalón community marked the introduction of a new technology and a new mode of production to the northern Maya lowlands. Statements by *encomenderos* in the *Relaciones* referred to the existence of what Wolf (1982: 84–85, 87) described as "putting-out" (or "commodity-peonage") industries in the northern Maya lowlands in the late sixteenth century. Putting-out industries thrived on coercing Maya households and communities to produce specialized commodities for sale to the *encomendero* who, in turn, sold them in the greater Indies market for profit. The *encomendero* extended control over the labor process in the towns of his charge by advancing tools, household articles, and prestige goods to the Maya for subsequent repayment in terms of the specialized commodity, thus securing future, and usually unequal, exchange. This combination of compulsory production with commercial enterprise functioned in the northern Maya lowlands outside of the Crown-sanctioned tribute network and was known in Yucatán, according to Farriss (1984: 43), as the *repartimiento*. These unauthorized industries and their products provided colonists a means of securing hard-to-obtain currency.

The two kilns at Ek Balám were part of this putting-out system that characterized mercantile capitalism in the sixteenth-century northern Maya lowlands (Hanson 1997b). In Valladolid province these extralegal industries produced salt, indigo (*añil*), and lime, among other commodities, each of which was abundant locally and in demand at both local and metropolitan markets. The two facilities could have produced any or all of these commodities, as heat is required for all three. Again, within the context of Stark's premise, this localized distribution of kilns in relation to two of the largest and most elaborate single-line structures demonstrates that their occupants controlled these production facilities. In other words, *principales* of the ranking Maya "house" in Tiquibalón in some manner cooperated with Juan Gutiérrez Picón in a mercantile-capitalist enterprise.

Similarly, single-line structures are located only in the *rejollada* zone. *Rejolladas* are nutrient- and water-rich features whose role in pre-Hispanic intensive agriculture and arboriculture has been well documented (Andrews et al. 1989: 91–92; Dunning 1996: 64–66; Fedick 1996: 9; Freidel and Sabloff 1984: 130, 183; Gómez-Pompa et al. 1990; Kepecs and Boucher 1996: 77–81; Roys 1957: 113). Within the context of Stark's premise, this localized distribution of single-line structures demonstrates that their occupants formed a residential corporate group which controlled the resources of, and production in, the *rejolladas* that surrounded them. The principle of first occupancy independently corroborates this conclusion. As mentioned above, the principle of first occupancy states that founders and their successors reside on the most productive land of a community and restrict access to it. This economic control leads to corporate group formation and its founders become the ranking "house" in a community. Given that Stark's premise is correct, the spatial distribution of single-line structures in relation to the kilns and *rejolladas* indicates that their occupants controlled these critical resources. Resource control is a primary feature of corporation.

Third, as discussed above, the repetitive strength of single-line architectural patterning is a robust archaeological indicator of residential corporation. Although the term "repetitive strength" is a relative measure, and although limited variation exists that ultimately reveals some internal differentiation among these structures and their occupants, I contend that the frequency, spatial distribution, and, above all, the consistency of their defining feature (the single alignment of stones) meets at least a minimal definition of "repetitive strength" in architectural patterning. I conclude, therefore, based on these three lines of evidence (historical records, resource control and production, and architectural patterning), that the single-line structures at Ek Balám were the residences of a ranking Maya corporate group during the latter half of the sixteenth century.

Conclusion

In the preceding I defined political economy as the production and flow of goods between households, communities, and nations and then discussed world-systems as a particular theory of political economic analysis that applies not only to post-, but also to pre-sixteenth-century history. I then demonstrated that a recent focus on households in world-systems theory mirrors a similar focus on household archaeology and settlement studies among Mayanists. I argued that household archaeology and world-systems theory complement each other in the manner of Chang's micro- and macrostructure in settlement studies. Given the significance of households for both fields, I turned to ethnoarchaeological methods of studying household remains. Employing three lines of independent evidence, I identified a Maya corporate group in the archaeological record of sixteenth-century Tiquibalón. This is significant because, according to ethnoarchaeological research, the archaeological remains of corporate-group dwellings represent the analytical level at which political and economic inferences become reliable and the analysis of households becomes meaningful. Meaningful inferences from household remains, in turn, permit analysis of the Maya political economy.

This contribution establishes a foundation for the identification of corporate groups in the pre-Hispanic archaeological record in accord with the methods of the direct historical approach. Analogies made by the direct historical approach provide the strongest claims about past behavior in relation to site content and structure (Hayden 1993: 127–129). In conjunction with organizing principles of world-systems theory, this chapter also provides a theoretical and methodological framework for the emergent paradigm whose goal is to model the pre-Hispanic Maya political economy. Despite complex variation in temporal and spatial productive strategies and transport and exchange mechanisms, pre-Hispanic Maya households, communities, and polities were woven into a single lowland political economy that did not exist apart from the Mesoamerican political economy. There were no closed corporate communities (Farriss 1984: 222; Wolf 1957) in either the Maya lowlands or across greater Mesoamerica during either pre-Hispanic or Hispanic horizons. All communities were bound to a greater or lesser degree to centers that had, as Redfield (1955: 114) put it, "their principal being elsewhere than in the village." After years of ethnographic fieldwork in the northern lowlands, he explained his statement in a clear example—in "Maya villages, the political organization, and the economic, are in large part controlled by authority and decision from outside the world of common cultural consciousness: from the world of the European or Europeanized townsman and cityman" (Redfield 1955: 121).

The case study from Ek Balám reported here substantiates and expands Redfield's statement. The distinctive nature of the intrusive architectural and artifactual complex at Ek Balám very clearly highlights the degree to which the households of a Maya community on the very periphery of the early modern world economy participated in it. The sixteenth-century artifacts are material markers of this interaction, which also can be understood as a historical analogy of pre-Hispanic conditions in the Maya lowlands: To the degree that European artifacts and architecture mark Tiquibalón's participation in the early modern world economy, to a similar or greater degree do nonlocal artifacts and architecture at Ek Balám mark its participation in the pre-Hispanic Mesoamerican world-system. Paraphrasing the *Annales* historian Marc Bloch,[4] we are too accustomed to perceiving European-derived communities as distant mirrors of ourselves and non-European-derived communities as cast from a radically different mold. They are not. Rather, history is to the study of "complex societies" as ethnoarchaeology is to household archaeology and settlement studies (Sabloff 1986: 116). One of the strengths of world-systems theory is its abnegation of the arbitrary, eurocentric, and, in the specific case of the lowland Maya, meaningless division between prehistory and history and, by implication, between prehistorical and historical archaeology (Houston 1989; Stuart 1993).

In conclusion, world-systems theory converges almost seamlessly with household archaeology in the Maya lowlands. Households are the central units of production and consumption and, therefore, they are critical to eliciting the Maya political economy. They form the specific sets of archaeological correlates with which to monitor variation in world-system structure and the articulations among its parts. I contend that expansion of Rathje's Core-Buffer Zone hypothesis to a more general world-systems framework offers a means of organizing household and settlement archaeology across the Maya lowlands with the goal of producing a standardized database for comparative purposes. Only such a database can substantiate our models for the pre-Hispanic political economy (Sabloff et al. 1974: 413). I do not advocate the theory uncritically or as an all-powerful explanatory device, but as a logical beginning point to elicit and explain the Maya (and Mesoamerican) political economy and render this relatively insular field of study accessible to a wider range of scholars (Sabloff 1977: 67). Ultimately, the utility of any theory "must be judged on its ability to explain the Maya archaeological record" (Phillips and Rathje 1977: 104) and Maya and Mesoamerican history.

Notes

1. I employ Chang's concepts with the following caveat: rather than the "social/cultural activities" and "cultural and social influences" that he highlights as critical to this interaction, I contend that economic exchange between households, communities, and nations governs or, at the very least, is critical to it.

2. A recent exception is García Targa's fieldwork at Tecoh in 2000.

3. The archaeological research at the sixteenth-century settlement of Tiquibalón was executed during three field seasons (with funding from the National Geographic Society [1992] and the National Science Foundation [1994–1995]). The research formed a subproject within the umbrella Ek Balám Archaeological Project (EKBAP), directed by William M. Ringle (Davidson College) and George J. Bey III (Millsaps College).

4. A subtle ethnocentrism has accustomed us to picture Europe's feudal-era history "as too like ourselves; but the comparative method in the hands of ethnographers has restored to us with a kind of mental shock this sense of the difference, the exotic element, which is the indispensable condition for a balanced understanding of the past" (Bloch 1967: 47).

References

Abu-Lughod, Janet L.
    1989 *Before European Hegemony: The World System* A.D. *1250–1350*. New York: Oxford University Press.
Alexander, Rani T.
    1998 "Afterword: Toward an Archaeological Theory of Culture Contact." Pp. 476–495 in *Studies in Culture Contact: Interaction, Culture Change, and Archaeology*, edited by James G. Cusick. Center for Archaeological Investigations Occasional Paper No. 25. Carbondale: Southern Illinois University.

1999a "Households and Communities in Yaxcabá, Yucatán, México." Pp. 175–179 in *At the Interface: The Household and Beyond*, edited by David B. Small and Nicola Tannenbaum, pp. 175–199. Monographs in Economic Anthropology No. 15. Lanham, Md.: University Press of America.

1999b "The Emerging World System and Colonial Yucatan: The Archaeology of Core-Periphery Integration, 1780–1847." Pp. 103–124 in *World Systems Theory in Practice: Leadership, Production, and Exchange*, edited by P. Nicholas Kardulias. Lanham, Md.: Rowman & Littlefield.

Algaze, Guillermo
1993 *The Uruk World System*. Chicago: University of Chicago Press.

Andrews, Anthony P., Tomás Gallareta Negrón, and Rafael Cobos Palma
1989 "Preliminary Report of the Cupul Survey Project." *Mexicon* 11(5): 91–95.

Arnold, Philip J. III
1990 "The Organization of Refuse Disposal and Ceramic Production within Contemporary Mexican Houselots." *American Anthropologist* 92: 915–932.

Arnold, Philip J. III, Christopher A. Pool, Ronald R. Kneebone, and Robert S. Santley
1993 "Intensive Ceramic Production and Classic-Period Political Economy in the Sierra de Los Tuxtlas, Veracruz, Mexico." *Ancient Mesoamerica* 4: 175–191.

Ashmore, Wendy, editor
1981 *Lowland Maya Settlement Patterns*. Albuquerque: University of New Mexico Press.

Ashmore, Wendy, and Richard R. Wilk
1988 "Household and Community in the Mesoamerican Past." Pp. 1–27 in *Household and Community in the Mesoamerican Past: Case Studies from the Maya Area and Oaxaca*, edited by Richard R. Wilk and Wendy Ashmore. Albuquerque: University of New Mexico Press.

Bey, George J. III, Tara M. Bond, William M. Ringle, Craig A. Hanson, Charles W. Houck, and Carlos Peraza L.
1998 "The Ceramic Chronology of Ek Balám, Yucatán, México." *Ancient Mesoamerica* 8: 101–120.

Blanton, Richard E., and Gary Feinman
1984 "The Mesoamerican World System: A Comparative Perspective." *American Anthropologist* 86: 673–682.

Blanton, Richard E., Gary M. Feinman, Stephen A. Kowalewski, and Peter N. Peregrine
1996 "A Dual-Processual Theory for the Evolution of Mesoamerican Civilization." *Current Anthropology* 37: 1–14.

Blanton, Richard E., Stephen A. Kowalewski, and Gary M. Feinman
1992 "The Mesoamerican World-System." *Review* 15: 419–426.

Bloch, Marc
1967 "A Contribution towards a Comparative History of European Societies." Pp. 44–81 in *Land and Work in Medieval Europe*. Berkeley: University of California Press.

Braswell, Geoffrey E., John E. Clark, Kazuo Aoyama, Heather I. McKillop, and Michael D. Glascock
2000 "Determining the Geological Provenance of Obsidian Artifacts from the Maya Region: A Test of the Efficacy of Visual Sourcing." *Latin American Antiquity* 11: 269–282.

Braudel, Fernand
1972–1973 *The Mediterranean and the Mediterranean World in the Age of Philip II.* 2 vols. New York: Harper and Row.
1980 "Toward a Serial History: Seville and the Atlantic, 1504–1650." Pp. 90–104 in *On History,* by Fernand Braudel. Chicago: University of Chicago Press.

Bullard, William R. Jr.
1960 "Maya Settlement Pattern in Northeastern Petén, Guatemala." *American Antiquity* 25: 355–372.

Bushnell, Amy Turner
1990 "The Sacramental Imperative: Catholic Ritual and Indian Sedentism in the Provinces of Florida." Pp. 475–490 in *Archaeological and Historical Perspectives on the Spanish Borderlands East,* edited by David Hurst Thomas. Columbian Consequences. Vol. 2. Washington, D.C.: Smithsonian Institution Press.

Chang, K. C.
1968 "Toward a Science of Prehistoric Society." Pp. 1–9 in *Settlement Archaeology,* edited by K. C. Chang. Palo Alto: National Press.

Deagan, Kathleen A.
1988 "Neither History nor Prehistory: The Questions that Count in Historical Archaeology." *Historical Archaeology* 22(1): 7–12.

Deal, Michael
1985 "Household Pottery Disposal in the Maya Highlands: An Ethnoarchaeological Interpretation." *Journal of Anthropological Archaeology* 4: 243–291.
1998 *Pottery Ethnoarchaeology in the Central Maya Highlands.* Salt Lake City: University of Utah Press.

Deetz, James
1991 "Introduction: Archaeological Evidence of Sixteenth- and Seventeenth-Century Encounters." Pp. 1–9 in *Historical Archaeology in Global Perspective,* edited by Lisa Falk. Washington, D.C.: Smithsonian Institution Press.

deFrance, Susan D.
1997 *Patterns of Sixteenth Century Faunal Use at Ek Balam, Yucatan.* Manuscript on file, Corpus Christi Museum of Science and History, Corpus Christi, Tex.

Demarest, Arthur A.
1996 "Closing Comment." *Current Anthropology* 37: 821–824.

Denmark, Robert A., Jonathan Friedman, Barry K. Gills, and George Modelski, editors
2000 *World System History: The Social Science of Long-Term Change.* New York: Routledge.

Drennan, Robert D.
1984 "Long-Distance Transport Costs in Pre-Hispanic Mesoamerica." *American Anthropologist* 86: 105–112.
1988 "Household Location and Compact Versus Dispersed Settlement in Prehispanic Mesoamerica." Pp. 273–293 in *Household and Community in the Mesoamerican Past: Case Studies from the Maya Area and Oaxaca*, edited by Richard R. Wilk and Wendy Ashmore. Albuquerque: University of New Mexico Press.

Dunning, Nicholas P.
1995 "Coming Together at the Temple Mountain: Environment, Subsistence and the Emergence of Lowland Maya Segmentary States." Pp. 61–69 in *The Emergence of Lowland Maya Civilization: The Transition from the Preclassic to the Early Classic*, edited by Nikolai Grube. Möckmühl: Verlag Anton Saurwein.
1996 "A Reexamination of Regional Variability in the Pre-Hispanic Agricultural Landscape." Pp. 53–68 in *The Managed Mosaic: Ancient Maya Agriculture and Resource Use*, edited by Scott L. Fedick. Salt Lake City: University of Utah Press.

Engels, Frederick
[1884]1954 *Origin of the Family, Private Property, and the State.* Moscow: Foreign Languages Publishing House.

Farriss, Nancy M.
1984 *Maya Society under Colonial Rule: The Collective Enterprise of Survival.* Princeton: Princeton University Press.

Fedick, Scott
1996 "Introduction: New Perspectives on Ancient Maya Agriculture and Resource Use." Pp. 1–14 in *The Managed Mosaic: Ancient Maya Agriculture and Resource Use*, edited by Scott L. Fedick. Salt Lake City: University of Utah Press.

Ford, Anabel
1996 "Critical Resource Control and the Rise of the Classic Period Maya." Pp. 1–14 in *The Managed Mosaic: Ancient Maya Agriculture and Resource Use*, edited by Scott L. Fedick. Salt Lake City: University of Utah Press.

Fox, John W., and Garrett W. Cook
1996 "Constructing Maya Communities: Ethnography for Archaeology." *Current Anthropology* 37: 811–821.

Frank, Andre Gunder
1967 *Capitalism and Underdevelopment in Latin America: Historical Studies of Chile and Brazil.* New York: Monthly Review Press.

Frank, Andre Gunder, and Barry K. Gills, editors
1993 *The World System: Five Hundred Years or Five Thousand?* New York: Routledge.

Freidel, David A.
1979 "Culture Areas and Interaction Spheres: Contrasting Approaches to the Emergence of Civilization in the Maya Lowlands." *American Antiquity* 44: 36–54.

1981 "The Political Economics of Residential Dispersion Among the Lowland Maya." Pp. 371–382 in *Lowland Maya Settlement Patterns*, edited by Wendy Ashmore. Albuquerque: University of New Mexico Press.

1983 "Lowland Maya Political Economy: Historical and Archaeological Perspectives in Light of Intensive Agriculture." Pp. 40–63 in *Spaniards and Indians in Southeastern Mesoamerica: Essays on the History of Ethnic Relations*, edited by Murdo J. MacLeod and Robert Wasserstrom. Lincoln: University of Nebraska Press.

1986 "Terminal Classic Lowland Maya: Successes, Failures, and Aftermaths." Pp. 409–430 in *Late Lowland Maya Civilization: Classic to Postclassic*, edited by Jeremy A. Sabloff and E. Wyllys Andrews, V. Albuquerque: University of New Mexico Press.

Freidel, David A., and Jeremy A. Sabloff
1984 *Cozumel: Late Maya Settlement Patterns*. New York: Academic Press.

Gallareta Negrón, Manuel Tomás
1984 *Coba: Forma y Funcion de una Comunidad Maya Prehispanica*. Tesis Profesional, Escuela de Ciencias Antropologicas, Universidad de Yucatán, Mérida.

García Targa, Juan
2000 "Análysis Histórico y Arqueológico del Asentamiento Colonial de Tecoh (Estado de Yucatán, México), Siglo XVI." *Ancient Mesoamerica* 11: 231–243.

Gómez-Pompa, Arturo, José Salvador Flores, and Mario Aliphat Fernández
1990 "The Sacred Cacao Groves of the Maya." *Latin American Antiquity* 1: 247–257.

Goodenough, Ward H.
1951 *Property, Kin, and Community on Truk*. Yale University Publications in Anthropology 66. New Haven, Conn.: Yale University Press.

Groenewegen, Peter
1987 "'Political Economy' and 'Economics.'" Pp. 904–907 in *The New Palgrave: A Dictionary of Economics*, Vol. 3, edited by John Eatwell, Murray Milgate, and Peter Newman. London: Macmillan.

Hammond, Norman
1997 Review of *The Managed Mosaic: Ancient Maya Agriculture and Resource Use*, edited by Scott L. Fedick. *Latin American Antiquity* 8: 274–276.

Hanson, Craig A.
1992 *Community Structure in the Chapel Group: A Report on the 1992 Ek Balám Field Season*. Manuscript on file, Department of Anthropology and Sociology, Davidson College.

1995a "The Hispanic Horizon in Yucatan: A Model of Franciscan Missionization." *Ancient Mesoamerica* 6: 15–28.

1995b "Testing the Occupation History: Excavations in the HS *Altillos*." Manuscript on file, Department of Anthropology and Sociology, Davidson College.

1997a *Settlement History in the Eastern Zone of Ek Balám: A Systematic Investigation*. Manuscript on file, Department of Anthropology and Sociology, Davidson College.

1997b "Incorporating the Sixteenth-Century Periphery: From Tributary to Capitalist Production in the Yucatecan Maya Cuchcabal of Tiquibalón (Ekbalám)."

Paper presented at the 30th annual meeting of the Society for Historical Archaeology, Corpus Christi.

1999 "Why a Dwelling?: A Summary of Archaeological and Ethnographical Research into the Lowland Maya Homestead." Unpublished manuscript.

Harrison, Peter D.

1989 "The Revolution in Ancient Maya Subsistence." Pp. 99–113 in *Vision and Revision in Maya Studies*, edited by Flora S. Clancy and Peter D. Harrison. Albuquerque: University of New Mexico Press.

Hauck, Forrest Richard

1975 "Preconquest Mayan Overland Routes on the Yucatan Peninsula and their Economic Significance." Ph.D. dissertation, Department of Anthropology, University of Utah. Ann Arbor: University Microfilms.

Hayden, Brian

1988 "The Coxoh Ethnoarchaeological Project." Pp. 1–4 in *Ethnoarchaeology among the Highland Maya of Chiapas, Mexico*, edited by Thomas A. Lee Jr. and Brian Hayden. Papers of the New World Archaeological Foundation no. 56. New World Archaeological Foundation. Provo: Brigham Young University.

1993 *Archaeology: The Science of Once and Future Things*. New York: W. H. Freeman and Company.

Hayden, Brian, and Aubrey Cannon

1982 "The Corporate Group as an Archaeological Unit." *Journal of Anthropological Archaeology* 1: 132–158.

1983 "Where the Garbage Goes: Refuse Disposal in the Maya Highlands." *Journal of Anthropological Archaeology* 2: 117–163.

1984 *The Structure of Material Systems: Ethnoarchaeology in the Maya Highlands*. SAA Papers No. 3. Washington, D.C.: Society for American Archaeology.

Hayden, Brian, and Rob Gargett

1990 "Big Man, Big Heart?: A Mesoamerican View of the Emergence of Complex Society." *Ancient Mesoamerica* 1: 3–20.

Henderson, John S., and Jeremy A. Sabloff

1993 "Reconceptualizing the Maya Cultural Tradition: Programmatic Comments." Pp. 445–468 in *Lowland Maya Civilization in the Eighth Century A.D.*, edited by Jeremy A. Sabloff and John S. Henderson. Washington, D.C.: Dumbarton Oaks.

Hicks, Frederick

1994 "Cloth in the Political Economy of the Aztec State." Pp. 89–112 in *Economies and Polities in the Aztec Realm*, edited by Mary Hodge and Michael E. Smith. Studies on Culture and Society Vol. 6. Albany: State University of New York Institute for Mesoamerican Studies.

Hirth, Kenneth G.

1993 "The Household as an Analytical Unit: Problems In Method and Theory." Pp. 21–36 in *Prehispanic Domestic Units in Western Mesoamerica: Studies of the Household, Compound, and Residence*, edited by Robert S. Santley and Kenneth G. Hirth. Boca Raton, Fla.: CRC Press.

Hopkins, Terence K., and Immanuel Wallerstein

1987 "Capitalism and the Incorporation of New Zones into the World-Economy." *Review* X: 763–779.

Houston, Stephen D.
1989 "Archaeology and Maya Writing." *Journal of World Prehistory* 3(1): 1–32.
Inomata, Takeshi, and Kazuo Aoyama
1996 "Central-Place Analyses in the La Entrada Region, Honduras: Implications for Understanding the Classic Maya Political and Economic Systems." *Latin American Antiquity* 7: 291–312.
Johnson, Matthew
1996 *An Archaeology of Capitalism.* Cambridge: Blackwell.
Kardulias, P. Nicholas, editor
1999 *World Systems Theory in Practice: Leadership, Production, and Exchange.* Lanham, Md.: Rowman & Littlefield.
Kepecs, Susan, and Sylviane Boucher
1996 "The Pre-Hispanic Cultivation of *Rejolladas* and Stone-Lands: New Evidence from Northeast Yucatán." Pp. 69–91 in *The Managed Mosaic: Ancient Maya Agriculture and Resource Use,* edited by Scott L. Fedick. Salt Lake City: University of Utah Press.
Kepecs, Susan, Gary Feinman, and Sylviane Boucher
1994 "Chichen Itza and Its Hinterland: A World-Systems Perspective." *Ancient Mesoamerica* 5: 141–158.
Killion, Thomas W.
1990 "Cultivation Intensity and Residential Site Structure: An Ethnoarchaeological Examination of Peasant Agriculture in the Sierra de los Tuxtlas, Veracruz, Mexico." *Latin American Antiquity* 1: 191–215.
1992a "The Archaeology of Settlement Agriculture." Pp. 1–13 in *The Archaeology of Settlement Agriculture in Greater Mesoamerica,* edited by Thomas W. Killion. Tuscaloosa: University of Alabama Press.
1992b "Residential Ethnoarchaeology and Ancient Site Structure: Contemporary Farming and Prehistoric Settlement Agriculture at Matacapan, Veracruz, Mexico." Pp. 119–149 in *Gardens of Prehistory: The Archaeology of Settlement Agriculture in Greater Mesoamerica,* edited by Thomas W. Killion. Tuscaloosa: University of Alabama Press.
Killion, Thomas W., Jeremy A. Sabloff, Gair Tourtellot, and Nicholas P. Dunning
1989 "Intensive Surface Collection of Residential Clusters at Terminal Classic Sayil, Yucatan, Mexico." *Journal of Field Archaeology* 16: 273–294.
Knapp, A. Bernard
1992 "Archaeology and *Annales*: Time, Space, and Change." Pp. 1–21 in *Archaeology, Annales, and Ethnohistory,* edited by A. Bernard Knapp. Cambridge: Cambridge University Press.
Kuhn, Thomas
1970 *The Structure of Scientific Revolutions.* 2d ed. Chicago: University of Chicago Press.
Kurjack, Edward B.
1974 *Prehistoric Lowland Maya Community and Social Organization: A Case Study at Dzibilchaltun, Yucatan, Mexico.* Middle American Research Institute Publication No. 38. New Orleans: Tulane University.

Lange, Frederick W.
1986 "Central America and the Southwest: A Comparison of Mesoamerica's Two Peripheries." Pp. 159–177 in *Research and Reflections in Archaeology and History: Essays in Honor of Doris Stone*, edited by E. Wyllys Andrews, V. Middle American Research Institute Publication No. 57. New Orleans: Tulane University.

Leone, Mark P.
1992 "Epilogue: The Productive Nature of Material Culture and Archaeology." *Historical Archaeology* 26(3): 130–133.

Leone, Mark P., and Parker B. Potter Jr.
1988 "Introduction: Issues in Historical Archaeology." Pp. 1–26 in *The Recovery of Meaning*, edited by Mark P. Leone and Parker B. Potter Jr. Washington, D.C.: Smithsonian Institution Press.

Lévi-Strauss, Claude
1982 "The Social Organization of the Kwakiutl." Pp. 163–187 in *The Way of the Masks*, by Claude Lévi-Strauss. Seattle: University of Washington Press.

Lister, Florence C., and Robert H. Lister
1982 *Sixteenth Century Maiolica Pottery in the Valley of Mexico*. Anthropological Papers of the University of Arizona No. 39. Tucson: University of Arizona Press.

Maine, Sir Henry
[1861]1960 *Ancient Law*. Everyman's Library 734. New York: E. P. Dutton.

Manzanilla, Linda, and Luis Barba
1990 "The Study of Activities in Classic Households: Two Case Studies from Coba and Teotihuacan." *Ancient Mesoamerica* 1: 41–49.

Marx, Karl, and Frederick Engels
[1846]1977 "Feuerbach: Opposition of the Materialistic and Idealistic Outlook." Pp. 16–80 in *Karl Marx and Frederick Engels: Selected Works in Three Volumes*, Vol. 1. Moscow: Progress Publishers.

McAnany, Patricia A.
1989 "Economic Foundations of Prehistoric Maya Society: Paradigms and Concepts." Pp. 347–372 in *Prehistoric Maya Economies of Belize*, edited by Patricia A. McAnany and Barry L. Isaac. Research in Economic Anthropology Supplement 4. Greenwich, Conn.: JAI Press.
1993 "The Economics of Social Power and Wealth among Eighth-Century Maya Households." Pp. 65–89 in *Lowland Maya Civilization in the Eighth Century A.D.*, edited by Jeremy A. Sabloff and John S. Henderson. Washington, D.C.: Dumbarton Oaks.
1995 *Living with the Ancestors: Kinship and Kingship in Ancient Maya Society*. Austin: University of Texas Press.

McCafferty, Sharisse D., and Geoffrey G. McCafferty
2000 "Textile Production in Postclassic Cholula, Mexico." *Ancient Mesoamerica* 11: 39–54.

Meillassoux, Claude
1981 *Maidens, Meal, and Money: Capitalism and the Domestic Community*. Cambridge: Cambridge University Press.

Mill, John Stuart
[1848]1965 "Principles of Political Economy with Some of Their Applications to Social Philosophy." In *Collected Works of John Stuart Mill*, Vol. 2 & 3, edited by John M. Robson. Toronto: University of Toronto Press.

Monaghan, John
1995 *The Covenants with Earth and Rain: Exchange, Sacrifice, and Revelation in Mixtec Sociality*. Norman: University of Oklahoma Press.

Morgan, Lewis Henry
[1881]1965 *Houses and House Life of the American Aborigines*. Chicago: University of Chicago Press.

Mrozowski, Stephen A.
1993 "The Dialectics of Historical Archaeology in a Post-Processual World." *Historical Archaeology* 27(2): 106–111.

Murdock, George P.
1949 *Social Structure*. New York: Macmillan.

Netting, Robert McC.
1971 "Maya Subsistence: Mythologies, Analogies, Possibilities." Pp. 299–333 in *The Origins of Maya Civilization*, edited by Richard E. W. Adams. Albuquerque: University of New Mexico Press.
1993 *Smallholders, Householders: Farm Families and the Ecology of Intensive, Sustainable Agriculture*. Stanford, Calif.: Stanford University Press.

Noble, Vergil E.
1999 Review of *Studies in Culture Contact: Interaction, Culture Change, and Archaeology*, edited by James G. Cusick. *Historical Archaeology* 33(4): 78–79.

Orme, Bryony
1973 "Archaeology and Ethnography." Pp. 481–492 in *The Explanation of Culture Change: Models in Prehistory*, edited by Colin Renfrew. Pittsburgh: University of Pittsburgh Press.

Parsons, Jeffrey R.
2000 Review of *Settlement Pattern Studies in the Americas: Fifty Years Since Virú*, edited by Brian R. Billman and Gary M. Feinman. *American Antiquity* 65: 579–581.

Phillips, David A. Jr., and William L. Rathje
1977 "Streets Ahead: Exchange Values and the Rise of the Classic Maya." Pp. 103–112 in *Social Process in Maya Prehistory: Studies in Honour of Sir Eric Thompson*, edited by Norman Hammond. New York: Academic Press.

Proskouriakoff, Tatiana
1950 *A Study of Classic Maya Sculpture*. Publication No. 593. Washington, D.C.: Carnegie Institution.

Pyburn, K. Anne
1996 "The Political Economy of Ancient Maya Land Use: The Road to Ruin." Pp. 236–247 in *The Managed Mosaic: Ancient Maya Agriculture and Resource Use*, edited by Scott L. Fedick. Salt Lake City: University of Utah Press.

Pyburn, K. Anne, Boyd Dixon, Patricia Cook, and Anna McNair
1998 "The Albion Island Settlement Pattern Project: Domination and Resistance in Early Classic Northern Belize." *Journal of Field Archaeology* 25(1): 37–62.

Rathje, William L.
1971 "The Origin and Development of Lowland Classic Maya Civilization." *American Antiquity* 36: 275–285.
1972 "Praise the Gods and Pass the Metates: An Hypothesis of the Rise and Fall of Lowland Rainforest Civilizations in Mesoamerica." Pp. 365–392 in *Contemporary Archaeology*, edited by Mark P. Leone. Carbondale: Southern Illinois University Press.
1973 "Classic Maya Development and Denouement." Pp. 405–454 in *The Classic Maya Collapse*, edited by T. Patrick Culbert. Albuquerque: School of American Research and the University of New Mexico.
1975 "The Last Tango in Mayapán: A Tentative Trajectory of Production-Distribution Systems." Pp. 409–448 in *Ancient Civilization and Trade*, edited by Jeremy A. Sabloff and C. C. Lamberg Karlovsky. Albuquerque: University of New Mexico Press.
1978 "Archaeological Ethnography . . . Because Sometimes It Is Better to Give than to Receive." Pp. 49–75 in *Explorations in Ethnoarchaeology*, edited by Richard A. Gould. Albuquerque: University of New Mexico Press.
1983 "To the Salt of the Earth: Some Comments on Household Archaeology among the Maya." Pp. 23–34 in *Prehistoric Settlement Patterns*, edited by Evon Z. Vogt and Richard M. Leventhal. Albuquerque: University of New Mexico Press.
Rathje, William L., David A. Gregory, and Frederick M. Wiseman
1978 "Trade Models and Archaeological Problems: Classic Maya Examples." Pp. 147–175 in *Mesoamerican Communication Routes and Cultural Contacts*, edited by Thomas A. Lee Jr. and Carlos Navarrete. Papers of the New World Archaeological Foundation No. 40. Provo, Utah: Brigham Young University.
Redfield, Robert
1955 *The Little Community: Viewpoints for the Study of a Human Whole*. Chicago: University of Chicago Press.
Relaciónes de Yucatán
[1579–1580]1898–1900 In *Colección de documentos inéditos relativos al descubrimiento, conquista y organización de las antiguas posesiones españolas de ultramar*. 2nd Series, Vols. 11 (RYI) and 13 (RYII). La Real Academia de la Historia, Madrid.
Restall, Matthew
1997 *The Maya World: Yucatec Culture and Society, 1550–1850*. Stanford, Calif.: Stanford University Press.
Rice, Prudence M.
1998 "Contexts of Contact and Change: Peripheries, Frontiers, and Boundaries." Pp. 44–66 in *Studies in Culture Contact: Interaction, Culture Change, and Archaeology*, edited by James G. Cusick. Center for Archaeological Investigations Occasional Paper No. 25. Carbondale: Southern Illinois University.
Roys, Ralph L.
1957 *The Political Geography of the Yucatan Maya*. Publication 613. Washington, D.C.: Carnegie Institution.

Sabloff, Jeremy A.
1977 "Old Myths, New Myths: The Role of Sea Traders in the Development of Ancient Maya Civilization." Pp. 67–95 in *The Sea in the Pre-Columbian World*, edited by Elizabeth P. Benson. Washington, D.C.: Dumbarton Oaks.
1986 "Interaction among Classic Maya Polities: A Preliminary Examination." Pp. 109–116 in *Peer Polity Interaction and Socio-Political Change*, edited by Colin Renfrew and John F. Cherry. Cambridge: Cambridge University Press.
Sabloff, Jeremy A., and William L. Rathje
1975 "The Rise of a Maya Merchant Class." *Scientific American* 233(4): 72–82.
Sabloff, Jeremy A., William L. Rathje, David A. Freidel, Judith G. Connor, and Paula L. W. Sabloff
1974 "Trade and Power in Postclassic Yucatan: Initial Observations." Pp. 397–416 in *Mesoamerican Archaeology: New Approaches*, edited by Norman Hammond. Austin: University of Texas Press.
Santley, Robert S.
1986 "Prehispanic Roadways, Transport Network Geometry, and Aztec Politico-Economic Organization in the Basin of Mexico." Pp. 223–244 in *Economic Aspects of Prehispanic Highland Mexico*, edited by Barry L. Isaac. Research in Economic Anthropology Supplement 2. Greenwich, Conn.: JAI Press.
1992 "A Consideration of the Olmec Phenomenon in the Tuxtlas: Early Formative Settlement Pattern, Land Use, and Refuse Disposal at Matacapan, Veracruz, Mexico." Pp. 150–183 in *Gardens of Prehistory: The Archaeology of Settlement Agriculture in Greater Mesoamerica*, edited by Thomas W. Killion. Tuscaloosa: University of Alabama Press.
Santley, Robert S., and Rani T. Alexander
1992 "The Political Economy of Core-Periphery Systems." Pp. 23–49 in *Resources, Power, and Interregional Interaction*, edited by Edward M. Schortman and Patricia A. Urban. New York: Plenum Press.
1996 "Teotihuacan and Middle Classic Mesoamerica: A Precolumbian World System?" Pp. 173–194 in *Arqueología Mesoamericana: Homenaje a William T. Sanders*, Vol. 1, edited by Alba Guadalupe Mastache, Jeffrey R. Parsons, Robert S. Santley, and Mari Carmen Serra Puche. Instituto Nacional de Antropología e Historia e Arqueología Mexicana, México.
Santley, Robert S., and Kenneth G. Hirth
1993 "Household Studies in Western Mesoamerica." Pp. 3–17 in *Prehispanic Domestic Units in Western Mesoamerica: Studies of the Household, Compound, and Residence*, edited by Robert S. Santley and Kenneth G. Hirth. Boca Raton, Fla.: CRC Press.
Santone, Lenore
1997 Transport Costs, Consumer Demand, and Patterns of Intraregional Exchange: A Perspective on Commodity Production and Distribution from Northern Belize." *Latin American Antiquity* 8: 71–88.
Schele, Linda
1992 "The Founders of Lineages at Copan and Other Maya Sites." *Ancient Mesoamerica* 3: 135–144.

Schmidt, Peter R., and Thomas C. Patterson
1995 "Introduction: From Constructing to Making Alternative Histories." Pp. 1–24 in *Making Alternative Histories: The Practice of Archaeology and History in Non-Western Settings*, edited by Peter R. Schmidt and Thomas C. Patterson. Santa Fe: School of American Research Press.
Schneider, Jane
1977 "Was There a Pre-capitalist World-System?" *Peasant Studies* VI(1): 20–29.
Schuyler, Robert L.
1978 "Historical and Historic Sites Archaeology as Anthropology: Basic Definitions and Relationships." Pp. 27–31 in *Historical Archaeology: A Guide to Substantive and Theoretical Contributions*, edited by Robert L. Schuyler. Farmingdale: Baywood Publishing Co.
Sheets, Payson
2000 "Provisioning the Ceren Household: The Vertical Economy, Village Economy, and Household Economy in the Southeastern Maya Periphery." *Ancient Mesoamerica* 11: 217–230.
Silva-Galdames, Osvaldo
1971 "Trade and the Concept of Nuclear and Marginal Culture Areas in Mesoamerica." *Cerámica de Cultura Maya* No. 7, Supplement: 5–63.
Simpson, Eyler N.
1937 *The Ejido: Mexico's Way Out.* Chapel Hill: University of North Carolina Press.
Smith, Joan, and Immanuel Wallerstein, editors
1992 *Creating and Transforming Households.* Cambridge: Cambridge University Press.
Smith, Joan, Immanuel Wallerstein, and Hans-Dieter Evers, editors
1984 *Households and the World-Economy.* Newbury Park, Calif.: Sage.
Smith, Michael E.
1992 "Braudel's Temporal Rhythms and Chronology Theory in Archaeology." Pp. 23–34 in *Archaeology, Annales, and Ethnohistory*, edited by A. Bernard Knapp. Cambridge: Cambridge University Press.
Smith, Robert E.
1971 *The Pottery of Mayapan, Including Studies of Ceramic Material from Uxmal, Kabah, and Chichen Itza.* 2 vols. Papers of the Peabody Museum of Archaeology and Ethnology Vol. 66. Cambridge, Mass.: Harvard University.
Smyth, Michael P.
1989 "Domestic Storage Behavior in Mesoamerica: An Ethnoarchaeological Approach." Pp. 89–138 in *Archaeological Method and Theory* Vol. 1, edited by Michael B. Schiffer. Tucson: University of Arizona Press.
1990 "Maize Storage among the Puuc Maya: The Development of an Archaeological Method." *Ancient Mesoamerica* 1: 51–69.
Soustelle, Jacques
1962 *The Daily Life of the Aztecs.* New York: Macmillan.
Spores, Ronald
1967 *The Mixtec Kings and Their People.* Norman: University of Oklahoma Press.

Stark, Barbara L.
1985 "Archaeological Identification of Pottery Production Locations: Ethnoarchaeological and Archaeological Data in Mesoamerica." Pp. 158–194 in *Decoding Prehistoric Ceramics*, edited by Ben A. Nelson. Carbondale: Southern Illinois University Press.

Steward, Julian H.
1942 "The Direct Historical Approach to Archaeology." *American Antiquity* 7: 337–343.

Stuart, David
1993 "Historical Inscriptions and the Maya Collapse." Pp. 321–354 in *Lowland Maya Civilization in the Eighth Century A.D.*, edited by Jeremy A. Sabloff and John S. Henderson. Washington, D.C.: Dumbarton Oaks.

Tourtellot, Gair
1988 "Peripheral Survey and Excavation and Settlement and Community Patterns." In *Excavations at Seibal, Department of Petén, Guatemala*, Memoirs of the Peabody Museum of Archaeology and Ethnology, Vol. 16, No. 1. Cambridge, Mass.: Harvard University.

Trigger, Bruce G.
1968 "The Determinants of Settlement Patterns." Pp. 53–78 in *Settlement Archaeology*, edited by K. C. Chang. Palo Alto, Calif.: National Press.

Vogt, Evon Z.
1969 *Zinacantan: A Maya Community in the Highlands of Chiapas*. Cambridge, Mass.: Harvard University.

Wallerstein, Immanuel
1974 *The Modern World System: Capitalist Agriculture and the Origins of the European World-Economy in the Sixteenth Century*. New York: Academic Press.

Wallerstein, Immanuel, William G. Martin, and Torry Dickinson
1982 "Household Structures and Production Processes: Preliminary Theses and Findings." *Review* 3: 437–458.

Wallerstein, Immanuel, and Joan Smith
1992a "Core-Periphery and Household Structures." Pp. 253–262 in *Creating and Transforming Households: The Constraints of the World-Economy*, edited by Joan Smith and Immanuel Wallerstein. Cambridge: Cambridge University Press.
1992b "Households as an Institution of the World-Economy." Pp. 3–23 in *Creating and Transforming Households: The Constraints of the World Economy*, edited by Joan Smith and Immanuel Wallerstein. Cambridge: Cambridge University Press.

Wauchope, Robert
1938 *Modern Maya Houses: A Study of Their Archaeological Significance*. Publication 502. Washington, D. C.: Carnegie Institution.

Weber, Max
1978 *Economy and Society: An Outline of Interpretive Sociology*. 2 vols. Berkeley: University of California Press.

Webster, David
1992 "Maya Elites: The Perspective from Copan." Pp. 135–156 in *Mesoamerican Elites: An Archaeological Assessment*, edited by Diane Z. Chase and Arlen F. Chase. Norman: University of Oklahoma Press.

Wesseling, Hank
1991 "Overseas History." Pp. 67–92 in *New Perspectives on Historical Writing*, edited by Peter Burke. University Park: Pennsylvania State University Press.
Whitecotton, Joseph W., and Richard A. Pailes
1986 "New World Precolumbian World Systems." Pp. 183–204 in *Ripples in the Chichimec Sea: New Considerations of Southwestern-Mesoamerican Interactions*. Carbondale: Southern Illinois University Press.
Wilk, Richard R.
1991 *Household Ecology: Economic Change and Domestic Life Among the Kekchi Maya in Belize*. Tucson: University of Arizona Press.
Wilk, Richard R., and William L. Rathje
1982 "Archaeology of the Household: Building a Prehistory of Domestic Life." *American Behavioral Scientist* 25: 611–724.
Willey, Gordon R.
1953 *Prehistoric Settlement Patterns in the Viru Valley, Peru*. Bureau of American Ethnology Bulletin No. 155. Washington, D.C.: Smithsonian Institution.
1956 "Problems Concerning Prehistoric Settlement Patterns in the Maya Lowlands." Pp. 107–114 in *Prehistoric Settlement Patterns in the New World*, edited by Gordon R. Willey. New York: Wenner Gren Foundation for Anthropological Research.
1974 "The Classic Maya Hiatus: A Rehearsal for the Collapse?" Pp. 417–430 in *Mesoamerican Archaeology: New Approaches*, edited by Norman Hammond. Austin: University of Texas Press.
1981 "Maya Lowland Settlement Patterns: A Summary Review." Pp. 385–415 in *Lowland Maya Settlement Patterns*, edited by Wendy Ashmore. Albuquerque: University of New Mexico Press.
1999 "Styles and State Formations." *American Antiquity* 10: 86–90.
Wolf, Eric R.
1957 "Closed Corporate Peasant Communities in Mesoamerica and Java." *Southwestern Journal of Anthropology* 13: 1–18.
1959 *Sons of the Shaking Earth*. Chicago: University of Chicago Press.
1982 *Europe and the People without History*. Berkeley: University of California Press.

Chapter Fourteen

Perspectives on Economy and Theory

Elizabeth Graham

Introduction

The centripetal force behind the papers in this volume was originally a tribute to William Rathje in the form of recognition of his contributions to our understanding of ancient Maya economy. In my presented paper (Graham 2000), I concentrated on those aspects of Rathje's perspective without which Maya research would have been much the poorer, and because of which we have been able to move forward to a greater understanding of local and regional economic integration.

This present volume has retained the original economic focus to bring together a range of chapters that provide new information on the changing faces of Maya economy. Rathje's focus went beyond economy, however, to include the role of economic forces in creating and sustaining Maya civilization. If economy figured largely in Rathje's theories, it was secondary to his interest in the explanation of societal change—the motivational force behind his work. Therefore the emphasis in this volume's title on "political" economy accurately reflects Rathje's legacy.

In the chapter that follows, I attempt to cover a range of issues that are critical to our perceptions of the way Maya economy formed, disintegrated, and re-formed through time. These are:

1. the question of explanation in theories of political economy—informing human action, economic integration, and ideology and elite behavior;

2. local and regional exchange;

3. the idea that resource diversity is in the eye of the beholder;

4. economic prosperity; and

5. the role of elites and their demands.

In the process, I will bring recent information from the excavations at Lamanai as well as excavation data from coastal sites to bear on questions of economic integration.

Explanation in Theories of Political Economy

Rathje's contributions (1972, 1975, 1983, chapter 2 this volume; Rathje et al. 1978) to our understanding of Maya economy are exceptional, in my view, in two major ways. The first is that they include the kind of explanation that can inform human action; and the second is that they attempt to explain Maya civilization in terms that require us to be knowledgeable about mechanisms of integration. Integration is given detailed attention in other explanatory paradigms, such as Flannery's cultural evolution of civilizations (1972); but Flannery's is a theory-for-all-seasons, whereas Rathje is well aware that mechanisms of integration have a momentum and a direction all their own, which he usually doesn't hesitate to define (chapter 2 this volume). In addition, Flannery's evolutionary paradigm, although it takes human action into account, is not designed to explain it.

Informing Human Action

My reference above to informing human action is a main criterion of mine in assessing the value of a theory, although I recognize that such a criterion is not universally significant for other scholars. For me, theory is inseparable from why I practice archaeology in the first place—because I believe we can learn from archaeology, and apply what we learn to solve contemporary socioeconomic problems. Therefore the key question I ask is, By what process do I learn from this theory?

There are theories that shed light on why things happen, but the clarity afforded can be gained only in hindsight, or exists on an analytical level that is irrelevant to individual action. For this kind of theory, understanding cannot be applied to individual decision-making. Much of evolutionary theory is like this (Dawkins 1976), as is systems theory (e.g., Flannery 1972). In terms of evolution, knowing that genes are selfish (Dawkins 1976) doesn't inform any decisions that I might make about the course of my life. It is interesting knowledge, and could be critical information in some deity's long-term planning, but it exists on a field that isn't relevant to me as a player. Therefore I cannot *learn* from it because learning involves modification of behavior, and knowing my genes are selfish doesn't provide me with particularly useful information about why I might choose to buy Farberware as opposed to Cuisinart. Nor will theories like it help me learn why, in Terminal Classic times at Lamanai and in contrast to the Petexbatun region (Foias, chapter 8 this volume), serving ware continued to be a hot item. The form and decoration of serving ware changed, but not the preference for vessels that were used to display food. This phenomenon reflects people's choices as well as responses to demands. To understand political economy, what we need are theories that help us evaluate the context of these choices.

In this volume, the contextual focus is political economy, and I will proceed to discuss aspects of political economy in more detail. I feel it important to begin at the level of explanation, because the subtext of every chapter in the volume includes choices the author or authors have already made about explanation and the purpose it serves. Although the focus on Rathje's work is not as explicitly highlighted in the volume as it was in the SAA session, I believe that it is the attention originally given by the authors to relating their data and conclusions about economy to some part of Rathje's work that makes the chapters work so well together. That is, we have agreed, in some cases explicitly and in others only implicitly, on the kinds of explanation that work, and the chapters address issues of political economy that work within this explanatory range.

Economic Mechanisms of Integration

It was Hanson's chapter (chapter 13) that made me aware of Rathje's work for its emphasis on integrative mechanisms. Hanson describes Rathje's core-buffer model as an explanation for the origin and historical development of Maya political economy. He sees Rathje's core-buffer framework as akin to a world-systems model in that it was developed to explain dependent economic development, with the surplus value of transactions accruing to the core. Hanson goes on to say that world-systems theory, and by implication the core-buffer zone model, is in effect a theory of historical change. Why should a theory of historical change appeal to archaeologists?

Be-cause theories of historical change are explanatory in ways that have implications for understanding human action.

Hanson elucidates another level of Rathje's work, which is also well developed by Dahlin and Ardren (chapter 9 this volume). This has to do with the frameworks for investigating households and household economy; specifically, the microstructure and macrostructure of households. Mayanists have, according to Hanson, devoted attention to households and their place within the community, but households have otherwise been neglected as institutions of critical importance in a world-systems or core-periphery frame. Some scholarly writing, in fact, still gives the impression that the household economy is indeed separate from economies operating at regional levels. But, as Hanson points out, Rathje recognized the household as *integral* to the structure of the larger economy, and thus tacitly recognized the interconnectedness of all aspects of Maya political economy.

Hanson, Dahlin and Ardren, and Braswell (chapters 13, 9, and 10, respectively, this volume) build on Rathje's work by amassing a wide range of detailed archaeological data on household and community internal patterning—based on architecture, traffic flow patterns, extra-household features, and, of course, artifacts. They then increase our understanding of the possible range of explanations for these patterns by providing coherent macrostructural models as frameworks of integration. In all three instances, the premises of the respective cases are laid out to facilitate testing of their hypotheses. This is critical in archaeological thought, in order that debates can move from what people might think are good or bad ideas to testing what is proposed.

Integration, Ideology, and Elite Behavior

Other contributions to this volume, such as that of Sullivan (chapter 7), Freidel et al. (chapter 3), and to some extent McAnany et al. (chapter 5), build on the integrative aspects of Rathje's theories by reference to elite behavior, and in particular elite exclusionary behavior, ideology, or cosmology. Both the core-buffer framework and Rathje's nouveau elite hypothesis (chapter 2 this volume) include integration at the level of ideology. Sullivan and McAnany et al. see economic and ideological factors as closely intertwined, and they present evidence—stronger in Sullivan's case because of the stage of the work—for exchange among elites being linked to shared ideologies and thereby the maintenance of elite ties. Sullivan sees ceramics in the Early Classic, and architecture in the Late Classic, as emblematic of elite power. McAnany et al. suggest that we consider cacao as an item of exchange among the elite, from which it follows that the growing of cacao is essentially a response to elite demands. Although McAnany et al.'s claims at this stage will be difficult to test, the ways in which elite activities and elite demands affected farmers and their priorities of production are critical to understanding the dynamics of Maya economy. Freidel et al. argue, in a different but closely related vein, that Maya political economy incorporated not only goods that had use-value, but goods that derived their value as much from their ideological or cosmological significance, such as jade or *Spondylus*. Prestige goods and elite control will be discussed in more detail below.

The implications of elite activities bring us directly back to Rathje's ideas (chapter 2) about the existence of a nouveau elite among the Maya. As with his earlier work on origins and development, the attractiveness of this hypothesis lies in the way it envisions—and stimulates thought about—the ideological and cultural factors that structure the character of social production. Rathje's argument about a growing hierarchy, and the early investment of elites in Monstrous Visual Symbols (with reference to Fletcher 1977) makes intuitive sense. Lamanai, certainly, can be said to represent this pattern (Pendergast 1981). The Late Preclassic construction of the 33m-high N10-43 is never again matched, and the acropolis-like platform affectionately known by us as Holiday House, which supports a dozen or so buildings the latest of which are Early Classic, is another example of early investment in monumental architecture with what appears to us to be a wasteful use of resources. The nouveau elite idea is additionally attractive to me at another level: It is an idea that attempts to explain the origins of Maya civilization by linking important changes in social state to the ways in which humans make decisions—in this case about the exercise of power—and therefore bears on our understanding of the use and abuse of power in a range of circumstances, both ancient and modern. I will examine the issue of elite power relations below, but will now turn to the ways in which economic integration is envisioned, and to tools of terminology that still need sharpening (Graham 1987: 761).

Local Exchange

Masson states in the introduction to this volume that "understanding local resources is critical for evaluating the value of commodities produced within subregions of the Maya area." She goes on to refer to McGuire (1989), who states that the more unevenly resources are distributed, the more likely communities will be dependent on others for items critical to their basic maintenance. I understand these observations to mean that local resources are important at the subregional level, both for their potential as basic subsistence items and for their potential commercial advantage (i.e., in exchange). I concur, but I have also argued strongly elsewhere (Graham 1987) that local resources and local exchange are critical in understanding interregional exchange, and even exchange over long distances (1987: 763). Most of the papers in this volume, in fact, prove the point that locally situating the resources and exchange patterns of the site one is investigating is the building block to understanding regional or long-distance exchange.

Can the Local Be Universal?

Despite my emphasis on the local, it is methodologically unsound to assume that there is a range of items that are universally "local" in the lowlands, such as chert, limestone, pottery, or forest products and game. What is local should in each case be established, not assumed. Masson's research (chapter 12 this volume) in northern Belize at the sites of Laguna de On and Caye Coco is doing exactly this: by carefully reconstructing local economies through analyses of all artifact categories, and by building knowledge of the locally available resources. Dahlin and Ardren's research, too, (chapter 9) includes a heavy emphasis on resource mapping. Masson has been able to reconstruct the details of community and intercommunity relationships and thus, with knowledge of what her communities have to offer through time, can assess the full implications of longer-distance relationships, and the layers of Postclassic political economy in particular.

What we should not do, however, is assume that there is a set of items that is local to Maya communities in the lowlands in general and attempt to build on this assumption. We cannot know what is exotic ("from another part of the world; foreign" [Soukhanov 1992]) until we know what is local, and as Mayanists we may even need to know more about the varieties of Maya subsistence patterns before we can be certain about what constitutes local subsistence items. For example, until about the fifth century, coastal Maya communities may have relied more heavily on root crops than on maize (Graham 1994: 269, 316). Salt is certainly not exotic to communities along the coast and for some distance inland, particularly in southern Belize where the river valleys run east-west, and in northern Belize where the rivers flow into Corozal Bay. Obsidian, too, was easier to acquire in areas of southern Belize than chert, which was not found locally owing to the absence of limestone deposits (Graham 1994: 9–18). Calabashes, probably widely used as household containers, grow in Belize in the "pine ridge" zones (savannas), and would be exotic to communities surrounded by broadleaf forests. Forest products and game, however, are exotic to many coastal and caye communities, as well as to those that occupied Belize's atolls, whereas *Spondylus americanus* and conch are local to communities that occupied the cayes and coast.

Although it is fruitful to develop the *concept* of local vs. nonlocal resources at a general level, it would be a mistake to assume that specific products or items will always fit the local or nonlocal bill. In fact, this would defeat our entire purpose, which is to sort out what people develop easy access to, and what they find hard to get but still worth getting.

As an example, I point to my work in the Stann Creek District in the 1970s (Graham 1994). Nothing I had done up to that time prepared me for the landscape in which I was to spend a good part of the next three years: virtually no limestone; highly acidic soils; slates, granites, and sandstones used as building material; white clay used as "plaster"; and plant communities I had not seen before. But I know all this now in hindsight; I did not know it then, and I approached the original excavations as I would have excavated in northern Belize. What were the most ubiquitous materials? No artifacts were found in great numbers, not even ceramics, but there were materials that were common to all sites in the district: chert, quartz, obsidian, granite, and slate. If I had gone into the area assuming in advance that chert was local and granite was nonlocal, I would have been in big trouble. Worse, what if no one had studied the area, but Mayanists continued to assume that chert is a local resource everywhere, and then reconstructed trade routes on this basis? They would have been completely off-base with regard to a good portion of the coast and hinterlands of southern Belize, which certainly figured, if not in the rise of civilization in the Petén, at least as locales of major transshipment points in both coastal and inland trade.

Chert is not found locally in this region because there is virtually no limestone (Graham 1994). It and obsidian had to be imported, and indications are that the supplies did not come from northern Belize, but from elsewhere (H. Shafer, personal communication 1976). Granite is accessible locally, although it depends on the location of the community. Those people living near river mouths either would have had to travel upriver to areas where granite boulders spill outward from deposits located in the foothills, or would have had to obtain the granite products from communities closer to the foothills. Recent work being carried out by Marc Abramiuk in Maya Mountains communities on local exchange of ground stone items suggests that it was probably the latter. There is a granite outcrop along the North Stann Creek River; any community based here would have been able to access the raw material more easily than those at the mouth of the river. As for obsidian, it occurred more commonly than chert; the small sample from the district included only 102 chert pieces vs. 282 obsidian pieces, although a small sample of chert from the 1973 season was lost (Graham 1994: 263–271). Because most of the communities in the district had easy access to the sea, it seems likely that obsidian reached them through coastal trade. Even with the lost chert sample, though, obsidian artifacts outnumber chert. Quartz chips (probably used in graters for root crops) and slate were found at all sites. Approximately 226 pieces were collected as possible artifacts, and 84 turned out to show use-wear (Graham 1994: 269). Quartz is found locally in almost all stream beds, but its use is difficult to detect without microscopic analysis. Slate is more restricted in distribution than quartz, although outcrops exist in the foothills and in at least one area, near a place called Alta Vista, along the North Stann Creek River.

At Lamanai, chert, obsidian, and granite artifacts occur (but no quartz chips), and slate is rare and occurs mainly in the form of mirror backs in caches. Lamanai is situated in an area dominated by limestone geology, so we assume that there are chert sources nearby; Chau Hiix (Pyburn 1998) is the nearest known source, and at least some chert at Lamanai comes from Colha (H. Shafer, personal communication to D. Pendergast, 1984). Obsidian distribution has not yet been studied, but obsidian sources lie far from Lamanai in comparison to the Stann Creek District sites. Obsidian nonetheless occurs in large amounts in Classic period caches, and in household deposits from Preclassic through Postclassic times. Granite sources lie distant from Lamanai, but are not as far away as the sources of obsidian in

volcanic regions, whereas granite occurs in the metamorphic highlands of Belize (Wright et al. 1959). Granite manos and metates occur throughout the site's history in household and midden deposits.
The proportion of granite to limestone ground stone artifacts has not
been measured, but granite artifacts are not uncommon.

The Many Faces of "The Region"

The term *region* may seem at first to be far less problematic than
the term local, but it, too, needs sharp definition, depending on the
circumstances (Graham 1987: 761–762). Does it have primarily an
environmental connotation in which zones of resource production are
distinguished from zones of resource distribution? Does it encompass
an area of production and distribution of a particular item of exchange, such as pottery, where a varied range of resources is found
within a delimited area? Or does it distinguish a political territory
defined on the basis of archaeological and epigraphic evidence (Graham 1987: 761)? West (chapter 6 this volume) has recognized the
subtleties of these distinctions and is careful to point out that the
distribution of the four ceramic paste groups in and around Palenque
corresponds with the distribution of Palenque's emblem glyph, and
this suggests congruence of Palenque's political and economic
spheres. Reese-Taylor and Walker (chapter 4 this volume) define
northern Belize as a geographic region, but the environmental features may define an area of cultural integration. Sullivan (chapter 7
this volume) considers northwestern Belize as a region by describing the geographic features that define it, but states explicitly that
political integration is not implied. The eastern river valleys of the
Caribbean watershed (McAnany et al., chapter 5 this volume) can be
seen as a region with regard to soil characteristics and agricultural
potential, at the same time that inferences can also be drawn, based
on architecture, about political status (Graham 1994: 13, 335–344;
McAnany et al. this volume). The Petexbatun region (Foias, chapter
8 this volume) we know from other publications to be primarily a
political entity (Houston 1993). Chunchucmil (Dahlin and Ardren,
chapter 9 this volume) is unusual in that it is defined as the center of
an economic region, whereas San Martín Jilotepeque (Braswell, chapter 10 this volume) and Andrews and Mock's region (chapter 11 this
volume) have the even rarer honor of being defined in relationship
to a specific regional resource: obsidian and salt, respectively.
This attention now given to regional definition and analysis signals

significant progress since the time I originally criticized Maya archaeology for its dull-edged terminological tools (Graham 1987: 761).

Some questionable conflation is still inherent in our usage nonetheless. The highlands and lowlands of Rathje's original model (1972) are basically environmentally conceived, whereas *core*, *periphery*, and *buffer* are terms that carry particular political and economic implications. The ease with which such broad environmental distinctions conflate with and feed into relationships of political economy should still be regarded by us with some suspicion. The highlands became politically peripheral more or less by the power of the pen, and the lowlands environment conveniently produced a division we already recognized on other terms. Seems too good to be true?

In any case, what is important is that the environmental terms we use, such as highlands and lowlands, among others, as well as the dichotomies we set up, such as local vs. nonlocal or exotic, are tools of analysis. As applied, they help us—outsiders in both space and time—as a kind of short-cut to figuring out what products or items might be found in a particular area (in the case of environmental terms), or to imagining how important it was and indeed whether it was even possible for people to obtain particular goods (subsistence vs. prestige), or how much effort might have been involved in getting the goods (local vs. nonlocal, regional, etc.). But we should be careful not to assume too much in advance.

Resource Diversity Is in the Eye of the Beholder

As alluded to above, the lowlands were at one time characterized as homogeneous in terms of resources, but that view subsequently changed (Graham 1987), and lowland environmental diversity now seems generally accepted (Masson, chapter 1 this volume). On the other hand, although resource diversity *can* act as a stimulus to exchange, there is a myriad of other factors that are equally important, so that resource diversity alone should not stand as the raison d'être for exchange. Both what constitutes a *resource* and the creation of a demand or need (concept of diversity) can reflect cultural characteristics, individual perceptions, and indeed local history. Generally, residents will see their home locale for its diversity rather than its sameness because they know it so well.

People living at Lamanai for their entire lives could have had no concept of a *highlands* being more diverse in resources if they had never been to a community we archaeologists characterize as being "in the highlands." And even then, people travel to communities to exchange goods or to make use of services or to visit relatives and friends. Except for some cases in modern tourism, people generally do not travel explicitly or solely for the purpose of visiting another environmental region. At the level of archaeological analysis, perceptions change based on familiarity. Many Mesoamericanists were born outside both the highlands and the lowlands of the Maya area. The less familiar we are with an area, the more we pick out only the obvious differences, and we categorize accordingly—usually simplistically (perhaps the source of the original perception of the lowlands as homogeneous).

Subsistence Goods: Are They Only Local?

Given that a single metate or mano could have lasted for several generations, and could have served an extended family, its frequency in deposits must be measured differently from that of chert or obsidian tools, for example, which broke readily and therefore had a different use and discard rate through time. This information, in addition to what I have discussed above concerning the Stann Creek sites, should caution us against saying that "few nonlocal subsistence goods have been found in the archaeological record of the Classic Maya lowlands" (West, chapter 6 this volume). Assuming that subsistence goods are those that most Maya families considered essential to the running of a household, and given the ubiquitous presence of chert and obsidian in household deposits, if in different proportions in different areas, then certainly chert destined for use as tools, and possibly obsidian destined for tool use, too, could be considered subsistence goods at Lamanai. I would also include granite in this category, because, based on preliminary data, households through time seem to have made efforts to obtain granite manos and metates in addition to their limestone inventory.

In Stann Creek, given the occurrence of chert, quartz, obsidian, and slate at all sites, and during all time periods, all these materials can be considered subsistence resources. Chert and obsidian in this case are *not* local. Quartz is local, but if it was a subsistence good to Stann Creek residents, who may have grown more root crops than elsewhere in the lowlands, it was not considered useful enough anywhere else to import. The same can be said of slate, which was commonly used as a tool for a variety of purposes in the Stann Creek

District, and at Tipu, along the Macal River—we found pieces that were ground down, notched, perforated, or with marks from being tied round with string—many forms of modification. In these cases it was clearly an abundant local resource (slate can be found along the upper reaches of the Macal River) that could serve a variety of purposes, including game boards (in Stann Creek) in the Postclassic, but it was not valued enough to export *except* when it was made into backs for mirrors. Here its contextual recovery in burials and caches at sites such as Lamanai suggests that it could also have served as a component, at least, of what has come to be called a prestige item.

To summarize, there is no purpose served in attempting to generalize broadly about local vs. nonlocal resources across the lowlands. The terms themselves are tools to help us envision the nature of the exchange relationships that might develop in an area. Questions of whether materials are abundant or restricted, found nearby or far away, considered essential or not so essential to families or in ritual, or destined to be made into different objects or used in different ways are all important criteria that should form our framework of analysis. Such terms should not be conflated universally with particular materials or items for several reasons:

1. materials found in some areas are not found in others;
2. materials found in some areas may be restricted and thereby exploited by single communities within a valley or subregion;
3. materials that are "far away" by land routes may be easily obtainable by sea routes;
4. materials are used in different ways and can be a subsistence item in one circumstance and a prestige item in another; this can be envisioned for a wide range of materials—slate, hematite and other minerals, shells (and shellfish), pottery, chert, obsidian, animal bones, stone, etc.

Can Prestige Items Be Local?

Freidel et al. (chapter 3 this volume) argue that Maya political economy incorporated not only goods that had use-value, but also goods that derived their value as much from their ideological or cosmological significance, such as jade or *Spondylus*. This observation is also particularly relevant for composite objects, such as slate-backed hematite mirrors, or to mosaics, which may incorporate materials that in another type of object would be considered mundane.

There are some problems, however, not with *Spondylus* as a new item in elite cosmology, but in Freidel et al.'s claims for its origins. If the Olmecs did not trade in *Spondylus*, may this not be because the bulk of the *Spondylus* shells and their products that appear from Maya Late Preclassic times onwards are *Spondylus americanus* and came from the Caribbean, along the coast of Belize, whereas the Olmecs' nearest access to the sea was the Gulf Coast? The bulk of the evidence from Belize during Preclassic through Postclassic times indicates that *Spondylus* occurred abundantly along the Belize coast. It occurs abundantly today, admittedly with the spines the worse for wear, washed up in mangrove swamps along the Belize coast. But the shells that appear in caches and burials with the spines in relatively good condition suggest that the Maya accessed *Spondylus* along the barrier reef. This organism occurs in specific microenvironmental zones on the reef, the parameters of which are known in marine biology, but not in great detail. *Spondylus* occurs on the reef at depths of 12 to 30 feet (Warmke and Abbott 1962) which means it is easily accessible to divers who know where to look. A recent survey carried out by Heidi Ritscher, Lisa Hilborn, Laura Howard, and I on Middle Caye, Glovers Reef Atoll, produced Maya pottery and numerous *Spondylus* shells—more than I have ever seen at a coastal site. I have not yet been able to excavate the atoll sites, but all indications are that one of the reasons the Maya journeyed to the atoll was to harvest *Spondylus* in a zone in which they occur in large numbers. *Spondylus* shells occur in deposits at all coastal sites I have excavated from Colson Point to Ambergris Caye. They seem to be the result of both gathering worn specimens in the mangrove swamps (these can be used for jewelry but, as noted above, have worn spines and seem not to have been used for caches) and reef harvesting, in which case the spines are longer and better preserved.

To look to West Mexico and Costa Rica, where *S. princeps* occurs, for the bulk of *Spondylus* that occurs at lowland sites seems illogical and unnecessary. However, that the Maya, perhaps in Late Preclassic times, were responsible for the extension of the idea of preciousness to include shell, and *Spondylus* in particular, makes a great deal of sense. The significance of *Spondylus americanus*, given its reef habitat in Belize, probably has deep roots in Maya cosmology that go back in time long before the Late Preclassic period. The Maya were in the lowlands long before the Late Preclassic (Hester et al. 1996), and indications from coastal sites I have excavated are that at least some ancient Maya groups had a long tradition of seafaring and coastal exploitation that extended at least back as far as the Late Preclassic period, and possibly to the Middle Preclassic (Graham 1989).

Spondylus is a good example of an item that crosscuts categories. Beads made from Spondylus formed bracelets and necklaces that could be highly elaborate and associated largely with tombs or very simple and associated with simple burials (Pendergast 1979, 1982, 1990). The common occurrence of Spondylus bead jewelry at Belize sites would remove Spondylus from the list of exotics and add it to the list of local resources for all Maya living on the atolls, on the cayes, along the coast, and in communities near the coast such as Altun Ha or Lamanai. I use this as an example to show that, although I believe Freidel and colleagues are right about the new importance of Spondylus in Maya ruling ideology in the Late Preclassic, Spondylus' cosmological significance has nothing whatsoever to do with it being an exotic or a long-distance trade item in the Maya lowlands, because, at least in the case of Spondylus americanus, it isn't. Its significance is more likely to lie in its origins in the sea, its delicate form and color, and its incorporation because of these features into Maya mythology, a mythology that all Maya shared but portions of which elites appropriated to themselves.

Economic Prosperity and Trade in Northern and Coastal Belize

Reese-Taylor and Walker (chapter 4 this volume) discuss power, economic prosperity, and trade in the Late Preclassic to Early Classic period in northern Belize. K'axob, Nohmul, and Cerros are all mentioned as early centers of power, with Cerros' role in trade a significant one. Whether control was involved or not is a moot point. I think it more likely that exchange and travel were widespread, and provided opportunities on a number of levels for people to acquire access to goods and to benefit from transporting the goods. Lamanai's monumentality suggests strongly that it was a leading center at the time. Structure N10-43 represents a massive Late Preclassic achievement (Pendergast 1981), and the Holiday House acropolis group, P9-25, represented at least triple the investment of labor and materials that went into N10-43 and appears to have spanned at least the period from the Late Preclassic to the early years of the Classic.

Although Reese-Taylor and Walker (chapter 4 this volume) report a state of decline in northern Belize from A.D. 200–400, it is not yet clear if such a decline is in evidence at Lamanai; more work is necessary on Holiday House, for example, to determine why construction ceased there in the Early Classic but not elsewhere on the site. N10-43, for example, continued to see major modifications in the eighth century. Lamanai's two Classic period tombs date to the mid- to late fifth century. One of the tombs, that of a woman laid against the N9-58 platform (Pendergast 1981: 40), contains a black-slipped, slab-footed cylinder tripod, which Reese-Taylor and Walker generally attribute to Teotihuacan influence, and a Tzakol 3 polychrome dish very similar to that found in the contemporaneous N9-56 tomb.

Along the coast at Marco Gonzalez and farther south at Colson Point (Graham 1989; Graham and Pendergast 1989; Graham 1994), there was an intensive period of resource procurement and transshipment of ceramics associated with the Early Classic period. I have dated the peak of activity from A.D. 100 to 300 at Colson Point, but this may turn out to be too conservative, because the latest ceramics to occur in the shell middens associated with this phase are, without doubt, Tzakol 3 polychromes (Graham 1994: 212, Fig. 5.31k–m; Graham 1989: 150, 154). This strongly suggests an end to this particular brand of coastal activity at around A.D. 500 to make way for the focus on the salt trade in the Late Classic. There is evidence in the form of unslipped jars, bowls, and other forms that occupation or at least utilization of coastal sites continued, but the kinds of activities were to change markedly.

How early in time people began focusing on salt-processing remains an estimate, but the only distinctive nonutilitarian pottery that shows up at all in these Late Classic deposits (at both Colson Point and Marco Gonzalez) is in the form of sherds from Tepeu 1 polychrome vases. There is little question, then, that the salt trade was in full swing by the seventh century, and very possible earlier. This conflicts with Andrews and Mock's conclusions (chapter 11 this volume) about the timing of the Belize salt trade, which they date to the Late to Terminal Classic transition. Radiocarbon dates from Colson Point (Graham 1989: 154) add support to the salt trade as predominantly a Late Classic phenomenon, although it may well have tapered off in Terminal Classic times. At Marco Gonzalez, the salt-processing levels are incorporated into house construction, with a series of burials, dug through house floors, that contain a Jaina-style whistle figurine, plumbate and Fine Orange pottery, a late polychrome dish, and local Terminal Classic to Early Postclassic-style vessels.

It does not seem to have taken long for people from Stann Creek to Ambergris Caye to rally economically after Classic upheavals, and to begin to produce salt for mainland communities, probably by constructing evaporation pans, and then further concentrating the salt by subjecting it to heating in standard-made bowls (Coconut Walk Unslipped) that also served as forms for the salt cakes (Graham 1994: 155–156, 247). What is interesting about these bowls is that on Ambergris Caye, the quartz sand temper used in their manufacture had to be imported from the mainland (Graham, Mazzullo, and Teal, in preparation), which suggests a degree of specialization not heretofore anticipated (McKillop, n.d.).

Are Elites Out of Control?

West (chapter 6 this volume) points out that elite control over resources is a problematic issue in archaeology, and that few archaeologists have developed adequate methods for identifying elite control of resource acquisition. In the previous section I have outlined the results of some excavations in which I have been involved in Belize, but it is my coastal experience above all that has made me cautious about the concept of elite control. In order to learn the extent to which an influx of goods and services to elites affected Maya economic organization, it is problematic to think in terms of elite *control*; it is more productive to think in terms of elite demands. *Control* implies a role for elites that cannot be supported on the basis of present evidence. Admittedly the term is often used metaphorically, but this does not make it less problematic.

In trying to understand the accumulation of power by elites, and the ways in which some societies have been able to limit the accumulation of elite power (Clastres 1989), I have been looking not at the elites themselves, but at what could be called social compliance: why the members of any group comply with power accumulation by individuals. I do not believe that the bulk of Maya society passively allowed power to accumulate in the hands of particular elites. I take the view that all of the Maya at all levels—other elites, craftsmen, framers, traders, fisherfolk—made decisions that bore on economic development. Some of these decisions fostered compliance with elite consolidation of power; others forced it into particular molds; still others consistently and pervasively weakened elite power. It is only when we consider power as a series of embedded and ever-changing relationships that involve society in its entirety in the Maya area (as do several chapters in this volume) that we will come to understand its growth or the complexities of power and economy.

How can we continue to broaden our view of power and its relationship to resource "control"? I have started in this chapter by challenging the complacency of some of our assumptions, such as exotic vs. local and subsistence vs. prestige. Not only did elites eat, sleep, and live their lives as part of households, but their production of polychromes, for example, involved more than elite interaction and control. If elites painted polychromes, they also needed body clays, slip clays, paints, brushes, holders, resins, cleaners, paper for designs, mineral pigments, stands, wooden rollers, tempers, kilns, firewood, and sponges, not to mention help in preparing surfaces, preparing ingredients, stoking fires, regulating air flow, getting lunch on time, settling clays, toting water, ordering supplies, keeping track of transactions, training and feeding apprentices, and cleaning up the mess at the end of the production day. In other words, when I try to envision production, it is hard to *see* a prestige economy in action as a phenomenon that is separate from other relationships. Prestige items represent a complex series of relationships, both synchronic and diachronic, and they rely on networks of acquisition in which so-called subsistence demands are embedded.

In another example, even Feldman's evidence (1985) drawn on by Foias (chapter 8 this volume) for certain prestige items being the privilege and property of elites in sixteenth-century highland Guatemala does not necessarily mean that the acquisition of raw materials or the processing or production of these items were actually *controlled* by elites. As noted above, elite luxury items are often composite items; they are not simply precious stones or shell, or even cacao, but instead consist of these materials made into something. This was true in Classic times as well. Therefore, though elite demands for mosaics, for example, may have been a reflection of the importance of jade and shell for them, the route that *Spondylus* or jade may have taken from their sources as raw materials to their final product as a prestige item was long and complicated, involved a number of different specialists along the way, and probably also involved multiple levels of exchange. Even the reality presented in the documents of something like the highland lords controlling cacao by owning cacao plantations does *not* mean that the concept of elite control thereby explains the economic profile.

The matter of control may seem like a small point, but one analogy I pointed to at the Society for American Archaeology meeting was the modern wine trade. A strong argument can be made for wine as a luxury good, and for the idea that its trade is controlled by elites, because the best wines in the world in any quantity go to the wealthy and the powerful. The procurement of cases of wine by wealthy families dominates transactions at the market level. The Rothschilds, some of whom are titled, grow and process wine, and could be seen as a parallel to the lords of highland Guatemala, or the Classic period lords of Tikal, who are said to have controlled cacao via trade or tribute. Either way, the involvement of elites is only part of a complex picture. Although it is possible to conceive that a market in wine might be controlled by elites in areas where grapes don't grow, this depends even in the modern world on the importance placed on wine culturally. In places such as France and Italy, where wine is culturally part of the subsistence diet, its consumption and distribution operate on a number of levels, even in areas where grapes do not grow, because of wine's cultural and culinary (and perhaps religious or symbolic) importance. Where Italians have moved to the Americas, even in areas where wine grapes cannot be grown, they acquire wine by a variety of means; many import grapes in order to make wine at home, as my grandparents did. And wine would be classed here as a subsistence item. In Mesoamerica, and particularly throughout the lowland tropical forest where cacao grows naturally, it is very difficult to imagine elite demands for cacao providing the sole structuring element of the cacao-growing economy. That elite demands for cacao in tribute *stimulated* production at a particular level within the economy is not debatable; but that their demands are the only paint in the picture of the economic (or culinary or ideological or cosmological) place of cacao in the lowlands is, in contrast, highly debatable.

Some scholars suggest that Maya polities were centralized and that ruling elites controlled the economy at all levels, whereas others see the Maya state as small-scale with little elite control. My point is that, either way, elites and nonelites both configured the structure of the economy, including the political economy, and that even in cases of what appear to be elite control, nonelites structure the product.

Control over Pottery Production

The data from Lamanai are being examined for information on how pottery production changed from the Classic to Postclassic period. To date, stylistic analysis of ceramics from middens and burials shows that, like the situation in the Petexbatun region (Foias, chapter 8 this volume), production of polychrome serving wares diminished in the Terminal Classic. However, unlike the Petexbatun, production of serving wares continues well into the thirteenth century, but the specifics of form and color change. Shallow serving bowls or dishes with polychrome painting overlap with and then give way to varieties of what Thompson originally called San José V redware outcurved bowls (Thompson 1939: 141), and what Gifford types as Roaring Creek Red (Gifford 1976: 241). Some are slipped red, whereas others have the characteristic Daylight Orange decoration (Gifford 1976: 301–302). The slips become orange, the pedestal increases in height, and by A.D. 1100, the serving inventory is orange-slipped, with incised decoration, and in forms that differ markedly from Classic times. Utilitarian vessels continue to be made, but their forms, and apparently their paste composition (L. Howie-Langs, personal communication), change as well. The indication is that demands had changed, but not enough evidence has been amassed yet to support claims of centralized production. Mass production is indicated by the widespread use of press-molds, but the transition from the Late Classic to Postclassic was so gradual—and the range of forms neither drastically reduced nor increased—that we cannot yet say what role centralization of production might have had.

A Final Note

To know the exotic, one must know the local; to know how prestige is manifested, we need to know the ideological and social factors that reinforce what we call prestige, but also the local economic compliancy factors: how agricultural production, trade, and exchange at multiple levels function to allow some resources to be directed to activities such as the production and painting of polychrome vases. The symbolism and social value of these vases may have been meaningful only within an elite context, but the vases nonetheless represent complex economic forces that include multiple levels of exchange. Without seeing economic production as a full set of social relationships of production, we cannot understand political economy.

References

Clastres, Pierre
  1989 *Society against the State*, translated by R. Hurley and A. Stein. New York: Zone Books.
Dawkins, Richard
  1976 *The Selfish Gene*. New York: Oxford University Press.

Feldman, Lawrence
1985 *A Tumpline Economy: Production and Distribution Systems in 16th-Century Eastern Guatemala*. Lancaster, Calif.: Labyrinthos.
Flannery, Kent V.
1972 "The Cultural Evolution of Civilizations." *Annual Review of Ecology and Systematics* 3: 399–426.
Fletcher, Roland
1977 "Settlement Studies (Micro and Semi-micro)." Pp. 47–162 in *Spatial Archaeology*, edited by D. L. Clarke. New York: Academic Press.
Gifford, James C.
1976 *Prehistoric Pottery Analysis and the Ceramics of Barton Ramie in the Belize Valley*. Memoirs of the Peabody Museum of Archaeology and Ethnology No. 18. Cambridge, Mass.: Harvard University.
Graham, Elizabeth
1987 "Resource Diversity in Belize and Its Implications for Models of Lowland Trade." *American Antiquity* 52(4): 753–767.
1989 "Brief Synthesis of Coastal Site Data from Colson Point, Placencia, and Marco Gonzalez, Belize." Pp. 135–154 in *Coastal Maya Trade*, edited by Heather McKillop and Paul F. Healy. Peterborough, Ontario: Trent University Occasional Papers in Anthropology, No. 8.
1994 *The Highlands of the Lowlands: Environment and Archaeology in the Stann Creek District, Belize, Central America*. Monographs in World Archaeology No. 19. Madison, Wis.: Prehistory Press.
2000 Discussion and comments for the session, "Ancient Maya Political Economies: Essays in Honor of William Rathje," organized by Marilyn Masson and David Freidel. 65th annual meeting, Society for American Archaeology, April 5–9, Philadelphia.
Graham, Elizabeth, and David M. Pendergast
1989 "Excavations at the Marco Gonzalez Site, Ambergris Cay, Belize, 1986." *Journal of Field Archaeology* 16: 1–16.
Hester, Thomas, H. Iceland, D. Hudler, and H. J. Shafer
1996 "The Colha Preceramic Project." *Mexicon* XVIII (3): 50.
Houston, Stephen D.
1993 *Hieroglyphs and History at Dos Pilas: Dynastic Politics of the Classic Maya*. Austin: University of Texas Press.
McGuire, Randall H.
1989 "The Greater Southwest as a Periphery of Mesoamerica." Pp. 40–66 in *Centre and Periphery: Comparative Studies in Archaeology*, edited by Timothy C. Champion. London: Unwin Hyman.
Pendergast, David M.
1979 *Excavations at Altun Ha, Belize, 1964–1970*, Volume 1. Archaeological Monographs ROM. Toronto: Royal Ontario Museum.
1981 "Lamanai, Belize: Summary of Excavation Results, 1974–1980." *Journal of Field Archaeology* 8(1): 29–53.
1982 *Excavations at Altun Ha, Belize, 1964–1970*, Volume 2. Archaeological Monographs ROM. Toronto: Royal Ontario Museum.

1990 *Excavations at Altun Ha, Belize, 1964–1970*, Volume 3. Archaeological Monographs ROM. Toronto: Royal Ontario Museum.

Pyburn, Anne

1998 "Smallholders in the Maya Lowlands: Homage to a Garden Variety Ethnographer." *Human Ecology* 26(2): 267–286.

Rathje, William

1972 "Praise the Gods and Pass the Metates: A Hypothesis of the Development of Lowland Rainforest Civilizations in Mesoamerica." Pp. 365–392 in *Contemporary Archaeology: A Guide to Theory and Contributions*, edited by Mark P. Leone. Carbondale: Southern Illinois University Press.

1975 "The Last Tango in Mayapan: A Tentative Trajectory of Production-Distribution Systems." Pp. 409–448 in *Ancient Civilization and Trade*, edited by J. A. Sabloff and C. C. Lamberg-Karlovsky. Albuquerque: University of New Mexico Press.

1983 "To the Salt of the Earth: Some Comments on Household Archaeology among the Maya." Pp. 23–34 in *Prehistoric Settlement Patterns: Essays in Honor of Gordon R. Willey*, edited by Evon Vogt and Richard Leventhal. Albuquerque: University of New Mexico Press.

Rathje, William L., David A. Gregory, and Frederick M. Wiseman

1978 "Trade Models and Archaeological Problems: Classic Maya Examples." Pp. 147–175 in *Mesoamerican Communication Routes and Culture Contacts*, edited by T. A. Lee and C. Navarrete. Papers of the New World Archaeological Foundation 40. Provo, Utah: Brigham Young University.

Soukhanov, Anne H., executive editor

1992 *The American Heritage Dictionary of the English Language, Third Edition.* Boston: Houghton Mifflin.

Thompson, J. Eric S.

1939 *Excavations at San José, British Honduras.* Publication No. 506. Washington, D.C.: Carnegie Institution of Washington.

Warmke, Germaine Le Clerc, and R. Tucker Abbott

1962 *Caribbean Seashells: A Guide to the Marine Molluscs of Puerto Rico and Other West Indian Islands, Bermuda, and the Lower Florida Keys.* Wynnewood, Penn.: Livingston Publishing Co.

Wright, A. C. S., D. H. Romney, R. H. Arbuckle, and V. E. Vial

1959 *Land in British Honduras, Report of the British Honduras Land Use Survey Team*, edited by D. H. Romney. London: Her Majesty's Stationery Office.

INDEX

Italicized entries refer to figures or tables.

Abrams, Elliot, 131, 233, 234-35
achiote, in northeastern Belize, 9
Actun Ik, 133
agrarian economic system. *See* bounded
    network; solar central place
agricultural product, 6, 9, 88
aguada, 226
Aguateca, 161, 162, 232, 235-36
Ahau, 271
ahaw, 46, 55, *56*, 58, *59*, 61, 68, 95, 98, 108,
    236
ah holpop, 226
Aizpuruia, Isaza, 42, 43
akbal, 49, 76
albarrada, 257, *258*, 262, 267
Alexander, Rani T., 370
Almarez, Russell, 272
Alta Mira Fluted urn, 113n3, 113n4
Altar de Sacrificios, 176
Altar 10 (Kaminaljuyu), 49, 52, *53*, 54, 55
Alta Verapaz, 312
Alta Vista, 407
altillos, 376, 379
Altun Ha, 238-39, 413
Ambergris Cay, 321-22, 412-13
Andrews, Anthony P., 14, 15, 271, 312,
    412
añil, 381
Arambala bowl, 164
archaeological ethnography, 372
architecture: astronomical significance of,
    114n7; at Caye Coco, 338-39, 340;
    Cerros Eight House of the North type
    structure, *93*; civic, 272; domestic,
    379-80, 381; at Dzibilchaltun, 272; and
    elite power, 203, 213-14, 340-42, 404;
    at Guijarral, 203; intensification of
    during Cycle 7, *93*-96, *94*; at Laguna
    de On, 338-39; at Rio Bravo, 203;
    ritual, 93-94, 271; at Wakna, 93-94
architecture, monumental: at Blue Creek,
    203, 212; at Chan Chich, 212; at Dos
    Hombres, 212; Holiday House, 402,
    411, 412; at Kinal, 212; at La

Honradez, 203, 212; at Lamanai, 411;
    at La Milpa, 203, 212; at Nakbe, 37; at
    Rio Azul, 89, 203, 212; at Three Rivers
    Region, 201-3, 212; use of, 80-81
Ardren, Traci, 10
arrow point, at Ek Balám, 377
ash temper, 168-74, *173*, *175*, 180, 183
Atiteco creation myth, 67-68
Atlas Arquiologico del Estado de Yucatan,
    267
au cuch cab, 226
axe, 45, *53*, 54, 377
Aztecs, 9, 143, 148, 183, 184, 356, 357

Bacalar, 9
Balam Ha, 132
Balanza Black, 106
Ball, Joseph W., 16, 141, 215, 233, 236
ball court, 90-91, 269, 338
bark, 13, 18
basal flange bowl, 107, 108, 214
batab, 226, 227
batabob, 227
Batllori, Eduardo, 307
Beach, Timothy, 266
Beaudry, Marilyn, 163-65
be/bi, 63
Becan, 94, 110
beeswax, 9
Bejucal, 110
Belize: ceramic at, 97, 98; economic
    prosperity/trade in coastal, 411-13;
    Kendal Axe in, *53*, 54; lack of ash
    temper in northern, 172; maritime
    trade in, 336-37; northwestern, 406
    (*See also* Three Rivers Region);
    obsidian distribution in, 149;
    resources of northeastern, 9-10; shell
    production/use in, 42. *See also*
    Coastal Belize, salinas of
Belize, northern, 178, 411-13. *See also*
    Caye Coco; Laguna de On
Belmopan Department of Archaeology,
    131

Bennyhof, James, 313, 314, 318
Berdan, Frances F., 8-9
Bezanilla, Clara, 311
Big Man, in Melanesia, 33
Big Man dispersal system, 31, 32, 33-37
Binford, Lewis R., 33
Bishop, Ronald L., et al., 145, 152-56,
    161, 162, 163, 176
Black-on-orange, 148, 184
Blake, Michael, 32
Blanton, Richard E., 5, 10, 161, 167-68
Blanton, Richard E., et al., 19, 21, 126
Bloch, Marc, 383
Blue Creek, 107, 110, 200, 201, 202, 203,
    212
Boas, Franz, 31, 38
Boat-billed Heron Pond, 132
Bohannon, Paul, 274
Bonampak, 127
Bonampak Stela 2, 76
Bond, Tara, 266
bone, 100, 101, 351, 353, 356, 377
Booth's River, 197, 200
border market exchange, 250
Boucher, Sylviane, 17
bounded network, 144-45, 147, 168, 184,
    291-92, 301
Brady, James, 102, 104
Brady, James E., et al., 98
Brandenburger, A. M., 270
Braswell, Geoffrey E., 15, 401
Braudel, Fernand, 368
Brenner, Mark, et al., 128
Brookfield, H. C., 33
Brumfiel, Elizabeth M., 7, 8
Brunton, R., 32
Buenavista, 166, 230, 231, 236
buffer, 407
buffer zone, 14
bul, 237-38
Bullard, William R., Jr., 371
burial: at Caye Coco, 340-41; at Colha,
    105; cyst, 213; at Laguna de On, 340,
    341; Middle Formative, 296; at North
    Acropolis, Tikal, 113n4; obsidian in
    elite, 151; at Santa Rita, 111, 341;
    Spondylus in, 77, 107. See also tomb

Cabbage Ridge, 318
cacao, 7, 9, 13, 18, 20; cultivation of, 20,
    124, 128-29, 131, 226; as currency, 20,
    42, 44, 225, 227; as exchange item, 88,
    123, 228, 232, 233, 357, 402; ideologi-
    cal significance of, 44; long-distance
    trade in, 226; in northeastern Belize,
    9; as prestige good, 229, 239, 402; as
    tribute, 7, 125, 127-28
Cakchiquel lords, 229
calabash, 404

Calakmul, 77, 214
callejones, 257, 259
callejuela, 257, 258-59, 261, 267
caluac, 226, 227
Canbalám, 271, 310, 325
Cannon, Aubrey, 373, 374
canoe, 9, 18
Caracol, 4, 76-79, 78, 96, 214, 235, 273
Caramba Red-on-orange, 97, 113n4
Carrasco, Ramon, 214
Catzin, José Serrano, 309
Caye Coco, 336, 403; architecture at,
    338-39, 440; artifact distribution by
    context at, 348-50; burial pattern at,
    340-41; ceramic trend at, 342, 345,
    347, 350-51; craft item/ornament at,
    350-52; craft production at, 354-56,
    355; Early/Late Facet deposits at, 351,
    352-53; economic trend at, 341-43,
    343-44; mercantile trend at, 337; sherd
    count by type/paste at, 346-47;
    similarity/difference with Laguna de
    On, 356-58; site of, 338, 339
Cayo Unslipped vessel, 213
cédula, 376
Celestial monster, 51
Celestún Salinas, 254, 309, 310-11
Cenote San Jose Chulchaca, 262
censer, 110, 115n11, 358
censer stand, 110-11
Central Mexico, 148, 161, 165
Central Peten, 233, 236. See also Peten
ceramic exchange, Classic, 152-62;
    exchange/consumption of Maya
    polychromes, 162-65; palace-school
    polychromes, 165-67; production/
    distribution of, 184; volcanic ash
    tempering, 168-74, 183
ceramic exchange, Postclassic, 174-75,
    183; fine paste ceramic, 176-78, 177;
    standardization of ceramic, 179
ceramic exchange system: at Palenque,
    152-56, 153, 154, 183; at Petexbatun
    region, 161-62, 184
ceramic/pottery: control of production
    of, 413-14; distribution of, 17-18,
    97-98, 142, 148-49, 160; effect of
    political landscape on, 16-18, 185;
    mass production of, 176, 180, 181,
    182; standardization of, 16, 17-18, 18,
    164-65, 175, 176, 178, 180, 181; trend
    at Caye Coco, 340, 343, 345, 348-49;
    trend at Laguna de On, 351, 354, 356
ceramic/pottery, polychrome, 12, 162-65,
    164, 166-67, 177, 184, 213, 232, 233,
    234, 235, 239, 412
ceramic/pottery workshop, 166, 230-31,
    236
Ceren, 5, 8

Cerritos Itzapa, 295
Cerros, 411; ceramic at, 97; decline/
    downfall of, 12, 100, 108-9, 110-11,
    215; diadem jewel at, 96, 97; eco-
    nomic change at, 100-101; Eight
    House of the North type structure at,
    93; expansion at, 90; iconographic
    program at, 95; and long-distance
    trade, 94; Peteltun Modeled censer
    stand at, 110; site location, 42, 90;
    Structure 6B at, 63-64; trade with
    Peten zone, 16; triadic arrangement
    at, 94; warfare at, 108-9
Cerros, Cache 1, Structure 6B, 68-70,
    68-72, 69, 71
Cerros Structure 52-2nd façade: ajaw
    glyph on, 95; diadem band on, 58,
    60-61; ear flare assemblage on, 51, 52,
    54, 61, 62-63, 64; eastern mask on, 49;
    flame brow on, 55, 57; iconographic
    program on, 48, 49, 51, 54-55, 64-66,
    75, 95; intentional preservation of, 48;
    jaguarian mask on, 48, 61, 64-65, 66;
    Principal Bird Deity on, 47, 48-49, 51;
    restoration drawings of, 47; symbolic
    use of jade/Spondylus on, 48, 54-55,
    58, 61, 63, 66; symbolic use of
    stairway on, 65, 76; trilobate motif
    on, 51, 52, 54, 64; upper east mask on,
    57, 58, 60, 61; upper west mask on,
    76; use of, 64-66; U-element on, 54,
    55, 57, 58, 61; Water Fowl on, 48, 49;
    western mask on, 49, 51
Chaakkax, 42
Chac Balam, 320
Chakah, 261
Chakah Group, 269
Chak ear flare, 53, 54, 57
Chak-Tok-Ich'aak I, 75, 107, 109, 110
Chalcatzingo, 252
Champion, Timothy C., 20, 127
Chan, Pina, 143
Chan Chich, 107, 197, 201, 202, 204, 212
Chang, K. C., 371, 372, 382, 384n1
Chanona Cave, 131
Charlie Chaplin greenstone figurine, 72
Chase, Arlen, 4, 10, 76, 183, 214-15
Chase, Diane, 76, 183, 214-15, 340
Chauaca, 10
Chau Hiix, 405
Chavín de Huántar, 38
chel, 114n6
Chenes region, 268
Chen Mul Modeled, 377
chert, 12-13, 90, 260, 274, 340, 341, 404-5,
    408
Chetumal Province, 338
Chicanel sphere ceramic, 16, 201

Chichen Itza, 17-18, 176, 178, 180, 181,
    183, 309-10, 325
Chikinchel region, 180, 181, 225, 310
Chimaltenango, 295, 302
China, 161, 183
CHOK, 75
Chontal Maya, 250
Chunchucmil, 10; agricultural productiv-
    ity/population at, 261-65; cityscape
    of, 253; construction at, 268-69, 271;
    economic model of, 267-75; economic
    region of, 254-57, 255; imported
    goods at, 260; mode of exchange at,
    250; physical connection with
    Canbalam, 271; political economy
    model of, 270-75; possible market-
    place at, 260-61; as region, 408;
    settlement distribution at, 255-56;
    specialized production at, 265-67;
    urban design of, 257-59, 258
Chunchucmil Archaeological Project, 310
Churchyard, 132
Cizan Chauaca-complex, 377
Clark, John E., 32, 37
Coastal Belize, salinas of, 313-19, 314
coatimundi effigy vessel, 204, 209, 210
Coba, 273
cochineal, 262
Coconut Walk Unslipped (CWU), 314,
    315-17, 318, 319-20, 321, 322
Codex-style ceramic, 167
codice, Postclassic Maya, 12
codification of world system, 125
Coe, Michael D., 115n11
Coggins, Clemency, 166
Colha, 13, 16, 90, 98, 105, 405
Colha Archaeological Project, 315
Colonial Yucatan, exchange in, 143
colono-plainware, 377
Colson Point region, 314, 412
Columbia Plain, 377
commodity-peonage. See putting-out
    industry
commodity trade items, 88
Conil, 10
conspicuous consumption, 33, 37-38
Contemporary Archaeology: A Guide to
    Theory and Contributions, 285
co-opetition, 270
Copador polychrome, 163-65
copal, 9, 168, 225, 303
Copan, 21, 55, 110
Copan Valley, 149, 184
copper bell, 20, 41, 377
core-periphery model, 3, 19, 44, 125, 127,
    285-86, 335, 367; and corporate group,
    374-75; and economy of San Martín
    Jilotepeque, 303; and rise/decline of
    Peten, 14-15, 21, 336-37; as theory of

historical change, 400-401; and world systems theory, 367, 368, 370, 383-84
Corozalito Northeast, 315
corporate group, definition of, 373-74
corporate group, residential, 382-83; and bounded network system, 291-92; indicator of presence of, 374-75. *See also* Ek-Balám
corporate political economy, 5
corridor site, 271
cosmological imagery, 64-66, 95
cosmology, Mayan, 133
Costa Rica, 410
Costin, Cathy L., 232
cotton, 13, 125; as trade item, 8, 9, 18, 232, 357; as tribute, 125
cotton mantle, 232, 233, 237, 238
Coxah Ethnoarchaeological Project, 372-73
Coyoacan, 9
Cozumel: coastal trade network at, 175; effigy censer at, 358; homogeneity at, 345; Olmec jade at, 43, 45; oracle at, viii-ix
Cozumel Island, Postclassic, viii; local power at, 340; pottery standardization at, 175
craft specialization, 147-49; at Aguateca, 235-36; at Chunchucmil, 265-67; in contact-period Yucatan, 225; in early modern England, 183; in highland Guatemala, 229; at K'axob, 90; levels of, 230-32; in Petexbatun region, 231-32; rise of during Cycle 7, 92
crystal, 351
Cuba, 309
cuchcabal, 375
Culbert, T. Patrick, 113n4, 162
cul de sac, 257
Cupul, 227
currency: axe as, 45; bead as, 20, 41, 227; cacao as, 20, 42, 44, 225, 227; copper bell as, 20, 41; feathers as, 42; as fungible, 42; greenstone as, 44, 225; ideological significance of, 43, 44; jade as, 16, 79; mammiform as, 103-5; metal bell as, 45; obsidian as, 16; red shell as, 41, 44; shell as, 7, 16, 41, 43-44, 225; sixteenth century, 227; *Spondylus* as, 20, 42, 43, 45, 79; textile as, 20
CWU. *See* Coconut Walk Unslipped
Cycle 7, Late Preclassic, beginning of, 88-92; homogeneity between sites of, 90-92, *91*; intensive agriculture during, 89-90; location of sites during, 90; long-distance trade networks of, 89-90; rise of craft specialization during, 92; rise of kingship during, 92

Cycle 7, Late Preclassic, intensification in: architecture during, 93-96, *94*; ceramic distribution during, 97-98; iconographic programs of, 94-95; increased social interaction during, 98; kingship during, 92, 95-96; long-distance trade during, 96-97; summary of, 98-99
Cycle 8, 96, 98, 99
cylinder tripod, 110, 209
cyst burial, 213

Dahlin, Bruce, 4, 10, 310
Dahlin, Bruce H., and Traci Ardren, 403
Dahlin, Bruce H., and William J. Litzinger, 273
Dahlin, Bruce H., et al., 256
Dalton, George, 270
D'Altroy, Thomas, 226, 228
Daylight Orange, 416
Deetz, James, 369
Demarest, Arthur A., 162, 259
deme, 380
dependicia, 368
diadem jewel: Cycle 7, 70-72, *71, 96, 97;* Late Preclassic, 61; Middle Preclassic, 45
Dillon, Brian, 312
directional exchange, *146*
distribution system: bounded network, *144-45*, 147, 168, 184, 291-92, 301; extended network, 290-91
Dore, 179
Dos Arroyos Orange Polychrome, *106, 107, 204, 206, 207*
Dos Barbaras, 202, 213
Dos Hombres, 110, 200, 201, 202; burials at, 213; coatimundi effigy vessel from, 204, 209, *210;* Early Classic construction at, 203; Early Classic tomb at, 204, *205;* monumental architecture at, 212
Dos Pilas, 161, 162, 214
Dos Pilas Hieroglyphic Stairway 1, 237
down-the-line exchange, *146*, 147
Dresden Codex, 104, 209
Dumbarton Oaks pectoral, 102
Dumbarton Oaks Plaque, 52-54, *53*
Dunning, Nicholas P., 271
Duranzo, 295
Durst, Jeff, 204
dwelling: pole-and-thatch, 377-78, 379-80; single-line structure, 379-80, 381
dye, 9, 18, 232, 262
Dzehkabtun, 268
Dzibilchaltun, 176, 271, 272
Dzilam Gonzalez, 271

ear flare: on Cerros Structure 52-2nd façade, 51-54, *52, 53,* 54, 61, *62-63, 64;* on El Zapote Stelae, 54; jade, 58, *60;* as portal, 63; shell, 54, *55;* on Structure 34 at El Mirador, 54
Earle, Timothy K., 226, 227
Early Classic, southern Maya lowland: political change during, 105-6; pottery production during, *106-8;* tomb building during, 106-7
Early Classic peccary head tetrapod, 114n6
economic model: bounded network system of distribution, *144-45,* 147, 168, 184, 291-92, 301; extended network system of distribution, 290-91; household industry, 288-89; household production, 288; workshop industry, 289-90, 301
economy: etymology of, 367; northern Belize (*See* Caye Coco; Laguna de On); Postclassic, 176, 357
economy, Classic period, 182-83; elite control of, 235, 238-39; level of specialization in, 229-30; market economy of, 272-73; scale of exchange of, 232-33; tax system of, 237-38; tribute payment, 237; types of exchange in, 233-34
economy, Mayan: as autonomous/ centralized, 2-3; scale/analysis of, 18-20; and social transformation, 20-21
effigy censor: at Cerros, 76; at Kaminaljuyu, 61; at Mayapan, 182; monumental, 61
effigy vessel, 209, *210*
Egypt, 79, 80
Eight House of the North, *93*
Eisenstadt, Shmuel N., 21
Ek Balám, 20; axe at, 377; description of, 375-76; domestic site structure at, 377-78; history of, 375-76; *principales* dwelling at, 379-80, 381; putting-out system at, 380-81; research method study of, 376-77; residential corporate group at, 378-82; single-line structure at, 379-80, 381
Ekholm, 68
Ek Luum, 320
Ek Wayeb, 65
El Arroyo, 202
El Cuyo, 310
elevated causeway, 37
El Intruso, 202, 203
elite control, problems in determining, 413-15
El Mirador, 16; ceramic at, 97; decline/ abandonment of, 12, 99-100; ear flare

on Structure 34 at, 54; and long-distance trade, 94; map of, *88;* relationship with Cerros, 90
El Mirador alliance, 111
El Perén, 299, 303
El Pilar, 13
El Salvador, 163, 311-12
El Tejar, 295
El Tigre, 100
El Zapote Stelae, 54
Emal, 180, *181,* 271, 310, 325
embedded social production, 33-34, 35-38
embroidered cloth, 9
encomendero, 379, 380
encomienda system, 124, 131
England, specialized production in, 183
Escuintla, 303
ethnoarchaeology, 372-73, 375
Ewald, Ursula, 309
exchange mechanism, in regional system: consumption patterns, 150-51; distribution, 145-47, *146;* production organization, 147-49; resource acquisition, 149-*50*
exotic item, difficulty in discerning, 404-5
extended network system, 290-91

falloff curve: for Late Classic ceramic near Tikal, *156-57;* Renfrow's predicted, *146,* 156-57
Farriss, Nancy M., 176, 272, 381
faunal bone, 354, 356
feather: as currency, 42; long-distance trade in, 226; as prestige good, 229; as trade item, 232; as tribute item, 125, 237, 238
Feinman, Gary M., 5, 10, 17, 21, 160
Feldman, Lawrence, 228, 233, 414
Fialko, Vilma, 108, 114n8
Fields, Virginia, 45, 61
Fine Gray (Grey), 177, 310, 345
Fine Orange paste, 182
Fine Orange ware, 177, 310, 345
finger ring, 377
Finsten, Laura M., 10, 20
First Father, 93, 95
fish, 9, 232
fishing, 317
flame brow, 55, *57-58, 59*
Flannery, Kent V., 399
Fletcher, Roland, 35
flint debitage, to seal tomb, 113n5-113n6
Floral Park, 201
Flor Cream bowl, 113n1
Foias, Antonia, 12, 161, 162, 414
Foliated Cross, 51, 65, 66-67, 75
Foliated Jaguar, 107, 114n10

Ford, Anabel, 13, 170, 171, 172
forest product, 9, 13, 18, 232, 404
Fox, John W., 141
Frank, Andre Gunder, 368
freelance exchange. See middlemen
    exchange
Freetown Sibun, 130, 133
Freidel, David A., 3, 4, 14, 62, 63, 65, 70,
    75, 92, 168, 183, 358, 409
Freidel, David A. et al., 15, 401
Frenchman's Green Vine Snake, 320
Fresh Kills Landfill, vii
Fry, Robert E., 16, 156-60, 161
funerary vessel, 12
fungible currency, 42

G-103, Rio Azul, 89
game, 9, 404
Gann, Thomas, 313
The Garbage Project, vii
Gargett, R., 32
gateway, characteristic of, 251-53
Geertz, Clifford, 48
Gibson, Eric C., 13
Gifford, James C., 416
gift exchange: in Colonial Yucatan, 143;
    in highland Guatemala, 228; in
    Postclassic Yucatan, 233-34
gift-exchange item: bead as, 233
Glicken, 170, 171, 172
glyph, statement of function in, 98
God D. See Itzamna
God N, 72
Graham, Elizabeth, 131, 214, 314-15,
    319-20, 402
Gran Cacao, 201, 202
granite, 404, 405
Greater Motul de San Jose area, 233
Greater Tikal-Uaxactun area, 233
Great Plaza, Tikal, 89
Greece, ancient, 151
greenstone: Charlie Chaplin greenstone,
    72; as currency, 44, 225; in diadem
    jewel, 61; as gift-exchange item, 233;
    ideological significance of, 44, 45;
    introduction in Maya lowlands, 45;
    long-distance trade in, 226; in Middle
    Preclassic sculpture, 57; in nonelite
    context, 5; use in burial, 61; use of by
    Olmec, 45
greenstone adze, 351, 357
greenstone bead, 351, 377
ground stone, 13, 350, 356, 405
Grove, David C., et al., 252
Grube, Nikolai, 67, 107, 108, 183, 214
Guaje, 261
Gualpopa bowl, 164
Guatemala, 156, 163. See also Petexbatun
    region; San Martín Jilotepeque

Guatemala, highland: economy/elite
    control in, 228-29, 414; merchant type
    in, 228; specialization in, 229
Guerrero, 320
Guijarral, 201, 202, 203

Hageman, Jon, 202, 209
hal, 77
halach uinic, 226, 227
hallucinogenic drug, 229, 232
Hammond, Norman, 68, 70, 72, 107,
    160-61
Hansen, Richard, 37, 43-44, 88-89, 90,
    100, 113n
Hanson, Craig, 19, 400-401
Harvard Arizona Cozumel Project, 43, 46
Hassig, Ross, 6
Hauberg Stela, 76
Hawaiian chiefdom, 227
Hayden, Brian, 32, 373, 374, 382
Hector Creek Lagoon, 319
Heider, Karl G., 269
Helms, Mary, 44
henequen, 262
hereditary aggrandizing elite, 36, 37, 38
hereditary social stratification, 32-33, 36,
    37, 38
Hershey site, 131-32
Hester, Thomas R., 13
Hidden Lagoon, 319
hide/skin, animal, 13
hierarchy of assemblage reliability,
    372-73
Hilborn, Lisa, 410
Hirth, Kenneth, 5, 141, 357
historical archaeology, 367, 369
Hodder, Ian, 146-47
Hodge, Mary G., et al., 184
Holiday House, 402, 411, 412
Holmul I burial, 106-7
Honduras, 163
honey, 9, 18, 168, 232, 357
Houk, Brett A., 212
household archaeology, 371, 372, 373
household industry, 288-89
household production, 288
Houston, Stephen, 42, 66, 74, 127
Howard, Laura, 410
Huaca Florida, 38
Huexotla, 183
Hunal, 43, 45, 46, 61, 66
Hunal trifurcate symbol, 70-72, 71
Hun Nal Ye, 66
huntan, 75
hypertrophic pottery, 233

Icacos Lagoon, 320
iconographic program: at Cerros
    Structure 52-2nd façade, 48, 49, 50-51,

54-55, 64-66, 75, 95; at G-103, Rio
   Azul, 89; at Kohunlich, 95; at
   Lamanai, 95; at North Acropolis,
   Tikal, 94-95; at Waxaktun, 95, 96
Ic period, craft production in, 183
ideo-technic artifact, 33
ikats, 128, 237, 238
i-ka-tsi, 125
Ik-period ceramic, 184
Imac-period ceramic, 184
imperial-style ceramic, 148, 182
Inca (Inka) Empire, 148, 227
incense burner, 12, 340
Inka Empire, 148
iron hardware, 377
Isla Cerritos, 325
Isla Cerritos Archaeological Project, 309
Itzamna, 209
Itzam Ye, 48, 64
Itza slate, 180
Ixcanrio Orange Polychrome, 102, 103,
   104-5, 107
Ix Chel, viii, 104
Ix Chel Oracle, viii-ix
Ixtepeque, 350
Izapa stelae, 55, 89

jade: in Blue Creek cache, 110; in burial,
   107; at Caye Coco, 351; at Copan, 55;
   and core-periphery dynamics, 14-15;
   correlation with breath, 66; at
   Cozumel, 43, 45; as currency, 16, 79;
   in diadem jewel, 61; in iconographic
   program, 46-48, 47, 55; ideological
   significance of, 44, 45-46, 402, 409;
   introduction of in Maya Lowlands,
   45; as luxury trade item, 88; as
   prestige good, 235, 239, 273; at Punta
   Canbalam, 260; reduction of trade in
   at Cerros, 100; ritual context of, 68-69,
   70, 72, 75, 76-77, 78, 79; symbolic use
   of, 54-55, 58, 61, 63, 66, 402, 409; as
   tribute item, 238; use of by Olmec, 45
jade ear flare, 58, 60
jade head, Olmec, 43, 46
jadeite, 125
jaguar, 65, 209
jaguarian mask, 48, 61, 64-65, 66
jaguar skin, 232
Jimbal, 184
Jones, Grant D., 176
Jones, John, 266
Jones, Tom, 114n9, 128, 131
Justeson, John S., 68, 72, 74

ka-bul, 237
kakaw, 125
Kaminaljuyu, 55, 61, 293, 294, 299, 303
k'an, 58, 63, 77

Kan B'alam II, 75
K'an Cross, 58, 60, 66, 67
Kappelman, Julia Guernsey, 51
Kaqchikel speaker, 296
K'atabche'kax, 42
k'atun, 107
K'awil, 63
K'axob, 42, 43, 89-90, 411
Kelly, Thomas, 315
Kendal Axe, 53, 54
Kepecs, Susan, 17, 180, 310
Kichpanha, 103, 105, 106
Kichpanha Bone, 100, 101
Kidder, Alfred V., 68
k'in, 48, 66
Kinal, 202, 212
K'inich Janab Pakal II, 63
knife blade, 377
Kohunlich, 95
Kowalewski, Stephen A., 5, 10, 21
Kraak porcelain, 377
Kuhn, Thomas, 365
k'uh-ul, 58
kula object, 274
Kurjack, Edward B., 371
Kwakiutl, 31, 32, 34-35

Laguna de On, 336, 403; architecture at,
   338-39; burial patterns at, 340, 341;
   ceramic trends at, 351, 354, 356;
   comparison of artifacts with Caye
   Coco, 354-56, 355; mercantile trends
   at, 337; similarities/differences with
   Caye Coco, 356-58; site of, 338, 339
Laguna Verde Incised, 103
La Honradez, 201, 202, 203, 212
Lamanai, 16, 131; Classic Period tomb at,
   412; growth of during Cycle 7, 89;
   iconographic program at, 95; local
   trade in, 402, 405-6; and long-distance
   trade at, 94, 108; monumentality at,
   411; possible decline at, 411-12;
   pottery production at, 415-16;
   prestige good at, 409; resource
   diversity in, 407-8; Spondylus at, 411;
   triadic arrangement at, 94
La Merced, 299
La Milpa, 200, 201, 202, 203, 209, 212
Landa, Friar Diego de, 143, 182, 239, 273
Laporte, Juan Pedro, 108, 114n8
Las Abejas, 201, 202, 213
Las Coloradas, 309, 310
Late Postclassic, ceramic and political
   landscape of, 18
Late Preclassic: appearance of Spondylus
   in, 44-45; architectural commonalties
   among, 90-91; ceramic and political
   landscape of, 16
La Venta, 287

Leach, J., and Edmund R. Leach, 274
LeCount, Lisa J., 172-74, 215
Leone, Mark, 285, 369
lithic artifact, 12-13
lithic flake/tool, 342, 350, 351, 354, 356, 377
local exchange: "region" in, 406-7; as universal, 403-6
local subsistence item, difficulty in discerning, 404-5
Loche, *181*
Loten, Stanley, 68
Love, Michael, 312
Lubaantun, 160-61, 182, 184
lumber, 225
luxury good: cotton as, 125; cotton mantle as, 232, 233, 237, 238; jade/jadeite as, 88, 125; *Spondylus* as, 88. *See also* cacao; feather

ma'at, 80
Ma'ax Na, 202, 212
macaw imagery, 204
MacKinnon, Jefferson, 320, 321
MacLeod, Barbara, 65, 66
Maine, Henry, 373
maize: at Chunchucmil, 261-62, 265, 266; market exchange of in highland Guatemala, 228; metaphor of, 80
Maize god, 51, 64-67, 72, 74, 75, 77
Mama Red, 377
mammiform tetrapod, 102-5, *103*, 107, 113n1, 114n6, 201
Mani, land division at, 233
mano, 13, 14, 408
Marco Gonzalez, 320, 412
Marcus, Joyce, 323
marine shell. *See* shell, marine
maritime trade, 18, 254, 256, 336-37
market fair model, 358
market function, 3-4
market system, 250; common characteristic of, 10; elite lack of control of, 6; open, 358; originations of, 168
Marlowe Cay, 325
Martin, Simon, 67, 107, 108, 183, 214
Marx, Karl, 367
Matacapan, 179
Matillas Fine Orange, 180
mat motif, 98
Maya, lowland: ceramic pottery/distribution in political economy of, 185; core of political power at, 127; embedded social production in, 37-38; introduction of jade/greenstone in, 45; introduction of *Spondylus* in, 45; map of selected sites/features, *124*; regal/ritual model of, 249-50

Maya civilization, origin of: jade, *Spondylus*, as ideology in, 45-46. *See also* Cerros Structure 52-2nd façade
Mayapan, 18, 175, 178, 182, 225, 358
mayordomo, 227
Mazanahau, 225
McAnany, Patricia, 3, 7, 16-17, 42, 43, 44, 142, 183, 233, 239
McAnany, Patricia et al., 19, 401-2
McGuire, Randall H., 10, 20, 403
McKillop, Heather, 319, 320
medicine, as trade item, 232
Meighan, Clement, 313, 314, 318
Meskill, Frances, 102, 104, 105
Mesopotamia, 79, 80
metal artifact, 229
metal bell, 45
metate, 13, 14, 88, 125, 265-67, 274, 408
Mexico, 38, 148, 161, 165, 312, 410
Miahuatlan, 9
mica, 350, 357
Middle Cay, 410
Middle Formative burial, 296
Middle Formative Ceremonial Complex, 45
middlemen exchange, *146*, 147, 149, 151; and ash-tempered ceramic, 174; in contact period Yucatan, 143; during Postclassic period, 176
Midwinter's Lagoon, 318
Milky Way, and rebirth of Maize God, 65-66, 75
Mill, John Stuart, 367
Miller, Mary, 127
Millet, C. Luis, 256
Minc, Leah D., 184
Mirador Basin, 37-38
Mock, Shirley B., 14, 15, 315-16, 317-19, 321, 322, 324-25, 412
Moho Cay, 319
Moho Cay-Toledo, 320
Moholy-Nagy, Hattula, 43
Monaghan, John, 312
monochrome pottery, 232, 233
Monstrous Visual Symbol (MVS), 15, 402; in Big Man dispersal system, 35-36; in Mayan Lowlands, 37-38; in Mexico, 38; at Mirador Basin, 37; in Peru, 38
Monte Alban, 142, 183
Montejo, Francisco (the Younger), 375
Mopan-Macal, 215
Mopan Maya, 132
Mora-Marín, David F., 14, 75
Morelos, 5
Morely model, 366
mosaics, 409, 414
Motul de San Jose, 236
Mundo Perdido, *103*, 104, 107-8, 109, 113n1

mural, 127
Mut Itzamna, 48
MVS. *See* Monstrous Visual Symbol

*na: s, 49
nab, 49
nacom, 226
Nahm, Werner, 64, 65
Naj Tunich Cave, 102, 104
Nakbe, 37, 44, 89, *91*, 167
Nalebuff, B. J., 270
Nance, Roger, 311
narcotic, 229, 232
Na Te' K'an, 65, 67
Navula Unslipped, 377
NBCP. *See* Northern Belize Coastal
    Project
net weight, 342, 350, 354, 356
new archaeology, 366
nivelación, 376, 377, 378
Nohmul, 107, 273, 411
Nohmul Structure 110 cache, 68, 72
nopal, 262
Norman, Garth V., 68, 72, 74
North Acropolis, Tikal, 89, 94-95, 100,
    113n4
North Coast Native American, 236
Northern Belize Coastal Project (NBCP),
    317-19
Northern River Lagoon (NRL), 315, 316,
    317, 318
North River Lagoon, clay cylinder from,
    315
nouveau elite mechanism of social
    change, 401, 402; embedding social
    production in, 33-34, 35-37; theoreti-
    cal structure of, 32
nouveau elite potlatch, 32, 34, 38
NRL. *See* Northern River Lagoon

Oaxaca Valley, 142, 148-49, 160, 183
obsidian: and core-periphery theory, 14;
    as cross-over item, 274; as currency,
    16; distance trade in, 18, 149;
    distribution of, 6, 10, 133, 149, 260,
    286-87, 354, 356; in elite burial, 151;
    local/long-distance context of, 404,
    405-6; in nonelite context, 5, 19; as
    prestige good, 273; as subsistence
    resource, 408; value of, over time, 6,
    10. *See also* San Martín Jilotepeque
obsidian blade, 88, 341, 342, 347, 351
obsidian core, 58, *60*, 149, 171-72
Ocós, 311
Ol, 49, 63, 72, 74, 209
olla, 12, 340
Olmec, 38, 45, 301, 410
Olmec style jade head, 43, *46*
Olson, Kirsten, 13

Oneness, 45
open market system, 358
oracle, viii-ix
orange-based Aguila series pottery, 106
O'sh'al K'abowil Siwan, 299-300
overlapping spheres of exchange, 8-9
Oxkintok, 267

Pailes, Richard A., 8
painted plaster, 350, 357
pajarique, 378-79
Pakal Na, 132
palace-school polychrome, 165-67
Palenque, 110; ash tempering at, 169;
    distribution of paste groups in, 406;
    Foliated Cross at, 65; K'inich Janab
    Pakal II at, 63; market-exchange at,
    145; Panel of the Foliated Cross at,
    51; peripheral market at, 273; regional
    ceramic exchange system at, 152-56,
    153, 154, 183; ritual paraphernalia
    production at, 182
Palenque area, utilitarian pottery use in,
    236
Palmar Orange-polychrome, 213
palm ash, 14, 323
Panel of the Foliated Cross, 51
paradigm/paradigm shift, 365-67
Paraíso, 38
Parker, Joy, 63
Parramos, 295
Parsons, Lee Allen, 61, 371
patan, 237
patio quadrangle, 268
Pawatuns, 72
Payil Red, 345
Peacock, David P. S., 230
peccary head tetrapod, 114n6
Pechtun Ha, 132
Pedro's Mound, 132
Pelican One Pot, 320
Peregrine, Peter N., 5
Pérez, Tomas, 37
periphery, 407
perishable trade item, 13, 168, 232
Peru, 38
Peten: ceramic at, 97; as core of Mayan
    political power, 127; effigy censer at,
    358; luxury item distribution at, 6;
    resources of, 9; shell currency at,
    43-44. *See also* Central Peten
Petexbatun region, 406; ash-tempering
    at, 172; location of, 223, *224*; pottery
    production at, 415; regional ceramic
    exchange system at, 161-62, 184;
    secondary elite at, 21. *See also*
    Petexbatun region, economy/elite
    control in

Petexbatun region, economy/elite control in: elite artisan in, 235-36; gifting in, 234; pottery specialization in, 231-32; production/distribution of polychrome by, 236; scale of exchange in, 233; subsistence item exchange in, 234-35. *See also* Petexbatun region
Picón, Juan Gutiérrez, 375, 381
Piedras Negras, 176
pigment, 351
pih, 127
pilgrimage-market fair model, 4
Piña Chan, Roman, 143
Placencia Lagoon, 320, 321
Pochkaak Red-on-orange censer dish, 110-12, *111*
polished stone, 357
political economy, Mayan: Classic period, 126-29; definition of, 2, 126, 367-68; role of elite in, 141-44; temporal trend in, 15-18, 21
political economy theory: and economic prosperity/trade, 411-13; and elite control, 413-16; as informing human action, 399-400; and integration/ideology/elite behavior, 401-2; and local exchange, 403-7; and resource diversity, 407-11
Polanyi, Karl, 143
polychrome. *See* ceramic/pottery, polychrome
pom, 303
Pomona Tomb 1, 68, 72-76, *73*
Pope, Kevin, 312
poph, 98
Popol Vuh, creation myth of, 67, 68, 75
Port Honduras/Wild Cane Cay area, 320
potlach, definition of, 31
Potter, Parker B., 369
Pott's Creek Lagoon, 313, 315
Pott's Landing, 315
Powell's Ridge, 318
pplom, 225
precious stone, 229
Preclassic icon, 49-*50*
prestige good: in ancient Greece, 151; cacao as, 229, 239, 402; context of, 150-51; feather as, 229; jade as, 235, 239, 273; marine shell as, 229, 235, 273; metal artifact as, 229; obsidian as, 273; resource diversity in, 409-11; slate as, 409
prestige-good economy, 5-6, 126
prestige-good exchange, 19-20; fall-off curve in, *146*, 147
prestige-goods theory, 126-27
Principal Bird Deity, 46, 204; on Altar 10, 49, 52, *53*, 54; on Altar 10 at Kaminaljuyu, 55; on Cerros Structure

52-2nd façade, *47*, 48-49, 51; Itzam Ye, 48, 64; Mut Itzamna, 48; on Panel of the Foliated Cross, 51
principales, dwellings of at Ek Balám, 379-80, 381
principle of first occupancy, 374, 381
Principles of Political Economy, 367
Pring, Duncan C., 102
production, modes of: household industry, 288-89; household production, 288; workshop industry, 289-90, 301
Programme for Belize Archaeological Project, 197
Protoclassic Horizon, southern Maya lowlands: ceramic/pottery of, 100, 102-4, *103*, 105; Homul I burial during, 107; political changes during, 99-101; political currency during, 103-5; ritual activity change during, 100
Protoclassic Phase pottery, 98
Puleston, Denny, 87
Punta Canbalam, 254, 256, 259-60
Putan Maya, 250
putting-out industry, 380-81
Puuc Red ware, 179
Puuc Slate ware, 179-80
Puuc Thin Slate ware, 179
Puuc Unslipped ware, 179
pyramid, 37, 268, 269
Pyramid at Acanceh, 55
pyrite, 88

Quadripartite Badge, 63, 75
quartz, 405, 408
quern, 266
quetzal feather, 88, 125
Quimal, 299
Quim Chi Hilan, 162
Quintal Unslipped, 209
Quintana Roo, 18, 178, 182, 337
Quirigua, 184, 230, 273
Quirigua Stela C, 67
Quiroz, Luis Marrón, 308, 311

Rands, Robert L., 145, 152-56, 161, 176
Rathje, William L., 10, 225, 366, 398, 399; on Buddhist Sutras, xi; cultural ecology model of lowland Maya by, ix-xi; discoveries at Cozumel Island by, 43; on far-flung trade, 18; household economy analysis of, 20, 335, 337, 338, 341; on long-distance salt trade, 307; mercantile model of, ix, xiii, 20, 175-77, 180-81, 335, 336, 340, 341, 347, 358; on origins of Maya civilization, 80; on recycling, viii; on

shrinking ceramic style zones, 17. *See also* core-periphery model
red bead, 233
Redfield, Robert, 369, 383
redistribution, 143
red shell, 41, 44
Reents-Budet, Dorie, 166, 230-31, 238-39
Reese-Taylor, Kathryn, 14, 64, 65, 87, 93, 215, 406, 411
region, defining, 4-6-407
Reilly, Kent, 57
Reina, Rubén, 312
rejollada, 128, 376, 377, 378, 380, 381
Relaciones Geográficas, 379, 380
Relacion of Campocolche, 41
Renfrew, Colin, 145-46, 157-58
repartimiento, 381
residential corporate group. *See* corporate group, residential
resin, 229
resource diversity, 407-8; in prestige good, 409-11; in subsistence good, 408-9
resource mapping, 403
Rice, Prudence M., 141
ring model, of economic structure, 3
Rio Azul, 89, 110, 201, 202; abandonment/destruction of, 212; funerary vessel at, 12; monumental architecture at, 89, 203, 212; tool production/agricultural intensification at, 90
Rio Bec, 214
Rio Bravo, 197, 200, 201, 203
Rio Bravo Escarpment, 209, 211
Rio Celestun, 254
rise of civilization, theories of, 31, 32
Rita Red, 345
Ritscher, Heidi, 410
Roaring Creek Red, 416
Robertson-Freidel, Robin, 97
Robinson, Eugenia J., 296
Rocky Point, 313, 325
royal palace glyph, 98
royal tomb, at Caracol, 96
Roys, Ralph L., 225, 226
Ruz, Alberto L., 43

Sabloff, Jeremy A., viii, ix, 18, 20-21, 175, 176, 225, 335, 336, 340, 341, 347, 358
Sacapulas, 312, 316, 317, 321
Sacatepéquez complex, 293
sacbe, 271
sacbeob, 257-59, 258, 261, 267, 268
Sacluc Black-on-orange, 97
Sagebiel, Kerry, 209
saggar, 232
Saktunja, 318, 319, 325
sal cocida, 311, 313, 319, 320, 321
Salinas de los Nueve Cerros, 14, 312-13, 323, 325

salt: consumption of, 323; as local subsistence item, 404; as perishable trade item, 13, 232. *See also* salt industry, prehispanic Maya; salt making; salt trade
Salt Creek Lagoon, 313, 318
salt industry, prehispanic Maya, 326; along North Central Belize Coast, 15, 313-19, 314, 412; in El Salvador, 311-12; in Guatemala, 14, 312-13, 323, 325; map of, 308; in Northern Yucatán, 308-11; in southern Coastal Brazil, 319-22
salt making: brine-cooking vessel for, 214, 315-17, 316, 320, 322; solar evaporation process in, 320, 321, 322; use of clay cylinder in, 315, 317, 318, 319-20, 321. *See also* salt; salt industry, prehispanic Maya; salt trade
salt trade: export routes for prehispanic Maya, 317-18; interregional trade in, 168; Late Classic Maya, 412-13; long-distance exchange of, 9, 14, 18, 88, 125; market exchange of, in highland Guatemala, 228; prehispanic Maya, 307, 322-26, 324; and prestige-goods exchange, 19, 20. *See also* salt; salt industry, prehispanic Maya; salt making
salt works, 254
Samuel Oshon site, 130, 133
San Andrés Itzapa, 295
Sánchez, Alicia Contreras, 309
Sanchez, Ramon Carillo, 265
Sanders, William T., 141, 142
San Fernando paste, 180, 181, 271
San Gervasio site, ix
San Jose, 169-71, 170, 175, 204
San José V red ware, 416
San Juan, 320
San Lorenzo, 295, 296
San Martín Jilotepeque, 15, 301-3; distribution of obsidian in, 286-88; dwelling at, 296, 297; Early Classic in, 295, 296, 298; Late Classic in, 298-99; Late Preclassic settlement in, 293-96, 294; location of obsidian in, 287; Middle Preclassic settlement in, 292-93; obsidian-exporting from, 15; Postclassic in, 299-300; as region, 406
San Mateo Ixtatán, 317
Santa Cruz, 320
Santa Rita, 108, 110, 111, 214-15, 340, 341
Santa Rita Corozal, 182
Santa Rita Ranch, shrine at, ix
Santa unslipped, 347
Santiago Atitlan, 67
Santley, Robert, 370
Sapote Striated vessel, 113n1

Sayil, 179-80, 273
Scarborough, Vernon L., 200
Scarlet Macaw, 46
Schele, Linda, 61, 63, 64, 65, 70, 92
Schmidt, Peter, 313
Schneider, Jane, 8, 369
Sechin Alto, 38
Seibal, 176
Selz Foundation Yaxuna project, 61
serpent-head emblem glyph, 214
Serpent Head polity, 214
settlement archaeology, 370-72
settlement pattern, definition of, 370
Sevilla Blue-on-blue, 377
Shafer, Harry J., 13
shaman, 95, 99
Sheets, Payson, 3
shell, marine: conch, 404; and core-
    periphery dynamics, 14-15; as
    currency, 7, 16, 41, 43-44, 225, 227; at
    Ek Balám, 377; as grave good, 341;
    long-distance trade in, 226; manufac-
    turing of, 9-10, 342, 350-54, 352, 353,
    355; as prestige good, 5, 229, 235, 273.
    See also Spondylus
shell bead, 77, 227, 350-51
Shephard, Anna, 169-70
Shook, Edwin M., 293
Sibun River, 129-30
Sibun River valley: archaeological sites
    at, 130; cacao production model of,
    134-35; Hershey site at, 131-32;
    pottery at, 133-34; ritual practice at,
    133; Samuel Oshon site at, 133
Siburn-Manatee Cone Karst, 129-30, 133
Sierra Group bowl, 98, 113n3
Sierra Red bowl, 112n1, 113n1
Sierra Red group, 102
Sierrita de Ticul, 272
Siho, 271
Silho Fine Orange ceramic, 178
silver coin, 377
Sinsimato, 225
sitio de paso, 257
Siyaj Chan K'awil I, 108
Siyaj Chan K'awill II, 114n10
Siyaj K'ak, 109
sky band, 114n6
slate: ash-tempered Itza slate at, 180; at
    Caye Coco, 350, 357; Itza, 409; local/
    export context of, 404, 405, 409; as
    prestige good, 409; Puuc Slate ware,
    179-80; Puuc Thin Slate ware, 179;
    standardization in, 180; as subsis-
    tence resource, 408-9; Ticul Thin
    Slate, 213
slate-backed mirror, 405, 409
slim (greenstone sculpture), 57
Smith, Adam, 367

Smith, Carol, 4, 141, 142, 144, 147, 160,
    165, 168, 290
Smith, M. Estellie, 2, 141
Smyth, Michael P., et al.,179
social compliance, 413
social production, definition of, 33
social production dispersal system, 33
socio-technic artifact, 33
socket, 320
Soconusco region, 180
solar central place, 17, 144, 145, 160, 184;
    in Caracol, 4; marketing in, 168;
    specialization in, 147
solares, 262
solar evaporation process, in salt
    making, 320, 321, 322
Sosa, Thelma Sierra, 311
Southwestern School, of Mayanist
    archaeology, 366-67
spacer, 320
spatial pattern, uncommercialized
    economy: bounded network system,
    184, 291-92; extended network
    system, 290
special exchange of the lords, highland
    Guatemala, 228-29
spice, 232
spindle whorl, 342, 350, 351, 354, 359
Spondylus: appearance in Late Preclassic,
    44-45; in burial, 77, 107; as currency,
    20, 42, 43, 45, 79; entrance into
    southern lowlands, 92; in icono-
    graphic program (See Cerros
    Structure 52-2nd façade); ideological/
    cosmological significance of, 44,
    45-46, 402, 409, 410-11; as jewel, 66; as
    local/exotic resource, 411; as luxury
    trade item, 88; occurrence of, 410;
    origins of, 410-11; reduction in trade
    at Cerros, 100; ritual context of, 68-71,
    69, 70, 72, 74-75, 76, 77, 78, 79
Spondylus americanus, 404, 410-11
Sta. Barbara, 267
staircase motif, 65, 76, 98, 237
Stann Creek District, 404, 408-9, 412-13
staple finance system, 226-27
Stark, Barbara L., 16, 380, 381
stone bead, 277, 350
Strombus, 61
Structure C-22-41-a, ix
Structure H-Sub 12, 49, 55
Stuart, David, 54, 74, 127-28
Subin Red bowl, 213
subsistence good, 234-35, 408-9
Suhler, Charles K., 70
Sullivan, Lauren A., 12, 401-2, 406
Sun God, 72-73, 75-76

Tabasco, México, 129

Targa, Garciá, 384n2
Taschek, Jennifer T., 233
Taube, Karl, 63, 66
Tecoh Red-on-Buff, 377
Tenochtitlan, 7
Teotihuacan: change in production/
  distribution at, 142; cylinder tripod
  at, 110, 209; decline of, 212; embedded system of social production at,
  33; relationship to Tikal, 109, 110
Tepeu 1 polychrome vase, 412
tetrapod vessel, 114n8
textile, 9, 13, 18, 20
theory of cultural evolution of civilizations, 399
Thompson, J. Eric S., 133, 416
Three Rivers Region, 215-16; chronological background of, 200-202; Early
  Classic Connections of, 202-11, 205-8,
  210; elites at, 203-4; Late Classic
  Independence, 211-14; location of,
  197-98; map of, 199; monumental
  architecture at, 201-3, 212; population
  decrease/increase in, 201, 202, 203,
  211-12; regional comparisons at,
  214-15; topography/vegetation of,
  200
Three Stone Place, 67, 77, 93
Ticul Thin Slate, 213
Tiger Mound, 320
Tigre Complex, at El Mirador, 89
Tikal: appearance of Spondylus shell at,
  43; ash-tempered ceramic at, 170, 172;
  Burial 85 at, 98, 113nn1 & 3; Burial
  125 at, 113n5-114n5; Burial 167 at, 98;
  ceramic at, 98; ceramic workshop at,
  166, 230; connection to Three Rivers
  Region, 204; decline of, 214; Early
  Classic burial site, 77; embedded
  system of social production at, 33;
  funerary vessel at, 12; fuschite mask
  at Bu 85, 61; heterogeneity/quality of
  ceramic at, 159-60; iconographic
  program at, 95; local/regional market
  at, 10; luxury item at, 6; market
  exchange at, 160; marketplace at, 273;
  North Acropolis at, 100, 109, 113n4,
  114n10; obsidian distribution in, 149;
  political transformation at, 109-10;
  polychrome vessel at, 162-63; regional
  ceramic exchange system at, 156-60,
  157, 158, 159; relative size of, 89;
  ritual activity changes at, 100; ruler
  of, 87, 99, 107, 108, 109-10, 114n10;
  Site 29 at, 108; Temple 1 at, 89;
  Temple 2 at, 89
Tikal area, use of utilitarian pottery in,
  236
Tikal cult, 209

Tikal-Teotihuacan confederacy, 110, 111
Tikal-Yaxha area, 170, 172
Tipu, 409
Tiquibalón. See Ek Balám
Tiwanaku, 236
Tohil Plumbate, 180
tok, 77
tomb: cenotaphic, 68, 72-76, 73; Classic,
  412; early Cimi phase, 113n5-114n5;
  Early Classic, 106-7, 204, 205, 209,
  211; Homul, 107; Pomona Tomb 1, 68,
  72-76, 73; royal, 96. See also burial
Tonsured Young Lord Maize god, 77
tool, at Ek Balám, 377
Tourteloot, Gair, 371
Tozzar, Alfred M., 41
tranchet adze, 90
tree, metaphor of, 67
triadic arrangement, Late Preclassic
  settlement, 90
tribute: cacao as, 7, 42, 125, 127-28; in
  contact-period Yucatán, 225-28; cotton
  as, 125; feather as, 125, 237, 238;
  glyph for, 125, 128, 237, 238;
  Spondylus as, 42
trifoil headdress design, 45, 46
trilobate motif, on Cerros Structure 52-
  2nd façade, 51-52
trilobate pendant, 51
Trobriand society, 4
Truinfo Striated, 209
Tulum, 12
Type III site, 296-99
Tzakol 3 polychrome, 412
Tzeme, 271

Uaxactun, 204; ash tempered ceramic at,
  170; coatimundi effigy vessel from,
  209, 210; demise of, 12; exterior of
  vessel from, 207; funerary vessel at,
  12; interior of vessel from, 206;
  macaw head handle from, 208;
  relationship with Three Rivers
  Region, 204
Uaymil, 265
Urrutia, Juan de, 379-80
u-element, 54, 55, 57, 58, 61, 63
Usulatan ceramic, 93, 96-97
Usumacinta drainage, 233, 323
utilitarian item, 5-7
utilitarian pottery: as both elite and
  commoner context, 12, 213; in Early
  vs. Late Classic period, 212-13; at East
  Plaza (Tikal), 234; in Palenque area,
  236; in Tikal area, 236
u-tohol, 237

Valdez, Fred, Jr., 89, 197, 322
Vallodolid province, 381

value/exchange system: exchange goods value, 10-13, *11*; intersecting spheres of exchange, 7-9; market variation in contact period Maya, 9-10
vanilla, wild, 9
varas, 376
Viejo, María Justina Sarabia, 309
village-tradition polychrome ceramic, 166, 167
visita, 131
Vleck, David T., et al., 263

Wak Chan Ahaw World Tree, 65, 66, 67, 75, 113n3
Wakna, 93-94, 96, 112n1-113n1
Walker, Debra, 115n12, 215, 406, 411
Wallerstein, Immanuel, 8, 19, 125, 135, 368
Watanabe, Takeshi, 265
Water Fowl, 48, 49, 51, 64, 76
water group prefix, 58, *59-60*
Waterlily Jaguar, 65
Watson's Island, 314, 315, 320
Waxaklajun Ubah K'awil, 75
Waxaktun: Eight House of the North type structure at, *93*; growth of during Cycle 7, 89; iconographic program at, 95, *96*; and long-distance trade, 94, 108; Peteltun Modeled censer stand at, 110; Structure H-Sub 12 at, 49, 55
Waxaktun Group E, 114n7
wealth finance system, 226
Webb, Malcom, 21
Webster, David, 141, 142
West, Georgia, 17, 406, 413
West Mexico, 410
Whitecotten, Joseph W., 8
Wild Cane, 320
Will Edward's Lagoon, 315
Willey, Gordon R., 370-71
wine trade, control of modern, 414-15
wi-te-na, 113n3
Wlley, Gordon R., 16
Wolf, Eric R., 135
wood, 9, 13, 18, 232
workshop industry, 289-90, 301
world economy, 19, 369
world empire, definition of, 19
world systems theory, 367, 368-70; and study of households, 375, 383; as theory of historical change, 400-401

XARP. *See* Xibun Archaeological Research Project
Xcalumkin, and gateway phenomenon, 271
Xcambó, 325
Xcambó-Xtampú, 311
Xibalba, 318
Xib'um. *See* Sibun River valley
Xibun, 20, 131, 133-34
Xibun Archaeological Research Project (XARP), 124-26, 132
Xico, 183
Xiu, 233
Xkichmook, 268
Xok Shell girdle, 67
Xpantzay faction, 300
Xtabay Hocaba-Tases, 377
Xunantunich, 170, 173, 174, *175*

Yacman Striated, 377
y-ajaw, 74
Yakal Chen, 268
Yalcihon, 271
Yaloche Cream-polychrome, 204, *208*
Yax Balam, 65
Yaxchilan, 21
Yax Ehb' Xook, 99, 115n10
Yaxha, 110
Yaxha-Sacnab area, 172
Yax Nuun Ayiin I, 109-10, 112, 113n3, 115n10
Yax P'otob, 132
Yoffee, Norman, 142-43
Young Tonsured Lord, 70, *71*
yubte', 237
Yucatán: ash tempering at, 169; cacao cultivation at, 128; as core of Mayan political power, 127; map of North-western, *251*; perishable goods trade in, 168; shell ear flare in, 54, *55*. *See also* Chunchucmil
Yucatán, contact-period: economy/tribute/elite control in, 225-28; elite control in, 225-26; frequency of feasting during, 239; markets in, 234-35; tribute/tax system in, 226-27
Yuncu Unslipped, 377
Yuxuna, 54, *55*

Zakpah Red, 345
Zapatista Trickle-on-cream brown, 97
Zender, Marc, 114n9
Zutuhil lord, 229

About the Authors

Anthony P. Andrews, Professor of Anthropology, has been teaching at New College of University of South Florida since 1981. He was raised in Yucatan, Mexico, where his father was also an archaeologist. He did his graduate work at the University of Arizona and has conducted field-work in Peru, Mexico, Guatemala, Belize, and El Salvador. For over thirty years his primary focus has been on the prehispanic and historic archae-ology, ethnohistory, and history of the lowland Maya coasts of Yucatán and Central America. He has published six books and monographs, and more than seventy articles, book chapters, and book reviews.

Traci Ardren is co-director of the Pakbeh Regional Economy Project cen-tered at the ancient Maya trading city of Chunchucmil, Yucatan, Mexico. Her research has focused on gender, iconography, architecture, and other forms of symbolic representation in the archaeological record. She is currently Assistant Professor of Anthropology at the University of Mi-ami.

Geoffrey E. Braswell received his Ph.D. in anthropology from Tulane University. Since then, he has conducted archaeological research at Chichen Itza (Mexico), Kaminaljuyu and Topoxte (Guatemala), Copan (Honduras), and Pusilha (Belize). He currently serves as Assistant Pro-fessor of Anthropology at the State University of New York at Buffalo.

Bruce Dahlin is in the Sociology/Anthropology Department at Howard University. He has taught at Catholic University and University of Colo-rado and has directed projects in Mexico, Belize, and Guatemala. His research interests include environmental archaeology, human ecology, and the origins of social stratification and complex political economies. He is currently a co-director of the Pakbeh Regional Economy Program which is centered on the Classic Maya site of Chunchucmil, Yucatan, Mexico.

.stant Professor of Anthropology at Williams Col-
. Harvard and Vanderbilt Universities and has done
.1ala over the last decade. She has worked on the Clas-
y of the Petexbatun region and has directed her own
Amelia and Motul de San Jose, both in northern Guate-
resent research at Motul focuses on the economic structure
.ssic Maya.

. A. Freidel is Professor of Anthropology at Southern Methodist
.versity. His Maya fieldwork includes surveying sites on Cozumel
.1and as a member of the Harvard-Arizona Cozumel Project, directing
research at the Late Preclassic site of Cerros in Belize, and serving as
project director at the ancient city of Yaxuna in Yucatan. He is initiating
research at the Classic period city of Wakah (El Peru) in Petén, Guatemala. He is co-author of A Forest of Kings and Maya Cosmos, both with
Linda Schele, and is preparing a book on Maya warfare.

Elizabeth Graham is a lecturer at the Institute of Archaeology, University College London. She has worked in Belize for thirty years, where
her research interests include Maya coastal trade, the long-term impact
of tropical urbanism, and Maya-Spanish relations at the time of the Conquest.

Craig Hanson is completing his doctorate at Tulane University. Among
his research interests are anthropological theory, world-systems approaches to archaeology, political economy, and sixteenth-century Maya
archaeology and history. He has directed Hispanic horizon investigations
at several sites in the northern Maya lowlands including Ek Balam,
Yucatan, the focus of his Ph.D. dissertation "The Late Mesoamerican
Village."

Eleanor Harrison, Department of Archaeology, Boston University, specializes in ancient Maya ritual economies, combining the energetics of
long-distance trade with the material basis of ritual expression, using as
her case study the settlements of the Sibun River Valley.

Patricia A. McAnany, Associate Professor of Archaeology at Boston University, has accumulated over twenty years of field experience in the
Maya lowlands. She is the principal i°nvestigator of the Xibun Archaeological Research Project and has long-abiding research interests in Maya
economies and ritual practices, employing a social history approach to
Maya archaeology.

Marilyn A. Masson is an assistant professor at the University at A SUNY. She has worked in northern Belize since 1983, and her res has focused specifically on Postclassic Maya social transforma since 1991 under the auspices of the Belize Postclassic Project as s marized in her recent book, *In the Realm of Nachan Kan* (Univers Press of Colorado, 2000). She recently started a new research project (collaboration with Carlos Peraza) at the Postclassic Maya city c Mayapán, which will facilitate comparisons of economic organization and integration of the Belize region and northwest Yucatan.

Shirley B. Mock has a Ph.D. in anthropology from the University of Texas and has carried out archaeological fieldwork in Latin America and North America. For more than ten years her research has been focused on the settlement pattern, economies, trade, and salt production of the north-central coast of Belize. She has published in peer-reviewed journals, edited *The Sowing and the Dawning: Dedication, Termination, and Transformation in the Archaeological and Ethnographic Record of Mesoamerica* (University of New Mexico Press, 1999), and coedited *New Horizons in Ceramics* (University Press of Florida, forthcoming).

David F. Mora-Marín has a Ph.D. in anthropology from the State University of New York at Albany. He is interested in historical anthropology, focusing on Mesoamerica, specializing in the application of various ethnohistorical methods, such as linguistics, epigraphy, art history, and archaeology, to the study of prehispanic Maya history. His dissertation deals with the grammar, orthography, content, and social context of Late Preclassic Mayan portable texts.

Steven Morandi, Department of Archaeology, Boston University, specializes in the osteology and paleopathology of ancient Maya populations. Currently he is researching the Formative through Classic period skeletal samples from K'axob, Belize.

Polly A. Peterson, Department of Archaeology, Boston University, specializes in ancient Maya ritual practices that were conducted in the underground caverns of the Sibun-Manatee karst system of Belize.

William L. Rathje graduated from the University of Arizona (B.A. 1967) and Harvard (Ph.D. 1971) in Anthropology. He was hired at the U.A. and focused his research on the interrelations between trade, burial positions, and paraphernalia, and the rise and fall of Maya civilization. By the late 1970s Rathje was inundated by the demands of the Garbage Project he ɔrs/ 435

ɔ to study the relationship between attitudes,
ɔany- ҳnains, and the environment. At present, Rathje still
ɔarɔh ﾉProject, but is also Professor Emeritus at the U.A.
ɔons ﾉssor at the Archaeology Center, Stanford.
ɔm-
ɔy
ɔ
ҳeese-Taylor is an Associate Profesor at the University of
ɔ began working in the southern Maya lowlands in 1983 and
ɔ has focused much of her research on the Late Preclassic pe-
ҳer current research interests include archaeological theory, land-
ﾉ studies, and ceramic analysis. She is presently directing a project
ҳorthwestern Belize that addresses questions of how the rural elite
ҳxpressed ideologies of power within their landscapes.

Lauren A. Sullivan teaches in the Department of Anthropology, University of Massachusetts at Boston, and has been involved in field research in the Maya lowlands since 1987. Her early interests included the development of complex society in northern Belize with a focus on Preclassic architecture and ceramics. More recently, she has focused on the analysis of ceramics recovered from a number of sites in northwestern Belize in order to develop a regional chronology and to examine patterns of trade, exchange, and social organization on intrasite as well as intersite levels.

Ben S. Thomas, Department of Archaeology, Boston University, specializes in Maya site hierarchies and political relations in the Sibun River Valley using the tool of Geographic Information Systems.

Debra S. Walker specializes in Maya ceramics. Her dissertation research focused on Terminal Classic and Postclassic pottery from Cerros, Belize. She subsequently directed further excavations at the site that led to a new focus on the Protoclassic era, on which her chapter is based. Walker is an Adjunct Professor at Florida International University in Miami. She lives in Key Largo, Florida, with her husband and two children. Elected to public office in 1994, she currently serves as Vice Chair of the Monroe County School Board.

Georgia West received a B.A. in history from the University of California at Berkeley and an M.A. in anthropology from the University at Albany–SUNY. She currently resides in New York City and works as a producer at The Merrow Report, a company that produces documentaries about youth and education for the Public Broadcasting System.